Praise for *Introduction to Game Design, Prototyping, and Development*

"*Introduction to Game Design, Prototyping, and Development* combines a solid grounding in evolving game design theory with a wealth of detailed examples of prototypes for digital games. Together these provide an excellent introduction to game design and development that culminates in making working games with Unity. This book will be useful for both introductory courses and as a reference for expert designers. I will be using this book in my game design classes, and it will be among those few to which I often refer."

—Michael Sellers
Professor of Practice in Game Design, Indiana University, former Creative Director at Rumble Entertainment, and General Manager at Kabam

"Prototyping and play-testing are often the most misunderstood and/or underutilized steps in the game design and development process. Iterative cycles of testing and refining are key to the early stages of making a good game. Novices will often believe that they need to know everything about a language or build every asset of the game before they can really get started. Gibson's new book prepares readers to go ahead and dive in to the actual design and prototyping process right away; providing the basics of process and technology with excellent "starter kits" for different types of games to jumpstart their entry into the practice."

—Stephen Jacobs
Associate Director, RIT Center for Media, Art, Games, Interaction and Creativity (MAGIC) and Professor, School of Interactive Games and Media

"Jeremy Gibson's *Introduction to Game Design, Prototyping, and Development* deftly combines the necessary philosophical and practical concepts for anyone looking to become a Game Designer. This book will take you on a journey from high-level design theories, through game development concepts and programming foundations in order to make your own playable video games. Jeremy uses his years of experience as a professor to teach the reader how to think with vital game design mindsets so that you can create a game with all the right tools at hand. A must-read for someone who wants to dive right into making their first game and a great refresher for industry veterans."

—Michelle Pun
Senior Game Designer, Zynga

Introduction to Game Design, Prototyping, and Development

The Addison-Wesley
Game Design and Development Series

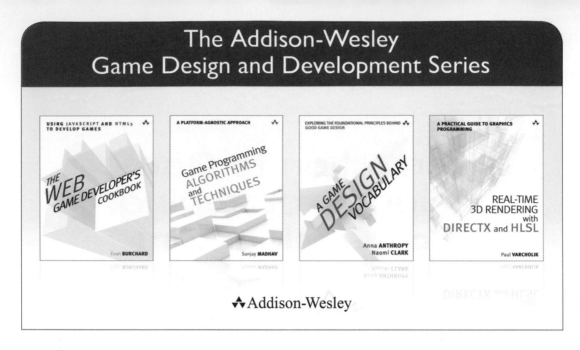

Visit **informit.com/series/gamedesign** for a complete list of available publications.

Essential References for Game Designers and Developers

These practical guides, written by distinguished professors and industry gurus, cover basic tenets of game design and development using a straightforward, common-sense approach. The books encourage readers to try things on their own and think for themselves, making it easier for anyone to learn how to design and develop digital games for both computers and mobile devices.

Make sure to connect with us!
informit.com/socialconnect

   ✦Addison-Wesley   **Safari**
the trusted technology learning source   Books Online

ALWAYS LEARNING   **PEARSON**

Introduction to Game Design, Protoyping, and Development

From Concept to Playable Game—with Unity® and C#

Jeremy Gibson

✦✦Addison-Wesley

Upper Saddle River, NJ • Boston • Indianapolis • San Francisco
New York • Toronto • Montreal • London • Munich • Paris • Madrid
Capetown • Sydney • Tokyo • Singapore • Mexico City

For information about buying this title in bulk quantities, or for special sales opportunities (which may include electronic versions; custom cover designs; and content particular to your business, training goals, marketing focus, or branding interests), please contact our corporate sales department at corpsales@pearsoned.com or (800) 382-3419.

For government sales inquiries, please contact governmentsales@pearsoned.com.

For questions about sales outside the U.S., please contact international@pearsoned.com.

Visit us on the Web: informit.com/aw

Library of Congress Control Number: 2014936195

ISBN-13: 978-0-321-93316-4
ISBN-10: 0-321-93316-8

Text printed in the United States on recycled paper at RR Donnelley in Crawfordsville, IN.

First printing, July 2014

Editor-in-Chief
Mark Taub

Senior Acquisitions Editor
Laura Lewin

Senior Development Editor
Chris Zahn

Managing Editor
Kristy Hart

Project Editor
Elaine Wiley

Copy Editor
Keith Cline

Indexer
Ken Johnson

Proofreader
Paula Lowell

Technical Editors
Marc Destefano
Charles Duba
Margaret Moser

Publishing Coordinator
Olivia Basegio

Cover Designer
Chuti Prasersith

Book Designer
Bumpy Design

Compositor
Nonie Ratcliff

This book is dedicated to:

My wife Melanie, the love of my life,
for her love, intellect, and support

My parents and sisters

And my many professors, colleagues, and students
who inspired me to write this book.

Contents at a Glance

Contents

FOREWORD

I have a theory about game designers and teachers. I think that, beneath the possible differences of our outer appearances, we're secretly the same; that many of the skills possessed by a good game designer are the same skills held by a great teacher. Have you ever had a teacher who held a class spellbound with puzzles and stories? Who showed you simple demonstrations of skills that were easy for you to understand and copy, but were difficult for you to master? Who gradually, cleverly, helped you put together pieces of information in your mind, maybe without your even realizing it, until one day your teacher was able to step aside and watch you do something amazing, something that you never would have thought was possible.

We video game designers spend a lot of our time finding ways to teach people the skills they need to play our games, while keeping them entertained at the same time. We sometimes don't want people to be aware that we're teaching them, though—the best tutorial levels that video games open with are usually the ones that simply seem like the beginning of a thrilling adventure. I was lucky to work at the award-winning game studio Naughty Dog for eight amazing years, where I was the Lead or Co-Lead Game Designer on all three PlayStation 3 games in the *Uncharted* series. Everyone at the studio was very happy with the sequence that opened our game *Uncharted 2: Among Thieves*. It effectively taught each player all the basic moves they would need to play the game, while keeping them on the edge of their seat because of the gripping predicament our hero Nathan Drake found himself in, dangling over the edge of a cliff in a ruined train carriage.

Video game designers do this kind of thing over and over again as they create digital adventures for us to play. Working on a sequence of player experiences like those found in the *Uncharted* games, I have to stay very focused on what the player has recently learned. I have to present my audience with interesting situations that use their new skills and that are easy enough that they won't get frustrated, but challenging enough that their interest will be held. To do this with complete strangers, through the channels of communication that a game provides—the graphics of the environments and the characters and objects within them, the sounds that the game makes, and the interactivity of the game's controls—is tremendously challenging. At the same time, it is one of the most rewarding things I know how to do.

Now that I've become a professor, teaching game design in a university setting, I've discovered firsthand just how many of the skills I developed as a game designer are useful in my teaching. I'm also discovering that teaching is just as rewarding as game design. So it came to me as no surprise when I discovered that Jeremy Gibson, the author of this book, is equally talented as a game designer and a teacher, as you're about to find out.

I first met Jeremy around ten years ago, at the annual Game Developers Conference in Northern California, and we immediately hit it off. He already had a successful career as a game developer, and his enthusiasm for game design struck a chord with me. As you'll see when you begin to read this book, he loves to talk about game design as a craft, a design practice and an emerging art. Jeremy and I stayed in touch over the years, as he went back to graduate school at Carnegie Mellon University's excellent Entertainment Technology Center to study under visionaries like Doctor Randy Pausch and Jesse Schell. Eventually, I came to know Jeremy as a professor and a colleague in the Interactive Media & Games Division of the School of Cinematic Arts at the University of Southern California—part of USC Games, the program in which I now teach.

In fact, I got to know Jeremy better than ever during his time at USC—and I did it by becoming his student. In order to acquire the skills that I needed to develop experimental research games as part of USC's Game Innovation Lab, I took one of Jeremy's classes, and his teaching transformed me from a Unity n00b with some basic programming experience into an experienced C# programmer with a strong set of skills in Unity, one of the world's most powerful, usable, adaptable game engines. Every single one of Jeremy's classes was not only packed with information about Unity and C#, but was also peppered with inspirational words of wisdom about game design and practical pieces of advice related to game development—everything from his thoughts about good "lerping," to great tips for time management and task prioritization, to the ways that game designers can use spreadsheets to make their games better. I graduated from Jeremy's class wishing that I could take it again, knowing that there was a huge amount more that I could learn from him.

So I was very happy when I heard that Jeremy was writing a book—and I became even happier when I read the volume that you now hold in your hands. The good news for both you and me is that Jeremy has loaded this book with everything that I wanted more of. I learned a lot in the game industry about best practices in game design, production, and development, and I'm happy to tell you that in this book, Jeremy does a wonderful job of summarizing those ways of making games that I've found work best. Within these pages, you'll find step-by-step tutorials and code examples that will make you a better game designer and developer in innumerable ways. While the exercises in this book might get complex—game design is among the most difficult things I know how to do—Jeremy won't ask you to do anything complicated without guiding you through it in clear, easy-to-follow language.

You'll also find history and theory in this book. Jeremy has been thinking deeply about game design for a long time and is very well-read on the subject. In the first part of this volume, you'll find an extraordinarily wide and deep survey of the state-of-the-art in game design theory, along with Jeremy's unique and strongly developed synthesis of the very best ideas he's encountered on his game design travels. Jeremy supports his discussion with interesting historical anecdotes and fascinating glimpses of the long traditions of play in human culture, all of which help to frame his conversation in valuable and progressive ways. He continually pushes you to question your assumptions about games, and to think beyond the console, the controller, the screen and the speakers, in ways that might just spur a whole new generation of game innovators.

Jeremy Gibson has moved on from USC, and now teaches at the University of Michigan Ann Arbor, and I'm very happy for the generations of U-M students that he'll lead to new understandings of the craft of game design in the coming years. This spring, when Jeremy walked into the restaurant at the annual GDC alumni dinner hosted by the USC Games program, the room full of our current and former students came alive with whoops and cheers and moments later broke out into applause. That tells you a lot about what Jeremy Gibson is like as a teacher. You're lucky that, thanks to this book, he can now be your teacher too.

The world of game design and development is changing at a rapid rate. You can be part of this wonderful world—a world unlike any other I know, and which I love with all my heart. You can use the skills you learn through reading this book to develop new prototypes for new kinds of games, and in doing so you might eventually create whole new genres of games, in expressive new styles, which appeal to new markets. Some of tomorrow's stars of game design are currently learning to design and program, in homes and schools all around the world. If you make good use of this book, by following the advice and doing the exercises you find in here, it might just help your chances of creating a modern game design classic.

Good luck, and have fun!

Richard Lemarchand
Associate Professor, USC Games

PREFACE

Welcome to *Introduction to Game Design, Prototyping, and Development*. This book is based on my work over many years as both a professional game designer and a professor of game design at several universities, including the Interactive Media and Games Division at the University of Southern California and the Department of Electrical Engineering and Computer Science at the University of Michigan Ann Arbor.

This preface introduces you to the purpose, scope, and approach of this book.

The Purpose of This Book

My goal in this book is quite simple: I want to give you all the tools and knowledge you need to get started down the path to being a successful game designer and prototyper. This book is the distillation of as much knowledge as I can cram into it to help you toward that goal. Unlike most books out there, this book combines the disciplines of game design and digital development (that is, computer programming) and wraps them both in the essential practice of iterative prototyping. The emergence of advanced, yet approachable, game development engines such as Unity has made it easier than ever before to create playable prototypes that express your game design concepts to others, and the ability to do so will make you a much more skilled (and employable) game designer.

The book is divided into four parts:

Part I: Game Design and Paper Prototyping

The first part of the book starts by exploring various theories of game design and the analytical frameworks for game design that have been proposed by several earlier books. This section then describes the Layered Tetrad as a way of combining and expanding on many of the best features of these earlier theories. The Layered Tetrad is explored in depth as it relates to various decisions that you must make as a designer of interactive experiences. This part also covers information about the interesting challenges of different game design disciplines; describes the process of paper prototyping, testing, and iteration; and gives you concrete information to help you become a better designer.

Part II: Digital Prototyping

The second part teaches you how to program. This part draws upon my many years of experience as a professor teaching nontechnical students how to express their game design ideas through digital code. If you have no prior knowledge or experience with programming or development, this part is designed for you. However, even if you do have some programming experience, you might want to take a look at this part to learn a few new tricks or get a refresher on some approaches.

Part III: Game Prototype Examples and Tutorials

The third part of the book encompasses several different tutorials, each of which guides you through the development of a prototype for a specific style of game. The purpose of this part is twofold: It reveals some best practices for rapid game prototyping by showing you how I personally approach prototypes for various kinds of games, and it provides you with a basic foundation on which to build your own games in the future. Most other books on the market that attempt to teach Unity (our game development environment) do so by taking the reader through a single, monolithic tutorial that is hundreds of pages long. In contrast, this book takes you through several much smaller tutorials. The final products of these tutorials are necessarily less robust than those found in some other books, but it is my belief that the variety of projects in this book will better prepare you for creating your own projects in the future.

Part IV: Appendices

This book has several important appendices that merit mention here. Rather than repeat information throughout the book or require you to go hunting through various chapters for it, any piece of information that is referenced several times in the book or that I think you would be likely to want to reference later (after you've finished reading the book once) is placed in the appendices. Appendix A is just a quick step-by-step introduction to the initial creation process for a game project in Unity. The second and longest appendix is Appendix B, "Useful Concepts." Though it has a rather lackluster name, this is the portion of the book that I believe you will return to most often in the years following your initial read through the book. "Useful Concepts" is a collection of several go-to technologies and strategies that I use constantly in my personal game prototyping process, and I think you'll find a great deal of it to be very useful. The third and final appendix is a list of very useful online references where you can find answers to questions not covered in this book. It is often difficult to know the right places to look for help online; this appendix lists those that I personally turn to most often.

There Are Other Books Out There

As a designer or creator of any kind, I think that it's absolutely essential to acknowledge those on whose shoulders you stand. There have been many books written on games and game design, and the few that I list here are those that have had the most profound effect on either my process or my thinking about game design. You will see these books referenced many times throughout this text, and I encourage you to read as many of them as possible.

Game Design Workshop by Tracy Fullerton

Initially penned by Tracy Fullerton, Chris Swain, and Steven S. Hoffman, *Game Design Workshop* is now in its third edition. More than any other text, this is the book that I turn to for advice on game design. This book was initially based on the Game Design Workshop class that Tracy and Chris taught at the University of Southern California, a class that formed the foundation for the entire games program at USC (and a class that I myself taught there from 2009–2013). The USC Interactive Media and Games graduate program has been named the number one school for game design in North America by Princeton Review every year that they have been ranking game programs, and the Game Design Workshop book and class were the foundation for that success.

Unlike many other books that speak volumes of theory about games, Tracy's book maintains a laser focus on information that helps budding designers improve their craft. I taught from this book for many years (even before I started working at USC), and I believe that if you actually attempt all the exercises listed in the book, you can't help but have a pretty good paper game at the end.

> Fullerton, Tracy, Christopher Swain, and Steven Hoffman, *Game Design Workshop: A Play-centric Approach to Creating Innovative Games,* 2nd ed. (Boca Raton, FL: Elsevier Morgan Kaufmann, 2008)

The Art of Game Design by Jesse Schell

Jesse Schell was one of my professors at Carnegie Mellon University and is a fantastic game designer with a background in theme park design gained from years working for Walt Disney Imagineering. Jesse's book is a favorite of many working designers because it approaches game design as a discipline to be examined through 100 different lenses that are revealed throughout the book. Jesse's book is a very entertaining read and broaches several topics not covered in this book.

> Jesse Schell, *The Art of Game Design: A Book of Lenses* (Boca Raton, FL: CRC Press, 2008)

The Grasshopper by Bernard Suits

While not actually a book on game design at all, *The Grasshopper* is an excellent exploration of the definition of the word *game*. Presented in a style reminiscent of the Socratic method, the book presents its definition of game very early in the text as the Grasshopper (from Aesop's fable *The Ant and the Grasshopper*) gives his definition on his deathbed, and his disciples spend the remainder of the book attempting to critique and understand this definition. This book also explores the question of the place of games and play in society.

> Bernard Suits, *The Grasshopper: Games, Life and Utopia* (Peterborough, Ontario: Broadview Press, 2005)

Game Design Theory by Keith Burgun

In this book, Burgun explores what he believes are faults in the current state of game design and development and proposes a much narrower definition of *game* than does Suits. Burgun's goal in writing this text was to be provocative and to push the discussion of game design theory forward. While largely negative in tone, Burgun's text raises a number of interesting points, and reacting to it helped me to refine my personal understanding of game design.

> Keith Burgun, *Game Design Theory: A New Philosophy for Understanding Games* (Boca Raton, FL: A K Peters/CRC Press, 2013)

Imaginary Games by Chris Bateman

Bateman uses this book to argue that games are a legitimate medium for scholarly study. He pulls from several scholarly, practical, and philosophical sources; and his discussions of books like *Homo Ludens* by Johan Huizinga, *Man, Play, and Games* by Roger Caillois, and the paper "The Game Game" by Mary Midgley are both smart and accessible.

> Chris Bateman, *Imaginary Games* (Washington, USA: Zero Books, 2011)

Level Up! by Scott Rogers

Rogers distills his knowledge from many years in the trenches of game development into a book that is fun, approachable, and very practical. When he and I co-taught a level design class, this was the textbook that we used. Rogers is also a comic book artist, and his book is full of humorous and helpful illustrations that drive home the concepts of level, character, narrative, and many other aspects of design.

> Scott Rogers, *Level up!: The Guide to Great Video Game Design* (Chichester, UK: Wiley, 2010)

Our Digital Prototyping Environment: Unity

All the digital game examples in this book are based on the Unity Game Engine and the C# programming language. I have taught students to develop digital games and interactive experiences for more than a decade, and in my experience, Unity is—by far—the best environment that I have found for learning to develop games. I have also found that C# is the best initial language for game prototypers to learn. Some other tools out there are easier to learn and require no real programming (Game Maker and Game Salad are two examples), but Unity allows you much more flexibility and performance in a package that is basically free (the free version of Unity includes nearly all the capabilities of the paid version, and it is the version used throughout this book). If you want to actually learn to program games, Unity is the engine you want to use.

Similarly, some programming languages are a little more approachable than C#. In the past, I have taught my students both ActionScript and JavaScript. However, C# is the one language I have used that continually impresses me with its flexibility and feature set. Learning C# means learning not only programming but also good programming practices. Languages such as JavaScript allow a lot of sloppy behaviors that I have found actually lead to slower development. C# keeps you honest (via things like strongly typed variables), and that honesty will not only make you a better programmer but will also result in your being able to code more quickly (for example, strong variable typing enables very robust code hinting and auto-completion, which makes coding faster and more accurate).

Who This Book Is For

There are many books about game design, and there are many books about programming. This book seeks to fill the gap between the two. As game development technologies like Unity become more ubiquitous, it is increasingly important that game designers have the ability to sketch their design ideas not only on paper but also through working digital prototypes. This book exists to help you learn to do just that:

- **If you're interested in game design but have never programmed,** this book is perfect for you. Part I introduces you to several practical theories of game design and presents you with the practices that can help you develop and refine your design ideas. Part II teaches you how to program from nothing to understanding object-oriented class hierarchies. Since I became a college professor, the majority of my classes have focused on teaching nonprogrammers how to program games. I have distilled all of my experience doing so into Part II of this book. Part III takes you through the process of developing eight different game prototypes across several different game genres. Each demonstrates fast methods to get from concept to working digital prototype. Lastly, the appendices will explain specific game development and programming concepts in-depth and guide you to resources to learn more once you've finished the book. This in-depth content was moved largely to Appendix B, "Useful Concepts," so that you could continue to use that section of the book as a reference in the years to come.

- **If you're a programmer who is interested in game design,** Parts I and III of this book will be of most interest to you. Part I introduces you to several practical theories for game design and presents you with the practices that can help you develop and refine your design ideas. You can skim Part II, which introduces C# and how it is used in Unity. If you are familiar with other programming languages, C# looks like C++ but has the advanced features of Java. Part III takes you through the process of developing eight different game prototypes across several different game genres. Game development in Unity is very different from what you may be used to from other game engines. Many elements of development are taken care of outside of the code. Each prototype will demonstrate the style of development that works best in Unity to get from concept to working digital prototype quickly. You will also want to look carefully at Appendix B, which is full of detailed information about various development concepts and is arranged as a reference that you can return to later.

Conventions

This book maintains several writing conventions to help make the text more easily understandable.

Any place that specific button names, menu commands, or other multi-word nouns are introduced in the text, they will be listed in *italics*. This includes terms like the *Main Camera* Game Object. An example menu command is *Edit > Project Settings > Physics*, which would instruct you to select the *Edit* menu from the menu bar, choose the *Project Settings* sub-menu, and then select *Physics*.

Book Elements

The book includes several different types of asides that feature useful or important information that does not fit in the flow of the regular body text.

> note
>
> Callouts in this format are for information that is useful but not critical. Information in notes will often be an interesting aside to the main text that provides a little bit more info about the topic.

> **tip**
> This element provides additional information that is related to the book content and can help you as you explore the concepts in the book.

> **warning**
> **BE CAREFUL**   Warnings cover information about things that you need to be aware of to avoid mistakes or other pitfalls.

> **SIDEBAR**
>
> The sidebar is for discussions of longer topics that are important to the text but should be considered separately from it.

Code

Several conventions apply to the code samples in this book. When specific elements from the code listing are placed in regular paragraph text, they appear in a `monospaced` font. The variable `variableOnNewLine` from the following code listing is an example of this.

Code listings also utilize a monospaced font and appear as follows:

```
1 public class SampleClass {
2     public GameObject       variableOnExistingLine;          // 1
3     public GameObject       variableOnNewLine;               // 2
4 }
```

1 Code listings are often annotated; in this case, additional information about the line marked with `// 1` would appear in this first annotation.
2 Some code listings will be expansions on code that you've already written or that already exists in the C# script file for another reason. In this case, the old lines will be at `normal weight`, and the new lines will be at **`bold weight`**.

Most of the code listings in the first two parts of the book will include line numbers (as seen in the preceding listing). You do not need to type the line numbers when entering the code into MonoDevelop (it will automatically number all lines). In the final part of the book, there are no line numbers due to the size of the code listings.

Book Website

The website for this book includes all of the files referenced in the chapters, lecturer notes, and finished versions of each tutorial prototype. It is available at **http://book.prototools.net**.

ACKNOWLEDGMENTS

A tremendous number of people deserve to be thanked here. First and foremost, I want to thank my wife, Melanie, whose help and feedback on my chapters throughout the entire process improved the book tremendously. I also want to thank my family for their many years of support, with special thanks to my father for teaching me how to program as a child.

As a new author, there were several people at Pearson who provided support to me and shepherded me through this process. Chief among them were Chris Zahn, Laura Lewin, Olivia Basegio, Elaine Wiley, and Keith Cline who each demonstrated laudable patience in working with me. I also had the support of some fantastic technical reviewers: Marc Destefano, Charles Duba, and Margaret Moser. Their keen eyes and minds found many places in the original text that could be clarified or improved.

I would also like to thank all the educators who have taught me and worked as my colleagues. Special thanks go to Dr. Randy Pausch and Jesse Schell. Though I had worked as a professor and game designer before meeting them, they each had a profound effect on my understanding of design and education. I also owe tremendous thanks to Tracy Fullerton, Mark Bolas, and Scott Fisher, who were friends and mentors to me in the years I taught at the University of Southern California's Interactive Media and Games Division. There were also many other brilliant faculty and friends at USC who helped me to flesh out the ideas in this book, including Adam Liszkiewicz, William Huber, Richard Lemarchand, Scott Rogers, Vincent Diamante, Sam Roberts, and Logan Ver Hoef.

Many of my friends in the industry have also helped me by giving me suggestions for the book and feedback on the ideas presented therein. These included Michael Sellers, Nicholas Fortugno, Jenova Chen, Zac Pavlov, Joseph Stevens, and many others.

Thanks as well to all the fantastic students whom I have taught over the past decade. It is you who inspired me to want to write this book and who convinced me that there was something important and different about the way that I was teaching game development. Every day that I teach, I find myself inspired and invigorated by your creativity, intelligence, and passion.

Finally, I would like to thank you. Thank you for purchasing this book and for your interest in developing games. I hope that this book helps you get started, and I would love to see what you make with the knowledge you gain here.

ABOUT THE AUTHOR

Jeremy Gibson is a lecturer teaching computer game design for the Electrical Engineering and Computer Science department at the University of Michigan Ann Arbor and is the founder of ExNinja Interactive, LLC. From 2009 to 2013, he was an Assistant Professor teaching game design and protyping for the Interactive Media and Games Division of the University of Southern California's School of Cinematic Arts, which was the number one game design school in North America throughout his tenure there. Jeremy serves the IndieCade independent game festival as the Chair for Education and Advancement, where he is responsible for the IndieXchange and GameU conference tracks, and he has spoken at the Game Developers Conference every year since 2009.

Jeremy earned a Master of Entertainment Technology degree from Carnegie Mellon University's Entertainment Technology Center in 2007 and a Bachelor of Science degree in Radio, Television, and Film from the University of Texas at Austin in 1999. Jeremy has worked as a programmer and prototyper for companies such as Human Code and froq design, has taught classes for Great Northern Way Campus (in Vancouver, BC), Texas State University, the Art Institute of Pittsburgh, Austin Community College, and the University of Texas at Austin, and has worked for Walt Disney Imagineering, Maxis, and Electronic Arts/Pogo.com, among others. While in graduate school, his team created the game *Skyrates*, which won the Silver Gleemax Award at the 2008 Independent Games Festival. Jeremy also apparently has the distinction of being the first person to ever teach game design in Costa Rica.

PART I

GAME DESIGN AND PAPER PROTOTYPING

CHAPTER 1

THINKING LIKE A DESIGNER

And thus your journey begins. This chapter presents the basic theories of design upon which the rest of the book is built. In this chapter, you will also encounter your first game design exercise and learn more about the underlying philosophy of this book.

You Are a Game Designer

As of this moment, you are a game designer, and I want you to say it out loud:[1]

> I am a game designer.

It's okay. You can say it out loud, even if other people can hear you. In fact, according to psychologist Robert Cialdini's book *Influence: The Psychology of Persuasion,*[2] if other people hear you commit to something, you're more likely to follow through. So, go ahead and post it to Facebook, tell your friends, tell your family:

> I am a game designer.

But, what does it mean to be a game designer? This book will help you answer that question and will give you the tools to start making your own games. Let's start with a design exercise.

Bartok: A Game Exercise

I first saw this exercise used by game designer Malcolm Ryan as part of a Game Design Workshop session at the Foundations of Digital Gaming conference. The goal of this exercise is to demonstrate how even a simple change to the rules of a game can have a massive effect on the experience of playing the game.

Bartok is a simple game played with a regular deck of playing cards that is very similar to the commercial game *Uno*. In the best case scenario, you would play this game with three friends who are also interested in game design; however, I've also made a digital version of the game so you can play the game solo. Either the paper or digital version will work fine for our purposes.[3]

GETTING THE DIGITAL VERSION OF *BARTOK*

There are two good ways to go about getting the digital version of this game. The first and simplest is to simply visit the website for this book:

> http://book.prototools.net

You will find the digital version of *Bartok* in the section of the website devoted to Chapter 1.

---

[1] I thank my former professor Jesse Schell for asking me to make this statement publicly in a class full of people. He also includes this request in his book *The Art of Game Design: A Book of Lenses* (Boca Raton, FL: CRC Press, 2008).

[2] Robert B. Cialdini. *Influence: The Psychology of Persuasion.* (New York: Morrow, 1993).

[3] The card images in this book and in the digital card games presented in the book are based on Vectorized Playing Cards 1.3, Copyright 2011, Chris Aguilar. Licensed under LGPL 3—http://www.gnu.org/copyleft/lesser.html, http://code.google.com/p/vectorized-playing-cards/.

The second way to get the game is to download the Unity build file for the game and compile it on your own machine. Although this isn't a very difficult task, you should probably only do so if you already know your way around Unity. If you are unfamiliar with Unity at this point, you can wait to download the build files until you've read the section of the book that covers digital prototyping.

The build files for the *Bartok* game are available at the same location:

   http://book.prototools.net

Later in this book, you will learn the steps to build a simple digital prototype for *Bartok* (in Chapter 32, "Prototype 5: *Bartok*").

You can, of course, also just grab a standard deck of playing cards and two to four friends and play the game in person, which will allow you to talk with your friends about the feel of the game and the changes you want to make to it.

Objective

Be the first player to get rid of all the cards in your hand.

Getting Started

Here are the basic rules for *Bartok*:

1. Start with a regular deck of playing cards. Remove the Jokers, leaving you with 52 cards (13 of each suit ranked Ace–King).
2. Shuffle the deck and deal seven cards to each player.
3. Place the rest of the cards face-down in a draw pile.
4. Pick the top card from the draw pile and place it on the table face-up to start the discard pile.
5. Starting with the player to the left of the dealer and proceeding clockwise, each player must play a card onto the discard pile if possible, and if she cannot play a card, the player must draw a single card from the draw pile (see Figure 1.1).
6. A player may play a card onto the discard pile if the card is either:
   a. The same suit as the top card of the discard pile. (For example, if the top card of the discard pile is a 2 of Clubs (2C), any other Club may be played onto the discard pile.)
   b. The same rank as the top card of the discard pile. (For example, if the top card of the discard pile is a 2C, any other 2 may be played onto the discard pile.)
7. The first player to successfully get rid of all her cards wins.

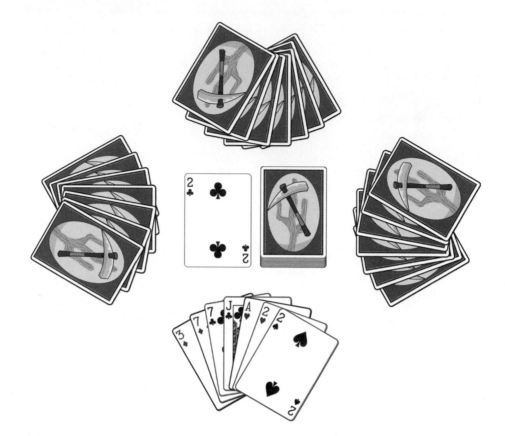

Figure 1.1   The initial layout of *Bartok*. In the situation shown, the player can choose to play any one of the cards highlighted with blue borders (7C, JC, 2H, 2S).

Playtesting

Try playing the game a couple of times to get a feel for it. Be sure to shuffle the cards thoroughly between each playthrough. Games will often result in a somewhat sorted discard pile, and without a good shuffle, subsequent games may have results weighted by the nonrandom card distribution.

> **tip**
>
> **DEBLOCKING**   *Deblocking* is the term for strategies used to break up blocks of cards (that is, groups of similar cards). In *Bartok*, each successful game ends with all the cards sorted into blocks of the same suit and blocks of the same rank. If you don't deblock those groups, the subsequent game will end much faster because players are more likely to be dealt cards that match each other.

Here are some standard strategies for deblocking a deck of cards if standard shuffling doesn't work:

- Deal the cards into several different piles. Then shuffle these piles together.

- Deal the cards out face-down into a large, spread-out pool. Then use both hands to move the cards around almost like mixing water. This is how dominoes are usually shuffled, and it can help break up your card blocks. Then gather all the cards into a single stack.

- Play 52 Pickup: Throw all the cards on the floor and pick them up.

According to mathematician and magician Persi Diaconis, seven good riffle shuffles should be sufficient for nearly all games;[4] if you run into issues, though, some of these deblocking strategies can help.

Analysis: Asking the Right Questions

After each playtest, it's important to ask the right questions, and each game will require slightly different questions, although many of them will be based on these general guidelines:

- Is the game of the appropriate difficulty for the intended audience? Is it too difficult, too easy, or just right?
- Is the outcome of the game based more on strategy or chance? Does randomness play too strong a role in the game, or, alternatively, is the game too deterministic so that once one player is in the lead, the other players don't have any chance to catch up?
- Does the game have meaningful, interesting decisions? When it's your turn, do you have several choices, and is the decision between those choices an interesting one?
- Is the game interesting when it's not your turn? Do you have any effect on the other players' turns, or do their turns have any immediate effect on you?

We could ask many other questions, but these are some of the most common.

Take a moment to think about your answers to these questions and write them down. If you're playing the paper version of this game with other human players, it's worthwhile to ask them to write down their own answers to the questions individually and then discuss them after they're written; this keeps their responses from being influenced by other players.

---

4   Persi Diaconis, "Mathematical Developments from the Analysis of Riffle Shuffling," *Groups, Combinatorics and Geometry,* edited by Ivanov, Liebeck, and Saxl. *World Scientific* (2003): 73–97. Also available online at http://statweb.stanford.edu/~cgates/PERSI/papers/Riffle.pdf.

Modifying the Rules

As you'll see throughout this book, the secret to good game design is iteration:

1. Decide how you want the game to feel during play.
2. Change the rules to achieve that feeling.
3. Play the game.
4. Analyze how the rule changes affected the feel of the game.
5. Return to step #1 and iteratively repeat this process until you're happy with the game.

Iterative design is this process of deciding on a small change to the game design, implementing that change, playtesting the game, analyzing how the change affected the gameplay, and then starting the process over again by deciding on another small change.

For the *Bartok* example, why don't you start by picking one of the following three rule changes and playtesting it:

- **Rule 1:** If a player plays a 2, the person to her left must draw two cards instead of playing.
- **Rule 2:** If any player has a card that matches the number and color (red or black) of the top card, she may announce "Match card!" and play it out of turn. Play then continues with the player to the left of the one who just played the out-of-turn card. This can lead to players having their turns skipped.

  For example: The first player plays a 3C (three of Clubs). The third player has the 3S, so she calls "Match card!" and plays the 3S on top of the 3C out-of-turn, skipping the second player's turn. Play then continues with the fourth player.
- **Rule 3:** A player must announce "Last card!" when she has only one card left. If someone else calls it first, she must draw two cards (bringing her total number of cards to three).

Choose only one of the rule changes from the previous listing and play the game through a couple of times with the new rule. Then have each player write their answers to the four playtest questions. You should also try playing with another one of the rules (although I would recommend still only using one of them at a time).

If you're playing the digital version of the game, you can use the check boxes on the menu screen to choose various game options.

> **warning**
>
> **WATCH OUT FOR PLAYTESTING FLUKES**   A weird shuffle or other external factor can sometimes cause a single play through the game to feel really different from the others. This is known as a *fluke*, and you want to be careful not to make game design decisions based on flukes. If a new rule seems to affect the game feel in a very unexpected way, be sure to play through the game multiple times with that rule to make sure you're not experiencing a fluke.

Analysis: Comparing the Rounds

Now that you've played through the game with some different rule options, it's time to analyze the results from the different rounds. Look back over your notes and see how each different rule set felt to play. As you experienced, even a simple rule change can greatly change the feel of the game. Here are some common reactions to the previously listed rules:

- **The original rules**

   Many players find the original version of the game to be pretty boring. There are no interesting choices to make, and as the players remove cards from their hands, the number of possible choices dwindles as well, often leaving the player with only one valid choice for most of the later turns of the game. The game seems to be largely based on chance, and players have no real reason to pay attention to other players' turns because they don't really have any way of affecting each other.

- **Rule 1:** *If a player plays a 2, the person to her left must draw two cards instead of playing.*

   This rule allows players to directly affect each other, which generally increases interest in the game. However, whether a player has 2s is based entirely on luck, and each player only really has the ability to affect the player on her left, which often seems unfair. However, this does make other players' turns a bit more interesting because players can actually affect each other.

- **Rule 2:** *If any player has a card that matches the number and color (red or black) of the top card, she may announce "Match card!" and play it out of turn. Play then continues with the player to the left of the one who just played the out-of-turn card.*

   This rule often has the greatest effect on player attention. Because any player has the opportunity to interrupt another player's turn, all players tend to pay a lot more attention to each other's turns. Games played with this rule often feel more dramatic and exciting than those played with the other rules.

- **Rule 3:** *A player must announce "Last card!" when she has only one card left. If someone else calls it first, she must draw two cards.*

   This rule only comes into play near the end of the game, so it doesn't have any effect on the majority of gameplay, however, it does change how players behave at the end. This can lead to some interesting tension as players try to jump in and say "last card" before the player who is down to only one card. This is a common rule in both domino and card games where the players are trying to empty everything from their hands because it gives other players a chance to catch up to the lead player if the leader forgets about the rule.

Designing for the Game Feel That You Want

Now that you've seen the effects of a few different rules on *Bartok*, it's time to do your job as a designer and make the game better. First, decide on the feel that you want the game to have: Do you want it to be exciting and cutthroat? Do you want it to be leisurely and slow? Do you want it to be based more on strategy or chance?

Once you have a general idea of how you want the game to feel, think about the rules that you tried out and try to come up with additional rules that can push the feel of the game in the direction that you wish. Here are some tips to keep in mind as you design new rules for the game:

- Change only one thing in between each playtest. If you change (or even tweak) a number of rules between each play through the game, it can be difficult to determine which rule is affecting the game in what way. Keep your changes simple, and you'll be better able to understand the effect that each is having.

- The bigger change you make, the more playtests it will take to understand how it changes the game feel. If you only make a subtle change to the game, one or two plays can tell you a lot about how that affects the feel. However, if it's a major rule change, you will need to test it more times to avoid being tricked by a fluke game.

- Change a number and you change the experience. Even a seemingly small change can have a huge effect on gameplay. For instance, think about how much faster this game would be if there were two discard piles to choose from or if the players started with five cards instead of seven.

Of course, adding new rules is a lot easier to do when playing the card game in person with friends than when working with the digital prototype. That's one of the reasons that paper prototypes can be so important, even when you're designing digital games. The first part of this book discusses both paper and digital design, but most of the examples and design exercises are done with paper games because they can be so much faster to develop and test than digital games.

The Definition of *Game*

Before moving too much further into design and iteration, we should probably clarify what we're talking about when we use terms such as *game* and *game design*. Many very smart people have tried to accurately define the word game. Here are a few of them in chronological order:

- In his 1978 book *The Grasshopper,* Bernard Suits (who was a professor of philosophy at the University of Waterloo) declares that "a game is the voluntary attempt to overcome unnecessary obstacles."[5]

- Game design legend Sid Meier says that "a game is a series of interesting decisions."

- In *Game Design Workshop,* Tracy Fullerton defines a game as "a closed, formal system that engages players in a structured conflict and resolves its uncertainty in an unequal outcome."[6]

---

[5] Bernard Suits, *The Grasshopper* (Toronto: Toronto University Press, 1978), 56.

[6] Fullerton, Tracy, Christopher Swain, and Steven Hoffman. *Game Design Workshop: A Playcentric Approach to Creating Innovative Games*, 2nd ed. (Boca Raton, FL: Elsevier Morgan Kaufmann, 2008), 43.

- In *The Art of Game Design,* Jesse Schell playfully examines several definitions for game and eventually decides on "a game is a problem-solving activity, approached with a playful attitude."[7]
- In the book *Game Design Theory,* Keith Burgun presents a much more limited definition of game: "a system of rules in which agents compete by making ambiguous, endogenously meaningful decisions."[8, 9]

As you can see, all of these are compelling and correct in their own way. Perhaps even more important than the individual definition is the insight that it gives us into each author's intent when crafting that definition.

Bernard Suits's Definition

In addition to the short definition "a game is the voluntary attempt to overcome unnecessary obstacles," Suits also offers a longer, more robust version: "To play a game is to attempt to achieve a specific state of affairs, using only means permitted by rules, where the rules prohibit use of more efficient in favor of less efficient means, and where the rules are accepted just because they make possible such activity." Throughout his book, Suits proposes and refutes various attacks on this definition; and having read the book, I am certainly willing to say that he has found the definition of "game" that most accurately matches the way that the word is used in day-to-day life.

However, it's also important to realize that this definition was crafted in 1978, and even though digital games and roleplaying games existed at this time, Suits was either unaware of them or intentionally ignored them. In fact, in Chapter 9 of *The Grasshopper,* Suits laments that there is no kind of game with rules for dramatic play through which players could burn off dramatic energy (much like children can burn off excess athletic energy via play of any number of different sports).[10]

Although this is a small point, it gets at exactly what is missing from this definition: Whereas Suits's definition of game is an accurate definition of the word, it offers nothing to designers seeking to craft good games for others.

For an example of what I mean, take a moment to play Jason Rohrer's fantastic game *Passage*: http://hcsoftware.sourceforge.net/passage/ (see Figure 1.2). The game only takes 5 minutes to

---

7   Schell, Jesse, *Art of Game Design: A Book of Lenses* (Boca Raton, FL: CRC Press, 2008), 37.

8   Burgun, Keith. *Game Design Theory: A New Philosophy for Understanding Games* (Boca Raton, FL: A K Peters/CRC Press, 2013), 10, 19.

9   *Endogenous* means inherent to or arising from the internal systems of a thing, so "endogenously meaningful decisions" are those decisions that actually affect the game state and change the outcome. Choosing the color of your avatar's clothing in *Farmville* is not endogenously meaningful, whereas choosing the color of your clothing in *Metal Gear Solid 4* is because the color of your clothing affects whether your avatar is visible to enemies.

10 Suits, *Grasshopper,* 95.

play, and it does a fantastic job of demonstrating the power that even short games can have. Try playing through it a couple of times.

Figure 1.2 *Passage* by Jason Rohrer (released December 13, 2007)

Suits's definition will tell you that yes, this is a game. In fact, it is specifically an "open game," which he defines as a game that has as its sole goal the continuance of the game.[11] In *Passage*, the goal is to continue to play for as long as possible...or is it? *Passage* has several potential goals, and it's up to the player to choose which of these she wants to achieve. These goals could include the following:

- Moving as far to the right as possible before dying (exploration)
- Earning as many points as possible by finding treasure chests (achievement)
- Finding a partner (socialization)

The point of *Passage* as an artistic statement is that each of these can be a goal in life, and the three goals are mutually exclusive to some extent. If you get married early in the game, it becomes more difficult to get treasure chests because the two of you are unable to enter areas that could be entered singly. If you choose to seek treasure, you will spend your time exploring the vertical space of the world and won't be able to see the different scenery to the right. If you choose to move as far to the right as possible, you won't rack up nearly as much treasure.

In this incredibly simple game, Rohrer exposes a few of the fundamental decisions that every one of us must make in life and demonstrates how even early decisions can have a major effect on the rest of our lives. The important thing here is that he is giving players choice and demonstrating to them that their choices matter.

This is an example of the first of a number of designer's goals that I introduce in this book: *experiential understanding*. Whereas a linear story like a book can encourage empathy with a character by exposing the reader to the character's life and the decisions that she has made, games can allow players not only to understand the outcome of decisions but also to be complicit in that outcome by giving the player the power and the responsibility of decision and then showing her the outcome wrought by her decisions. Chapter 8, "Design Goals," explores these in much greater depth.

---

[11] Suits contrasts these with closed games, which have a specific goal (for example, crossing a finish line in a race or ridding yourself of all your cards in *Bartok*). Suits's example of an open game is the games of make-believe that children play.

Sid Meier's Definition

By stating that "a game is a series of interesting decisions," Meier is saying very little about the definition of the word *game* (there are many, many things that could be categorized as a series of interesting decisions and yet are not games) and quite a bit about what he personally believes makes for a good game. As the designer of games such as *Pirates*, *Civilization*, *Alpha Centauri*, and many more, Sid Meier is one of the most successful game designers alive, and he has consistently produced games that presented players with interesting decisions. This, of course, raises the question of what makes a decision *interesting*. An interesting decision is generally one where:

- The player has multiple valid options from which to choose
- Each option has both positive and negative potential consequences
- The outcome of each option is predictable but not guaranteed

This brings up the second of our designer's goals: to create *interesting decisions*. If a player is presented with a number of choices, but one choice is obviously superior to the others, the experience of deciding which to choose doesn't actually exist. If a game is designed well, players will often have multiple choices from which to choose, and the decision will often be a tricky one.

Tracy Fullerton's Definition

As she states in her book, Tracy is much more concerned with giving designers tools to make better games than she is with the philosophical definition of *game*. Accordingly, her definition of a game as "a closed, formal system that engages players in a structured conflict and resolves its uncertainty in an unequal outcome" is not only a good definition of *game* but also a list of elements that designers can modify in their games:

- **Formal elements:** The elements that differentiate a game from other types of media: rules, procedures, players, resources, objectives, boundaries, conflict, and outcome.
- **Dynamic systems:** Methods of interaction that evolve as the game is played.
- **Conflict structure:** The ways in which players interact with each other.
- **Uncertainty:** The interaction between randomness, determinism, and player strategy.
- **Unequal outcome:** How does the game end? Do players win, lose, or something else?

Another critical element in Fullerton's book is her continual insistence on *actually making games*. The only way to become a better game designer is to make games. Some of the games you'll design will probably be pretty awful—some of mine certainly have been—but even designing a terrible game is a learning process, and every game you create will improve your design skills and help you better understand how to make great games.

Jesse Schell's Definition

Schell defines a game as "a problem-solving activity, approached with a playful attitude." This is similar in many ways to Suits's definition, and like that definition, it approaches the definition of game from the point of view of the player; it is the playful attitude of the player that makes something a game. In fact, Suits argues in his book that two people could both be involved in the same activity, and to one, it would be a game, whereas to the other, it would not be. His example is a foot race where one runner is just running because he wants to take part in the race and where the other knows that at the finish line there is a bomb she must defuse before it explodes. According to Suits, although the two runners would both be running in the same foot race, the one who was simply racing would follow the rules of the race because of what Suits calls his lusory attitude. The other runner would break the rules of the game the first chance she got because she would have a serious attitude (as is required to defuse a bomb) and would not be engaged in the game. *Ludus* is the Latin word for play, so Suits proposes the term *lusory attitude* to describe the attitude of one who willingly takes part in playing a game. It is because of the lusory attitude that players will happily follow the rules of the game even though there may be an easier way to achieve the stated goal of the game (what Suits would call the pre-lusory goal). For example the stated goal of golf is to get the golf ball into the cup, but there are many easier ways to do so than to stand hundreds of yards away and hit the ball with a bent stick. When people have a lusory attitude, they set challenges for themselves just for the joy of overcoming them.

So, another design goal is to encourage a *lusory attitude*. Your game should be designed to encourage players to enjoy the limitations placed on them by the rules. Think about why each rule is there and how it changes the player experience. If a game is balanced well and has the proper rules, players will enjoy the limitations of the rules rather than feel exasperated by them.

Keith Burgun's Definition

Burgun's definition of a game as "a system of rules in which agents compete by making ambiguous, endogenously meaningful decisions" is his attempt to narrow the meaning of game down to something that can be better examined and understood in order to push the discourse on games forward from the rut that he feels it has fallen into. The core of this definition is that the player is making choices and that those choices are both ambiguous (the player doesn't know exactly what the outcome of the choice will be) and endogenously meaningful (the choice is meaningful because it has a noticeable effect upon the game system).

Burgun's definition is intentionally limited and purposefully excludes several of the things that many people think of as games, including foot races and other competitions based on physical skill as well as *reflective* games like *The Graveyard*, by Tale of Tales, in which the player experiences wandering through a graveyard as an old woman. Both of these are excluded because the decisions in them lack ambiguity and endogenous meaning.

Burgun chooses such a limited definition because he wants to get down to the essence of games and what makes them unique. In doing so, he makes several good points, including his statement that whether an experience is fun has little to do with the question of whether it is a game. Even a terribly boring game is still a game; it's just a bad game.

In my discussions with other designers, I have found that there can be a lot of contention about this question of what types of things should fall under the term *game*. Games are a medium that has experienced a tremendous amount of growth, expansion, and maturation over the last couple of decades, and the current explosion of independent game development has only hastened the pace. Today, more people with disparate voices and backgrounds are contributing work to the field of games than ever before, and as a result, the definition of the medium is expanding, which is understandably bothersome to some people because it can be seen as blurring the lines of what is considered a *game*. Burgun's response to this is his concern that it is difficult to rigorously advance a medium if we lack a good definition of what the medium is.

Why Care About the Definition of Game?

In his 1953 book *Philisophical Investigations,* Ludwig Wittgenstein proposed that the term *game* as it is used colloquially had come at that time to refer to several very different things that shared some traits (which he likened to a family resemblance) but couldn't be encapsulated in a single definition. In 1978, Bernard Suits attacked this idea by using his book, *The Grasshopper,* to argue very stringently for the specific definition of game that you read earlier in this chapter. However, as Chris Bateman points out in his book *Imaginary Games,* though Wittgenstein used the word *game* as his example, he was really trying to make a larger point: Words are created to define things rather than things being created to meet the definition of words.

In 1974 (between the publications of *Philosophical Investigations* and *The Grasshopper*), the philosopher Mary Midgley published a paper titled "The Game Game" in which she explored and refuted the "family resemblance" claim by Wittgenstein not by arguing for a specific definition of game herself but instead by exploring why the word *game* existed. In her paper, she agrees with Wittgenstein that the word *game* came into being long after games existed, but she makes the statement that words like *game* are not defined by the *things* that they encompass but instead by the *needs* that they meet. As she states

> Something can be accepted as a chair provided it is properly made for sitting on, whether it consists of a plastic balloon, a large blob of foam, or a basket slung from the ceiling. Provided you understand the need you can see whether it has the right characteristics, and aptness for that need *is* what chairs have in common.[12]

In her paper, Midgley seeks to understand some of the needs that games fulfill. She completely rejects the idea that games are closed systems by both citing many examples of game outcomes that have effects beyond the game and pointing out that games cannot be closed because humans have a reason for entering into them. To her, that reason is paramount. The following are just a few reasons for playing games:

- **Humans desire structured conflict:** As Midgley points out, "The Chess Player's desire is not for general abstract intellectual activity, curbed and frustrated by a particular set of rules. It is a desire for a particular kind of intellectual activity, whose channel is the rules of chess." As Suits pointed out in his definition, the rules that limit behavior are there precisely because the challenge of those limitations is appealing to players.

---

[12] Mary Midgley. "The Game Game," *Philosophy 49,* no. 189 (1974): 231–53.

- **Humans desire the experience of being someone else:** We are all acutely aware that we have but one life to live (or at least one at a time), and play can allow us to experience another life. Just as a game of *Call of Duty* allows a player to pretend to experience the life of a soldier, so too does *The Graveyard* allow the player to pretend to experience the life of an old woman, and playing the role of Hamlet allows the actor to pretend to experience the life of a troubled Danish prince.

- **Humans desire excitement:** Much popular media is devoted to this desire for excitement, be it action films, courtroom dramas, or romance novels. The thing that makes games different in this regard is that the player is actively taking part in the excitement rather than vicariously absorbing it as is the case for the majority of linear media. As a player, you aren't watching someone else be chased by zombies, you're being chased yourself.

Midgley found it critical to understand the needs that are fulfilled by games in order to understand both their importance in society and the positive and negative effects that games can have on the people who play them. Both Suits and Midgley spoke about the potentially addictive qualities of games in the 1970s, long before video games became ubiquitous and concern emerged about players becoming addicted to massively multiplayer online games (MMOGs). As game designers, it is useful for us to understand these needs and respect their power.

The Nebulous Nature of Definitions

As Midgley pointed out, it is useful to think of the word *game* as being defined by the need that it fills. However, she also stated that a chess player doesn't want to play just any kind of game; he specifically wants to play chess. Not only is it difficult to come up with an all-encompassing definition for game, it's also true that the same word will mean different things to different people at different times. When I say that I'm going to play a game, I usually mean a console or video game; when my wife says the same thing, though, she usually means *Scrabble* or another word game. When my parents say they want to play a game, it means something like Alan R. Moon's *Ticket to Ride* (a board game that is interesting but doesn't require players to be overly competitive with each other), and my in-laws usually mean a game of cards or dominoes when they use the word. Even within our family, the word has great breadth.

The meaning of the word *game* is also constantly evolving. When the first computer games were created, no one could have possibly imagined the multi-billion-dollar industry that we now have or the rise of the fantastic indie renaissance that we've seen over the past several years. All that they knew was that these things people were doing on computers were kind of like tabletop war board games (I'm thinking of *Space War* here), and they were called "computer games" to differentiate them from the preexisting meanings of *game*.

The evolution of digital games was a gradual process with each new genre building in some way on the ones which had come before, and along the way, the term *game* expanded further and further to encompass all of them.

Now, as the art form matures, many designers are entering the field from various other disciplines and bringing with them their concepts about what can be created with the technologies and design methodologies that have been created to make digital games. (You may even be one of them.) As these new artists and designers enter the space, some of them are making things that are very different from what we think of as the stereotypical game. That's okay; in fact, I think it's fantastic! And, this isn't just my opinion. IndieCade, the international festival of independent games, seeks every year to find games that push the envelope of what is meant by *game*. According to Festival Chair Celia Pearce and Festival Director Sam Roberts, if an independent developer wants to call the interactive piece that she has created a game, IndieCade will accept it as one.[13]

Summary

After all these interwoven and sometimes contradictory definitions, you may be wondering why this book has spent so much time exploring the definition of the word *game*. I have to admit that in my day-to-day work as an educator and game designer, I don't spend a lot of time wrestling with the definitions of words. As Shakespeare points out, were a rose to be named something else, it would still smell as sweet, still have thorns, and still be a thing of fragile beauty. However, I believe that an understanding of these definitions can be critical to you as a designer in the following three ways:

- Definitions help you understand what people expect from your games. This proves especially true if you're working in a specific genre or for a specific audience. Understanding how your audience defines the term will help you to craft better games for them.

- Definitions can lead you to understand not only the core of the defined concept but also the periphery. As you read through this chapter, you encountered several different definitions by different people, and each had both a core and a periphery (i.e., games that fit the definition perfectly (the core) and games that just barely fit the definition (the periphery). The places where these peripheries don't mesh can be hints at some of the interesting areas to explore with a new game. For example, the area of disagreement between Fullerton and Midgley about whether a game is a closed system highlights the previously untracked ground that in the 2000s grew into alternate reality games (ARGs), a genre centered on perforating the closed magic circle of play.[14]

- Definitions can help you speak eloquently with others in the field. This chapter has more references and footnotes than any other in the book because I want you to be able to explore the philosophical understanding of games in ways that are beyond the scope of

---

[13] This was stated during the "Festival Submission Workshop" given by Celia Pearce and Sam Roberts at IndieCade East 2014 and is paraphrased on the IndieCade submissions website at: http://www.indiecade.com/submissions/faq/.

[14] The first large-scale ARG was *Majestic* (Electronic Arts, 2001), a game that would phone players in the middle of the night and send them faxes and emails. Smaller-scale ARGs include the game *Assassin*, which is played on many college campuses, where players can "assassinate" each other (usually with Nerf or water guns) any time that they are outside of classes. One of the fun aspects of these games is that they are always happening and can interfere with normal life.

this one book (especially since this book is really focused on the practicalities of actually making digital games). Following these footnotes and reading the source material can help improve the critical thinking that you do about games.

The Core Lessons of This Book

This book will actually teach you how to design a lot more than just games. In fact, it will teach you how to craft any kind of *interactive experience*. As I define it, an interactive experience is any experience created by a designer, inscribed into rules, media, or technology and decoded by people through play. That makes *interactive experience* a pretty expansive term. In fact, any time that you attempt to craft an experience for people—whether you're designing a game, planning a surprise birthday party, or even planning a wedding—you're using the same tools that you will learn as a game designer. The processes that you will learn in this book are more than just the proper way to approach game design. They are a meaningful way to approach any design problem, and the iterative process of design that is introduced in Chapter 7, "Acting Like a Designer," is *the* essential method for improving the quality of any design.

No one bursts forth from the womb as a brilliant game designer. My friend Chris Swain[15] is fond of saying that "Game design is 1% inspiration and 99% iteration," a play on the famous quote by Thomas Edison. He is absolutely correct, and one of the great things about game design (unlike the previously mentioned examples of the surprise party and the wedding) is that you get the chance to iterate on your designs, to playtest the game, make subtle tweaks, and play it again. With each different prototype you make, and with each iteration of those prototypes, your skills as a designer will improve. Similarly, once you reach the parts of this book that teach digital development, be sure to keep experimenting and iterating. The code samples and tutorials are designed to show you how to make a playable game prototype, but every tutorial in this book will end where your work as a designer should begin. Each one of these prototypes could be built into a larger, more robust, better balanced game, and I encourage you to do so.

Next Steps

Now that you've experienced a bit of game design and explored various definitions of *game,* it's time to move on to a more in-depth exploration of a few different analytical frameworks that game designers use to understand games and game design. The next chapter explores various frameworks that have been used over the past several years, and the chapter that follows synthesizes those into the framework used throughout the remainder of this book.

---

[15] Chris Swain co-wrote the first edition of *Game Design Workshop* with Tracy Fullerton and taught the class of the same name at the University of Southern California for many years. He is now an entrepreneur and independent game designer.

CHAPTER 2

GAME ANALYSIS FRAMEWORKS

Ludology is the fancy name for the study of games and game design. Over the past decade, ludologists have proposed various analytical frameworks for games to help them understand and discuss the structure and fundamental elements of games and the impact of games on players and society.

This chapter presents a few of the most commonly used frameworks that you should know as a designer.

The following chapter will synthesize ideas from these common frameworks into the Layered Tetrad framework used throughout this book.

Common Frameworks for Ludology

The frameworks presented in this chapter are:

- **MDA:** First presented by Robin Hunicke, Marc LeBlanc, and Robert Zubek, *MDA* stands for mechanics, dynamics, and aesthetics. It is the framework that is most familiar to designers working in the field and has important things to say about the difference in the relationships of the designer and the player to the game.

- **Formal, dramatic, and dynamic elements:** Presented by Tracy Fullerton and Chris Swain in the book *Game Design Workshop,* the FDD framework focuses on concrete analytical tools to help designers make better games and push their ideas further. It owes a lot to the history of film studies.

- **Elemental tetrad:** Presented by Jesse Schell in his book *The Art of Game Design,* the elemental tetrad splits games into four core elements: mechanics, aesthetics, story, and technology.

Each of these frameworks has benefits and drawbacks, and each has contributed to the Layered Tetrad presented in this book. They are covered here in the order that they were published.

MDA: Mechanics, Dynamics, and Aesthetics

First proposed at the Game Developers Conference in 2001 and formalized in the 2004 paper "MDA: A Formal Approach to Game Design and Game Research,"[1] MDA is the most commonly referenced analytical framework for ludology. The key elements of MDA are its definitions of mechanics, dynamics, and aesthetics; its understanding of the different perspectives from which the designer and player view a game; and its proposal that designers should first approach a game through the lens of aesthetics and then work back toward the dynamics and mechanics that will generate those aesthetics.

Definitions of Mechanics, Dynamics, and Aesthetics

One of the things that can be confusing about the three frameworks presented in this chapter is that they each reuse some of the same words, and each framework defines them slightly differently. MDA defines these terms as follows:[2]

---

[1] Robin Hunicke., Marc LeBlanc, and Robert Zubek, "MDA: A Formal Approach to Game Design and Game Research," in *Proceedings of the AAAI workshop on Challenges in Game AI Workshop* (San Jose, CA: AAAI Press, 2004), http://www.cs.northwestern.edu/~hunicke/MDA.pdf.

[2] Ibid. p. 2.

- **Mechanics:** The particular components of the game at the level of data representation and algorithms
- **Dynamics:** The runtime behavior of the mechanics acting on player inputs and each other's outputs over time
- **Aesthetics:** The desirable emotional responses evoked in the player when she interacts with the game system

Designer and Player Views of a Game

According to MDA, designers tend to consider games first in terms of the aesthetics, the emotions that the designer wants players to feel while playing the game. Once a designer has decided on the aesthetics, she will work backwards to the kinds of dynamic play that would prompt those feelings and finally to the gameplay mechanics that will create those dynamics. Players tend to view the game in the opposite way: first experiencing the mechanics (e.g., the written rules for the game), then experiencing the dynamics by playing the game, and finally (hopefully) experiencing the aesthetics that were initially envisioned by the designer (see Figure 2.1)

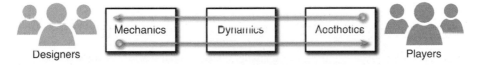

Figure 2.1   According to MDA, designers and players view a game from different directions.[3]

Design from Aesthetics to Dynamics to Mechanics

Based on these differing views, MDA proposes that designers should first approach a game by deciding on the emotional response (aesthetics) that they want to engender in the player and then work backward from that to create dynamics and mechanics that fit this chosen aesthetic.

For example, children's games are often designed to make each player feel like they're doing well and have a chance to win up until the very end. To have this feeling, players must feel that the end of the game is not inevitable and must be able to hope for good luck throughout the game. Keep this in mind when looking at the layout of a *Snakes and Ladders* game.

Snakes and Ladders

Snakes and Ladders is a board game for children that originated in ancient India where it was known as *Moksha Patamu*.[4] The game requires no skill and is entirely based on chance. Each

---

[3]   Adapted from: Hunicke, LeBlanc, and Zubek, "MDA: A Formal Approach to Game Design and Game Research," 2.

[4]   Jack Botermans, *The Book of Games: Strategy, Tactics, & History* (New York / London: Sterling, 2008), 19.

turn, a player rolls one die and moves *his* counter the number of spaces shown. Counters are not placed on the board initially, so if a player rolls a 1 on her first turn, she lands on the first space of the board. The goal is to be the first player to reach the end of the board (space 100). If a player lands on a space at the start of a green arrow (a ladder), she can move to the space at the end of the arrow (for example, a player landing on the 1 space can move her piece to the 38). If a player lands on the start of a red arrow (a snake), she must move her piece to the space at the end of the arrow (for example, a player landing on space 87 must move her piece all the way down to 24).

In the board layout depicted in Figure 2.2, the position of the snakes and ladders is very important. Here are just a few examples of how:

- There is a ladder from 1 to 38. This way, if a player rolls a 1 on her first turn (which would normally feel unlucky), the player can move immediately to 38 and gain a strong lead.
- There are three snakes in the final row of the game (93 to 73, 95 to 75, and 98 to 79). These serve to slow a player who is ahead of the others.
- The snake 87 to 24 and the ladder 28 to 84 form an interesting pair. If a player lands on 28 and moves to 84, her opponents can hope that she will subsequently land on 87 and be forced back to 24. Contrastingly, if a player lands on 87 and moves to 24, she can then hope to land on 28 and be moved back up to 84.

Each of these examples of snake and ladder placement are based on building hope in players and helping them to believe that dramatic changes in position are possible in the game. If the snakes and ladders were absent from the board, a player who was significantly behind the others would have little hope of catching up.

In this original version of the game, the desired aesthetic is for the players to experience hope, reversal of fortune, and excitement in a game in which the players never make any choices. The mechanic is the inclusion of the snakes and the ladders, and the dynamic is the intersection of the two where the act of the players encountering the mechanics leads to the aesthetic feelings of hope and excitement.

Modifying *Snakes and Ladders* for More Strategic Play

Young-adult and adult players are often looking for more challenge in games and want to feel that they have won a game not by chance but by making strategic choices along the way. Given that we as designers want the game to feel more strategic and intentional, it is possible to modify the rules (an element of the mechanics) without changing the board to achieve this aesthetic change. One example of this would be accomplished by adding the following rules:

1. Players each control two pieces instead of one.
2. On her turn, each player rolls two dice.
3. She may either use both dice for one piece or one die for each piece.
4. She may alternatively sacrifice one die and use the other to move one opponent's piece backward the number of spaces shown on the die.

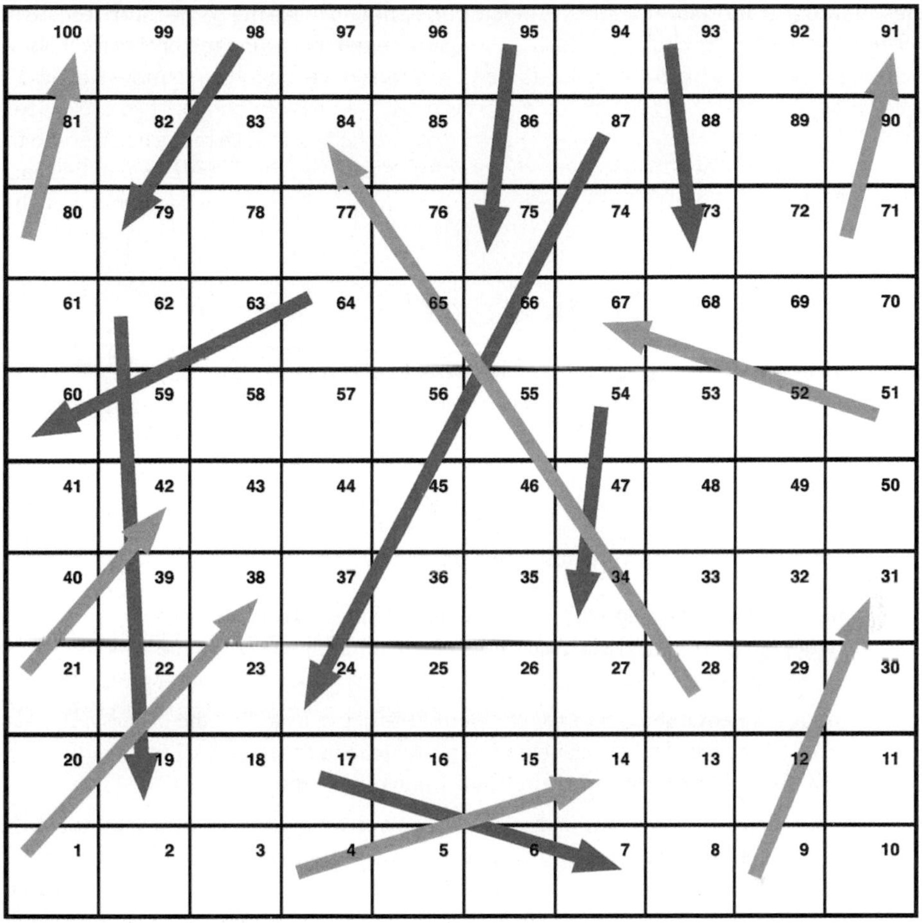

Figure 2.2   A layout for the classic game *Snakes and Ladders*

5. If a player's piece lands on the same space as any opponent's piece, the opponent's piece is knocked down one row (e.g., a piece knocked off of 48 would fall to 33, and a piece knocked off 33 would fall to 28 and then take the ladder up to 84!).

6. If a player's piece lands on the same space as her own other piece, the other piece is knocked up one row (e.g., a piece knocked off of 61 could be knocked up to 80 and then follow the ladder to 100!).

These changes allow for a lot more strategic decision making on the part of the players (a change to the dynamic play of the game). With rules 4 and 5 in particular, it is possible to directly hurt or help other players,[5] which can lead to players forming alliances or grudges.

---

[5] An example of how this could be used to help another player would be a situation in which knocking another player's piece down a row would land the piece on the beginning of a ladder.

Rules 1 through 3 also allow for more strategic decisions and make the game much less suscep-tible to chance. With the choice of which die to use for either piece and the option for a player to choose to not move her own pieces, a smart player will never be forced to move her own piece onto a snake.

This is but one of many demonstrations of how designers can modify mechanics to change dynamic play and achieve aesthetic goals.

Formal, Dramatic, and Dynamic Elements

Where MDA seeks to help both designers and critics better understand and discuss games, the framework of formal, dynamic, and dramatic elements,[6] or FDD, was created by Tracy Fuller-ton and Chris Swain to help students in their Game Design Workshop class at the University of Southern California more effectively design games.

This framework breaks games down into three types of elements:

- **Formal elements:** The elements that make games different from other forms of media or interaction and provide the structure of a game. Formal elements include things like rules, resources, and boundaries.
- **Dramatic elements:** The story and narrative of the game, including the premise. Dramatic elements tie the game together, help players understand the rules, and encourage the player to become emotionally invested in the outcome of the game.
- **Dynamic elements:** The game in motion. Once players turn the rules into actual game-play, the game has moved into dynamic elements. Dynamic elements include things like strategy, behavior, and relationships between game entities. It's important to note that this is related to the use of the term *dynamics* in MDA but is broader because it includes more than just the runtime behavior of the mechanics.

Formal Elements

Game Design Workshop proposes seven formal elements of games:

- **Player interaction pattern:** How do the players interact? Is the game single-player, one-on-one, team versus team, multilateral (multiple players versus each other, as is the case in most board games), unilateral (one player versus all the other players like some *Mario Party* minigames or the board game *Scotland Yard*), cooperative play, or even multiple individual players each working against the same system?

---

[6] Tracy Fullerton, *Game Design Workshop: A Playcentric Approach to Creating Innovative Games* (Burlington, MA: Morgan Kaufmann Publishers, 2008).

- **Objective:** What are the players trying to achieve in the game? When has someone won the game?

- **Rules:** Rules limit the players' actions by telling them what they may and may not do in the game. Many rules are explicitly written and included in the game, but others are implicitly understood by all players (e.g., no rule says so, but it's implicitly understood that you can't steal money from the bank in *Monopoly*).

- **Procedures:** The types of actions taken by the players in the game. A rule in *Snakes and Ladders* tells you to roll the die and move the number of spaces shown. The procedure dictated by the rule is the actual action of rolling the die and moving the piece. Procedures are often defined by the interaction of a number of rules. Some are also outside of the rules: Though it is not explicitly defined by the rules of poker, bluffing is an important procedure in the game.

- **Resources:** Resources are elements that have value in the game. These include things like money, health, items, and property.

- **Boundaries:** Where does the game end and reality begin? In his book *Homo Ludens*, Johan Huizinga introduces the term "magic circle" as one of several examples of a play-ground within which special rules apply. Katie Salen and Eric Zimmerman appropriated the term in their book *Rules of Play* and further defined a magic circle as a temporary world where the rules of the game apply rather than the rules of the ordinary world. Their use of the term gave rise to its common use in the gaming community today. In a sport like football or ice hockey, the magic circle is defined by the boundaries of the playing field; but in an alternative reality game like *I Love Bees* (the ARG for *Halo 2*), the boundaries are more vague.

- **Outcome:** How did the game end? There are both final and incremental outcomes in games. In a game of chess, the final outcome is that one player will win, and the other will lose. In a pen and paper roleplaying game like *Dungeons & Dragons*, there are incremental outcomes when a player defeats an enemy or gains a level, and even death is often not a final outcome since there are ways to resurrect players.

According to Fullerton, another way to look at formal elements is that the game ceases to exist when they are removed. If one removes the rules, outcome, or any of the others from a game, it really ceases to be a game.

Dramatic Elements

Dramatic elements help make the rules and resources more understandable to players and can give players greater emotional investment in the game.

Fullerton presents three types of dramatic elements:

- **Premise:** The basic story of the game world. In *Monopoly*, the premise is that each of the players is a real-estate developer trying to get a monopoly on corporate real estate in Atlantic City, New Jersey. In *Donkey Kong*, the player is trying to single-handedly save his girlfriend from a gorilla that has kidnapped her. The premise forms the basis around which the rest of the game's narrative is built.

- **Character:** Characters are the individuals around whom the story revolves, be it the nameless and largely undefined silent first-person protagonist of games like *Quake* or a character like Nathan Drake from the *Uncharted* series of games who is as deep and multidimensional as the lead characters in most movies. Unlike movies, where the goal of the director is to encourage the audience to have empathy for the film's protagonist, in games, the player actually *is* the protagonist character, and designers must choose whether the protagonist will act as an avatar for the player (conveying the emotions, desires, and intentions of the player into the world of the game and following the wishes of the player) or as a role that the player must take on (so that instead the player acts out the wishes of the game character). The latter is the most common of the two and is much more straightforward to implement.

- **Story:** The plot of the game. Story encompasses the actual narrative that takes place through the course of the game. The premise sets the stage on which the story takes place.

One of the central purposes of dramatic elements is that of helping the player to better understand the rules. In the board game *Snakes and Ladders*, the fact that the green arrows in our diagram are called "ladders" in the game implies that players are meant to move up them. In 1943, when Milton Bradley began publishing the game in the United States, they changed the name to *Chutes and Ladders*.[7] Presumably, this helped American children to better grasp the rules of the game because the chutes (which look like playground slides) were a more obvious path downward than the original snakes, just as the ladders were an obvious path upward.

In addition to this, many versions of the game have included images of a child doing a good deed at the bottom of a ladder and an image of her being rewarded for doing so at the top of the ladder. Conversely, the top of chutes depicted a child misbehaving, and the bottom of the chute showed her being punished for doing so. In this way, the narrative embedded in the board also sought to encourage the moral standards of 1940s America. Dramatic elements cover both the ability of the embedded narrative to help players remember rules (as in the case of the snakes being replaced by chutes) and the ability of the game narrative to convey meaning to the players that persists outside of the game (as was intended by the images of good and bad deeds and their consequences).

Dynamic Elements

Dynamic elements are those changes that occur only when the game is being played. There are a few central things to understand about dynamics in games:

- **Emergence:** Collisions of seemingly simple rules can lead to unpredictable outcomes. Even an incredibly simplistic game like *Snakes and Ladders* can lead to unexpected dynamic experiences. If one player of the game happened to exclusively land on ladders throughout the game where another exclusively landed on snakes, each would have a very different experience of the game. If you consider the six additional proposed rules, it's easy to

---

[7] About.com entry on *Chutes and Ladders* versus *Snakes and Ladders*: http://boardgames.about.com/od/gamehistories/p/chutes_ladders.htm. Last accessed March 1, 2014.

imagine that the range of gameplay experienced by players would expand in size due to the new rules (e.g., now, instead of fate being against player A, perhaps player B would choose to attack A at every possible opportunity, leading to a very negative play experience for A). Simple rules lead to complex and unpredictable behavior. One of a game designer's most important jobs is to attempt to understand the emergent implications of the rules in a game.

- **Emergent narrative:** In addition to the dynamic behavior of mechanics covered in the MDA model, Fullerton's model recognizes that narrative can also be dynamic with a fantastic breadth of narratives emerging from the gameplay itself. Games, by their nature, put players in extra-normal situations, and as a result, they can lead to interesting stories. This is the central appeal of pen and paper roleplaying games like *Dungeons & Dragons*, in which a single player acts as the Dungeon Master and crafts a scenario for the other players to experience and characters for them to interact with. This is different from the embedded narrative covered by Fullerton's dramatic elements and is one of the entertainment possibilities that is unique to interactive experiences.

- **Playtesting is the only way to understand dynamics:** Experienced game designers can often make better predictions about dynamic behavior and emergence than novice designers, but no one understands exactly how the dynamics of a game will play out without playtesting them. The six additional rules proposed for *Snakes and Ladders* seem like they would increase strategic play, but it is only through several rounds of playtests that one could determine the real effect the rules changes would have on the game. Repeated playtesting reveals information about the various dynamic behaviors that a game could have and helps designers understand the range of experiences that could be generated by their game.

The Elemental Tetrad

In *The Art of Game Design*,[8] Jesse Schell describes the elemental tetrad, through which he presents his four basic elements of games:

- **Mechanics:** The rules for interaction between the player and the game. Mechanics are the elements in the tetrad that differentiate games from all noninteractive forms of media (like film or books). Mechanics contain things like rules, objectives, and the other formal elements described by Fullerton. This is different from the *mechanics* presented by MDA because Schell's use of the term differentiates between game mechanics and the underlying technology that enables them.

- **Aesthetics:** Aesthetics describe how the game is perceived by the five senses: vision, sound, smell, taste, and touch. Aesthetics cover everything from the soundtrack of the game to the character models, packaging, and cover art. This is different from MDA's use of the word *aesthetics* because MDA used the word to refer to the emotional response

---

[8] Jesse Schell, *The Art of Game Design: A Book of Lenses* (Boca Raton, FL: CRC Press, 2008).

engendered by the game, while Schell uses the word to refer to things that are crafted by the game developers like actual game art and sound.

- **Technology:** This element covers all the underlying technology that makes the game work. While this most obviously refers to things such as console hardware, computer software, rendering pipelines, and such, it also covers technological elements in board games. Technology in board games can include things like the type and number of dice that are chosen, whether dice or a deck of cards are used as a randomizer, and various stats and tables used to determine the outcome of actions. In fact, the Technology Award at the IndieCade game conference in 2012 went to Zac S. for *Vornheim*, a collection of tools—in the form of a printed book—to be used by game masters when running tabletop roleplaying games set in a city.[9]

- **Story:** Schell uses the term story to convey everything covered by Fullerton's dramatic elements, not just what she terms *story*. *Story* is the narrative that occurs in your game and includes both premise and characters as well.

Schell arranges these elements into the tetrad shown in Figure 2.3.

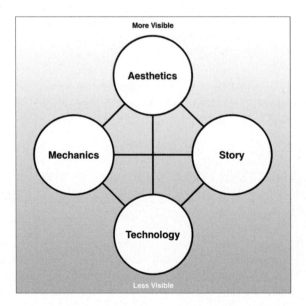

Figure 2.3   The elemental tetrad by Jesse Schell[10]

The tetrad shows how the four elements all interrelate with each other. In addition, Schell points out that the aesthetics of the game are always very visible to the player (although, this

---

[9] http://www.indiecade.com/2012/award_winners/.

[10] Adapted from: Schell, *The Art of Game Design,* 42.

is different from the aesthetic feelings described in MDA), and the technology of the game is the least visible with players generally having a better understanding of the game mechanics (e.g., the way that snakes and ladders affect the position of the player) than game technology (e.g., the probability distribution of a pair of six-sided dice). Schell's tetrad does not touch on dynamic play of the game and is more about the static elements of the game as it comes in a box (in the case of a board game) or on disk. Schell's elemental tetrad is discussed and expanded considerably in the next chapter, as it forms the inscribed layer of the Layered Tetrad.

Summary

Each of these frameworks for understanding games and other interactive experiences approach that understanding of games from a different perspective:

- MDA seeks to demonstrate and concretize the idea that players and designers approach games from different directions and proposes that designers can be more effective by learning to see their games from the perspective of their players.

- Formal, dramatic, and dynamic elements breaks game design into specific components that can each be considered and improved. It is meant to be a designer's toolkit and to enable designers to isolate and examine all the parts of their games that could be improved. FDD also asserts the importance of narrative in player experience.

- The elemental tetrad is more of a game developer's view on games. It separates the basic elements of a game into the sections that are generally assigned to various teams: Game designers handle mechanics, artists handle aesthetics, writers handle story, and programmers handle technology.

In the following chapter, the Layered Tetrad is presented as a combination of and expansion on the ideas presented in all of these frameworks. It is important to understand these frameworks as the underlying theory that led to the Layered Tetrad, and I strongly recommend reading the original paper and books in which they were presented.

CHAPTER 3

THE LAYERED TETRAD

The previous chapter presented you with various analytical frameworks for understanding games and game design. This chapter presents the Layered Tetrad, a combination and extension of many of the best aspects of those frameworks, and it is expanded upon throughout the following chapters.

The Layered Tetrad is a tool to help you understand and create the various aspects of a game. It will help you to analyze games that you love and will help you to look at your game holistically, leading to an understanding of not only the game's mechanics but also their implications in terms of play, socialization, meaning, and culture.

The Layered Tetrad is an expansion and combination of the ideas expressed by the three game analysis frameworks presented in the previous chapter. The Layered Tetrad does not define what a game is. Rather, the Layered Tetrad is a tool to help you understand all the different elements that need to be designed to create a game and what happens to those elements both during play and beyond as the game becomes part of culture.

The Layered Tetrad is composed of four elements—as was Schell's elemental tetrad—but those four elements are experienced through three layers. The first two, inscribed and dynamic, are based on the division between Fullerton's formal and dynamic elements. In addition, a third cultural layer is added that covers the game's life and effects outside of play, providing a link between game and culture that is critical to understand for us to be responsible game designers and creators of meaningful art.

Each of the layers is described briefly in this chapter, and each of the next three chapters is devoted to a layer of the tetrad.

The Inscribed Layer

The inscribed layer of the tetrad (see Figure 3.1) is very similar to Schell's elemental tetrad.

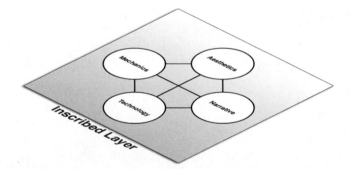

Figure 3.1   The inscribed layer of the Layered Tetrad[1]

The definitions of the four elements are similar to Schell's, but they are limited to the aspects of the game that exist even when it is not being played.

- **Mechanics:** The systems that define how the player and the game will interact. This includes the rules of the game and the following formal elements from Fullerton's book: player interaction patterns, objectives, rules, resources, and boundaries.

---

[1] Adapted from: Jesse Schell, *The Art of Game Design: A Book of Lenses* (Boca Raton, FL: CRC Press, 2008), 42.

- **Aesthetics:** Aesthetics describe how the game looks, sounds, smells, tastes, and feels. Aesthetics cover everything from the soundtrack of the game to the character models, packaging, and cover art. This definition differs from MDA's (mechanics, dynamics, and aesthetics approach) use of the word *aesthetics* because MDA used the word to refer to the emotional response engendered by the game, whereas Schell and I use the word to refer to inscribed elements like actual game art and sound.

- **Technology:** Just as with Schell's technology element, this element covers all the underlying technology that makes the game work for both paper and electronic games. For digital games, the technology element is primarily developed by programmers, but it is critical for designers to understand this element because the technology written by programmers forms the possibility space of decisions that can be made by game designers. This understanding is also vital because a seemingly simple design decision (for example, "let's move this level from solid ground onto a rocking ship in a massive storm") can require thousands of hours of development time to implement.

- **Narrative:** Schell uses the term *story* in his elemental tetrad, but I've chosen to use the broader term *narrative* to encompass the premise and characters in addition to the plot and to be more in-line with Fullerton's use of the terms. The inscribed narrative includes all prescripted story and pregenerated characters that are in the game.

The Dynamic Layer

As in Fullerton's book *Game Design Workshop,* the dynamic layer (see Figure 3.2) arises when the game is played.

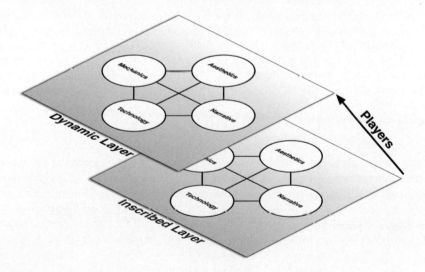

Figure 3.2   The dynamic layer positioned relative to the inscribed layer

As you can see, it is players who take the static inscribed layer of the game and from it construct the dynamic layer. Everything in the dynamic layer arises from the game during play, and the dynamic layer is composed of both elements in the player's direct control and of the results of her interaction with the inscribed elements. The dynamic layer is the realm of *emergence*, the phenomenon of complex behavior arising from seemingly simple rules. The emergent behavior of a game is often difficult to predict, but one of the great skills of game design that you will build over time is the ability to do so. The four dynamic elements are:

- **Mechanics:** Whereas inscribed mechanics covered rules, objectives, and so on, the dynamic mechanics cover how the players interact with those inscribed elements. Dynamic mechanics include procedures, strategies, emergent game behavior, and eventually the outcome of the game.

- **Aesthetics:** Dynamic aesthetics cover the way that aesthetic elements are created for the player during play. This includes everything from procedural art (digital game art or music generated on the fly by computer code) to the physical strain that can result from having to mash a button repeatedly over a long period of time.

- **Technology:** Dynamic technology describes the behavior of the technological components of a game during play. This covers how a pair of dice never actually seems to generate the smooth bell curve of results predicted by math. It also covers nearly everything that is done by computer code in digital games. One specific example of this could be the performance of the game's artificial intelligence code for enemies, but dynamic technology actually covers everything that a digital game's code does once the game is launched.

- **Narrative:** Dynamic narrative refers to stories that emerge procedurally out of the game's systems. This can mean an individual player's path through a branching scripted narrative such as *L.A. Noire* or *Heavy Rain*, the family story created by a play through *The Sims*, or the stories generated by team play with other human players. In 2013, the Boston Red Sox baseball team went "from worst to first" in a story that mirrored the city of Boston's recovery from the bombing at the 2013 Boston Marathon. That kind of story, enabled by the rules of the game, also fits under dynamic narrative.

The Cultural Layer

The third and final layer of the Layered Tetrad is cultural (see Figure 3.3), and it describes the game beyond play. The cultural layer covers both the impact of culture upon the game and the impact of the game upon culture. It is the community of players around the game that moves it into the cultural layer, and it is at this point that the players actually have more control and ownership over the game than the designers, but it is also through this layer that our societal responsibility as designers becomes clear.

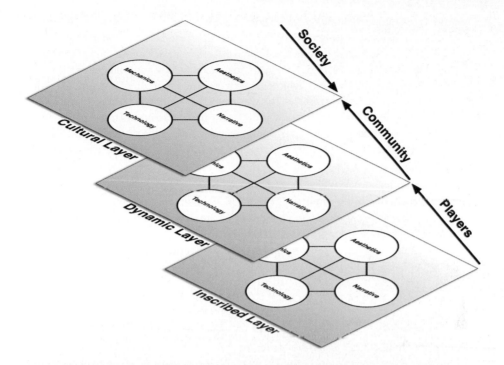

Figure 3.3 The cultural layer exists at the collision of the game and society.

The delineations between the four elements are much blurrier in the cultural layer, but it's still worthwhile to approach this layer through the lens of the four elements:

- **Mechanics:** The simplest form of cultural mechanics is represented by things like game mods (modifications to a game that are made by players and affect the inscribed mechanics of the game). This also covers things as complex as the impact that the emergent play of a game can have on society. For instance, the much maligned ability for the player character in *Grand Theft Auto 3* to sleep with a prostitute and then kill her to get his money back was a result of emergent dynamic mechanics in the game, but it had a massive impact on the perception of the game by the general public (which is part of the cultural layer).

- **Aesthetics:** As with the mechanics, cultural aesthetics can cover things like fan art, remixes of the music for the game, or other aesthetic fan activities like cosplay (short for "costume play," when fans of the game dress in costume to resemble game characters). One key point here is that authorized transmedia properties (i.e., a conversion of the game's intellectual property to another medium, such as the movie version of *Tomb Raider*, a Pokemon lunchbox, etc.) are not part of the cultural layer. This is because authorized transmedia properties are controlled by the original owners of the game's intellectual property, while cultural aesthetics are controlled and created by the community of players of the game.

- **Technology:** Cultural technology covers both the use of game technologies for nongame purposes (e.g., flocking algorithms for game characters could also be used in robotics) and the ability of technology to affect the game experience. Back in the days of the NES (Nintendo Entertainment System), having an Advantage or Max controller gave the player the ability to press turbo buttons (which was an automated method of pressing the regular A or B controller buttons very rapidly). This was a massive advantage in some games and had an effect on the game experience. Cultural technology also covers the expansion of possibilities of what *game* can mean by continually expanding the possibility space of gaming and the technological aspects of mods made by players to alter the inscribed elements of a game.

- **Narrative:** Cultural narrative encompasses the narrative aspects of fan-made transmedia properties created from the game (e.g., fan fiction, the narratives of fan-made tribute movies, and the fan-made characters and premises that are part of some game mods). It also covers the stories told about the game in culture and society, including both the stories that vilify games like *Grand Theft Auto* and the stories that extol the virtues and artistic merit of games like *Journey* and *Ico*.

The Responsibility of the Designer

All designers are aware of their responsibility for the formal layer of the game. It's obvious that the developers of the game must include clear rules, interesting art, and so on to enable and encourage the game to be played.

At the dynamic layer, some designers get a little muddier about their responsibility. Some designers are surprised by the behavior that emerges out of their games and want to pass responsibility for that behavior on to the players. For example, a few years ago, Valve decided to give hats to players of their game *Team Fortress 2*. The mechanic they chose was to randomly reward hats to players that were logged in. Because the distribution of hats was based exclusively on whether the player was logged in to a game at the right time, servers sprouted up that had players camping in them, not actually playing the game, just waiting for hat drops. Valve saw this behavior and chose to punish the players for it by taking hats back from any player that they suspected of having camped on a server rather than actually playing the game.

One way of seeing this is to see the players as trying to cheat the game. However, another is to realize that the players were just engaging in the most efficient method for obtaining hats as defined by the rules for hat drops that Valve had created. Because the system was designed to give players hats any time they were online regardless of whether they were actually doing anything, the players settled on the easiest path to get the hats. The players may have cheated the intent of the designers of the hat drop system, but they didn't cheat the system itself. Their dynamic behavior was exactly what was implied by the rules of the system that Valve set in place. As you can see from this example, the designer is also responsible for the experience at the dynamic layer through the implications of the systems she designs. In fact, one of the most important aspects of game design is the anticipation and crafting of the dynamic player experience. Of course, doing so is a very difficult task, but that's part of what makes it interesting.

So, what is the designer's responsibility at a cultural level? As a result of most game designers rarely if ever considering the cultural layer, video games are generally regarded in society as puerile and vulgar, selling violence and misogyny to teenage boys. You and I know that this doesn't have to be the case and that it isn't actually true of many or even most games, but this is the ubiquitous perception among the general public. Games can teach, games can empower, and games can heal. Games can promote pro-social behavior and help players learn new skills. A ludic attitude and some quickly devised rules can make even the most dull task enjoyable. As a designer, you are responsible for what your game says to society about gaming and for the impact that it has on players. We have become so good at making games compelling that some players are addicted to them to their detriment. Some designers have even made games that attempt to scam children into spending hundreds or thousands of dollars. This kind of behavior by designers damages the reputation of games in society and prevents many people from considering games worthy of their time or of being regarded as art, and that's truly sad. I believe that it is our responsibility as designers to promote pro-social, thoughtful behavior through our games and to respect our players and the time that they dedicate to experiencing what we create.

Summary

As demonstrated in this chapter, it's important to explicitly realize that the three layers of the Layered Tetrad represent a transition of ownership from the developers of the game to the players of the game. Everything in the inscribed layer is owned, developed, and implemented by the game designers and developers. The inscribed layer is completely within the developers' control.

The dynamic layer is the point at which the game is actually experienced, so game designers require that players take action and make decisions for the games inscribed by the designers to actually be experienced. Through the players' decisions and their effect on game systems, players take some ownership of the experience, yet that experience is still subject to the inscribed decisions of the developers. Thus, the ownership over the dynamic layer is shared between the developers and the players.

At the cultural layer, the game is no longer under the developers' control. This is why things like game mods fit in the cultural layer: Through a game mod, a player is taking control of and changing inscribed aspects of the game. Of course, most of the inscribed game still remains, but it is the player (as mod developer) who determines which inscribed elements she chooses to leave and which she chooses to replace; the player is in control. This is also why I have excluded authorized transmedia from the cultural layer. The developers and owners of the inscribed game maintain ownership over the authorized transmedia, and the cultural layer is defined by the shift of ownership to the players and the communities that surround the game.

Additionally, the aspect of the cultural layer that covers the perception of the game by non-players in society is also largely controlled by the player community's representation of their gameplay experience. People who don't play a game have their opinion of that game shaped by the media they read which was (hopefully) written by people who did actually play the game. However, even though the cultural layer is largely controlled by players, the developers and designers of a game still have an important influence over and responsibility for the game and its effect on society.

The following three chapters each tackle one layer of the Layered Tetrad and reveal it in more detail.

CHAPTER 4

THE INSCRIBED LAYER

This is the first of three chapters that explore the layers of the Layered Tetrad in greater depth.

As you learned in Chapter 3, "The Layered Tetrad," the inscribed layer covers all elements that are directly designed and encoded by game developers.

In this chapter, we look at the inscribed aspects of all four elements: mechanics, aesthetics, narrative, and technology.

Inscribed Mechanics

The inscribed mechanics are most of what one would think of as the traditional job of the game designer. In board games, this includes designing the board layout, the rules, the various cards that might be used and any tables that could be consulted. Much of the inscribed mechanics are described very well in Tracy Fullerton's book *Game Design Workshop* in her chapter on formal elements of games, and for the sake of lexical solidarity (and my distaste for every game design book using different terminology), I reuse her terminology throughout this section of the chapter as much as the Layered Tetrad framework allows.

As mentioned in Chapter 2, "Game Analysis Frameworks," Tracy Fullerton lists seven formal elements of games in her book: player interaction patterns, objectives, rules, procedures, resources, boundaries, and outcomes. In the formal, dramatic, and dynamic elements framework, these seven formal elements are defined as the things that make games different from other media.

Inscribed mechanics are a bit different from this, although there is a lot of overlap because mechanics is the element of the tetrad that is unique to games. However, the core of the inscribed layer is that everything in it is intentionally designed by a game developer, and the mechanics are no exception. As a result of this, inscribed mechanics does not include procedures or outcomes (although they are part of Fullerton's formal elements) because both are controlled by the player and therefore part of the dynamic layer. We'll also add a couple of new elements to give us the following list of inscribed mechanical elements:

- **Objectives:** Objectives cover the goals of the players in the game. What are the players trying to accomplish?
- **Player relationships:** Player relationships define the ways that players combat and collaborate with each other. How do the players' objectives intersect, and does this cause them to collaborate or compete?
- **Rules:** Rules specify and limit player actions. What can and can't the players do to achieve their objective?
- **Boundaries:** Boundaries define the limits of the game and relate directly to the magic circle. Where are the edges of the game? Where does the magic circle exist?
- **Resources:** Resources include assets or values that are relevant within the boundaries of the game. What does the player own in-game that enables her in-game actions?
- **Spaces:** Spaces define the shape of the game space and the possibilities for interaction therein. This is most obvious in board games, where the board itself is the space of the game.
- **Tables:** Tables define the statistical shape of the game. How do players level up as they grow in power? What moves are available to a player at a given time?

All of these inscribed mechanical elements interact with each other, and overlap certainly exists between them (e.g., the tech tree in *Civilization* is a table that is navigated like a space). The purpose of dividing them into these seven categories is to help you as a designer think about the various possibilities for design in your game. Not all games have all elements, but as with the "lenses" in Jesse Schell's book *The Art of Game Design: A Book of Lenses*, these inscribed mechanical elements are seven different ways to look at the various things that you can design for a game.

Objectives

While many games have an apparently simple objective—to win the game—in truth, every player will be constantly weighing several objectives every moment of your game. These can be categorized based on their immediacy and their import to the player, and some objectives may be considered very important to one player while being less important to another.

Immediacy of Objectives

As shown in the image in Figure 4.1 from the beautiful game *Journey* by thatgamecompany, nearly every screen of a modern game presents the player with short-, mid-, and long-term objectives.

Figure 4.1   Short-, mid-, and long-term objectives in the first level of *Journey* with objectives highlighted green, blue, and purple respectively

In the short term, the player wishes to charge her scarf (which enables flying in *Journey*), so she's shouting (the white sphere around her), which draws the highlighted scarf pieces to her. She also is drawn to explore the nearby building. For mid-term goals, there are three additional structures near the horizon. Because the rest of the desert is largely barren, the player is attracted to the ruins on the horizon (this indirect guidance strategy is used several times throughout *Journey* and is analyzed in Chapter 13, "Guiding the Player"). And, for long-term goals, the player is shown the mountain with the shaft of light (in the top-left corner of Figure 4.1) in the first few minutes of the game, and it is her long-term goal throughout the game to reach the top of this mountain.

Importance of Objectives

Just as objectives vary in immediacy, they also vary in importance to the player. In an open-world game like *Skyrim* by Bethesda Game Studios, there are both primary and optional objectives. Some players may choose to exclusively seek the primary objectives and can play through *Skyrim* in as little as 10 to 20 hours, whereas others who wish to explore various side quests and optional objectives can spend more than 400 hours in the game without exhausting the content (and even without finishing the primary objectives). Optional objectives are often tied to specific types of gameplay; in *Skyrim*, there is a whole series of missions for players who wish to join the Thieves Guild and specialize in stealth and theft. There are also other series of missions for those who wish to focus on archery or melee[1] combat. This ensures that the game could adapt to the varying gameplay styles of different players.

Conflicting Objectives

As a player, the objectives that you have will often conflict with each other or compete for the same resources. In a game like *Monopoly*, the overall objective of the game is to finish the game with the most money, but you must give up money to purchase assets like property, houses, and hotels that will eventually make you more money later. Looking at the design goal of presenting the player with interesting choices, a lot of the most interesting choices that a player can make are those that will benefit one objective while hurting another.

Approaching it from a more pragmatic perspective, each objective in the game will take time to complete, and a player may only have a certain amount of time that she is willing to devote to the game. Returning to the *Skyrim* example, many people (myself included) never finished the main quest of *Skyrim* because they spent all of their time playing the side quests and lost track of the urgency of the main story. Presumably, the goal of *Skyrim*'s designers was to allow each player to form her own story as she played through the game, and it's possible that the designers wouldn't care that I hadn't finished the main quest as long as I enjoyed playing the game, but as a player, I felt that the game ended not with a bang but a whimper as the layers upon layers of quests I was given had seemingly smaller and smaller returns. If, as a designer, it's important to you that your players complete the main quest of the game, you need to make sure that the player is constantly reminded of the urgency of the task and (unlike many open world games) you may need to have consequences for the player if she does not complete the main quest in a timely manner. As an example, in the classic game *Star Control*, if the player did not save a certain alien species within a given amount of time from the start of the game, the species' planet actually disappeared from the universe.

Player Relationships

Just as an individual player has several objectives in mind at any given time, the objectives that players have also determine relationships between them.

---

[1] This is a word that is often mispronounced by gamers. The word *melee* is pronounced "may-lay." The word "mealy" (pronounced "mee-lee") means either pale or in some other way like grain meal (e.g., cornmeal).

Player Interaction Patterns

In *Game Design Workshop,* Fullerton lists seven different player interaction patterns:

- **Single player versus game:** The player has the objective of beating the game.
- **Multiple individual players versus game:** Several co-located players each have the objective of beating the game, but they have little or no interaction with each other. This can often be seen in MMORPGs (massively multiplayer online roleplaying games) like *World of Warcraft* when players are each seeking to succeed at their missions in the same game world but not interacting with each other.
- **Cooperative play:** Multiple players share the common objective of beating the game together.
- **Player versus player:** Each of two players has the objective of defeating the other.
- **Multilateral competition:** The same as player versus player, except that there are more than two players, and each player is trying to beat all of the others.
- **Unilateral competition:** One player versus a team of other players. This can be seen in the board game *Scotland Yard* (also called *Mr. X*), where one player plays a criminal trying to evade the police and the other 2 to 4 players of the game are police officers trying to collaborate to catch the criminal.
- **Team competition:** Two teams of players, each with the objective of beating the other.

Some games, like *Mass Effect* by BioWare, provide computer-controlled allies for the player. In terms of designing player interaction patterns, these computer-controlled allies can either be thought of as an element of the single player's abilities in the game or as proxies for other players that could play the game, so a single-player game with computer-controlled allies could be seen either as single player versus game or as cooperative play.

Player Relationships and Roles Are Defined by Objectives

In addition to the interaction patterns listed in the preceding section, there are also various combinations of them, and in several games, one player might be another player's ally at one point and their competitor at another. For example, when trading money for property in a game like *Monopoly*, two players make a brief alliance with each other, even though the game is primarily multilateral competition.

At any time, the relationship between each player and both the game and other players is defined by the combination of all the players' layered objectives. These relationships lead each player to play one of several different roles:

- **Protagonist:** The protagonist role is that of the player trying to conquer the game.
- **Competitor:** The player trying to conquer other players. This can be either to win the game or on behalf of the game (e.g., in the 2004 board game *Betrayal at House on the Hill*, partway through the game, one of the players is turned evil and then must try to kill the other players).
- **Collaborator:** The player working to aid other players.

■ **Citizen:** The player in the same world as other players but not really collaborating or competing with them.

In many multiplayer games, all players will play each of these roles at different times, and as you'll see when we look into the dynamic layer, there are different types of players who prefer different roles.

Rules

Rules limit the players' actions. Rules are also the most direct inscription of the designer's concept of how the game should be played. In the written rules of a board game, the designer is attempting to inscribe and encode the experience that she wants for the players to have when they play the game. Later, the players decode these rules and hopefully experience something like what the designer intended.

Unlike paper games, digital games usually have very few inscribed rules that are read directly by the player; however, the programming code written by the game developers is another way of encoding rules that will be decoded through play. Because rules are the most direct method through which the game designer communicates with the player, rules act to define many of the other elements. The money in *Monopoly* only has value because the rules declare that it can be used to buy assets and other resources.

Explicitly written rules are the most obvious form of rules, but there are also implicit rules. For example, when playing poker, there is an implicit rule that you shouldn't hide cards up your sleeve. This is not explicitly stated in the rules of poker, but every player understands that doing so would be cheating.[2]

Boundaries

Boundaries define the edges of the space and time in which the game takes place. Within the boundaries, the rules and other aspects of the game apply: poker chips are worth something, it's okay to slam into other hockey players on the ice, and it matters which car crosses a line on the ground first. Sometimes, boundaries are physical, like the wall around a hockey rink. Other times, boundaries are less obvious. When a player is playing an ARG (alternate reality game), the game is often surrounding the player during her normal day. As mentioned in Chapter 1, "Thinking Like a Designer," players of *Majestic* gave Electronic Arts their phone number, fax number, email address, and home address; and they would receive phone calls, faxes, and so on at all times of the day from characters in the game. The intent of the game was to blur the boundaries between gaming and everyday life.

---

[2] This is a good example of one of the differences between single-player and multiplayer game design. In a multiplayer poker game, concealing a card would be cheating and could ruin the game. However, in the game *Red Dead Redemption* by Rockstar Studios, the in-game poker tournaments become much more interesting and entertaining once the player acquires the suit of clothes that allows her character to conceal and swap poker cards at will (with a risk of being discovered by NPCs).

Resources

Resources are things of value in a game. These can be either things like assets or nonmaterial attributes. Assets in games include things such as the equipment that Link has collected in a *Legend of Zelda* game; the resource cards that players earn in the board game *Settlers of Catan*; and the houses, hotels, and property deeds that players purchase in *Monopoly*. Attributes often include things such as health, amount of air left when swimming under water, and experience points. Because money is so versatile and so ubiquitous, it is somewhere between the two. A game can have physical money assets (like the cash in *Monopoly*), or it can have a nonphysical money attribute (like the amount of money that a player has in *Grand Theft Auto*).

Spaces

Designers are often tasked with creating navigable spaces. This includes both designing the board for a board game and designing virtual levels in a digital game. In both cases, you want to think about both flow through the space and making the areas of the space unique and interesting. Things to keep in mind when designing spaces include the following:

- **The purpose of the space:** Architect Christopher Alexander spent years researching why some spaces were particularly well suited to their use and why others weren't. He distilled this knowledge into the concept of *design patterns* through his book *A Pattern Language*,[3] which explored various patterns for good architectural spaces. The purpose of the book was to put forward a series of patterns that others could use to make a space that correctly matched the use for which it was intended.

- **Flow:** Does your space allow the player to move through it easily, or if it does restrict movement, is there a good reason? In the board game *Clue*, players roll a single die each turn to determine how far they can move. This can make it very slow to move about the gameboard. (The game board is 24x25 spaces, so with an average roll of 3.5, it could take 7 turns to cross the board.) Realizing this, the designers added secret passages that allow players to teleport from each corner of the board to the opposite corner, which helped flow through the mansion quite a bit.

- **Landmarks:** It is more difficult for players to create a mental map of 3D virtual spaces than actual spaces through which they have walked in real life. Because of this, it is important that you have landmarks in your virtual spaces that players can use to more easily orient themselves. In Honolulu, Hawaii, people don't give directions in terms of compass directions (north, south, east, and west) because these are not terribly obvious unless it's sunrise or sunset. Instead, the people of Honolulu navigate by obvious landmarks: *mauka* (the mountains to the northeast), *makai* (the ocean to the southwest), Diamond Head (the landmark mountain to the southeast), and *Ewa* (the area to the northwest). On other parts of the Hawaiian Islands, *mauka* means inland and *makai* means towards the ocean, regardless of compass direction (the islands being circular). Making landmarks that players can easily

---

[3] Christopher Alexander, Sara Ishikawa, and Murray Silverstein, *A Pattern Language: Towns, Buildings, Construction* (New York: Oxford University Press, 1977).

see will limit the number of times your players need to consult the map to figure out where they are.

- **Experiences:** The game as a whole is an experience, but the map or space of the game also needs to be sprinkled with interesting experiences for your players. In *Assassin's Creed 4: Black Flag*, the world map is a vastly shrunken version of the Caribbean Sea. Even though the actual Caribbean has many miles of empty ocean between islands that would take a sailing vessel hours or days to cross, the Caribbean of AC4 has events sprinkled throughout it that ensure that the player will encounter a chance to have an experience several times each minute. These could be small experiences like finding a single treasure chest on a tiny atoll, or they could be large experiences like coming across a fleet of enemy ships.

- **Short-, medium-, and long-term objectives:** As demonstrated in the shot from *Journey*, shown in Figure 4.1, your space can have multiple levels of goals. In open-world games, a player is often shown a high-level enemy early on so that she has something to aspire to defeat later in the game. Many games also clearly mark areas of the map as easy, medium, or high difficulty.

Tables

Tables are a critical part of game balance, particularly when designing modern digital games. Put simply, tables are grids of data that are often synonymous with spreadsheets, but there are many different things that tables can be used to design and illustrate:

- **Probability:** Tables can be used to determine probability in very specific situations. In the board game *Tales of the Arabian Nights*, the player selects the proper table for the individual creature she has encountered, and it gives her a list of possible reactions that she can have to that encounter and the various results of each of her possible reactions.

- **Progression:** In paper roleplaying games (RPGs) like *Dungeons & Dragons*, tables show how the players' abilities increase and change as the player character's level increases.

- **Playtest Data:** In addition to tables that players use to enable the game, you as a designer will also create tables to hold playtest data and information about player experiences.

Of course, tables are also a form of technology in games, so they cross the line between mechanics and technology. Tables as technology include the storage of information and any transformation of information that can happen in the table (e.g., formulae in spreadsheets). Tables as mechanics include the design decisions that game designers make and inscribe into the table.

Inscribed Aesthetics

Inscribed aesthetics are those aesthetic elements that are crafted by the developers of the game. These cover all the five senses, and as a designer, you should be aware that throughout the time that your player is playing the game, she will be sensing with all five of her senses.

The Five Aesthetic Senses

Designers must consider all five of the aesthetic senses when inscribing games. These five senses are:

- **Vision:** Of the five senses, vision is the one that gets the most attention from most game development teams. As a result, the fidelity of the visual experience that we can deliver to players has seen more obvious improvement over the past several years than that of any other sense. When thinking about the visible elements of your game, be sure to think beyond the 3D art in the game or the art of the board in a paper game. Realize that everything that players (or potential players) see that has anything to do with your game will affect their impression of it as well as their enjoyment of it. Some game developers in the past have put tremendous time into making their in-game art beautiful only to have the game packaged in (and hidden behind) awful box art.

- **Hearing:** Audio in games is second only to video in the amazing level of fidelity that can be delivered to players. All modern consoles can output 5.1-channel sound, and some can do even better than that. Game audio is composed of sound effects, music, and dialogue. Each will take a different amount of time to be interpreted by the player, and each has a different best use. In addition, on a medium to large team, each of these three will usually be handled by a different artist.

Audio Type	Immediacy	Best For
Sound effects	Immediate	Alerting the player; conveying simple information
Music	Medium	Setting the mood
Dialogue	Medium / Long	Conveying complex information

Another aspect of audio to consider is background noise. For mobile games, you can almost always expect that the player is going to be in a nonoptimal audio situation when playing your game. Though audio can always add to a game, it's just not prudent to make it a vital aspect of a mobile game unless it's the core feature of the game (e.g., games like *Papa Sangre* by Somethin' Else or *Freeq* by Psychic Bunny). There is also background noise in computer and console games to consider. Some cooling fans are very loud, and that needs to be considered when developing quiet audio for digital games.

- **Touch:** Touch is very different between board games and digital games, but in both cases, it's the most direct contact that you have with the player. In a board game, touch comes down to the feel of the playing pieces, cards, board, and so on. Do the pieces for your game feel high quality or do they feel cheap? Often you want them to be the former, but the latter isn't terrible. James Ernst, possibly the most prolific board game designer in the world for several years, ran a company called Cheap Ass Games, the mission of which was to get great games to players at as low a cost to them as possible. In order to cut costs, playing pieces were made of cheap materials, but this was fine with players because the games from his company cost less than $10 each instead of the $40–$50 that many board games cost. All design decisions are choices; just make sure that you're aware of the options and know that you're making a choice.

One of the most exciting recent technological advancements for board game prototyping is 3D printing, and many board game designers are starting to print pieces for their game prototypes. There are also several companies online now that will print your game board, cards, or pieces.

There are also aspects of touch in digital games. The way that the controller feels in a player's hands and the amount of fatigue that it causes are definitely aspects that the designer needs to consider. When the fantastic PlayStation 2 game *Okami* was ported to the Nintendo Wii, the designers chose to change the attack command from a button press (the X on the PlayStation controller) to a waggle of the Wiimote (which mimicked the attack gesture from *The Legend of Zelda: Twilight Princess* that had done very well on the Wii). However, while attacks in the heat of battle in *Twilight Princess* happen about once every couple of seconds, attacks in *Okami* happen several times per second, so the attack gesture that worked well in *Twilight Princess* instead caused player fatigue in *Okami*. With the rise of tablet and smartphone gaming, touch and gesture are elements that every game designer must consider carefully.

Another aspect of touch in digital games is rumble-style player feedback. As a designer, you can choose the intensity and style of rumble feedback in most modern console controllers.

- **Smell:** Smell is not often a designed aspect of inscribed aesthetics, but it is there. Just as different book printing processes have different smells, so too do different board and card game printing processes. Make sure that you get a sample from your manufacturer before committing to printing 1,000 copies of something that might smell strange.

Aesthetic Goals

When designing and developing the inscribed aesthetic elements of a game, we as game developers are taking advantage of hundreds of years of cultural understanding of other forms of art. Humankind has been making art and music since long before the dawn of written history. Interactive experiences have the advantage of being able to pull from all of that experience and of allowing us as designers to incorporate all of the techniques and knowledge of aesthetic art into the games that we create. However, when we do so, it must be done with a reason, and it must mesh cohesively with the other elements of the game. These are some of the goals that aesthetic elements can serve well in our games:

- **Mood:** Aesthetics do a fantastic job of helping to set the emotional mood of a game. While mood can definitely be conveyed through game mechanics, both visual art and music can do a fantastic job of influencing a player's mood much faster than mechanics are able to.

- **Information:** Several informational colors are built in to our psyche as mammals. Things like the color red or alternating yellow and black are seen by nearly every species in the animal kingdom as indicators of danger. In contrast, cool colors like blue and green are usually seen as peaceful.

  In addition, players can be trained to understand various aesthetics as having specific meaning. The LucasArts game *X-Wing* was the first to have a soundtrack that was procedurally generated by the in-game situation. The music would rise in intensity to warn the player that enemies were attacking. Similarly, as described in Chapter 13, the colors bright blue and yellow are used throughout the Naughty Dog game *Uncharted 3* to help the player identify handholds and footholds for climbing.

Inscribed Narrative

As with all forms of experience, dramatics and narrative are an important part of many interactive experiences. However, game narratives face challenges that are not present in any form of linear media, and as such, writers are still learning how to craft and present interactive narratives. This section will explore the components of inscribed dramatics, purposes for which they are used, methods for storytelling in games, and differences between game narratives and linear narratives.

Components of Inscribed Narrative

In both linear and interactive narrative, the components of the dramatics are the same: premise, setting, character, and plot.

- **Premise:** The premise is the narrative basis from which the story emerges:[4]

    A long time ago in a galaxy far, far away, an intergalactic war is brought to the doorstep of a young farmer who doesn't yet realize the importance of his ancestry or himself.

    Gordon Freeman has no idea about the surprises that are in store for him on his first day of work at the top secret Black Mesa research facility.

    Edward Kenway must fight and pirate his way to fortune on the high seas of the Caribbean while discovering the secret of the mysterious Observatory, sought by Templars and Assassins alike.

- **Setting:** The setting expands upon the skeleton of the premise to provide a detailed world in which the narrative can take place. The setting can be something as large as a galaxy far, far away or as small as a tiny room beneath the stairs, but it's important that it is believable within the bounds of the premise and that it is internally consistent; if your characters will choose to fight with swords in a world full of guns, you need to have a good reason for it.

    In *Star Wars*, when Obi Wan Kenobi gives the light saber to Luke, he answers all of these questions by stating that it is "not as clumsy or random as a blaster; an elegant weapon for a more civilized age."

- **Character:** Stories are about characters, and the best stories are about characters we care about. Narratively, characters are composed of a backstory and one or more objectives. These combine to give the character a role in the story: protagonist, antagonist, companion, lackey, mentor, and so on.

---

[4] These are the premises of *Star Wars: A New Hope*, *Half-Life*, and *Assassin's Creed 4: Black Flag*.

- **Plot:** Plot is the sequence of events that take place in your narrative. Usually, this takes the form of the protagonist wanting something but having difficulty achieving it because of either an antagonist or an antagonistic situation getting in the way. The plot then becomes the story of how the protagonist attempts to overcome this difficulty or obstruction.

Traditional Dramatics

Though interactive narrative offers many new possibilities to writers and developers, it still generally follows traditional dramatic structures.

Five-Act Structure

German writer Gustav Freytag wrote about five-act structure in his 1863 book *Die Technik des Dramas* (*The Technique of Dramas*). It described the purpose of the five acts often used by Shakespeare and many of his contemporaries (as well as Roman playwrights) and proposed what has come to be known as Freytag's pyramid (see Figure 4.2). The vertical axis in Figures 4.2 and 4.3 represents the level of audience excitement at that point in the story.

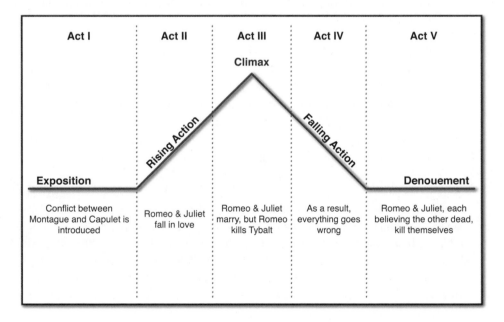

Act I	Act II	Act III	Act IV	Act V

Climax

Rising Action

Falling Action

Exposition

Denouement

| Conflict between Montague and Capulet is introduced | Romeo & Juliet fall in love | Romeo & Juliet marry, but Romeo kills Tybalt | As a result, everything goes wrong | Romeo & Juliet, each believing the other dead, kill themselves |

Figure 4.2 Freytag's pyramid of five-act structure showing examples from *Romeo and Juliet* by Shakespeare

According to Freytag, the acts work as follows:

- **Act I: Exposition:** Introduces the narrative premise, the setting, and the important charac-ters. In Act I of William Shakespeare's *Romeo and Juliet*, we are introduced to Verona, Italy, and the feud between the powerful Montague and Capulet families. Romeo is introduced as the son of the Montague family and is infatuated with Rosaline.

- **Act II: Rising action:** Something happens that causes new tension for the important characters, and the dramatic tension rises. Romeo sneaks into the Capulet's ball and is instantly smitten with Juliet, the daughter of the Capulet family.

- **Act III: Climax:** Everything comes to a head, and the outcome of the play is decided. Romeo and Juliet are secretly married, and the local friar hopes that this may lead to peace between their families. However, the next morning, Romeo is accosted by Juliet's cousin Tybalt. Romeo won't fight, so his friend Mercutio fights in his stead, and Tybalt accidentally kills Mercutio (because Romeo got in the way). Romeo is furious and chases Tybalt, eventually killing him. Romeo's decision to kill Tybalt is the moment of climax of the play because before that moment, it seems like everything might work out for the two lovers, and after that moment, the audience knows that things will end horribly.

- **Act IV: Falling action:** The play continues toward its inevitable conclusion. If it's a comedy, things get better; if it's a tragedy, they may appear to be getting better, but it just gets worse. The results of the climax are played out for the audience. Romeo is banished from Verona. The friar concocts a plan to allow Romeo and Juliet to escape together. He has Juliet fake her death and sends a message to Romeo to let him know, but the messenger never makes it to Romeo.

- **Act V: Denouement (pronounced "day-new-maw"):** The play resolves. Romeo enters the tomb believing Juliet to be truly dead and kills himself. She immediately awakens to find him dead and then kills herself as well. The families become aware of this tragedy, and everyone weeps, promising to cease the feud.

Three-Act Structure

In his books and lectures, American screenwriter Syd Field has proposed another way of understanding traditional narrative in terms of three acts.[5] Between each act, a plot point changes the direction of the story and forces the characters' actions. Figure 4.3 provides an example that is further explained in the following list:

- **Act I: Exposition:** Introduces the audience to the world of the narrative and presents the premise, setting, and main characters. In Act I of *Star Wars*, Luke is a young, idealistic kid who works on his uncle's moisture farm. There's a galactic rebellion happening against a fascist Empire, but he's just a simple farmer dreaming of flying starfighters.

- **Hook:** Gets the audience's attention quickly. According to Field, an audience decides in the first few minutes whether they're going to watch a film, so the first few minutes should be really exciting, even if the action in them has nothing to do with the rest of the film (e.g., the beginning of any James Bond film). In *Star Wars*, the opening scene of Princess Leia's ship being attacked had some of the best special visual effects that 1977 audiences had ever seen and a fantastic score by John Williams, both of which helped make it an exciting hook.

---

[5] Syd Field, *Screenplay: The Foundations of Screenwriting* (New York: Delta Trade Paperbacks, 2005).

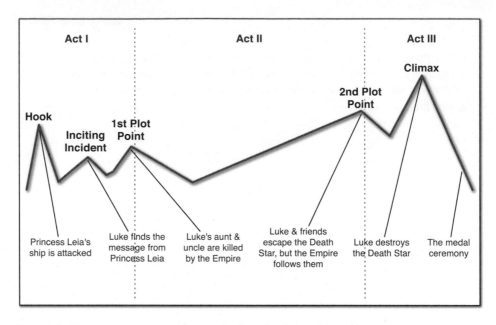

Figure 4.3   Three-act structure, with examples from *Star Wars: A New Hope*

- **Inciting Incident:** An event enters the life of the main character, causing her to start the adventure. Luke is leading a pretty normal life until he finds Leia's secret message stored inside of R2-D2. This discovery causes him to seek out "Old Ben" Kenobi, who changes his life.

- **First Plot Point:** The first plot point ends the first act and pushes the protagonist down the path toward the second. Luke has decided to stay home and not help Obi-Wan Kenobi, but when he finds that the Empire has killed his aunt and uncle, he changes his mind and decides to join Obi-Wan and train to become a Jedi.

- **Act II: Antagonism:** The protagonist starts on her journey, but a series of obstacles get in her way. Luke and Obi-Wan hire Han Solo and Chewbacca to help them deliver the secret plans carried by R2-D2 to Alderaan, however when they arrive, Alderaan has been destroyed, and their ship is captured by the Death Star.

- **Second Plot Point:** The second plot point ends the second act and pushes the protagonist into her decision of what she will attempt in the third act. After much struggle, Luke and his friends escape from the Death Star with both the princess and the plans, but his mentor, Obi-Wan Kenobi, is killed in the process. The Death Star follows them to the rebel's secret base, and Luke must choose whether to aid in the attack on the Death Star or leave with Han Solo.

- **Act III: Resolution:** The story is concluded, and the protagonist either succeeds or fails. Either way, she emerges from the story with a new understanding of who she is. Luke chooses to help attack the Death Star and ends up saving the day.

- **Climax:** The moment when everything comes to a head, and the main question of the plot is answered. Luke is alone in the Death Star trench having lost both his wingmen and R2-D2. Just as he is about to be shot down by Darth Vader, Han and Chewbacca appear to save him, allowing him a clean shot. Luke chooses to trust the Force over technology and shoots with his eyes closed, making an extremely difficult shot and destroying the Death Star.

In most modern movies and in nearly all video games, the climax is very close to the end of the narrative with very little time for falling action or denouement. One marked example of this not being the case is the game *Red Dead Redemption* by Rockstar Games. After the big climax where the main character, John Marston, finally defeats the man the government hired him to kill, he is allowed to go home to his family, with the game playing its only sung musical track as John rides home slowly in the snow. Then, the player is subjected to a series of rather dull missions where John clears crows out of their grain silo, teaches his petulant son to wrangle cattle, and does other chores around the house. The player feels the boredom of these missions much like John does. Then, the same government agents that initially hired John come to his farm to kill him, eventually succeeding in their task. Once John dies, the game fades to black and fades back in on the player in the role of Jack (John's son) three years after his father's death. The game returns to more action-based missions as Jack attempts to track down the agents who killed his father. This kind of falling action is rare and refreshing to see in games, and it made the narrative of *Red Dead Redemption* one of the most memorable that I've played.

Differences Between Interactive and Linear Narrative

At their core, interactive and linear narratives are quite different because of the difference in the role of the audience versus the player. Though an audience member of course brings her own background and interpretations to any media that she consumes, she is still unable to change the actual media itself, only her perception thereof. However, a player is constantly affecting the media in which she is taking part, and therefore a player has actual agency in the interactive narratives that she experiences. This means that authors of interactive narrative must be aware of some core differences in how they can craft their narratives.

Plot Versus Free Will

One of the most difficult things to give up when crafting interactive narratives is control over the plot. Both authors and readers/viewers are accustomed to plots with elements like fore-shadowing, fate, irony, and other ways in which the intended outcome of the plot actually influences earlier parts of the story. In a truly interactive experience, this would be impossible because of the free will of the player. Without knowing what choices the player will make, it is very difficult to intentionally foreshadow the results of those choices. There are several possibilities for dealing with this dichotomy, some of which are used often and others of which are used in situations like pen-and-paper RPGs but have not yet been implemented in many digital games:

- **Limited possibilities:** Limited possibilities are actually a part of nearly all interactive narrative experiences. In fact, most games, at their inscribed level, are not actually interactive narratives. All the most popular series of games over the past decade (*Prince of Persia*, *Call of Duty*, *Halo*, *Uncharted*, and so on) have exclusively linear stories at their core. No matter what you do in the game, your choices are to either continue with the narrative or quit the game. In fact, *Spec Ops: The Line* by Yager Development explored this issue beautifully, placing the player and main character of the story in the same position of having only two real choices: continue to perform increasingly horrific acts or just stop playing the game. In *Prince of Persia: The Sands of Time*, this is handled by having the narrator (the prince of the title and the protagonist) say "No, no, no; that's not the way it happened. Shall I start again?" whenever the player dies and the game has to back up to the most recent check point. In the *Assassin's Creed* series, this is handled by stating that you have become "desynchronized" from your ancestor's story if (through lack of player skill) the ancestor is allowed to die.

  There are also several examples of games that limit choices to only a few possibilities and base those on the player's actions throughout the game. Both *Fable*, by Lionhead Studios, and *Star Wars: Knights of the Old Republic*, by Bioware, claimed to be watching the player throughout the game to determine the final game outcome, but though each did track the player on a good versus evil scale throughout the game, in both cases (as in many other games), a single choice made at the end of the game could override an entire game of good or evil behavior.

  Other games like the Japanese RPGs *Final Fantasy VII* and *Chrono Trigger* have more subtle and varied possibilities. In *Final Fantasy VII*, there is a point where the main character, Cloud, goes on a date with someone at the Golden Saucer amusement part. The default is for Cloud to go out with Aeris; however, if the player has ignored Aeris throughout the game and kept her out of their battle party, Cloud will instead go out with Tifa. The possibilities for the date are the characters Aeris, Tifa, Yuffie, and Barrett, although it takes resolute effort to have the date with Barrett. The game never explains that this math is happening in the background but it is always there, and the Final Fantasy team used a similar strategy in *Final Fantasy X* to determine who the protagonist, Tidus, would ride on a snowmobile within a romantic scene. *Chrono Trigger* uses several metrics to determine which of the game's thirteen endings to choose (and some of those endings have multiple possibilities within them). Again, the calculations for this are largely invisible to the player.

- **Allow the player to choose from several linear side quests:** Many of Bethesda Softwork's open-world games use this strategy, including the recent games *Fallout 3* and *Skyrim*. While the main quest is generally pretty linear for these games, it is only a small fraction of the game's total content. In *Skyrim*, for instance, the main quest takes about 12 to 16 hours to complete, but the game has over 400 hours of additional side quests. A player's reputation and history in the game lead to some side quests being unlocked and exclude her from playing others. This means that each individual who plays the game has the potential to have a different combination of linear experiences that add up to a different overall game experience from other players.

- **Foreshadowing multiple things:** If you foreshadow several different things that might happen, some of them probably will happen. Players will generally ignore the foreshadowing that is not paid off while noticing that which does. This happens often in serial television shows where several possibilities for future plots are put in place but only a few are ever actually executed (e.g., the Nebari plot to take over the universe that is revealed in the *Farscape* episode "A Clockwork Nebari" and the character of the Doctor's daughter from the *Doctor Who* episode "The Doctor's Daughter" who never returns to the show).

- **Develop minor nonplayer characters (NPCs) into major ones:** This is a tactic used often by game masters of pen-and-paper RPGs. An example of this would be if the players were attacked by a group of ten bandits, and the players defeated the bandits, but one got away. The game master (GM) could then choose to have that bandit return at some point with a vendetta against the players for killing his friends. This differs significantly from games like *Final Fantasy VI* (originally titled *Final Fantasy III* in the U.S.), where it is pretty obvious from early in the game that Kefka will be a recurring, annoying, and eventually wholly evil nemesis character. Though the characters in the player's party don't realize this, just the fact that the developers chose to give Kefka a special sound effect for his laugh makes it apparent to the player.

> ## tip
>
> Pen-and-paper RPGs still offer players a unique interactive gaming experience, and I highly recommend them. In fact, when I taught at the University of Southern California, I required all of my students to run an RPG and play in a couple run by their peers. Roughly 40% of the students each semester listed it as their favorite assignment.
>
> Because pen-and-paper RPGs are run by a person, that game master (GM) can craft the narrative in real time for the players in a way that computers have yet to match. All of the strategies listed earlier are used by GMs to guide their players and make their experiences seem fated, foreshadowed, or ironic in ways that are usually reserved for linear narrative.
>
> The perennial RPG *Dungeons & Dragons*, by Wizards of the Coast, is a good place to get started, and there are a tremendous number of source books for it. However, I have found that D&D campaigns tend to be very combat focused. For an experience that allows you to most easily create and experience interactive stories, I recommend the *FATE* system by Evil Hat Productions.

Empathetic Character Versus Avatar

In linear narratives, the protagonist is often a character with whom the audience is expected to empathize. When the audience watches Romeo and Juliet make stupid decisions, they remember being young themselves and empathize with the feelings that lead the two lovers down their fatal path. In contrast, the protagonist in an interactive narrative is not a character separate from the player but instead the player's *avatar* in the world. (*Avatar* is a word from Sanskrit that refers to the physical embodiment of a god on Earth; in games, it is the virtual embodiment of the player in the game world.) This can lead to a dissonance between the actions and personality that the player would like to have in the world and the personality of the player-character (PC). For me, this was driven home by my experience with Cloud Strife as the protagonist of *Final Fantasy VII*. Throughout the game, Cloud was a little more petulant than I would have liked, but in general, his silence allowed me to project my own character on to him. However, after a pivotal scene where Cloud loses someone close to him, he chose to sit, unresponsive in a wheelchair instead of fighting to save the world from Sephiroth, as I wanted to. This dichotomy between the PC's choice and the choice that I as the player wanted to make was extremely frustrating for me.

A fantastic example of this dichotomy being used to great effect happens in the Clover Studio game *Okami*. In *Okami*, the player character is Amaterasu, a reincarnation of the female god of the sun in the form of a white wolf. However, Amaterasu's powers have diminished over the past 100 years, and the player must work to reclaim them. About a quarter of the way through the narrative, the main antagonist, the demon Orochi, chooses a maiden to be sacrificed to him. Both the player and Amaterasu's companion, Issun, know that Amaterasu has only regained a few of her powers at this point, and the player feels wary of facing Orochi in such a weakened state. However, despite Issun's protests, Amaterasu runs directly to the fight. As the music swells in support of her decision, my feelings as a player changed from trepidation to temerity, and I actually felt like a hero because I knew that the odds were against me, but I was still doing what needed to be done.

This character versus avatar dichotomy has been approached several ways in games and interactive narrative:

- **Role fulfillment:** By far, the most common approach in games is to have the player roleplay the game character. When playing character-driven games like the *Tomb Raider* or *Uncharted* series, the player is playing not themselves but instead Lara Croft or Nathan Drake. The player sets aside her own personality to fulfill the inscribed personality of the game's protagonist.

- **The silent protagonist:** In a tradition reaching at least as far back as the first *Legend of Zelda* game, many protagonists are largely silent. Other characters talk to them and react as if they've said things, but the player never sees the statements made by the player character. This was done with the idea that the player could then impress her own personality on the protagonist rather than being forced into a personality inscribed by the game developers. However, regardless of what Link says or doesn't say, his personality is demonstrated rather clearly by his actions, and even without Cloud saying a word, players can still experience a dissonance between their wishes and his actions as described in the preceding example.

- **Multiple dialogue choices:** Many games offer the player multiple dialogue choices for her character, which can certainly help the player to feel more in control of the character and her personality. However, there are a couple of important requirements:

- *The player must understand the implications of her statement:* Sometimes, a line that may seem entirely clear to the game's writers does not seem to have the same connotations to the player. If the player chooses dialogue that seems to her to be complimentary, but the writer meant for it to be antagonistic, the NPC's reaction can seem very strange to the player.

- *The choice of statement must matter:* Some games offer the player a fake choice, anticipating that she will make the choice that the game desires. If, for instance, she's asked to save the world, and she just says "no," it will respond with something like "oh, you can't mean that," and not actually allow her a satisfactory choice.

One fantastic example of this being done well is the dialog wheel in the *Mass Effect* series by Bioware. In these games, the player is presented with a wheel of dialog choices, and the sections of the wheel are coded with meaning. A choice on the left side of the wheel will extend the conversation, while one on the right side will shorten it. A choice on the top of the wheel will be friendly, while one on the bottom will be surly or antagonistic. By positioning the dialog options in this way, the player is granted important information about the connotations of her choice and is not surprised by the outcome.

Another very different but equally compelling example is *Blade Runner* by Westwood Studios. The designers felt that choosing dialog options interrupted the flow of the player experience, so instead of offering the player a choice between dialogue options at every statement, the player was able to choose a mood for her character (friendly, neutral, surly, or random). The protagonist would act and speak as dictated by his mood without any interruption in the narrative flow, and the player could change the mood at any time to alter her character's response to the situation.

- **Track player actions and react accordingly:** Some games now track the player's relationships with various factions and have the faction members react to the player accordingly. Do a favor for the Orcs, and they may let you sell goods at their trading post. Arrest a member of the Thieves Guild, and you may find yourself mugged by them in the future. This is a common feature of open-world western roleplaying games like those by Bethesda Softworks and is in some ways based on the morality system of eight virtues and three principles that was introduced in *Ultima IV*, by Origin Systems, one of the first examples of complex morality systems in a digital game.

Purposes for Inscribed Dramatics

Inscribed dramatics can serve several purposes in game design:

- **Evoking emotion:** Over the past several centuries, writers have gained skill in manipulating the emotions of their audiences through dramatics. This holds true in games and interactive narrative as well, and even purely linear narrative inscribed over a game can focus and shape the player's feelings.

- **Motivation and justification:** Just as dramatics can shape emotions, they can also be used to encourage the player to take certain actions or to justify actions if those actions seem distasteful. This is very true of the fantastic retelling of Joseph Conrad's *Heart of Darkness* in the game *Spec Ops: The Line*. A more positive example comes from *The Legend of Zelda: The Wind Waker*. At the beginning of the game, Link's sister Aryll lets him borrow her telescope for one day because it's his birthday. On the same day, she is kidnapped by a giant bird, and the first part of the game is driven narratively by Link's desire to rescue her. The inscribed storytelling of her giving something to the player before being kidnapped increases the player's personal desire to rescue her.

- **Progression and reward:** Many games use cut scenes and other inscribed narrative to help the player know where she is in the story and to reward her for progression. If the narrative of a game is largely linear, the player's understanding of traditional narrative structure can help her to understand where in the three-act structure the game narrative currently is, and thereby, she can tell how far she has progressed in the overall plot of the game. Narrative cut scenes are also often used as rewards for players to mark the end of a level or other section of the game. This is true in the single-player modes of nearly all top-selling games with linear narratives (e.g., the *Modern Warfare*, *Halo*, and *Uncharted* series).

- **Mechanics reinforcement:** One of the most critical purposes of inscribed dramatics is the reinforcement of game mechanics. The German board game *Up the River* by Ravensburger is a fantastic example of this. In the game, players are trying to move their three boats up a board that is constantly moving backward. Calling the board a "river" reinforces the backward movement game mechanic. A board space that stops forward progress is called a "sandbar" (as boats often get hung up on sandbars), the space that pushes the player forward is called a "high tide." Because each of these elements has dramatics associated with it, it is much easier to remember than, for instance, if the player were asked to remember that space number 3 stopped the boat and number 7 moved the boat forward.

Inscribed Technology

Much like inscribed mechanics, inscribed technology is largely understood only through its dynamic behavior. This is true whether considering paper or digital technology. The choice of how many dice of how many sides each to be thrown by the player only really matters when those dice are in play just as the code written by a programmer is only really understood by the player when she sees the game in action. This is one of the reasons that technology is the least visible of the inscribed elements.

In addition, a large overlap exists between inscribed mechanics and technology. Technology enables mechanics, and mechanical design decisions can lead to a choice of which technology to use.

Inscribed Paper Game Technology

Inscribed paper technologies in paper games are often used for randomization, state tracking, and progression:

- **Randomization:** Randomization is the most common form of technology in paper games. This ranges from dice, to cards, to dominoes, to spinners, and so on. As a designer, you have a lot of control over which of these you choose and how the randomization works. Randomization can also be combined with tables to do things like generate random encounters or characters for a game. In Chapter 11, "Math and Game Balance," you can read about the various types of randomizers and when you might want to use them.

- **State tracking:** State tracking can be everything from keeping track of the scores of the different players of the game (like a cribbage board) or tables like the complex character sheets used in some roleplaying games.

- **Progression:** Progression is often inscribed via charts and tables. This includes things such as player progression of abilities when the player levels up, the progression of various technologies and units in the technology tree of a game like *Civilization*, progression of resource renewal in the board game *Power Grid*, and so on.

Inscribed Digital Game Technology

The latter sections of this book extensively cover digital game technology in the form of programming games using Unity and the C# programming language. Just as with inscribed paper game technology, the art of game programming is that of encoding the experience you want the player to have into inscribed rules (in the form of programming code) that will then be decoded by the player as she plays the game.

Summary

The four elements of the inscribed layer make up everything that players receive when they download or purchase your game, and therefore the inscribed layer is the only one over which the game developers have complete control. In the next chapter, we allow players to move our games from the static form of the inscribed layer up to the emergence of the dynamic layer.

CHAPTER 5

THE DYNAMIC LAYER

Once players start actually playing a game, it moves from the inscribed layer into the dynamic layer of the Layered Tetrad. Play, strategy, and meaningful player choices all emerge in this layer.

This chapter explores the dynamic layer, various qualities of emergence, and how designers can anticipate the dynamic play that emerges from their inscribed design decisions.

The Role of the Player

A fellow designer once told me that a game isn't a game unless someone is playing it. Although this might sound initially like a rehash of "if a tree falls in the woods, and there's no one to hear it, does it make a sound?" it's actually much more important for interactive media than any other medium. A film can still exist and show in a theater if there's no one to watch it.[1] Television can be sent out over the airwaves and still be television, even if no one is tuned to that station. Games, however, just don't exist without players, for it is through the actions of players that games transform from a collection of inscribed elements into an experience (see Figure 5.1).

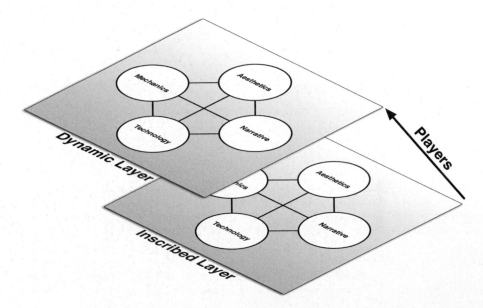

Figure 5.1   Players move the game from the inscribed layer into the dynamic layer

There are, of course, some edge cases to this, as there are to all things. The game *Core War* is a hacking game where players each try to write a computer virus that will propagate and take over a fake computer core from the viruses of their competitors. Players submit their viruses and wait for them to fight each other for memory and survival. In the yearly RoboCup tournament, various teams of robots compete against each other in soccer without any interference by the programmers during the game. In the classic card game *War*, players make no decision beyond the choice of which of the two decks to take at the beginning of the game, and the game plays out entirely based on the luck of the initial shuffle. Though in each of these cases, the player has

---

[1]   Some films, like the *Rocky Horror Picture Show,* owe a lot of their cult fandom to presentations in which the audience takes part, and the audience reactions in those films do alter the viewing experience of the other audience members. However, the film itself is completely unaffected by the audience. The dynamism in games comes from the ability of the medium to react to the player.

no input and makes no choices during the actual play of the game, the play is still influenced by player decisions made before the official start of the match, and the players certainly have interest in and are waiting for the outcome of the game. In all of these cases, it still takes players to set up the game and to make the choices that determine its outcome.

Though players have a tremendous effect on the game and gameplay (including influences on the tetrad elements), players sit outside of the tetrad as the engine that makes it work. Players cause games to come into being and allow them to become the experience that has been encoded into the inscribed layer of the game by the game developers. As designers, we rely on players to aid us in helping the game to become what we intend. There are several aspects that are completely beyond our control as designers, including whether the player is actually trying to follow the rules, whether the player cares about winning or not, the physical environment in which the game is played, the emotional state of the players, etc. Because players are so important, we as developers need to treat them with respect and take care to ensure that the inscribed elements of the game, like rules, are clear enough to the players that they can decode them into the game experience that we intend.

Emergence

The most important concept in this chapter is *emergence*, the core of which is that even very simple rules can beget complex dynamic behaviors. Consider the game of *Bartok* that you played and experimented with in Chapter 1, "Thinking Like a Designer." Though *Bartok* had very few rules, complex play emerged from them. And, once you started changing rules and adding your own, you were able to see that even simple, seemingly innocuous rule changes had the potential to lead to large changes in both the feel and the play of the game.

The dynamic layer of the Layered Tetrad encompasses the results of the intersection of player and game across all four elements of the tetrad: mechanics, aesthetics, dramatics, and technology.

Unexpected Mechanical Emergence

My colleague Scott Rogers, author of two books on game design,[2] once told me that he didn't believe in emergence. After discussing it with him for a while, we came to the conclusion that he did believe in emergence, but he didn't believe that it was legitimate for game designers to use emergence as an excuse for irresponsible design. Scott felt, and I believe, that as the designer of the systems within a game, you are responsible for the play that emerges from those systems. Of course, it's extremely difficult to know what possibilities will emerge from the rules that you put in place, which is why playtesting is so critically important. As you develop your games, playtest early, playtest often, and take special care to note unusual things that happen in only one playtest. Once your game gets out in the wild, the sheer number of people

---

[2] Scott Rogers, *Level up!: The Guide to Great Video Game Design* (Chichester, UK: Wiley, 2010) and Scott Rogers, *Swipe this! The Guide to Great Tablet Game Design* (Hoboken, NJ: John Wiley & Sons, 2012).

playing will cause those unusual flukes to happen a lot more often than you would expect. Of course, this happens to all designers—look at some of the cards that have been declared illegal in *Magic: The Gathering*—but as Scott says, it's important that designers own these issues and take care to resolve them.

Dynamic Mechanics

Dynamic mechanics are the dynamic layer of the elements that separate games and interactive media from other media; the elements that make them games. Dynamic mechanics include procedures, meaningful play, strategy, house rules, player intent, and outcome. As with the inscribed mechanics, many of these are an expansion of elements described in Tracy Fullerton's book *Game Design Workshop.*[3]

Procedures

Mechanics in the inscribed layer included rules: instructions from the designer to the players about how to play the game. Procedures are the dynamic actions taken by the players in response to those rules. Another way to say this is that procedures emerge from rules. In the game *Bartok*, if you added the rule about a player needing to announce when they had only one card left, there was an explicit procedure presented in the rules that the active player needed to do so (once she had only one card left). However, there was also an implicit procedure in that rule: the procedure of other players watching the hand of the active player so that they could catch her if she forgot to announce it. Prior to this rule, there was no real reason for a player to pay attention to the game during another person's turn, but this simple rule change altered the procedures of playing the game.

Meaningful Play

In *Rules of Play*, Katie Salen and Eric Zimmerman define meaningful play as play that is both discernable to the player and integrated into the larger game.[4]

- **Discernable:** An action is discernable to the player if the player can tell that the action has been taken. For example, when you press the call button for an elevator, the action is discernable because the call button lights up. If you've ever tried to call an elevator when the light inside the button was burned out, you know how frustrating it can be to take an action and yet not be able to discern whether the game interpreted your action.

- **Integrated:** An action is integrated if the player can tell that it is tied to the outcome of the game. For example, when you press the call button for the elevator, that action is integrated because you know that doing so will cause the elevator to stop on your floor.

---

[3] Tracy Fullerton, Christopher Swain, and Steven Hoffman, *Game Design Workshop: A Playcentric Approach to Creating Innovative Games* (Burlington, MA: Morgan Kaufmann Publishers, 2008), chapters 3 and 5.

[4] Katie Salen and Eric Zimmerman, *Rules of Play: Game Design Fundamentals* (Cambridge, MA: MIT Press, 2003), 34.

In *Super Mario Bros.*, the decision of whether to stomp an individual enemy or just avoid it is generally not very meaningful because that individual action is not integrated into the overall outcome of the game. *Super Mario Bros.* never gives you a tally of the number of enemies defeated; it only requires that you finish each level before the time runs out and finish the game without running out of lives. In HAL Laboratories' series of *Kirby* games, however, the player character Kirby gains special abilities by defeating enemies, so the decision of which enemy to defeat is directly integrated into the acquisition of abilities, and the decision is made more meaningful.

If a player's actions in the game are not meaningful, she can quickly lose interest. Salen and Zimmerman's concept of meaningful play reminds designers to constantly think about the mindset of the player and whether the interactions of their games are transparent or opaque from the player's perspective.

Strategy

When a game allows meaningful actions, players will usually create strategies to try to win the game. A strategy is a calculated set of actions to help the player achieve a goal. However, that goal can be anything of the player's choosing and does not necessarily need to be the goal of winning the game. For instance, when playing with a young child or with someone of a lower skill level in a game, the player's goal might be to make sure that the child enjoys playing the game and learns something, sometimes at the expense of the player winning the game.

Optimal Strategy

When a game is very simple and has few possible actions, it is possible for players to develop an optimal strategy for the game. If both players of a game are playing rationally with the goal of winning, an optimal strategy is the possible strategy with the highest likelihood of winning. Most games are too complex to really have an optimal strategy, but some games like *Tic-Tac-Toe* are simple enough to allow one. In fact, *Tic-Tac-Toe* is so simple that chickens have been trained to play it and force a draw or a win almost every time.[5]

An optimal strategy is more often a fuzzy idea of the kind of thing that would likely improve a player's chance of winning. For instance, in the board game *Up the River* by Manfred Ludwig, players are trying to move three boats up a river to dock at the top of the game board, and arriving at the dock is worth 12 points to the first boat to arrive, then 11 points for the second boat, and down to only 1 point for the twelfth boat. Every round (that is, every time that all players have taken one turn), the river moves backward 1 space, and any boat that falls off the end of the river (the waterfall) is lost. Each turn, the player rolls 1d6 (a single six-sided die) and chooses which boat to move. Because the average roll of a six-sided die is 3.5, and the player must choose from among her three boats to move every turn, each boat will move an average of 3.5 spaces every three of her turns. However, the board will move backward 3 spaces every

---

5 Kia Gregory, "Chinatown Fair Is Back, Without Chickens Playing Tick-Tack-Toe," *New York Times*, June 10, 2012.

three turns, so each boat only makes an average forward progression of 0.5 spaces every three turns (or 0.1666, (or 1/6) spaces every turn).[6]

In this game, the optimal strategy is for the player to never move one of her boats and just let it fall off the waterfall. Then each boat would move forward an average of 3.5 spaces every two turns instead of three. With the board moving backward 2 spaces in two turns, this would give each of her boats an average movement forward of 1.5 spaces every two turns (or 0.75 spaces each turn), which is much better than the 0.1666 afforded to the player if she tries to keep all of her boats. Then this player would have a better chance of getting to the dock in first and second place, giving her 23 total points (12 + 11). In a two-player game, this strategy wouldn't work because the second player would tie up at 10, 9, and 8 for 27 points, but in a three or four-player game, it's the closest thing to an optimal strategy in this game. However, the other players' choices, randomized outcomes of the dice, and other factors mean that it won't always ensure a win; it will just make a win more likely.

Designing for Strategy

As a designer, you can do several things to make strategy more important in your game. For now, the main thing to keep in mind is that presenting the player with multiple possible ways to win will require her to make more difficult strategic decisions during play. In addition, if some of these goals conflict with each other while others are complementary (i.e., some of the requirements for the two goals are the same), this can actually cause individual players to move into certain roles as the game progresses. Once a player can see that she is starting to fulfill one of the goals, she will pick its complementary goals to pursue as well, and this will lead her to make tactical decisions that fulfill the role for which those goals were designed. If these goals cause her to take a specific type of action in the game, it can alter her in-game relationship with other players.

An example of this comes from the game *Settlers of Catan*, designed by Klaus Teuber. In this game, players acquire resources through random die rolls and trade, and some of the five game resources are useful in the early game while others are useful at the end. Three that are less useful at the beginning are sheep, wheat, and ore; however, together, the three can be traded for a development card. The most common development card is the soldier card, which can move the robber token onto any space, allowing the player moving it to steal from another player. Therefore, an excess of ore, wheat, and sheep at the beginning of the game can lead the player to purchase development cards, and because having the largest number of soldier cards played can earn the player victory points, the combination of that resource and that potential goal can influence the player to rob the other players more often and actually make her play the role of the bully in the game.

House Rules

House rules occur when the players themselves intentionally modify the rules. As you saw in the *Bartok* game example, even a simple rule change can have drastic effects on the game. For

---

[6] There are additional rules of the game that I'm omitting for the sake of simplicity in the explanation.

instance, most players of *Monopoly* have house rules that cut the auction of property (which happens if someone lands on an unowned property and chooses not to buy it) and add collection of all fines to the Free Parking space to be picked up by a player who lands on that space. The removal of the auction rule removes nearly all potential strategy from the beginning of *Monopoly* (converting it into an extremely slow random property distribution system), and the second rule removes some determinism from the game (since it could benefit any player, either the one in the lead or in last place). Not all house rules are bad, of course, and some make games considerably more fun.[7] In all cases, however, they are an example of the players beginning to take some ownership of the game, making it a little more theirs and a little less the designer's. The fantastic thing about house rules is that they are many people's first experimentation with game design.

Player Intent: Bartle's Types, Cheaters, Spoilsports

Something that you will have little or no control over is the intent of your players. While most players will be playing your game rationally to win, you may also have to contend with cheaters and spoilsports. Even within legitimate players of games, you will find four distinct personality types as defined by Richard Bartle, one of the designers of the first MUD (multi-user dungeon, a text-based online ancestor of modern massively multiplayer online roleplaying games). The four types of players that he defined have existed since his early MUD and carry through all multiplayer online games today. His 1996 article "Hearts, Clubs, Diamonds, Spades: Players Who Suit MUDs"[8] contains fantastic information on how these types of players interact with each other and the game as well as information about how to grow your community of players in positive ways.

Bartle's four types (which he also identified with the four suits of a deck of cards) are as follows:

- **Achiever (Diamond):** Seeks to get the highest score in the game. Wants to dominate the game.
- **Explorer (Spade):** Seeks to find all the hidden places in the game. Wants to understand the game.
- **Socializer (Heart):** Wants to play the game with friends. Wants to understand the other players.
- **Killer (Club):** Wants to provoke other players of the game. Wants to dominate the other players.

---

[7] If you're ever playing the game *Lunch Money* by Atlas Games, try allowing players to attack another player, heal themselves, **and** discard any cards they don't want each turn (rather than having to choose one of the three). It makes the game a lot more frantic!

[8] Richard Bartle, "Hearts, Clubs, Diamonds, Spades: Players Who Suit Muds," http://www.mud.co.uk/richard/hcds.htm, accessed February 2, 2014.

These can be understood as belonging to a 2x2 continuum (also from Bartle's article). Figure 5.2 represents this graphically.

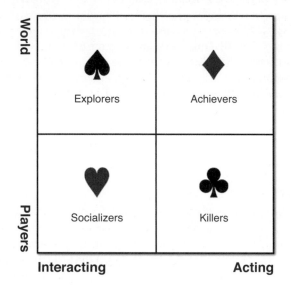

Figure 5.2   Richard Bartle's four players who suit MUDs[9]

There are certainly other theories of player motivation and player types,[10] but Bartle's are the most widely recognized and understood in the game industry.

The other two player types that you may encounter are cheaters and spoilsports:

- **Cheaters:** Care about winning but don't care about the integrity of the game. Cheaters will bend or break the rules to win.

- **Spoilsports:** Don't care about winning or about the game. Spoilsports will often break the game to ruin other players' experiences.

Neither of these are players that you want in your game, but you need to understand their motivations. For instance, if a cheater feels that she has a chance of winning legitimately, she may not feel as driven to cheat. Spoilsports are much more difficult to deal with since they don't care about the game or winning, but you rarely have to deal with spoilsports in digital single-player games, because they would have no reason to play the game if they weren't interested in it in the first place. However, even great players can sometimes become spoilsports when they encounter terrible game mechanics...often right before they choose to turn the game off.

---

9   Adapted from: Richard Bartle, "Hearts, Clubs, Diamonds, Spades: Players Who Suit Muds," http://www.mud.co.uk/richard/hcds.htm, accessed February 2, 2014.

10 See Nick Yee's "Motivations of Play in MMORPGs: Results from a Factor Analytic Approach," http://www.nickyee.com/Daedalus/motivations.pdf.

Outcome

Outcome is the result of playing the game. All games have an outcome. Many traditional games are *zero sum,* meaning that one player wins and the other loses. However, this is not the only kind of outcome that a game can have. In fact, every individual moment in a game has its own outcome. There are several different levels of outcome in most games:

- **Immediate outcome:** Each individual action has an outcome. When a player attacks an enemy, the outcome of that attack is either a miss or a hit and the resultant damage to the enemy. When a player purchases property in *Monopoly*, the outcome is that the player has less money available but now owns the potential to earn more money.

- **Quest outcome:** In many games, the player will be sent on missions or quests and will gain some sort of reward for completing that quest. Missions and quests often have narratives constructed around them (e.g., a little girl has lost her balloon in *Spider-man 2*, so Spider-man must retrieve it for her), so the outcome of the quest also marks the end of the tiny narrative surrounding it.

- **Cumulative outcome:** When the player has been working toward a goal over time and finally achieves it, that is a cumulative outcome. One of the most common examples of this is leveling up in a game with experience points (XP). Everything that the player does accrues a few experience points, and once the total number of XP has reached a threshold, the player's in-game character gains a new level, which grants the character a boost in stats or abilities. The main difference between this and a quest outcome is that the cumulative outcome usually doesn't have a narrative wrapped around it, and the player often reaches the cumulative outcome passively while actively doing something else (e.g., a player of *Dungeons & Dragons 4th Edition* actively takes part in a game session and then, while adding up earned XP at the end of the evening, notices that she has reached 10,000 XP and achieved level 7).[11]

- **Final outcome:** Most games have an outcome that ends the game: A player wins chess (and the other loses), a player finishes *Final Fantasy VII* and saves the world from Sephiroth, and so on. There are a few games where the final outcome doesn't end the game (e.g., in *Skyrim*, even when the player has finished the main quest, she can still continue to play in the world and experience other quests). Interestingly, the death of the player character is very rarely a final outcome in games.

  In the few games where death is a final outcome (e.g., the game *Rogue*, where a single loss will cause the player to lose all progress in the game), the individual game session is usually relatively short so that the player doesn't feel a tremendous loss at the death of the player character. In most games, however, death is just a temporary setback and in-game checkpoints usually ensure that the player never loses more than five minutes of progress in the game.

---

[11] Rob Heinsoo, Andy Collins, and James Wyatt, *Dungeons & Dragons Player's Handbook: Arcane, Divine, and Martial Heroes: Roleplaying Game Core Rules* (Renton, WA: Wizards of the Coast, 2008).

Dynamic Aesthetics

Just as with dynamic mechanics, dynamic aesthetics are those that emerge when playing the game. There are two different primary categories:

■ **Procedural aesthetics:** Aesthetics that are programmatically generated by digital game code (or via the application of mechanics in a paper game). These include procedural music and art that emerge directly from inscribed aesthetics and technology.

■ **Environmental aesthetics:** These are the aesthetics of the environment in which the game is played, and they are largely beyond the control of the game developers.

Procedural Aesthetics

Procedural aesthetics, as we generally think of them, are created programmatically by combining technology and inscribed aesthetics. These are called *procedural* because they arise from procedures (also known as functions) that have been written programming code. If you look at the cascading waterfall of objects that is created in the first programming chapter (Chapter 18, "Hello World: Your First Program"), that could be considered procedural art because it is an interesting visual that emerges from C# programming code. In professional games, two of the most common forms of procedural aesthetics are music and visual art.

Procedural Music

Procedural music has become very common in modern videogames, and it is currently created through three different techniques:

■ **Horizontal Re-Sequencing (HRS):** HRS rearranges the order of several precomposed sections of music according to the emotional impact that the designers wish for the current moment in the game. An example of this is LucasArts' iMUSE (Interactive MUsic Streaming Engine), which was used in the *X-Wing* game series as well as many of LucasArts adventure games. In *X-Wing*, the pre-composed music is sections of John William's score for the *Star Wars* films. Using iMUSE, designers are able to play peaceful music when the player is just flying through space, ominous music when enemy forces are about to attack, victory music whenever a player destroys an enemy craft or achieves an objective, and so on. There are also longer sections of music that are meant to loop and provide a single mood as well as very short sections of music (one or two measures in length) that are used to mask the transition from one mood to the next. This is currently the most common type of procedural music technology and harkens at least as far back as *Super Mario Bros.*, which played a transitional musical string and then switched background music when the player had less than 99 seconds to complete the current level.

■ **Vertical Re-Orchestration (VRO):** VRO includes recordings of various tracks of a single song that can be individually enabled or disabled. This is used very commonly in rhythm games like *PaRappa the Rapper* and *Frequency*. In *PaRappa*, there are four different tracks of music representing four different levels of success for the player. The player's success is ranked every few measures, and if she either drops or increases in rank, the background music switches to a worse- or better-sounding track to reflect this. In *Frequency* and its sequel *Amplitude*, the player controls a craft traveling down a tunnel, the walls of which represent various tracks in a studio recording of a song. When the player succeeds at the rhythm game on a certain wall, that track of the recording is enabled. *Amplitude* includes a mode where players can choose which tracks to enable at any point in the song to create their own remix of the tracks included with the game. This is nearly ubiquitous in rhythm games—with the fantastic Japanese rhythm game *Osu Tatake Ouendan!* and its Western successor *Elite Beat Agents* as marked exceptions—and has also become common in other games to give the player musical feedback on the health of their character, speed of their vehicle, and so on.

- **Procedural Composition (PCO):** PCO is the most rare form of procedural music because it takes the most time and skill to execute. In PCO, rather than rearrange various precomposed tracks of music or enable and disable precomposed tracks, the computer program actually composes music from individual notes based on programmed rules of composition, pacing, etc. One of the earliest commercial experiments in this realm was *C.P.U. Bach* by Sid Meier and Jeff Brigs, a title for the 3DO console. In *C.P.U. Bach*, the player was able to select various instruments and parameters, and the game would craft a Bach-like musical composition based on procedural rules.

  Another fantastic example of procedural composition is the music created by composer and game designer Vincent Diamante for the game *Flower* by thatgamecompany. For the game, Diamante created both precomposed sections of music and rules for procedural composition. During gameplay, background music is usually playing (some of which is re-arranged based on the situation using HRS) as the player flies over flowers in a field and opens them by passing near. Each flower that is opened creates a single note as it blooms, and Diamante's PCO engine chooses a note for that flower that will blend harmoniously with the precomposed music and create a melody along with other flower notes. Regardless of when the player passes over a flower, the system will choose a note that fits well with the current audio soundscape, and passing over several flowers in sequence will procedurally generate pleasing melodies.

Procedural Visual Art

Procedural visual art is created when programming code acts dynamically to create in-game visuals. There are a few forms of procedural visuals with which you are probably already familiar:

- **Particle systems:** As the most common form of procedural visuals, particle systems are seen in almost every game these days. The dust cloud that rises when Mario lands a jump in *Super Mario Galaxy*, the fire effects in *Uncharted 3*, and the sparks that appear when cars crash into each other in *Burnout* are all various versions of particle effects. Unity has a very fast and robust particle effects engine (see Figure 5.3) that you will use to create a fire spell in Chapter 35, "Prototype 8: Omega Mage."

- **Procedural animation:** Procedural animation covers everything from flocking behavior for groups of creatures to the brilliant procedural animation engine in Will Wright's *Spore* that created walk, run, attack, and other animations for any creature that a player could design. With traditional animation, the animated creatures always follow the exact paths inscribed by the animator. In procedural animation, the animated creatures follow procedural rules that emerge into complex motion and behavior. You will get some experience with the flocking behavior known as *boids* in Chapter 26, "Object-Oriented Thinking" (see Figure 5.4).

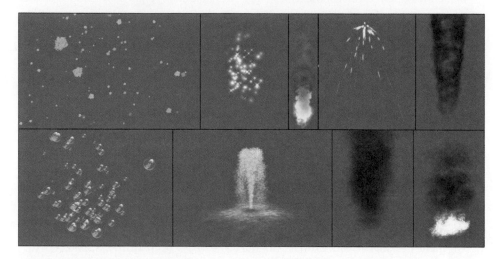

Figure 5.3   Various particle effects that are included with Unity

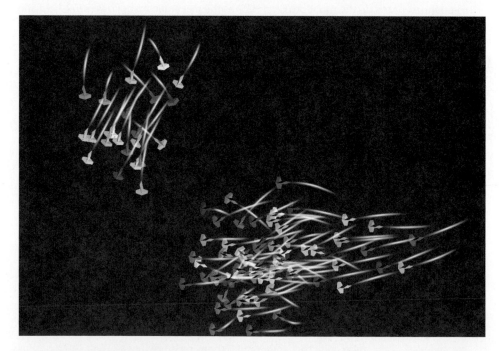

Figure 5.4   Boids, an example of procedural animation from Chapter 26

- **Procedural environments:** The most obvious example of a procedural environment in games is the world of *Minecraft* by Mojang. Each time a player starts a new game of *Minecraft*, an entire world (billions of square kilometers in size) is created for her to explore from a single seed number (known as the *random seed*). Because digital random number generators are never actually random, this means that anyone who starts from the same seed will get the same world.

Environmental Aesthetics

The other major kind of dynamic aesthetics are those controlled by the environment in which the game is played. While these are beyond the control of the game designer, it is still the designer's responsibility to understand what environmental aesthetics might arise and accommodate them as much as possible.

Visual Play Environment

Players will play games in a variety of settings and on a variety of equipment, so it's necessary as a designer to be aware of the issues that this may cause. You should accommodate two elements in particular:

- **Brightness of the environment:** Most game developers tend to work in environments where the light level is carefully controlled to make the images on their screen as clear as possible. Players don't always interact with games in environments with perfect lighting. If your player is on a computer outside, playing on a projector, or playing anywhere else with imperfect control of lighting, it can be very difficult for them to clearly see scenes in your game that are meant to be taking place in a dark setting. Remember to make sure that your visual aesthetic either has a lot of contrast in it between light and dark or allows the player the ability to adjust the gamma or brightness level of the visuals. This is especially important if designing for a phone or other mobile device, since these can easily be played outside in direct sunlight.

- **Resolution of the player's screen:** If you are developing for a fixed-screen device like the iPad or PSVita, this won't be an issue. However, if you're designing for a computer or game console, you have very little control over the resolution or quality of your player's screen, particularly if it's a console game. You cannot assume that your player will have a 1080p or even 720p screen. All modern consoles before the PS4 and Xbox One could still output the standard composite video signal that has existed for standard-definition television since the '50s. If you're dealing with a player on a standard-def television, you will need to use a much larger font size to make it at all legible. Even AAA games like *Mass Effect*, *The Last of Us*, and *Assassin's Creed* don't accommodate this well, and it is impossible to read critical text in these games on any television made more than 10 years ago. You never know when someone might be trying to play your game on older equipment, but you can detect whether this is the case and change the font size to help them out.

Auditory Play Environment

As with the visual play environment, you rarely have control over the audio environment in which your game is played. Though this is essential to understand when making a mobile game, it's also important to keep in mind for any game. Things to consider include the following:

- **Noisy environments:** Any number of things may be happening at the same time as your game, so you need to make sure that your player can still play even if they miss or can't hear some of the audio. You also need to make sure that the game itself doesn't create an environment so noisy that the player misses critical information. In general, important dialog and spoken instructions should be the loudest sounds in your game, and the rest of the mix should be kept a little quieter. You will also want to avoid subtle, quiet audio cues for anything important in the game.

- **The player controls the volume:** The player might mute your game. This is especially true with mobile games where you can never count on the player to be listening. For any game, make sure that you have alternatives to sound. If you have important dialogue, make sure to allow the player to turn on subtitles. If you have sound cues to inform players of where things are, make sure to also include visual cues as well.

Player Considerations

Another critical thing to consider about the environment in which your game will be played is the player herself. Not all players have the optimal ability to sense all five aesthetics. A player who is deaf should really be able to play your game with little trouble, especially if you follow the advice in the last few paragraphs. However, there are two other considerations in particular that many designers miss:

- **Colorblindness:** About 7% to 10% of Caucasian men have some form of colorblindness. There are several different forms of deficiency in color perception, the most common of which causes a person to be unable to differentiate between similar shades of red and green. Because colorblindness is so common, you should be able to find a colorblind friend that you can ask to playtest your game and make sure that there isn't key information being transmitted by color in a way that they can't see. Another fantastic way to check for your game is to take a screen shot and bring it into Photoshop. Under the *View* menu in Photoshop is a submenu called *Proof Setup*, and in there, you can find settings for the two most common types of color blindness. This will enable you to view your screen shot as it would be viewed by your colorblind players.

- **Epilepsy and migraine:** Both migraines and epileptic seizures can be caused by rapidly flashing lights, and children with epilepsy are particularly prone to having seizures triggered by light. In 1997, an episode of the Pokemon television show in Japan triggered simultaneous seizures in hundreds of viewers because of flickering images in one scene.[12] Nearly all games now ship with a warning that they may cause epileptic seizures, but the occurrence of that is now very rare because developers have accepted the responsibility to consider the effect their games might have on their players and have removed rapidly flashing lights from their games.

---

[12] Sheryl WuDunn, "TV Cartoon's Flashes Send 700 Japanese Into Seizures," *New York Times*, December 18, 1997.

Dynamic Narrative

There are several ways of looking at narrative from a dynamic perspective. The epitome of the form is the experience of players and their game master when playing a traditional pen-and-paper roleplaying game. While there have certainly been experiments into crafting truly interactive digital narratives, after over 30 years, they still haven't reached the level of interaction in a well-run game of *Dungeons & Dragons* (D&D). The reason that *D&D* can create such fantastic dynamic narratives is that the dungeon master (DM: the player running the game for the others) is constantly considering the desires, fears, and evolving skills of her players and crafting a story around them. As mentioned earlier in this book, if the players run into a low-level enemy that (due to random die rolls working in its favor) is very difficult to fight, the DM can choose to have that enemy escape at the last minute and then return as a nemesis for the players to fight later. A human DM can adapt the game and the game narrative to the players in a way that is very difficult for a computer to replicate.

Interactive Narrative Incunabula

In 1997, Janet Murray, a professor at the Georgia Institute of Technology, published the book *Hamlet on the Holodeck*[13] in which she examined the early history of interactive narrative in relation to the early history of other forms of narrative media. In her book, Murray explores the incunabular stage of other media, which is the stage when that medium was between its initial creation and its mature form. For instance, in the incunabular stage of film, directors were attempting to shoot 10-minute versions of *Hamlet* and *King Lear* (due to the 10-minute length of a single reel of 16mm film), and incunabular television was largely just televised versions of popular radio programs. Having many examples from other media, Murray proceeds to talk about the growth of interactive digital fiction and where it is currently in its incunabular stage. She covers early Infocom text adventure games like the *Zork* series and *Planetfall* and points out two very compelling aspects that make interactive fiction unique.

Interactive Fiction Happens to the Player

Unlike nearly every other form of narrative, interactive fiction is happening directly to the player. The following happens near the beginning of the game *Zork*. (The lines preceded by a right angle bracket [e.g., > open trap door] are the commands entered by the player.)

```
...With the rug moved, the dusty cover of a closed trap door appears.

> open trap door

The door reluctantly opens to reveal a rickety staircase descending
into darkness.

> down
```

---

[13] Janet Horowitz Murray, *Hamlet on the Holodeck* (New York: Free Press, 1997).

```
It is pitch dark. You are likely to be eaten by a grue.

> light lamp

The lamp is now on.
You are in a dark and damp cellar with a narrow passageway leading
east and a crawlway to the south. To the west is the bottom of a
steep metal ramp which is unclimbable.
The door crashes shut, and you hear someone barring it.14
```

The key element here is that *you* hear someone barring it. *You* are now trapped. Interactive fiction is the only narrative medium where the player/reader is the character taking actions and suffering consequences in the narrative.

Relationships Are Developed Through Shared Experience

Another compelling aspect of interactive fiction is that it allows the player to develop a relationship with other characters through shared experience. Murray cites *Planetfall*,[15] another Infocom text adventure, as a fantastic example of this. Following the destruction of the spaceship on which she was a janitor, the player is largely alone for the first section of *Planetfall*. Eventually, she comes across a machine to make warrior robots, but when she engages it, it malfunctions and produces a child-like, mostly useless robot named Floyd. Floyd follows the player around for the remainder of the game and does little more than provide comic relief. Much later in the game, there is a device locked in a bio-lab that the player must retrieve, but the lab is full of both radiation and vicious aliens. Immediately, Floyd simply says "Floyd go get!" and enters the lab to retrieve the item. Floyd soon returns, but he is leaking oil and barely able to move. He dies in the player's arms as she sings the *Ballad of the Starcrossed Miner* to him. Many players reported to the designer of *Planetfall*, Steven Meretzky, that they cried when Floyd died, and Murray cites this as one of the first examples of a tangible emotional connection between a player and an in-game character.

Emergent Narrative

True dynamic narrative emerges when the players and game mechanics contribute to the story. Several years ago, I was playing in a *Dungeons & Dragons* 3.5 edition game with some friends. The game master had us in a pretty tight spot. We had just retrieved an artifact from some forces of evil in another dimension and were being chased by a large balrog[16] as we fled down a narrow cave on our flying carpet toward the portal back to our dimension. It was gaining on us quickly, and our weapons were having little effect. However, I remembered a little-used property of the Rod of Splendor that I possessed. Once per week, I could use the Rod of Splendor

---

[14] *Zork* was created at the Massachusetts Institute of Technology in 1977–79 by Tim Anderson, Marc Blank, Bruce Daniels, and Dave Lebling. They formed Infocom in 1979 and released *Zork* as a commercial product.

[15] *Planetfall* was designed by Steve Meretzky and published by Infocom in 1983.

[16] A balrog is the giant winged demon of fire and smoke that faced Gandalf in the "you shall not pass" scene of *The Fellowship of the Ring* by J. R. R. Tolkien.

to create a huge pavilion of silk, 60 feet across, inside of which were the furnishings and food for a party to entertain 100 people.[17] Usually, we would use this capability of the rod to throw a party when we'd finished a mission, but this time I cast the tent directly behind us in the tunnel. Because the tunnel was only 30 feet wide, the balrog crashed into the tent and became entangled, allowing us to escape without anyone dying.

This kind of unexpected story emerges from a combination of the situation created by the game master, the game's rules, and the creativity of individual players. I have encountered many similar stories through the roleplaying campaigns that I have been part of (as both a player and game master), and you can do several things to encourage this kind of collaborative storytelling in roleplaying campaigns that you run. For more information about roleplaying games and how to run a good campaign, see the "Roleplaying Games" section of Appendix B, "Useful Concepts."

Dynamic Technology

As with the previous chapter, because other large sections of this book are devoted to game technology it is covered very little in this chapter. The core concept for you to know at this point is that the game code you author (your inscribed technology) will be a system that runs as the player is experiencing the game. As with all dynamic systems, emergence will occur, and this means that there is both the opportunity for wonderful, unexpected things to happen and the danger of horrible, unexpected things to happen. Dynamic technology covers all of the runtime behavior of your code and the ways in which it affects the player. This could be anything from a system to simulate physics to artificial intelligence code to anything else that is implemented in your code.

To find information on the dynamic behavior of paper game technologies such as dice, spinners, cards, and other randomizers, look to Chapter 11, "Math and Game Balance." For information on digital game technologies, you can look to the latter two parts of the book as well as Appendix B.

Summary

Dynamic mechanics, aesthetics, narrative, and technology all emerge from the act of players playing a game. While the elements that emerge can be challenging to predict, it is the responsibility of designers to playtest in order to understand the envelope of that emergence.

The next chapter will explore the cultural layer of the Layered Tetrad, the layer beyond gameplay. It is in the cultural layer that players gain more control over the game than the original game developers, and it is the cultural layer that is experienced by members of society who do not ever play the game themselves.

---

[17] The Dungeons & Dragons 3.5e System Reference Document entry for the Rod of Splendor is at http://www.d20srd.org/srd/magicItems/rods.htm#splendor.

CHAPTER 6

THE CULTURAL LAYER

As the final layer in the Layered Tetrad, the cultural layer is the furthest from the designer's hand, yet it is still critical to a holistic understanding of game design and the implications of game development.

This chapter explores the cultural layer, the space where player communities and society take control of the game and make it their own.

Beyond Play

The inscribed and dynamic layers are obvious to all game designers, as they are both integral to the concept of interactive experiences. The cultural layer, however, is a little less obvious. The cultural layer exists at the intersection of the game and society. The players of a game become a community united by their shared experience of play, and that community takes the concepts and intellectual property of the game out into the world. The cultural layer of the game is seen from one side by the community of players who have intimate knowledge of the game and from the other by the members of society in general who have no prior knowledge of the game and first encounter it not through play but through the artifacts created by this community of players (see Figure 6.1).

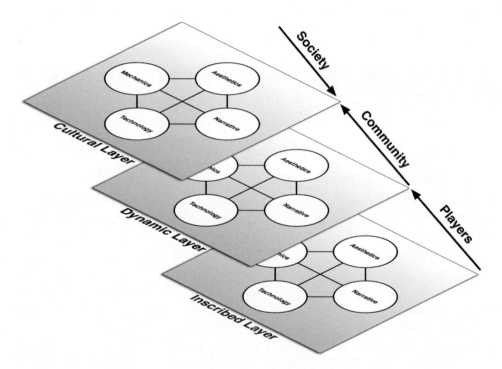

Figure 6.1   The cultural layer, created by the community of game players and witnessed by society

As Constance Steinkuehler points out in her paper "The Mangle of Play,"[1] the dynamic play of a game—particularly a massively multiplayer game—is an "interactively stabilized mangle of practice." In saying so, she points out that, as discussed in the preceding chapter, the dynamic layer of a game is composed not only of the intents of the game developers but also of the intents of the players, and the overall responsibility for and control over the experience is

---

[1]   Constance Steinkuehler. "The Mangle of Play." *Games and Culture 1*, no. 3 (2006): 199–213.

shared between players and developers. Extending this concept, it is in the cultural layer that the players (and society in general) have more control and agency than the original developers. The cultural layer is where player communities actually change the inscribed game though game mods (that is, modifications to the game through software that changes the inscribed game elements), it is where player communities seize ownership of the game narrative by writing their own fan fiction, and it is where players create their own game-related aesthetics through fan art and music.

Unlike the inscribed layer, where the four elements (mechanics, aesthetics, narrative, and technology) are distinctly assigned to different members of the development team, there is much more overlap and fuzziness of borders between elements when they are examined through the lens of the cultural layer. Fan-made game mods, which feature prominently in the cultural layer, are often combinations of all four elements with the responsibility for each element within the mod often shared by the players and communities who make them.[2]

In the sections that follow, the four elemental divisions are maintained to provide consistency with the preceding chapters and to encourage you to look at the examples listed through the lens of that particular element. However, many of the examples listed under one cultural element could also have been listed under another.

Cultural Mechanics

Cultural mechanics occur when players take the mechanics of the game into their own hands, sometimes even crafting a new experience out of the game. The most common examples of this include the following:

- **Game mods:** Players repurpose the game to accommodate their own mechanics. This is most extensive in games for Windows-based personal computers. Players modded *Quake 2* by Id to make dozens if not hundreds of new games that all used the technology of *Quake 2* but replaced the mechanics with gameplay and levels of their own (often also replacing the aesthetics and dramatics).

  Several fantastic game mods have become commercial products in their own right. *Counter Strike* started as a mod for *Half-Life* and was subsequently purchased by Valve, the *Half-Life* developers.[3] Similarly, *Defense of the Ancients* (*DotA*) started as a fan mod for Blizzard's

---

[2] I definitely do not mean to disparage the developers of game mods by continuing to refer to them throughout this chapter as *players*. By doing so, I am only attempting to be clear so that there is no confusion between the *developers* (i.e., developers of the inscribed content) and *players* (i.e., those who played the game and who may develop game mods). Many fantastic game designers and developers have started by making game mods, and doing so is a fantastic way to practice the craft.

[3] http://www.ign.com/articles/2000/11/23/counter-strike-2 and http://en.wikipedia.org/wiki/Counter-Strike

game *Warcraft III* and eventually popularized the entire genre of multi-user online battle arenas (MOBAs).[4]

In addition, many companies have released editors for their games that encourage and allow players to create custom content for the game. For example, Bethesda Softworks has released Creation Kit for their game *The Elder Scrolls V: Skyrim*. Creation Kit allows players to create their own levels, quests, NPCs (nonplayer characters), etc. Bethesda has done this before for other games, including *Fallout 3* and earlier games in the *Elder Scrolls* series.

- **Custom game levels:** Even without changing the other mechanics, some games accommodate player-made levels. In fact, some games rely on players to make levels for the game. *Little Big Planet* by Media Molecule and *Sound Shapes* by Queasy Games both include simple level-editor tools and expect some of their players to create levels for the game. Both games also include systems for players to distribute the levels they create and to rate levels created by other players. The game editors and mod creation kits like those released for *Skyrim* and *Fallout 3* also include level editors, and the level editing community for Epic's first-person shooter *Unreal* is one of the broadest and most mature in modern gaming.

The major aspect that differentiates cultural mechanics like game mods from house rules (a dynamic mechanic) is whether the inscribed mechanics of the game are actually changed. If the inscribed mechanics remain the same but players choose to apply their own goals to the game (e.g., players choosing to do a "speed run" and finish the game as quickly as possible or attempting to play through a usually violent game like *Skyrim* without directly killing any enemies), that behavior still fits within the realm of dynamic mechanics. It is when players take control from the designers by modifying the inscribed elements of the game that the behavior moves into the cultural layer.

Cultural Aesthetics

Cultural aesthetics occur when the community of players creates their own aesthetics that relate to the game. This is often in the form of their own versions of the character art, music, or other aesthetics of the game, but it also can take the form of the community using the game engine to achieve their own aesthetic purposes:

- **Fan art:** Many artists take games and game characters as inspiration for their work and create new art that depicts those characters.
- **Cosplay:** Similar to fan art, cosplay (a portmanteau of costume and play) is the practice of a fan of a game (or comic, anime, manga, or film) dressing up as one of the characters from the game. In cosplay, the cosplayer takes on the role and personality of the game character in the real world, just as she did in the virtual world of the game. Cosplay is most commonly seen at game, anime, and comic fan conventions.

---

[4] According to http://en.wikipedia.org/wiki/Multiplayer_online_battle_arena and http://themittani.com/features/dota-2-history-lesson, DotA was originally a *Warcraft III* remake of a mod for *Starcraft* known as *Aeon of Strife*. Both *Warcraft III* and *Starcraft* were created by Blizzard.

- **Gameplay as art:** As was mentioned in an earlier chapter, in Keith Burgun's book *Game Design Theory*, he proposes that some game developers should be seen in much the same way as those who make musical instruments: artisans who craft tools that performers can use to make art. According to him, there is an art not only to crafting games but also to gameplay itself, and the elegance with which some highly skilled players can play a game should be regarded as an aesthetic in and of itself.

Cultural Narrative

Sometimes, the community of players of a game will use the game or the world of the game to tell their own stories and create their own narratives. With pen and paper roleplaying games such as *Dungeons & Dragons*, this is a necessary part of the dynamics of play. However, there are also examples of players doing this far outside of the standard or expected dynamics of gameplay:

- **Fan fiction:** Just as with film, television, or any other form of narrative media, some fans of games will write their own stories about the game's characters or world.

- **Narrative game mods:** Some games like *Skyrim* and *Neverwinter Nights* allow the players to use authorized tools to create their own interactive narratives within the game world. This allows players to tell their own stories with the game's characters, and because they are built with tools similar to those used by the game developers, these stories can have the same depth and branching as the narratives originally inscribed in the game.

  One particularly inspiring narrative game mod was just a simple change made by Mike Hoye, a father and fan of *The Legend of Zelda: The Windwaker*. Hoye had been playing the game with his daughter, Maya, and she absolutely loved it, but he was bothered by the game constantly referring to Link (as played by Maya) as a boy. Mike hacked the game to create a version that referred to Link as a girl. In Hoye's words, "As you might imagine, I'm not having my daughter growing up thinking girls don't get to be the hero and rescue their little brothers." This small change by a player of the game allowed his daughter to feel empowered as the hero of the story in a way she couldn't have playing the original, gender-biased game.[5]

- **Machinima:** Another interesting example of narrative in the cultural layer is *machinima*, which are linear videos made by taking screenshots of a game. One of the most famous of these is the *Red vs. Blue (RvB)*, a comedy series by Rooster Teeth Productions that takes place entirely within the world of Bungie's first-person shooter, *Halo*. In its original incarnation, the videos were all asymmetrically letterboxed with a thin bar at the top and a thick black bar at the bottom. The bottom bar was there to cover the gun that would have been in the scene because the creators of *Red vs. Blue* originally used footage exactly as seen by players in the game. In those early videos, you can still see the aiming reticle of the gun.

---

[5] You can read Mike Hoye's original blog post about this and download the custom patch that he made at http://exple.tive.org/blarg/2012/11/07/flip-all-the-pronouns/.

Red vs. Blue began in April 2003 and has become much more successful and polished over the years, eventually even receiving direct support from the Bungie team. A bug in the original version of *Halo* caused a character's head to pop back up to looking straight forward when the character's gun was aimed all the way down. This was used by Rooster Teeth to make it look like the characters were nodding their heads while talking (without their guns pointing at each other). In *Halo 2*, Bungie fixed this bug but enabled a non-aiming posture for characters to make machinima like *RvB* easier to make.

Other game engines have also embraced machinima. *Quake* by Id was one of the earliest heavily used machinima engines. *Uncharted 2: Drake's Deception* by Naughty Dog had a multiplayer online Machinima Mode that encouraged players to make machinima with the game engine and enabled several changes to camera angles, animation, and more.

Cultural Technology

As mentioned in the note earlier in this chapter, there is a lot of fuzziness between the four elements in the cultural layer, and therefore, most of the examples of cultural technology have already been listed under the other three elements (e.g., game mods, which are listed under cultural mechanics but also require technology for their implementation). As with the other three elements, the core of cultural technology is twofold; it covers both the effect that the game's technology has on the lives of players once they have stopped playing and the technology that player communities develop to alter the inscribed technology in the game or the dynamic game experience:

- **Game technology beyond games:** Over the past couple of decades, game technology has expanded by leaps and bounds. The increasing resolution of displays (e.g., the transition of television from 480i to 1080p and 4K) and the appetite of players for progressively better-looking games have driven developers to constantly improve their techniques for rendering high-quality graphics quickly. These real-time techniques, developed for games, have found their way into everything from medical imaging to previsualization of films (the practice of using game-like animations and real-time graphics to carefully plan complicated shots).

- **Player-made external tools:** External tools, created by players, that can change a player's game experience but don't count as game mods because they don't alter any of the inscribed mechanics of the game are part of the technical layer. Examples include the following:

    - Map applications for *Minecraft* enable players to see a large-area map of their game, giving them the ability to search for specific geographic features or minerals.

    - Damage per second (DPS) calculators for massively multiplayer online games (MMOGs), like *World of Warcraft*, that can help players determine the best ways to level their characters and the best equipment to obtain to do the most average damage per second in combat.

- Any of several tools for the MMOG *Eve Online* that are available on iOS. These include tools to manage skill training, assets, in-game mail, and so on.[6]

- Fan-made game guides like those available at http://gamefaqs.com. These guides help players understand the game better and can improve a player's ability to play a game well, but they don't actually modify the inscribed game.

Authorized Transmedia Are Not in the Cultural Layer

The word *transmedia* refers to narrative or intellectual property that exists across more than one medium. An excellent example of this is *Pokemon*, which has been extremely successful as a television show, a card game, a series of handheld games for portable Nintendo consoles, and a manga series since its creation in 1996. There are many other examples of this, including the video games made to accompany the release of nearly every new Disney film and the movies that have been made from famous games like *Resident Evil* and *Tomb Raider*.

Transmedia can be an important part of the brand of a game and can be a strategy to increase market penetration and duration of that brand. However, it's important to draw a distinction between authorized transmedia (like the *Pokemon* example) and unauthorized fan-made transmedia. The latter belongs in the cultural layer, but the former does not (see Figure 6.2).

The inscribed, dynamic, and cultural layers of the Layered Tetrad are separated based on the progression from the elements inscribed by the game's creators through the dynamic play of the game by players and out to the cultural impact that playing the game has on the players and society. In contrast, authorized transmedia are the re-inscribing of the game's brand into something else by the owners of that brand and intellectual property (the ID owners). This places authorized transmedia firmly on the inscribed layer; each individual transmedia property is another product on the inscribed layer that has the possibility of its own dynamic and cultural layers. The important distinction is one of who has control. In both the inscribed layer of a game and an authorized transmedia companion product to a game, the control is held by the company that develops the game. When the game moves into the dynamic layer, the control is shared between technologies and mechanics put in place by the developers and the actual actions, procedures, strategies, and such executed by the players. In the cultural layer, the control has shifted completely from the developers of the game to the community of players of the game. For this reason, fan fiction, cosplay, game mods, and fan-made transmedia all belong in the cultural layer, but authorized transmedia products do not.

To learn more about transmedia, I recommend reading Professor Henry Jenkins' books and papers on the topic.

---

[6] In *Eve Online*, skills are trained in real time regardless of whether the player is currently logged in; so, having an alarm to tell the player that a skill is done and she can now select a new one to train is very useful (information from http://pozniak.pl/wp/?p=4882 and https://itunes.apple.com/us/app/neocom/id418895101).

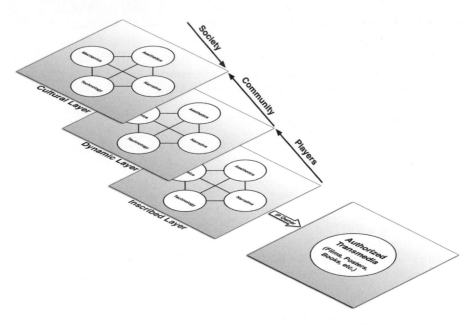

Figure 6.2 The location of transmedia relative to the Layered Tetrad

The Cultural Impact of a Game

So far, we've looked at the cultural layer as the way in which players take ownership of a game and move it out into society at large. Another very different way of looking at this is to consider the impact that gameplay has on players. Disappointingly, the game industry over the past several decades has been quick to acknowledge and promote psychological studies that found evidence of the positive effects of game playing (e.g., improved multitasking skills, improved situational awareness), while simultaneously denying studies that found evidence of the negative impact of gaming (e.g., addiction to games and the negative effects of violence in video games).[7] In the case of violent video games in particular, it's probable that this was largely defensive. Nearly every company that belongs to the Entertainment Software Association (the lobbying group for video game companies) has made games where the core mechanic is some type of violence, and it seems that "violent video games" are often one of the first culprits that

---

[7] Even a cursory perusal of the Entertainment Software Association's (ESA's) archive of noteworthy news (at http://www.theesa.com/newsroom/news_archives.asp) reveals a plethora of articles about the positive benefits of gameplay and almost none about the potential negative effects.

journalists tend to blame when unstable people commit horrible acts.[8] However, in 2011, the landscape for this discussion changed in a critical way when the Supreme Court of the United States decided in *Edmund G. Brown, Jr., Governor of California, et al., Petitioners v. Entertainment Merchants Association et al.,* 564 U.S. (2011), that games are art and are therefore protected by the First Amendment to the United States Constitution. Up to this point, members of the ESA and other game developers had good reason to fear government action to ban violent games. Now, just like most other forms of media, games are protected as art, and developers can make games about whatever they want without fear of government bans.

Of course, with this liberty also comes a responsibility to acknowledge the effects that the games we make have upon society, and this isn't limited exclusively to the violence in games. In the 2011 class-action suit *Meguerian v. Apple Inc.,*[9] Apple paid more than $100 million in settlements because games developed by third-party companies and approved by Apple had been designed with mechanics that encouraged children to pay hundreds of dollars for in-app purchases as part of gameplay. Though Apple settled the suit and thereby avoided a judgment, the complaint was that the games had been designed to prey on children's underdeveloped understanding of real money, and some children had charged over $1,000 in less than a month without their parents' knowledge or approval. It has also been shown that the peak time that people play casual social network games (e.g., Facebook games) is during work hours, and many of these games are designed with "energy" and "spoilage" mechanics that encourage players to return to the game every fifteen minutes, which certainly has a negative effect on workplace productivity.

Summary

The inscribed and dynamic layers of the Layered Tetrad have been discussed in several books prior to this one, but the cultural layer has received far less attention. In fact, even in my personal practice as a game designer and game design professor, though I think very concretely about the inscribed and dynamic layers on a daily basis, I spend much less time than I should considering the cultural impact of my work and the changes that players might make to my games.

It is largely beyond the scope of this book to cover game design ethics in meaningful detail, but it is important that designers think about the consequences of the games they create, particularly because after a player has finished playing a game and set it aside, the cultural layer is all that remains.

---

[8] Dave Moore and Bill Manville. "What role might video game addiction have played in the Columbine shootings?" *New York Daily News,* April 23, 2009 and Kevin Simpson and Jason Blevins. "Did Harris preview massacre on *DOOM?*" *Denver Post,* May 4, 1999.

[9] Meguerian v. Apple Inc., case number 5:11-cv-01758, in the U.S. District Court for the Northern District of California.

CHAPTER 7

ACTING LIKE A DESIGNER

Now that you've learned something about how to take a designer's approach to thinking about and analyzing games, it's time to look at the way that game designers go about crafting interactive experiences.

As mentioned in previous chapters, game design is a practice, and therefore, the more design you do, the better you will get at it. However, you also need to make sure that you're starting with the kinds of actions that will yield you the greatest gains over time. That is the purpose of this chapter.

Iterative Design

"Game design is 1% inspiration and 99% iteration." —Chris Swain

Remember this saying from the first chapter? In this section, we explore it further.

The number one key to good design—the most important thing that you can learn from this book—is the process of iterative design shown in Figure 7.1. I have seen iterative design take some games that were initially terrible and make them great, and I've seen it at work across all forms of design from furniture to illustration to game design.

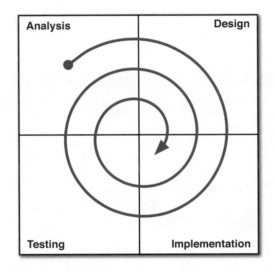

Figure 7.1   The iterative process of design[1]

The four phases of the iterative process of design are:

- **Analysis:** The analysis phase is all about understanding where you are and what you want to accomplish. Understand the problem that you're trying to solve (or opportunity that you're trying to take advantage of) with your design. Understand the resources that you can bring to bear on the project. Understand the amount of time you have.

- **Design:** Now that you have a clear idea where you are and what you're trying to accomplish with your design, create a design that will solve the problem/opportunity with the resources you have available to you. This phase starts with brainstorming and ends with a concrete plan for implementation.

- **Implementation:** You have the design in hand; now execute it. There's an old adage: "It's not a game until people are playing it." The implementation phase is about getting from

---

[1]   Based on: Tracy Fullerton, Christopher Swain, and Steven Hoffman, *Game Design Workshop: A Playcentric Approach to Creating Innovative Games* (Burlington, MA: Morgan Kaufmann Publishers, 2008), 36.

game design idea to playable prototype as quickly as possible. As you'll see in the digital game tutorials later in this book, the earliest implementations are sometimes just moving a character around the screen—with no enemies or objectives—and seeing if the movement feels responsive and natural. It's perfectly fine to implement just a small part of the game before testing; a test of just a portion of the game can often be more focused than a large-scale implementation could be. At the end of implementation, you're ready to run a playtest.

■ **Testing:** Put people in front of your game and get their reactions. As your experience as a designer grows, you will get better at knowing how the various game mechanics you design will play out once the game is being tested, but even with years of experience, you will never know for sure. Testing will tell you. You always need to test early, when it's still possible to make changes to the game and get it on the right track. Testing must also be done very frequently so that you can best understand the causes of the changes in player feedback that you witness.

Let's look at each phase in more detail.

Analysis

Every design seeks to solve a problem or take advantage of an opportunity, and before you can start to design, you need to have a clear idea of what that problem or opportunity is. You may be saying to yourself "I just want to make a great game," which is true of most of us, but even with that as your initial statement, you can dig deeper and analyze your problem further.

To start, try asking yourself these questions:

1. **For whom am I designing the game?** Knowledge of your target audience can dictate many other elements of design. If you're creating a game for children, it is more likely that their parents would let them use a mobile device than a computer connected to the Internet. If you're designing a game for people who like strategy games, they will most likely be used to playing on a PC. If you're designing a game for men, you should be aware that nearly 10% of Caucasian men are colorblind.

   One thing that you should always be aware of is the danger of designing a game for yourself. If you just make a game for you, there's a legitimate possibility that only *you* will want to play it. Researching your intended audience and understanding what makes them tick can tell you a tremendous amount about where your game design should go and help you to make your game better.

   It's also important to realize that what players think they want and what they will actually enjoy are sometimes two different things. In your research, it's important to try to differentiate between your audience's stated desires and the things that actually motivate and engage them.

2. **What are my resources?** Most of us don't have a budget of tens of millions of dollars with which to employ a studio of 200 people to make a game over the span of two years. But you do have some time and talent and maybe even a group of talented friends as well. Being honest with yourself about your resources, strengths, and weaknesses can help

shape your design. As an independent developer, your primary resources are talent and time. Money can help you purchase either of these through hiring contractors or purchasing assets, but especially if you're working on a small indie game team, you want to make sure that the game you're developing makes the best use of the resources on your team. When working on a game, you should treat your time and that of your team members as a precious resource; be sure to not waste it.

3. **What prior art exists?** This is the single question that is most often ignored by my students (often to their detriment). *Prior art* is the term used to describe existing games and other media that are related to yours in some way. No game comes from a vacuum, and as a designer, it is up to you to know not only the other games that have inspired you (which, of course, you know), but also what other games exist in the same space that came before or after your primary inspirations.

   For instance, if you were to design a first-person shooter for console, of course you'd look at *Titanfall* and the *Call of Duty: Modern Warfare* series, but you would also need to be familiar with *Halo* (the first game that made the first-person shooter [FPS] genre work on a console when conventional wisdom held that it was impossible to do so), *Marathon* (Bungie's game prior to *Halo*, which forms the basis for a lot of the design decisions and mythology in *Halo*), and the other FPSs that were precursors for *Marathon*.

   You must research prior art because you need to be sure to know everything you can about the ways that other people have tried to approach the design problem that you're tackling. Even if someone else had the exact same idea as you, it's almost certain that they approached it in a different way, and from their successes and mistakes, you can learn to make your game better.

4. **What is the fastest path to a playable game that demonstrates what I want to test?** Though often-overlooked, this question is critical for obvious reasons. You only have 24 hours available to you each day, and if you're at all like me, only a small fraction can be devoted to game development. Knowing this, it is critical that your time is used as efficiently as possible if you want to get your game made. Think about the *core mechanic* of the game you want to create—the thing that the player does most throughout the game (for example, in *Super Mario Bros.*, the core mechanic is jumping)—and make sure that you design and test that first. From that, you'll know whether it's worth it to make more of the game. Art, music, and all other aesthetic elements are of course critical to your final game, but at this point, you must focus on the mechanics—on gameplay—and get that working first. That is your goal as a game designer.

Of course, you'll have many more questions of your own to add to these, but regardless of the game you're making, these four are critical to keep in mind during the analysis phase.

Design

A large portion of this book is about design, but in this section, I'm going to focus on the attitude of a professional designer. (Chapter 14, "The Digital Game Industry," covers this in more detail.)

Design isn't about getting your way, it's not about being a great genius or auteur who is followed by everyone else on the team, and it's not even about doing a great job of communicating your vision to the rest of the team. Design isn't about you; it is about the project. Working as a game designer is about collaborating with the rest of the team, compromising, and above all listening.

In the first few pages of his book *The Art of Game Design,* Jesse Schell states that listening is the most important skill that a game designer can have, and I emphatically agree. Schell lists five kinds of listening that you need to develop:[2]

- **Listen to your audience:** Whom do you want to play your game? Whom do you want to buy your game? As mentioned previously, these are questions that you must answer, and after you have answered them, you need to listen to the kinds of experiences that your audience wants to have. The whole purpose of the iterative process of design is to make something, throw it out to playtesters, and get their feedback. Make sure you're listening to that feedback when they give it, even (especially!) if it's not what you expected or what you want to hear.

- **Listen to your team:** On most game projects, you'll be working with a team of other talented people. Your job as the designer is to listen to all of their thoughts and ideas and work with them to unearth the ideas that will create the best game for your audience. If you surround yourself with people who are willing to speak up when they disagree with you, you will have a better game. Your team should not be contentious; rather, it should be a team of creative individuals who all care passionately about the game.

- **Listen to your client:** A lot of the time, as a professional game designer, you'll be working for a client (boss, committee, etc.), and you're going to need to take their input. They aren't usually going to be expert game designers—that's why they hired you—but they will have specific needs that you must meet. At the end of the day, it will be your job to listen to them at several levels: what they tell you they want, what they think they want but don't say out loud, and even what they really want deep down but might not even admit to themselves. With clients, you need to listen very carefully in order to leave them with an excellent impression of working with you and an excellent game.

- **Listen to your game:** Sometimes certain elements of a game design fit together like a hand in a glove, and sometimes, it's more like a wolverine in a Christmas stocking (p.s.: *bad idea*). As the designer, you'll be closest to the gameplay, and it will be up to you to understand the game from a gestalt (holistic) perspective. Even if a certain aspect of a game is brilliant design, it might not fit well with the rest. Don't worry; if it is a great bit of design, there's a good chance you can find a place for it in another game... you'll make a lot of games in your career.

---

[2] Jesse Schell, *The Art of Game Design: A Book of Lenses* (Boca Raton, FL: CRC Press, 2008), 4–6.

- **Listen to yourself:** There are several important aspects of listening to yourself:

  - **Listen to your gut:** Sometimes you'll get a gut feeling about something, and sometimes these will be wrong, but other times they'll be very right. When your gut tells you something about a design, give it a try. It may be that some part of your mind figured out the answer before your conscious mind had a chance to.

  - **Listen to your health:** Take care of yourself and stay healthy. Seriously. There is a tremendous amount of research out there showing that pulling all-nighters, being stressed, and not exercising have a tremendously negative effect on your ability to do creative work. To be the best designer you can be, you need to be healthy and well rested. Don't let yourself get caught in a cycle of one crisis after another that you try to solve by working crazy hours into the night.

  - **Listen to how you sound to other people:** When you say things to your colleagues, peers, friends, family, and acquaintances, take a moment every once in a while to really listen to how you sound. I don't want you to get a complex about it or anything, but I do want you to listen to yourself and ask these questions: Do I sound respectful? Do I sound like I care about the other person? Do I sound like I care about the project? All other things being equal, the people who do best in life are those who consistently demonstrate respect and care for others. I've known some really talented people who didn't get this; they did all right initially, but without fail, their careers sputtered and failed as fewer and fewer people wanted to work with them. Game design is a community of shared respect.

There are, of course, many more aspects to acting like a professional designer than just listening, but Schell and I agree that it is one of the most important. The rest of this book covers more nuts-and-bolts aspects of being a designer, but all of it must be approached with the humble, healthy, collaborative, and creative attitude I've outlined here.

Implementation

The latter two-thirds of this book are about digital implementation, but it's important to realize that the key to effective implementation in the process of iterative design is to get from design to playtest in the most efficient way possible. If you're testing the jump of a character in a platform game like *Super Mario Bros.* or *Mega Man*, you will need to make a digital prototype. However, if you're testing a graphical user interface (GUI) menu system, you don't need to build a fully working digital version; it's perfectly fine to print out images of the various states of the menu and ask testers to navigate through them with you acting as the computer (and swapping the printed images by hand).

For instance, the diagram in Figure 7.2 shows some different screens from a GUI mockup of an options menu. Each playtester would only be shown one screen at a time, starting with #1, the Options Menu. While shown screen #1, the playtester would be instructed to "Press the selections you would make to turn the subtitles on." (You would encourage the playtesters to actually touch the paper as if they were touching a touchscreen.)

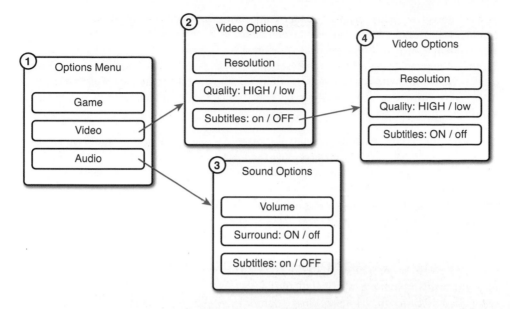

Figure 7.2 A simple paper GUI prototype.

Some playtesters might press the *Video* button, whereas others might press *Audio* (and a few might press *Game*). Once the user made a selection, the #1 sheet of paper would be replaced with the menu of their selection (for example, #2 Video Options). Then, presumably, the play-tester would press the *Subtitles: on / OFF* button to switch the subtitles on, which would cause #2 to be replaced with #4 Video Options.

One important thing to note here is that subtitles are available to be changed on both the video and sound options screens. For testing this works well because regardless of which of the two options are chosen by the player (Video or Audio), you can then subsequently test whether the "on / OFF" capitalization clearly conveys that the subtitles are currently turned off.

Paper prototyping is covered further in Chapter 9, "Paper Prototyping."

Testing

As you've just seen, paper prototyping can be the fastest way to get to playtesting when you're in the early phases of a project. Chapter 10, "Game Testing," covers several different aspects of testing. The key thing to keep in mind now is that regardless of what you think about your game, you won't really know anything until a player (who is not you) has tested it and given you feedback. The more people who play your game, the more legitimate that feedback will be.

In my Game Design Workshop class at the University of Southern California, each of our board game projects took place over four weeks of labs. In the first lab, the students were placed in teams and given time to brainstorm their game ideas. Every subsequent lab was devoted entirely to playtesting the current version of their game. By the end of a 4-week project, each student team had completed nearly 6 hours of in-class playtesting and had drastically improved their designs as a result. The best thing you can do for your designs is to have people playing them and giving you feedback as often as possible. And, for the sake of all that is good, please write down what your playtesters tell you. If you forget their feedback, the playtest is a waste.

It is also important to make sure that your playtesters are giving you honest feedback. Sometimes, playtesters will give you overly positive feedback because they don't want to hurt your feelings. In *The Art of Game Design,* Jesse Schell recommends telling your testers something like "I need your help. This game has some real problems, but we're not sure what they are. Please, if there is anything at all you don't like about this game, it will be a great help to me if you let me know"[3] to encourage them to be honest with you about flaws they see in the game.

Analysis/Design/Implementation/Testing/Repeat!

After you have run your playtest, you should have a lot of feedback written down from your testers. Now it's time to analyze again. What did the players like? What didn't they like? Were there places in the game that were overly easy or difficult? Was it interesting and engaging?

From all of these questions, you will be able to determine a new problem to solve with your design. For instance, you might decide that you need to make the second half of the first level more exciting, or you may decide that the game has too much randomness.

After each playtest session, I review the feedback from my players and fill out the chart shown in Figure 7.3 with a line for each issue on which players have given feedback.

Where	Feedback	Underlying Issue	Severity	Proposed Solution
Boss1	"I didn't know what to do after the first boss." "Where do I go now?" "Ok, now what?"	Players are not sure what the next step is after the first boss fight. The play has been really directed up to this point, but now they don't know what to do.	High	The mentor character could return after the boss is defeated and give the player her 2nd mission.

Figure 7.3   One line from a playtest analysis chart

This is only a single sample line from the chart that could be dozens or hundreds of lines long. The first thing I do when creating this chart is to collect similar feedback together. You need to make sure that all testers are talking about the same part of the game, so you should have some sort of system for marking where they were in the game when they made the comment

---

[3] Jesse Schell, *The Art of Game Design: A Book of Lenses* (Boca Raton, FL: CRC Press, 2008), 401.

(e.g., Boss1). Then, place all similar comments in the same Feedback cell. Next, analyze these comments as a whole and attempt to understand what is causing the players to feel this way. Then decide how serious you think this underlying issue is and if it is an issue of Medium or High severity, propose a solution that might fix the problem. After you have all of your pro-posed solutions it's time to take them into the design phase and continue the cycle of iterative design. Each subsequent iteration of the design should include some changes, but not all of those you have proposed. The most important thing is to get to the next playtest quickly and determine whether the solutions that you *have* implemented solved the problems they were meant to solve.

Innovation

In his book *The Medici Effect*,[4] author Frans Johansson writes about two kinds of innovation: incremental and intersectional. Incremental innovation is making something a little better in a predictable way. The progressive improvement of Pentium processors by Intel throughout the 1990s was incremental innovation; each year, a new Pentium processor was released that was larger and had more transistors than the previous generation. Incremental innovation is reliable and predictable, and if you're looking for investment capital, it's easy to convince investors that it will work. However, as its name would suggest, incremental innovation can never make great leaps forward precisely because it is exactly what everyone expects.

The other kind of innovation is intersectional innovation. Intersectional innovation occurs at the collision of two disparate ideas, and it is where a lot of the greatest ideas can come from. However, because the results of intersectional innovation are novel and often unpredictable, it is more difficult to convince others of the merit of the ideas generated through intersectional innovation.

In 1991, Richard Garfield was trying to find a publisher for his game *RoboRally*. One of the people he approached was Peter Adkison, founder and CEO of Wizards of the Coast. Though Adkison liked the game, he didn't feel that Wizards had enough resources to publish a game like *RoboRally* that had so many different pieces, but he mentioned to Richard that they had been looking for a new game that could be played with very little equipment and resolve in 15 minutes.

Richard intersected this idea of a fast-play, low-equipment card game with another idea that had been kicking around in his head for a while of playing a card game with cards that were collected like baseball cards, and in 1993, Wizards of the Coast released *Magic: The Gathering*, which started the entire genre of collectible card games (CCGs).

Though Garfield had been thinking about a card game that was collectible for a little while before his meeting with Adkison, it was the intersection of that idea with Adkison's specific

---

4   Frans Johansson, *The Medici Effect: What Elephants and Epidemics Can Teach Us about Innovation* (Boston, MA: Harvard Business School Press, 2006).

needs for a fast-play game that gave birth to the collectible card game genre, and nearly all CCGs that have come since have the same basic formula: a basic rule set, cards that have rules on them which override the basic rules, deck construction, and fast play.

The brainstorming procedure described in the next section takes advantage of both kinds of innovation to help you create better ideas.

Brainstorming and Ideation

"The best way to have a good idea is to have a lot of ideas and throw out all the bad ones."
—Linus Pauling, sole winner of both the Nobel Prize in Chemistry and the Nobel Peace Prize

Just like anyone else, not all of your ideas are going to be great ones, so the best you can do is to generate a lot of ideas and then sift through them later to find the good ones. This is the whole concept behind brainstorming. This section covers a specific brainstorming process that I have seen work very well for many people, especially in groups of creative individuals.

For this process, you will need: a whiteboard, a stack of 3x5 note cards (or just a bunch of slips of paper), a notebook for jotting down ideas, and various whiteboard markers, pens, pencils, and so on. The process works best with five to ten people, but you can alter it to work for fewer people by repeating tasks, and I've modified it in the past to work for a classroom of 65 students. (For instance, if you're by yourself, and it says that each person should do something once, just do it a few times until you're satisfied.)

Step 1: Expansion Phase

Let's say that you are just starting a 48-hour game jam with a few friends. The theme of the game jam is *uroboros* (the symbol of a snake eating its own tail symbol). This was the theme of the Global Game Jam in 2012. Not much to go on, right? So, you start with the kind of brainstorming that you learned in grade school. Draw an uroboros in the middle of a white board, draw a circle around it, and start free associating. Don't worry about what you're writing at this point—don't censor anything—just write whatever comes to mind as you go. Figure 7.4 shows an example.

> ### warning
>
> **BEWARE THE TYRANNY OF THE MARKER**   If you have more people taking part in the brainstorm than you have whiteboard markers, you should always be careful to make sure that everyone is being heard. Creative people come in all types, and the most introverted person on your team may have some of the best ideas. If you're managing a creative team, try to make sure that the more introverted members of your team are the ones holding the whiteboard markers. They may be willing to write something on the board that they aren't willing to say out loud.

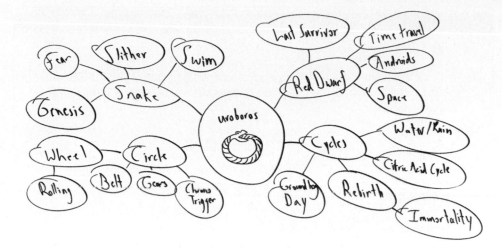

Figure 7.4 The expansion phase of brainstorming a game for uroboros

When you're done, take a picture of the whiteboard. I have hundreds of pictures of whiteboards in my phone, and I've never regretted taking one. Once you have captured it, email it out to everyone in the group.

Step 2: Collection Phase

Collect all of the nodes of the brainstorming expansion phase and write them each down on one 3x5 note card. These are called idea cards (see Figure 7.5).

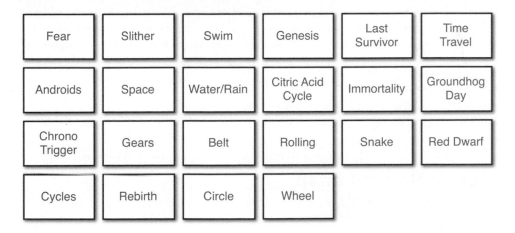

Figure 7.5 Uroboros idea cards

A QUICK ASIDE AND A BAD JOKE OR TWO

Let's start with the bad joke:

There are two lithium atoms walking along, and one says to the other, "Phil, I think I lost an electron back there." So Phil says, "Really Jason, are you sure?" And Jason replies, "Yeah, I'm positive!"

Here's another:

Why was six afraid of seven?

Because seven eight nine!

Sorry, I know. They're terrible.

You may be wondering why I'm subjecting you to bad jokes. I'm doing so because jokes like these work on the same principle as intersectional innovation. Humans are creatures that love to think and combine weird ideas. Jokes are funny because they lead our minds down one track and then throw a completely different concept into the mix. Your mind makes the link between the two disparate, seemingly unrelated concepts, and the joy that this mental link causes comes across as humor.

The same thing happens when you intersect two ideas, and this is why it's so pleasurable for us to get the eureka moment of intersecting two common ideas into a new uncommon one.

Step 3: Collision Phase

Here's where the fun begins. Shuffle all the idea cards that you've made and deal two to each person in the group. Each person takes their two cards up to the whiteboard and reveals them to everyone. Then the group collectively comes up with three different game ideas inspired by the collision of the two cards. (If the two cards either are too closely paired or just don't work together at all, it's okay to skip them.) Figure 7.6 presents a couple of examples.

Now, the examples in Figure 7.6 are just the first ideas that came to me, as they should be for you. We're still not doing a lot of filtering in this phase. Write down all of the different ideas that you come up with in this phase.

Step 4: Rating Phase

Now that you have a lot of ideas, it's time to start culling them. Each person should write on the whiteboard the two ideas from Step 3 that she thinks have the most merit.

Groundhog Day	Gears

1. Gardener building crazy contraptions to trap a groundhog that's been eating her garden.
2. Gears of War-style shooter where soldiers must relive a battle until they get it perfect (like in the movie *Groundhog Day*).
3. A time-management game (e.g., *Diner Dash* by Nick Fortugno) where the player must manage the weather so that each season accomplishes its goals and transitions to the next on time.

Belt	Snake

1. Classic game of *Snake* (snake eats apples and grows but must avoid running into itself), but on a moving conveyor belt.
2. A snake must move across a room camouflaged as people's belts by jumping from waist to waist.
3. A snake hypnotizes a person but can only control them to do very simple things. As the person's belt, the snake must swing and platform them through a dangerous level to escape the zoo.

Figure 7.6 Uroboros idea collisions

Once everyone has done this, then all people should simultaneously put a tick mark next to the three ideas written on the board that they like the most. You should end up with some ideas with lots of tick marks and some with very few.

Step 5: Discussion

Now that you have lots of ideas, it's time to boil them down and combine them into good ideas. With dozens of different crazy ideas to choose from, you should be able to find a couple that sound really good and to combine them into a great starting point for your design.

Changing Your Mind

Changing your mind is a key part of the iterative design process. As you work through the different iterations of your game, you will inevitably make changes to your design.

As shown in Figure 7.7, no one ever has an idea and turns it directly into a game with no changes at all (as shown in the top half of the figure), or if anyone ever does, it's almost certain to be a terrible game. In reality, what happens is a lot more like the bottom half of the figure. You have an idea and make an initial prototype. The results of that prototype give you some ideas, and you make another prototype. Maybe that one didn't work out so well, so you backtrack and make another. You continue this process until you've forged your idea over time into a great game, and if you stick to the process and engage in listening and creative collaboration, it'll be a much better game than the original one you set out to make.

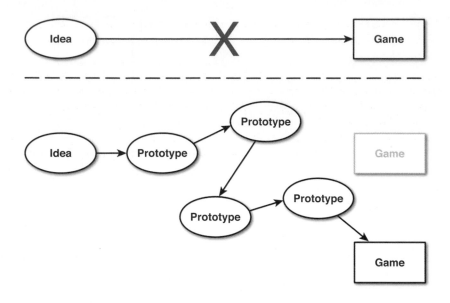

Figure 7.7 The reality of game design

As the Project Progresses, You're More Locked In

The process just described is fantastic for small projects or the preproduction phase of any project, but after you have a lot of people who have put a lot of time into something, it's much more difficult and expensive to change your mind. A standard professional game is developed in several distinct phases:

- **Preproduction:** This is the phase covered by most of this book. In the preproduction phase, you're experimenting with different prototypes, and you're trying to find something that is demonstrably enjoyable and engaging. During preproduction, it is perfectly fine to change your mind about things. On a large industry project, there would be between 4 and 16 people on the project during preproduction, and at the end of this phase, you typically would want to have created a *vertical slice*, which is a short, five-minute section of your game at the same level of quality as the final game. This is like a demo level for the executives to play and decide whether or not to move the game into production. Other sections of your game should be designed at this point, but for the most part, they won't be implemented.

- **Production:** In the industry, when you enter the production phase of a game, your team will grow considerably in size. On a large console game title, there could be well over 100 people working on the game at this point, many of whom might not be in the same city or even country as you. During production, all of the *systems design* (i.e., the game mechanics) need to be locked down very early, and other design aspects (like level design, tuning character abilities, and such) will be progressively locked down throughout production as the team finalizes them. From an aesthetics side, the production phase is when all of the modeling, texturing, animation, and other implementation of aesthetic elements take place. The production phase expands the high quality of the vertical slice out across the rest of the project.

- **Alpha:** Once you've reached the alpha phase of your game, all the functionality and game mechanics should be 100% locked down. At this point, there are no more changes to the systems design of the game, and the only changes you should make to things like level design will be in response to specific problems discovered through playtesting. This is the phase where playtesting transitions to quality assurance (QA) testing in an effort to find problems and bugs (See Chapter 10 for more information). When you start alpha, there may still be some bugs (i.e., errors in programming), but you should have identified all of them and know how to reproduce them.

- **Beta:** Once you're in beta, the game should be effectively done. At beta, you should have fixed any bugs that had the potential to crash your game, and the only remaining bugs should be minor. The purpose of the beta period is to find and fix the last of the bugs in your game. From the art side, this means making sure that every texture is mapped properly, that every bit of text is spelled properly, etc. You are not making any changes in the beta phase, just fixing any final problems that you can find.

- **Gold:** When your project goes gold, it is ready to ship. This is a holdover from the days of CD-ROM production when the master for all the CDs was actually a disc made of gold that the CDs were pressed onto. Now that even disc-based console games have updates delivered online, gold has lost some of its finality, but gold is still the name for the game being ship-ready.

- **Post-release:** With the ubiquity of the Internet today, all games that aren't on cartridges (e.g., Nintendo DS games and some 3DS games are delivered on cartridges) can be tuned[5] after they're released. The post-release period can also be used for development of downloadable content (DLC). Because DLC is often composed of new missions and levels, each DLC release goes through the same phases of development as the larger game (though on a much smaller scale): preproduction, production, alpha, beta, and gold.

Scoping!

One critical concept you must understand to act like a game designer is how to scope your work. Scoping is the process of limiting the design to what can reasonably be accomplished with the time and resources that you have available, and overscoping is the number one killer of amateur game projects.

I'll say that again: *Overscoping is the number one killer of game projects.*

Most of the games you see and play took dozens of people months and months of full-time work to create. Some large console games cost nearly $500 million to develop. The teams on

---

5 *Tuning* is the term for the final stages of adjustments to game mechanics where only tiny changes are made.

these projects are all composed of fantastic people who have been doing their jobs well for years.

I'm not trying to discourage you, but I am trying to convince you to think small. For your own sake, don't try to make the next *Titanfall* or *World of Warcraft* or any other large, famous game you can think of. Instead find a small, really cool core mechanic and explore it deeply in a small game.

If you want some fantastic inspiration, check out the games that are nominated each year at the IndieCade Game Festival. IndieCade is the premier festival for independent games of various sizes, and I think it represents the vanguard of where independent games are going.[6] If you take a look at their website (http://indiecade.com), you can see tons of fantastic games, each of which pushes the boundaries of gaming in a cool new way. Each of these was someone's passion project, and many of them took hundreds or thousands of hours of effort for a small team or an individual to create.

As you look at them, you might be surprised by how small in scale they are. That's okay. Even though the scope of these games is pretty small, they are still fantastic enough to be considered for an IndieCade award.

As you progress in your career, you may go on to make massive games like *Starcraft* or *Grand Theft Auto*, but remember that everyone got their start somewhere. Before George Lucas made *Star Wars,* he was just a talented kid in the film program at the University of Southern California. In fact, even when he made *Star Wars,* he scoped it down so perfectly that he was able to make one of the highest-grossing movies of all time for only $11 million. (It went on to make over $775 million at the box office and many, many times that in toy sales, home movie sales, and so on.)

So for now, think small. Come up with something that you know you can make in a short amount of time and make it. If you make something great, you can always add on to it later.

Summary

The tools and theories you've read in this chapter are the kinds of things that I teach to my students and use in my personal design. I have seen the brainstorming strategies that I listed work in both big and small groups to create interesting, off-the-wall, yet implementable ideas, and every experience that I have had in the industry and academia has led me to feel that iterative design, rapid prototyping, and proper scoping are the key processes that you can implement to improve your designs. I cannot more highly recommend them to you.

---

6 For purposes of full disclosure, since 2013, I have served as IndieCade's Chair for Education and Advancement, and I am very proud to belong to such a great organization.

CHAPTER 8

DESIGN GOALS

This chapter explores several important goals that you may have for your games. It covers everything from the deceptively complex goal of *fun* to the goal of *experiential understanding*, which may be unique to interactive experiences.

As you read this chapter, think about which of these goals matter to you. The relative importance of these goals to each other will shift as you move from project to project and will often even shift as you move through the various phases of development, but you should always be aware of all of them, and even if one is not important to you, that should be due to deliberate choice rather than unintentional omission.

Design Goals: An Incomplete List

You could have any number of goals in mind when designing a game or interactive experience, and I'm sure that each of you has one that won't be covered in this chapter. However, I am going to try to cover most of the goals that I see in my personal work as a designer and in the design work of my students and friends.

Designer-Centric Goals

These are goals that are focused on you as the designer. What do you want to get out of designing this game?

- **Fortune:** You want to make money.
- **Fame:** You want people to know who you are.
- **Community:** You want to be part of something.
- **Personal expression:** You want to communicate with others through games.
- **Greater good:** You want to make the world better in some way.
- **Becoming a better designer:** You simply want to make games and improve your craft.

Player-Centric Goals

These goals are focused on what you want for the players of your game:

- **Fun:** You want players to enjoy your game.
- **Lusory attitude:** You want players to take part in the fantasy of your game.
- **Flow:** You want players to be optimally challenged.
- **Structured conflict:** You want to give players a way to combat others or challenge your game systems.
- **Empowerment:** You want players to feel powerful both in the game and in the metagame.
- **Interest/attention/involvement:** You want players to be engaged by your game.
- **Meaningful decisions:** You want players' choices to have meaning to them and the game.
- **Experiential understanding:** You want players to gain understanding through play.

Now let's explore each in detail.

Designer-Centric Goals

As a game designer and developer, there are some goals for your life that you hope the games you make might help you achieve.

Fortune

My friend John "Chow" Chowanec has been in the game industry for years. The first time I met him, he gave me some advice about making money in the game industry. He said "You can literally make hundreds of...dollars in the game industry."

As he hinted through his joke, there are a *lot* of faster, better ways to make money than the game industry. I tell my programming students that if they want to make money, they should go work for a bank; banks have lots of money and are very interested in paying someone to help them keep it. However, the game industry is just like every other entertainment industry job: There are fewer jobs available than people who want them, and people generally enjoy doing the work; so, game companies can pay less than other companies for the same kind of employees. There are certainly people in the game industry who make a lot of money, but they are few and far between.

It is absolutely possible—particularly if you're a single person without kids—to make a decent living working in the game industry. This is especially true if you're working for a larger game company where they tend to have good salaries and benefits. Smaller companies (or starting your own small company) are generally a lot riskier and usually pay worse, but you may have a chance to earn a percentage ownership in the company, which could have a small chance of eventually paying out very nicely.

Fame

I'll be honest: Very, very few people become famous for game design. Becoming a game designer because you want to be famous is a little like becoming a special effects artist in film because you want to be famous. Usually with games, even if millions of people see your work, very few will know who you are.

Of course, there are some famous names like Sid Meier, Will Wright, and John Romero, but all of those people have been making games for years and have been famous for it for equally long. There are also some newer people whom you might know like Jenova Chen, Jonathan Blow, and Markus "Notch" Persson, but even then, many more people are familiar with their games (*Flow/Flower/Journey*, *Braid*, and *Minecraft*, respectively) than with them.

However, what I find to be far better than fame is community, and the game industry has that in spades. The game industry is smaller than anyone on the outside would ever expect, and it's a great community. In particular, I have always been impressed by the acceptance and openness of the independent game community and the IndieCade game conference.

Community

There are, of course, many different communities within the game industry, but on the whole, I have found it to be a pretty fantastic place filled with great people. Many of my closest friends are people whom I met through working in the game industry or in games education. Though a sad number of high-budget, AAA games appear sexist and violent, in my experience, most of the people working on these games are genuinely good people. There is also a large and vibrant community of developers, designers, and artists who are working to make games that are more progressive and created from more varied perspectives. Over the past couple of years of the IndieCade independent game conference, there have been very well attended panels on diversity in both the games we make and the development teams who are making those games. The independent game community in particular is a meritocracy; if you make great work, you will be welcomed and respected by the indie community regardless of race, gender, sexual orientation, religion, or creed. There is certainly still room to improve the openness of the game development community, but it is full of people who want to make it a welcoming place for everyone.

Personal Expression and Communication

This goal is the flip side of the player-centric goal of experiential understanding. However, personal expression and communication can take many more forms than experiential understanding (which is the exclusive domain of interactive media). Designers and artists have been expressing themselves in all forms of media for hundreds of years. If you have something that you wish to express, there are two important questions to ask yourself:

> What form of media could best express this concept?

> What forms of media are you adept at using?

Somewhere between these two questions you'll find the answer of whether an interactive piece will be the best way for you to express yourself. The good news is that there is a very eager audience seeking new personal expressions in the interactive realm. Very personal interactive pieces like *That Dragon, Cancer*; *Mainichi*; and *Papo y Yo* have received a lot of attention and critical acclaim recently, signaling the growing maturity of interactive experiences as a conduit for personal expression.[1]

Greater Good

A number of people make games because they want to make the world a better place. These games are often called *serious games* or *games for change* and are the subject of several developer's conferences. This genre of games can also be a great way for a small studio to get off the ground and do some good in the world; there are a number of government agencies, companies, and nonprofit organizations who offer grants and contracts for developers interested in making serious games.

---

[1] *That Dragon, Cancer* (2014, by Ryan Green and Josh Larson) relates the experience of a couple learning that their young son has terminal cancer, and creating it helped Ryan come to terms with his own son's cancer. *Mainichi* (2013, by Mattie Brice) was designed to express to a friend of hers what it was like to be a transgender woman living in San Francisco. *Papo y Yo* (2014, by Minority Media) places the player in the dream world of a boy trying to protect himself and his sister from a sometimes-helpful, sometimes-violent monster that represents his alcoholic father.

There are many names used to describe games for the greater good. Three of the biggest are:

- **Serious games:** This is one of the oldest and most general names for games of this type. These games can of course still be fun; the "serious" moniker is just to note that there is a purpose behind the game that is more than just playful. One common example of this category is educational games.

- **Games for social change:** This category of games for good is typically used to encompass games that are meant to influence people or change their minds about a topic. Games about things like global warming, government budget deficits, or the virtues or vices of various political candidates would fall into this category.

- **Games for behavioral change:** The intent of these games is not to change the mind or opinion of the player (as in games for social change) but instead to change a player's behavior outside of the game. For example, many medicinal games have been created to discourage childhood obesity, improve attention spans, combat depression, and detect things like childhood amblyopia. There is a large and growing amount of research out there demonstrating that games and game play can have significant effects (both positive and negative) on mental and physical health.

Becoming a Better Designer

The number one thing you can do to become a great game designer is make games...scratch that, make *a lot* of games. The purpose of this book is to help you get started doing this, and it's one of the reasons that the tutorials at the end of the book cover several different games rather than having just one monolithic tutorial that meanders through various game development topics. Each tutorial is focused on making a prototype for a specific kind of game and covering a few specific topics, and the prototypes you make are meant to serve not only as learning tools but also as foundations upon which you can build your own games in the future.

Player-Centric Goals

As a game designer and developer, there are some goals for your game that are centered on the effects that you want the game to have on your player.

Fun

Many people regard fun as the only goal of games, although as a reader of this book, you should know by now that this is not true. As discussed later in this chapter, players are willing to play something that isn't fun as long as it grabs and holds their attention in some way. This is true with all forms of art; I am glad to have watched the movies *Schindler's List, Life is Beautiful,* and *What Dreams May Come,* but none of them were at all "fun" to watch. Even though it is not the only goal of games, the elusive concept of fun is still critically important to game designers.

In his book *Game Design Theory,* Keith Burgun proposes three aspects that make a game fun. According to him, it must be enjoyable, engaging, and fulfilling:

- **Enjoyable:** There are many ways for something to be enjoyable, and enjoyment in one form or another is what most players are seeking when they approach a game. In his 1958 book *Les Jeux et Les Hommes,*[2] Roger Caillois identified four different kinds of play:
  - Agon: Competitive play (e.g., chess, baseball, *Uncharted*)
  - Alea: Chance-based play (e.g., gambling and rock, paper, scissors)
  - Ilinx: Vertiginous play (e.g., roller coasters, children spinning around until they're dizzy, and other play that makes the player feel vertigo)
  - Mimicry: Play centered on make-believe and simulation (e.g., playing house, playing with action figures)

  Each of these kinds of play are enjoyable in their own way, and as Chris Bateman points out in his book *Imaginary Games,* a fine line exists between excitement and fear in games of ilinx, the only difference being the lusory attitude of the player.[3]

- **Engaging:** The game must grab and hold the player's attention. In his 2012 talk, "Attention, Not Immersion," at the Game Developers Conference in San Francisco, Richard Lemarchand, co-lead game designer of the *Uncharted* series of games, referred to this as "attention," and it's a very important aspect of game design. I discuss his talk in greater detail later in this chapter.

- **Fulfilling:** Playing the game must fill some need or desire of the player. As humans, we have many needs that can be met through play in both real and virtual ways. The need for socialization and community, for instance, can be met both through playing a board game with friends or experiencing the day-to-day life of *Animal Crossing* with the virtual friends who live in your town. The feeling of *fiero* (the Italian word for personal triumph over adversity)[4] can be achieved by helping your team win a soccer match, defeating a friend in a fighting game like *Tekken,*[5] or by eventually defeating the final level in a difficult rhythm game like *Osu! Tatake! Ouendan.* Different players have different needs, and the same player can have drastically different needs from day to day.

Lusory Attitude

In *The Grasshopper,* Bernard Suits talks at length about the lusory attitude: the attitude one must have to take part in a game. When in the lusory attitude, players happily follow the rules of the game for the joy of eventually winning via the rules (and not by avoiding them). As Suits points out, neither cheaters nor spoilsports have a lusory attitude; cheaters want to win but

---

[2] Roger Caillois, *Le Jeux et Les Hommes (Man, Play, & Games)* (Paris: Gallimard, 1958).

[3] Chris Bateman, *Imaginary Games.* (Washington, USA: Zero Books, 2011), 26-28.

[4] Nicole Lazzaro discusses *fiero* often in her talks at GDC about emotions that drive players.

[5] Thanks to my good friends Donald McCaskill and Mike Wabschall for introducing me to the beautiful intricacies of Tekken 3 and for the thousands of matches we've played together.

not to follow the rules, and spoilsports may or may not follow the rules but have no interest in winning the game.

As a designer, you should work toward games that encourage players to maintain this lusory attitude. In large part, I believe that this means you must show respect for your players and not take advantage of them. In 2010, my colleague Bryan Cash and I gave two Game Developers Conference talks about what we termed *sporadic-play* games,[6] games that the player plays sporadically throughout her day. Both talks were based on our experience designing *Skyrates*[7] (pronounced like pirates), a graduate school project for which our team won a few design awards in 2008. In designing *Skyrates* we sought to make a persistent online game (like the massively multiplayer online games [MMOs] of the time; e.g., Blizzard's *World of Warcraft*) that could easily be played by busy people. Skyrates set players in the role of privateers of the skies, flying from skyland (floating island) to skyland trading goods and battling pirates. The sporadic aspect of the game was that each player was able to check in for a few minutes at a time throughout her day, set orders for her skyrate character, fight a few pirate battles, upgrade her ship or character, and then let her skyrate play out the orders while the player herself went about her day. At various times during the day, she might receive a text message on her phone letting her know that her skyrate was under attack, but it was her choice whether to jump into combat or to let her skyrate handle it on his own.

As designers in the industry at the time, we were witnessing the rise of social media games like *FarmVille* and the like that seemed to have little or no respect for their players' time. It was commonplace for games on social networks to demand (through their mechanics) that players log in to the game continually throughout the day, and players were punished for not returning to the game on time. This was accomplished through a few nefarious mechanics, the chief of which were *energy* and *spoilage*.

In social network games with energy as a resource, the player's energy level built slowly over time regardless of whether she was playing or not, but there was a cap on the energy that could be earned by waiting, and that cap was often considerably less than the amount that could be accrued in a day and less than the amount needed to accomplish the optimal player actions each day. This required players to log in several times throughout the day to spend the energy that had accrued and not waste potential accrual time on capped-out energy. Of course, players

---

[6]   Cash, Bryan and Gibson, Jeremy. "Sporadic Games: The History and Future of Games for Busy People" (presented as part of the Social Games Summit at the Game Developers Conference, San Francisco, CA, 2010). Cash, Bryan and Gibson, Jeremy "Sporadic Play Update: The Latest Developments in Games for Busy People" (presented at the Game Developers Conference Online, Austin, TX, 2010).

[7]   *Skyrates* was developed over the course of two semesters in 2006 while we were all graduate students at Carnegie Mellon University's Entertainment Technology Center. The developers were Howard Braham, Bryan Cash, Jeremy Gibson, Chuck Hoover, Henry Clay Reister, Seth Shain, and Sam Spiro, with character art by Chris Daniel. Our faculty advisors were Jesse Schell and Dr. Drew Davidson. After *Skyrates* was initially released, we continued development as a hobby and added the developers Phil Light and Jason Buckner. You can play the game now at http://skyrates.net.

were also able to purchase additional energy that was not capped and did not expire, and this drove a large amount of the sales in these games.

The spoilage mechanic is best explained through *FarmVille*, in which players could plant crops and were required to harvest them later. However, if a crop was left unharvested for too long, it would spoil, and the player would lose her investment in both the seeds and the time spent to grow and nurture the crop. For higher-value crops, the delay before spoilage was drastically less than that of low-value, beginner-level crops, so habitual players found themselves required to return to the game within increasingly small windows of time to get the most out of their investments.

Bryan and I hoped through our GDC talks to counter these trends or at least offer some alternatives. The idea of a sporadic-play game is to give the player the most agency (ability to make choices) in the least amount of time. Our professor, Jesse Schell, once commented that *Skyrates* was like a friend who reminded him to take a break from work every once in a while, but after several minutes of play also reminded him to get back to work. This kind of respect caused our game to have a conversion rate of over 90%, meaning that over 90% of the players who initially tried the game became regular players.

The Magic Circle

As was mentioned briefly in Chapter 2, "Game Analysis Frameworks," in his 1938 book *Homo Ludens,* Johan Huizinga proposed an idea that has come to be known as the *magic circle*. The magic circle is the space in which a game takes place, and it can be mental, physical, or some combination of the two. Within the magic circle, the rules hold sway over the players, and the amount that certain actions are encouraged or discouraged is different from the world of everyday life.

For example, when two friends are playing poker against each other, they will often bluff (or lie) about the cards that they have and how certain they are that they will win the pot. However, outside of the game, these same friends would consider lying to each other to be a violation of their friendship. Similarly, on the ice in the game of hockey, players routinely shove and slam into each other (within specific rules, of course), however these players will still shake hands and sometimes be close friends outside of the boundaries of the game.

As Ian Bogost and many other game theorists have pointed out, the magic circle is a porous and temporary thing. Even children recognize this and will sometimes call "time out" during make-believe play. Time out in this sense denotes a suspension of the rules and a temporary cessation of the magic circle, which is often done so that the players can discuss how the rules should be shaped for the remainder of the game. Once the discussion is complete, "time in" is called, and both play and the magic circle continue where they left off.

Not only is it possible to halt and resume the magic circle, it is also sometimes difficult to maintain the integrity of the magic circle. During long delays of football games (for example, if the game is delayed 30 minutes for weather in the middle of the second quarter), commentators will often discuss how difficult it is for players to either maintain the game mindset through the delay or get back into the game mindset once play resumes.

Flow

As described by psychologist Mihaly Csíkszentmihályi (pronounced chick-sent-me-high), flow is the state of optimal challenge, and it has been discussed frequently at the Game Developers Conference because it relates so closely to what many game designers are trying to create. In a flow state, a player is focused intently on the challenge before her and very often loses awareness of things that are outside of the flow experience. You have probably felt this at times when you have played or worked so intently on something that time seems distorted, either passing faster or more slowly than normal.

Flow in this sense was the subject of Jenova Chen's MFA thesis paper at the University of Southern California as well as the subject of his thesis game, appropriately titled *Flow*.[8] Jenova also spoke about this concept in a couple of talks at GDC.

As you can see in Figure 8.1, the flow state exists between boredom and frustration. If the game is too challenging for the player's skill level, she will feel frustrated; conversely, if the player is too skilled for the game, she will feel bored.

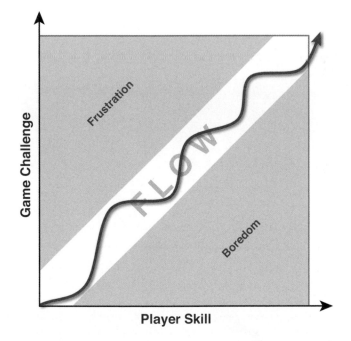

Figure 8.1 Flow as described by Csíkszentmihályi

---

[8] The original Flash-based version of *Flow* can be played at http://interactive.usc.edu/projects/cloud/flowing/. The updated and expanded PlayStation 3 version can be downloaded from the PlayStation Store.

According to the 2002 article, "The Concept of Flow," by Jeanne Nakamura and Mihaly Csíkszent-mihályi, the experience of flow is the same across cultures, genders, ages, and various kinds of activity, and it relies on two conditions:[9]

- Perceived challenges, or opportunities for action, that stretch (neither overmatching nor underutilizing) existing skills; a sense that one is engaging challenges at a level appropriate to one's capacities
- Clear proximal goals and immediate feedback about the progress that is being made

This is what much of the discussion of flow has centered on in the realm of game design. Both of these conditions are concrete enough for designers to understand how to implement them in their games, and through careful testing and player interviews, it's easy to measure whether your game is doing so. However, since 1990, when Csíkszentmihályi published his book *Flow: The Psychology of Optimal Experience,* research has expanded our understanding of flow as it relates to games in one very important way: Designers realized that flow is tiring to maintain. It turns out that while players enjoy flow—and moments of flow are some of the most memorable of your games—it is difficult to maintain flow for more than 15 or 20 minutes. In addition, if the player is always kept in a perfect state of flow, she may never actually see that her skill is improving. So, for many players, you actually want a flow diagram like the one shown in Figure 8.2.

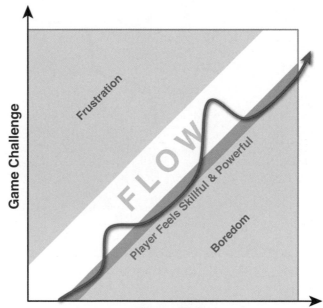

Figure 8.2 Updated flow

---

[9] Jeanne Nakamura and Mihaly Csíkszentmihályi, "The Concept of Flow." *Handbook of positive psychology* (2002): 89–105, 90.

There is a border between flow and boredom where the player feels powerful and skillful (i.e., they feel awesome!), and players actually need that. While the flow state is powerful and successful, it's also important to let your players out of the flow state so that they can reflect on what they accomplished while within flow. Think about the best boss fight you've ever had in a game. When in a flow state, by definition, you lose track of everything outside of the moment because flow requires total attention. If you are like me, it wasn't until you had actually defeated the boss that you had a moment to breathe and realize how amazing the fight had been. Players need not only these moments but also moments to revel in their increased skill.

Like many other games, the original *God of War* game did this very well. It would consistently introduce the player to a single opponent of a new type, and this often felt like a mini boss fight because the player hadn't yet figured out the strategies for defeating that type of enemy. The player eventually learned the strategy for that particular enemy and over several encounters with single enemies of this type, perfected her skill. Then, several minutes later, the player was required to fight more than one of this enemy type simultaneously, though because she had increased in skill, this was actually less of a challenge than the single opponent had been originally. Her ability to easily dispatch several copies of the enemy that had given her trouble singly demonstrated to her that she had increased in skill and made her feel awesome.

As you design your games, remember that it's not just about giving the player an optimal challenge, it's also about giving her the understanding that she is getting better and granting her time to just be awesome. After a difficult fight, give the player some time to just be powerful. This encourages feelings of empowerment.

Structured Conflict

As you saw in Chapter 1, "Thinking Like a Designer," structured conflict is one of the human needs that can be fulfilled by games. One of the primary differences between play and game is that game always involves struggle or conflict, which can be conflict against other players or conflict against the systems of the game (see the section on player relationships in Chapter 4, "The Inscribed Layer"). This conflict gives players a chance to test their skill (or that of their team) against others, against systems, against chance, or against themselves.

This desire for structured conflict is also evident in the play of animals. As Chris Bateman points out in *Imaginary Games:*

> When our puppy plays with other dogs, there are clear limits as to what is acceptable behavior. When play fighting with another puppy, there is much gentle biting, climbing upon one another and general rolling around in frenzied mock violence; there are rules of a kind here.[10]

Even in some actual wars, there have been game-like rules. In the memoir of his life, Chief Plenty-Coups of the Native American Crow tribe relates some of the rules of counting coup in

---

[10] Chris Bateman, *Imaginary Games*. (Washington, USA: Zero Books, 2011), 24.

battle. Coup was counted for getting away with dangerous actions on the battlefield. Striking an armed and able enemy warrior with a coup-stick, quirt (short riding whip), or bow before otherwise harming him; stealing an enemy's weapons while he was still alive; stealing horses or weapons from an enemy camp; and striking the first enemy to fall in battle (before he was killed) all counted for coup. Doing so while avoiding injury to oneself counted more. Plenty-coups also spoke of rules regarding the two symbolic sticks of tribal fraternities:

> One of these sticks in each society was straight and bore one eagle's feather on its smaller end. If in battle its carrier stuck this stick into the ground, he must not retreat or leave the stick. He must drop his robe [die] there unless relieved by a brother member of his society riding between him and the enemy. He might then move the stick with honor, but while it was sticking in the ground it represented the Crow country. The bearers of the crooked sticks, each having two feathers, might at their discretion move them to better stands after sticking them to mark a position. But they must die in losing them to the enemy. By striking coup with any of these society coup-sticks, the bearers counted double, two for one, since their lives were in greater danger while carrying them.[11]

After the battle, coup was counted, as each warrior related the tales of his exploits during the battle. For escaping from a coup without being harmed, the warrior would receive an eagle feather that could be worn in the hair or attached to a coup-stick. If he had been injured, the feather was painted red.

The activity of counting coup among the Native American tribes of the plains lent additional meaning to the wars between nations and provided a structured way for acts of bravery on the battlefield to translate into increased respect once the battle was complete.

Many of today's most popular games provide for structured conflict between teams of players, including most traditional sports (soccer, football, basketball, and hockey being the most popular worldwide) as well as online team competitions like *League of Legends*, *Team Fortress 2*, and *Counter Strike*. But even without teams, games as a whole provide ways for players to engage in conflict and triumph over adversity.

Empowerment

The earlier section on flow covered one kind of empowerment (giving the player the feeling that she is powerful in the game world). This section covers another kind of empowerment: giving the player power over what she chooses to do in the game. I mean this in two senses: autotelic and performative.

Autotelic

The term *autotelic* comes from the Latin words for self (auto) and goal (telos). A person is auto-telic when she is determining her own goals for herself. When Csíkszentmihályi initially started

---

[11] Frank Bird Linderman, *Plenty-coups, Chief of the Crows*, New ed. (Lincoln, NE: University of Nebraska Press, 2002), 31–32.

developing his theory of flow, he knew that autotelisis would have a major role in it. According to his research, autotelic individuals get the most pleasure out of flow situations, whereas non-autotelic individuals (that is, those who don't enjoy setting their own goals) tend to get more pleasure out of easy situations where they perceive their skill level to be much higher than the difficulty level of the challenge.[12] Csíkszentmihályi believes that it is an autotelic personality that enables a person to find happiness in life regardless of situation.[13]

So, what kinds of games encourage autotelic behavior? One fantastic example is *Minecraft*. In this game, the player is dropped into a randomly generated world where her only real goal is survival. (Zombies and other monsters will attack the player at night.) However, she is also given the ability to mine the environment for resources and then use those resources to make both tools and structures. Players of *Minecraft* have not only built castles, bridges, and a full-scale model of the Star Trek *Enterprise NCC-1701D* but also roller coasters that run for many kilometers and even simple working computers with RAM.[14] This is the true genius of *Minecraft*: it gives players the opportunity to choose their own path as players and provides them with flexible game systems that enable that choice.

While most games are less flexible than *Minecraft*, it is still possible to allow the player multiple ways to approach a problem. One of the reasons for the loss in popularity of both text-based adventures (e.g., *Zork*, *Planetfall*, and *The Hitchhiker's Guide to the Galaxy* by Infocom) and the point-and-click adventure games that followed them (e.g., the *King's Quest* and *Space Quest* series by Sierra OnLine) is that they often only allowed a single (often obtuse) approach to most problems. In *Space Quest II*, if you didn't grab a jockstrap from a random locker at the very beginning of the game, you couldn't use it as a sling much later in the game, and you would have to restart the game from the beginning. In Infocom's game version of *The Hitchhiker's Guide to the Galaxy* when a bulldozer approached your house, you had to lie down in the mud in front of it and then "wait" three times. If you didn't do this *exactly,* you would die and have to restart the game.[15] Contrast this with more modern games like *Dishonored*, where nearly every problem has at least one violent and one nonviolent solution. Giving the player choice over how she will accomplish her goals builds player interest in the game and player ownership over successes.[16]

---

[12] Nakamura and Csíkszentmihályi, "The Concept of Flow," 98.

[13] Mihaly Csíkszentmihályi, *Flow: The psychology of optimal experience* (New York: Harper & Row, 1990), 69.

[14] http://www.escapistmagazine.com/news/view/109385-Computer-Built-in-Minecraft-Has-RAM-Performs-Division.

[15] One of the major reasons that this was done was because of the multiplicative explosions of content that would occur if the player were allowed to do anything in the game narrative. The closest thing that I have seen to a truly open, branching narrative is the interactive drama *Façade* by Michael Mateas and Andrew Stern.

[16] However, you must also keep development cost and time in perspective. If you're not careful, every option that you give your player could increase the cost of development, both in terms of monetary cost and in terms of time. It's a careful balance that you must maintain as a designer and developer.

Performative

The other kind of empowerment that is important to games is performative empowerment. In *Game Design Theory,* Keith Burgun states that not only are game designers creating art, they're creating the ability for players to make art. The creators of passive media can be thought of as composers; they create something to be consumed by the audience. But, as a game designer, you're actually somewhere between a composer and an instrument maker. Instead of just creating the notes that others will play, you're also creating the instrument that they can use to make art. One of the best examples of this kind of game thus far is *Tony Hawk's Pro Skater*, where the player has a large vocabulary of moves to draw from and must choose how to string them together in harmony with the environment to get a high score. Just as the cellist Yo-yo Ma is an artist, a game player can be an artist when empowered by a game designer who crafts a game for her that she can play artistically. This can also be seen in other games with large vocabularies of moves or strategies like fighting and real-time strategy games.

Attention and Involvement

As mentioned earlier in this chapter, the fantastic game designer Richard Lemarchand spoke at GDC about attention in his 2012 talk, "Attention, Not Immersion: Making Your Games Better with Psychology and Playtesting, the Uncharted Way." The purpose of his talk was to expose confusion about the use of the word *immersion* in game design, and to demonstrate that talking about getting and holding an audience's *attention* was a much clearer way of describing what game designers usually seek to do.

Prior to Lemarchand's talk, many designers sought to increase immersion in their games. This led to things like the reduction or removal of the HUD (heads-up onscreen display) and the minimization of elements that could pull the player out of the experience of the game. But as Lemarchand pointed out in his talk, gamers never truly achieve immersion, nor would they want to. If a gamer actually believed that he was in Nathan Drake's position halfway through *Uncharted 3*, being shot at while clinging to a cargo net that was hanging out of the open door of a transport plane thousands of feet above a desert, the player would be absolutely terrified! One of the critical aspects of the magic circle is that both entry into the circle and remaining in the circle are choices made by the player, and she is always aware that the game is voluntary. (As Suits points out, once participation is no longer voluntary, the experience is no longer a game.)

Instead of immersion, Lemarchand seeks to initially gain the player's attention and then to maintain hold over it. For the sake of clarity, I will use *attention* to describe immediate interest that can be grabbed and *involvement* to describe long-term interest that needs to be held (though Lemarchand chose to use the word attention to describe both states). Lemarchand also differentiates between reflexive attention (the involuntary response that we have to stimuli around us) and executive attention (which occurs when we choose to pay attention to something).

According to his talk, the elements of beauty, aesthetics, and contrast are great at grabbing attention. James Bond films always open with an action scene for this very reason. They begin *in medias res* (in the middle of things) because doing so creates a marked contrast between the boredom of sitting in the theater waiting for the film to start and the excitement of the beginning of the film. This kind of attention grab exploits reflexive attention, the attention shift that is evolutionarily hard-wired into you. When you see something moving out of the corner of your eye, it will grab your attention regardless of whether you wish it to or not. Then, once the Bond movie has your attention, it switches to the rather tedious exposition required to set up the rest of the film. Because the viewer is already hooked by the film, she will choose to use executive attention (that is, attention by choice) to listen to this exposition.

In *The Art of Game Design,* Jesse Schell presents his theory of the interest curve. The interest curve is also about grabbing attention, and according to Schell, a good interest curve looks like Figure 8.3.

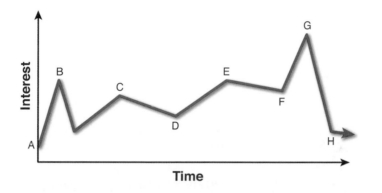

Figure 8.3 Interest curve from Jesse Schell's book

According to Schell, in a good interest curve, the audience will enter with a little interest (A), and then you want to grab them with a "hook" that piques their interest (B). After you have them interested, you can drop it back down and steadily build interest with little peaks and val-leys (C, D, E, and F) that should slowly build to the highest point of interest: the climax (G). After the climax, the audience's interest is let back down to (H) in a denouement as the experience comes to a close. This is actually very similar to Syd Field's standard three-act dramatic curve diagram that describes most stories and film, and it has been shown to work well for time spans between a few minutes and a couple of hours. Schell tells us that this interest curve can be repeated in fractal fashion to cover longer periods of time. One way this could be accomplished is by having a mission structure within a larger game and making sure that each mission has its own good interest curve within the larger interest curve of the entire game. However, it's more complex than that because the interest that Schell discusses is what I'm calling attention, and we still need to account for involvement if we want to interest the player for long periods of time.

Taking a closer look at attention and involvement, attention is directly paired with reflexive attention (the involuntary response), while involvement is almost exclusively executive atten-tion. Having thought about this for a while, I've created the diagram shown in Figure 8.4 as a synthesis of Lemarchand's concepts and my personal experience as both a designer and player.

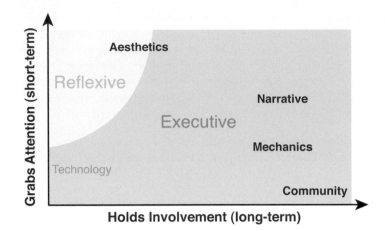

Figure 8.4   The four elements in relation to attention and involvement (because technology is largely invisible to the player it doesn't register much on this graph)

As you can see in the diagram, aesthetics (in terms of the aesthetic element in the tetrad) are best at grabbing our attention, and in the case of aesthetics, that attention is largely reflexive. This is because aesthetics deal directly with our senses and call for attention.

Narrative and mechanics both require executive attention. As pointed out by Lemarchand, narrative has a greater ability to grab our attention, but I disagree with Lemarchand and Jason Rohrer when they state that mechanics have a greater ability to sustain involvement than narrative. While a single movie tends to last only a couple of hours, that is also relatively true of the mechanics in a single session of play. And, in my personal experience, I have found that just as great mechanics can hold my involvement for over 100 hours, so can a series of narratives hold my attention through over 100 episodes of a serial television show. The major difference between mechanics and narrative here is that narrative must be ever evolving while gameplay mechanics can exist unchanged for years and still hold interest due to the different circumstances of play. (Consider a player's lifelong devotion to chess or go.)

The one thing that I have seen outlast both narrative and mechanics in terms of long-term involvement is community. When people find that a community exists around a game, movie, or activity, and they feel part of that community, they will continue to take part long after the hold of narrative or mechanics have lost their sway. Community is what kept many guilds together in *Ultima Online* long after most people had moved on to other games. And when the members of the community did eventually move on, they more often than not chose as a community which new game to play together, thus continuing the same community through multiple different online games.

Interesting Decisions

As you read in Chapter 1, Sid Meier has stated that games are (or should be) a series of interesting decisions, but we questioned at that time what exactly was meant by *interesting*.

Throughout the book thus far, we have seen several concepts presented that can help illuminate this.

Katie Salen and Eric Zimmerman's concept of meaningful play as presented in Chapter 5, "The Dynamic Layer," gives us some insight into this. To be meaningful, a decision must be both discernible and integrated:[17]

- **Discernible:** The player must be able to tell that the game received and understood her decision (i.e., immediate feedback).
- **Integrated:** The player must believe that her decision will have some effect on the long-term outcome of the game (i.e., long-term impact).

In his definition of *game*, Keith Burgun points out the importance of decisions being ambiguous:

- **Ambiguous:** A decision is ambiguous for the player if she can guess at how it might affect the system but can never be sure. The decision to wager money in the stock market is ambiguous. As a savvy investor, you should have a pretty decent guess about whether the value of the stock will go up or down, but the market is so volatile that you can never know for sure.

Almost all interesting decisions are also double-edged (as in the saying *a double-edged sword*):

- **Double-edged:** A decision is double-edged when it has both an upside and a downside. In the previous stock purchase example, the upside is the longer-term potential to make money, and the downside is the immediate loss of the resource (money) used to purchase the stock as well as the potential for the stock to lose value.

Another aspect involved in making a decision interesting is the novelty of the decision.

- **Novel:** A decision is novel if it is sufficiently different from other decisions that the player has made recently. In the classic Japanese roleplaying game (JRPG) *Final Fantasy VII*, combat with a specific enemy changes little once the encounter has begun. If the enemy is weak to fire, and the player has enough mana and fire magic, she will generally attack every round with fire magic until the enemy is defeated. In contrast, the excellent combat in the JRPG *Grandia III* makes positioning and location important for most special attacks but the player's characters move around the field independent of player input. Whenever the player is able to make a decision, time freezes for her, and she must reevaluate the positions of allies and enemies before making each decision. This movement of her characters and the importance of position make every combat decision novel.

---

[17] Katie Salen and Eric Zimmerman, *Rules of Play* (Cambridge, MA: MIT Press, 2003), 34.

The final requirement for interesting decisions is that they must be clear.

- **Clear:** Although it is important for the outcomes of a choice to have some ambiguity, the choice itself must be clear, and there are many ways that choices can lack clarity:
    - A choice can be unclear if there are too many options to choose from at a given time; the player can have difficulty discerning the differences between them. This leads to *choice paralysis*, the inability to choose because there are too many options.
    - A choice can be unclear if the player can't intuit the likely outcome of the choice. This was often a problem with the dialog trees in games, which for years just listed the possible statements that a player could make without any information about the implied meaning of the statement. In contrast, the dialog tree decision wheel in *Mass Effect* included information about whether a statement would extend or shorten a conversation and whether it would be said in a friendly or antagonistic way. This allowed the player to choose an attitude rather than specific wording of a statement and removed the ambiguity from the dialog tree.
    - A choice can also be unclear if the player doesn't understand the significance of the choice. One of the great advances in the combat system of *Grandia III* over *Grandia II* allowed threatened characters to automatically call for help during another character's turn. If Character A is about to be hit by an attack, and Character B can prevent it by acting on this turn, Character A will cry for help during Character B's turn. The player may still choose to have Character B do something other than prevent the attack, but the game has made it clear to her that this is her last chance to prevent the attack on A.

These six aspects can all be combined together into a decent understanding of the things that make a decision interesting. An interesting decision is one that is discernible, integrated, ambiguous, double-edged, novel, and clear. By making your decisions more interesting, you can increase the appeal of your mechanics and thereby the player's long-term involvement in your game.

Experiential Understanding

The final goal for players that we'll discuss in this chapter is experiential understanding, a design goal that is far more accessible to game designers than designers of any other kind of media.

In 2013, game critic and theorist Mattie Brice released *Mainichi*, the first game that she had designed and developed (see Figure 8.5).

As described by Brice, *Mainichi* is a personal letter from her to a friend to help her friend understand what her daily life is like. In her real life, Brice is a transgender woman living in the Castro district of San Francisco. In *Mainichi*, the player takes on the role of Mattie Brice and must choose what to do to prepare to go out for coffee with a friend: Does she dress nicely, put on makeup, eat a bite? Each of these decisions change how some (but not all) of the people around town react to her as she walks to the coffee shop and orders her drink. Even a simple decision like whether to pay with a credit card or cash has meaning in the game. (Paying with a credit card will cause the barista to refer to you as "Ms...er...Mr. Brice" because he reads Brice's old, male name on the credit card.)

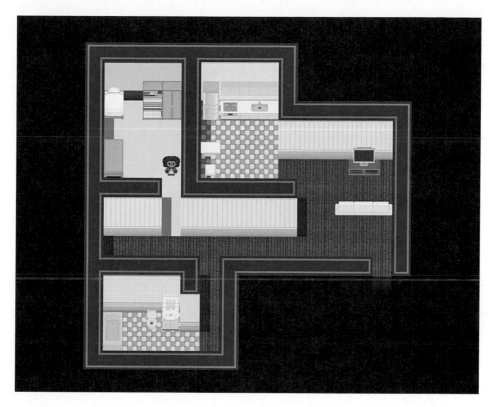

Figure 8.5 *Mainichi* by Mattie Brice (2013)

The game is very short, and as a player, you are compelled to try again and see what happens differently based on the seemingly small choices that you make throughout the game. Because the player's decisions change how the character of Mattie is perceived, you feel complicit in her being treated well or poorly by the people around her. Though some kind of branching chart or a story structured like the movie *Groundhog Day* (in which Bill Murray's character must relive the same day hundreds of times until he finally gets it right) could convey the same information about the large implications of the tiny choices that Brice makes every day, neither would convey a sense of responsibility to the audience. At this time, it is only through a game (be it a video game, make-believe, or roleplaying) that a person can actually walk in the shoes of another and gain insight into what it must be like to make the decisions that she makes. This experiential understanding is one of the most interesting goals that we can seek to achieve as game designers.

Summary

Everyone making games has different feelings about each of these design goals. Some people just want to make fun experiences, some people want to give players interesting puzzles, some people want to encourage players to think deeply about a specific topic, and some people want to give players an arena in which to be empowered. Regardless of what your reasons are for wanting to make a game, it is time now to start making them.

The next two chapters are about paper prototyping and playtesting. Together, prototyping and playtesting form the core of the real work of game design. In almost any game, especially a digital game, there will be hundreds of small variables that you can tweak to change the experience. However, in digital games, even seemingly small changes can take considerable development time to implement. The paper prototyping strategies presented in the next chapter can help you get from concept to playable (paper) prototype very quickly and then get you from one prototype to the next even more rapidly. For many games, this paper prototyping phase can save you a lot of time in digital development because you will have already run several paper playtests to find the fun before writing a single line of code.

CHAPTER 9

PAPER PROTOTYPING

In this chapter, you learn about paper prototyping, one of the best tools available to game designers to rapidly test and iterate on game ideas. Although simple to implement, paper prototypes can teach you a tremendous amount about various aspects of your game, even if that game will eventually be digital.

By the end of the chapter, you will know the best practices for implementing paper prototypes and understand the parts of a digital game that can best be understood and tested through paper.

The Benefits of Paper Prototypes

While digital technologies have enabled a whole new world of possibilities for game development, many designers still find themselves exploring their initial ideas using traditional paper methods. With computers able to calculate and display information much faster than a person could draw or calculate by hand, you may be wondering why this is. It largely comes down to two factors: speed and ease of implementation. However, there are many benefits that you should consider, including:

- **Initial development speed:** For quickly throwing together a game, nothing beats paper. You can grab some dice and some 3x5 note cards and make a game in very little time. Even when you have a lot of experience as a game designer, starting on a new digital game project can take quite a bit of time if it's completely different from anything you've done before.

- **Iteration speed:** It's also very fast to make changes to paper games; in fact, it's even possible to make changes to the games while you're playing. Because of the ease of changes, paper prototypes are a great fit for game brainstorming at the beginning of preproduction on a project (when large changes to the project can happen often). If a paper prototype isn't working, making a change can take as little as a few minutes.

- **Low technical barrier to entry:** Because very little technical knowledge or artistic talent is required to make a paper prototype, anyone on the game development team can take part in the process. This is a way to get great ideas from people on your team who would be less able to effectively contribute to a digital prototype.

- **Collaborative prototyping:** Because of the low barrier to entry and the rapid iteration, it's possible to collaboratively create and modify a paper prototype in a way that is not yet possible for digital prototypes. A group of people from across your team can work together on a paper prototype and share ideas quickly. As an added benefit, bringing people from across your game development team into the design process in this way can help to increase their buy-in for the entirety of the project and can serve as a fantastic team-building activity.

- **Focused prototyping and testing:** To even a complete novice, it is obvious that a paper prototype of a digital game is going to be very different from the final digital product. This allows you to test specific elements of your game without your testers getting hung up on details. Many years ago, an internal document to user interface designers at Apple Computer recommended that they make rough sketches of the buttons for their interfaces on paper, scan the paper, and then make their UI prototypes from the scanned images. Because the sketched and scanned images of UI elements like buttons and menus were so obviously not the final look that Apple would choose for the UI, testers didn't get hung up on the look of the buttons and instead focused on the usability of the interface, which is what Apple was interested in testing. A paper prototype can help direct the attention of your testers in the same way so that they don't get hung up on the look of the prototype but instead focus on the specific aspect of gameplay that you intend to test.

Paper Prototyping Tools

You might want to have several paper prototyping tools on hand. You can make a paper proto-type from almost anything, but some tools can help make the process go faster:

- **Large sheets of paper:** At most office supply stores, you can get easel-sized sheets of paper (something like 24 inches wide by 36 inches tall). These often come in a pad of several sheets, and some have a mild adhesive on the back of each sheet to stick them to walls and such. You can also often find large sheets of paper inscribed with a square or hexagonal grid. See the "Movement on Different Grid Types" sidebar for information about why you may want to choose a hexagonal or square grid and how to handle free movement on an open grid game board.

MOVEMENT ON DIFFERENT GRID TYPES

As shown in Figure 9.1, you need to make choices about how players can move across the grid in your game. As depicted in image A, on a square grid diagonal movement moves the player almost 50% further than orthogonal movement. (According to the Pythagorean theorem, the diagonal distance is $\sqrt{2}$ or roughly 1.414.) However, movement to any adjacent hex in a hexagonal grid is the same, regardless of which hex you choose (image B).

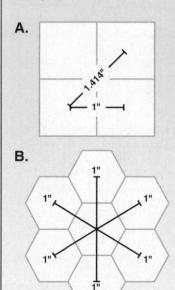

Figure 9.1 Movement systems

Image C shows a simple alternative movement system across a square grid that can be used in board games to still allow diagonal movement yet prevent abuse thereof. Players are allowed to move diagonally with every other movement. This evens out the distances somewhat and makes the possible movement within a specific number of moves roughly circular. The purple lines on diagram C show two different possible paths of four moves each.

Hexagonal grids are often used for military simulation board games where an accurate representation of distances and movement is critical. However, most buildings in the real world are rectangular, so they don't fit as well on a hexagonal board. The choice of which to use is up to you as a designer.

- **Dice:** Most people have some d6 dice (normal six-sided dice) sitting around. As a game designer, it's also really good to have some of the other varieties. Your local game store should have sets for sale that include all the dice normally used for d20 roleplaying games including 2d6 (2 six-sided dice), 1d8, 1d12, 1d20, and percentile dice (2d10 with one marked 0–9 and the other marked 00–90; rolled together, they give you a number between 00 and 99). Chapter 11, "Math and Game Balance," includes a lot of information about different kinds of dice and what the probability space of their randomness looks like. For example, with 1d6, you have an even chance of any number from 1 to 6, but with 2d6 there are 6 different ways to roll a 7 (a 6/36 chance) but only one way to roll a 12 (a 1/36 chance).

- **Cards:** Cards are a fantastic prototyping tool because they are so malleable. Create cards numbered 1–6, and you have a 1d6 deck. If you shuffle before every draw, it acts just like a 1d6, but if you draw all the cards before reshuffling, then you're guaranteed to get one each of 1, 2, 3, 4, 5, and 6 before seeing any number for a second time.

- **Card sleeves:** Most gaming stores sell several different styles of card sleeves. Card sleeves were initially developed to protect baseball cards, and they were extended to the gaming industry with the rise of collectible card games like *Magic: The Gathering* in the '90s. Each card sleeve is a protective plastic cover for an individual card, and there's enough room inside of them for both a regular card and a slip of paper. This is great for prototyping because it means that you can print the cards for your prototype on regular printer paper and then put them into a sleeve in front of a regular playing card. The regular card will give the card enough stiffness to be shuffled without the time and expense of writing or printing on card stock. The card sleeves can also ensure that all the card backs look uniform, or alternatively, several sets of card sleeves can be used to keep different decks of designed cards separate.

- **3x5 note cards:** Cut in half, 3x5 note cards are a great size for a deck of cards. At their regular size, they're fantastic for brainstorming. Some stores now sell 3x5 cards that have already been cut in half (to 3x2.5).

- **Post-It notes:** These simple little sticky notes are fantastic for quickly arranging and sorting ideas.

- **Whiteboard:** Nothing says brainstorming like a white board. Be sure to have lots of colors of markers available. White boards tend to get erased often, so be sure to snap a digital photo of anything you write on one that is at all worth keeping. If you have a whiteboard tabletop or a vertical whiteboard that is magnetic, you can also draw a game board on it, but I tend to prefer large sheets of paper for game boards because they don't get erased as often.

- **Pipe cleaners / LEGO blocks:** Both of these can be used for the same purpose: quickly building little things. These could be playing pieces, set pieces, or really anything you can think of. LEGO blocks are a lot more sturdy, but pipe cleaners are much cheaper and more flexible.

- **A notebook:** As a designer, you should always have a notebook handy. I like the pocket-size Moleskine with unlined paper, but there are several types. The key element of your notebook is that it needs to be small enough to carry with you and have enough pages that you won't be filling it up and replacing it every few weeks. Any time someone plays your game prototype, you should be taking notes. You always think you'll remember the important things, but that's often not the case.

An Example of a Paper Prototype

In this section of the chapter, I'll explain the paper prototype for an upcoming tactical combat game that I'm developing. For this paper prototype to work, one person—referred to as the game master (GM)—will need to take on the role of the computer artificial intelligence (AI). The other takes the role of the player.

Initial Game Concept

The eventual game will be a touchscreen tablet expansion of the type of turn-based tactical combat exemplified by the Blitz system developed by SEGA for the *Valkyria Chronicles* series of games. The game will pit a squad of player-controlled characters against a computer-controlled enemy squadron. Because this is a paper prototype for a digital game, I started by making some sketches of how I thought the final digital game might work.

Figure 9.2 shows a very rough mockup of gameplay for the tactics game. In the touchscreen version, the player starts each turn looking at a top-down map of the space and draws a line to show the path that she wants the character to follow. Each character can only move a certain distance on each turn. The character will then run along the line, and as the character approaches various cover points (areas of the map where a character can hide from incoming enemy attacks), the player has the option to tap on the cover point and have her character detour to that cover. The player can then swipe away from the cover to have the character hop out from behind cover and continue on the original path. Pressing *Attack!* at any time during the move will give the player a short amount of time to line up a shot and fire on an enemy. The player may tap *Done* to end the turn.

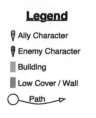

Legend

- Ally Character
- Enemy Character
- Building
- Low Cover / Wall
- Path

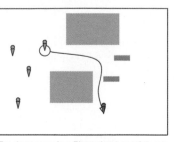

Top-down map view. Player draws a path to set movement for an ally.

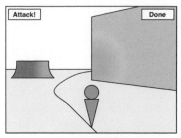

As the ally moves, the camera is 3rd person over-the-shoulder. Areas glow green to show possible cover.

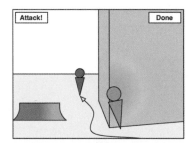

Tapping on a green cover area will cause the ally to go into cover. While in cover, enemy shots will hit less frequently, and the ally can see around corners

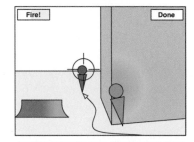

Any time during the move, the player can press the Attack! button. Then she has until the yellow timer runs out to line up her shot and press Fire!

Figure 9.2   Mockup images of the tactics game

Several elements of this game can be prototyped with paper:

- **Map layout:** I hope to procedurally generate the level maps for this game, but I don't yet know what kind of maps will be best suited to the style of game. This paper prototype will help me understand this better.

- **Artificial intelligence:** The final game will involve artificial intelligence to decide enemy goals, movements, and attacks. By paying attention to the choices made by the person playing the GM for the enemy forces in the game, we can learn how to design this AI.

- **Weapon designs:** Various weapons in the game will have different chances of hitting, damage amounts per shot, and so on. The paper prototype can help define what weapons are interesting in this space and how to balance them against each other.

- **Finding the fun:** While some of the fun of the final game will be the graphics, movement, and touch-based interaction (all of which can only really happen in a digital prototype), the core mechanic and the core fun in the game should come from the interesting tactical decisions that the player must make every turn and the necessity of guiding a small team to overcome challenging obstacles and a larger enemy force. All of these can be discovered through the paper prototype.

Constructing the Prototype

The prototype starts with a large sheet of hex grid paper. You can search online for a pad of ½" hex grid paper, or you can find a PDF of a hex grid and print it yourself. For the size map we're talking about, if you're printing, you'll probably want to tape four pieces of paper together.

Making the Map

The first thing you need to do is to decide what kind of mission you want this to be. There are several possible mission types:

- **Rout:** The player must destroy at least 80% of the enemy forces, causing them to retreat.
- **Assassination:** The player must find and eliminate a single enemy target.
- **Sabotage:** The player must sneak into an enemy base and reach a specific target (that will be sabotaged in some way).
- **Infiltration/exfiltration:** The player must sneak in to the enemy base, reach a specific space, and then retreat without triggering an alarm.
- **Capture:** The player must take and hold certain goal points to control the map area.

For this first prototype, we'll set up a capture mission, since it has a nice mix of strategic goals for both the player and the AI. (Once the player has captured a goal point, the AI may try to recapture it.)

Starting from the center of the map, place some small buildings by drawing shaded boxes on the map (or by placing pieces of colored paper over parts of the map). To make movement, visibility, and cover easier to handle, characters will not be able to enter buildings in this prototype. You should also place some low walls around the map along the borders between spaces. These walls will be about waist high in the prototype and can be used by characters for cover. Finally, place about three control points by shading areas in red. These areas are usually surrounded by walls, and the player's goal during play is to capture all three control points. When you're done, your map should look something like the one in Figure 9.3.

Copy the building locations onto a smaller version of the map that will be held by the GM. (I recommend also printing a sheet of ¼" hex graph paper for this.) Then, the GM should secretly place a number of markers to indicate enemy soldier locations on her map. The indicators should show not only position but also facing as shown in Figure 9.4. These enemy unit locations are not revealed to the player until one of her units is in a position to see the enemy (as covered shortly). When placing enemy units, remember that the goal of the GM is not to beat the player but rather to create an experience that feels fun and challenging. For example, placing a lot of units together in each control point and facing them each in different directions makes a lot of strategic sense, but that kind of arrangement would be less enjoyable for the player. The player will want to be able to do things like sneak up on an enemy, and as a designer, the GM should support this.

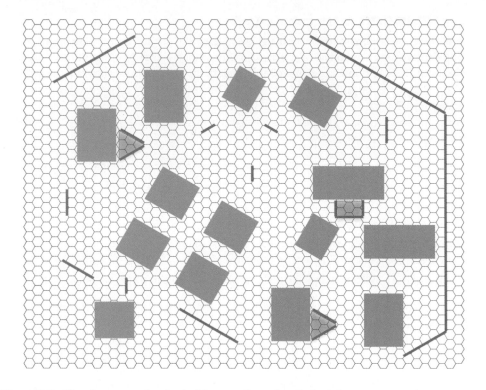

Figure 9.3 The player map showing buildings, walls, and control points

Gameplay

Establishing the gameplay for the prototype comes next. This section covers the required elements of the gameplay for our example.

Objective

The player's objective is to capture all three control points.

Required Equipment

The required equipment includes the following:

- Hex-grid paper map.
- Smaller hex-grid GM map.
- Several six-sided dice.
- Unit markers that can fit within a single hex and face in an obvious direction. Units should also be colored and numbered for easy reference (for example, Red-4, Blue-2, and so on). Player units should be blue, and enemy units red. (Colors don't really matter; all that matters is that you can tell the units apart, and it's obvious which belong to the player.)
- A sheet of paper to track unit health and another to take playtest notes.

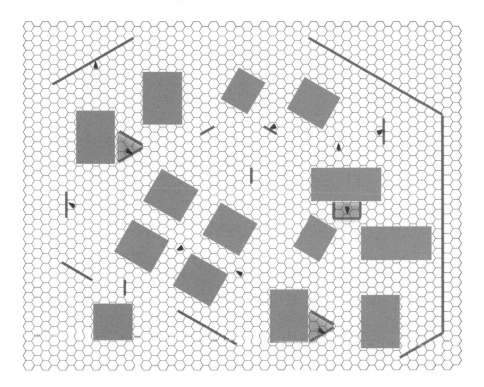

Figure 9.4   The GM map showing enemy unit placement and facing

Setup

In the initial version of the prototype, the player is given four units, all of which have the same capabilities. (In later revisions of the prototype, the capabilities of the units will vary.)

The player may select any hex on the edge of the map as her starting position. She places her first unit on that hex and then must place the other units on adjacent hexes.

Visibility

Visibility is critically important in this game. Any unit can see a distance of ten spaces in an arc in front of it. The arc is shown in Figure 9.5. Units can also share information, so once a unit of the enemy side sees one of the player's units, all enemy units are aware of its presence. Units must have *line of sight* to see each other, and buildings block line of sight. If any part of a building Is in between two units, they cannot see each other (with the exception of building corners described in the section on "Cover" that follows.

The GM is responsible for tracking visibility. During movement, if an enemy unit comes into view of one of the player's units, the GM must place that unit on the player map (regardless of whether it is the player's unit or the enemy unit that is moving). Whenever an enemy unit is no longer in sight of a player, its token is removed from the board. Alternatively, you can just flip that unit token over to show that it's no longer being updated (that is, the enemy unit could be moving, but since the player can't see it, the token stays in the same place), and then, when the enemy unit comes back into view of the player, you can flip the token right side up again and move it to the updated location.

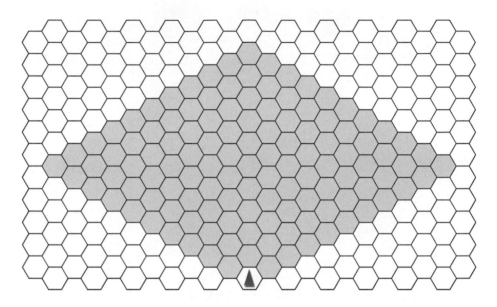

Figure 9.5 The area shaded red shows visibility for the enemy unit.

Player Movement

On the player's turn, she has 4 action points to spend. For each action point, she can activate one unit, so she could move each unit once or one unit four times. However, each time that a unit is moved in a single turn, that unit's movement amount decreases. A unit can move 8 hexes on its first action each turn; on subsequent actions it can move 6, 4, and finally 2 hexes for a single action point. Players can move any direction, and while moving, players should be considered to be seeing up to 10 hexes in all directions for the purposes of visibility (though units are still unable to see through buildings).

Weapons and Firing

Each unit in the game can be outfitted with one of the weapons that are depicted in Figure 9.6. For the first time you play the prototype, I recommend giving all units pistols and then experimenting with other weapons in later playtests. A unit can shoot at any other unit that is visible to it, and a unit may choose to fire once per action (even during the middle of movement). To calculate the odds of hitting, count the number of spaces from the firing unit to the target and consult Figure 9.6. For example, if a unit with a pistol were shooting at another unit five spaces away, the to-hit value would be 3. The player controlling the firing unit would then roll four six-sided dice (one for each of the pistol's four shots), and any die with a result of 3 or higher would hit (which is a 66% chance of hitting for each die). The unit attacked would then take 2 points of damage for each shot that hit.

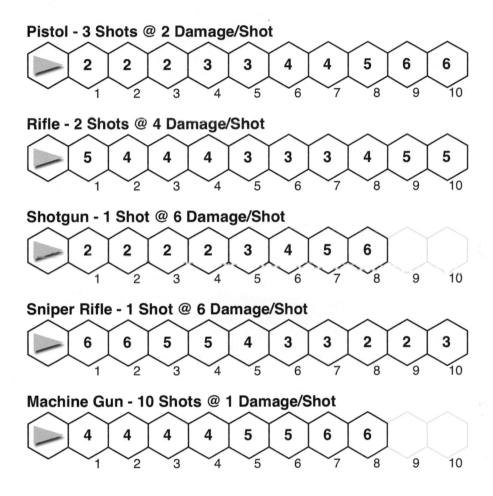

Figure 9.6   Weapon statistics and chance to hit

In Chapter 11, you will build the spreadsheet that I used to explore the initial balance of the weapons in Figure 9.6.

Counterattacks

If a unit has been attacked and survives the attack, it will immediately turn to face its attacker (placing the attacker within the survivor's visibility arc) and return fire using standard attack rules. This means that attacking is risky if the attacked unit isn't killed by the attacker.

Cover

Cover protects units. If a unit is in a hex that is adjacent to either a short wall or the corner of a building, that unit is considered to be in cover. While in cover, the damage taken by a unit is halved (round down). So, if a unit was shot, and the total damage from the attack was 7 points, the damage would be rounded down to 3 points if the target were in cover.

If a unit is in cover around the corner of a building, that unit is treated as having visibility around both sides of the corner as shown in Figure 9.7. This is done to simulate the ability of the unit to peek around the corner and is similar to the advantage that a unit would have in the digital game.

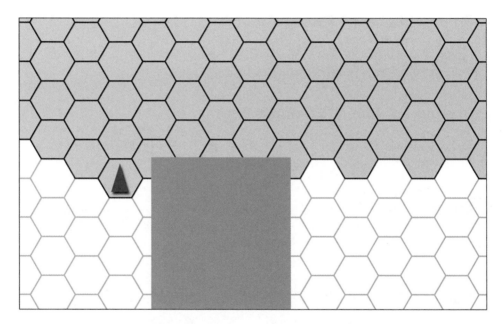

Figure 9.7   Unit visibility when in corner cover

Health

Each unit starts with 6 points of health. If a unit's health drops to 0, that unit is knocked out and can no longer take actions or react at all. Health is not allowed to go below 0; so once a unit is knocked unconscious, it is immune to further damage. Another unit can revive the knocked-out unit through the use of a health pack.

Health Packs

Each unit carries one health pack that can be used either on itself or a unit in an adjacent hex. Using a health pack consumes a unit's single attack during its action and will heal 4 points of health. A health pack can only be used once and is then depleted.

Interception Fire

Other units can fire on a unit that is moving in certain special circumstances:

- A stationary unit may fire on a moving unit when the moving unit enters its visibility.
- A stationary unit may fire on a moving unit when the unit exits its visibility.
- If the moving unit is visible to the stationary unit but it is outside the range of the stationary unit's weapon, the stationary unit instead fires when the moving unit enters or exits the range of the stationary unit's weapon (while still visible).
- A stationary unit may fire on a moving unit that ends its move within view of the stationary unit.

Interception fire is calculated like a regular attack, except that only half the normal number of dice are rolled (rounded up). This means that shotguns, rifles, and sniper rifles each get one interception shot die, while a pistol would get 2 interception shot dice.

When units are stationary, they can only see in the arc in front of them; however, once a moving target has moved into the stationary unit's visible arc, the stationary unit will rotate facing to follow the moving target until the target leaves its visibility.

If there is a moment when both the moving unit and the stationary unit wish to fire at the same time, the moving unit shoots first.

Capturing Control Points

If a unit ends its turn within the shaded area of a control point and there are no enemy units also conscious within the same control point, the control point is captured. The opposing team can recapture a control point through the same rules.

GM Strategy

As mentioned previously, one of the major goals of this prototype is to determine the best strategy for the digital game's AI. Here are some things to consider:

- GM units should generally not be moved until they are either seen by the player or become aware of the player in some other way. (For example, if a red unit sees the player, you can imagine that it might notify other nearby red units.) Because the player has fewer numbers than the red forces, this gives her a chance for surprise attacks.
- Once the player has taken a control point, all GM units are aware of this. So, even if a red unit has not yet been activated by seeing or being seen by a player unit, the GM unit could choose to move toward the control point in the hopes of retaking it.
- Remember to keep track not only of which GM units the player can see but also which player units the GM units can see. As a GM try not to act on information about player units that individual GM units shouldn't have.
- The GM should take notes about which strategies work well against the player and which are too difficult or too easy. Remember that the GM's goal is for the player to have fun and succeed without it being overly easy for the player.

Playtest

Play the prototype a few times with different friends and see what you think. Be sure to keep these questions in mind:

- Does the initial building placement that you chose work? If not, why not? If it does work, why do you think it does?
- Are the weapons balanced to each other? If not, rebalance them to find something that feels right. (You can use the spreadsheet covered in Chapter 11 to do so.)
- Do the units start with the right amount of health? Does the health pack heal the right amount of damage?
- Is your strategy as a GM sound? Is the player having fun?

Be sure to write down both your answers to these questions and your players' answers every time you play the game. You may find that your opinions change over time, and you may find that your opinions differ from those of the player. Writing all of these down can help you to gain perspective on which playtests went better or worse than others and give you more awareness of trends over time.

Best Uses for Paper Prototyping

As you saw in the example prototype, there are both strengths and weaknesses of paper proto-typing for digital games. Here are some things that paper prototypes are particularly good at:

- **Understanding player movement through space:** Through various building and wall layouts, you will find that players tend to choose similar paths through space. Understanding player flow through space will help you in all types of level design.
- **Balancing simple systems:** The weapons in the prototype are all based on three simple variables: accuracy over distance, number of shots, and damage per shot. Although there are only three of these, balancing each weapon against the others is more complex than it may originally seem. For example, consider the shotgun and the machine gun relative to each other:
    - **Shotgun:** At 6 points of damage per shot, the shotgun will kill an enemy with one shot, and at a range of 1 to 4, it will hit on any roll other than a 1 (for a 5/6 chance of hitting). However, because it has only one shot, if that shot misses, the enemy will take no dam-age at all.
    - **Machine Gun:** The machine gun only does 1 point of damage per shot, so six shots must hit to kill the enemy. At a range of 1 to 4, any roll above 3 will hit (for a 3/6 chance of hitting). With ten shots, it is much more likely that you will get close to the aver-age damage of the gun at that distance (5 points) rather than the all or nothing of the shotgun.

    With these stats, the shotgun is risky but powerful while the machine gun is reliable but a little less powerful. We'll look into all the math behind these statements in Chapter 11.

- **Graphical user interface:** It is very easy to print several mock-ups of a GUI (i.e., buttons, menus, input fields) and then ask testers which on-screen button they would press to accomplish a certain task (e.g., pausing the game, picking a character).

- **Trying wild ideas:** Because of the rapid iteration and development speed of paper proto-types, it is easy to just try a crazy rule every once in a while to see how it changes game-play. What if interception fire happened once for every step taken by a moving player? What if attackers got a damage or to-hit bonus for firing on a target that was unaware of them (that is, that couldn't see them)? These are easy questions to answer using a paper prototype.

Poor Uses for Paper Prototyping

As you have probably been able to tell playing the example prototype, paper prototyping is not very good at some things:

- **Tracking lots of information:** Several things in the prototype could have been handled better by a computer. These include visibility calculations, tracking health, counting how many spaces an attacker is from a target, and so on. For the paper prototype, you want to focus on the simple systems in your game and get a good idea of things like the layout of the level and the general feel of each weapon (e.g., the "risky" shotgun and the "reliable" machine gun). You'll then fine-tune this information with the digital prototype.

- **Game rhythm for fast or slow games:** Paper prototypes can also give you a false impres-sion of game rhythm and feel if the game will be played much more quickly or more slowly than the paper prototype. For instance, if this were an action game rather than a turn-based strategy game, the player would have a lot less time for thought and strategizing in the real game than the prototype, so it could give you some false ideas about how strategic the player would be. In another example, I once saw a team put too much stock in a paper prototype for a game that would be played by players around the world over the span of a month. The paper prototype had a number of interesting revenge mechanics where players could directly taunt and compete with each other. These worked really well with all players in the same room and the paper prototype lasting only an hour or so. However, with players distributed around the world and the actual game lasting weeks or months, the revenge mechanics were less immediate and didn't work very well.

- **Physical interface:** While paper prototypes can work well for GUIs, they have very little to tell us about physical interfaces (e.g., gamepad controllers, touchscreens, keyboard, and mouse). Until you have a digital prototype working with the actual physical interface that will be used by the player, you really won't know anything about how well the physical control scheme maps to your game. This is a tough issue as can be evidenced by the subtle changes to controls for most game series (for example, all the changes over the years to the controls of the various *Assassin's Creed* games).

Summary

I hope that this chapter has demonstrated to you the power and ease of paper prototyping. At some of the best university game design programs, game design students spend their first semester working primarily on board games and card games to build their skills in paper pro- totyping, game balance, and tuning. Not only can paper prototypes help you rapidly explore concepts for your digital games, they can also help you build skills in iterative design and deci- sion making that will be invaluable to you when you start making digital games.

Each time you start designing a new game (or a new system for a game you're already devel- oping), ask yourself the question of whether that game or system could benefit from a paper prototype. For example, the game that is prototyped in this chapter took me just a couple hours to develop and implement as an initial paper prototype, yet it took me over a week to program all the different logic, camera moves, artificial intelligence, controls, and so on in the digital version.

Another thing that you can learn from paper prototypes is to not be discouraged when a design decision you make backfires. We all make bad design decisions throughout our careers as designers, and it's okay to do so. The benefit of a bad decision in a paper prototype is that you can quickly discover that it is a bad decision, toss it out, and move on to the next idea.

In the next chapter, you will learn about various forms of playtesting and usability testing. This knowledge can help you get more valid and specific information from your playtests. Then, in Chapter 11, you'll explore some of the math behind game design and look at how to use a spreadsheet program to help you balance your games.

CHAPTER 10

GAME TESTING

Inherent in the concepts of prototyping and iteration is an understanding that high-quality testing is absolutely necessary to good game design. But the question becomes how exactly should this testing be performed?

In this chapter, you learn about various methods of playtesting for games, how to implement them properly, and at what stage in development each method is appropriate.

Why Playtest?

Once you've analyzed your goals, designed a solution, and implemented a prototype, it's time to test that prototype and get some feedback on your design. I understand that this can be a frightening proposition. Games are difficult to design, and it's going to take a lot of experience for you to get good at it. Even when you become an experienced designer, you'll still probably have some trepidation when you think about people playing your game for the first time. That's okay. The number one thing to keep in mind is that every person who plays your game is making it better; every comment you get, whether positive or negative, can help steer you in a direction that will improve player experience and hone your design.

Refining the design is what it's all about, and you absolutely must have external feedback to do so. I have served as a judge for several game design festivals, and it always amazes me how easy it is to tell whether a dev team has done sufficient playtesting. Without enough playtesting the goals of the game are often not clearly specified, and the difficulty of the game often ramps up very quickly. These are both common indications that the game was most often played by people who already knew how to play and knew how to get through the difficult parts, so they couldn't see the ambiguity or the rise in difficulty the way that a naïve tester would have.

This chapter will give you the knowledge and skills to run meaningful playtests and get the information from them that you need to make your games better.

> ## note
>
> **INVESTIGATORS VERSUS PLAYTESTERS**   Oftentimes in the game industry, we refer to both the people running the playtests and the participants in the tests as *playtesters*. For clarity, in this book, I will use these terms as follows:
>
> - **Investigator:** A person administering a playtest
>
> - **Playtester:** A person taking part in a playtest by playing games and giving feedback

Being a Great Playtester Yourself

Before getting into how to run various types of playtests for your games or what to look for in playtesters, let's examine how you can be a great playtester for other people.

- **Think out loud:** One of the best things you can do as a playtester is to describe your internal thought processes out loud while playing. Doing so will help the investigator running the test to correctly interpret the thoughts behind your actions. This can be especially helpful if it's the first time that you've ever encountered the game.

- **Reveal your biases:** All players are all biased by their experiences and tastes, and it's often difficult for investigators to know where their playtesters are coming from. As you're playing, talk about other games, films, books, experiences, etc. that the game reminds you of. This will help the investigators understand the background and biases that you bring with you to the playtest.

- **Self-analyze:** Try to help the investigators understand why you're experiencing the reactions that you're having to the game. Instead of just saying something like "I feel happy," it's better to say "I feel happy because the jumping mechanic makes me feel powerful and joyful."

- **Separate elements:** As a playtester, once you've given overall feedback on the game experience, try to see each element separately; analyze art, game mechanics, game feel, sound, music, etc. as individual elements. This can be very helpful to investigators and is akin to saying "the cellos sound out of tune" rather than "I didn't like that symphony." As a designer, your insight into games can allow you to give more specific feedback than most players, so take advantage of it.

- **Don't worry if they don't like your ideas:** As a designer, you should tell the investigators any ideas you have to make their game better, but you also shouldn't be at all offended if they don't use them. A lot of game design is about checking your ego at the door; it turns out that playtesting has an element of that as well.

The Circles of Playtesters

The game testing you do will go through several expanding circles of playtesters, starting with you and expanding outward through your friends and acquaintances to eventually encompass many people you have never met. Each circle of people can help with different aspects of your playtesting.

You

As a game designer, the first and last playtester of the games you design will most likely be you. You will be the first person to try out each of your ideas, and you'll be the first person to decide whether the game mechanics and interface feel right.

A central theme of this book is that you always want to get a prototype of your game working as soon as possible. Until you have a working prototype, all you have is a jumble of ideas, but after you have a prototype, you have something concrete to react to.

Later in this book, you'll be making digital game prototypes in Unity. Every time you press the *Play* button in Unity to run your game, you're acting as a playtester. Even if you're working in a team and are not the primary engineer on the project, as a designer, it will be your job to determine whether the game is heading toward the kind of experience your team wants to create. Your skills as a playtester are most useful in the very early stages of prototyping when you may need a great prototype to help other team members understand the design or when you may be still trying to discover the core mechanic or core experience of the game.

Eventually, there is a point at which you need to branch out and show your game to other people. You can never get a first impression of your own game; you know too much about it. Once you feel that your game is anything better than terrible, it's time to find a few other people and show it to them.

Trusted Friends

Once you've playtested your game, iterated, made improvements, and actually crafted something that approximates the experience that you want, it's time to show it to others. The first of these should be trusted friends and family members, preferably those either in your target audience or in the game development community. Members of your target audience will give you good feedback from the point of view of your future players (and hopefully future paying customers), and game developers can help by sharing their considerable insight and experience. Game developers will often have the experience to overlook aspects of the game that are obviously unfinished, which can also be very useful for relatively early prototypes.

TISSUE PLAYTESTERS

Tissue playtester is an industry term to describe playtesters that are brought in to play the game and give their feedback once and are then discarded. They are one-use, like a facial tissues. This kind of tester is important because they can give you a naïve reaction to your game. Once anyone has played your game even a single time, they know something about it, and that knowledge biases subsequent playtest sessions. This kind of naïve perspective is critically important when testing:

- The tutorial system
- The first few levels
- The emotional impact of any plot twists or other surprises
- The emotional impact of the end of the game

Everyone Is a Tissue Playtester Only Once

Your game never gets a second chance to make a first impression. When Jenova Chen was working on his brilliant game, *Journey*, he and I were housemates. However, he asked me to wait until more than a year into the development of the game before I playtested it. Later, he expressed to me that he specifically wanted my feedback on the polish level of the game and whether it was achieving its intended emotional arc. As such, it would have ruined the experience for me to have played it in the early stages of development before any of that polish existed. Keep this in mind when playtesting with close friends. Think about the most valuable kinds of feedback that each person can give and make sure to show them the game at the best time for each individual.

That being said, never use that point as an excuse for hiding your game from everyone "until it's ready." Hundreds of people playtested *Journey* before I saw it. You will find that

---

in the initial stages of playtesting, most people will tell you the same things in slightly different ways. You need that feedback, and even very early in the development process, you need tissue playtesters to tell you which of your game mechanics are confusing or need work for a variety of reasons. Just save a couple of trusted people for later when you know that their specific feedback will be most useful.

Acquaintances and Others

After you've been iterating on your game for a while and you have something that seems pretty solid, it's time to take it out into the wild. This isn't yet the time to post a beta to the Internet and expose your game to the rest of the world, but this is when feedback from others that you don't normally associate with can be helpful. The people you call your friends and family often share your background and experiences, meaning that they will also often share some of your tastes and biases. If you only test with them, you will get a biased understanding of your game. A corollary to this would be someone in Austin, Texas, being surprised that the state of Texas voted for a Republican presidential candidate. Most people in Austin are liberal, while the rest of the state is primarily conservative. If you only polled people in Austin and didn't break out of that left-leaning bubble, you'd never know the opinion of the state as a whole. Similarly, you're going to need to get out of your normal social circles to find more playtesters for your game and to understand a larger audience's reaction to your game.

So, where do you look for more people to playtest your game? Here are some possibilities:

- **Local universities:** Many college students love playing games. You could try setting up your game in the student center or quad and showing it to groups of people. Of course, you'll want to check with campus security before doing so.

  You could also look into whether your local university has a game development club or a group that meets for weekly game nights and ask if they would mind you bringing a game for them to playtest.

- **Local game stores/malls:** People head to these places to buy games, so it could be a fantastic place to get some playtest feedback. Each of these places will have different corporate policies on these kinds of things, so you need to talk with them first.

- **Farmers markets/community events/parties:** These kinds of public gatherings of people can have incredibly diverse audiences. I've gotten some great feedback on games from people I met at parties.

The Internet

The Internet can be a scary place. Anonymity ensures that there is little or no accountability for actions or statements, and some people online will be mean just for kicks. However, the Internet also contains the largest circle of playtesters that you can possibly get. If you're developing an online game, you're eventually going to have to reach out to the Internet and see what happens. However, before you do so, you will need to have considerable data and user tracking in place, which you can read about in the later section, "Online Playtesting."

Methods of Playtesting

There are several different methods of playtesting, each of which is most appropriate for different phases of your game. The following pages explore various methods of playtesting that I have found to be useful in my design process.

Informal Individual Testing

As an independent developer this is how I tend to do most of my testing. I've been focusing on mobile tablet games lately, so it's easy to carry my device around with me and show my games to people. More often than not, during a break in conversation I'll ask if the person I'm speaking with would mind taking a look at my game. This is, of course, most useful in the early stages of development or when you have a specific new feature that you want to test. Things to keep in mind during this kind of testing include the following:

- **Don't tell the player too much:** Even in the early stages, it's important to learn whether your interface is intuitive and the goals of your game are clear. Try giving your game to players and watching what they do before they've had any instruction. This can tell you a lot about what interactions your game implies on its own. Eventually, you'll learn the specific short sentences you need to say to people to help them understand your game, and these will become the basis for your in-game tutorial.

- **Don't lead the playtester:** Be sure you don't ask leading questions that may inadvertently bias your player. Even a simple question like "Did you notice the health items?" informs your playtester that health items exist and implies that it is important for her to collect them. Once your game is released, most players won't have you there to explain the game to them, and it's important to let your playtesters struggle a bit to help you learn which aspects of your game are unintuitive.

- **Don't argue or make excuses:** As with everything in design, your ego has no place in a playtest. Listen to the feedback that playtesters are giving you, even (or possibly especially) if you disagree with it. This isn't the time to defend your game; it's the time to learn what you can from the person who is taking time out of her day to help the design improve.

- **Take notes:** Keep a small notebook with you and take notes on the feedback you get, especially if it's not what you expected or wanted to hear. Later, you can collate these notes and look for statements that you heard multiple times. You shouldn't really put too much stock in what is said by a single playtester, but you should definitely pay attention if you hear the same feedback from many different people.

Formal Group Testing

For many years, this is how playtesting was done at large studios, and when I was working at Electronic Arts, I took part in many of these playtests for other teams. Several people are brought into a room full of individual stations at which they can play the game. They are given little or no instruction and allowed to play the game for a specific amount of time. After this time, the playtesters are given a written survey to fill out, and investigators sometimes interview them individually. This is a great way to get feedback from a high volume of people, and it can get you a large number of answers to some important questions.

Some example post-playtest survey questions include:

- "What were your three favorite and three least favorite parts of the game?"
- Provide the playtester with a sequential list of various points in the game (or even better a series of images) and ask them, "How would you describe the way you felt at each of these points in the game?"
- "How do you feel about the main character (or other characters) in the game? / Did your feelings about the main character change over the course of the game?"
- "How much would you pay for this game? / How much would you charge for this game?"
- "What were the three most confusing things about the game?"

Formal group testing is often administered by investigators outside of the core development team, and there are even companies that provide testing services like this.

All Formal Testing Requires a Script

Any time you are doing formal testing, either with investigators from inside or outside the team, you will want to have a script. The script should include the following information:

- What should investigators say to the playtesters to set up the game? What instructions should they give?
- How should investigators react during the playtest? Should they ask questions if they see a playtester do something interesting or unusual? Should they provide any hints to playtesters during the test?
- What should the environment be like for the playtest? How long should the playtester be allowed to play?
- What specific survey questions should be asked of the playtester once the playtest is complete?

Formal Individual Testing

Where formal group testing seeks to gather small bits of information from many different people and grant investigators a gestalt understanding of how playtesters react to a game, formal individual testing seeks to understand the fine details of a single playtester's experience. To accomplish this goal, investigators carefully record the details of a single individual's experience with the game and then review the recordings later to make sure that they haven't missed anything. There are several different data streams that you should record when doing formal individual testing:

- **Record the game screen:** You want to see what the player is seeing.

- **Record the playtester's actions:** You want to see the input attempted by the player. If the game is controlled with mouse and keyboard, place a camera above them. If the game is tested on a touchscreen tablet, you should have a shot of the player's hands touching the screen.

- **Record the playtester's face:** You want to see the player's face so that you can read her emotions.

- **Record audio of what the playtester says:** Even if the player doesn't vocalize her stream of consciousness, hearing utterances she makes can give you more information about her internal thought process.

- **Log game data:** Your game should also be logging time stamped data about its internal state. This can include information about: input from the player (e.g., button presses on the controller), the player's success or failure at various tasks, the location of the player, time spent in each area of the game, and so on. See the "Automated Data Logging" sidebar later in this chapter for more information.

All of these various data streams are later synched to each other so that designers can clearly see the relationships between them. This allows you to see the elation or frustration in a player's face while simultaneously viewing exactly what the player was seeing on-screen at the time and the input her hands were attempting on the controls. Though this is a considerable amount of data, modern technology has actually made it relatively cheap to create a reasonably good lab for individual testing. See the sidebar for more information.

SETTING UP A LAB FOR FORMAL INDIVIDUAL PLAYTESTING

You can easily spend tens of thousands of dollars setting up a lab for formal individual testing, and many game studios have, but you can also mock up a pretty decent one for not a lot of money.

For most game platforms, you should be able to capture all of the data streams listed in the chapter with just three consumer cameras: one on the screen, one on the player's face, and one on the player's hands. All cameras can record audio, which can help you to synchronize them. The game data log should also be time stamped to allow for synchronization.

Synchronizing Data

Many software packages out there enable you to sync several video streams, but often the oldest methods are the easiest, and in this case, you can use a digital version of the slate from the early days of sound in film. In a film, the slate is the little clap board that is shown at the beginning of a take. A member of the crew holds the slate, which shows the name of the film, the scene number, and the take number. She reads these three things out loud and then claps the slate together. This enables the editor to match the visual film frame where the clapper closed with the moment in the audio tape that the sound was made, synching the separate video and audio tracks.

You can do the same thing by making a digital slate part of your game. At the beginning of a playtest session, the game screen can show a digital slate containing a unique ID number for the session. An investigator can read the ID number out loud and then press a button on the controller. Simultaneously, the software can show a digital clapper closing, make a clapper sound, and log game data with the time stamp according to the internal clock on your playtest machine. All of these can be used to sync the various video streams later (with the clapper sound used to sync streams which cannot see the screen), and it's even possible to sync the game data log. Most even half-decent video editing programs will allow you to put each of these videos into one quarter of the screen and fill the fourth quarter with the date, time, and unique ID of the playtest session. Then you can see all of this data synchronized in a single video.

Privacy Concerns

In modern times, many people are concerned about their personal privacy. You will need to be upfront with your playtesters and let them know that they will be recorded. However, you should also promise them that the video will only be used for internal purposes and will never be shared with anyone outside of the company.

Running a Formal Individual Playtest

Investigators should seek to make the individual playtest as similar as possible to the experience a player who had bought the game would have at home. The player should be comfortable and at ease. You might want to provide snacks or drinks, and if the game is designed for tablet or console, you might want to give the player a couch or other comfortable seat to sit on. (For computer games, a desk and office chair are often more appropriate.)

Start the playtest by telling the playtester how much you appreciate the time she has set aside to test your game and how useful it will be for you to get her feedback. You should also request that she please speak out loud while playing. Few playtesters will actually do so, but it can't hurt to ask.

Once the playtester has finished the section of the game that you want her to play, an investigator should sit with her and discuss her experience with the game. The questions asked by the investigator should be similar to those that are asked at the end of formal group testing, but the one-on-one format will allow the investigator to frame meaningful follow-up questions and get better information. The post-playtest question and answer sessions should also be recorded, though audio recording is more important than video for the post-play interview.

As with all formal playtesting, it is best if the investigator is not part of the game development team. This helps the investigator's questions and perceptions to not be biased by personal investment in the game. However, after you have found a good investigator, it is very useful to work with the same investigator throughout the development process so that they can provide you information about the progression of playtesters' reactions to the game.

Online Playtesting

As mentioned previously, the largest circle of playtesters is composed of online playtest communities. Your game must be in the beta phase before you attempt this, so these are colloquially known as *beta tests,* and they come in a few forms:

- **Closed:** An invite-only test with a limited number of people. This is where your online tests should start. Initially, you should have only a few trusted people serve as online playtesters. This gives you a chance to find any bugs with your server architecture or any aspects of your game that are unclear before a larger audience sees it.

  For *Skyrates,*[1] our first closed online beta started eight weeks into the project and was composed of the four members of the dev team and only twelve other people, all of whom had offices in the same building as the development team. After two weeks of fixing both game and server issues and adding a few more features, we expanded the playtest group to 25 people, all of whom were still in the same building. Two weeks later, we expanded to 50. Up until this point, a member of the dev team had individually sat down with each player and taught her how to play the game.

  Over the next two weeks, we developed an online game tutorial document and entered the limited beta phase.

- **Limited:** A limited beta is generally open to anyone who signs up, though there are often a few specific limitations in place. The most common limitation is the number of players.

  When *Skyrates* first entered the limited beta phase, we capped the number of players at 125 and told our players that they could invite one friend or family member to join the game. This was a much larger number of concurrent players than we'd had in prior rounds, and we wanted to make sure that the server could handle it. After that, we limited the next round to 250 before moving on to our first open beta.

- **Open:** Open betas will allow anyone online to play. This can be fantastic because you can watch your game gain popularity halfway around the globe, but it can also be terrifying because a spike in players can threaten to overload your server. Generally, you want to make sure that your game is near completion before you do an online, open beta.

  Skyrates entered open beta at the end of the first semester of development. We didn't expect to work on the game for a second semester, so we left our game server running over the summer. To our surprise, even though *Skyrates* was initially developed as a two-week game experience, several people played the game throughout the summer, and our total numbers for the summer were somewhere between 500 and 1,000 players. However, this

---

[1] *Skyrates* (Airship Studios, 2006) is a game that was introduced in Chapter 8, "Design Goals." It made extensive use of the concept of sporadic play, where players interacted with the game for only a few minutes at a time throughout their day. Though this is now common behavior for Facebook games, at the time we were developing it, this was an unusual concept, and it required many rounds of playtesting to refine it.

all happened in 2006 before Facebook became a game platform and before the ubiquity of gaming on smartphones and tablets. While 99% of all games on these platforms don't gain much popularity at all, be aware that a game released on any of them has the potential to go from only a few players to millions in just a few days. Be wary of open betas on social platforms, but know that you need to open up the game eventually.

AUTOMATED DATA LOGGING

You should include automated data logging (ADL) in your game as early as possible. ADL occurs when your game automatically records information about player performance and events any time someone plays your game. This is often recorded to a server online, but can just as easily be stored as local files and then output by your game later.

At Electronic Arts in 2007, I designed and produced the game *Crazy Cakes* for Pogo.com. *Crazy Cakes* was the first Pogo game to ever use ADL, but afterward it became a standard part of production. The ADL for *Crazy Cakes* was really pretty simple. For each level of the game that was played, we recorded several pieces of data:

- Timestamp: The date and time that the round started

- Player username: This allowed us to talk to players with very high scores and ask them what strategies they employed or contact them if something unusual happened during gameplay

- Difficulty level and round number: We had a total of five difficulty levels, each of which contained four progressively more challenging rounds

- Score

- Number and type of power-ups items used during the round

- Number of tokens earned

- Number of patrons served

- Number of desserts served to patrons: Some patrons requested multiple desserts, which this helped us track

At the time, Pogo.com had hundreds of beta testers, so three days after releasing *Crazy Cakes* to our closed beta group, we had recorded data from over 25,000 playtest sessions! I culled this data to 4,000 randomly selected rows and brought it into a spreadsheet application that I used to balance the game based on real data rather than conjecture. Once I thought that the game was well balanced relative to the data, I selected another 4,000 random rows and confirmed the balance with them.[2]

---

[2] The data was limited to 4,000 rows because at the time, Excel had difficulty handling more than 4,000 rows of data.

Other Important Types of Testing

In addition to playtesting, other important types of game testing include the following five types.

Focus Testing

Focus testing involves gathering a group of people from your game's core demographic (a *focus group*) and getting their reaction to the look, premise, music, or other aesthetic and narrative elements of your game. This is sometimes done by large studios to determine whether there is a good business case for developing a certain game.

Interest Polling

It is now possible to use social networks like Facebook or crowdfunding sites like Kickstarter to poll the level of interest that your game could generate in the online public. On these websites, you can post a pitch video for a game and receive feedback, either in the form of likes on a social media site or pledges on a crowdfunding site. If you are an independent developer with limited resources, this may be a way to secure some funding for your game, but of course, the results are incredibly varied.

Usability Testing

Many of the techniques now used in formal individual testing grew out of the field of usability testing. At its core, usability testing is about understanding how well testers can understand and use the interface for a piece of software. Because understanding is so important to usability, data gathering of the screen, interaction, and face of the tester are common practices. In addition to the playtesting of your game, it is also important to engage in some individual usability testing that investigates how easily the playtester can interact with and gain critical information from your game. This can include testing of various layouts for on-screen information, several different control configurations, etc.

Quality Assurance (QA) Testing

Quality assurance testing is focused specifically on finding bugs in your game and ways to reliably reproduce them. There is an entire industry devoted to this kind of testing, and it's largely outside the scope of this book, but the core elements are as follows:

1. Find a bug in the game (a place where the game breaks or doesn't react properly).
2. Discover and write down the steps required to reliably reproduce the bug.
3. Prioritize the bug. Does it crash the game? How likely is it to occur for a normal player? How noticeable is it?
4. Tell the engineering team so that they can fix it.

QA is most often done by the development team and a group of game testers hired for the final phase of a project. It's also possible to set up ways for players to submit bugs that they find, but most players don't have the training to generate really good bug reports that include clear steps for reproducing the bug. Many free bug-tracking tools are available and can be deployed on your project website, including *Bugzilla*, *Mantis Bug Tracker*, and *Trac*.

Automated Testing

Automated testing (AT) occurs when a piece of software attempts to find bugs in your game or game server without requiring human input. For a game, AT could simulate rapid user input (like hundreds of clicks per second all over the screen). For a game server, AT could inundate the server with thousands of requests per second to determine the level of load that could cause the server to fail. While AT is complex to implement, it can effectively test your game in ways that are very difficult for human QA testers to accomplish. As with other forms of testing, there are several companies who make their living through automated testing.

Summary

The intent of this chapter was to give you a broad understanding of various forms of testing for your games. As a new game designer, you should find the ones that seem most useful to you and try to implement them. I have had success with several different forms of testing, and I believe that all the forms covered in this chapter can provide you with important information that can improve your game.

In the next chapter, you'll be shown some of the math that lies beneath the surface of the fun in games. You'll also learn about how to use a spreadsheet application to aid you in game balancing.

CHAPTER 11

MATH AND GAME BALANCE

In this chapter, we explore various systems of probability and randomness and how they relate to paper game technologies. You also learn a little about OpenOffice Calc to help us explore these possibilities.

Following the mathematical explorations (which I promise are as clear and easy to understand as possible), we cover how these systems can be used in both paper and digital games to balance and improve gameplay.

The Meaning of Game Balance

Now that you've made your initial game prototype and experimented with it a few times through playtests, you will probably need to *balance* it as part of your iteration process. Balance is a term that you will often hear when working on games, but it means different things depending on the context.

In a multiplayer game, balance most often means fairness: each player should have an equal chance of winning the game. This is most easily accomplished in *symmetric* games where each player has the same starting point and abilities. Balancing an *asymmetric* game is considerably more difficult because player abilities or start positions that may seem balanced could demonstrate a bias toward one player in practice. This is one of the many reasons why playtesting is critically important.

In a single-player game, balance usually means that the game is at an appropriate level of difficulty for the player and the difficulty changes gradually. If a game has a large jump in difficulty at any point, that point becomes a place where the game will tend to lose players. This relates to the discussion of flow as a player-centric design goal in Chapter 8, "Design Goals."

In this chapter, you learn about several disparate aspects of math that are all part of game design and balance. This includes understanding probability, an exploration of different randomizers for paper games, and the concepts of weighted distribution, permutations, and positive and negative feedback. Throughout this exploration, you use Apache OpenOffice Calc, a spreadsheet program, to better explore and understand the concepts presented. At the end of the chapter, you will see how Calc was used to balance the weapons used in the paper prototype example in Chapter 9, "Paper Prototyping."

Installing Apache OpenOffice Calc

To start our exploration into game math, I'd like you to download and install Apache OpenOffice. OpenOffice is a suite of applications that is comparable to Microsoft Office but is free and open source. You can download it from http://openoffice.org. The current version as of this writing is 4.1.0. Please visit the website and download Open Office now; we'll be using it throughout this chapter.[1]

---

[1] If you are using OS X, it may not allow you to run the OpenOffice app because it was not downloaded directly from the Apple App Store. If this is the case, you should read the support article for Apple Gatekeeper at http://support.apple.com/kb/HT5290 or read the OpenOffice Install Guide at http://www.openoffice.org/download/common/instructions.html.

> **note**
>
> For this book, I have chosen to use OpenOffice Calc because it is free, cross-platform, and easily available. Many other spreadsheet programs have the same capabilities as Calc (e.g., Microsoft Excel, Google Docs Spreadsheet, and LibreOffice Calc Spreadsheet), but each program is subtly different from the others, so attempting to follow the directions in this chapter in an application other than OpenOffice Calc may lead to frustration.

For some of the things that we'll be doing in this chapter, a spreadsheet program like Calc isn't strictly necessary—you could get the same results with a piece of scratch paper and a calculator—however, I feel it's important to introduce spreadsheets as an aspect of game balance for a few reasons:

- A spreadsheet can help you quickly grasp gestalt information from numerical data. In Chapter 9, I presented you with several different weapons that each had different stats. At the end of this chapter, we will recreate the process that I went through to balance those weapons to each other, contrasting weapon stats that I created initially based on gut feeling with those that I refined through use of a spreadsheet.

- Charts and data can often be used to convince nondesigners of the validity of a game design decision that you have made. To develop a game, you will often be working with many different people, some of whom will prefer to see numbers behind decisions rather than instinct. That doesn't mean that you should always make decisions with numbers, I just want you to be able to do so if it's necessary.

- Many professional game designers work with spreadsheets on a daily basis, but I have seen very few game design programs that teach students anything about how to use them. In addition, the classes at universities that do cover spreadsheet use tend to be more interested in business or accounting than game balance, and therefore focus on different spreadsheet capabilities than I have found useful in my work.

As with all aspects of game development, the process of building a spreadsheet is an iterative and somewhat messy process. Rather than show you perfect examples of making spreadsheets from start to finish with every little thing planned ahead of time, the tutorials in this chapter are designed to demonstrate not only the steps to make a spreadsheet but also a realistic iterative process of both building and planning the spreadsheet.

Examining Dice Probability with Calc

A large portion of game math comes down to probability, so it's critical that you understand a little about how probability and chance work. We'll start by using OpenOffice Calc to help us understand the probability distribution of rolling various numbers using two six-sided dice (2d6).

On a single roll of a single six-sided die (1d6), you will have any even chance of getting a 1, 2, 3, 4, 5, or 6. That's pretty obvious. However, things get much more interesting when you're talking about adding the results of two dice together. If you roll 2d6, then there are 36 different possibilities for the outcome, all of which are shown here:

Die A: 1 2 3 4 5 6 1 2 3 4 5 6 1 2 3 4 5 6 1 2 3 4 5 6 1 2 3 4 5 6 1 2 3 4 5 6

Die B: 1 1 1 1 1 1 2 2 2 2 2 2 3 3 3 3 3 3 4 4 4 4 4 4 5 5 5 5 5 5 6 6 6 6 6 6

It's certainly possible to write all of these by hand, but I'd like you to learn how to use Calc to do it as an introduction to using a spreadsheet to aid in game balance. Open OpenOffice and create a new Spreadsheet. (Doing so will open the Calc part of OpenOffice.) You should see a new document like the one shown in Figure 11.1.

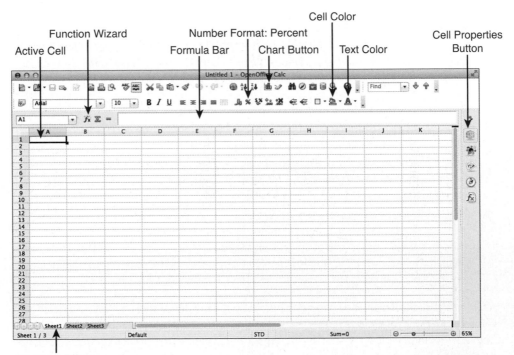

Figure 11.1   A new OpenOffice Calc spreadsheet showing important parts of the interface

Getting Started with Calc

The cells in a spreadsheet are each named with a column letter and a row number. The top-left cell in the spreadsheet is A1. In Figure 11.1, cell A1 is highlighted with a black border and a small black box in its bottom-right corner, showing that it is the Active Cell.

The directions that follow will show you how to get started using Calc:

1. Select cell A1 in OpenOffice by clicking it.

2. Type the number **1** on your keyboard and press Return. A1 will now hold the value 1.

3. Click in cell B1 and type **=A1+1** and press Return. This creates a formula in B2 that will constantly calculate its value based on A1. All formulas start with an =. You'll see that the value of B1 is now 2 (the number you get when you add 1 to the value in A1). If you change the value in A1, B1 will automatically update.

4. Click B1 and copy the cell (Choose *Edit > Copy* from the menu bar or Command-C on an OS X keyboard or Control+C on a PC keyboard).

5. Hold Shift on the keyboard and Shift-click cell K1. This will highlight the cells from B1 to K1.

6. Paste the formula from B1 into the highlighted cells (*Edit > Paste* from the menu bar, Command-V on OS X, or Ctrl+V on PC). This will paste the formula that you copied from B1 into the cells from B1 to K1 (that is, the formula =A1+1).

> ## note
>
> Because the cell reference A1 in the formula is a *relative reference,* it will update based on the position of the new cell into which it has been pasted. In other words, the formula in K1 will be =J1+1 because J1 is one cell to the left of K1 just as A1 was one to the left of B1.
>
> As a relative reference in the formula of cell B1 (=A1+1), A1 is storing the position of the cell *relative* to B1 rather than the specific cell location A1. To create an *absolute reference* (that is, a cell reference that *will not* change if the formula is copied to another cell), put a $ (dollar sign) in front of both the column (A) and row (1). This would give you the formula =$A$1+1 that contains an absolute reference to cell A1. You can also make just the column or row absolute by putting the $ in front of one or the other instead of both.

Creating a Row of Numbers from 1 to 36

The preceding instructions should leave you with the numbers 1 through 11 in the cells A1:K1 (in other words, the cells from A1 to K1; the colon is used to define a range between the two listed cells). Next, we will extend the numbers to count all the way from 1 to 36 (for the 36 possible die rolls):

1. Click B1 to select it.

2. Another way that you can copy the contents of a single cell over a large range is to use the black square in the lower-right corner of a selected cell (which you can see at the lower-right corner of cell A1 in Figure 11.1). Click and drag the black square from the corner of B1 to the right until you have highlighted cells B1:AJ1. When you release the mouse button, you will now see that A1:AJ1 are filled with the series of numbers from 1 to 36.

Setting Column Widths

This has filled the cells A1:AJ1 with the correct data, however these 36 columns are much wider than they actually need to be. We'll now narrow them to a more appropriate width:

1. Click cell A1.

2. On your keyboard, hold Shift and Command (on Windows, Shift and Control) and press the right-arrow key. This will select all of the cells from A1:AJ1. When holding the Command key, pressing any of the arrow keys will cause the cell highlight to jump to the last filled cell in that direction before an empty cell.

3. From the menu bar, choose *Format > Column > Optimal Width*. This will open a small dialog box asking you the amount of padding you would like to have (that is, extra space between each column). Leave it set to 0.1" and click the *OK* button. The columns A through AJ will now narrow to hold their numbers plus 0.1" of extra space. This should make it much easier to fit all of them on your screen at once.

Another way to set column width is to position your mouse directly above the border between two column headings (as is shown in Figure 11.2) and click and drag the border left or right. This will shrink or expand the width of the column. Release the mouse button to set the column to the new width.

If you have multiple columns selected (which will highlight them blue as they are in Figure 11.2), this will allow you to set the width of all of them to the same value, but you must select the entire column, not just cells within the column (to do so, click the A column heading and then Shift-click the AJ column heading). Double-clicking the border at the right of a column will set it to the optimal width.

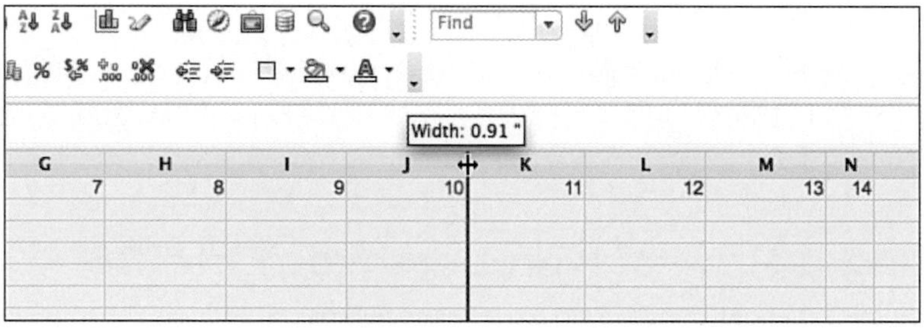

Figure 11.2   Adjusting the column width penOffice Calc using the mouse

Making the Row for Die A

Now, we have a series of numbers, but what we really want is two rows like those for Die A and Die B that were listed earlier in this chapter. We can achieve this with some simple formulas:

1. Click A2 to select it.

2. Click the *Function Wizard* button shown in Figure 11.1. This will bring up Calc's Function Wizard, a dialog box listing all the functions available in Calc.

3. Scroll through the functions to find MOD and click it. The Function Wizard gives you a brief description of the MOD() function, but this description lacks a lot of key information.

4. Click the *Help* button in the dialog box and then type **MOD** in the search box and press Return (Enter on PC) to cause the help file to display more information about how MOD works. As the Help states, MOD() returns the remainder when one integer is divided by another. This means that MOD(5;3) would return the value 2 (which is the remainder of 5/3). MOD(6;3) would return 0 because there is no remainder when 6 is divided by 3.

5. Close the Help window, and switch back to the Calc program if necessary.

6. Type **=MOD(A1;6)** into the Formula field of the Function Wizard. You should see the Result field update to show 1 (the remainder when 1 is divided by 6).

7. Click the *OK* button in the Function Wizard. This will enter the function from the Function Wizard into cell A2.

8. Copy cell A2 and paste it into cells A2:AJ2 (the colon [:] denotes the range of cells from A2 to AJ2). This will give you the numbers 1 2 3 4 5 0 repeated six times across cells A2:AJ2. Because the reference to A1 in the formula is a relative reference, each cell from A2:AJ2 is taking the value of the cell directly above it and modding it by 6 (i.e., finding the remainder of that value divided by 6).

The results of this formula are very close to what we wanted for Die A. It gives us the numbers 1 2 3 4 5 0 repeating, but we wanted the numbers 1 2 3 4 5 6, so we'll need to iterate a bit.

Adjusting the Mod Formula

We need to fix two issues through modification to the formulae in A2:AJ2. First, the lowest number should be in columns A, F, L, and so on; and second, the numbers should range from 1 to 6, not 0 to 5. Both of these can be fixed by simple adjustments:

1. Select cell A1 and change its value from 1 to 0. This will cascade through the formulae in B1:AJ1 and give you a series of numbers on row 1 from 0 to 35. Now, the formula in A2 returns 0 (the remainder when 0 is divided by 6), and the numbers in A2:AJ2 will be six series of 0 1 2 3 4 5, which fixes the first issue.

2. To fix the second issue, select A2 and change the formula in A2 to **=MOD(A1;6)+1**. This will simply add one to the result of the previous formula, which increases the formula result in A2 from 0 to 1. This may seem like we've gone in a circle, but once you complete step 3, you'll see the reason for doing so.

3. Copy A2 and paste it over A2:AJ2. Now, the row for Die A is complete and you have six series of the numbers 1 2 3 4 5 6. The mod values still range from 0 to 5, but now they are in the correct order, and adding 1 to them has generated the numbers that we wanted for Die A.

Making the Row for Die B

The row for Die B includes six repetitions of each number on the die. To accomplish this, we will use the division and floor functions in Calc. Divisions works as you would expect it to (for example, =3/2 will return the result 1.5), however, floor may be a function that you have not encountered before.

1. Select cell A3.

2. Click the *Function Wizard* button and scroll through the list of functions to find FLOOR. As the Function Wizard shows, FLOOR is used to round decimal numbers to integers, but FLOOR always rounds down. For example, `=FLOOR(5.1;1)` returns 5 and `=FLOOR(5.9;1)` also returns 5. The second argument to the FLOOR function (i.e., the `;1` in the preceding examples) sets the significance of the floor. To floor to a whole integer, this argument should always be 1.

3. Enter **=FLOOR(A1/6;1)** into the Formula field. You will see that the Result field updates to show a result of 0.

4. As was needed with the Die A row, we must add one to the result of the formula. Change the formula to **=FLOOR(A1/6;1)+1**, and you will see that the result is now 1.

5. Click *OK* to close the Function Wizard.

6. Copy the contents of A3 and paste them into A3:AJ3.

Your spreadsheet should now look like the top image in Figure 11.3. However, it would be much easier to understand if it were labeled as is shown in the bottom image of Figure 11.3.

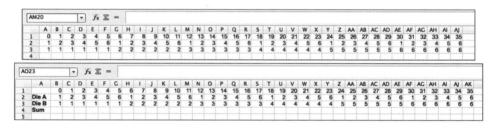

Figure 11.3   Adding clarity with labels

Adding Clarity with Labels

To add the labels shown in the second image of Figure 11.3, you will need to insert a new column to the left of column A:

1. Right-click on any cell in column A and choose *Insert* from the menu. If you're on OS X and don't have a right-click button, you can Control-click. See the section "Right-Click on OS X" in Appendix B, "Useful Concepts," for more information.

2. From the dialog box that appears, choose *Entire column* and click *OK*. This will place a new column A to the left of the existing columns. Note that all of the functions update properly and none of your data or formulae are damaged.

3. Click on the new, empty cell A2 and enter **Die A**. This won't fit in the narrow column, but you can easily adjust a column width while typing by holding the Option key (the Alt key on PC) and pressing the right- and left-arrow keys.

4. Enter **Die B** into A3. Then select A2:A3 and make them bold by either pressing Command-B (Ctrl+B on PC) or clicking the **B** formatting button above the function bar.

5. Type **Sum** in A4 and make it bold as well. Your spreadsheet should now look like the second image in Figure 11.3.

Summing the Results of the Two Dice

Another formula will allow you to sum the results of the two dice.

1. Click B4 and enter the formula **=SUM(B2;B3)**, which will sum the values in the cells from B2 to B3 (the formula =B2+B3 would also work equally well). This will put the value 2 into B4.

2. Copy B4 and paste it into B4:AK4. Now, row 4 shows the results of all 36 possible rolls of 2d6.

Counting the Sums of Die Rolls

Row 4 now shows all the results of the 36 possible rolls of 2d6. However, although the data is there, it is still not very easy to interpret it. This is where we can really use the strength of a spreadsheet. To start the data interpretation, we'll create formulae to count the occurrences of each sum (that is, count how many times we roll a 7 on 2d6):

1. Select cells A7:A17 and from the menu bar choose *Edit > Fill > Series*. This allows you to fill cells with a series of numbers.

2. Set the *Direction* to *Down*, the *Start value* to **2**, and the *End value* to **12** with an increment of 1.

3. Click *OK*. This will fill A7:A17 with the numbers from 2 to 12.

4. Select cell B7 and type **=COUNTIF(** but don't press the Return or Enter key.

5. Use your mouse to click and drag from B4 to AK4. This will draw a box around B4:AK4 and enter **B4:AK4** into your in-progress formula.

6. Type **;**.

7. Click A7. This will enter A7 into the formula. At this point, the entire formula should be =COUNTIF(B4:AK4;A7).

8. Type **)** and press Return (Windows, Enter). Now, the formula in B7 will be =COUNTIF(B4:AK4;A7).

The COUNTIF function counts the number of times within a series of cells that a certain criterion is met. In cell B7, the COUNTIF function looks at all the cells B4:AK4 and counts the number of times that the number 2 occurs (because 2 is the number in A7).

Next, you will want to extend this from just counting the number of twos to counting the number of rolls of all numbers from 2 to 12:

1. Copy the formula from B7 and paste it into B7:B17.

   You will notice that this doesn't work properly. The counts for all the numbers other than two are 0. Let's explore why this is happening.

2. Select cell B7 and then click once in the formula bar. This will highlight all of the cells that are used in the calculation of the formula in cell B7.

3. Press the Esc (Escape) key. This is a critical step because it returns you from the cell-editing mode. If you were to click another cell without pressing Esc first, that cell's reference would be entered into the formula. See the following warning for more information.

> ## warning
>
> **EXITING FORMULA EDITING**   When working in Calc, you need to press either Return or Esc (Enter or Esc on PC) to exit from editing a formula. Return or Enter will accept the changes that you have made, and Escape will cancel them. If you don't properly exit from formula editing, any cell you click will be added to the formula (which you don't want to do accidentally). If this does happen to you, you can press Esc to exit editing without changing the actual formula.

4. Select cell B8 and click once in the formula bar. Now, you should see the problem with the formula in B8. Instead of counting the occurrence of threes in B4:AK4, it is looking for threes in B5:AK5. This is a result of the automatic updating of relative references that was covered earlier in this chapter. Because B8 is one cell lower than B7, all of the references in B8 were updated to be one cell lower. This update of the relative reference is correct for the second argument in the formula (i.e., B8 should be looking for the number in A8 and not A7), but needs to be fixed for the first argument.

5. Press Esc to exit from editing B8.

6. Select B7 and change the formula to =**COUNTIF(B\$4:AK\$4;A7)**.

7. Copy the formula from B7 and paste it into B7:B17. Now you will see that the numbers update correctly, and each formula in B7:B17 properly queries the cells B\$4:AK\$4.

Charting the Results

Now, the cells B7:B17 show you the data we wanted. Across the 36 possible rolls of 2d6, there are six possible ways to roll a 7 but only one way to roll a 2 or a 12. This information can be read in the numbers in the cells, but this kind of thing is much easier to understand in a chart:

1. Select cells A7:B17.

2. Click the Chart button (shown in Figure 11.1). This will bring up the Chart Wizard and show you an unrefined version of the chart.

3. The chart type should already be set to *Column* by default.

4. On the left side of the Chart Wizard, click *2. Data Range* and choose the options *Data in Columns* and *First column as label*. This will remove the first column (the numbers 2–12) from the chart itself and make them instead the labels at the bottom of the chart.

5. Click *4. Chart Elements* and deselect *Display Legend*. This will remove the legend that had contained Column B from the right side of the chart.

6. Click *Finish*, and you'll have a nice chart of the 2d6 data as shown in Figure 11.4. If you click something other than the chart and then click the chart again, you can move it to another location.

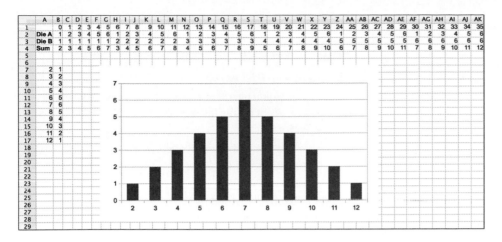

Figure 11.4 A probability distribution chart for 2d6

I know that this was a pretty exhausting way to get this data, but I wanted to introduce you to Calc because it can be an extremely important tool in helping you to balance your games.

The Math of Probability

At this point, you are probably thinking that there must be an easier way to learn about the probability of rolling dice than just enumerating all of the possibilities. Happily, there is an entire branch of mathematics that deals with probability, and this section of the chapter will cover several of the rules that it has taught us.

First, let's try to determine how many possible different combinations there can be if you roll 2d6. Because there are two dice, and each has 6 possibilities, there are 6 x 6 = 36 different possible rolls of the 2 dice. For 3d6, there are 6 x 6 x 6 = 216, or 6^3 different combinations. For 8d6, there are 6^8 = 1,679,616 possibilities! This means that we would require a ridiculously large spreadsheet to calculate the distribution of results from 8d6 if we used the enumeration method that we employed for 2d6.

In *The Art of Game Design,* Jesse Schell presents "Ten Rules of Probability Every Game Designer Should Know,"[2] which I have paraphrased here:

■ **Rule 1: Fractions are decimals are percents:** Fractions, decimals, and percents are interchangeable, and you'll often find yourself switching between them when dealing with probability. For instance, the chance of rolling a 1 on 1d20 is 1/20 or 0.05/1 or 5%. To convert from one to the other, follow these guidelines:

---

[2] Schell, *The Art of Game Design*, 155–163.

- Fraction to Decimal: Type the fraction into a calculator. (Typing 1 ÷ 20 = will give you the result 0.05.)

- Percent to Decimal: Divide by 100 (5% = 5 / 100 = 0.05).

- Decimal to Percent: Multiply by 100 (0.05 = (0.05 * 100)% = 5%).

- Anything to Fraction: This is pretty difficult; there's often no easy way to convert a decimal or percent to a fraction except for the few equivalencies that most people know (e.g., 0.5 = 50% = 1/2, 0.25 = 1/4).

- **Rule 2: Probabilities range from 0 to 1 (which is equivalent to 0% to 100% and 0/1 to 1/1):** There can never be less than a 0% chance or higher than a 100% chance of something happening.

- **Rule 3: Probability is "sought outcomes" divided by "possible outcomes":** If you roll 1d6 and want to get a 6, that means that there is 1 sought outcome (the 6) and 6 possible outcomes (1, 2, 3, 4, 5, or 6). The probability of rolling a 6 is 1/6 (which is roughly equal to 0.16666 or about 17%). There are 13 spades in a regular deck of 52 playing cards, so if you pick one random card, the chance of it being a spade is 13/52 (0.25 or 25%).

- **Rule 4: Enumeration can solve difficult mathematical problems:** If you have a very low number of possible outcomes, enumerating all of them can work fine, as you saw in the 2d6 example in Calc. If you have a larger number (something like 10d6, which has 60,466,176 possible rolls), you could write a computer program to enumerate them. Once you've gotten some programming under your belt, you should check out the program to do so that is included in Appendix B.

- **Rule 5: When sought outcomes are mutually exclusive, add their probabilities:** Schell's example of this is figuring the chance of drawing either a face card *OR* an ace from the deck. There are 12 face cards (3 per suit) and 4 aces in the deck. Aces and face cards are mutually exclusive, meaning that there is no card that is both an ace and a face card. Because of this, if you ask the question, "What is the probability of drawing a face card *OR* an ace from the deck?" then you can add the two probabilities. 12/52 + 4/52 = 16/52 (0.3077 ≈ 31%). What is the probability of rolling a 1, 2, or 3 on 1d6? 1/6 + 1/6 + 1/6 = 3/6 (0.5 = 50%). Remember, if you use an *OR* to combine mutually exclusive sought outcomes, you can add their probabilities.

- **Rule 6: When sought outcomes are not mutually exclusive, multiply their probabilities:** If you want to know the probability of choosing a card that is both a face card *AND* a spade, you can multiply the two probabilities together. There are 13 spades (13/52) and 12 face cards (12/52). Multiplied together, you get the following:

  13/52 x 12/52

  = (13x12) / (52x52)

  = 156/2704   *both sides are divisible by 52*

  = 3/52 (0.0577 ≈ 6%)

We know this is correct because there are actually 3 spades that are face cards in the deck (which is 3 out of 52). Another example would be the probability of rolling a 1 on 1d6 *AND* a 1 on another 1d6. This would be 1/6 x 1/6 = 1/36 (0.0278 ≈ 3%), and as we saw in the enumerated example in Calc, there is exactly a 1/36 chance of getting a 1 on both dice when you roll 2d6.

Remember, if you use an *AND* to combine non-mutually exclusive sought outcomes, you can multiply their probabilities.

Corollary: When sought outcomes are independent, multiply their probabilities: If two actions are completely independent of each other (which is a subset of their not being mutually exclusive), the probability of them both happening is the multiplication of their individual probabilities. For instance, the probability of rolling a 6 on 1d6 is 1/6. The two dice in a 2d6 roll are completely independent of each other, so the probability of getting 6 on both dice is the multiple of the two independent probabilities (1/6 x 1/6 = 1/36) as we saw in our enumerated example in Calc. The probability of getting a 6 on 2d6 *AND* getting heads on two coin tosses is (1/6 x 1/6 x 1/2 x 1/2 = 1/184).

- **Rule 7: One minus "does" = "doesn't":** The probability of something happening is 1 minus the probability of it not happening. For instance the chance of rolling a 1 on 1d6 is 1/6, as you know. This means that the chance of *not* rolling a 1 on 1d6 is 1 − 1/6 = 5/6 (0.8333 ≈ 83%). This is useful because it is sometimes easier to figure out the chance of something not happening than something happening.

For example, what if you wanted to calculate the odds of rolling a 6 on at least one die when you roll 2d6? If we enumerate, we'll find that the answer is 11/36 (the sought outcomes being 6_x, x_6, *AND* 6_6 where the x could be any number other than 6). You can also count the number of columns with at least one 6 in them in the Calc chart we made. However, we can also use rules 5, 6, and 7 to figure this out mathematically.

The possibility of rolling a 6 on 1d6 is 1/6. The possibility of rolling a non-6 on 1d6 is 5/6, so the possibility of rolling 6 *AND* a non-6 (6_x) is 1/6 x 5/6 = 5/36. (Remember, *AND* means multiply from Rule 6.) Because this can be accomplished by either rolling 6_x *OR* x_6, we add those two possibilities together: 5/36 + 5/36 = 10/36. (Rule 5: *OR* means add.)

The possibility of rolling a 6 *AND* a 6 (6_6) is 1/6 x 1/6 = 1/36. Because this is another possible mutually exclusive case from 6_x *OR* x_6, they can be added together: 5/36 + 5/36 + 1/36 = 11/36 (0.3055 ≈ 31%).

This got complicated pretty quickly, but we can actually use Rule 7 to simplify it. If you reverse the problem and look for the chance of *not* getting a 6 in two rolls, that can be restated "What is the chance of getting a non-6 on the first roll *AND* a non-6 on the second roll?" These two sought possibilities are not mutually exclusive, so you can multiply them! So, the chance of getting a non-6 on both rolls is just 5/6 x 5/6 or 25/36. 1 − 25/36 = 11/36, which is pretty awesome and a lot easier to figure out!

Now, what if you were to roll 4d6 and sought at least one 6? This is now simply:

$$1 - (\, 5/6 \times 5/6 \times 5/6 \times 5/6 \,)$$

$$= 1 - (\, 5^4 / 6^4 \,)$$

$$= 1 - (\, 625 / 1{,}296 \,)$$

$$= (\, 1{,}296 / 1{,}296 \,) - (\, 625 / 1{,}296 \,) \qquad \textit{1,296/1,296 is equal to 1}$$

$$= (\, 1{,}296 - 625 \,) / 1{,}296 \qquad \textit{Because both are divisible by 1,296, they can be combined}$$

$$= 671 / 1{,}296 \qquad (\, 0.5177 \approx 52\% \,)$$

There is about a 52% chance of rolling at least one 6 on 4d6.

- **Rule 8: The sum of multiple dice is not a linear distribution:** As we saw in the enumerated Calc example of 2d6, though each of the individual dice has a linear distribution. That is, each number 1–6 has an equal chance of happening on 1d6, and when you sum multiple dice together, you get a weighted distribution of probability. It gets even more complex with more than two dice, as shown in Figure 11.5.

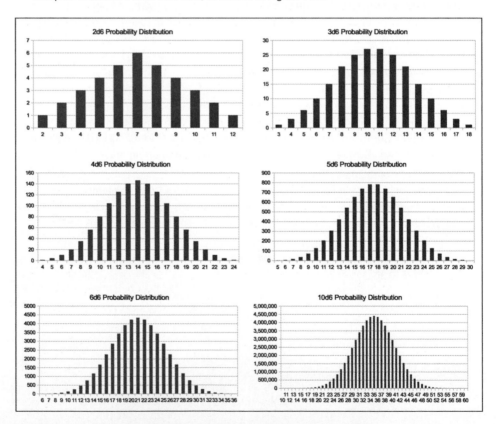

Figure 11.5 Probability distribution for 2d6, 3d6, 4d6, 5d6, 6d6, and 10d6

As you can see in the figure, the more dice you add, the more severe the bias is toward the average sum of the dice. In fact, with 10d6, you have a 1/60,466,176 chance of rolling all 6s, but a 4,395,456/60,466,176 (0.0727 ≈ 7%) chance of rolling exactly 35 or a 41,539,796/60,466,176 (0.6869922781 ≈ 69%) chance of rolling a number from 30 to 40. There are a couple of complex math papers about how to calculate these values with a formula, but I followed Rule 4 and wrote a program to do so.

As a game designer, it's not important for you to understand the exact numbers of these probability distributions. The thing that it *is* very important for you to remember is this: The more dice you have the player roll, the more likely they are to get a number near the average.

- **Rule 9: Theoretical versus practical probability:** In addition to the theoretical probabilities that we've been talking about, it is sometimes easier to approach probability from a more practical perspective, or to put this another way, the results of rolling actual dice don't always match the theoretical peredictions. There are both digital and analog ways in which this can be done.

Digitally, you could write a simple computer program to do millions of trials and determine the outcome. This is often called the Monte Carlo method, and it is actually used by several of the best artificial intelligences that have been devised to play *Chess* and *Go*. *Go* is so complex that the best a computer can do is to calculate the results of millions of random plays by both the computer and its human opponent and determine the play that statistically leads to the best outcome for it. This can also be used to determine the answers to what would be very challenging theoretical problems. Schell's example of this is a computer program that could rapidly simulate millions of rolls of the dice in *Monopoly* and let the programmer know which spaces on the board players were most likely to land on.

Another aspect of this rule is that not all dice are created equal. For instance, if you wanted to publish a board game and were looking for a manufacturer for your dice, it would be very worthwhile to get a couple dice from each potential manufacturer and roll each of them a couple hundred times, recording the result each time. This might take an hour or more to accomplish, but it would tell you whether the dice from the manufacturer were properly weighted or if they would instead roll a certain number more often than the others.

- **Rule 10: Phone a friend:** Nearly all college students who major in computer science or math will have to take a probability class or two as part of their studies. If you run into a difficult probability problem that you can't figure out on your own, try asking one of them. In fact, according to Schell, the study of probability began in 1654 when the Chevalier de Méré couldn't figure out why he seemed to have a better than even chance of rolling at least one 6 on four rolls of 1d6 but seemed to have a less than even chance of rolling at least one 12 on 24 rolls of 2d6. The Chevalier asked his friend Blaise Pascal for help. Pascal wrote to his father's friend Pierre de Fermat, and their conversation became the basis for probability studies.[3] Now, using the 10 rules here, you should be able to figure out why.

---

[3] Schell, *The Art of Game Design*, 154.

In Appendix B, I have included a Unity program that will calculate the distribution of rolls for any number of dice with any number of sides (as long as you have enough time to wait for it to calculate).

Randomizer Technologies in Paper Games

Some of the most common randomizers used in paper games include dice, spinners, and decks of cards.

Dice

We've already covered a lot of information about dice in this chapter. The important elements are as follows:

- A single die generates randomness with a linear probability distribution.
- The more dice you add together, the more the result is biased toward the average (and away from a linear distribution).
- Standard die sizes include: d4, d6, d8, d10, d12, and d20. Commonly available packs of dice for gaming usually include 1d4, 2d6, 1d8, 2d10, 1d12, and 1d20.
- 2d10 are sometimes called *percentile dice* because one will be used for the 1s place (marked with the numbers from 0–9) and the other for the 10s place (marked with the multiples of 10 from 00–90), giving an even distribution of the numbers from 00 to 99 (where a roll of 0 and 00 is usually counted as 100%).

Spinners

There are a couple of different kinds of spinners, but all have a rotating element and a still element. In most board games, the spinner is composed of a cardboard base that is divided into sections with a spinning arrow mounted above it (see image A in Figure 11.6). Larger spinners (for example, the wheel from the television show *Wheel of Fortune*) often have the sections on the spinning wheel and the arrow on the base (see Figure 11.6, image B). As long as players spin the spinner with enough force, a spinner is effectively the same as a die from a probability standpoint.

Spinners are often used in children's games for two major reasons:

- Young children lack the motor control to throw a die within a small area, so they will often accidentally throw dice in a way that they roll off of the gaming table.
- Spinners are a lot more difficult for young children to swallow.

Though they are less common in games for adults, spinners provide interesting possibilities that are not feasible with dice:

- Spinners can be made with any number of slots. However, it is difficult (though not impossible) to construct a die with 3, 7, 13, or 200 sides.

- Spinners can be weighted very easily so that not all possibilities have the same chance of happening. Image C of Figure 11.6 shows a hypothetical spinner to be used by a player when attacking. On this spinner, the player would have a 3/16 chance of a Miss, 5/16 chance of Hit 1, 3/16 chance of Hit 2, 2/16 chance of Hit 3, and 1/16 chance of Hit 4, Hit 5, or Crit!

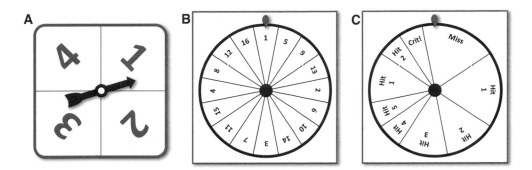

Figure 11.6 Various spinners. In all diagrams, the red elements are static, and the black element rotates.

Decks of Cards

A standard deck of playing cards includes 13 cards of 4 different suits and sometimes two jokers (see Figure 11.7). This includes the ranks 1 (also called the Ace) through 10, Jack, Queen, and King in each of the four suits: Clubs, Diamonds, Hearts, and Spades.

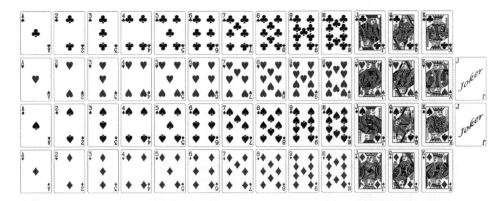

Figure 11.7 A standard deck of playing cards with two jokers

Playing cards are very popular because of both their compactness and the many different ways that they can be divided.

In a draw of a single card from a deck without Jokers, you have the following probabilities:

- **Chance of drawing a particular single card:** 1/52 (0.0192 ≈ 2%)
- **Chance of drawing a specific suit:** 13/52 = 1/4 (0.25 = 25%)
- **Chance of drawing a face card (J, Q, or K):** 12/52 = 3/13 (0.2308 ≈ 23%)

Custom Card Decks

A deck of cards is one of the easiest and most configurable randomizers that can be made for a paper game. You can very easily add or remove copies of a specific card to change the probability of that card appearing in a single draw from the deck. See the section on weighted distributions later in this chapter for more information.

TIPS FOR MAKING CUSTOM CARD DECKS

One of the difficulties in making custom cards is getting material for them that you can easily shuffle. 3x5 note cards don't work particularly well for this, but there are a couple of better options:

- Use marker or stickers to modify an existing set of cards. Sharpies work well for this and don't add thickness to the card like stickers do.

- Buy a deck of card sleeves, and insert a slip of paper along with a regular card into each, as described in Chapter 9.

The key thing you want to avoid when making a deck (or any element of a paper prototype) is putting too much time into any one piece. After you've devoted time to making a lot of nice cards (for instance) you may be less willing to remove any of those cards from the prototype or to scrap them and start over.

When to Shuffle a Deck

If you shuffle the entire deck of cards before every draw, then you will have an equal likelihood of drawing any of the cards (just like when you roll a die or use a spinner). However, this isn't how most people use decks of cards. In general, people will draw until the deck is completely exhausted and then shuffle all the cards. This leads to very different behavior from a deck than from an equivalent die. If you had a deck of six cards numbered 1–6, and you drew every card before reshuffling, you would be guaranteed to see each of the numbers 1–6 once for every six times you drew from the deck. Rolling a die six times will not give you this same consistency. An additional difference is that players could count cards and know which have and have not been drawn thus far, giving them insight into the probability of a certain card being drawn next. For example, if the cards 1, 3, 4, and 5 have been drawn from the six-card deck, there is a 50% chance that the next card will be a 2 and a 50% chance that it will be a 6.

This difference between decks and dice came up in the board game *Settlers of Catan* where some players got so frustrated at the difference between the theoretical probability of the 2d6 rolls in the game versus the actual numbers that came up in play that the publisher of the game now sells a deck of 36 cards (marked with each of the possible outcomes of 2d6) to replace the dice in play, ensuring that the practical probability experienced in the game is the same as the theoretical probability.

Weighted Distributions

A weighted distribution is one in which some options are more likely to come up than others. Most of the examples that we've looked at so far involved linear distributions of random possibilities, but it is a common desire as a designer to want to weight one option more heavily than another. For example, in the board game *Small World*, the designers wanted an attacker to get a random bonus on her final attack of each turn about half of the time, and they wanted that bonus to range from +1 to +3. To do this, they created a die with these six sides (see Figure 11.8).

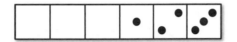

Figure 11.8 The attack bonus die from *Small World* with weighted bonus distribution

With this die, the chance of getting no bonus is 3/6 = 1/2 (0.5 = 50%), and the chance of getting a bonus of 2 is 1/6 (0.1666 ≈ 17%), so the chance of no bonus is weighted much more heavily than the other three choices.

What if instead, you still wanted the player to get a bonus only half of the time, but you wanted for the bonus of 1 to be three times more likely than the 3, and the 2 to be twice as likely as the 3. This would give us the weighted distribution shown in Figure 11.9.

Figure 11.9 Die with 1/2 chance of 0, 1/4 chance of 1, 1/6 chance of 2, and 1/12 chance of 3

Luckily, this adds up to 12 total possible sides for a die (a common die size). However, if it didn't add up to a common size, you could always create a spinner or a deck of cards with the same probabilities (though the card deck would need to be shuffled each time before drawing a card). It's also possible to model weighted distributions with randomized outcomes in Calc. Doing so is very similar to how you will deal with random numbers later in Unity and C#.

Weighted Probability in Calc

Weighted probability is commonplace in digital games. For instance, if you wanted an enemy who encounters the player to attack her 40% of the time, adopt a defensive posture 40% of the time, and run away 20% of the time, you could create an array of values [Attack, Attack, Defend, Defend, Run][4] and have the enemy's artificial intelligence code pull a random value from it when the player was first detected.

Following these steps will give you a Calc worksheet that can be used to randomly select from a series of values. Initially, it will pick a random number between 1 and 12, and once the worksheet is made, you can replace choices in column A with any that you choose.

1. Open a new document in Calc.

2. Fill in everything shown in columns A and B of Figure 11.10 but leave column C empty for now. To right-align the text in column B, select cells B1:B4 and choose *Format > Alignment > Right* from the Calc menu bar.

C2	▼	fx Σ =	=RAND0		
	A		B		C
1	1		# Choices:		12
2	2		Random:		0.08807831
3	3		Index:		2
4	4		Roll:		2
5	5				
6	6				
7	7				
8	8				
9	9				
10	10				
11	11				
12	12				

Figure 11.10   OpenOffice Calc table for weighted random number selection

3. Select cell C1 and enter the formula **=COUNTIF(A1:A100;"<>")**. This will count the number of cells in the range A1:A100 that are not empty (in Calc, <> means "different from," and not following it with a specified value means "different from nothing"). This gives us the number of valid choices that are listed in column A (we currently have 12).

4. In cell C2 enter the formula **=RAND()**, which will generate a number from 0 to 1 (including 0, but never actually reaching 1).

---

[4] Square brackets ([ ]) are used in C# to define arrays (a group of values), so I'm using them here to group the five possible action values.

5. Select cell C3 and enter the formula **=FLOOR(C2*C1;1)+1**. The number we're flooring is the random number between 0 and 0.9999 multiplied by the number of possible choices, which is 12 in this case. This means that we're flooring numbers between 0 and 11.9999 to give us the integers from 0 to 11. Then we add 1 to the result to give us the integers 1 to 12.

6. In cell C4, enter the formula **=INDEX(A1:A100;C3)**. INDEX() takes a range of values (e.g., A1:A100) and chooses from them based on an index (C3 in this case, which can range from 1 to 12). Now, C4 will choose a random value from the list in column A.

To get a different random value, press *F9* on your keyboard. (If you're on OS X, you probably need to hold the *fn* key and then press *F9*.) This will cause Calc to recalculate all formulas on the page (including the RAND() formula) and give you another random number.

You can put either numbers or text into the cells in column A as long as you don't skip any rows. Try replacing the numbers in cells A1:A12 with the weighted values from Figure 11.9 (that is, [0, 0, 0, 0, 0, 0, 1, 1, 1, 2, 2, 3]). If you do so and try recalculating the random value in C3 several times, you will see that zero comes up about half of the time. You can also fill the values A1:A5 with [Attack, Attack, Defend, Defend, Run] and see the weighted enemy A1 choice that was used as an example at the beginning of this section.

Permutations

There is a traditional game called *Bulls and Cows* (see Figure 11.11) that served as the basis for the board game *Master Mind* (1970 by Mordecai Meirowitz). In this game, each player starts by writing down a secret four-digit code (where each of the digits are different). Players take turns trying to guess their opponent's code, and the first person to guess correctly wins. When a player guesses, her opponent responds with a number of bulls and a number of cows. The guesser gets a bull for each number she guessed that is in the correct position and a cow for each number that is part of the code but in an incorrect position. In the diagram below, red represents a bull, and white represents a cow.

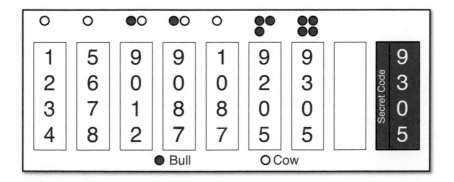

Figure 11.11   An example game of *Bulls and Cows*

From the perspective of the guesser, the secret code is effectively a series of random choices. Mathematicians call series like these permutations. In *Bulls and Cows*, the secret code is a permutation of the ten digits 0–9, where four are chosen with no repeating elements. In the game *Master Mind*, there are eight possible colors, of which four are chosen with no repetition. In both cases, the code is a permutation and not a combination because the positions of the elements matter (9305 is not the same as 3905). A combination is a selection of choices where the position doesn't matter. For example, 1234, 2341, 3421, 2431, and so on are all the same thing in a combination.

Permutations with Repeating Elements

We'll start with permutations that allow repetition because the math is a little easier. If there were four digits with repetition allowed, there would be 10,000 possible combinations (the numbers 0000 through 9999). This is easy to see with numbers, but we need a more general way of thinking about it (for cases where there are not exactly 10 choices per slot). Because each digit is independent of the others and each has 10 possible choices, according to probability Rule 6, the probability of getting any one number is $1/10 \times 1/10 \times 1/10 \times 1/10 = 1/10,000$. This also tells us that there are 10,000 possible choices for the code (if repetition is allowed).

The general calculation for permutations with repetition allowed is to multiply the number of choices for each slot by each other. With four slots and ten choices each, this is $10 \times 10 \times 10 \times 10 = 10,000$. If you were to make the code from six-sided dice instead of digits, then there would be six choices per slot, making $6 \times 6 \times 6 \times 6 = 1296$ possible choices.

Permutations with No Repeating Elements

But what about the actual case for *Bulls and Cows* where you're not allowed to repeat any digits? It's actually simpler than you might imagine. Once you've used a digit, it's no longer available. So, for the first slot, you can pick any number from 0–9, but once a digit (e.g., 9) has been chosen for the first slot, there are only 9 choices remaining for the second slot (0–8). This continues for the rest of the slots, so the calculation of possible codes for *Bulls and Cows* is actually $10 \times 9 \times 8 \times 7 = 5040$. Almost half of the possible choices are eliminated by not allowing repeating digits.

Positive and Negative Feedback

One of the most important concepts to understand about game balancing is that of positive and negative feedback. In a game with *positive* feedback, a player who takes an early lead gains an advantage over the other players and is more likely to win the game. In a game with *negative* feedback, the players who are losing have an advantage.

Poker is an excellent example of a game with positive feedback. If a player wins a big pot and has more money than the other players, individual bets matter less to her, and she has more freedom to do things like bluff (because she can afford to lose). However, a player who loses money early in the game and has little left can't afford to take risks and has less freedom when playing. *Monopoly* has a strong positive feedback mechanism where the player with the best property consistently gets more money and is able to force other players to sell her their property if they can't afford the rent when they land on her spaces. Positive feedback is generally frowned upon in multiplayer games, but it can be very good if you want the game to end quickly. Single-player games also often have positive feedback mechanisms to make the player feel increasingly powerful throughout the game.

Mario Kart is a great example of a game with negative feedback in the form of the random items that it awards to players when they drive through item boxes. The player in the lead will usually only get a banana (a largely defensive weapon), a set of three bananas, or a green shell (one of the weakest attacks). A player in last place will often get much more powerful items like a lightning bolt that slows every other player in the race. Negative feedback makes games feel more fair to the players who are not in the lead and generally leads to both longer games and to all players feeling that they have still have a chance of winning even if they're pretty far behind.

Using Calc to Balance Weapons

Another use of math and programs like OpenOffice Calc in game design is the balance of various weapons or abilities. In this section, we'll look at the process that went into balancing the weapons for the paper prototype example in Chapter 9. As you saw in Chapter 9, each weapon has values for three things:

- The number of shots fired at a time
- The damage done by each shot
- The chance that each shot will hit at a given distance

As we balance these weapons, we want them to feel roughly equal to each other in power, though we want each weapon to have a distinct personality. For each weapon, this would be as follows:

- **Pistol:** A basic weapon; pretty decent in most situations but doesn't excel in any
- **Rifle:** A good choice for mid and long range
- **Shotgun:** Deadly up close but its power falls off quickly; only one shot, so a miss really matters
- **Sniper Rifle:** Terrible at close range but fantastic at long range
- **Machine Gun:** Fires many shots, so even if some miss, the others will usually hit; this should feel like the most reliable gun, though not the most powerful

Figure 11.12 shows the values for the weapons as I initially imagined they might work. The ToHit value is the minimum roll on 1d6 that would hit at that range. For example, in cell K3, you can see that the ToHit for the pistol at a range of 7 is 4, so if shooting a target 7 spaces away, any of 4 or above would be a hit. This is a 50% chance of hitting on 1d6 (because it would hit on a roll of 4, 5, or 6).

	A	B	C	D	E	F	G	H	I	J	K	L	M	N	O	P	Q	R	S	T	U	V	W	X	Y	Z
1	Weapon	Shots	D/Shot	ToHit												Percent Chance										
2	Original				1	2	3	4	5	6	7	8	9	10		1	2	3	4	5	6	7	8	9	10	
3	Pistol	4	2		2	2	2	3	3	4	4	5	5	6												
4	Rifle	3	3		4	3	2	2	3	3	3	4	4													
5	Shotgun	1	10		2	2	3	3	4	5	6															
6	Sniper Rifle	1	8		6	5	4	4	3	3	2	2	3	4												
7	Machine Gun	6	1		3	3	4	4	5	5	6	6														

Figure 11.12   Initial values for the weapons balance spreadsheet

Create a new spreadsheet document in Calc and enter all of the data shown in Figure 11.12. To change the background color of a cell, you can use the *Cell Color* button shown in Figure 11.1.

Determining the Percent Chance for Each Bullet

In the cells under the heading Percent Chance, we want to calculate the chance that each shot of a weapon will hit at a certain distance. To do so, follow these steps.

1. In cell E3, you can see that each shot from a pistol will hit at a distance of 1 if the player rolls a 2 or better on 1d6. This means that it will miss on a 1 and hit on 2, 3, 4, 5, or 6. This is a 5/6 chance (or ≈83%), and we need a formula to calculate this. Looking at probability rule #7, we know that there is a 1/6 chance of it missing (which is the same as the ToHit number minus 1). Select cell P3 and enter the formula **=(E3-1)/6**. This will cause P3 to display the chance of the pistol *missing* at a range of one.

2. Using Rule 7 again, we know that 1-miss = hit, so change the formula in P3 to **=1-((E3-1)/6)**. Order of operations works in Calc, so divide operations happen before minus operations. To enforce the order in which I want the operations to occur, I've added parentheses. Once you've done this, P3 will hold the value 0.8333333.

3. To convert P3 from showing decimal numbers to showing a percentage, click the *Number Format: Percent* button shown in Figure 11.1. You will also probably want to click the *Number Format: Delete Decimal Place* button a couple times. It is the button to the right of *Number Format: Percent* that shows .000 with a red *X* above it.

4. Copy the formula in P3 and paste it into all the cells in the range P3:Y7. You'll see that everything works perfectly except for the blank ToHit cells, which now have a percent chance of %117! The formula needs to be altered to ignore blank cells.

5. Select P3 again and change the formula to **=IF(E3="";"";1-((E3-1)/6))**. The IF statement has three parts, which are divided by semicolons.

    ■ **E3="":** The first part is a question: Is E3 equal to "". That is, is E3 equal to an empty cell.

    ■ **"":** The second part is what to put in the cell if the question evaluates to true. That is, if E3 is empty, make cell P3 empty as well.

    ■ **1-((E3-1)/6):** The third part is what to put in the cell if the question evaluates to false. (That is, if E3 is not empty, then use the same formula we had before.)

6. Copy the new formula from P3 and paste it into P3:Y7. You will see that the empty cells in the ToHit area now cause empty cells in the Percent Chance area. (For example, L5:N5 are empty, so W5:Y5 are empty as well.) It should now look like the Percent Chance section in Figure 11.13.

	M	N	O	P	Q	R	S	T	U	V	W	X	Y	Z	AA	AB	AC	AD	AE	AF	AG	AH	AI	AJ	AK
1				Percent Chance											Average Damage										
2	9	10		1	2	3	4	5	6	7	8	9	10		1	2	3	4	5	6	7	8	9	10	
3	5	6		83%	83%	83%	67%	67%	50%	50%	33%	33%	17%		6.7	6.7	6.7	5.3	5.3	4.0	4.0	2.7	2.7	1.3	
4	4	4		50%	67%	83%	83%	83%	67%	67%	67%	50%	50%		4.5	6.0	7.5	7.5	7.5	6.0	6.0	6.0	4.5	4.5	
5				83%	83%	67%	67%	50%	33%	17%					8.3	8.3	6.7	6.7	5.0	3.3	1.7				
6	3	4		17%	33%	50%	50%	67%	67%	83%	83%	67%	50%		1.3	2.7	4.0	4.0	5.3	5.3	6.7	6.7	5.3	4.0	
7				67%	67%	50%	50%	33%	33%	17%	17%				4.0	4.0	3.0	3.0	2.0	2.0	1.0	1.0			

Figure 11.13 The Percent Chance and Average Damage sections of the weapons spreadsheet. You will be making the Average Damage section next. (Note that the spreadsheet has been scrolled to the right to show columns M through AK.)

Calculating Average Damage

The next step in the balancing process is to determine how much average damage each gun will do at a certain distance. Because some guns fire multiple shots and each shot has a certain amount of damage, the average damage will be equal to the number of shots fired * the amount of damage per shot * the chance that each shot will hit:

1. Select cell AA3 and enter the formula **=IF(P3="";"";$B3*$C3*P3)**. Just like in the formula for P3, the IF statement here ensures that only non-empty cells are calculated. The formula includes absolute column references for cells $B3 and $C3 because B3 is the number of shots, and C3 is the damage per shot. We don't want those references moving to other columns (though we do want them able to move to other rows, so only the column reference is absolute).

2. Copy cell AA3 and paste it into AA3:AJ7. Now your Average Damage section should look like the one shown in Figure 11.13.

Charting the Average Damage

The next important step is to chart the average damage. While it's possible to look carefully at the numbers and interpret them, it's much easier to have Calc do the job of charting information, allowing you to visually assess what is going on. Follow these steps to do so:

1. Click and drag to select cells AA3:AJ7.

2. Click the *Chart* button (see Figure 11.1) to bring up the Chart Wizard. This chart will be a little more complex than the previous one.

3. In step *1. Chart Type*, choose *Line* from the list of chart types. This will give you four options of line charts as icons to the right of the list of cart types.

4. Choose the *Lines Only* type of line chart, which is the third option.

5. Click *2. Data Range* in the list of steps at the left of the Chart Wizard.

6. The data for each weapon is stored in a row, so choose the *Data series in rows* option. Now, the chart will start to look a little more like you might have expected.

7. To use the names of the weapons as labels, they must be part of the data range of the chart. Change the text in the *Data range* field to **$A$3:$A$7;$AA$3:$AJ$7**. This will include the gun names in A3:A7 as the first column of the data range.

8. Check the *First column as label* option. This will now use the gun names as labels for the five lines in the chart.

9. Click the *Finish* button to complete the chart.

10. To move the chart when it is selected, move your mouse near the border of the chart, and the mouse icon will change to a hand. Then you can click and drag to move the chart. You can also drag the small green boxes around the border to resize the chart.

You can see the results of the chart in the bottom of Figure 11.14. As you can see, there are some problems with the weapons. Some, like the sniper rifle and shotgun, have personalities as we had hoped (the shotgun is deadly at close range, and the sniper rifle is better at long range), but there are a lot of other problems:

- The machine gun is ridiculously weak.

- The pistol may be too strong.

- The rifle is also overly strong compared to the other weapons.

In short, the weapons are not balanced well to each other.

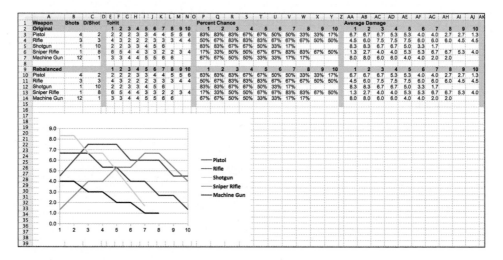

Figure 11.14   The weapon balance at the halfway point showing the chart of initial weapon stats. The Original and Rebalanced sections of the spreadsheet are also shown with Rebalanced currently showing a duplicate of the original values.

Duplicating the Weapon Data

To rebalance the weapons, it will be very helpful to have the original and rebalanced information next to each other (as is shown in Figure 11.14):

1. Start by moving the chart to the location shown in Figure 11.14.

2. Next, you need to make a copy of the data and formulas that you've already worked out. Select the cells A2:AK8 and copy them. Click cell A9 and paste. This should create a full copy of all the data you just created.

3. Change the heading in A9 from Original to Rebalanced, and your worksheet should now look like Figure 11.14. This second set of data will be where you make the changes and try out new numbers.

4. Next, you'll want to make a chart for the new data that is identical to the one for the original weapon stats. Select AA10:AJ14. Choose a *Line chart* of the type *Line Only* again as you did for the previous chart.

5. Set the *Data range* for the chart to **$A$10:$A$14;$AA$10:$AJ$14** and select the *Data series in rows* and *First column as label* options as you did in the previous chart.

6. Click *Finish* and move the new chart to the right of the original one so that you can see both charts and the data above them.

Showing Overall Damage

One final stat that you might want to track is overall damage. This sums the average damage that a weapon can do at all ranges to give you an idea of the overall power of the weapon. To do this, we will take advantage of a trick that will allow us to make a simple bar chart within the spreadsheet (and not in a chart).

1. Select cell AL3 and enter the formula **=SUM(AA3:AJ3)**. This will add up the average damage done by the pistol at all ranges (it should equal 45.33333).

2. For the bar chart trick, we need to be working with integers, not decimal numbers, so the SUM will need to be rounded. Change the formula in AL3 to **=ROUND(SUM(AA3:AJ3))**. The result will now be 45.

3. Select cell AM3 and enter the formula **=REPT("|";AL3)**. The REPT function repeats text a certain number of times. The text in this case is the pipe character (which you type by holding Shift and pressing the backslash key, which is above the Return/Enter key on most U.S. keyboards), and it is repeated 45 times because the value in AL3 is 45. After you've done this, you will see a little bar of pipe characters extending to the right in cell AM3.

4. Select cells AL3:AM3 and copy them. Paste them into cells AL3:AM7 and AL10:AM14. This will give you a text-based total damage bar chart for all weapons, both original and balanced.

Be sure to save your worksheet before starting to rebalance the weapons.

Rebalancing the Weapons

Now that you have two sets of data and two charts, you can try rebalancing the weapons. How will you make the machine gun more powerful? Will you increase its number of shots, its chance to hit, or its damage per shot? Keep the following things in mind as you balance:

- Units in the game have only 6 health, so they will fall unconscious if 6 or more damage is dealt to them.

- In the paper prototype, if an enemy was not downed by an attacking soldier, the enemy could counterattack. This makes dealing 6 damage in an attack much more powerful than dealing 5 damage because it also protects the attacker from counterattack.

- Weapons with many shots (e.g., the machine gun) will have a much higher chance of dealing the average amount of damage in a single turn, whereas guns with a single shot will feel much less reliable (e.g., the shotgun and sniper rifle). Figure 11.5 shows how the probability distribution shifts toward the average when you start rolling dice for multiple shots instead of a single one.

- Even with all this information, some aspects of weapon balance will not be shown in this chart. This includes things like the point made previously about multishot weapons having a much higher chance of dealing the average amount of damage as well as the benefit of the sniper rifle to deal damage to enemies who are too far away to effectively shoot back.

Try your hand at balancing the stats for these weapons. You should only change the values in the range B10:N14. Leave the original stats alone, and don't touch the Percent Chance and Average Damage cells; they will update to reflect the changes you make to the ToHit, Shots, and D/Shot cells. Once you've played with this for a while, continue reading.

The Balance Chosen for Chapter 9

In Figure 11.15, you can see the weapon stats that I chose for the prototype in Chapter 9. This is absolutely not the only way to balance these weapons or even the best way to balance them, but it does achieve many of the design goals.

- The weapons each have a personality of their own, and none is too overpowered or underpowered.

- Though the shotgun may look a little too similar to the machine gun in its chart, the two guns will feel very different due to two factors: 1. a hit with the 6-damage shotgun is an instant knockout, and 2. the machine Gun fires many bullets, so it will deal average damage much more often.

- The pistol is pretty decent at close range and is more versatile than the shotgun or machine gun with its ability to attempt to hit enemies at longer range.

- The rifle really shines at mid-range.

- The sniper rifle is terrible at close range, but it dominates long distance. A hit with the sniper rifle is 6 points of damage like the shotgun, so it will also take down an enemy in one shot.

Even though this kind of spreadsheet-based balancing doesn't cover all possible implications of the design of the weapons, it's still a critical tool to have in your game design arsenal because it can help you understand large amounts of data quickly. Several designers of free-to-play games spend most of their day modifying spreadsheets to make slight tweaks in game balance, so if you're interested in a job in that field, spreadsheets and data-driven design (like you just did) are very important skills.

	A	B	C	D	E	F	G	H	I	J	K	L	M	N	AK	AL	AM
9	Rebalanced				1	2	3	4	5	6	7	8	9	10			
10	Pistol	3	2		2	2	2	3	3	4	4	5	6	6	33		|||||||||||||||||||||||||
11	Rifle	2	4		5	4	4	3	3	3	4	5	5		40		|||||||||||||||||||||||||||||
12	Shotgun	1	6		2	2	2	2	3	4	5	6			30		|||||||||||||||||||||||
13	Sniper Rifle	1	6		6	6	5	5	4	3	3	2	2	3	31		|||||||||||||||||||||||
14	Machine Gun	10	1		4	4	4	4	5	5	6	6			30		|||||||||||||||||||||||

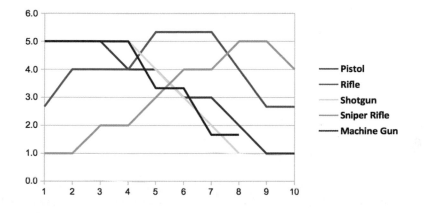

Figure 11.15   The weapon balance chosen for Chapter 9

Summary

There was a lot of math in this chapter, but I hope you saw that learning a little about math can be very useful for you as a game designer. Most of the topics covered in this chapter could merit their own book or course, so I encourage you to look into them further if your interest has been piqued.

In the next chapter, you learn about the specific discipline of puzzle design. Though games and puzzles are similar, there are some key differences that make puzzle design worth separate consideration.

CHAPTER 12

PUZZLE DESIGN

Puzzles are an important part of many digital games as well as an interesting design challenge in their own right. This chapter starts by exploring puzzle design through the eyes of one of the greatest living puzzle designers, Scott Kim.

The latter part of the chapter explores various types of puzzles that are common in modern games, some of which might not be what you would expect.

Puzzles Are Almost Everywhere

As you'll learn through this chapter, most single-player games have some sort of puzzle in them. However, multiplayer games often do not. The primary reason for this is that both single-player games and puzzles rely on the game system to provide challenge to the player, where multiplayer digital games (that are not cooperative) more often rely on other human players to provide the challenge. Because of this parallel between single-player games and puzzles, learning about how to design puzzles will help you with any game that you intend to have a single-player or cooperative mode.

Scott Kim on Puzzle Design

Scott Kim is one of today's leading puzzle designers. He has written puzzles for magazines such as *Discover, Scientific American,* and *Games* since 1990 and has designed the puzzle modes of several games including *Bejeweled 2*. He has lectured about puzzle design at both the TED conference and the Game Developers Conference. His influential full-day workshop, The Art of Puzzle Design[1]—which he delivered with Alexey Pajitnov (the creator of *Tetris*) at the 1999 and 2000 Game Developers Conferences—has shaped many game designers ideas about puzzles for over a decade. This chapter explores some of the content of that workshop.

What Is a Puzzle?

Kim states that his favorite definition of puzzle is also one of the simplest: "A puzzle is fun, and it has a right answer."[2] This differentiates puzzles from toys, which are fun but don't have a right answer, and from games, which are fun but have a goal rather than a specific correct answer. Kim sees puzzles as separate from games, though I personally see them as more of a highly developed subset of games. Though this definition of puzzles is very simple, some important subtleties lie hidden therein.

A Puzzle Is Fun

Kim states that there are three elements of fun for puzzles:[3]

- **Novelty:** Many puzzles rely on a certain specific insight to solve them, and once the player has gained that insight, finding the puzzle's solution is rather simple. A large part of the fun of solving a puzzle is that flash of insight, the joy of creating a new solution. If a puzzle lacks novelty, the player will often already have the insight required to solve it before even starting the puzzle, and thus that element of the puzzle's fun is lost.

- **Appropriate difficulty:** Just as games must seek to give the player an adequate challenge, puzzles must also be matched to the player's skill, experience, and type of creativity. Each

---

[1] Scott Kim and Alexey Pajitnov, "The Art of Puzzle Game Design" (presented at the Game Developers Conference, San Jose, CA, March 15, 1999), http://www.scottkim.com/thinkinggames/GDC99/index.html

[2] Scott Kim, "What Is a Puzzle?" Accessed January 17, 2014, http://www.scottkim.com/thinkinggames/whatisapuzzle/.

[3] Ibid.

player approaching a puzzle will have a unique level of experience with puzzles of that type and a certain level of frustration that she is willing to experience before giving up. Some of the best puzzles in this regard have both an adequate solution that is of medium difficulty and an expert solution that requires advanced skill to discover. Another great strategy for puzzle design is to create a puzzle that appears to be simple though it is actually quite difficult. If the player perceives the puzzle to be simple, she'll be less likely to give up.

- **Tricky:** Many great puzzles cause the player to shift her perspective or thinking to solve them. However, even after having that perspective shift, the player should still feel that it will require skill and cunning to execute her plan to solve the puzzle. This is exemplified in the puzzle-based stealth combat of Klei Entertainment's *Mark of the Ninja*, in which the player must use insight to solve the puzzle of how to approach a room full of enemies and then, once she has a plan, must physically execute that plan with precision.[4]

And It Has a Right Answer

Every puzzle needs to have a right answer, and some puzzles have several right answers. One of the key elements of a great puzzle is that once the player has found the right answer, it is clearly obvious to her that she is right. If the correctness of the answer isn't easily evident, the puzzle can seem muddled and unsatisfying.

Genres of Puzzles

Kim identifies four genres of puzzle (see Figure 12.1),[5] each of which causes the player to take a different approach and use different skills. These genres are at the point of intersection between puzzles and other activities. For example, a story puzzle is the mixture of a narrative and a series of puzzles.

- **Action:** Action puzzles like *Tetris* have time pressure and allow players a chance to fix their mistakes. They are the combination of an action game with a puzzle mindset.

- **Story:** Story puzzles like *Myst*, the *Professor Layton* series, and most hidden-object games[6] have puzzles that players must solve to progress through the plot and explore the environment. They combine narrative and puzzles.

---

4 Nels Anderson, "Of Choice and Breaking New Ground: Designing Mark of the Ninja" (presented at the Game Developers Conference, San Francisco, CA, March 29, 2013). Nels Anderson, the lead designer of *Mark of the Ninja*, spoke in this talk about narrowing the gulf between intent and execution. They found that making it easier for a player to execute on her plans in the game shifted the skill of the game from physical execution to mental planning, making the game more puzzle-like and more interesting to players. He has posted a link to his slides and his script for the talk on his blog at http://www.above49.ca/2013/04/gdc-13-slides-text.html, accessed March 6, 2014.

5 Scott Kim and Alexey Pajitnov, "The Art of Puzzle Game Design," slide 7.

6 *Myst* was one of the first CD-ROM adventure games, and was the number one best-selling CD-ROM game until *The Sims* took that title. The *Professor Layton* series of games is an ongoing series for Nintendo's handheld platforms that wraps many individual puzzles inside an overarching mystery story. Hidden-object games are a popular genre of game where a player is given a list of objects to find hidden in a complicated scene. They often have mystery plots that they player is attempting to solve by finding the objects.

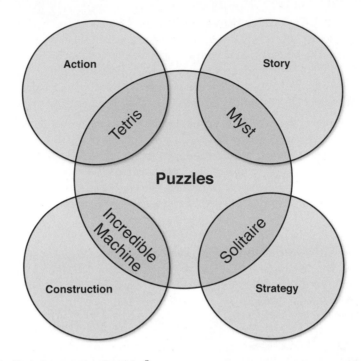

Figure 12.1   Kim's four genres of puzzles[7]

- **Construction:** Construction puzzles invite the player to build an object from parts to solve a certain problem. One of the most successful of these was *The Incredible Machine*, in which players built Rube Goldberg-like contraptions to cause the cats in each scene to run away. Some construction games even include a *construction set* that allows the player to devise and distribute her own puzzles. Construction puzzles are the intersection of construction, engineering, and spatial reasoning with puzzles.

- **Strategy:** Many strategy puzzle games are the solitaire versions of the kinds of puzzles that players encounter in games that are traditionally multiplayer. These include things like bridge puzzles (which present players with various hands in a bridge game and ask how play should proceed) and chess puzzles (which give players a few chess pieces positioned on a board and ask how the player could achieve checkmate in a certain number of moves). These combine the thinking required for the multiplayer version of the game with the skill building of a puzzle to help players train to be better at the multiplayer game.

Kim also holds that there are some pure puzzles that don't fit in any of the other four genres. This would include things like *Sudoku* or crossword puzzles.

---

7   Scott Kim and Alexey Pajitnov, "The Art of Puzzle Game Design," slide 7.

The Four Major Reasons that People Play Puzzles

Kim's research and experience have led him to believe that people primarily play puzzles for the following reasons:[8]

- **Challenge:** People like to feel challenged and to feel the joy of overcoming those challenges. Puzzles are an easy way for players to feel a sense of achievement, accomplishment, and progress.

- **Mindless distraction:** Some people seek big challenges, but others are more interested in having something interesting to do to pass the time. Several puzzles like *Bejeweled* and *Angry Birds* don't provide the player with a big challenge but rather a low-stress interesting distraction. Puzzle games of this type should be relatively simple and repetitive rather than relying on a specific insight (as is common in puzzles played for challenge).

- **Character and environment:** People like great stories and characters, beautiful images, and interesting environments. Puzzle games like *Myst*, *The Journeyman Project*, the *Professor Layton* series, and *The Room* series rely on their stories and art to propel the player through the game.

- **Spiritual journey:** Finally, some puzzles mimic spiritual journeys in a couple of different ways. Some famous puzzles like *Rubik's Cube* can be seen as a rite of passage—either you've solved one in your life or you haven't. Many mazes work on this same principle. Additionally, puzzles can mimic the archetypical hero's journey:[9] the player starts in regular life, encounters a puzzle that sends her into a realm of struggle, fights against the puzzle for a while, gains an epiphany of insight, and then can easily defeat the puzzle that had stymied her just moments earlier.

Modes of Thought Required by Puzzles

Puzzles require players to think in different ways to solve them, and most players have a particular mode of thought that they prefer to engage in (and therefore a favorite class of puzzle). Figure 12.2 illustrates these concepts, and the list that follows explains each mode.

- **Word:** There are many different kinds of word puzzles. Most rely on the player having a large and varied vocabulary.

- **Image:** Image puzzle types include jigsaw, hidden-object, and 2D/3D spatial puzzles. Image puzzles tend to exercise the parts of the brain connected to visual/spatial processing and pattern recognition.

---

[8] Scott Kim and Alexey Pajitnov, "The Art of Puzzle Game Design," slide 8.

[9] The concept of the *hero's journey* was presented by Joseph Campbell in his book *The Hero With a Thousand Faces*. Campbell's theory is that there is a single monomyth that is shared by all cultures of a young person leaving the world that is comfortable to her, experiencing trials and difficulties, overcoming a great foe, and then returning to her home with the skills to lead her people to new heights. (The hero's journey traditionally focuses exclusively on male protagonists, but there's no reason to continue that gender bias.)

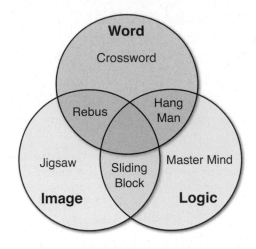

Figure 12.2   The modes of thought that Scott Kim has found are often used in puzzles including examples of each mode and of puzzles that use two modes of thought simultaneously[10]

- **Logic:** Logic puzzles like *Master Mind/Bulls & Cows* (described in Chapter 11, "Math and Game Balance"), riddles, and deduction puzzles cause the player to exercise their logical reasoning. Many games are based on *deductive* reasoning: the top-down elimination of several false possibilities, leaving only one that is true (e.g., a player reasoning "I know that all of the other suspects are innocent, so Colonel Mustard must have killed Mr. Boddy"). These include *Clue*, *Bulls & Cows*, and *Logic Grid* puzzles. There are far fewer games that use *inductive* reasoning: the bottom-up extrapolation from a specific certainty to a general probability (e.g., a player reasoning "The last five times that John bluffed in *Poker*, he habitually scratched his nose; he's scratching his nose now, so he's probably bluffing"). Deductive logic leads to certainty, while inductive logic makes an educated guess based on reasonable probability. The certainty of the answers has traditionally made deductive logic more attractive to puzzle designers.

- **Word/Image:** Many games like *Scrabble*, rebuses (like the one in Figure 12.3), and word searches incorporate both the word and image modes of thought to solve. *Scrabble* is a mixed-mode puzzle, but crossword puzzles are not, because in *Scrabble* the player is determining where to place the word and attempting to arrange it over score multipliers on the board. These are two acts of visual/spatial reasoning and decision-making that are not needed to play a crossword puzzle.

- **Image/Logic:** Sliding block puzzles, laser mazes, and puzzles like those shown in the second category of Figure 12.3 fit this category.

- **Logic/Word:** Most riddles fall into this category, including the classic Riddle of the Sphinx, which is the first riddle in Figure 12.3. It was given by the sphinx to Oedipus in the classic Greek tragedy *Oedipus Rex* by Sophocles.

---

10 Scott Kim and Alexey Pajitnov, "The Art of Puzzle Game Design." Slide 9.

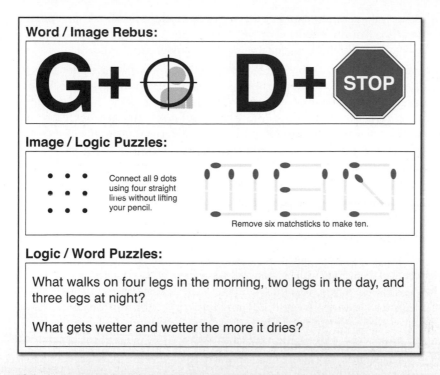

Figure 12.3 Various mixed-mode puzzles (solutions are at the end of the chapter)

Kim's Eight Steps of Digital Puzzle Design

Scott Kim describes eight steps that he typically goes through when designing a puzzle:[11]

1. **Inspiration:** Just like a game, inspiration for a puzzle can come from anywhere. Alexey Pajitnov has stated that his inspiration for *Tetris* was the mathematician Solomon Golomb's concept of pentominoes (12 different shapes, each made of five blocks, that could be fit together into an optimal space-filling puzzle) and the desire to use them in an action game. However, there were too many different five-block pentomino shapes, so he reduced it to the seven four-block tetrominoes found in *Tetris*.

2. **Simplification:** Usually you need to go through some form of simplification to get from your original inspiration to a playable puzzle.

    a. Identify the core puzzle mechanic, the essential tricky skill required.

    b. Eliminate any irrelevant details; narrow the focus.

    c. Make pieces uniform. For example, if you're dealing with a construction puzzle, move the pieces onto a uniform grid to make it easier for the player to manipulate.

---

11 Scott Kim and Alexey Pajitnov, "The Art of Puzzle Game Design," slide 97.

    d. Simplify the controls. Make sure that the controls for the puzzle are appropriate to the interface. Kim talks about how great a *Rubik's Cube* feels in real life but how terrible it would be to manipulate a digital version with a mouse and keyboard.

3. **Construction set:** Build a tool that makes construction of puzzles quick and easy. Many puzzles can be built and tested as paper prototypes, but if that isn't the case for your puzzle, this is the first place that you will need to do some programming. Regardless of whether it is paper or digital, an effective construction set can make the creation of additional levels much, much easier for you. Determine which tasks are repetitive time-wasters in the puzzle construction process and see if you can't make reusable parts or automated processes for them.

4. **Rules:** Define and clarify the rules. This includes defining the board, the pieces, the ways that they can move, and the ultimate goal of the puzzle or level.

5. **Puzzles:** Make some levels of the puzzle. Make sure that you create different levels that explore various elements of your design and game mechanics.

6. **Testing:** Just like a game, you don't know how players will react to a puzzle until you place it in front of them. Even with his many years of experience, Kim still finds that some puzzles he expects to be simple are surprisingly difficult, while some he expects to be difficult are easily solved. Playtesting is key in all forms of design. Usually, step 6 leads the designer to iteratively return to steps 4 and 5 and refine previous decisions.

7. **Sequence:** Once you have refined the rules of the puzzle and have several levels designed, it's time to put them in a meaningful sequence. Every time you introduce a new concept, it should be done in isolation, requiring the player to use just that concept in the most elementary way. Then you can progressively increase the difficulty of the puzzle that must be solved using that concept. Finally, you can create puzzles that mix that concept with other concepts that the player already understands. This is very similar to the sequencing in Chapter 13, "Guiding the Player," that is recommended for teaching any new game concept to a player.

8. **Presentation:** With the levels, rules, and sequence all created, it's now time to refine the look of the puzzle. Presentation also includes refinements to the interface and to the way that information is displayed to the player.

Seven Goals of Effective Puzzle Design

You need to keep several things in mind when designing a puzzle. Generally, the more of these goals that you can meet, the better puzzle you will create:

- **User friendly:** Puzzles should be familiar and rewarding to their players. Puzzles can rely on tricks, but they shouldn't take advantage of the player or make the player feel stupid.

- **Ease of entry:** Within one minute, the player must understand how to play the puzzle. Within a few minutes, the player should be immersed in the experience.

- **Instant feedback:** The puzzle should be "juicy" in the way that Kyle Gabler (co-creator of *World of Goo* and *Little Inferno*) uses the word:[12] The puzzle should actively react to player input in a way that feels physical, active, and energetic.

- **Perpetual motion:** The player should constantly be prodded to take the next step, and there should be no clear stopping point. When I worked at Pogo.com, all of our games ended with a *Play Again* button instead of a game over screen. Even a simple thing like that can keep players playing for longer.

- **Crystal-clear goals:** The player should always clearly understand the primary goal of the puzzle. However, it's also useful to have advanced goals for players to discover over time. The puzzle games *Hexic* and *Bookworm* are examples of puzzles that have very clear initial goals and also include advanced expert goals that veteran players can discover over time.

- **Difficulty levels:** The player should be able to engage the puzzle at a level of difficulty that is appropriate to her skill. Just like all games, appropriate difficulty is critical to making the experience fun for players.

- **Something special:** Most great puzzle games include something that makes them unique and interesting. Alexey Pajitnov's game *Tetris* combines apparent simplicity with the chance for deep strategy and steadily increasing intensity. Both *World of Goo* and *Angry Birds* have incredibly juicy, reactive gameplay.

Puzzle Examples in Action Games

There are a huge number of puzzles within modern AAA game titles. Most of these fall into one of the following categories.

Sliding Block / Position Puzzles

These puzzles usually take place in third-person action games and require the player to move large blocks around a gridded floor to create a specific pattern. An alternative version of this used in some games involves positioning mirrors that are used to bounce light or laser beams from a source to a target. One variation that is commonly introduced is a slippery floor that causes the blocks to move continuously until they hit a wall or other obstacle.

- **Game examples:** *Soul Reaver, Uncharted, Prince of Persia: The Sands of Time, Tomb Raider, The Legend of Zelda*

---

[12] Kyle Gray, Kyle Gabler, Shalin Shodan, and Matt Kucic. "How to Prototype a Game in Under 7 Days" Accessed May 29, 2014. http://www.gamasutra.com/view/feature/130848/how_to_prototype_a_game_in_under_7_.php

Physics Puzzles

These puzzles all involve using the physics simulation built in to the game to move objects around the scene or hit various targets with either the player character or other objects. This is the core mechanic in the *Portal* series and has become increasingly popular as reliable physics engines like Havok and the Nvidia PhysX system (built in to Unity) have become ubiquitous in the industry.

- **Game examples:** *Portal, Half-Life 2, Super Mario Galaxy, Rochard, Angry Birds*

Traversal

These puzzles show you a place in the level that you need to reach but often make it less than obvious how to get there. The player must frequently take detours to unlock gates or open bridges that will allow her to reach her objective. Racing games like *Gran Turismo* can also be seen as traversal puzzles; the player must discover the perfect racing line that will enable her to complete each lap as efficiently and quickly as possible. This is critically important in the Burning Lap puzzles of the *Burnout* series in which players are asked to traverse a racecourse that includes sections of oncoming traffic and hairpin turns without making a single mistake.

- **Game examples:** *Uncharted, Tomb Raider, Assassin's Creed, Oddworld: Abe's Oddyssee, Gran Turismo, Burnout, Portal*

Stealth

An extension of traversal puzzles that became important enough to merit its own genre, stealth puzzles ask the player to traverse a level while also avoiding detection by enemy characters, who are usually patrolling a predetermined path or following a specific schedule. Players usually have a way to disable the enemy characters, though this can also lead to detection if performed poorly.

- **Game examples:** *Metal Gear Solid, Uncharted, Oddworld: Abe's Oddyssee, Mark of the Ninja, Fallout 3, The Elder Scrolls V: Skyrim, Assassin's Creed*

Chain Reaction

These games include physics systems in which various components can interact, often to create explosions or other mayhem. Players use their tools to set traps or series of events that will either solve a puzzle or gain them an advantage over attacking enemies. The *Burnout* series of racing games include a Crash Mode that is a puzzle game where the player must drive her car into a specific traffic situation and cause the greatest amount of monetary damage through a fantastic multicar collision.

- **Game examples:** *Pixel Junk Shooter, Tomb Raider (2013), Half-Life 2, The Incredible Machine, Magicka, Red Faction: Guerilla, Far Cry 2, Bioshock, Burnout*

Boss Fights

Many boss fights, especially in classic games, involve some sort of puzzle where the player is required to learn the pattern of reactions and attacks used by a boss and determine a series of actions that exploit this pattern to defeat the boss. This is especially common in third-person action games by Nintendo like those in the *Zelda*, *Metroid*, and *Super Mario* series. One element that is very common in this kind of puzzle is the *rule of three:* The first time the player performs the correct action to damage the boss, it is often a surprise to her, the second time, she is experimenting to see if she now has the insight to defeat the puzzle/boss, and the third time, she is demonstrating her mastery over the puzzle and defeats the boss. Most bosses through-out the *Legend of Zelda* series since *The Ocarina of Time* can be defeated in three attacks, as long as the player understands the solution to the puzzle of that boss.

- **Game examples:** *The Legend of Zelda, God of War, Metal Gear Solid, Metroid, Super Mario 64/Sunshine/Galaxy, Guacamelee, Shadow of the Colossus*, multiplayer cooperative raids in *World of Warcraft*

Summary

As you've seen in this chapter, puzzles are an important aspect of many games that have single-player modes. As a game designer, puzzle design is not a large departure from the skills you've already learned, but there are some subtle differences. When designing a game, the most important aspect is the moment-to-moment gameplay, whereas in puzzle design, the solution and the moment of insight are of primary importance. (In an action puzzle like *Tetris*, however, insight and solution happen with the drop and placement of every piece.) In addition, when the player solves a puzzle, it is important that she can tell that she has found the right answers; in games interesting decisions rely on there being uncertainty in the player's mind about the outcome or correctness of decisions.

Regardless of the differences between designing puzzles and games, the iterative design process is as critical for puzzles as it is for all other kinds of interactive experiences. As a puzzle designer, you will want to make prototypes and playtest just as you would for a game; how-ever, with puzzles, it is even more critical that your playtesters have not seen the puzzle before (because they will have already had the moment of insight).

To close, Figure 12.4 shows the solutions to the puzzles in Figure 12.3. I didn't want to give away the answer by saying so, but the insight of the matchstick puzzle is that it actually requires all three modes of thought: logic, image, and word.

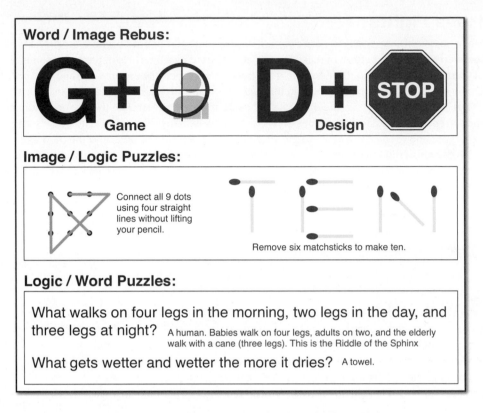

Figure 12.4   Mixed-mode puzzle solutions for the puzzles shown in Figure 12.4

CHAPTER 13

GUIDING THE PLAYER

As you've read in earlier chapters, your primary job as a designer is to craft an experience for players to enjoy. However, the further you get into your project and your design, the more obvious and intuitive your game appears to you. This comes from your familiarity with the game and is entirely natural.

However, this means that you need to keep a wary eye on your game, making sure that players who have never seen your game before also intuitively understand what they need to do to experience the game as you intended. This requires careful, sometimes invisible guidance, and it is the topic of this chapter.

This chapter covers two styles of player guidance: *direct*, where the player knows that she is being; and *indirect*, where the guidance is so subtle that players often don't even realize that they are being guided. The chapter concludes with information about *sequencing*, a style of progressive instruction to teach players new concepts or introduce them to new game mechanics.

Direct Guidance

Direct guidance methods are those that the player is explicitly aware of. Direct guidance takes many forms, but in all of them, quality is determined by immediacy, scarcity, brevity, and clarity:

- **Immediacy:** The message must be given to the player when it is immediately relevant. Some games try to tell the player all the possible controls for the game at the very beginning (sometimes showing a diagram of the controller with all of the buttons labeled), but it is ridiculous to think that a player will be able to remember all of these controls when the time comes that she actually needs to use them. Direct information about controls should be provided immediately the first time that the player needs it. In the PlayStation 2 game *Kya: Dark Lineage*, a tree falls into the path of the player character that she must jump over, and as it is falling, the game shows the player the message "Press X to jump" at exactly the time she needs to know that information.

- **Scarcity:** Many modern games have lots of controls and lots of simultaneous goals. It is important that the player not be flooded with too much information all at one time. Making instructions and other direct controls more scarce makes them more valuable to the player and more likely to be heeded. This is also the case with missions. A player can only really concentrate on a single mission at once, and some otherwise fantastic open world games like *Skyrim* inundate the player with various missions to the point that after several hours of gameplay, the player could potentially be in the middle of dozens of different missions, many of which will just be ignored.

- **Brevity:** Never use more words than are necessary, and don't give the player too much information at one time. In the tactical combat game *Valkyria Chronicles*, if you wanted to teach the player to press O to take cover behind some sandbags, the least you would need to say is "When near sandbags, press O to take cover and reduce damage from enemy attacks."

- **Clarity:** Be very clear about what you're trying to convey. In the previous example, you might be tempted to just tell the player "When standing near sandbags, press O to take cover," because you might assume that players should know that cover will shield them from incoming bullets. However, in *Valkyria Chronicles*, cover not only shields you but also drastically reduces the amount of damage you take from bullets that do hit (even if the cover is not between the attacker and the target). For the player to understand everything she needs to know about cover, she must also be told about the damage reduction.

Methods of Direct Guidance

There are a number of methods of direct guidance:

- **Instructions:** The game explicitly tells the player what to do. These can take the form of text, dialogue with an authoritative non-player character (NPC), or visual diagrams and often incorporate combinations of the three. Instructions are one of the clearest forms of direct guidance, but they also have the greatest likelihood of either overwhelming the player with too much information or annoying her by pedantically telling her information she already knows.

- **Call to action:** The game explicitly gives the player an action to perform and a reason to do so. This often takes the form of missions that are given to the player by NPCs. A good strategy is to present the player with a clear long-term goal and then give her progressively smaller medium- and short-term goals that must be accomplished on the way to the long-term goal.

  The *Legend of Zelda: Ocarina of Time* begins with the fairy Navi waking Link to tell him that he has been summoned by the Great Deku Tree. This is then reinforced by the first person Link encounters upon leaving his home, who tells him that it is a great honor to be summoned and that he should hurry. This gives Link a clear long-term goal of seeking the Great Deku Tree (and the Great Deku Tree's conversation with Navi before Link is awoken hints to the player that Link will be assigned a much longer-term goal once he arrives). Link's path to the Great Deku Tree is blocked by Mido, who tells him that he will need a sword and shield before venturing into the forest. This gives the player two medium-term goals that are required before she can achieve her long-term goal. Along the way to obtaining both, Link must navigate a small maze, converse with several people, and earn at least 40 rupees. These are all small-term, clear goals that are directly tied to the long-term goal of reaching the Great Deku Tree.

- **Map or guidance system:** Many games include a map or other GPS-style guidance system that directs the player toward her goals or toward the next step in her mission. For example, *Grand Theft Auto V* has a radar/mini-map in the corner of the screen with a highlighted route for the player to follow to the next objective. The world of *GTA V* is so vast that missions will often take the player into an unfamiliar part of the map, where the player relies very heavily on the GPS. However, be aware that this kind of guidance can lead to players spending most of their time just following the directions of the virtual GPS rather than actually thinking about a destination and choosing a path of their own, and this can increase the time it takes for the player to learn the layout of the game world.

- **Pop-ups:** Some games have contextual controls that change based on the objects near the player. In *Assassin's Creed IV: Black Flag*, the same button controls such diverse actions as opening doors, lighting barrels of gunpowder on fire, and taking control of mounted weapons. To help the player understand all the possibilities, pop-ups with the icon for the button and a very short description of the action appear whenever an action is possible.

Indirect Guidance

Indirect guidance is the art of influencing and guiding the player without her actually knowing that she is being controlled. Several different methods of indirect guidance can be useful to you as a designer. I was first introduced to the idea of indirect guidance by Jesse Schell, who presents it as "indirect control" in Chapter 16 of his book *The Art of Game Design: A Book of Lenses*. This list is an expansion of his six methods of indirect control.[1]

Constraints

If you give the player limited choices, she will choose one of them. This seems elementary, but think about the difference between a question that asks you to fill in the blank and one that gives you four choices to pick from. Without constraint, players run the risk of choice paralysis, which occurs when a person is presented with so many choices that she can't weigh them all against each other and instead just doesn't make a choice. This is the same reason that a restaurant menu might have 100 different items on it but only feature images of 20. The restaurant owners want to make it easier for you to make a decision about dinner.

Goals

In the previous section of this chapter, we discussed ways that goals can be used for direct guidance. Goals can also be used to guide the player indirectly. As Schell points out, if the player has a goal to collect bananas and has two possible doors to go through, placing clearly visible bananas behind one of the doors will encourage the player to walk through the door with bananas.

Players are also often willing to create their own goals, to which you can guide them by giving them the materials to achieve those goals. In the game *Minecraft* (the name of which includes the two direct instructions "mine" and "craft"), the designers defined which items the player are able to craft from various materials, and these design choices in turn imply the goals that players are able to create for themselves. Because most of the simplest recipes allow the player to make building materials, simple tools, and weapons, these recipes start the player down the path toward building a defensible fort to make her home. That goal then causes her to explore for materials. In particular, the knowledge that diamond makes the best tools will lead a player to explore deeper and deeper tunnels to find diamond (which is rare and only occurs at depths of about 50–55 meters below ground) and encourage her to expand the amount of the world that she has seen.

Physical Interface

Schell's book covers information about how the shape of a physical interface can be used to indirectly guide the player: If you give a player of *Guitar Hero* or *Rock Band* a guitar-shaped controller, she will generally expect to use it to play music. Giving a *Guitar Hero* player a regular game controller might lead her to think that she could control her character's movement

---

[1] Jesse Schell, *The Art of Game Design: A Book of Lenses* (Boca Raton, FL: CRC Press, 2008), pp. 283–298.

around the stage (because a standard game controller usually directs character movement), but with a guitar, her thoughts focus on making music.

Another way in which physical interface can be used for indirect guidance is through the rumble feature on most game controllers, which enables the controller to vibrate in the player's hands at various intensities. Actual automobile racetracks include red and white rumble strips on the inside of turns. The rumble strips alternate height along with color, allowing the driver to feel rumbling in the steering wheel if her wheel goes too far to the inside of the turn and makes contact with the rumble strip. This is helpful because racers are often trying to be as close to the inside of a turn as possible to be on the perfect racing line, and it's not possible to see exactly where the wheels are touching the road from inside the car. This same method is used in many racing games, rumbling the controller when the player is at the extreme inside edge of a turn. Expanding on this, you could imagine keeping the controller still when the player is on the track but causing it to rumble erratically if the player goes off the track into some grass. The tactile sensation would help the player understand that she should return to the track.

Visual Design

Visuals are used in several different ways to indirectly guide the player:

- **Light:** Humans are naturally drawn to light. If you place a player in a dark room with a pool of light at one end, she will usually move toward that light before exploring anything else.

- **Similarity:** Once a player has seen that something in the world is good in some way (helpful, healing, valuable, etc.), she will seek out similar things.

- **Trails:** Similarity can lead to a breadcrumb-trail-like effect where the player picks up a certain item and then follows a trail of similar items to a location that the designer wishes her to explore.

- **Landmarks:** Larger interesting objects can be used as landmarks. At the beginning of *Journey* by thatgamecompany, the player starts in the middle of a desert next to a sand dune. Everything around her is roughly the same color (sand) except for a dark stone marker at the top of the tallest nearby dune (see Figure 13.1, left). Because this marker is the only thing in the landscape that stands out, the player is driven to move up the dune toward it. Once she reaches the top, the camera rises above her, revealing a towering mountain with light bursting from the top (see Figure 13.1, right). The camera move causes the mountain to emerge from directly behind the stone marker, signifying to the player that the mountain is her new goal. The camera move directly transfers the goal state from the marker to the mountain.

When initially designing Disneyland, Walt Disney Imagineering (which at the time was named WED Enterprises) designed various landmarks to guide guests around the park and keep them from bunching up in the main hub. When guests first enter the park, they are located on Main Street USA, which looks like an idealized small American town from the early twentieth century. However, very soon into their journey down Main Street, they notice Sleeping Beauty's Castle at the end of the street and are immediately drawn to it. Upon finally reaching the castle, guests notice that it is much smaller than it initially appeared and that there's really nothing to do there. Now that they are in the main hub of Disneyland, they can see the mountain of the Matterhorn rising in front of them, the space-age statue at the entrance to Tomorrowland to their right, and the fort wall of Frontierland to their left. From their position in the hub, these new landmarks look much more interesting than the small castle, and guests disperse through the park toward these new landmarks.[2]

Figure 13.1   Landmarks in *Journey*

Landmarks are also used throughout the *Assassin's Creed* series. Whenever a player first enters a new part of the map, she will see that there are a few structures that are taller than the others in the area. In addition to the natural attraction of these landmarks, each is also a *view point* in the game from which the player can *synchronize*, which updates her in-game map with detailed information about the area. Because the designers have given the player both a landmark and a goal (filling in her map), they can guess that players will often seek a view point as their first activity in a new part of the world.

- **Arrows:** The annotated image in Figure 13.2 shows examples of subtle arrows used to direct the player in the game *Uncharted 3: Drake's Deception* by Naughty Dog. In these images, the player (as Drake) is chasing an enemy named Talbot.

  A. As the player vaults up to the roof of a building, there are numerous lines formed by physical edges and contrasting light that direct the player's attention to the left. These lines include the ledge she is vaulting, the short half-wall in front of her, the boards on the left, and even the facing of the gray chair.

  B. Once the player is on top of the roof, the camera angle rotates, and now the ledge, the wall, and the wooden planks all point directly at the next location where the player must jump (the roof of the building at the top of the frame). The cinderblock next to the wall in shot B even forms the head of an arrow made by the wall.

  This is particularly important in this moment of the chase because the landing area will collapse when the player hits it, which could cause the player to doubt whether jumping on that roof was the correct direction for her to have gone. The arrows in the environment minimize this doubt.

  The *Uncharted 3* dev team referred to wooden planks like those shown in this image as *diving boards*, and they were used throughout the game to guide players to make leaps in a specific direction. Emilia Schatz, the designer of this chase sequence, cited the usability research of Donald Norman as the inspiration for these diving boards.

[2] This was first pointed out to me by Scott Rogers, who covers it in more detail in Level 9 (i.e., Chapter 9) of his book *Level Up!: The Guide to Great Video Game Design* (Chichester, UK: Wiley, 2010).

In his books, Norman writes about the "affordances" implied by objects;[3] an edge of a platform implies that a person should be careful to stand back, but a diving board affords a person the ability to jump off of it. You can see another diving board in image A of Figure 13.3.

Figure 13.2 Arrows created by line and contrast in *Uncharted 3* provide subtle but powerful indirect guidance.

C. In this part of the same chase, Talbot has run through a gate and slams it in the player's face. The blue fabric on the short wall draws the player's eye to the left, and the folds in the fabric form an arrow to the left as well. Schatz also points out that the fabric here forms a continuance over the edge formed by the wall, causing the player to see the covered wall as less of a barrier.

D. The camera has now panned to the left, and from this perspective, the blue fabric forms an arrow pointing directly at the yellow window frame (the player's next goal). Bright blue and yellow colors like those seen in this image are used throughout the game to show the correct path to the player, so their presence here confirms the player's decision to head through the yellow window.

■ **Camera:** Many games that involve traversal puzzles use the camera to guide the player. By showing the player the next objective or next jump, the camera guides her in areas where she might otherwise be confused. This is demonstrated in the shots from *Uncharted 3* that are shown in Figure 13.3.

In shot A, the camera is directly behind the player; however, once the player jumps to the handholds in front of her, the camera pans to the left, directing her to the left (shot B). The camera continues to face left (shot C) until the player reaches the far left ladder, at which point the camera faces forward and moves down to reveal the yellow rungs going forward (shot D).

---

3   Norman, Donald. *The Design of Everyday Things* (New York: Basic Books, 1988).

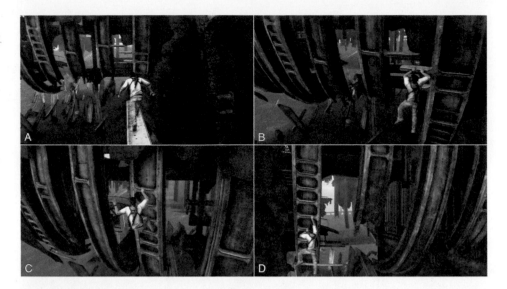

Figure 13.3   Camera-based guidance in Uncharted 3

- **Contrast:** The shots in Figures 13.2 and 13.3 each also demonstrate the use of contrast to guide player attention. There are several forms of contrast demonstrated in Figures 13.2 and 13.3 that contribute to player guidance:

  - **Brightness:** In shots A and B of Figure 13.2, the ledge and the wall that form the arrows have the highest range of brightness contrast in the image. The dark areas alongside light areas cause the lines to stand out visually.

  - **Texture:** In shots A and B of Figure 13.2, the wooden planks are smooth while the surrounding stone textures are rough.

  - **Color:** In shots C and D of Figure 13.2, the blue fabric, yellow window frame, and yellow bars contrast with the other colors (or lack thereof) in the scene. In shot D of Figure 13.3, the yellow rung at the bottom stands out because the rest of the scene is mostly blue and gray.

  - **Directionality:** Though it is not as commonly used as the other three, contrast in directionality can also be used effectively to draw the eye. In shot A of Figure 13.3, the horizontal rungs stand out because every other line in that part of the screen is vertical.

Audio Design

Schell states that music can be used to influence the player's mood and thereby her behavior.[4] Certain types of music have become linked to various types of activity: Slow, quiet, somewhat jazzy music is often linked to activities like sneaking or searching for clues, whereas loud,

---

[4] Schell, *Art of Game Design*, 292–293.

fast, powerful music like that in an action movie is better suited to scenes where the player is expected to brazenly fight through enemies and feel invincible.

Sound effects can also be used to influence player behavior by drawing attention to possible actions that the player can take. In the *Assassin's Creed* series, a shimmering, ringing sound effect plays whenever the player is near a treasure chest. This informs the player that she could choose to take the action of looking for the chest and, because it only happens with a chest is nearby, it tells her that it wouldn't be too far out of her way to do so. With a guaranteed reward in close proximity, the player is usually guided to search for the chest unless she is already engaged in another more important activity.

Player Avatar

The model of the player's avatar (that is, player character) can have a strong effect on player behavior. If the player character looks like a rock star and is holding a guitar, the player might expect for her character to be able to play music. If the player character has a sword, the player would expect to be able to hit things and run into combat. If the player character walks around in a wizard hat and long robe while holding a book instead of a weapon, the player would be encouraged to stay back from direct combat and focus on spells.

Non-Player Characters

Non-player characters (NPCs) in games are one of the most complex and flexible forms of indirect player guidance, and that guidance can take many forms.

Modeling Behavior

NPC characters can model several different types of behavior. In games, behavior modeling is the act of demonstrating a specific behavior and allowing the player to see the consequences of that behavior. Figure 13.4 shows various examples of behavior modeling in the game *Kya: Dark Lineage* by Atari. Types of modeling include:

- **Negative behavior:** In modeling negative behavior, the NPC does something that the player should avoid doing and demonstrates the consequences. In image A of Figure 13.4, one of the Nativs (circled in red) has stepped onto a circular trap on the ground and has been caught (it then lifted the Nativ up and flew him back toward pursuing enemies).

- **Positive behavior:** The other Nativ in image A (circled in green) jumped over a trap, showing how to avoid it. This is modeling positive behavior, showing the player how to act properly in the game world. Image B shows another example; the Nativ has stopped immediately before a place in the level where air currents blow swiftly from left to right in timed pulses, even though the air isn't blowing yet. The Nativ waits for the air current to blow, and once it stops, he continues running. This models for the player that she should stop before these air current areas, get the timing right, and then continue.

- **Safety:** In images C and D, the Nativ is jumping onto or into something that looks quite dangerous. However, because of his willingness to jump, the player knows that it is safe to follow.

Figure 13.4   NPC Nativs modeling behavior in *Kya: Dark Lineage*

Emotional Connections

Another way in which NPCs influence player behavior is through the emotional connections that the player develops with them.

In the *Journey* images shown in Figure 13.5, the player is following the NPC because of an emotional connection. The beginning of Journey is very lonely, and the NPC in these images is the first emotive creature that the player has encountered on her journey through the desert. It is also possible to cause the player to follow an NPC because of a negative emotional connection. For example, the NPC could steal something from the player and run, causing the player to chase him in order to retrieve her property. In either case, the reaction of the player is to follow the NPC, and this can be used to guide the player to another location.

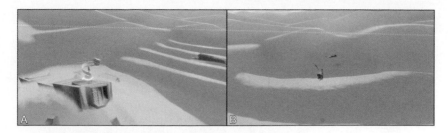

Figure 13.5 Emotional connections in *Journey*

Teaching New Skills and Concepts

While direct and indirect guidance usually focus on moving the player through the virtual locations of the game; this final section is devoted to guiding the player to a better understanding of how to play the game.

When games were simpler, it was possible to present the player with a simple diagram of the controls or even to just let them experiment. In *Super Mario Bros.*, one button caused Mario to jump, and the other button caused him to run (and to shoot fireballs once he picked up a fire flower). Through just a small amount of experimentation, the player could easily understand the functions of the A and B buttons on the Nintendo Entertainment System (NES) controller. Modern controllers, however, typically have two analog sticks (that can also be clicked like buttons), one 8-direction D-Pad, eight face buttons, two shoulder buttons, and two triggers. Even with all of these possible controls, many modern games have so many possible interactions allowed to the player that individual controller buttons have different uses based on the current context, as was mentioned when discussing pop-ups in the direct guidance section.

With so much complexity in some modern games, it becomes critical to teach the player how to play the game as she is playing. An instruction booklet won't cut it anymore; now the player needs to be guided though experiences that are properly sequenced.

Sequencing

Sequencing is the art of gently presenting new information to the player, and most examples follow the basic style shown in Figure 13.6. The figure shows several steps in the sequence from *Kya: Dark Lineage* that first introduces the player to a hovering mechanic that is used many times throughout the game.

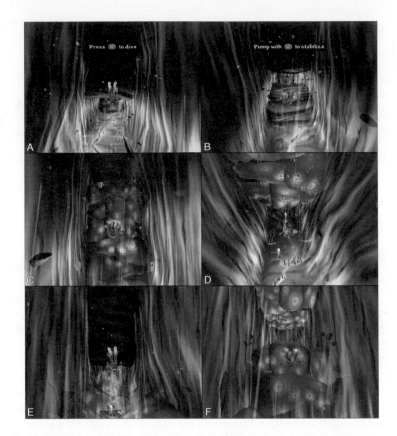

Figure 13.6 The sequence teaching hovering in *Kya: Dark Lineage*

- **Isolated introduction:** The player is introduced to the new mechanic such that she must use it to continue. In image A of Figure 13.6, air is constantly blowing upward, and the player must press and hold X to drop down far enough to go under the upcoming wall. There is no time pressure here, and nothing progresses until she holds X and passes under the wall.

- **Expansion:** Image B of Figure 13.6 shows the next step of this sequence. Here, the player is presented with walls blocking both the top and the bottom of the tunnel, so she must learn to tap the X button to hover in the middle of the tunnel. However, there is still no penalty for failing to do so correctly.

- **Adding danger:** In image C of Figure 13.6., some danger has been added. The red surface of the floor will harm the player if she gets too close; however, the roof is still completely safe, so not pressing X will keep the player safe. Next, in image D, the ceiling is dangerous, and the floor is completely safe, so if the player is still building her skills, she can simply hold the X button and glide forward along the floor.

■ **Increased difficulty:** Images E and F of Figure 13.6 show the final stages of this introduction sequence. In image E, the ceiling is still safe, but the player must navigate through the narrow channel ahead. Image F also requires navigation through a narrow channel, but now the danger has been expanded to both ceiling and floor. The player must demonstrate mastery of the X tapping mechanic to hover safely through the tunnel.[5]

I've used several images from *Kya: Dark Lineage* in this chapter because it is one of the best examples I have ever seen of this kind of sequencing. In the first six minutes of gameplay, the player learns about movement, jumping, avoiding traps, avoiding thorns, the ability to dribble and kick ball-like animals to disarm traps, avoiding horizontal air gusts, base jumping, hovering, stealth, and about a dozen other mechanics. All of them are taught using sequencing, and at the end of playing through the introduction for the first time, I remembered all of them.

This is common in many different games. In the *God of War* series, every time Kratos receives a new weapon or spell, he is told how to use it through pop-up text messages, but then he is immediately shown as well. If it's a spell like a lightning strike that could either be used to power devices or electrocute enemies, the player is first asked to use it for the non-combat purpose (e.g., the player receives the lightning spell in a room with locked doors and must use the lightning to activate devices to open the doors). Then, the player is presented with a combat that is easily won using the new spell. This not only gives the player experience using the spell in combat but also demonstrates the strength of the spell, making the player feel powerful.

Integration

Once the player understands how to use the new game mechanic in isolation (as described in the previous examples), it's time to teach her how to combine it with other mechanics. This can be done explicitly (for example, the player could be told that casting the lightning spell in water will expand its range from 6 feet to the size of the entire pool of water) or implicitly (for example, the player could be placed in combat in a pool of water and would notice herself that when she used the lightning spell, everything in the water was electrocuted, not just those enemies in range). When later in the game the player attained a spell that allowed her to drench her enemies and cause a temporary pool of water, she would immediately realize that this also allowed her to expand the reach of her lightning spell.

---

[5] Figure 13.6 also shows the use of color contrast to convey information about safety. The color of the tunnel shifts from green to red to show increasing danger, and in image F, the purple light at the end of the tunnel signifies to the player that this gauntlet will be ending soon.

Summary

There are many more methods of player guidance than could fit in this chapter, but I hope that it gave you a good introduction not only to some specific methods but also the reasoning behind why those methods are used. As you design your games, remember to keep player guidance in mind at all times. This can be one of the toughest things to do because to you, as the designer, every game mechanic will seem obvious. It is so difficult to break out of your own perspective that most game companies will seek dozens or hundreds of one-time testers to play their game throughout the development process. It is critically important as a designer to always find new people to test your game and give you feedback on the quality of the guidance from the perspective of someone who has never seen the game before. Games developed in isolation without the benefit of naïve testers will often either be too difficult for new players or at least have uneven, staggered rises in difficulty that cause frustration. Test early, test often, and test with new people whenever you can.

CHAPTER 14

THE DIGITAL GAME INDUSTRY

If you're taking the time to read this book and learn about prototyping games, it's probably safe to assume that you might have some interest in joining the game industry.

This chapter presents a little information about the current state of the industry. Then I talk a little about university games education programs. I give you some tips on meeting people, networking, and looking for work. Finally, I tell you about how to prepare for your own independent game projects.

About the Game Industry

The most definitive thing that I can tell you about the game industry right now is that it is changing. A lot of big names like Electronic Arts and Activision are still around, as they have been for the last three decades, but we've also seen the rise of new startups like Riot Games (which went from just a few employees in 2008 to having the most played online game world-wide today). Even just a few years ago, no one would have believed that a cell phone could be one of the most successful game platforms, but sales of games for Apple's iOS devices alone are now worth billions of dollars. Because everything is changing so quickly, I'm not going to give you specific numbers for most things. Instead, I'll point you to resources that can (and that will be updated yearly).

Entertainment Software Association Essential Facts

The ESA (http://theesa.com) is the trade association and lobbying organization for most large game development companies, and it was the ESA that successfully argued before the United States Supreme Court for games to be protected by the first amendment. The ESA releases a yearly "Essential Facts" report on the state of the game industry that you can find by searching for "ESA essential facts" on Google. There are certainly some bias issues with the reports (it's the ESA's job to see the game industry through rose-colored glasses), but it's still a good way to get an idea of what the overall industry looks like. Here are ten facts from their Essential Facts 2013 report:[1]

1. Fifty-eight percent of Americans play video games.
2. Consumers spent $20.77 billion on video games, hardware, and accessories in 2012.
3. Purchases of digital content, including games, add-on content, mobile apps, subscriptions, and social networking games accounted for 40% of game sales in 2012.
4. The average game player is 30 years old and has been playing games for 13 years.
5. The average age of the most frequent game purchaser is 35 years old.
6. Forty-five percent of all game players are women. Women over the age of 18 represent a larger portion of the game-playing population (31%) than boys age 17 or younger (19%).
7. Fifty-one percent of U.S. households own a dedicated game console, and those that do own an average of two.
8. Thirty-six percent of gamers play games on their smartphone, and 25% play games on their wireless device.
9. Ninety-one percent of games rated by the ESRB (Entertainment Software Ratings Board) in 2012 received a rating of "E" for Everyone, "E10+" for Everyone 10+, or "T" for Teen. (See www.esrb.org for more information on game ratings.)
10. Parents are present when games are purchased or rented 89% of the time.

---

[1] http://www.theesa.com/facts/pdfs/ESA_EF_2013.pdf

Things That Are Changing

The things that are changing in the industry have to do with working conditions, the costs of producing games, freemium games, and the renaissance independent game development.

Working Conditions at Game Companies

If you know nothing about the game industry, you might think that working at a game company would be fun and easy. If you know a little about it, you might have heard that game company employees routinely work 60-hour weeks with mandatory overtime for no additional pay. Though the real story now for most companies is better than that, the stories you may have heard were based on fact, and I do have friends in the industry who still have mandatory 70-hour workweeks (10 hours/day, no weekends) during "crunch time" on their projects, but luckily that trend has diminished greatly over the past decade. Now, most companies, especially larger companies, will still ask you to work overtime sometimes, but the stories of game developers who haven't seen their partners or kids for a week are more and more rare (though sadly, they do still exist). However, when interviewing with any game company, you should definitely ask about their overtime policy and history of crunch time on projects.

Rising Costs of AAA Development

Each generation of gaming consoles has seen a rise in the cost of developing a top title (also known as a "AAA" game, pronounced "triple-a") This was especially true with the PlayStation 3 and Xbox 360 versus the PlayStation 2 and Xbox, and the trend will continue for the Xbox One and PlayStation 4 as well. Teams for AAA titles are now routinely over 100 or 200 people, and even some with apparently small teams actually have outsourced several aspects of the game's development to other studios with hundreds of their own employees. It is still unusual—but no longer unheard of—for a AAA game budget to exceed $100 million and have a combined total team of over 1,000 people spread across several studios.

The effect of all of this on the game industry has been the same as the effect that budget inflation had on the film industry: The more money that a company will be spending on a project, the less willing they are to take risks. This is why in the ESA's list of the top 20 best-selling games of 2012 you will not find a single game that isn't a sequel (see Figure 14.1).

1 CALL OF DUTY: BLACK OPS II	**11** JUST DANCE 3
2 MADDEN NFL 13	**12** SKYLANDERS GIANTS
3 HALO 4	**13** MASS EFFECT 3
4 ASSASSIN'S CREED III	**14** NBA 2K12
5 JUST DANCE 4	**15** NCAA FOOTBALL 13
6 NBA 2K13	**16** NEW SUPER MARIO BROS. 2
7 CALL OF DUTY: MODERN WARFARE 3	**17** BATTLEFIELD 3
8 BORDERLANDS 2	**18** ELDER SCROLLS V: SKYRIM
9 LEGO BATMAN 2: DC SUPER HEROES	**19** BATMAN: ARKHAM CITY
10 FIFA SOCCER 13	**20** MARIO KART 7

Figure 14.1   The 20 top-selling games in 2012 by units sold (according to ESA Essential Facts 2013)

The Rise (and Possible Fall) of Freemium Games

According to Flurry Analytics, there was a six-month period between January and June of 2011 when free-to-play games rapidly overtook paid games in terms of iOS revenue.[2] In January of 2011, *premium* games (which are purchased upfront) accounted for 61% of the game revenue on the iOS App Store. By June, that number had crashed down to 35%, with 65% of revenue then coming from *freemium* games. The freemium model—where the player gets the game for free but is asked to pay small amounts of money to gain gameplay advantages or customization— catapulted Zynga from a two-person start-up to over 2,000 employees in just a few years. However, this model has been shown to work much better for casual games than more traditional genres, and some developers of more traditional genres who are now creating mobile games have chosen to return to the premium model because they believe that their market is averse to the freemium model.

A few freemium games have done well with a more core (that is, less-casual) audience of gamers. The primary differentiating factor between these and the casual freemium games is that many of the casual games allow and encourage players to purchase a competitive edge in the game (i.e., pay more to win more), whereas core games like *Team Fortress 2* (*TF2*) only allow players to purchase aesthetic items (e.g., clothing) or items that change game mechanics without making them imbalanced (e.g., the Black Box rocket launcher for Soldiers that has −25% clip size yet grants the Soldier +15 health whenever it hits an enemy). In addition, nearly every item that is purchasable in *TF2* can alternatively be crafted by players from items gained through gameplay. The critical element in this is that core players don't want to feel that someone else has bought a gameplay advantage over them.

Whether you choose to go for freemium or premium for your game relies largely on the genre of game you want to develop and the market and type of players that you are seeking. Look at other games in the market and see what the standards are, then decide whether you want to go along with them or buck the trend.

The Rise of the Indie Scene

While AAA games have become much more expensive to create, the ubiquity of free or cheap game development tools like Unity, GameMaker, and Unreal Engine has led to the rise of a worldwide independent development community to an extent that has never been seen before. As you'll see when you read the rest of this book, almost anyone can learn to program, and dozens of developers have now proven that all you need to make a game is a great idea, some talent, and a lot of time. Many of the most famous independent game projects started as the passion project of a single person, including *Minecraft*, *Spelunky*, and *The Stanley Parable*. IndieCade is a game festival that started in 2005 and is dedicated exclusively to independent games. Beyond that, there are dozens of other conferences that either focus on independent development or have a track or contest for indie developers.[3] It is now easier than it has ever been to make video games, and the rest of this book will teach you how.

---

[2] "Free-to-play Revenue Overtakes Premium Revenue in the App Store" by Jeferson Valadares (Jul 07, 2011), http://blog.flurry.com/bid/65656/Free-to-play-Revenue-Overtakes-Premium-Revenue-in-the-App-Store.

[3] Full disclosure: Since IndieCade 2013, I have been the IndieCade Chair of Education and Advancement and programmed the IndieXchange and Game U conference tracks. I'm honored to be part of such a fantastic organization and conference.

Game Education

Over the past decade, game design and development education at the university level has gone from a curiosity to a legitimate field of study. *The Princeton Review* now ranks the top graduate and undergraduate game programs yearly, and there are now even programs offering Ph.D. degrees in games.

There are generally two top questions that people have about these programs:

- Should I attend a games education program?
- Which games education program should I attend?

I will attempt to answer these questions in the next two sections.

Should I Enroll in a Games Education Program?

As a professor who has spent the last several years of my life teaching in these programs, I can say that my answer to this question is a qualified yes. There are several clear benefits to game education programs:

- You have a concentrated space and time in which to build your design and development skills in a structured way.
- You'll be surrounded both by faculty who can give you honest, meaningful feedback on your work and peers who can become great collaborators. In addition, many faculty in these programs have worked in the game industry and have connections to several game companies.
- Many game companies actively recruit from the top schools. Being at one of them means that you could have the chance to interview for an internship with one of your favorite studios.
- When new employees are hired out of university game programs—especially master-level programs—they usually enter the company at a higher level than others. Traditionally, people got into game companies by working in QA (quality assurance) and testing games. If they excelled at QA, they could get noticed and move up into one of the other positions. Although this is still a very valid way to enter the industry, I have seen new people coming out of university programs often get hired above talented people with several years of seniority who came up through QA.
- Higher education in general will push you to grow and become a better person.

However, there are some definite caveats. School takes both time and money. If you don't have a bachelor's degree, I personally think that you should absolutely get one. Throughout your life, it will open more doors and grant you more opportunities than not having one. A master's degree is much less necessary in the industry, but programs at the graduate level are able to offer a much more focused education and can be truly transformative. Masters programs generally take between 2 and 3 years and can cost $60,000 or more. However, as my professor Dr. Randy Pausch was fond of saying, you can always make more money, and loans or scholarships can help pay for school; the thing you can't get back is time. You shouldn't ask yourself whether grad school is worth the money; it's much more important to ask yourself whether it's worth the time.

Which Games Education Program?

There are many, many games education programs out there, and new ones are being added every year. *The Princeton Review*'s list of the top schools is generally well respected, but it's much more important that you pick a school that is right for you and what you want to do in the industry. Take time to research the program and learn about their classes and faculty. Investigate how much emphasis they put on the different aspects of game development: design, art, programming, management, and so on. Are the program's faculty currently working in the game industry, or do they focus entirely on teaching? Each school will have certain aspects that are their particular strengths.

As a student, I attended Carnegie Mellon University's Entertainment Technology Center (ETC) for my Master of Entertainment Technology degree. At its core, the ETC is based around teamwork and client work. In the first semester (which was for me the best educational semester I have ever experienced), each incoming student works on five collaborative two-week assignments with a randomly selected team of peers in a class called Building Virtual Worlds (BVW). The incoming class size is generally more than 60 students, and this helps them experience working with new people continuously throughout the semester. In that semester, each person works about 80 hours each week on her team assignment in addition to taking two or three other classes that supplement BVW. Then, for the remaining three semesters, each student is assigned to a single project team for the full semester and takes only one additional class. Most of these semester-long projects have a real client for whom they are being produced, so ETC students learn first-hand how to manage client expectations, work with peers, handle internal disputes and external change orders, and generally get several years' worth of industry experience in two years of school. The goal of the ETC is to prep game designers, producers, programmers, and technical artists for work on industry teams.

In contrast, the #1 ranked Master of Fine Arts program in the Interactive Media & Games Division (IMGD) at the University of Southern California (where I taught for four years) is structured very differently. The size of the incoming cohort each year is generally 15 or less, and all students take several different classes together in the first year. Though there are group projects, the students do several independent assignments as well. In the second year, students are encouraged to branch out and explore their personal interests. Roughly half of the classes in the second year are taken with their cohort, but the other half can be selected from across the university. The third year in the IMGD is devoted almost entirely to each student's work on her individual thesis project. Though each student leads a thesis project, students very rarely work alone. Most thesis teams are 6 to 10 people in size, and the other team members are pulled from interested students across the university. Each thesis project also has a thesis committee composed of mentors from industry and academia who are interested in the project and led by a thesis chair from the IMGD faculty. The goal of the IMGD is to "create thought leaders." It is more important to this program that the individual students grow and produce something innovative than that they are prepared for industry jobs.

As you can imagine, each of these programs benefit students in very different ways. I have chosen these two to illustrate the point because they are the two with which I am most familiar, but every single school is different, and you owe it to yourself to learn the goals that each school has for their students and how they hope to achieve them through the classes they teach.

Getting into the Industry

The content in this section is condensed from the "Networking with the Pros" talk that I gave at the 2010 Game Developers Conference Online. If you'd like to see the expanded version, you can find the slides on the website for this book.[4]

Meeting People in the Industry

The best way to meet people in the game industry is to go where they are. If you're interested in board games, this means Gen Con; if you are interested in AAA development, this means the Game Developers Conference in San Francisco; and if you're interested in independent game development, this means IndieCade. Many other conferences out there are quite good, but those are the three that have the biggest draw from each of those groups.[5]

However, being at a dev conference only really means that you are *co-located* with game developers. In order to meet them, you need to find a way to go up and say hello. Some good times to do so include parties, after a talk that they've given, when they're working the Expo floor, and so on. However, in each of these cases, you need to be courteous, concise, and respectful both to the developer and especially to the other people who want to talk to her. Game developers are busy people, and they each have a reason to be at the conference; they too want to meet people, expand their networks, and talk shop with other developers. So don't take too much of their time, don't ever make them feel trapped in a conversation with you, and always have something to bring to the table. That is, make sure that you have something to say that will be interesting to them before you start the conversation.

When meeting people for the first time, don't act like a fawning fan. Every game designer from Will Wright to Jenova Chen is a regular person, and very few of them have any interest in being idolized. Along these lines, avoid saying things like "I love you! I'm your biggest fan!" Frankly, that's pretty damn creepy. Instead, it's much better to say things like "I really enjoyed playing *Journey*." That way, you're complimenting the game—a game that several people worked on— rather than complimenting the individual person, whom you actually know very little about.

Of course, the very best time to meet someone new is when you're introduced. This gives you an in as well as something to talk about (your mutual friend). However, when this happens, you have a critical responsibility to the friend that introduced you—the responsibility to not make her look bad. Whenever someone introduces you, she is vouching for you, and if you do something embarrassing, it reflects badly on her.

---

[4] The complete slides from the talk are available at http://book.prototools.net.
[5] E3 and PAX are other famous game conferences, but you're less likely to meet actual game developers there.

Also, don't just focus on meeting famous game developers. Everyone at these conferences loves games, and students and volunteers at the conference are some of the most passionate and creative people you can talk to. Plus, who knows, it's possible that anyone you meet at a dev conference could be the next great designer that everyone is talking about, and later they'll be a great person to have take a look at your games as you develop them.

Things to Take to the Game Conference

If you're going to meet people, you should always have business cards on you. You can put whatever you want on the front, as long as you make sure it's legible. I usually recommend leaving the back blank so that the person to whom you give the card can write notes on it that will remind her later of what you talked about.

Other things I tend to take with me include the following:

- Breath mints and toothpicks. Seriously.
- A pocket tool like a small Leatherman. It's nice to be the person in the room who can fix little things that break.
- A resume. I don't carry these with me anymore, since I'm very happy with my current job, but if you're seeking a job, you really want to have a few copies with you.

Following Up

So, you've met someone at the conference and gotten her business card. What's the next step?

About two weeks after the conference, write the person an email. You generally want to wait a couple of weeks because everyone is completely flooded with emails and work when they get back from a dev conference. Your email should generally follow a format similar to that shown in Figure 14.2.

Send the letter and wait a couple of weeks. If you don't hear anything back, write them one more time with a lead in like "I'm willing to bet that you were pretty busy after the conference, so I wanted to write again and make sure that you got my email."

Interviewing

If everything goes well, you'll have a chance to interview at the studio. Now, how do you prepare?

Questions to Ask Before the Day of the Interview

When you interview, you'll be talking to people who are actually on game development teams. Before the interview, the person you talk to will be a recruiter. Part of the recruiter's job is to make sure that candidates are properly prepared for the interview, and her evaluation at the end of the year will be partially based on the quality of candidates she brings in. This means that it is in her best interest for you to be perfect for the job, and she is more than willing to answer any questions that will help you better prepare for the interview.

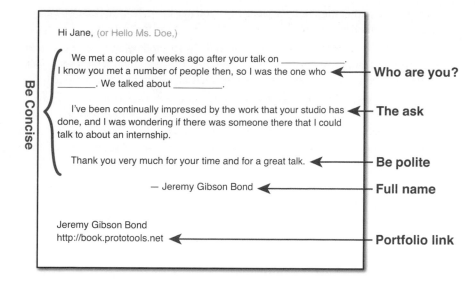

Figure 14.2 An example letter

Questions to ask include:

- **What would my job be?** You want to know the answer to this as specifically as possible so that you can prep, though you don't want to ask for any information that is already made clear in the job posting.

- **On which project would I be working?** This will also answer whether they're interviewing you for a specific position or if they're interested in hiring good people without a specific project in mind.

- **What is the company culture like?** Each company culture is different, particularly in the game industry. A question like this can also lead to a discussion of things like overtime and crunch time. You don't really need to know the answer to working conditions questions like those at this point, but you definitely need to know them before you sign a contract.

- **What would be appropriate for me to wear to the interview?** Many, many people skip this simple but important question. In general, I tend to dress more formally than I would on a normal workday, but for most game companies, that doesn't mean wearing a suit (and it almost never means wearing a tie). Remember, you're not going to a nice dinner, a party, a date, or a religious ceremony. My wife, a professional costume designer and professor, recommends this: You want to look nice, but you want to make sure that the focus is on your skills and mind, not how you look.

Another thing to consider is that while you definitely want to wear something that makes you feel comfortable, you also want to wear something that makes the interviewers feel comfortable. Every studio talks at some point to investors, the press, publishers, and other people who tend to work in more formal cultures than a game development studio. One of the things that the studio needs to know about you is whether you can be part of those discussions or whether they would have to hide you in a back room so you don't embarrass them when guests visit. Be sure that they place you in the former category.

There are a lot of different opinions out there on the web about what is appropriate to wear, so the best thing you can do is ask the recruiter. The recruiter will have seen every candidate who comes in, and she'll know what works and what doesn't.

- **Are there any games I should make sure to play before the interview?** You absolutely must play games made by the studio where you're interviewing before you go in, and if you're interviewing to work on a specific game, it is unforgivable to have not played it or its prequels. This question is more about which of their competitor's games they think you should have played.

- **Can you tell me who will be interviewing me?** If you know ahead of time who you'll be speaking with, you can do some research into their background. Knowing other projects that your interviewers worked on before coming to the current studio or other studios where they worked previously can give you more insight into their background and more things to talk about.

There are also questions you should definitely not ask. Questions to *not* ask include the following:

- **What games has the studio made? / How long has the studio been around?** The answers to these questions are easily available online. Asking something like this makes it seem like you haven't done your research before coming to the interview (and consequently like you don't really care much about the interview or job).

- **How much will I get paid?** Though this will eventually be a very important question to ask, it's inappropriate to ask this of an interviewer or recruiter. Instead, it will be part of your negotiations after you have been offered the job. For information on industry averages, you can look to the Game Developer Salary Survey at GameCareerGuide.com.[6]

After the Interview

After the interview, it's best to send handwritten thank you notes to the people with whom you spoke. Try to take notes throughout the actual interview so that you can comment on something specific to each individual. "Thank you very much for walking me through the studio and especially for introducing me to Team X" is much better than "It was great to me you, and I'm glad we talked about things." Just like items in games, handwritten letters are valuable because they are rare. Every month, I get thousands of emails, over 100 printed letters through postal mail, and less than 1 handwritten thank you note. Handwritten notes are never spam.

---

[6] The salary surveys were traditionally a yearly article in *Game Developer Magazine,* which has the same owners as GameCareerGuide.com. However, the magazine ceased publication in 2013. The salary survey that was published in 2013 can still be seen at http://gamecareerguide.com/features/1279/game_developer_salary_survey_.php.

Don't Wait to Start Making Games!

Just because you're not yet a game company employee doesn't mean that you can't make games. After you've finished this book and gotten some experience programming and developing prototypes, you'll probably be looking for a game to work on. Here are some tips for that time.

Join a Project

I'm sure you've got a ton of great ideas for games bouncing around in your head, but the best thing you can do if you're new to development is to join a team that already has some experience developing a game. Working with a team of other developers, even if they're still learning like you are, is one of the best ways to quickly grow your skills.

Start Your Own Project

Once you've either gotten some experience on a team or if you just can't find a team to work with, it's time to start creating your own games. To do so, you will need five critical elements.

The Right Idea

There are millions of different game ideas out there. You need to pick one that will actually work. It needs to be something that you know you won't lose interest in, something that doesn't just copy a game you love, something that other people find interesting, and most importantly, something that you know you can make. This leads us to...

The Right Scope

The number one thing that stops teams from finishing games is overscoping. Most new developers don't understand how long it can take to make a game, so their game concepts are drastically overscoped. Scoping-down is the process of getting the game down to its bare essentials and eliminating fluff. For a game to have good scope, you must have a true and realistic understanding of the amount of effort it will take to implement the game, and you must make sure—you must be absolutely certain—that you have the team and the time to finish it.

It is drastically better to make a tiny game and expand upon it than to start by trying to make something huge. Remember that most games you have played took a large team of professionals about two years and millions of dollars to make. Even indie games often take years of work by an extremely talented team. When you're just starting out, think small. You can always add more to the game later, and having a small, finished game is much more impressive to people in the industry than having a large, unfinished one.

The Right Team

Working on a game with someone is a long-term relationship, and you need to treat it that way. It's also sadly true that the things that make you great friends with someone might not be the same things that are required to make you great team members. When you're thinking about working with people, you want to make sure that they have similar work habits to yours, and it's best if they tend to work at similar times of day as well. Even if you're part of a remote team, it can really help to be text or video chatting with your teammates while you work.

While creating your team, you also need to have a conversation about ownership of the intellectual property (IP) of the game. If there is no agreement in place, the default is that everyone who had anything to do with the project owns an equal share.[7] IP issues are really sticky, and they may seem kind of ridiculous to talk about before any game exists, but it is a critical conversation to have. However, the flip side of this is that I have actually seen game teams never get started because people were bickering about the IP ownership of a game that didn't exist. You definitely don't want to get stuck in that trap.

The Right Schedule

In Chapter 27, "The Agile Mentality," I cover agile development practices and burndown charts. Make sure that you read it before you start a project. Though your mileage may vary, I have found that for the vast majority of my student teams, burndown charts are a fantastic tool to keep them on track and aware of where each person is in their individual development tasks. In addition, burndown charts do a fantastic job of helping you to understand the difference between how long you estimate a task will take and how long it actually takes you to accomplish it. By looking at the difference between the two in the chart up to the point where you are currently, you can get a more realistic estimate of how long it will take you to complete the remaining tasks.

The Will to Finish

As you make progress on your project, you will come to a point where you clearly see all the things that you could have done better. You'll see that your code is a mess, your art could be better, and the design has some holes in it. A lot of teams get to this point surprisingly close to the end of the project. If you are near the end, you need to push on through. *You must have the will to finish your game.* If the number one killer of games is bad scoping, the number two killer is that the last 10% of the project is always the hardest climb. Keep pushing, because even if the game isn't perfect—and trust me, no game ever is—even if the game isn't all you hoped, even if it is far less than what you hoped, it will be done. You will be a game developer with a finished title, and that means a tremendous amount to everyone you hope to work with in the future.

Summary

There is much more to be learned about the game industry than was able to fit in this single chapter. Luckily, many websites and publications cover the game industry, and there are often talks at conferences about both what it takes to join the industry and the process of starting a company. A simple web search should surface many of them.

If you do choose to start a company, be sure that you find a lawyer and an accountant that you can trust to help you before you actually run into any bumps in the process. Lawyers and accountants have years of training in how to build and protect companies, and having them available to consult with can make your path to incorporation much, much easier.

---

[7] I am not a lawyer, and I am not trying to give legal advice. I'm just sharing my personal understanding of the situation. If you have any friends who are lawyers, I recommend asking them about it or looking for information online.

PART II

DIGITAL PROTOTYPING

CHAPTER 15

THINKING IN DIGITAL SYSTEMS

If you've never programmed before, this chapter will be your introduction to a new world: one where you have the ability and skills to make digital prototypes of the games you imagine.

This chapter describes the mindset you need to have when approaching programming projects. It gives you exercises to explore that mindset and helps you think about the world in terms of systems of interconnected relationships and meaning.

At the conclusion of this chapter, you will be in the right mindset to explore the challenges of the "Digital Prototyping" part of this book.

Systems Thinking in Board Games

In the first part of the book, you learned that games are created from interconnected systems. In games, these systems are encoded into the rules of the game and the players themselves; all players bring certain expectations, abilities, knowledge, and social norms to the games that they play. For example, when you think about a standard pair of six-sided dice, there are specific expected and unexpected behaviors that the dice carry with them in most board games:

- **Common expected behaviors of 2d6 (two six-sided dice) in board games**
    1. Each die is rolled to generate a random number between 1 and 6 (inclusive).
    2. The dice are often rolled together, especially if they are the same color and size.
    3. When rolled together, the dice are usually summed. For example, a 3 on one die and a 4 on the other would sum to a total of 7.
    4. If "doubles" are rolled (that is, both dice show the same value), there is sometimes a special benefit for the player.
- **Common unexpected behaviors of 2d6 in board games**
    1. A player will not just place the dice on the values that she would prefer to have.
    2. The dice must stay on the table and must land completely flat on a side to be considered a valid roll. Otherwise, they are rerolled.
    3. Once rolled, the dice are generally not touched for the rest of that player's turn.
    4. Dice are generally not thrown at other players.

While it may seem somewhat pedantic to explore such simple, often unwritten, rules in detail, it serves to show how many of the rules of board games are not actually written in the rule book, rather they are based on the shared understanding of *fair play* among the players. This idea is incumbent in the concept of the magic circle, and it's a large part of what makes it so easy for a group of children to make up a game that they all intuitively understand how to play. Most human players carry within them massive preconceptions about how games are played.

Computer games, however, rely on specific instructions to do absolutely everything. At their core, regardless of how powerful they have become over the past several decades, computers are mindless machines that follow very specific instructions several million times per second. It is up to you, the programmer, to provide the computer with a semblance of intelligence by encoding your ideas into very simple instructions for it to follow.

An Exercise in Simple Instructions

One classic exercise for budding computer science students to help them understand how to think in terms of very simple instructions involves telling another person how to stand up from a prone position. You'll need a friend for this.

Ask your friend to lie on his back on the floor, and once he is there, tell him to only follow your exact instructions to the letter. Your goal is to give your friend instructions that will move him into a standing position, however, you cannot use any complex commands like "stand up." Instead, you must only use the kind of simple commands that you might imagine giving to a robot. For example:

- Bend your left elbow closed 90 degrees.
- Extend your right leg halfway.
- Place your left hand on the ground with your palm facing downward.
- Point your right arm at the television.

In reality, even these simple instructions are drastically more complex than anything that could be sent to most robots, and they're pretty open to interpretation. However, for the sake of this exercise, this level of simplicity will suffice.

Give it a try.

How long did it take you to give your friend the right instructions to stand up? If you and your friend try to follow both the rules and the spirit of the exercise, it will take quite a while. If you try it with different people, you'll find that it takes much, much longer if your friend doesn't know ahead of time that you are trying to get him to stand up.

How old were you the first time you were asked by a member of your family to set the table for a meal? I think I was only about four when my parents decided that I could handle that complex task with my only instruction being "please set the table for dinner." Based on the exercise that you just completed, imagine how many simple instructions you would have to give to a person to recreate the complex task of setting the table, yet many children are able to do this before they start elementary school.

What This Means to Digital Programming

Now, of course, I didn't give you that exercise to discourage you. In fact, the following two chapters are meant to be really inspirational! Rather, it was given to help you understand the mentality of computers and to set up several metaphors for aspects of computer programming. Let's take a look.

Computer Language

When I gave you the list of four example commands that you could give, I was outlining the parameters of the language that you could use to talk to your friend. Obviously, this was a pretty loose language definition. Throughout this book, we will be using the programming language C# (pronounced "see sharp"), and luckily, its language definition is far more specific. We explore C# much more later in this part of the book, but suffice to say that I have taught hundreds of students several different programming languages over more than a decade, and my experience has shown me that C# is one of the best languages for someone to learn as their first programming language. Though it requires slightly more diligence than simpler languages like Processing or JavaScript, it gives learners a far better understanding of core development concepts that will help them throughout their game prototyping and development careers, and it enforces good coding practices that eventually make code development faster and easier.

Code Libraries

In the previous exercise, you can see that it would have been much easier to have been able to tell your friend to "stand up" rather than going through the trouble of having to give so many low-level commands. In that case, "stand up" would have been a multipurpose high-level instruction that could be used to tell your friend what you wanted regardless of the starting position that he was in. Similarly, "please set the table" is a common, high-level instruction that generates the desired outcome regardless of what meal is bring prepared, how many people will be eating, or even what household you are in. In C#, collections of high-level instructions for common behaviors are called *code libraries*, and there are hundreds of them available to you as a C# and Unity developer.

The most common code library that you will use is the collection of code that tailors C# to work properly with the Unity development environment. In your code, this extremely powerful library will be imported under the name `UnityEngine`. The `UnityEngine` library includes code for the following:

- Awesome lighting effects like fog and reflections
- Physics simulations that cover gravity, collisions, and even cloth simulation
- Input from mouse, keyboard, gamepad, and touch-based tablets
- Thousands of other things

In addition, there are hundreds of thousands of free (and paid) code libraries out there to help make your coding easier. If the thing you want to do is pretty common (e.g., moving an object across the screen smoothly over the course of one second), there's a good chance that someone has already written a great code library to do so (in this case, the free library iTween by Bob Berkebile, http://itween.pixelplacement.com/index.php).

The prevalence of great code libraries for Unity and C# means that you can concentrate on writing code for the new, unique aspects of your games rather than reinventing the wheel every time you start a new game project. In time, you will also start collecting commonly used bits of your own code into libraries that you will use across multiple projects. In this book, we will start doing so by creating a code library called `ProtoTools` that will grow in capability across several projects in this book.

Development Environment

The Unity game development environment is an essential part of your development experience. The Unity application can best be thought of as an environment in which to collect and compose all of the assets that you create for a game. In Unity, you will bring together 3D models, music and audio clips, 2D graphics and textures, and the C# scripts that you author. None of these assets are created directly within Unity, rather it is through Unity that they are all brought together into a cohesive computer game. Unity will also be used to position game objects in three-dimensional space, handle user input, set up a virtual camera in your scene, and finally compile all of these assets together into a working, executable game. The capabilities of Unity are discussed extensively in Chapter 16, "Introducing Our Development Environment: Unity."

Breaking Down Complex Problems into Simpler Ones

One of the key things you must have noticed in the exercise is that the exclusion from giving complex commands like "stand up" meant that you needed to think about breaking complex commands down into smaller, more discrete commands. Although this activity was difficult in the exercise, in your programming, you will find the skill of breaking complex tasks into simpler ones to be one of the greatest tools that you have for tackling the challenges that you face and helping you make the games you want one small piece at a time. This is a skill that I use every day in the development of my games, and I promise that it will serve you well. As an example, let's break down the *Apple Picker* game that you will make in Chapter 28, "Prototype 1: *Apple Picker*" into simple commands.

Game Analysis: *Apple Picker*

Apple Picker is the first prototype that you will make in this book (built in Chapter 28. It is based on the game play of the classic Activision game *Kaboom!*, which was designed by Larry Kaplan and was published by Activision in 1981.[1] Many clones of *Kaboom!* have been made through the years, and ours is a somewhat less violent version. In the original game, the player moved buckets back and forth in an attempt to catch bombs being dropped by a "Mad Bomber." In our version, the player uses a basket to collect apples that are falling from a tree (see Figure 15.1).

Figure 15.1   The *Apple Picker* game made in Chapter 28

---

[1] http://en.wikipedia.org/wiki/Kaboom!_(video_game)

In this analysis, we will look at each of the GameObjects in *Apple Picker*, analyze each of their behaviors, and break those behaviors down to simple commands in flowchart form. This will demonstrate how simple commands can lead to complex behavior and fun gameplay. I recommend searching for "play Kaboom!" online to see whether you can find an online version of the game to play before digging into this analysis, but the game is simple enough that doing so is not necessary. You can also find a version of the *Apple Picker* game prototype on the http://book.prototools.net website under Chapter 15, though the *Apple Picker* game is only a single endless level, whereas *Kaboom!* had eight difficulty levels.

Apple Picker Basic Gameplay

The player controls the three baskets at the bottom of the screen and is able to move them left and right using the mouse. The apple tree moves back and forth rapidly while dropping apples, and the player must catch the apples using her baskets before they hit the ground. For each apple that the player catches, she earns points, but if even a single apple hits the ground, it and all other remaining apples will disappear, and the player will lose a basket. When the player loses all three baskets, the game is over. (There are a few other rules in the original *Kaboom!* game about the number of points earned per bomb [apple] and how the various levels progress, but those are unimportant for this analysis.)

Apple Picker GameObjects

In Unity terminology, any object in the game—usually meaning anything that you see on screen—is a GameObject. We can also use this term in discussing the elements seen in Figure 15.2. For later consistency with our Unity projects, I will capitalize the name of all GameObjects (e.g., Apples, Baskets, and AppleTree) in the following list .

A. **Baskets:** Controlled by the player, the Baskets move left and right following the player's mouse movements. When a Basket hits an Apple, the Apple is caught, and the player gains points.

B. **Apples:** The Apples are dropped by the AppleTree and fall straight down. If an Apple collides with any of the three Baskets, it is caught and disappears from the screen (granting the player some points). If an Apple hits the bottom of the play window, it disappears, and it causes all other Apples on screen to disappear as well. This destroys one of the Baskets (starting at the bottom), and then the AppleTree starts dropping Apples again.

C. **AppleTree:** The AppleTree moves left and right randomly while dropping Apples. The Apples are dropped at a regular interval, so the only randomness in the behavior is the left and right movement.

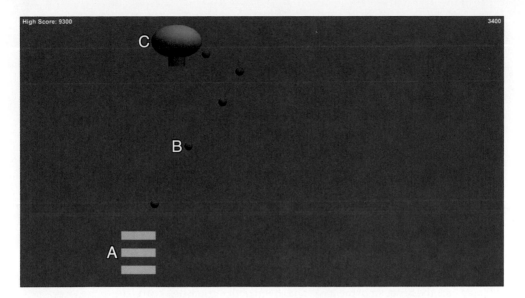

Figure 15.2   *Apple Picker* with GameObjects labeled

Apple Picker GameObject Action Lists

In this analysis, we're not going to consider the difficulty level or the round structure that are present in the original *Kaboom!* game. Instead we will focus on the moment-to-moment actions taken by each GameObject.

Basket Actions

Basket actions include the following:

- Move left and right following the player's mouse.
- If any Basket collides with an Apple, catch the Apple.[2]

That's it! The Baskets are very simple.

Apple Actions

Apple actions include the following:

- Fall down.
- If an Apple hits the ground, it disappears and causes other Apples to disappear.

The Apples are also very simple.

---

[2] It would also be possible to make this reaction to collisions part of the Apple actions, but I have chosen to make it part of Basket.

AppleTree Actions

AppleTree actions include the following:

- Move left and right randomly.
- Drop an Apple every 0.5 seconds.

The AppleTree is pretty simple too.

Apple Picker GameObject Flowcharts

A flowchart is often a good way to think about how the flow of actions and decisions works in your game. Let's look at some for *Apple Picker*. Though the following flowcharts refer to things like adding points and ending the game, right now, we're just looking at the actions that take place in a single round, so we're not worrying about how those kinds of scoring and round actions actually work.

Basket Flowchart

In Figure 15.3 the behavior of the Basket has been outlined in a flowchart. The game loops through this flowchart every *frame* (which is at least 30 times every second). This is shown by the oval that is at the top left of the chart. Actions are shown in boxes (e.g., *Match Left/Right Mouse Movement*), and decisions are shown as diamonds. See the sidebar "Frames in Computer Games" to learn more about what constitutes a frame.

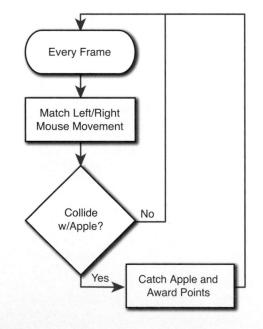

Figure 15.3   Basket flowchart

FRAMES IN COMPUTER GAMES

The term *frame* comes from the world of film. Historically, films were composed of strips of celluloid containing thousands of individual pictures (known as frames). When those pictures were shown in quick succession (at either 16 or 24 frames per second [fps]), it produced the illusion of movement. In television, the movement was constructed from a series of electronic images projected onto the screen, which were also called frames (and operated at about 30 fps).

When computer graphics became fast enough to show animation and other moving images, each individual image shown on the computer screen was also called a frame. In addition, all of the computation that takes place leading up to showing that image on screen is also part of that frame. When Unity runs a game at 60 fps, it is not only displaying a different image on screen 60 times per second, in that time, it is also calculating the tremendous amount of math required to properly move objects from one frame to the next.

Figure 15.3 shows a flowchart of all the computation that would go into moving the Basket from one frame to the next.

Apple Flowchart

The Apple has a pretty simple flowchart as well (see Figure 15.4).

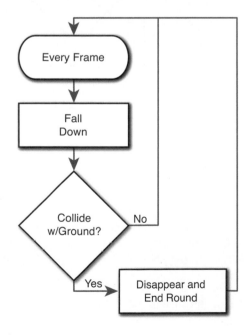

Figure 15.4 Apple flowchart

AppleTree Flowchart

The AppleTree flowchart is slightly more complex (see Figure 15.5) because the AppleTree has two decisions to make each frame:

- Does it change direction?
- Does it drop an Apple?

The decision of whether to change direction could just as easily come before or after the actual movement. For the purposes of this chapter, either would have worked.

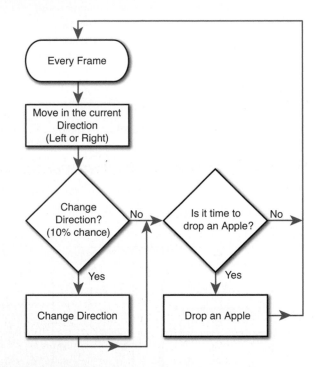

Figure 15.5   AppleTree flowchart

Summary

As you've now seen, digital games can be broken down into a set of very simple decisions and commands. This task is implicit in how I approached creating the prototypes for this book, and it is something that you will do yourself when you approach your own game design and development projects.

In Chapter 28, we expand upon this analysis and show how these action lists can be converted into lines of code that make your Baskets move, your Apples fall, and your AppleTrees run around like a Mad Bomber dropping Apples.

CHAPTER 16

INTRODUCING OUR DEVELOPMENT ENVIRONMENT: UNITY

This is the start of your programming adventure.

In this chapter, you download Unity, the game development environment that you will use throughout the rest of this book. We talk about why Unity is a fantastic game development tool for any budding game designer or developer and why we've chosen C# as the language for you to learn.

You also take a look at the sample project that ships with Unity, learn about the various window panes in the Unity interface, and move these panes into a logical arrangement that will match the examples you see in the rest of the book.

Downloading Unity

First things first, let's start downloading Unity. The Unity installer is over 1 GB in size, so depending on your Internet speed, this could take anywhere from a few minutes to a couple of hours. After you've gotten this process started, we can move on to talking about Unity.

As of this writing, the latest major version of Unity is Unity 4. Because Unity is under constant development, the current minor version should be something like 4.x.y, with the x and y being sub-version numbers. Regardless of version, Unity is always available for free from Unity's official website:

> http://unity3d.com/unity/download

This should take you to a page that provides the latest download link for your system (see Figure 16.1). Unity is available for both PC and OS X, and it is nearly identical on both platforms.

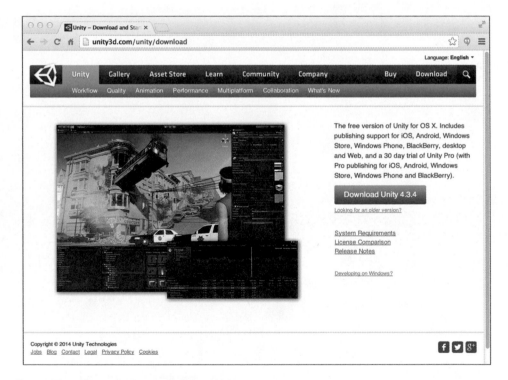

Figure 16.1   The web page to download Unity

> tip
>
> Unity is free, but you will still need to acquire a license, and this requires that you have an available Internet connection the first time that you run the application.

Introducing Our Development Environment

Before you can begin prototyping in earnest, you first need to become familiar with Unity, our chosen development environment. Unity itself can really be thought of as a synthesis program; while you will be bringing all the elements of your game prototypes together in Unity, the actual production of the assets will largely be done in other programs. You will program in MonoDevelop; model and texture in a 3D modeling program like Maya, Autodesk 3ds Max, or Blender; edit images in a photo editor such as Photoshop or GIMP; and edit sound in an audio program such as Pro Tools or Audacity. Because a large section of this book is about programming and learning to program in C# (pronounced "see-sharp"), you'll be spending most of the time with tutorials using MonoDevelop, but it's still critically important to understand how to use Unity and how to effectively set up your Unity environment.

Why Choose Unity?

There are many game development engines out there, but we've chosen to focus on Unity for several reasons:

- **Unity is free:** With the free version of Unity, you can create and sell games that run on OS X, PC, the Web, Linux, iOS, Android, BlackBerry, Windows Phone, Windows Store, and more. While the Pro version of Unity includes a few additional useful features, for a game designer just learning to prototype, the free version is really all that you need. The Pro version normally costs $1,500 (or $75/month), but if you're a student, a one-year license for Unity Pro is about ten times less!

> ### tip
>
> **STUDENT PRICING**   If you are a student, you can purchase a 1-year educational license for Unity Pro at a tremendous discount (about $150 instead of $1,500). This license does prevent you from being able to sell your game directly to players, but it lets you use the full power of Unity Pro to develop your game and make excellent portfolio pieces. After you're done developing, if you know you've got a hit on your hands, you can purchase the commercial version of Pro before attempting to sell your game. Unity has also recently added Pro student licenses that do allow you to sell your games, but those have a higher cost.
>
> To find the latest student pricing for Unity, I recommend searching the Web for "unity educational student pricing." That will make sure that you're looking at the latest.

- **Write once, deploy anywhere:** The free version of Unity can build applications for OS X, PC, the Web, Linux, iOS, Android, BlackBerry, Windows Phone, Windows Store, and more, all from the same code and files. This kind of flexibility is at the core of Unity; in fact, it's what the product and company are named for. There are also paid extensions to Unity Pro that professionals can use to create games for the PlayStation 3, Xbox 360, and several other game consoles.

- **Great support:** In addition to excellent documentation, Unity has an incredibly active and supportive development community. Hundreds of thousands of developers are using Unity, and many of them contribute to the discussions on Unity forums across the web.

- **It's awesome!:** My students and I have joked that Unity has a "make awesome" button. Although this is not strictly true, there are several phenomenal features built in to Unity that will make your games both play and look better by simply checking an option box. Unity engineers have already handled a lot of the difficult game programming tasks for you. Collision detection, physics simulation, pathfinding, particle systems, draw call batching, shaders, the game loop, and many other tough coding issues are all included. All you need to do is make a game that takes advantage of them!

Why Choose C#?

Within Unity, you have the choice to use any of three programming languages: UnityScript, C#, or Boo. Very, very few people actually use Boo, so you're really left with two choices.

UnityScript, A Version of JavaScript

JavaScript is often seen as a language for beginners; it's easy to learn, the syntax is forgiving and flexible, and it's also used for scripting web pages. JavaScript was initially developed in the mid-1990s by Netscape as a "lite" version of the Java programming language. It was used as a scripting language for web pages, though early on that often meant that various JavaScript functions worked fine in one web browser but didn't work at all in another. The syntax of Java Script was the basis for HTML5 and is very similar to Adobe Flash's ActionScript 3. Despite all of this, it is actually JavaScript's flexibility and forgiving nature that make it an inferior language for this book. As one example, JavaScript uses weak typing, which means that if we were to create a variable (or container) named bob, we could put anything we wanted into that variable: a number, a word, an entire novel, or even the main character of our game. Because the variable bob doesn't have a variable type, Unity never really knows what kind of thing bob is, and that could change at any time. These flexibilities in JavaScript make scripting more tedious and prevent programmers from taking advantage of some of the most powerful and interesting features of modern languages.

C#

C# was developed in 2000 as Microsoft's response to Java. They took a lot of the modern coding features of Java and put them into a syntax that was much more familiar to and comfortable for traditional C++ developers. This means that C# has all the capabilities of a modern language. For you experienced programmers, these features include function virtualization and delegates, dynamic binding, operator overloading, lambda expressions, and the powerful Language INtegrated Query (LINQ) query library among many others. For those of you new to programming, all you really need to know is that working in C# from the beginning will make you a better programmer and prototyper in the long run. In my prototyping class at the

University of Southern California, I taught using both UnityScript and C# in different semesters, and I found that students who were taught C# consistently produced better game prototypes, exhibited stronger coding practices, and felt more confident about their programming abilities than their peers who had been taught UnityScript in prior semesters of the class.

RUNTIME SPEED OF EACH LANGUAGE

If you've had some experience programming, you might assume that C# code in Unity would execute faster than code written in JavaScript or Boo. This assumption would come from the understanding that C# code is usually compiled while JavaScript and Boo are interpreted (meaning that compiled code is turned into a computer's machine language by a compiler as part of the coding process, while interpreted code is translated on-the-fly as the player is playing the game, making interpreted code generally slower). However, in Unity, every time you save a file of C#, UnityScript, or Boo code, Unity imports it, converts any of the three languages to the same Common Intermediate Language (CIL), and then compiles that CIL into machine language. So, regardless of the language you use, your Unity game prototypes will execute at the same speed.

On the Daunting Nature of Learning a Language

There's no way around it, learning a new language is tough. I'm sure that's one of the reasons that you bought this book rather than just trying to tackle things on your own. Just like Spanish, Korean, Mandarin, French, or any other human language, there are going to be things in C# that don't make any sense at first, and there are places that I'm going to tell you to write something that you don't immediately understand. There will also probably be a point where you are just starting to understand some things about the language but feel utterly confused by the language as a whole (which is the exact same feeling you'd have if you took one semester of Spanish class and then tried to watch soap operas on Telemundo). This feeling comes for almost all of my students about halfway through the semester, and by the end of the semester, every one of them feels much more confident and comfortable with both C# and game prototyping.

Rest assured, this book is here for you, and if you read it in its entirety, you will emerge with not only a working understanding of C# but also several simple game prototypes that you can use as foundations on which to build your own projects. The approach that I take in this book comes from many semesters of experience teaching "nonprogrammers" how to find the hidden coder within themselves and, more broadly, how to convert their game ideas into working prototypes. As you'll see throughout this book, that approach is composed of three steps:

1. **Concept introduction:** Before asking you to code anything for each project, I'll tell you what we're doing and why. This general concept of what you're working toward in each tutorial will give you a framework on which to hang the various coding elements that are introduced in the chapter.

2. **Guided tutorial:** You'll be guided step by step through a tutorial that will demonstrate these concepts in the form of a playable game. Unlike some other approaches, we will be compiling and testing the game throughout the process so that you can identify and repair bugs (problems in the code) as you go, rather than trying to fix all of them at the end. Additionally, I'll even guide you to create some bugs so that you can see the errors they cause and become familiar with them; this will make it easier when you encounter your own bugs later.

3. **Lather, rinse, repeat:** In many tutorials, you'll be asked to repeat something. For instance, in a top-down shooter game like *Galaga*, the tutorial would guide you through the process of making one single enemy type, and then it would ask you to create three others on your own. Don't skip this part! This repetition will really drive the concept home, and it will help your understanding solidify later.

pro tip

90% OF BUGS ARE JUST TYPOS   I've spent so much time helping students fix bugs that now I can very quickly spot a typo in code. The most common include the following:

- **Misspellings:** If you type even one letter wrong, the computer won't have any idea what you're talking about.

- **Capitalization:** To your C# compiler, `A` and `a` are two completely different letters, so `variable`, `Variable`, and `variAble` are all completely different words.

- **Missing semicolons:** Just like almost every sentence in English should end in a period, nearly every statement in C# should end in a semicolon (;). If you leave the semicolon out, it will often cause an error on the next line. FYI: A semicolon is used because the period was needed for decimal numbers and what's called *dot syntax* in variable names and subnames (e.g., varName. subVarName.subSubVarName).

Earlier, I mentioned that most of my students feel confused and daunted by C# at about the midway point of the semester, and it's at exactly that time that I assign them the Classic Games Project. They are asked to faithfully recreate the mechanics and game feel of a classic game over the course of four weeks. Some great examples have included *Super Mario Bros.*, *Metroid*, *Castlevania*, *Pokemon*, and even the original *Legend of Zelda*. By being forced to work things out on their own, to schedule their own time, and to dig deeply into the inner workings of these seemingly simple games, the students come to realize that they understand much more C# than they thought, and that is the time that everything really falls into place. The key component here is that the thought process changes from "I'm following this tutorial" to "I want to do this...now how do I make it happen?" At the end of this book, you will be prepared to tackle your own game projects (or your own Classic Game Project, if you want). The tutorials in this book can be a fantastic starting point on which to build your own games.

Running Unity for the First Time

Hopefully reading all of that will have given Unity enough time to download in the background. Congratulations! You're about to embark on a challenging but rewarding journey.

Installing Unity

Depending on your personal system settings, the Unity installer should have placed itself in a *Downloads* folder somewhere on your hard drive. I'm sure you've done this kind of thing several times before, so find the file, run the installer with all default options, and let's get to work. This is a big install, so it could take a while. In the final bit of the installation, it may look like it has frozen; but don't worry, just give it some time to complete.

Your First Launch: Licensing

The first time you run Unity, it will open a built-in web page that will ask you to create a license and register (see Figure 16.2), but it's really quite painless, and it shouldn't take much time at all. You will need to choose between the free license and a 30-day trial of Unity Pro. At this time, I recommend activating the free version of Unity, especially if you plan to work through this book slowly. The Pro version will be nice to have for the prototype you'll make in Chapter 34, "QuickSnap," so I recommend waiting until then to start the 30-day trial of Unity Pro. However, choosing the 30-day Unity Pro trial now would allow you to see the beautiful reflections and depth-of-field shaders in Figure 16.4.

You can choose to activate the 30-day trial any time, although you can only activate it once, and once the trial is over, you will be reverted to the free version. If you choose the free version now, you can always go back and upgrade to the Pro trial by selecting *Unity > Manage License* from the menu bar on OS X (on PC, choose *Help > Manage License*).

Once you click *OK*, you are prompted to create a Unity account. They'll send you an email to confirm this (so you need to give them a valid email address). Then, you may be asked to take part in a survey, which you can choose to skip if you want (through a link at the bottom of the survey).

After this, Unity will automatically open the *AngryBots* demo project. This is a large project, so it may take several seconds to load. It may appear that Unity has frozen or is unresponsive, but if you wait a bit, everything will show up.

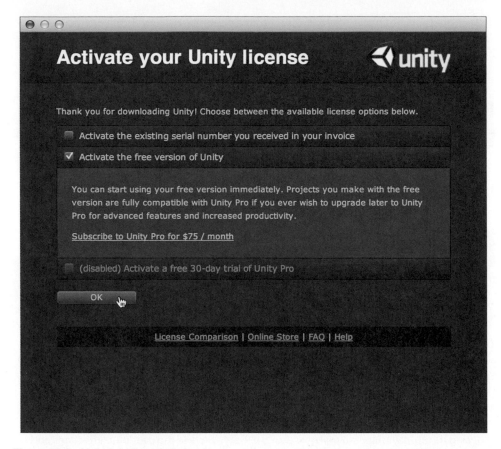

Figure 16.2   Unity licensing window

Example Project: *AngryBots*

When you first launch Unity, it will open a demo project and will show you a *Welcome to Unity* window that pops up over the main Unity window. For now, close the *Welcome to Unity* window, but feel free to explore the introductory videos and other links there later if you want more of an introduction to Unity than is provided in this chapter.

Unless you tell it not to (by holding the Option key at launch), Unity will open an existing project every time you launch it. The default project for this is *AngryBots* (see Figure 16.3), a game created internally by the Unity team to show off the capabilities of the engine. If for some reason the default scene doesn't open automatically, you will need to double-click the *Angry-Bots* Scene Asset to open it; it should be the first one listed in the Project window pane in the bottom half of the screen. You'll see Project and several other window panes on screen that I'll explain later, but for now, just click the large *Play* button at the top of the Unity window (the tri-angle pointing to the right in the top, center of the Unity window) and enjoy playing this game for a while. You can read about the controls for this game in the nearby tip.

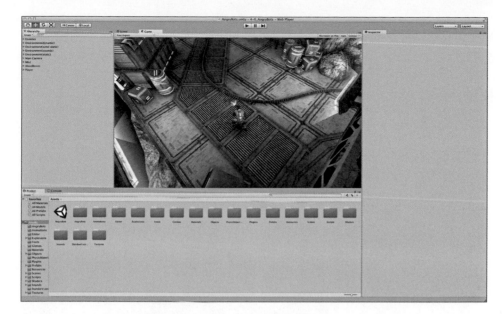

Figure 16.3   The Unity window when it opens for the first time

tip

ANGRYBOTS CONTROLS

- Movement is controlled by the W, A, S, and D or arrow keys.

- The gun will always aim at your mouse pointer.

- Hold down the left mouse button to fire.

You must stand very close to any circular door for a couple of seconds for it to
open.

There are several computers that you need to stand in front of in order to unlock
them (turn the color of electric wires coming out of them from red to green).

Here are some things to notice while you're playing:

- **Shaders:** AngryBots is rife with *shaders* (see Figure 16.4), code written specifically for the
graphics card with the sole purpose of making the game look amazing. Special ones to
check out include the following:
  - A. The depth-of-field image effect that makes some parts of the scene in-focus while
others are out-of-focus (see letter *A* in Figure 16.4). This will only appear in Unity Pro.

B. The reflections on the floors (especially of the laser sight) (see letter *B* in Figure 16.4). This will only appear in Unity Pro.

C. The animated water droplets on the floor when outside (see letter *C* in Figure 16.4). This appears regardless of whether you are using Unity Pro or free.

As explained earlier, if you chose to activate the free license rather than the 30-day Unity Pro trial, you will not see the most advanced shaders. This is one of the few differences between the free and Pro versions of Unity.

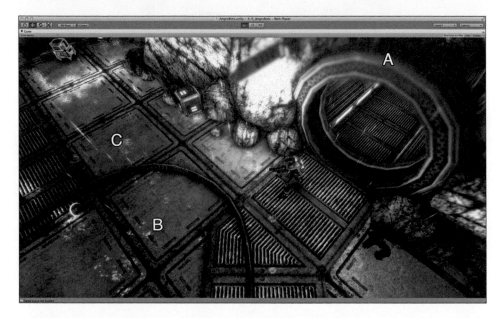

Figure 16.4   Screen showing the effects of various shaders

- **Character rigging and animation:** Unity makes use of animation blending to enable the player character to walk in one direction while looking and shooting in another.

- **AI pathing:** Enemies will move around objects in a room to find and attack the player.

Feel free to explore the whole space and see what elements of AngryBots you might want to use in your own project. Go ahead, I'll wait.

...

...

So, what did you think? Did you blow up the base, or did you escape the exploding station? Did you find the white museum? The controls of this game are a little unusual, but regardless, it's a good showcase for how beautiful Unity can look.

Now, let's do something really cool.

Compile and Deploy AngryBots for the Web

Once you've clicked the blue Stop button at the top of the Unity window (the square next to the Play button), choose *File > Build Settings* from the menu bar (meaning that you should choose the item *Build Settings* from the File menu, as shown in Figure 16.5).

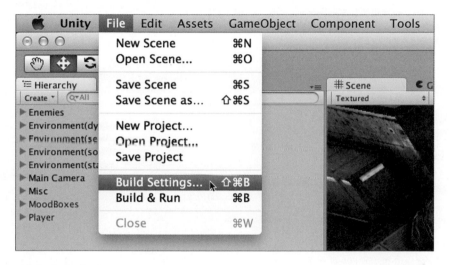

Figure 16.5 Build Settings menu selection

You should see the *Build Settings* window shown in Figure 16.6.

From here, be sure to click *Web Player* on the left and then check *Offline Deployment* in the *Web Player* options area. Click *Build and Run*, and Unity will ask you where to save the files. Type **AngryBots Web Build** for the filename and click *Save*.

Unity will process this for a while and build a web version of the game for you. Once it's built, your web browser will automatically be opened and sent to the page you just made as shown in Figure 16.7. Depending on your browser, you may be prompted to give the Unity plug-in permission to run.

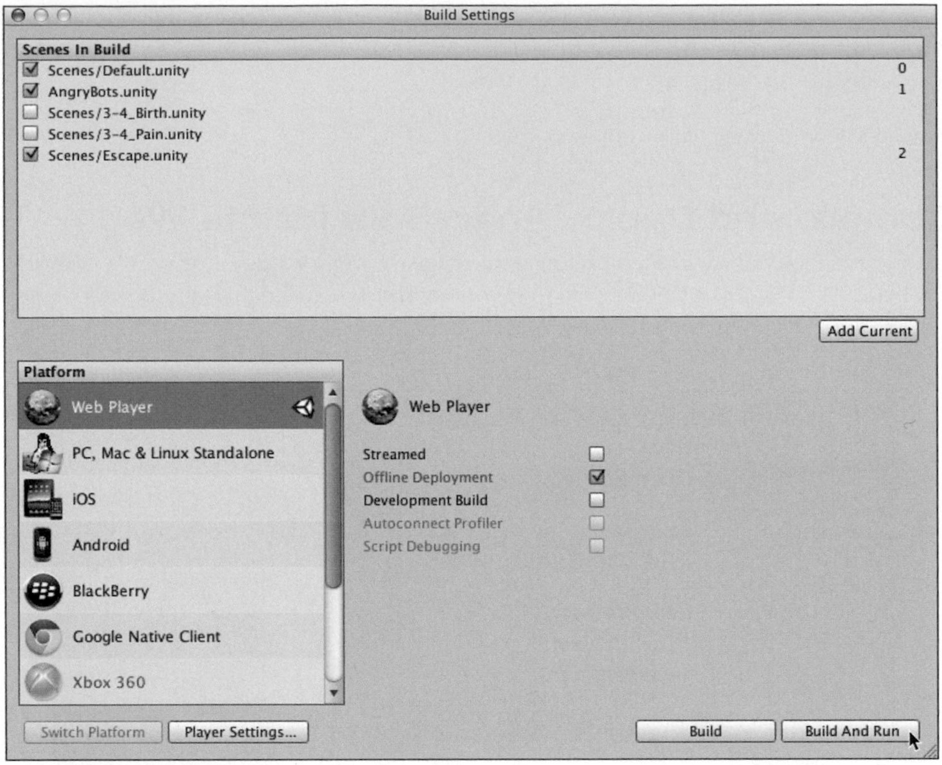

Figure 16.6 Unity build settings for the web player

And there you go. You've compiled *AngryBots* for the web. Unity makes things like this very easy so that you can focus on the interesting work: game design and development.

Setting Up the Unity Window Layout

The last thing we need to do before we start actually making things in Unity is to get our environment laid out properly. Unity is very flexible, and one of those flexibilities is that it allows you to arrange its window panes however you like. You can see several window layouts by choosing various options from the *Layout* pop-up menu in the top-right corner of the Unity window (see Figure 16.8).

Figure 16.7   *AngryBots* running in a browser window

Figure 16.8   Position of the *Layout* pop-up menu and selection of the *2 by 3* layout

Choose *2 by 3* from this pop-up menu. This will be the starting point for making our layout.

Before doing anything else, let's make the Project pane look a little cleaner. Click on the options pop-up for the Project pane (shown in the black circle in Figure 16.9) and choose *One Column Layout*.

Figure 16.9   Choosing the One Column Layout for the Project pane

Unity enables you to both move window panes around and adjust the borders between them. As shown in Figure 16.10, you can move a pane by dragging its tab (the arrow cursor) or adjust a border between panes by dragging the border between them (the left-right resize cursor).

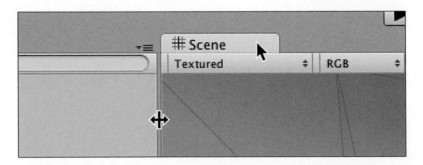

Figure 16.10   Two types of cursors for moving and resizing Unity's window panes

When you drag a pane by its tab, a small ghosted version will appear (see Figure 16.11). Some locations will cause the pane to snap into place. When this happens, the ghosted version of the tab will appear in the new location.

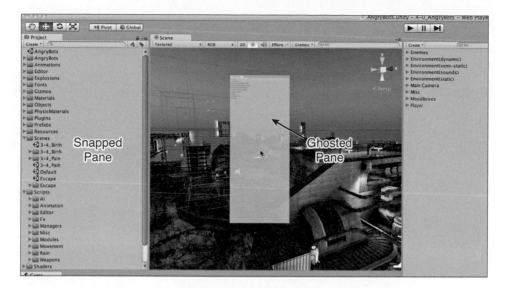

Figure 16.11 Ghosted and snapped panes when moving them around the Unity window

Play around with moving the window panes until your window looks like Figure 16.12.

Figure 16.12 Proper layout for the Unity window...but it's still missing something

Now the last thing we need to add is the Console pane. From the menu bar, choose *Window > Console*. Then drag the Console pane below the Hierarchy pane. You'll also need to move the Project pane after you've done this to create the final layout shown in Figure 16.13.

Figure 16.13   Final layout of the Unity window, including the Console pane

Now you just need to save this layout in the Layout pop-up menu so that you don't have to go through all that again. Click the Layout pop-up menu and choose *Save Layout*, as shown in Figure 16.14.

Figure 16.14   Saving the layout

Save this layout with the name *Game Dev*, with a leading space before the G in Game (i.e., " Game Design"). By putting a space at the beginning of the name, you make sure that this layout is sorted to the top of the menu. Now, any time you need to return to this layout, you can simply choose it from this pop-up menu.

Learning Your Way Around Unity

Before we can really get into coding things, you need to get to know the various window panes that you've just arranged. Refer back to Figure 16.13 as we discuss each pane:

- **Scene pane:** The Scene pane allows you to navigate around your scene in 3D and to select, move, rotate, and scale objects.
- **Game pane:** The Game pane is where you will preview your actual gameplay; it's the window in which you played *AngryBots* before compiling the web build. This pane also shows you the view from the *Main Camera* in your scene.
- **Hierarchy pane:** The Hierarchy pane shows you every GameObject that is included in your current scene. For now, you can think of each scene as a level of your game. Everything that exists in your scene, from the camera to your player-character, is a GameObject.
- **Project pane:** The Project pane contains all of the assets that are included in your project. An asset is any kind of file that is part of your project, including images, 3D models, C# code, text files, sounds, fonts and so on. The Project pane is a reflection of the contents of the Assets folder within your Unity project folder on your computer hard drive. These assets are not necessarily in your current scene.
- **Inspector pane:** Any time you click on an asset in the Project pane or a GameObject in the Scene or Hierarchy panes, you will be able to see and edit information about it in the Inspector pane.
- **Console pane:** The Console pane will allow you to see messages from Unity about errors or bugs in your code as well as messages from yourself that will help you understand the inner workings of your own code.[1] We will use the Console pane extensively in Chapter 18, "Hello World: Your First Program," and Chapter 19, "Variables and Components."

Summary

That's it for setup. Now, let's move on to actually developing! As you've seen in this chapter, Unity can create some pretty stunning visuals and compelling gameplay. Though the process of making beautiful 3D models and shaders is outside the scope of this book, it's important for you to know the extent of Unity's graphical capabilities. In the next chapter, you'll learn more about C#, the language you'll be using for game development.

---

[1] Unity's `print()` and `Debug.Log()` functions allow you to print messages to the Console pane.

CHAPTER 17

INTRODUCING OUR LANGUAGE: C#

This chapter introduces you to the key features of C# and describes some important reasons why it was chosen as the language for this book. It also examines the basic syntax of C#, explaining what is meant by the structure of some simple C# statements.

By the end of this chapter, you will better understand C# and be ready to tackle the more in-depth chapters that follow.

Understanding the Features of C#

As covered in Chapter 15, "Thinking in Digital Systems," programming consists of giving the computer a series of simple commands, and C# is the language through which we do so. However, there are lots of different programming languages out there, each of which has benefits and drawbacks. Some of the features of C# are that it is

- A compiled language
- Managed code
- Strongly typed
- Function-based
- Object-oriented

Each of these features is described further in the following sections, and each will help you in various ways.

C# Is a Compiled Language

When most people write computer programs, they are not actually writing in a language that the computer itself comprehends. In fact, each computer chip on the market has a slightly different set of very simple commands that it understands, known as machine language. This language is very, very fast for the chip to execute, but it is incredibly difficult for a person to read. For example, the machine language line `000000 00001 00010 00110 00000 100000` would certainly mean something to the right computer chip, but it means next to nothing to human readers. You might have noticed, however, that every character of that machine code is either a 0 or 1. That's because all the more complex types of data—numbers, letters, and so on—have been converted down to individual *bits* of data (i.e., ones or zeros). If you've ever heard of people programming computers using punch cards, this is exactly what they were doing: For some formats of binary punch cards, physically punching a hole in card stock represented a one, while an unpunched hole represented a zero.

For people to be able to write code more easily, human-readable programming languages—sometimes called authoring languages—were created. You can think of an authoring language as an intermediate language meant to act as a go-between from you to the computer. Authoring languages like C# are logical and simple enough for a computer to interpret while also being close enough to written human languages to allow programmers to easily read and understand them.

There is also a major division in authoring languages between *compiled* languages such as BASIC, C++, C#, and Java and *interpreted* languages such as JavaScript, Perl, PHP, and Python (see Figure 17.1).

In an *interpreted* language, authoring and executing code is a two-step process: The programmer writes the code; and then, each time any player plays the game, the code is converted from the authoring language to machine language in real time on the player's machine. The good thing about this is that it enables code portability, because the authoring code can be interpreted specifically for the type of computer on which it is running. For example, the Java Script of a given web page will run on almost any modern computer regardless of whether the computer is running OS X, Windows, Linux, or even many mobile operating systems like iOS, Android, Windows Phone, and so on. However, this flexibility also causes the code to execute more slowly due to: the time it takes to interpret the code on the player's computer, the authoring language not being well optimized for the device on which it will run, and a host of other reasons. Because the same interpreted code is run on all devices, it is impossible to optimize for the specific device on which it happens to be running. It is for this reason that the 3D games created in an interpreted language like JavaScript run so much more slowly than those created in a compiled language, even when running on the same computer.

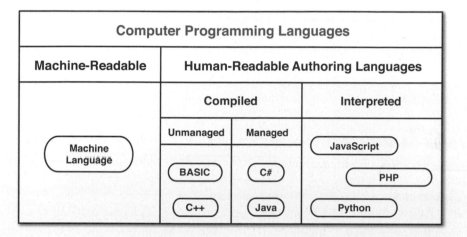

Figure 17.1 A simple taxonomy of programming languages

When using a *compiled* language, such as C#, there are three separate steps to the programming process: authoring the code, compiling the code, and executing the compiled program. This added middle process of compilation converts the code from the authoring language into an executable (that is, an application or app) that can be run directly by a computer without the need for an interpreter. Because the compiler has both a complete understanding of the program and a complete understanding of the execution platform on which the program will run, it is possible to incorporate many optimizations into the process. In games, these optimizations translate directly into higher frame rates, more detailed graphics, and more responsive games. Most high-budget games are authored in a compiled language because of this optimization and speed advantage, but this means that a different executable must be compiled for each execution platform.

In many cases, compiled authoring languages are only suited for a single execution platform. For instance, *Objective C* is Apple Computer's proprietary authoring language for making applications for both OS X and iOS. This language is based on C (a predecessor of C++), but it includes a number of features that are unique to OS X or iOS development. Similarly, XNA was a flavor of C# developed by Microsoft specifically to enable students to author games for both Windows-based personal computers and the Xbox 360.

As mentioned in Chapter 16, "Introducing Our Development Environment: Unity," Unity enables C# (as well as Boo and a JavaScript flavor named UnityScript) to be used to create games. Any of these three languages are compiled into a Common Intermediate Language (CIL) in an additional compilation step, and that CIL is then compiled to target any number of platforms, from iOS to Android, Mac, Windows PC, game consoles such as the Wii and Xbox, and even interpreted languages such as WebGL. This additional CIL step ensures that Unity programs are able to be compiled even if they are written in UnityScript or Boo, but I still find C# to be vastly superior to the other two.

The ability to write once and compile anywhere is not unique to Unity, but it is one of Unity Technologies' core goals for Unity and is better integrated into Unity than any other game development software I have seen. However, as a game designer, you will still need to think seriously about the design differences between a game meant for a handheld phone controlled by touch and one meant to run on a personal computer controlled by mouse and keyboard, so you will usually have slightly different code for the different platforms.

C# Is Managed Code

More traditional compiled languages such as BASIC, C++, and Objective-C require programmers to directly manage memory, obliging a programmer to manually allocate and de-allocate memory any time she creates or destroys a variable.[1] If a programmer doesn't manually de-allocate RAM in these languages, her programs will have a "memory leak" and eventually allocate all the computer's RAM, causing it to crash.

Luckily for us, C# is *managed code*, which means that the allocation and de-allocation of memory is handled automatically. You can still cause memory leaks in managed code, but it is more difficult to do so accidentally.

C# Is Strongly Typed

Variables are covered much more in later chapters, but there are a couple things that you should know now. First, a variable is just a named container for a value. For instance, in algebra, you may have seen an expression like this:

```
x = 5
```

---

[1] Memory allocation is the process of setting aside a certain amount of random-access memory (RAM) in the computer to enable it to hold a chunk of data. While computers now often have hundreds of gigabytes (GB) of hard drive space, they still usually have less than 20GB of RAM. RAM is *much* faster than hard drive memory, so all applications pull assets like images and sounds from the hard drive, allocate some space for them in RAM, and then store them in RAM for fast access.

In this one line, we have created a variable, named it x, and assigned it the value 5. Later, if asked the value of $x + 2$, I'm sure you could tell me that the answer is 7 because you remember that x was holding the value 5. That is exactly what variables do for you in programming.

In most interpreted languages, like JavaScript, a single variable can hold any kind of data. The variable x could hold the number 5 one minute, an image the next, and a sound file thereafter. This capability to hold any kind of value is what is meant when we say that a programming language is *weakly typed*.

C#, in contrast, is *strongly typed*. This means that when we initially create a variable, we tell it at that moment what kind of value it can hold:

```
int x - 5;
```

In the preceding statement, we have created a variable, named it x, told it that it is exclusively allowed to hold integer values (that is, numbers without a decimal point), and assigned it the integer value 5. Although this might seem like it would make it more difficult to program, strong typing enables the compiler to make many optimizations and makes it possible for the authoring environment, MonoDevelop, to perform real-time syntax checking on the code you write (much like the grammar checking that is performed by Microsoft Word). This also enables and enhances code-completion, a technology in MonoDevelop that enables it to predict the words you're typing and provide you valid completion options based on the other code that you've written. With code-completion, if you're typing and see MonoDevelop suggest the correct completion of the word, you simply press Tab to accept the suggestion. Once you're used to this, it can save you hundreds of keystrokes every minute.

C# Is Function Based

In the early days of programming, a program was composed of a single series of commands. These programs were run directly from beginning to end much like the directions you would give to a friend who was trying to drive to your house:

1. From school, head north on Vermont.
2. Head west on I-10 for about 7.5 miles.
3. At the intersection with I-405, take the 405 south for 2 miles.
4. Take the exit for Venice Blvd.
5. Turn right onto Sawtelle Blvd.
6. My place is just north of Venice on Sawtelle.

Later, repeatable sections were added to programming in the form of things like *loops* (a section of code that repeats itself) and *subroutines* (an otherwise inaccessible section of code that is jumped to, executed, and then returned from).

Functional languages allow programmers to name chunks of code and thereby encapsulate functionality (that is, group a series of actions under a single function name). For example, if in addition to giving someone detailed directions to your house as previously described, you also asked him to pick up some milk for you on the way, he would know that if he saw a grocery store on the way, he should stop the car, get out, walk to find milk, pay for it, return to his car, and continue on his way to your house. Because your friend already knows how to buy milk, you just need to request that he do so rather than giving him explicit instructions for every tiny step. This could look something like this:

"Hey man, if you see a store on the way, could you please `BuySomeMilk()`?"

In this statement, you have encapsulated all of the instructions to buy milk into the single function named `BuySomeMilk()`. The same thing can be done in any functional language. When the computer is processing C# and encounters a function name followed by parentheses, it will *call* that function (that is, it will execute all of the actions encapsulated in the function). You will learn much more about functions in Chapter 23, "Functions and Parameters."

The other fantastic thing about functions is that when you have written the code for the function `BuySomeMilk()` once, you shouldn't have to write it again. Even if you're working on a completely different program, you can often copy and paste functions like `BuySomeMilk()` and reuse them without having to write the whole thing again from scratch. Throughout the tutorial chapters of this book, you will be writing a C# script named `Utils.cs` that includes several reusable functions.

C# Is Object-Oriented

Many years after functions were invented, the idea of *object-oriented* code (OOC) was created. In OOC, not only functionality but also data are encapsulated together into something called an *object*, or more correctly a *class*. This is covered extensively in Chapter 25, "Classes," but here's a metaphor for now.

Consider some various animals. Each animal has specific information that it knows about itself. Some examples of this data could be its species, age, size, emotional state, level of hunger, current location, and so on. Each animal also has certain things that it can do: eat, move, breath, etc. The data about the animal are analogous to variables in code, while the actions that can be performed by the animal are analogous to functions.

Before OOC, an animal represented in code could hold information (i.e., variables) but could not perform any actions. Those actions were performed by functions that were not directly connected to the animal. A programmer could write a function named `Move()` that could move any kind of animal, but she would have to write several lines of code in that function that determined what kind of animal it was and what type of movement was appropriate for it. For example, dogs walk, fish swim, and birds fly. Any time a new animal was added to the program, `Move()` would need to be changed to accommodate the new type of locomotion, and `Move()` would consistently grow larger and more complex.

Object orientation changed all of this by introducing the ideas of *classes* and *class* inheritance. A *class* combines both variables and functions into one whole object. In OOC, instead of having a huge `Move()` function that can handle any animal, there is instead a much smaller, more specific `Move()` function attached to each species of animal. This eliminates the need for you to rewrite `Move()` every time a new species is added, and it eliminates the need for all of the species checking in the non-OOC version of `Move()`. Instead, each new animal species class is given its own small `Move()` function when it is created.

Object orientation also includes the concept of *class inheritance*. This enables classes to have subclasses that are more specific, and it allows the subclasses to either inherit or override functions in their superclasses. Through inheritance, a single `Animal` class could be created that included declarations of the data types that are shared by all animals. This class would also have a `Move()` function, but it would be nonspecific. In subclasses of `Animal`, like `Dog` or `Fish`, the function `Move()` could be overridden to cause specific behavior like walking or swimming. This is a key element of modern game programming, and it will serve you well when you want to create something like a basic `Enemy` class that is then further specified into various subclasses for each individual enemy type that you want to create.

Reading and Understanding C# Syntax

Just like any other language, C# has a specific syntax that you must follow. Take a look at these example statements in English:

- The dog barked at the squirrel.
- At the squirrel the dog barked.
- The dog at the squirrel. barked
- barked The dog at the squirrel.

Each of these English statements has the same words and punctuation, but they are in a different order, and the punctuation and capitalization is changed. Because you are familiar with the English language, it is easy for you to tell that the first is correct and the others are just wrong. Another way of examining this is to look at it more abstractly as just the parts of speech:

- [Subject] [verb] [object].
- [Object] [subject] [verb].
- [Subject] [object]. [verb]
- [verb] [Subject] [object].

When parts of speech are rearranged like this, doing so alters the syntax of the sentence, and the latter three sentences are incorrect because they have *syntax errors*.

Just like any language, C# has specific syntax rules for how statements must be written. Let's examine this simple statement in detail:

```
int x = 5;
```

As explained earlier, this statement does several things:

- Declares a variable named x of the type int

  Any time a statement starts with a variable type, the second word of the statement becomes the name of a new variable of that type (see Chapter 19, "Variables and Components"). This is called *declaring* a variable.

- Defines the value of x to be 5

  The = symbol is used to *assign* values to variables, which is also called *defining* the variable. When doing so, the variable name is on the left, and the value assigned is on the right.

- Ends with a semicolon (;)

  Every simple statement in C# must end with a semicolon (;). This is similar in use to the period at the end of sentences in the English language.

> **note**
>
> Why not end C# statements with a period? Computer programming languages are meant to be very clear. The period is not used at the end of statements in C# because it is already in use in numbers as a decimal point (for example, the period in 3.14159). For clarity, the only use of the semicolon in C# is to end statements.

Now, let's add a second simple statement:

```
int x = 5;
int y = x * ( 3 + x );
```

You already understand the first statement, so now we'll examine the second. The second statement does the following:

- Declares a variable named y of the type int
- Adds 3 + x (which is 3 + 5, for a result of 8)

  Just like in algebra, *order of operations* follows parentheses first, meaning that 3 + x is evaluated first because it is surrounded by parentheses. The sum is 8 because the value of x was set to 5 in the previous statement. In Appendix B, "Useful Concepts Reference," read the section "Operator Precedence and Order of Operations," to learn more about order of operations in C#, but the main thing to remember for your programs is that if there is *any* doubt in your head about the order in which things will occur, you should use parentheses to remove doubt (and increase the readability of your code).[2]

---

[2] If there had been no parentheses, order of operations would handle multiplication and division *before* addition and subtraction. This would have resulted in x * 3 + 5, which would become 5 * 3 + 5, then 15 + 5, and finally 20.

- Multiplies x * 8 (x is 5, so the result is 40)
- Defines the value of y to be 40
- Ends with a semicolon (;)

This chapter finishes with a breakdown of one final couplet of C# statements. In this example, the statements are now numbered. Line numbers can make it much simpler to reference a specific line in code, and it is my hope that they will make it easier for you to read and understand the code in this book when you're typing it into your computer. The important thing to remember is that **you do not need to type the line numbers** into MonoDevelop. MonoDevelop will automatically number (and renumber) your lines as you work:

```
1    string greeting = "Hello World!";
2    print( greeting );
```

These statements deal with strings (a series of characters like a word or sentence) rather than integers. The first statement (numbered 1):

- Declares a variable named greeting of the type string

  string is another type of variable just like int.

- Defines the value of greeting to be "Hello World!"

  The double quotes around "Hello World!" tell C# that the characters in between them are to be treated as a *string literal* and not interpreted by the compiler to have any additional meaning. Putting the string literal "x = 10" in your code will **not** define the value of x to be 10 because the compiler knows to ignore all string literals between quotes.

- Ends with a semicolon (;)

The second statement (numbered 2):

- Calls the function print()

  As discussed earlier, functions are named collections of actions. When a function is *called*, the function executes the actions it contains. As you might expect, print() contains actions that will output a string to the Console pane. Any time you see a word in code followed by parentheses, it is either calling or defining a function. Writing the name of a function followed by parentheses calls the function, causing that functionality to execute. You'll see an example of defining a function in the next chapter.

- Passes greeting to print()

  Some functions just do things and don't require parameters, but many require that you *pass* something in. Any variable placed between the parentheses of a function call is passed into that function as an *argument*. In this case, the string greeting is passed into the function print(), and the characters Hello World! are output to the Console pane.

- Ends with a semicolon (;)

  Every simple statement ends with a semicolon.

Summary

Now that you understand a little about C# and about Unity, it's time to put the two together into your first program. The next chapter takes you through the process of creating a new Unity project, creating C# scripts, adding code to those scripts, and manipulating 3D GameObjects.

CHAPTER 18

HELLO WORLD: YOUR FIRST PROGRAM

Welcome to coding.

By the end of this chapter, you'll have created your own new project and written your first bits of code. We start with the classic Hello World project that has been a traditional first program since long before I started coding, and then we move on to something with more of a Unity flair to it.

Creating a New Project

Now that we've got the Unity window set up properly (in the previous chapter), let's leave *AngryBots* behind and make our own program. Not surprisingly, you start this by creating a new project.

Appendix A, "Standard Project Setup Procedure," contains detailed instructions that show you how to set up Unity projects for the chapters in this book. At the start of each project, you will see a sidebar like the one here. Please follow the directions in the sidebar to create the project for this chapter.

SET UP THE PROJECT FOR THIS CHAPTER

Following the standard project setup procedure, create a new Project in Unity. For information on the standard project setup procedure, see Appendix A.

- **Project name:** Hello World
- **Scene name:** (none yet)
- **C# Script names:** (none yet)

You should read the whole procedure in Appendix A, but for now, you only need to create the project. The scene and C# scripts will be created as part of this chapter.

When you create a project in Unity, you're actually just making a folder that will hold all the files that comprise your project. As you can see, once Unity has finished creating the project, the new project comes with an open scene containing only a *Main Camera* and absolutely nothing in the Project pane. Before doing anything else, save your scene by choosing *File > Save Scene* from the menu bar. Unity will automatically choose the correct place to save the scene, so just name it *_Scene_0* and click *Save*.[1] Now your scene appears in the Project pane.

Right-click the Project pane and choose *Reveal in Finder* (or *Show in Explorer* for Windows) as shown in Figure 18.1.

> **tip**
>
> **RIGHT-CLICK ON OS X**   Performing a right-click on an OS X mouse or trackpad is not as straightforward as doing so on a Windows PC. For information on how to do so, check out the "Right-Click on OS X" section of Appendix B, "Useful Concepts Reference."

---

[1] The underscore (_) at the beginning of the scene name _Scene_0 will cause the scene to always be sorted to the top of the Project pane. I also often change the name of *Main Camera* to *_MainCamera* to achieve the same sorting benefit in the Hierarchy pane.

Selecting *Reveal in Finder* will open a Finder window (or Explorer window) showing you the contents of your Project folder (see Figure 18.2).

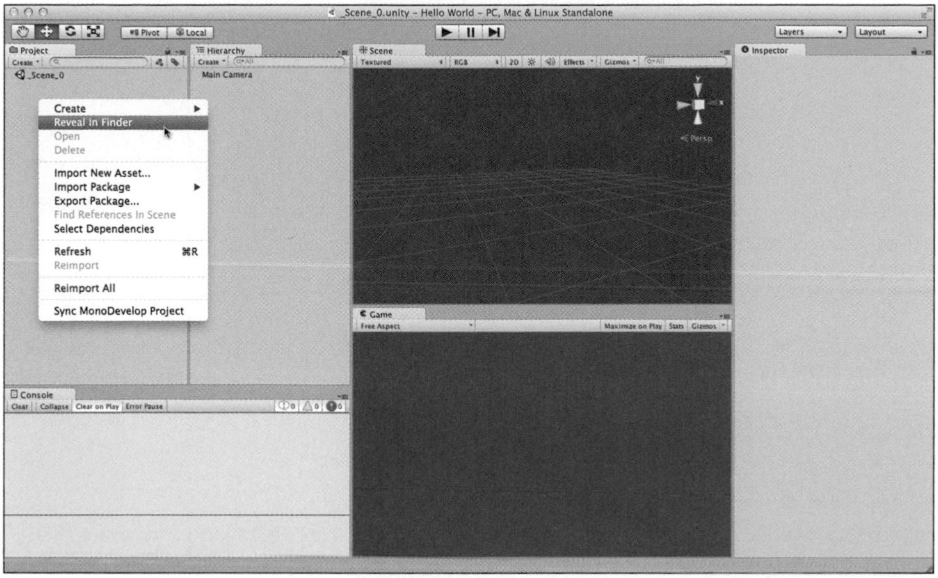

Figure 18.1   The blank canvas of a new Unity project (showing Reveal in Finder in the Project pane pop-up menu)

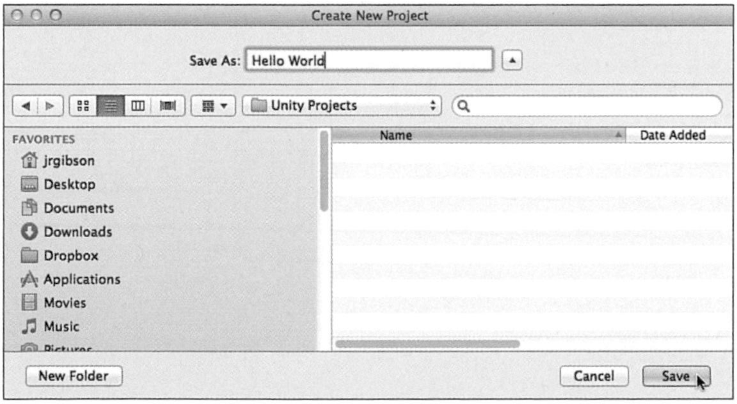

Figure 18.2   The project folder for Hello World as it appears in the OS X Finder

As you can see in the image in Figure 18.2, the Assets folder holds everything that appears in the Project pane inside of Unity. In theory, you can use the Assets folder and the Project pane interchangeably (for example, if you drop an image into the Assets folder, it appears in the Project pane and vice versa), but I highly recommend working exclusively with the Project pane rather than the Assets folder. Making changes in the Assets folder directly can sometimes lead to problems, and the Project pane is generally safer. In addition, it is very important that you never touch the Library, ProjectSettings, or Temp folders. Doing so could cause unexpected behavior from Unity and could possibly even damage your project.

> ### warning
>
> **NEVER CHANGE THE NAME OF YOUR PROJECT FOLDER WHILE UNITY IS RUNNING**   If you change the name of the project folder while Unity is running, it will crash in a very ungraceful way. Unity does a lot of file management in the background while it's running, and changing a folder name on it will almost always cause a crash. If you want to change your project folder name, quit Unity, change the folder name, and launch Unity again.

Switch back to Unity now.

Making a New C# Script

It is time. Now you're going to write your first chunk of code. We'll be talking a lot more about C# in later chapters, but for now, just copy what you see here. Click the *Create* button in the Project pane and choose *Create > C# Script* (as shown in Figure 18.3). A new script will be added to the Project pane, and its name will automatically be highlighted for you to change. Name this script *HelloWorld* (make sure there's no space between the two words) and press Return (or Enter on PC) to set the name.

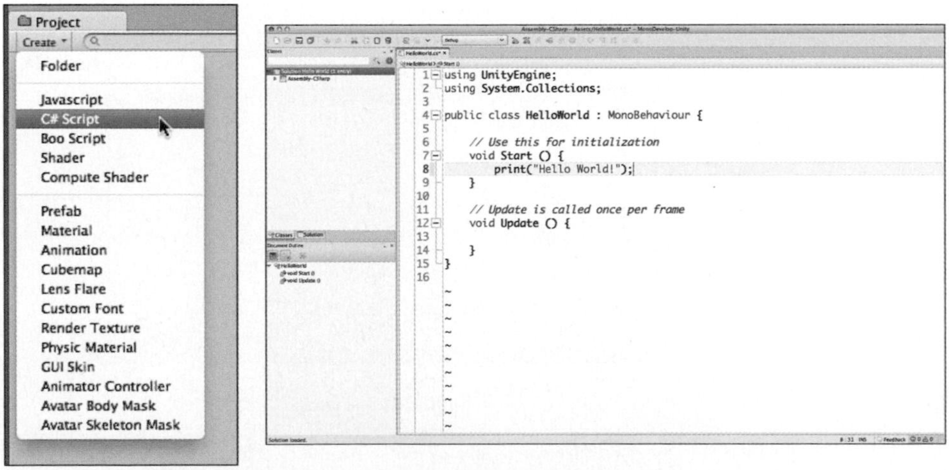

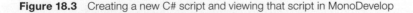

Figure 18.3   Creating a new C# script and viewing that script in MonoDevelop

Double-click the name or the icon of the HelloWorld script to launch MonoDevelop, our C# editor. Your script should look exactly like the one in Figure 8.3 except for line 8. Type two tabs and the code `print ("Hello World");` into line 8 of your script in MonoDevelop. Make sure to spell and capitalize everything correctly and to put a semicolon (`;`) at the end of the line. Your HelloWorld script should now look exactly like the following code listing. In code listings throughout the book, anything new that you need to type will be in **bold weight**, and code that is already there is in normal weight.

Each line in the following code syntax also has a line number preceding it. As you can see in Figure 18.3, MonoDevelop will automatically show you line numbers for your code, so you do not need to type them yourself. They are just here in the book to help make the code listings more clear.

```
 1 using UnityEngine;
 2 using System.Collections;
 3
 4 public class HelloWorld : MonoBehaviour {
 5
 6     // Use this for initialization
 7     void Start () {
 8         print("Hello World");
 9     }
10
11     // Update is called once per frame
12     void Update () {
13
14     }
15 }
```

> **note**
>
> Your version of MonoDevelop may automatically add extra spaces in some parts of the code. For example, it may have added a space between `print` and `(` in line 8 of the `Start()` function. This is okay, and you shouldn't be too concerned about it. In general, while capitalization matters tremendously to programming, spaces are more flexible. In addition, a series of several spaces (or several line breaks/returns) will be seen by the computer as just one, so you can add extra spaces and returns if it makes your code more readable (though extra returns may make your line numbers different from those in the code listings).
>
> You should also not be too upset if your line numbers differ from the ones in the examples. As long as the code is the same, the line numbers don't really matter.

Now, save this script by choosing *File > Save* from the MonoDevelop menu bar and switch back to Unity.

This next part's a bit tricky, but you'll soon be used to it because it is so often done in Unity. Click and hold on the name of the HelloWorld script in the Project pane, drag it over on top of *Main Camera* in the scene Hierarchy pane, and release the mouse button as is shown in Figure 18.4. When you are dragging the script, you will see the words *HelloWorld (Monoscript)* following the mouse, and when you release the mouse button over *Main Camera*, the *HelloWorld (Monoscript)* words will disappear.

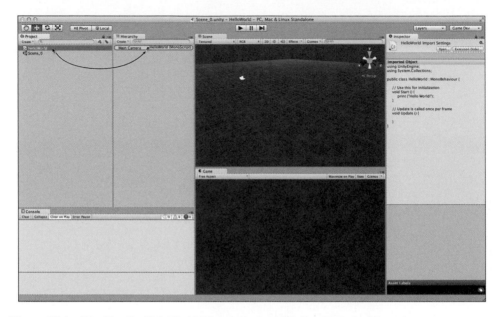

Figure 18.4 Attaching the HelloWorld C# script to the Main Camera in the Hierarchy pane

Dragging the HelloWorld script onto Main Camera *attaches* the script to Main Camera as a *component*. All objects that appear in the scene hierarchy pane (for example, Main Camera) are known as GameObjects, and GameObjects are made up of components. If you now click Main Camera in the Hierarchy pane, you should see *HelloWorld (Script)* listed as one of Main Camera's components in the Inspector pane. As you can see in Figure 18.5, the Inspector pane shows several components of the Main Camera, including its Transform, Camera, GUILayer, Flare Layer, Audio Listener, and HelloWorld (Script). GameObjects and components are covered in much more detail in later chapters.

Now, just click the *Play* button (the triangle facing to the right at the top of the Unity window) and watch the magic!

The script we wrote printed *Hello World!* to the Console pane, as shown in Figure 18.6. You'll notice that it also printed *Hello World!* to the small gray bar at the bottom-left corner of the screen. This probably isn't the most magical thing that's ever happened in your life, but you have to start somewhere, and that we have. As a wise old man once said, you've taken your first step into a larger world.

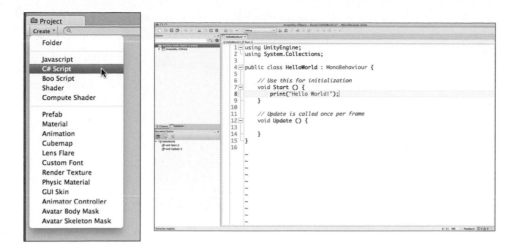

Figure 18.5   The HelloWorld script now appears in the Inspector pane for Main Camera.

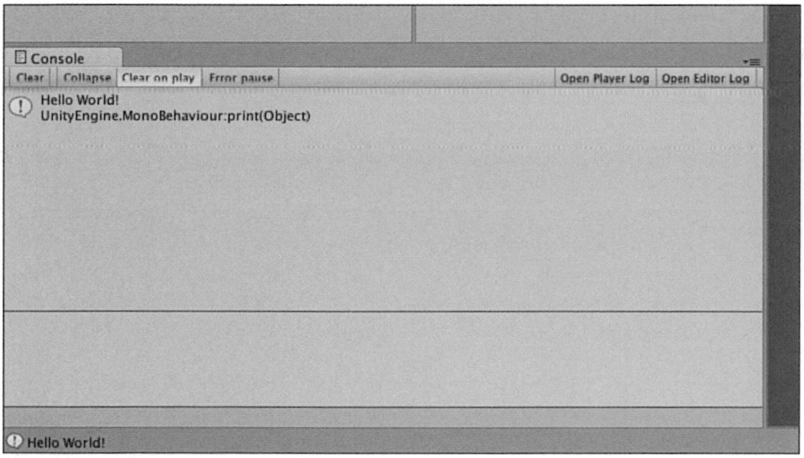

Figure 18.6   *Hello World!* printed to the Console pane

Start() **Versus** Update()

Now let's try moving the print() function call from Start() to Update(). Go back to MonoDevelop and edit your code as shown in the following code listing.

Adding the two forward slashes (//) to the beginning of line 8 converts everything on line 8 that follows the slashes to a *comment*. Comments are completely ignored by the computer and are used to either disable code (as you are now doing to line 8) or to leave messages for other humans reading the code (as you can see on lines 6 and 11). Adding two slashes before a line (as we've done to line 8) is referred to as *commenting out* the line. Type the statement `print("Hello World!");` into line 13 to make it part of the `Update()` function.

```
1 using UnityEngine;
2 using System.Collections;
3
4 public class HelloWorld : MonoBehaviour {
5
6     // Use this for initialization
7     void Start () {
8         // print("Hello World!"); // This line is now ignored.
9     }
10
11     // Update is called once per frame
12     void Update () {
13         print("Hello World!");
14     }
15 }
```

Save the script (replacing the original version) and try clicking the Play button again. You'll see that *Hello World!* is now printed many, many times in rapid succession (see Figure 18.7). You can click the Play button again to stop execution now, and you'll see that Unity stops spitting out *Hello World!* messages.

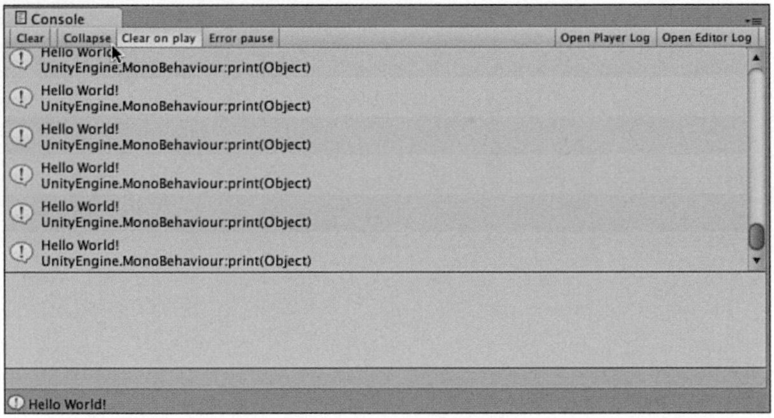

Figure 18.7   `Update()` has caused *Hello World!* to be printed once every frame

`Start()` and `Update()` are both special functions in Unity's version of C#. `Start()` is called once on the first frame that an object exists, whereas `Update()` is called every frame, hence the single message of Figure 18.6 versus the multiple messages of Figure 18.7. Unity has a whole list of these special functions that are called at various times. Many of them will be covered later in the book.

> ### tip
>
> If you want to see each repeat of the same message only once, you can click the *Collapse* button of the Console pane (indicated by the arrow cursor in Figure 18.7), and it will ensure that each different message text appears only once.

Making Things More Interesting

Now, we're going to add some Unity style to your first program. In this example, we're going to create many, many copies of a cube. Each of these cube copies will independently bounce around and react to physics. This will demonstrate both the speed at which Unity runs and the ease with which it enables you to create content.

Start by creating a new scene. *Choose File > New Scene* from the menu bar. You won't notice much of a difference because we didn't really have much in _Scene_0 other than the script on the camera, but if you click the Main Camera, you'll see it no longer has a script attached, and you'll also notice that the title bar of the Unity window has changed from *_Scene_0.unity - Hello World - PC, Mac, & Linux Standalone* to *Untitled - Hello World - PC, Mac, & Linux Standalone*. As always, the first thing you should do is save this new scene. Choose *File > Save Scene* from the menu bar and name this *_Scene_1*.

Now, choose *GameObject > Create Other > Cube* from the menu bar. This will place a Game Object named *Cube* in the Scene pane (and in the Hierarchy pane). If it's difficult to see Cube in the Scene pane, try double-clicking its name in the Hierarchy pane, which should focus the scene on Cube. For more information, read the "Changing the Scene View" sidebar later in this chapter that covers how to manipulate the view of the Scene pane.

If you click Cube in the hierarchy, you should see it selected in the Scene pane and see its components appear in the Inspector pane (see Figure 18.8). The primary purpose of the Inspector pane is to enable you to view and edit the components that comprise any GameObject. This Cube GameObject has Transform, Mesh Filter, Box Collider, and Mesh Renderer components:

- **Transform:** The Transform component sets the position, rotation, and scale of the GameObject. This is the only component that is required in every GameObject.
- **Cube (Mesh Filter):** The Mesh Filter component gives the GameObject its three-dimensional shape, which is modeled as a mesh composed of triangles. 3D models in games are generally a surface that is hollow inside. Unlike a real egg (which is filled with a yolk and albumen), a 3D model of an egg would just be a mesh simulating the eggshell. The Mesh Filter component attaches a 3D model to the GameObject. In the case of Cube, the Mesh Filter is using a simple 3D cube model that is built into Unity, but you can also

import complex 3D models into the Project pane to bring more complex meshes into your game.

- **Box Collider:** Collider components enable a GameObject to interact with other objects in the physics simulation that Unity runs. There are several different kinds of colliders, the most common of which are: Sphere, Capsule, Box, and Mesh (in increasing order of computational complexity). A GameObject with a collider component (and no Rigidbody component) acts as an immovable object in space that other GameObjects can run into.

- **Mesh Renderer:** While the Mesh Filter provides the actual geometry of the GameObject, the Mesh Renderer component makes that geometry appear on screen. Without a renderer, nothing in Unity will appear on screen. Renderers work with the Main Camera to convert the 3D geometry of the Mesh Filter into the pixels you actually see on screen.

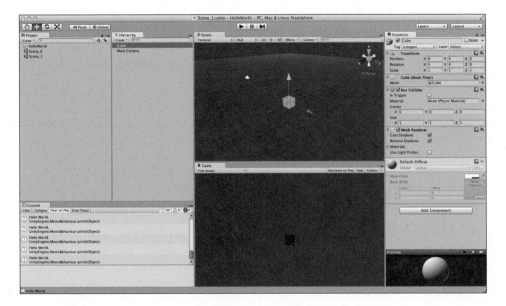

Figure 18.8   Creating a new Cube GameObject

Now we're going to add one more component to this GameObject: a *Rigidbody*. With the Cube still selected in the hierarchy, choose *Component > Physics > Rigidbody* from the menu bar, and you'll see a Rigidbody component added to the Inspector:

- **Rigidbody:** The Rigidbody component tells Unity that we want physics to be simulated for this GameObject. This includes physical forces like gravity, friction, collisions, and drag. A Rigidbody enables a GameObject with a collider to move through space. Without a Rigidbody, even if the GameObject is moved by adjusting its transform, the Collider component of the GameObject will not move. You must attach a Rigidbody component to any GameObject that you want to both move and properly collide with other colliders.

Now, if you click the Play button, you'll see the box fall due to gravity.

All the physical simulations in Unity are based on the metric system. This means that

- 1 unit of distance = 1 meter (for example, the units for the position of a transform). I will sometimes refer to one unit of distance in Unity as *1m*.
- 1 unit of mass = 1 kilogram (for example, the units of mass of a Rigidbody).
- The default gravity of −9.8 = 9.8 m/s^2 in the downward (negative y) direction.
- An average human character would be about 2 units (2 meters) tall.

Click the Play button again to stop the simulation.

Currently, your scene is a little dark, so let's add some light. Choose *GameObject > Create Other > Directional Light* from the menu bar. This will add a directional light to the scene, enabling you to see the cube more clearly. We'll talk more about the various kinds of lights in later chapters.

Making a Prefab

Now, we're going to make Cube into a *prefab*. A prefab is a reusable element in a project that can be instantiated (cloned into existence) any number of times. You can think of a prefab as a mold for a GameObject, and each GameObject made from that prefab is called an *instance* of the prefab (hence the word *instantiate*). To make a prefab, click Cube in the Hierarchy pane, drag it over to the Project pane, and release the mouse button (see Figure 18.9).

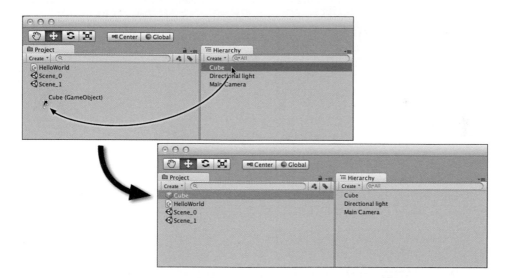

Figure 18.9 Making Cube into a prefab

You'll see that a couple of things have just happened:

1. A prefab named Cube has been created in the Project pane. You can tell it's a prefab by the blue cube icon next to it. (The prefab icon is always a cube regardless of the shape of the prefab itself.)

2. The name of the Cube GameObject in the Hierarchy has turned blue. If a GameObject has a blue name in the Hierarchy it means that that GameObject is an instance of a prefab (which is a copy made from the prefab mold).

Just for the sake of clarity, let's rename the Cube prefab in the Project pane to *Cube Prefab*. Click once on the Cube prefab to select it. Then click a second time to rename it (you can also try pressing Return [or F2 on PC] once it's selected to rename it) and then change the name to *Cube Prefab*. You'll see that because the instance in the Hierarchy pane is just a copy of this, its name changes as well. If you had renamed the instance in the Hierarchy to be different from the name of the prefab, the instance name would not have been affected.

Now that we've got our prefab set up, we don't actually need the instance in the scene any more. Click Cube Prefab in the Hierarchy pane (not the Project pane!). Then choose *Edit > Delete* from the menu bar.

It's time to get our hands dirty with some more code.

Choose *Assets > Create > C# Script* from the menu bar and rename the newly created script *CubeSpawner* (making sure that there are two capital letters and no spaces in the name). Double-click the CubeSpawner script to open MonoDevelop, add the bolded code shown here, and save it:

```
 1 using UnityEngine;
 2 using System.Collections;
 3
 4 public class CubeSpawner : MonoBehaviour {
 5     public GameObject        cubePrefabVar;
 6
 7     // Use this for initialization
 8     void Start () {
 9         Instantiate( cubePrefabVar );
10     }
11
12     // Update is called once per frame
13     void Update () {
14
15     }
16 }
```

As with our previous script, this needs to be attached to something to run, so in Unity, drag the CubeSpawner script over to Main Camera just as you did previously in Figure 18.4.

Now, click the Main Camera in the Hierarchy pane. You'll see that a *Cube Spawner (Script)* component has been added to the Main Camera GameObject (see Figure 18.10).

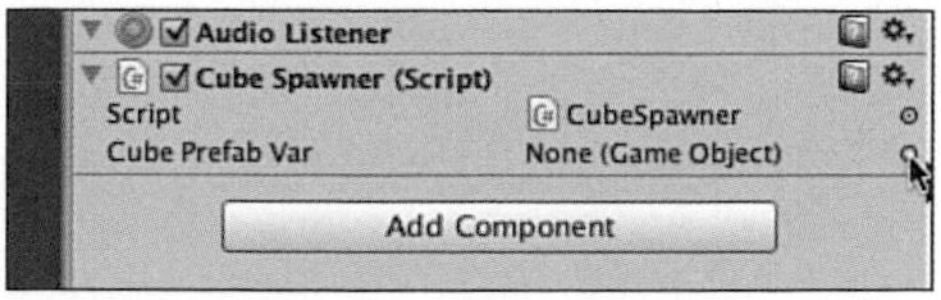

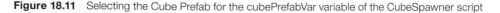

Figure 18.10   The CubeSpawner script component in the Inspector pane for Main Camera

You can also see that there is a variable called *Cube Prefab Var* in this component (though it really should be *cubePrefabVar*, as explained in the following warning). That comes from the `"public GameObject cubePrefabVar;"` statement you typed on line 5. If a variable of a script is labeled `"public"`, it will appear in the Inspector pane.

> ## warning
>
> **VARIABLE NAMES LOOK DIFFERENT IN THE INSPECTOR**   Someone at Unity thought it would look nice to change the capitalization and spacing of variable names in the Inspector pane. I have no idea why this has lasted into the current version, but it means that your variable names like `cubePrefabVar` will incorrectly appear in the Inspector as *Cube Prefab Var*. Be careful to always refer to your variable names properly in your programming and please ignore the strange capitalization and spacing that you see in the Inspector. Throughout the book, I refer to variables by their proper name in code rather than the names that appear in the Inspector.

As you can see in the Inspector, cubePrefabVar currently has no value assigned. Click the circular target to the right of the cubePrefabVar variable value (as shown by the arrow cursor in Figure 18.10), and this will bring up the *Select GameObject* dialog box from which you can select a prefab to be assigned to this variable. Make sure that the *Assets* tab is selected. (The Assets tab shows GameObjects in your Project pane, while the Scene tab shows GameObjects in your Hierarchy.) Double-click CubePrefab to select it (see Figure 18.11).

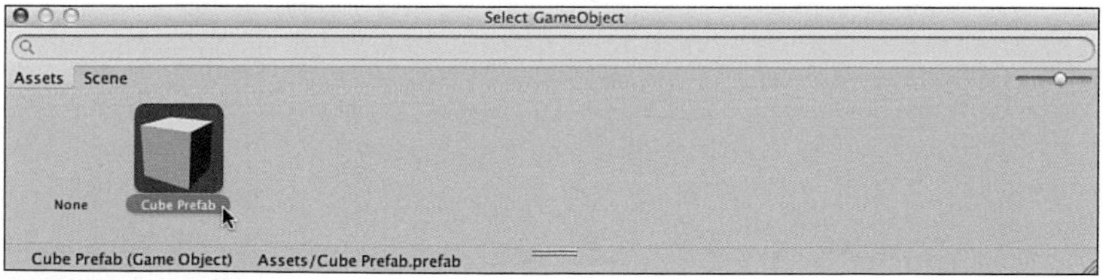

Figure 18.11   Selecting the Cube Prefab for the cubePrefabVar variable of the CubeSpawner script

Now, you can see in the Inspector that the value of cubePrefabVar is Cube Prefab from the Project pane. To double-check this, click the value *Cube Prefab* in the Inspector, and you'll see that Cube Prefab is highlighted yellow in the Project pane.

Click the *Play* button.

You'll see that a single Cube Prefab (Clone) GameObject is instantiated in the Hierarchy. Just like we saw in the Hello World script, the Start() function is called once, and it creates a single instance (or clone) of the Cube Prefab. Now, switch to MonoDevelop, comment out the Instantiate() call on line 9 in the Start() function and add an Instantiate (cubePrefabVar); statement to line 14 in the Update() function, as shown in the following code.

```
 1 using UnityEngine;
 2 using System.Collections;
 3
 4 public class CubeSpawner : MonoBehaviour {
 5     public GameObject        cubePrefabVar;
 6
 7     // Use this for initialization
 8     void Start () {
 9         // Instantiate( cubePrefabVar );
10     }
11
12     // Update is called once per frame
13     void Update () {
14         Instantiate( cubePrefabVar );
15     }
16 }
```

Save the CubeSpawner script, switch back to Unity, and press *Play* again. As shown in Figure 18.12, this will give you cubes galore.

This is an example of the power of Unity. Very quickly, we were able to get up to speed and make something cool and interesting. Now, let's add some more objects to the scene for the cubes to interact with.

In the Hierarchy, click the *Create* pop-up menu and choose *Cube*. Rename this cube *Ground*.

With a GameObject selected in the Scene pane or Hierarchy pane, pressing the W, E, or R keys will allow you to translate (move), rotate, or scale the GameObject. This will show gizmos (the arrows, circles, and such shown around the cube in Figure 18.13) around Ground. In translation mode, clicking and dragging on one of the arrows will move the cube exclusively along the axis of that arrow (x, y, or z). The colored elements of the rotation and scale gizmos lock the transformation to a specific axis in similar ways. See the "Changing the Scene View" sidebar for information about how to use the hand tool shown in Figure 18.13.

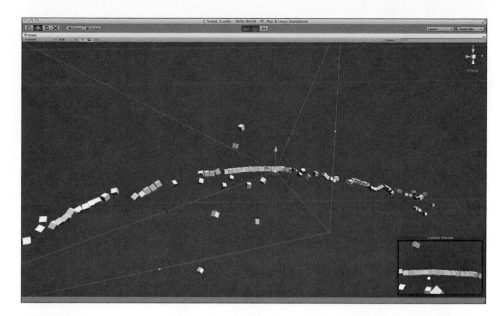

Figure 18.12   Creating a new instance of the CubePrefab every `Update()` quickly adds up to a lot of cubes!

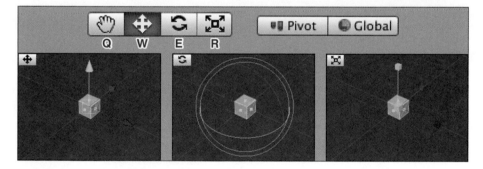

Figure 18.13   The translate (position), rotate, and scale gizmos. Q, W, E, and R are the keys that select each tool. Unity has *just* added another icon after the scale one (R) in their current beta for version 4.6, but that's not common knowledge yet.

CHANGING THE SCENE VIEW

The first tool on the toolbar shown in Figure 18.13—known as the *hand tool*—is used to manipulate the view shown in the Scene pane. The Scene pane has its own invisible *scene camera* that is different from the Main Camera in the Hierarchy. The hand tool has several different abilities. Select the hand tool (by either clicking it or pressing Q on your keyboard) and try the following:

- Left-dragging (that is, clicking and dragging using the left mouse button) in the Scene pane will move the position of the scene camera without changing the position of any of the objects in the scene. To be technical, the scene camera is moved in a plane perpendicular to the direction that the camera is facing (that is, perpendicular to the camera's forward vector).

- Right-dragging in the Scene pane will rotate the scene camera to look in the direction of your drag. The scene camera stays in the same position when right-dragging.

- Holding the Option key (or Alt key on PC) will change the cursor over the Scene pane from a hand to an eye, and left-dragging with the Option key held will cause the Scene view to rotate around objects in the Scene pane (this is known as orbiting the camera around the scene). When Option-left-dragging, the position of the scene camera changes, but the location that the scene camera is looking at does not.

- Scrolling with the scroll wheel on your mouse will cause the scene camera to zoom in and out of the scene. Zooming can also be done by Option-right-dragging in the Scene pane.

The best way to get a feel for the hand tool is to try moving around the scene using the different methods described in this sidebar. After you have played with it a little, it should become second nature to you.

Try moving Ground to a Y position of -4 and setting its scale in the X and Z dimensions to 10. Throughout the book, I will suggest positions, rotations, and scales using this format.

> Ground (Cube)   P:[0,-4,0]   R:[0,0,0]   S:[10,1,10]

Ground here is the name of the GameObject, and *(Cube)* is the type of the GameObject. *P:[0,-4,0]* means to set the X position to 0, the Y position to -4, and the Z position to 0. Similarly, R:[0,0,0] means to keep the X, Y, and Z rotations set to 0. *S:[10,1,10]* means to set the X scale to 10, the Y scale to 1, and the Z scale to 10. You can either use the tools and gizmos to make these changes or just type them into the Transform component of the Ground's Inspector.

Feel free to play around with this and add more objects. The instances of Cube Prefab will bounce off of the static objects that you put into the scene (see Figure 18.14). As long as you don't add a Rigidbody to any of the new shapes, they should be *static* (i.e., solid and immovable). When you're done, be sure to save your scene!

Figure 18.14   The scene with static shapes added

Summary

In about 20 pages, you've gone from nothing to having a working Unity project with a little programming in it. Admittedly, this project was pretty small, but I hope that it has served to show you the raw speed at which Unity can operate as well as the speed at which you can get something running in Unity.

The next chapter will continue your introduction to C# and Unity by introducing you to variables and increasing your knowledge of the most common components that can be added to a GameObject.

CHAPTER 19

VARIABLES AND COMPONENTS

This chapter introduces you to the many variable and component types used throughout Unity C# programming. By the end of the chapter, you will understand many of the common types of C# variables and some important variable types that are unique to Unity.

This chapter also introduces you to Unity's GameObjects and components. Any object in a Unity scene is a GameObject, and the components that comprise them enable everything from the positioning of a GameObject to physics simulation, special effects, displaying a 3D model on screen, and character animation.

Introducing Variables

To recap a bit of Chapter 17, "Introducing our Language: C#," a *variable* is just a name that can be defined to be equal to a specific value. This is actually a concept that comes from the study of algebra. In algebra, for instance, you can be given the definition:

```
x = 5
```

This *defines* the *variable* x to be equal to the *value* 5. In other words, it assigns the value 5 to the name x. Then, if later, you encounter the definition:

```
y = x + 2
```

Then you now know that the value of the variable y is 7 (because x = 5 and 5 + 2 = 7). x and y are called *variables* because their value can be redefined at any time; however, the order in which these definitions occur does matter. Take a look at these definitions. (*Comments* are included after two slashes [//] in the following code listing to help explain what the code is doing.)

```
x = 10       // x is now equal to the value 10
y = x - 4    // y is now 6 because 10-4 = 6
x = 12       // x is now equal to the value 12, but y is still 6
z = x + 3    // z is now 15 because 12+3 = 15
```

After this sequence of definitions, the values assigned to x, y, and z are 12, 6, and 15, respectively. As you can see, even though x changed value, y was not affected because y is defined as the value 6 before x is assigned the new value 12, and y is not retroactively affected.

Strongly Typed Variables in C#

Instead of being able to be assigned any kind of value, C# variables are *strongly typed*, meaning that they can only accept a specific type of value. This is necessary because the computer needs to know how much space in memory to allocate to each variable. A large image can take up many megabytes or even gigabytes of space, while a Boolean value (which can only hold either a 1 or a 0) only really requires a single bit. Even just a single megabyte is equivalent to 8,388,608 bits!

Declaring and Defining Variables in C#

In C#, a variable must be both declared and defined for it to have a usable value.

Declaring a variable creates it and gives it a name and type. However, this does not give the variable a value.

```
bool    bravo;
int     india;
float   foxtrot;
char    charlie;
```

Defining a variable gives that variable a value. Here are some examples using the declared variables:

```
bravo = true;
india = 8;
foxtrot = 3.14f; // The f makes foxtrot a float, as described later
charlie = 'c';
```

Literals

Whenever you write a specific value in your code (e.g., `true`, `8`, or `'c'`), that specific value is called a *literal*. In the previous code listing, `true` is a bool literal, `8` is an int literal, `3.14f` is a float literal, and `'c'` is a char literal. By default, MonoDevelop shows these literals in a bright magenta color, and each variable type has certain rules about how its literals are represented. Check out each of the variable types in the following sections for more information on this.

Declaration Before Definition

You must first declare a variable before you can define it, although this is often done on the same line:

```
string   sierra = "Mountain";
```

In general, Unity will complain and throw a compiler error if you try to access (i.e., read) a variable that has been declared but has not yet been defined.

Important C# Variable Types

Several different types of variables are available to you in C#. Here are a few important ones that you'll encounter frequently. All of these basic C# variable types begin with a lowercase letter, whereas most Unity data types begin with an uppercase letter. For each, I've listed information about the variable type and an example of how to declare and define the variable.

bool: A 1-Bit True or False Value

The term *bool* is short for Boolean. At their heart, all variables are composed of bits that can either be set to true or false. A bool is 1 bit in length, making it the smallest possible variable.[1] Bools are extremely useful for logic operations like `if` statements and other conditionals, which are covered in the next two chapters. In C#, bool literals are limited to the lowercase keywords `true` and `false`:

```
bool verified = true;
```

---

[1] Though a bool only requires a single bit of memory for storage, C# actually uses at least 1 byte (which is 8 bits) to store each bool. On a 32-bit system, the smallest possible memory chunk is 32 bits, and on a 64-bit system, it's 64 bits or 8 bytes.

int: A 32-Bit Integer

Short for integer, an *int* can store a single integer number (integers are numbers without any fractional value like 5, 2, & –90). Integer math is very accurate and very fast. An int in Unity can store a number between –2,147,483,648 and 2,147,483,647 with 1 bit used for the positive or negative sign of the number and 31 bits used for the numerical value. An int can hold any integer value between these two numbers (inclusive):

```
int nonFractionalNumber = 12345;
```

float: A 32-bit Decimal Number

A floating-point number,[2] or *float*, is the most common form of decimal number used in Unity. It is called "floating point" because it is stored using a system similar to scientific notation. Scientific notation is the representation of numbers in the form $a \cdot 10^b$ (for example, 300 would be written $3 \cdot 10^2$, and 12,345 would be written $1.2345 \cdot 10^4$). Floating point numbers are stored in a similar format with $a \cdot 2^b$. When storing numbers this way in memory, 1 bit represents whether the number is positive or negative, 23 bits are allocated to the significand (the number itself and the *a* part above), and 8 are allocated to exponent to which the number is raised or lowered (the *b* part). This means that there will be significant gaps in the precision of very large numbers and any number between 1 and –1. For instance, there is no way to accurately represent 1/3 using a float.

Most of the time, the imprecise nature of floats doesn't matter much in your games, but it can cause small errors in things like collision detection; so in general, keeping elements in your game larger than 1 unit and smaller than several thousand units in size will make collisions a little more accurate. Float literals must be either a whole number or a decimal number followed by an f. This is because C# assumes that any decimal literal without a trailing f is a *double* (which is a float with double the precision) instead of the single-precision floats that Unity uses. Floats are used in all built-in Unity functions instead of doubles to bring about the fastest possible calculation, though this comes at the expense of accuracy:

```
float notPreciselyOneThird = 1.0f/3.0f;
```

> **tip**
>
> If you see the following compile-time error in your code
>
> ```
> error CS0664: Literal of type double cannot be implicitly converted to
> type 'float'. Add suffix 'f' to create a literal of this type
> ```
>
> it means that somewhere you have forgotten to add the f after a float literal.

---

2 http://en.wikipedia.org/wiki/Floating_point

char: A 16-Bit Single Character

A *char* is a single character represented by 16 bits of information. Chars use Unicode[3] values for storing characters, enabling the representation of over 110,000 different characters from over 100 different character sets and languages (including, for instance, all the characters in Simplified Chinese). A char literal is surrounded by single-quote marks (a.k.a. apostrophes):

```
char theLetterA = 'A';
```

string: A Series of 16-Bit Characters

A string is used to represent everything from a single character to the text of an entire book. The theoretical maximum length of a string in C# is over 2 billion characters, but most computers will encounter memory allocation issues long before that limit is reached. To give some context, there are a little over 175,000 characters in the full version of Shakespeare's play *Hamlet*,[4] including stage directions, line breaks, and so on. This means that *Hamlet* could be repeated over 12,000 times in a single string. A string literal is surrounded by double-quote marks:

```
string theFirstLineOfHamlet = "Who's there?";
```

It's also possible to access the individual chars of a string using *bracket access*:

```
char theCharW = theFirstLineOfHamlet[0]; // W is the 0th char in the string
char theChart = theFirstLineOfHamlet[6]; // t is the 6th char in the string
```

Placing a number in brackets after the variable name retrieves the character in that position from the string (without affecting the original string). When using bracket access, counting starts with the number 0; so in the preceding code, W is the 0th (pronounced "zeroth") character of the first line of "Hamlet," and t is the 6th character. You will encounter bracket access much more in Chapter 22, "Lists and Arrays."

> **tip**
>
> If you see any of the following compile-time errors in your code
>
> ```
> error CS0029: Cannot implicitly convert type 'string' to 'char'
> error CS0029: Cannot implicitly convert type 'char' to 'string'
> error CS1012: Too many characters in character literal
> error CS1525: Unexpected symbol '<internal>'
> ```
>
> it usually means that somewhere you have accidentally used double quotes (" ") for a char literal or single quotes (' ') for a string literal. String literals always require double quotes, and char literals always require single quotes.

---

[3] http://en.wikipedia.org/wiki/Unicode
[4] http://shakespeare.mit.edu/hamlet/full.html

class: The Definition of a New Variable Type

A *class* defines a new type of variable that can be best thought of as a collection of both variables and functionality. All the Unity variable types and components listed in the "Important Unity Variable Types" section of this chapter are examples of classes. Chapter 25, "Classes," covers classes in greater detail.

The Scope of Variables

In addition to variable type, another important concept for variables is *scope*. The scope of a variable refers to the range of code in which the variable exists and is understood. If you declare a variable in one part of your code, it might not have meaning in another part. This is a complex issue that will be covered throughout this book. If you want to learn about it progressively, just read the book in order. If you want to get a lot more information about variable scope right now, you can read the section "Variable Scope" in Appendix B, "Useful Concepts."

Naming Conventions

The code in this book follows a number of rules governing the naming of variables, functions, classes, and so on. Although none of these rules are mandatory, following them will make your code more readable not only to others who try to decipher it but also to yourself if you ever need to return to it months later and hope to understand what you wrote. Every coder follows slightly different rules—my personal rules have even changed over the years—but the rules I present here have worked well for both me and my students, and they are consistent with most C# code that I've encountered in Unity:

1. Use *camelCase* for pretty much everything (see the camelCase sidebar).

CAMELCASE

camelCase is a common way of writing variable names in programming. It allows the programmer or someone reading her code to easily parse long variable names. Here are some examples:

- aVariableNameStartingWithALowerCaseLetter

- AClassNameStartingWithACapitalLetter

- aRealLongNameThatIsEasierToReadBecauseOfCamelCase

The key feature of camelCase is that it allows multiple words to be combined into one with a medial capital letter at the beginning of each original word. It is named camelCase because it looks a bit like the humps on a camel's back.

2. Variable names should start with a lowercase letter (e.g., `someVariableName`).

3. Function names should start with an uppercase letter (e.g., `Start()`, `Update()`).

4. Class names should start with an uppercase letter (e.g., `GameObject`, `ScopeExample`).

5. Private variable names can start with an underscore (e.g., `_hiddenVariable`).

6. Static variable names can be all caps with snake_case (e.g., `NUM_INSTANCES`). As you can see, snake_case combines multiple words with an underscore in between them.

For your later reference, this information is repeated in the "Naming Conventions" section of Appendix B.

CLASS INSTANCES AND STATIC FUNCTIONS

Just like the prefabs that you saw in Chapter 18, "Hello World: Your First Program," classes can also have *instances*. An instance of any class (also known as a *member* of the class) is a data object that is of the type defined by the class.

For example, you could define a class `Human`, and everyone you know would be an instance of that class. Several functions are shared by all humans (for example, `Eat()`, `Sleep()`, `Breathe()`).

Just as you differ from all other humans around you, each instance of a class differs from the other instances. Even if two instances have perfectly identical values, they are stored in different locations in computer memory and seen as two distinct objects. (To continue the human analogy, you could think of them as identical twins.) Class instances are referred to by *reference*, not value. This means that if you are comparing two class instances to see whether they are the same, the thing that is compared is their *location in memory*, not their values (just as two identical twins have different names).

It is, of course, possible to reference the same class instance using different variables. Just as the person I might call "daughter" would also be called "granddaughter" by my parents, a class instance can be assigned to any number of variable names yet still be the same data object, as is shown in the following code:

```
1 using UnityEngine;
2 using System.Collections;
3
4 // Defining the class Human
5 public class Human {
6     public string    name;
7     public Human     partner;
8 }
9
10 public class Family : MonoBehaviour {
11     // public variable declaration
12     public Human husband;
13     public Human wife;
```

```
14
15    void Start() {
16        // Initial state
17        husband = new Human();
18        husband.name = "Jeremy Gibson";
19        wife = new Human();
20        wife.name = "Melanie Schuessler";
21
22        // My wife and I get married
23        husband.partner = wife;
24        wife.partner = husband;
25
26        // We change our names
27        husband.name = "Jeremy Gibson Bond";
28        wife.name = "Melanie Schuessler Bond";
29
30        // Because wife.partner refers to the same instance as husband,
31        //  the name of wife.partner has also changed
32        print(wife.partner.name);
33        // prints "Jeremy Gibson Bond"
34    }
35 }
```

It is also possible to create *static functions* on the class Human that are able to act on one or more instances of the class. The following static function Marry() allows you to set two humans to be each other's partner with a single function.

```
35  // This replaces line 35 from the previous code listing
36
37    static public void Marry(Human h0, Human h1) {
38        h0.partner = h1;
39        h1.partner = h0;
40    }
41 }
```

With this function, it would now be possible to replace lines 23 and 24 from the initial code listing with the single line Human.Marry(wife, husband); . Because Marry() is a static function, it can be used almost anywhere in your code. You will learn more about static functions and variables later in the book.

Important Unity Variable Types

Unity has a number of variable types that you will encounter in nearly every project. All of these variable types are examples of classes and follow Unity's naming convention that all class types start with an uppercase letter. For each of the Unity variable types, you will see information about how to create a new *instance* of that class (see the sidebar on class instances) followed by listings of important variables and functions for that data type. For most of the Unity classes listed in this section, the variables and functions are split into two groups:

- **Instance variables and functions:** These variables and functions are tied directly to a single instance of the variable type. If you look at the Vector3 information that follows, you will see that x, y, z, and `magnitude` are all instance variables of Vector3, and each one is accessed via *dot syntax*, which is the name of a Vector3 variable, a period, and then the name of the instance variable (for example, `position.x`). Each Vector3 instance can have different values for these variables. Similarly, the `Normalize()` function acts on a single instance of Vector3 and sets the `magnitude` of that instance to 1.

- **Static class variables and functions:** Static variables are tied to the class definition itself rather than being tied to an individual instance. These are often used to store information that is the same across all instances of the class (for example, `Color.red` is always the same red color) or to act on multiple instances of the class without affecting either (for example, `Vector3.Cross( v3a, v3b )` is used to calculate the cross product of two Vector3s and return that value as a new Vector3 without changing either v3a or v3b).

For more information on any of these Unity types, check out the Unity documentation links referenced in the footnotes.

Vector3: A Collection of Three Floats

Vector3[5] is a very common data type for working in 3D. It is used most commonly to store the three-dimensional position of objects in Unity. Follow the footnote for more detailed information about Vector3s.

```
Vector3 position = new Vector3( 0.0f, 3.0f, 4.0f ); // Sets the x, y, & z values
```

Vector3 Instance Variables and Functions

As a class, each Vector3 instance also contains a number of useful built-in values and functions:

```
print( position.x ); // 0.0, The x value of the Vector3
print( position.y ); // 3.0, The y value of the Vector3
print( position.z ); // 4.0, The z value of the Vector3
print( position.magnitude ); // 5.0, The distance of the Vector3 from 0,0,0
                             //  Magnitude is another word for "length".
position.Normalize(); // Sets the magnitude of position to 1, meaning that the
                      //  x, y, & z values of position are now [0.0, 0.6, 0.8]
```

---

[5] http://docs.unity3d.com/Documentation/ScriptReference/Vector3.html

Vector3 Static Class Variables and Functions

In addition, several static class variables and functions are associated with the Vector3 class itself:

```
print( Vector3.zero );    // (0,0,0), Shorthand for: new Vector3( 0, 0, 0 )
print( Vector3.one );     // (1,1,1), Shorthand for: new Vector3( 1, 1, 1 )
print( Vector3.right );   // (1,0,0), Shorthand for: new Vector3( 1, 0, 0 )
print( Vector3.up );      // (0,1,0), Shorthand for: new Vector3( 0, 1, 0 )
print( Vector3.forward ); // (0,0,1), Shorthand for: new Vector3( 0, 0, 1 )
Vector3.Cross( v3a, v3b );// Computes the cross product of the two Vector3s
Vector3.Dot( v3a, v3b );  // Computes the dot product of the two Vector3s
```

This is only a sampling of the fields and methods affiliated with Vector3. To find out more, check out the Unity documentation referenced in the footnote.

Color: A Color with Transparency Information

The Color[6] variable type can store information about a color and its transparency (alpha value). Colors on computers are mixtures of the three primary colors of light: red, green, and blue. These are different from the primary colors of paint you may have learned as a child (red, yellow, and blue) because color on a computer screen is *additive*, rather than *subtractive*. In a subtractive color system like paint, mixing more and more different colors together will move the mixed color toward black (or a really dark, muddy brown). By contrast, in an additive color system (like a computer screen, theatrical lighting design, or HTML colors on the Internet), adding more and more colors together will get brighter and brighter until the final mixed color is eventually white. The red, green, and blue components of a color in C# are stored as floats that range from 0.0f to 1.0f with 0.0f representing none of that color channel and 1.0f representing as much of that color channel as possible:[7]

```
// Colors are defined by floats for the Red, Green, Blue, Alpha channels
Color darkGreen = new Color( 0f, 0.25f, 0f); // If no alpha info is passed in,
                                             //  the alpha value is assumed to
                                             //  be 1 (fully opaque)
Color darkRedTransparent = new Color( 0.25f, 0f, 0f, 0.5f );
```

As you can see, there are two different ways to define a color, one with three parameters (red, green, and blue) and one with four parameters (red, green, blue, and alpha).[8] The alpha value sets the transparency of the color. A color with an alpha of 0.0f is fully transparent, and a color with an alpha of 1.0f is fully opaque.

---

[6] http://docs.unity3d.com/Documentation/ScriptReference/Color.html

[7] In the Unity color picker, the four channels of a color are defined as whole numbers between 0 and 255. These numbers match the possible color values of HTML but are automatically converted to a float from 0–1 in Unity.

[8] The ability of the new Color() function to take different numbers of variables is called *function overloading*, and you can read more about it in Chapter 23, "Functions and Parameters."

Color Instance Variables and Functions

Each channel of a color can be referenced through instance variables:

```
print( Color.yellow.r ); // 1, The red value of the Color
print( Color.yellow.g ); // 0.92f, The green value of the Color
print( Color.yellow.b ); // 0.016f, The blue value of the Color
print( Color.yellow.a ); // 1, The alpha value of the Color
```

Color Static Class Variables and Functions

Several common colors are predefined in Unity as static class variables:

```
// Primary Colors: Red, Green, and Blue
Color.red     = new Color(1, 0, 0, 1); // Solid red
Color.green   = new Color(0, 1, 0, 1); // Solid green
Color.blue    = new Color(0, 0, 1, 1); // Solid blue

// Secondary Colors: Cyan, Magenta, and Yellow
Color.cyan    = new Color(0, 1, 1, 1); // Cyan, a bright greenish blue
Color.magenta = new Color(1, 0, 1, 1); // Magenta, a pinkish purple
Color.yellow  = new Color(1, 0.92f, 0.016f, 1); // A nice-looking yellow
// As you can imagine, a standard yellow would be new Color(1,1,0,1),
//  but in Unity's opinion, this yellow looks better.

// Black, White, and Clear
Color.black   = new Color(0, 0, 0, 1); // Solid black
Color.white   = new Color(1, 1, 1, 1); // Solid white
Color.gray    = new Color(0.5f, 0.5f, 0.5f, 1) // Gray
Color.grey    = new Color(0.5f, 0.5f, 0.5f, 1) // British spelling of gray
Color.clear   = new Color(0, 0, 0, 0); // Completely transparent
```

Quaternion: Rotation Information

Explaining the inner workings of the Quaternion[9] class is far beyond the scope of this book, but you will be using them often to set and adjust the rotation of objects through the quaternion `GameObject.transform.rotation`, which is part of every GameObject. Quaternions define rotations in a way that avoids gimbal lock, a problem with standard x, y, z (or Euler, pronounced "oiler") rotations where one axis can align with another and limit rotation possibilities. Most of the time, you will be defining a quaternion by passing in Euler rotations and allowing Unity to convert them into the equivalent quaternion:

```
Quaternion lookUp45Deg = Quaternion.Euler( -45f, 0f, 0f );
```

In cases like this, the three floats passed into `Quaternion.Euler()` are the number of degrees to rotate around the x, y, and z axes (respectively colored red, green, and blue in Unity). GameObjects, including the Main Camera in a scene, are initially oriented to be looking down

---

[9]　http://docs.unity3d.com/Documentation/ScriptReference/Quaternion.html

the positive z-axis. The rotation in the preceding code would rotate the camera -45 degrees around the red x-axis, causing it to then be looking up at a 45° angle relative to the positive z-axis. If that last sentence was confusing, don't worry about it too much right now. Later, you can try going into Unity and changing the x, y, and z rotation values in the Transform Inspector for a GameObject and see how it alters the object's orientation.

Quaternion Instance Variables and Functions

You can also use the instance variable `eulerAngles` to cause a quaternion to return its rotation information to you in Euler angles:

```
print( lookUp45Deg.eulerAngles ); // ( -45, 0, 0 ), the Euler rotation
```

Mathf: A Library of Mathematical Functions

Mathf[10] isn't really a variable type as much as it's a fantastically useful library of math functions. All of the variables and functions attached to Mathf are static; you cannot create an instance of Mathf. There are far too many useful functions in the Mathf library to list here, but a few include the following:

```
Mathf.Sin(x);           // Computes the sine of x
Mathf.Cos(x);           // .Tan(), .Asin(), .Acos(), & .Atan() are also available
Mathf.Atan2( y, x );    // Gives you the angle to rotate around the z-axis to
                        //      change something facing along the x-axis to face
                        //      instead toward the point x, y.11
print(Mathf.PI);        // 3.141593; the ratio of circumference to diameter
Mathf.Min( 2, 3, 1 );   // 1, the smallest of the three numbers (float or int)
Mathf.Max( 2, 3, 1 );   // 3, the largest of the three numbers (float or int)
Mathf.Round( 1.75f );   // 2, rounds up or down to the nearest number
Mathf.Ceil( 1.75f );    // 2, rounds up to the next highest integer number
Mathf.Floor( 1.75f );   // 1, rounds down to the next lowest integer number
Mathf.Abs( -25 );       // 25, the absolute value of -25
```

Screen: Information about the Display

Screen[12] is another library like Mathf that can give you information about the specific computer screen that your Unity game is using. This works regardless of device, so screen will give you accurate info whether you're on a PC, OS X, an iOS device, or an Android tablet:

```
print( Screen.width );   // Prints the width of the screen in pixels
print( Screen.height );  // Prints the height of the screen in pixels
Screen.showCursor = false; // Hides the cursor
```

---

[10] http://docs.unity3d.com/Documentation/ScriptReference/Mathf.html

[11] http://docs.unity3d.com/Documentation/ScriptReference/Mathf.Atan2.html

[12] http://docs.unity3d.com/Documentation/ScriptReference/Screen.html

SystemInfo: Information about the Device

SystemInfo[13] will tell you specific information about the device on which the game is running. It includes information about operating system, number of processors, graphics hardware, and more. I recommend following the link in the footnote to learn more:

```
print( SystemInfo.operatingSystem ); // Mac OS X 10.8.5, for example
```

GameObject: The Type of Any Object in the Scene

GameObject[14] is the base class for all entities in Unity scenes. Anything you see on screen in a Unity game is a subclass of the GameObject class. GameObjects can contain any number of different *components*, including all of those referenced in the next section: "Unity GameObject Components." However, GameObjects also have a few important variables beyond what is covered there:

```
GameObject gObj = new GameObject("MyGO"); // Creates a new GameObject named MyGO
print( gObj.name );    // MyGO, the name of the GameObject gObj
Transform trans = gObj.GetComponent<Transform>(); // Defines trans to be
                                        a reference to the Transform
                                        Component of gObj
Transform trans2 = gObj.transform; // A shortcut to access the same Transform
gObj.SetActive(false);   // Makes gObj inactive, rendering it invisible
                         // and preventing it from running code.
```

The method[15] gObj.GetComponent<Transform>() shown here is of particular importance because it can enable you to access any of the components attached to a GameObject. You will sometimes see methods with angle brackets <> like GetComponent<>(). These are called *generic methods* because they are designed to be used on many different data types. In the case of GetComponent<Transform>(), the data type is Transform, which tells GetComponent<>() to find the Transform component of the GameObject and return it to you. This can also be used to get any other component of the GameObject by typing that component type inside the angle brackets instead of Transform. Examples include the following:

```
Renderer rend = gObj.GetComponent<Renderer>(); // Gets the Renderer Component
Collider coll = gObj.GetComponent<Collider>(); // Gets the Collider Component
HelloWorld hwInstance = gObj.GetComponent<HelloWorld>();
```

As shown in the third line of the preceding code listing, GetComponent<>() can also be used to return the instance of any C# class that you've attached to the GameObject.

---

[13] http://docs.unity3d.com/Documentation/ScriptReference/SystemInfo.html

[14] http://docs.unity3d.com/Documentation/ScriptReference/GameObject.html

[15] "Function" and "method" have the same basic meaning. The only difference is that "function" is used to describe a standalone function while "method" refers to a function that is part of a class.

If there were an instance of the HelloWorld C# script class attached to gObj, then
`gObj.Getcomponent<HelloWorld>()` would return it. This technique is used several times
throughout this book.

Unity GameObjects and Components

As mentioned in the previous section, all on-screen elements in Unity are GameObjects, and
all GameObjects are composed of components. When you select a GameObject in either the
Hierarchy pane or the Scene pane, the components of that GameObject are displayed in the
Inspector pane, as shown in Figure 19.1.

Figure 19.1   The Inspector pane showing various important components.

Transform: Position, Rotation, and Scale

Transform[16] is a mandatory component that is present on all GameObjects. Transform handles
critical GameObject information like position (the location of the GameObject), rotation
(the orientation of the GameObject), and scale (the size of the GameObject). Though the

---

[16] http://docs.unity3d.com/Documentation/Components/class-Transform.html

information is not displayed in the Inspector pane, Transform is also responsible for the parent/child relationships in the Hierarchy pane. When one object is the child of another, it moves with that parent object as if attached to it.

MeshFilter: The Model You See

A MeshFilter[17] component attaches a 3D mesh in your Project pane to a GameObject. To see a model on screen, the GameObject must have both a MeshFilter that handles the actual 3D mesh information and a MeshRenderer that combines that mesh with a shader or material and displays the image on screen. The MeshFilter creates a skin or surface for a GameObject, and the MeshRenderer determines the shape, color, and texture of that surface.

Renderer: Allows You to See the GameObject

A Renderer[18] component—in most cases, a MeshRenderer—allows you to see the GameObject in the Scene and Game panes. The MeshRenderer requires a MeshFilter to provide 3D mesh data as well as at least one Material if you want it to look like anything other than an ugly magenta blob (Materials apply textures to objects). Renderers bring the MeshFilter, the Material(s), and lighting together to show the GameObject on screen.

Collider: The Physical Presence of the GameObject

A Collider[19] enables a GameObject to have a physical presence in the game world and collide with other objects. There are four different kinds of Collider components in Unity:

- Sphere Collider:[20] The fastest collision shape. A ball or sphere.
- Capsule Collider:[21] A pipe with spheres at each end. The second fastest type.
- Box Collider:[22] A rectangular solid. Useful for crates, cars, torsos, and so on.
- Mesh Collider:[23] A collider formed from a 3D mesh. Although useful and accurate, they are much, much slower than any of the other three. Also, only Mesh Colliders with Convex set to true can collide with other Mesh Colliders.

[17] http://docs.unity3d.com/Documentation/Components/class-MeshFilter.html

[18] http://docs.unity3d.com/Documentation/Components/class-MeshRenderer.html

[19] http://docs.unity3d.com/Documentation/Components/comp-DynamicsGroup.html

[20] http://docs.unity3d.com/Documentation/Components/class-SphereCollider.html

[21] http://docs.unity3d.com/Documentation/Components/class-CapsuleCollider.html

[22] http://docs.unity3d.com/Documentation/Components/class-BoxCollider.html

[23] http://docs.unity3d.com/Documentation/Components/class-MeshCollider.html

Physics and collision are handled in Unity via the NVIDIA PhysX engine. Although this does usually provide very fast and accurate collisions, be aware that all physics engines have limitations, and even PhysX will sometimes have issues with fast-moving objects or thin walls.

Colliders are covered in much more depth later in this book, and you can also learn more about them from the Unity documentation.

Rigidbody: The Physics Simulation

The Rigidbody[24] component controls the physics simulation of your GameObject. The Rigidbody component simulates acceleration and velocity every FixedUpdate (generally every 50th of a second) to update the position and rotation of the Transform component over time. It also uses the Collider component to handle collisions with other GameObjects. The Rigidbody component can also model things like gravity, drag, and various forces like wind and explosions. Set *isKinematic* to true if you want to directly set the position of your GameObject without using the physics provided by Rigidbody.

For the position of a Collider component to move with its GameObject, the GameObject *must* have a Rigidbody. Otherwise, as far as Unity's PhysX physics simulation is concerned, the collider will not move. In other words, if a Rigidbody is not attached, the GameObject will appear to move across the screen, but in PhysX, the location of the Collider component will not be updated and will therefore remain in the same location.

Script: The C# Scripts That You Write

All C# scripts are also GameObject components. One of the benefits of scripts being components is that you can attach more than one script to each GameObject, a capability that we will take advantage of in some of the tutorials in Part III of this book. Later in the book, you will read much more about Script components and how to access them.

> **warning**
>
> **VARIABLE NAMES WILL CHAGE IN THE INSPECTOR**   In Figure 19.1, you can see that the name of the script is *Scope Example (Script)*, but that breaks the naming rules for classes, because class names cannot have spaces in them.
>
> The actual script name in my code is a single word in camelCase: `ScopeExample`. I'm not sure why exactly, but in the Inspector, the spelling of class and variable names is changed from their actual spelling in the C# scripts you write by the following rules:
>
> - The class name `ScopeExample` becomes *Scope Example (Script)*.
> - The variable `trueOrFalse` becomes *True Or False*.

---

[24] http://docs.unity3d.com/Documentation/Components/class-Rigidbody.html

- The variable `graduationAge` becomes *Graduation Age*.

- The variable `goldenRatio` becomes *Golden Ratio*.

This is an important distinction, and it has confused some of my students in the past. Even though the names appear differently in the Inspector, the variable names in your code have not been changed.

Summary

This was a long chapter with a lot of information in it, and you may need to read it again or refer back to it later once you've had some more experience with code. However, all of this information will prove invaluable to you as you continue through this book and as you start writing your own code. Once you understand the GameObject/Component structure of Unity and how to take advantage of the Unity Inspector to set and modify variables, you'll find that your Unity coding moves a lot faster and more smoothly.

CHAPTER 20

BOOLEAN OPERATIONS AND CONDITIONALS

Most people have heard that computer data is, at its base level, composed entirely of 1s and 0s, bits that are either true or false. However, only programmers really understand how much of programming is about boiling a problem down to a true or false value and then responding to it.

In this chapter, you learn about Boolean operations like AND, OR, and NOT; you learn about comparison statements like >, <, ==, and !=; and you come to understand conditionals like `if` and `switch`. These all lie at the heart of programming.

Booleans

As you learned in the previous chapter, a bool is a variable that can hold a value of either true or false. Bools were named after George Boole, a mathematician who worked with true and false values and logical operations (now known as "Boolean operations"). Though computers did not exist at the time of his research, computer logic is fundamentally based upon it.

In C# programming, bools are used to store simple information about the state of the game (for example, `bool gameOver = false;`) and to control the flow of the program through the `if` and `switch` statements covered later in this chapter.

Boolean Operations

Boolean operations allow programmers to modify or combine bool variables in meaningful ways.

!—The NOT Operator

The `!` (either pronounced "not" or "bang") operator reverses the value of a bool. False becomes true, or true becomes false:

```
print( !true );      // Outputs: false
print( !false );     // Outputs: true
print( !(!true) );   // Outputs: true    (the double negative of true is true)
```

`!` is also sometimes referred to as the *logical negation operator* to differentiate it from ~ (the bitwise not operator), which is explained in the "Bitwise Boolean Operators and Layer Masks" section of Appendix B, "Useful Concepts."

&&—The AND Operator

The `&&` operator returns true only if both operands are true:

```
print( false && false );    // false
print( false && true  );    // false
print( true  && false );    // false
print( true  && true  );    // true
```

||—The OR Operator

The `||` operator returns true if either operand is true as well as if both are true:

```
print( false || false );    // false
print( false || true  );    // true
print( true  || false );    // true
print( true  || true  );    // true
```

Shorting Versus Non-Shorting Boolean Operators

The standard forms of AND and OR (`&&` and `||`) are *shorting* operators, which means that if the shorting operator can determine its return value from the first argument, it will not bother to evaluate the second argument. By contrast, a non-shorting operator (`&` and `|`) will always evaluate both arguments completely. The following code listing includes several examples that illustrate the difference. In the code listing, a double slash followed by a number (e.g., `// 1`) to the right of a line indicates that there is an explanation of that line following the code listing.

```
1  // This function prints "--true" and returns a true value.
2  bool printAndReturnTrue() {
3      print( "--true" );
4      return( true );
5  }
6
7  // This function prints "--false" and returns a false value.
8  bool printAndReturnFalse() {
9      print( "--false" );
10      return( false );
11  }
12
13  void ShortingOperatorTest() {
14      // The first half of this test uses the shorting && and ||
15      bool tfAnd = ( printAndReturnTrue() && printAndReturnFalse() );      // 1
16      print( "tfAnd: "+tfAnd );
17
18      bool tfAnd2 = ( printAndReturnFalse() && printAndReturnTrue() );     // 2
19      print( "tfAnd2: "+tfAnd2 );
20
21      bool tfOr = ( printAndReturnTrue() || printAndReturnFalse() );       // 3
22      print( "tfOr: "+tfOr );
23
24      bool tfOr2 = ( printAndReturnFalse() || printAndReturnTrue() );      // 4
25      print( "tfOr2: "+tfOr2 );
26
27
28      // The second half of this test uses the non-shorting & and |
29      bool tfAnd3 = ( printAndReturnFalse() & printAndReturnTrue() );      // 5
30      print( "tfAnd3: "+tfAnd3 );
31
32      bool tfOr3 = (printAndReturnTrue() | printAndReturnFalse() );        // 6
33      print( "tfOr3: "+tfOr3 );
34
35  }
```

The numbers in the list below refer to lines in the preceding code that are marked with `// 1` and `// 2` to the right of the line.

1. This line will print `--true` and `--false` before setting `tfAnd` to false. Because the first argument that the shorting `&&` operator evaluates is true, it must also evaluate the second argument to determine that the result is false.

2. This line only prints `--false` before setting `tfAnd2` to false. Because the first argument that the shorting `&&` operator evaluates is false, it returns false without evaluating the second argument at all. On this line, `printAndReturnTrue()` is *not* executed.

3. This line only prints `--true` before setting `tfOr` to true. Because the first argument that the shorting `||` operator evaluates is true, it returns true without evaluating the second.

4. This line prints `--false` and `--true` before setting `tfOr2` to true. Because the first argument that the shorting `||` operator evaluates is false, it must evaluate the second argument to determine which value to return.

5. The non-shorting `&` operator will evaluate both arguments regardless of the value of the first argument. As a result, this line prints `--false` and `--true` before setting `tfAnd3` to false.

6. The non-shorting `|` operator will evaluate both arguments regardless of the value of the first argument. This line prints `--true` and `--false` before setting `tfOr3` to true.

It is useful to know about both shorting and non-shorting operators when writing your code. Shorting operators (`&&` and `||`) are much more commonly used because they are more efficient, but `&` and `|` can be used when you want to ensure that you evaluate all of the arguments of a Boolean operator.

If you want, I recommend entering this code into Unity and running the debugger to step through the behavior and really understand what is happening. To learn about the debugger, read Chapter 24, "Debugging."

Bitwise Boolean Operators

`|` and `&` are also sometimes referred to as bitwise OR and bitwise AND because they can also be used to perform bitwise operations on integers. These are useful for a few esoteric things having to do with collision detection in Unity; and you can learn more about them in the "Bitwise Boolean Operators and Layer Masks" section of Appendix B.

Combination of Boolean Operations

It is often useful to combine various Boolean operations in a single line:

```
bool tf = true || false && true;
```

However, care must be taken when doing so because order of operations extends to Boolean operations as well. In C#, the order of operations for Boolean operations is as follows:

```
!  - NOT
&  - Non-shorting AND / Bitwise AND
|  - Non-shorting OR  / Bitwise OR
&& - AND
|| - OR
```

This means that the previous line would be interpreted by the compiler as:

```
bool tf = true || ( false && true );
```

The `&&` comparison is executed before the `||` comparison every time.

> **tip**
>
> Regardless of the order of operations, you should always use parentheses for clarity in your code as often as possible. Good readability is critical in your code if you plan to ever work with someone else (or even if you want to read the same code yourself months later). I code by a simple rule: If there's any chance at all that something might be misunderstood later, I use parentheses and add comments to clarify what I am doing in the code and how it will be interpreted by the computer.

Logical Equivalence of Boolean Operations

The depths of Boolean logic are beyond the scope of this book, but suffice to say, some very interesting things can be accomplished by combining Boolean operations. In the examples that follow a and b are bool variables, and the rules hold true regardless of whether a and b are true or false, and they are true regardless of whether the shorting or non-shorting operators are used:

- `( a & b )` is the same as `!( !a | !b )`
- `( a | b )` is the same as `!( !a & !b )`
- Associativity: `( a & b ) & c` is the same as `a & ( b & c )`
- Commutativity: `( a & b )` is the same as `( b & a )`
- Distributivity of AND over OR:
  `a & ( b | c )` is the same as `( a & b ) | ( a & c )`
- Distributivity of OR over AND:
  `a | ( b & c )` is the same as `( a | b ) & ( a | c )`

If you're interested in more of these equivalencies and how they could be used, you can find many resources about Boolean logic online.

Comparison Operators

In addition to comparing Boolean values to each other, it is also possible to create a Boolean result value by using comparison operators on any other values.

== (Is Equal To)

The equality comparison operator checks to see whether the values of any two variables or literals are equivalent to each other. The result of this operator is a Boolean value of either true or false.

```
 1 int i0 = 10;
 2 int i1 = 10;
 3 int i2 = 20;
 4 float f0 = 1.23f;
 5 float f1 = 3.14f;
 6 float f2 = Mathf.PI;
 7
 8 print( i0 == i1 );     // Outputs: True
 9 print( i1 == i2 );     // Outputs: False
10 print( i2 == 20 );     // Outputs: True
11 print( f0 == f1 );     // Outputs: False
12 print( f0 == 1.23f );  // Outputs: True
13 print( f1 == f2 );     // Outputs: False                              // 1
```

1. The comparison in line 13 is false because Math.PI is far more accurate than 3.14f, and == requires that the values be exactly equivalent.

> ## warning
>
> **DON'T CONFUSE = AND ==**   There is sometimes confusion between the assignment operator (=) and the equality operator (==). The assignment operator (=) is used to set the value of a variable while the equality operator (==) is used to compare two values. Consider the following code listing:
>
> ```
> 1 bool f = false;
> 2 bool t = true;
> 3 print( f == t ); // prints: False
> 4 print( f = t );  // prints: True
> ```
>
> On line 3, f is compared to t, and because they are not equal, false is returned and printed. However, on line 4, f is assigned the value of t, causing the value of f to now be true, and true is printed.
>
> Confusion is also sometimes an issue when talking about the two operators. To avoid confusion, I usually pronounce i=5; as "i equals 5," and I pronounce i==5; as "i is equal to 5."

See the "Testing Equality by Value or Reference" sidebar for more detailed information about how equality is handled for several different variable types.

TESTING EQUALITY BY VALUE OR REFERENCE

Unity's version of C# will compare most simple data types by value. This means that as long as the values of the two variables are the same, they will be seen as equivalent. This works for all of the following data types:

- bool
- int
- float
- char
- string
- Vector3
- Color
- Quaternion

However, with more complex variable types like GameObject, Material, Renderer, and so on, C# no longer checks to see whether all the values of the two variables are equal but instead checks to see if the *references* of the two variables are equal. In other words, it checks to see whether the two variables are referencing (or pointing to) the same single object in the computer's memory. (For the following example we'll assume that boxPrefab is a preexisting variable that references a GameObject prefab.)

```
1 GameObject go0 = Instantiate( boxPrefab ) as GameObject;
2 GameObject go1 = Instantiate( boxPrefab ) as GameObject;
3 GameObject go2 = go0;
4 print( go0 == go1 ); // Output: false
5 print( go0 == go2 ); // Output: true
```

Even though the two instantiated boxPrefabs assigned to the variables go0 and go1 have the same values (they have the exact same default position, rotation, and so on) the == operator sees them as different because they are actually two different objects, and therefore reside in two different places in memory. go0 and go2 are seen as equal by == because they both refer to the exact same object. Let's continue the previous code:

```
6 go0.transform.position = new Vector3( 10, 20, 30)
7 print( go0.transform.position); // Output: (10.0, 20.0, 30.0)
8 print( go1.transform.position); // Output: ( 0.0,  0.0,  0.0)
9 print( go2.transform.position); // Output: (10.0, 20.0, 30.0)
```

Here, the position of go0 is changed. Because go1 is a different GameObject instance, its position remains the same. However, since go2 and go0 reference the same GameObject instance, go2.transform.position reflects the change as well.

!= (Not Equal To)

The inequality operator returns true if two values are not equal and false if they are equal. It is the opposite of ==. (For the remaining comparisons, literal values will be used in the place of variables for the sake of clarity and space.)

```
print ( 10 != 10 );          // Outputs: False
print ( 10 != 20 );          // Outputs: True
print ( 1.23f != 3.14f );    // Outputs: True
print ( 1.23f != 1.23f );    // Outputs: False
print ( 3.14f != Mathf.PI ); // Outputs: True
```

> (Greater Than) and < (Less Than)

> returns true if the value on the left side of the operator is greater than the value on the right:

```
print ( 10 > 10 );           // Outputs: False
print ( 20 > 10 );           // Outputs: True
print ( 1.23f > 3.14f );     // Outputs: False
print ( 1.23f > 1.23f );     // Outputs: False
print ( 3.14f > 1.23f );     // Outputs: True
```

< returns true if the value on the left side of the operator is less than the value on the right:

```
print ( 10 < 10 );           // Outputs: False
print ( 20 < 10 );           // Outputs: True
print ( 1.23f < 3.14f );     // Outputs: True
print ( 1.23f < 1.23f );     // Outputs: False
print ( 3.14f < 1.23f );     // Outputs: False
```

The characters < and > are also sometimes referred to as *angle brackets,* especially when they are used as tags in languages like HTML and XML or in generic functions in C#. However, when they are used as comparison operators, they are always called *greater than* and *less than.*

>= (Greater Than or Equal To) and
<= (Less Than or Equal To)

>= returns true if the value on the left side is greater than or equivalent to the value on the right:

```
print ( 10 >= 10 );          // Outputs: True
print ( 10 >= 20 );          // Outputs: False
print ( 1.23f >= 3.14f );    // Outputs: False
print ( 1.23f >= 1.23f );    // Outputs: True
print ( 3.14f >= 1.23f );    // Outputs: True
```

`<=` returns true if the value on the left side is less than or equal to the value on the right:

```
print( 10 <= 10 );          // Outputs: True
print( 10 <= 20 );          // Outputs: True
print( 1.23f <= 3.14f );    // Outputs: True
print( 1.23f <= 1.23f );    // Outputs: True
print( 3.14f <= 1.23f );    // Outputs: False
```

Conditional Statements

Conditional statements can be combined with Boolean values and comparison operators to control the flow of your programs. This means that a true value can cause the code to generate one result while a false value can cause it to generate another. The two most common forms of conditional statements are `if` and `switch`.

`if` Statements

An `if` statement will only execute the code inside its braces { } if the value inside its parentheses () evaluates to true.

```
if (true) {
    print( "The code in the first if statement executed." );
}
if (false) {
    print( "The code in the second if statement executed." );
}

// The output of this code will be:
//    The code in the first if statement executed.
```

The code inside the braces { } of the first `if` statement executes, yet the code inside the braces of the second `if` statement does not.

---

note

Statements enclosed in braces do not require a semicolon after the closing brace. Other statements that have been covered all require a semicolon at the end:

```
float approxPi = 3.14159f; // There's the standard semicolon
```

Compound statements (that is, those surrounded by braces) do not require a semicolon after the closing brace:

```
if (true) {
    print( "Hello" );  // This line needs a semicolon.
    print( "World" );  // This line needs a semicolon.
}                      // No semicolon required after the closing brace!
```

The same is true for *any* compound statement surrounded by braces.

Combining `if` Statements with Comparison Operators and Boolean Operators

Boolean operators can be combined with `if` statements to react to various situations in your game:

```
bool night = true;
bool fullMoon = false;

if (night) {
    print( "It's night." );
}
if (!fullMoon) {
    print( "The moon is not full." );
}
if (night && fullMoon) {
    print( "Beware werewolves!!!" );
}
if (night && !fullMoon) {
    print( "No werewolves tonight. (Whew!)" );
}


// The output of this code will be:
//      It's night.
//      The moon is not full.
//      No werewolves tonight. (Whew!)
```

And, of course, `if` statements can also be combined with comparison operators:

```
if (10 == 10 ) {
    print( "10 is equal to 10." );
}
if ( 10 > 20 ) {
    print( "10 is greater than 20." );
}
if ( 1.23f <= 3.14f ) {
    print( "1.23 is less than or equal to 3.14." );
}
if ( 1.23f >= 1.23f ) {
    print( "1.23 is greater than or equal to 1.23." );
}
if ( 3.14f != Mathf.PI ) {
    print( "3.14 is not equal to "+Mathf.PI+"." );
    // + can be used to concatenate strings with other data types.
    // When this happens, the other data type is converted to a string.
}
```

```
// The output of this code will be:
//      10 is equal to 10.
//      1.23 is less than or equal to 3.14.
//      1.23 is greater than or equal to 1.23.
//      3.14 is not equal to 3.141593.
```

---

warning

AVOID USING = IN AN IF STATEMENT   As was mentioned in the previous warning, == is a comparison operator that determines whether two values are equivalent. = is an assignment operator that assigns a value to a variable. If you accidentally use = in an `if` statement, the result will be an assignment instead of a comparison.

Sometimes Unity will catch this by giving you an error about not being able to implicitly convert a value to a Boolean. You will get that error from this code:

```
float f0 = 10f;
if ( f0 = 10 ) {
    print( "f0 is equal to 10.");
}
```

Other times, Unity will actually give you a warning stating that it found an = in an `if` statement and asking if you meant to type ==.

---

if...else

Many times, you will want to do one thing if a value is true and another if it is false. At these times, an `else` clause is added to the `if` statement:

```
bool night = false;

if (night) {
    print( "It's night." );
} else {
    print( "It's daytime. What are you worried about?" );
}

// The output of this code will be:
//      It's daytime. What are you worried about?
```

In this case, because night is false, the code in the `else` clause is executed.

if...else if...else

It's also possible to have a chain of `else` clauses:

```
bool night = true;
bool fullMoon = true;
```

```
if (!night) {                // Condition 1 (false)
    print( "It's daytime. What are you worried about?" );
} else if (fullMoon) {       // Condition 2 (true)
    print( "Beware werewolves!!!" );
} else {                     // Condition 3 (not checked)
    print( "It's night, but the moon is not full." );
}

// The output of this code will be:
//     Beware werewolves!!!
```

Once any condition in the `if...else if...else` chain evaluates to true, all subsequent conditions are no longer evaluated (the rest of the chain is shorted). In the previous listing, Condition 1 is false, so Condition 2 is checked. Because Condition 2 is true, the computer will completely skip Condition 3.

Nesting `if` Statements

It is also possible to nest `if` statements inside of each other for more complex behavior:

```
bool night = true;
bool fullMoon = false;

if (!night) {
    print( "It's daytime. What are you worried about?" );
} else {
    if (fullMoon) {
        print( "Beware werewolves!!!" );
    } else {
        print( "It's night, but the moon is not full." );
    }
}

// The output of this code will be:
//     It's night, but the moon is not full.
```

`switch` Statements

A `switch` statement can take the place of several `if...else` statements, but it has some strict limitations:

1. Switch statements can only compare for equality.

2. Switch statements can only compare a single variable.

3. Switch statements can only compare that variable against literals (not other variables).

Here is an example:

```
int num = 3;

switch (num) {  // The variable in parentheses (num) is the one being compared
case (0):  // Each case is a literal number that is compared against num
    print( "The number is zero." );
    break;  // Each case must end with a break statement.
case (1):
    print( "The number is one." );
    break;
case (2):
    print( "The number is two." );
    break;
default:  // If none of the other cases are true, default will happen
    print( "The number is more than a couple." );
    break;
}  // The switch statement ends with a closing brace.

// The output of this code is:
//      The number is more than a couple.
```

If one of the cases holds a literal with the same value as the variable being checked, the code in that case is executed until the `break` is reached. Once the computer hits the `break`, it exits the switch and does not evaluate any other cases.

It is also possible to have one case "fall through" to the next if there are no lines of code between the two:

```
int num = 4;

switch (num) {
case (0):
    print( "The number is zero." );
    break;
case (1):
    print( "The number is one." );
    break;
case (2):
    print( "The number is a couple." );
    break;
case (3):
case (4):
case (5):
    print( "The number is a few." );
    break;
```

```
default:
    print( "The number is more than a few." );
    break;
}

// The output of this code is:
//      The number is a few.
```

In the previous code, if `num` is equal to 3, 4, or 5, the output will be `The number is a few.`

Knowing what you know about combining conditionals and `if` statements, you might question when `switch` statements are used, since they have so many limitations. They are used quite often to deal with the different possible states of a GameObject. For instance, if you made a game where the player could transform into a person, bird, fish, or wolverine, there might be a chunk of code that looked like this:

```
string species = "fish";
bool   inWater = false;

// Each different species type will move differently
public function Move() {
    switch (species) {
    case ("person"):
        Run(); // Calls a function named Run()
        break;
    case ("bird"):
        Fly();
        break;
    case ("fish"):
        if (!inWater) {
            Swim();
        } else {
            FlopAroundPainfully();
        }
        break;
    case ("wolverine"):
        Scurry();
        break;
    default:
        print( "Unknown species type: "+species );
        break;
    }
}
```

In the preceding code, the player (as a fish in water) would `Swim()`. It's important to note that the `default` case here is used to catch any species that the `switch` statement isn't ready for and that it will output information about any unexpected species it comes across. For instance, if `species` were set to `"lion"`, the output would be:

```
Unknown species type: lion
```

In the preceding code syntax, you also see the names of several functions that are not yet defined (e.g., `Run()`, `Fly()`, `Swim()`). Chapter 23, "Functions and Parameters," covers the creation of your own functions.

Summary

Though Boolean operations may seem a bit dry, they form a big part of the core of programming. Computer programs are full of hundreds, even thousands, of branch points where the computer can do either one thing or another, and these all boil down in some way to Booleans and comparisons. As you continue through the book, you may want to return to this section from time to time if you're ever confused by any comparisons in the code you see.

CHAPTER 21

LOOPS

Computer programs are usually designed to do the same thing repeatedly. In a standard game loop, the game draws a frame to the screen, takes input from the player, considers that input, and then draws the next frame, repeating this behavior at least 30 times every second.

A loop in C# code causes the computer to repeat a certain behavior several times. This could be anything from looping over every enemy in the scene and considering the AI of each to looping over all the physics objects in a scene and checking for collisions. By the end of this chapter, you'll understand all you need to know about loops, and in the next chapter, you'll learn how to use them with Lists and arrays.

Types of Loops

C# has only four kinds of loops: `while`, `do...while`, `for`, and `foreach`. Of those, you'll be using `for` and `foreach` much more often than the others because they are generally safer and more adaptable to the challenges you'll encounter while making games:

- `while` loop: The most basic type of loop. Checks a condition before each loop to determine whether to continue looping.

- `do...while` loop: Similar to the while loop, but checks a condition *after* each loop to determine whether to continue looping.

- `for` loop: A loop statement that includes an initial statement, a variable that increments with each iteration, and an end condition. The most commonly used loop structure.

- `foreach` loop: A loop statement that automatically iterates over every element of an enumerable object or collection. This chapter contains some discussion of `foreach`, and it is covered more extensively in the next chapter as part of the discussion of C# Lists and Arrays.

Set Up a Project

In Appendix A, "Standard Project Setup Procedure," detailed instructions show you how to set up Unity projects for the chapters in this book. At the start of each project, you will also see a sidebar like the one here. Please follow the directions in the sidebar to create the project for this chapter.

SET UP THE PROJECT FOR THIS CHAPTER

Following the standard project setup procedure, create a new project in Unity. For information on the standard project setup procedure, see Appendix A.

- **Project name:** Loop Examples
- **Scene name:** _Scene_Loops
- **C# Script names:** Loops

Attach the script Loops to the Main Camera in the scene.

`while` Loops

The `while` loop is the most basic loop structure. However, this also means that it lacks the safety of using a more modern form of loop. In my coding, I almost never use `while` loops because of the danger that using one could create an *infinite loop*.

The Danger of Infinite Loops

An infinite loop occurs when a program enters a loop and is unable to escape it. Let's write one to see what happens. Open the Loops C# script in MonoDevelop (by double-clicking it in the Project pane) and add the following bolded code.

```
 1 using UnityEngine;
 2 using System.Collections;
 3
 4 public class Loops : MonoBehaviour {
 5
 6     void Start () {
 7         while (true) {
 8             print( "Loop" );
 9         }
10     }
11
12 }
```

Save this script by choosing *File > Save* from the MonoDevelop menu bar. After you've done this, switch back to Unity and click the triangular Play button at the top of the Unity window. See how nothing happens... see how nothing happens *forever?* In fact, you're probably going to have to Force Quit Unity now (see the sidebar for instructions). What you have just encountered is an infinite loop, and as you can see, an infinite loop will completely freeze Unity. It is lucky that we all run multithreaded computer operating systems now, because in the old days of single-threaded systems, infinite loops wouldn't just freeze a single application, they'd freeze the entire computer and require a restart.

HOW TO FORCE QUIT AN APPLICATION

On OS X

Implement a force quit by doing the following:

1. Press Command-Option-Esc on the keyboard. This brings up the Force Quit window.

2. Find the application that is misbehaving. Its name will often be followed by "(not responding)" in the applications list.

3. Click that application, and then click Force Quit. You may need to wait a few seconds for the force quit to happen.

On Windows

Implement a force quit by doing the following:

1. Press Shift+Control+Esc on the keyboard. This brings up the Windows Task Manager.

> **2.** Find the application that is misbehaving.
>
> **3.** Click that application and then click End Task. You may need to wait a few seconds for the force quit to happen.
>
> If you have to force quit Unity while it is running, you will lose any work that you've done since your last save. Because you must constantly save C# scripts, they shouldn't be an issue, but you might have to redo unsaved changes made to your scene. For example, in _Scene_Loops, if you did not save the scene after adding the Loops C# script to the Main Camera, you will need to attach it to the Main Camera again.

So, what happened there that caused the infinite loop? To discover that, take a look at the `while` loop.

```
7            while (true) {
8                print( "Loop" );
9            }
```

Everything within the braces of a `while` loop will be executed repeatedly as long as the *condition clause* within the parentheses is true. On line 7, the condition is always true, so the line `print( "Loop" );` will repeat infinitely.

But, you may wonder, if this line was repeating infinitely, why did you never see "Loop" printed in the Console pane? Though the `print()` function was called many times (probably millions of times before you decided to force quit Unity), you were never able to see the output in the Console pane because Unity was trapped in the infinite `while` loop and was unable to redraw the Unity window (which would have needed to happen to see the changes to the Console pane).

A More Useful `while` Loop

Open the Loops C# script in MonoDevelop and modify it to read as follows:

```
1 using UnityEngine;
2 using System.Collections;
3
4 public class Loops : MonoBehaviour {
5
6     void Start () {
7         int i=0;
8         while ( i<3 ) {
9             print( "Loop: "+i );
10            i++;        // See the sidebar on Increment and Decrement Operators
11        }
12    }
13
14 }
```

INCREMENT AND DECREMENT OPERATORS

On line 10 of the code listing for the "more useful" while loop is the first instance in this book of the *increment* operator (++). The increment operator increases the value of the variable that it follows by 1. So, if i=5, then the i++; statement would set the value of i to 6.

There is also a *decrement* operator (--). The decrement operator decreases the value of the variable by 1.

---

tip

In most of the examples in this chapter, the *iteration variable* used will be named i. The variable names i, j, and k are often used by programmers as iteration variables (i.e., the variable that increments in a loop), and as a result, they are rarely used in any other code situations. Because these variables are created and destroyed so often in various loop structures, you should generally avoid using the variable names i, j, or k for anything else.

Save your code, switch back to Unity and click Play. This time, Unity does not get stuck in an infinite loop because the while condition clause (i<3) eventually becomes false. The output from this program to the console (minus all the extra stuff Unity throws in) is as follows:

```
Loop: 0
Loop: 1
Loop: 2
```

That is because it calls print (i) every time the while loop iterates. It's important to note that the condition clause is checked *before* each iteration of the loop.

do...while Loops

A do...while loop works in the same manner as a while loop, except that the condition clause is checked *after* each iteration. This guarantees that the loop will run at least once. Modify the code to read as follows:

```
1 using UnityEngine;
2 using System.Collections;
3
4 public class Loops : MonoBehaviour {
5
6     void Start () {
7         int i=10;
```

```
8          do {
9              print( "Loop: "+i );
10             i++;
11         } while ( i<3 );
12     }
13
14 }
```

Make sure that you change line 7 of the `Start()` function to `int i=10;`. Even though the `while` condition is not ever true (10 is never less than 3), the loop still goes through a single iteration before testing the condition clause on line 11. Had `i` been initialized to `0` here as it was in the `while` loop example, the console output would have looked the same, so we set `i=10` in line 7 to demonstrate that a `do...while` loop will always run at least once regardless of the value of `i`. It is important to place a trailing semicolon (`;`) after the condition clause in a `do...while` loop (as is shown on line 11).

Save this script and try it out in Unity to see the result.

`for` Loops

In both the `while` and `do...while` examples, we needed to declare and define a variable `i`, increment the variable `i`, and then check the condition clause on the variable `i`; and each of these actions was performed by a separate statement. The `for` loop handles all of these actions in a single line. Write the following code in the Loops C# script, and then save and run it in Unity.

```
1 using UnityEngine;
2 using System.Collections;
3
4 public class Loops : MonoBehaviour {
5
6     void Start() {
7         for ( int i=0; i<3; i++ ) {
8             print( "Loop: "+i );
9         }
10    }
11
12 }
```

The `for` loop in this example sends the same output to the Console pane as was sent by the preceding "more useful" `while` loop, yet it does so in fewer lines of code. The structure of a `for` loop requires an *initialization* clause, a *condition* clause, and an *iteration* clause to be valid. In the preceding example, the three clauses are as follows:

Initialization clause:	`for ( int i=0; i<3; i++ ) {`
Condition clause:	`for ( int i=0; i<3; i++ ) {`
Iteration clause:	`for ( int i=0; i<3; i++ ) {`

The initialization clause (`int i=0;`) is executed before the `for` loop begins. It declares and defines a variable that is scoped locally to the `for` loop. This means that, the variable `int i` will cease to exist once the `for` loop is complete. For more information on variable scoping, see the "Variable Scope" section of Appendix B, "Useful Concepts."

The condition clause (`i<3`) is checked before the first iteration of the `for` loop (just as the condition clause is checked before the first iteration of a `while` loop). If the condition clause is true, the code between the braces of the `for` loop is executed.

Once an iteration of the code between the braces of the `for` loop has completed, the iteration clause (`i++`) is executed (that is, after `print( i );` has executed once, `i++` is executed). Then the condition clause is checked again, and if the condition clause is still true, the code in the braces is executed again, and the iteration clause is executed again. This continues until the condition clause evaluates to false, and then the `for` loop ends.

Because `for` loops mandate that each of these three clauses be included and that they all be on the same line, it is easier to avoid writing infinite loops when working with `for` loops.

> ### warning
>
> **DON'T FORGET THE SEMICOLONS BETWEEN EACH CLAUSE OF THE FOR STATEMENT**   It is critical that the initialization, condition, and iteration clauses be separated by semicolons. This is because each is an independent clause that must be terminated by a semicolon like any independent clause in C#. Just as most lines in C# must be terminated by a semicolon, so must the independent clauses in a `for` loop.

The Iteration Clause Doesn't Have to Increment

Though the iteration clause is commonly an increment statement like `i++`, it doesn't have to be. Any operation can be used in the iteration clause.

Decrement

One of the most common alternate iteration clauses is counting down rather than counting up. This is accomplished by using a decrement operator in a `for` loop.

```
6     void Start() {
7         for ( int i=5; i>2; i-- ) {
8             print( "Loop: "+i );
9         }
10    }
```

And the output to the Console pane would be as follows:

```
Loop: 5
Loop: 4
Loop: 3
```

foreach Loops

A foreach loop is kind of like an automatic for loop that can be used on anything that is enumerable. In C#, most collections of data are enumerable, including the Lists and arrays covered in the next chapter as well as strings (which are a collection of chars). Try this example in Unity.

```
1 using UnityEngine;
2 using System.Collections;
3
4 public class Loops : MonoBehaviour {
5
6     void Start() {
7         string str = "Hello";
8         foreach( char chr in str ) {
9             print( chr );
10        }
11    }
12
13 }
```

The Console output will print a single char from the string str on each iteration, resulting in:

```
H
e
l
l
o
```

The foreach loop guarantees that it will iterate over all the elements of the enumerable object. In this case, it iterates over each character in the string "Hello". foreach loops are covered further in the next chapter as part of the discussion of Lists and arrays.

Jump Statements within Loops

A jump statement is any statement that causes code execution to jump to another location in the code. One example that has already been covered is the break statement at the end of each case in a switch statement.

break

break statements can also be used to prematurely break out of any kind of loop structure. To see an example, change your Start() function to read as follows:

```
6    void Start() {
7        for ( int i=0; i<10; i++ ) {
8            print( i );
9            if ( i==3 ) {
10               break;
11           }
12       }
13   }
```

Note that in the this code listing, lines 1–5 and the final line containing only a closing brace } (which was formerly line 13) have been omitted because they are identical to the lines in previous code listings. They should still be there in your script in MonoDevelop, and you should just replace the foreach loop from lines 7–10 of the preceding foreach code listing with lines 7–12 of this code listing.

Run this in Unity, and you will get this output:

```
0
1
2
3
```

The break statement exits the for loop prematurely. A break can also be used in while, do...while, and foreach statements.

Code examples:	**Console output from that code:**

```
7 for ( int i=0; i<10; i++ ) {
8     print( i );                      0
9     if ( i==3 ) {                    1
10        break;                       2
11    }                                3
12 }
```

```
7 int i = 0;
8 while (true) {                       0
9     print( i );                      1
10    if ( i > 2 ) break;    // 1      2
11    i++;                             3
12 }
```

```
 7 int i = 3;
 8 do {                                       3
 9     print ( i );                            2
10     i--;
11     if ( i==1 ) break;        // 2
12 } while ( i > 0 );

 7 foreach (char c in "Hello") {
 8     if (c == 'l') {                         H
 9         break;                              e
10     }
11     print ( c );
12 }
```

The numbers in the following list refer to lines in the preceding code that are marked with // 1 and // 2 to the right of the line (these have been bolded in the preceding code for emphasis).

1. This line shows the single-line version of an if statement. If there is only one line, the braces are not necessary.

2. This code only outputs 3 and 2 because on the second iteration of the loop, the i-- decrement reduces i to 1, and then the condition clause for the if statement on line 11 is true and breaks out of the loop.

Take the time to look at each preceding code example and make sure you understand why each is generating the output shown. If any look confusing, type the code into Unity and then run through it with the debugger. (The debugger is explained in detail in Chapter 24, "Debugging.")

continue

continue is used to force the program to skip the remainder of the current iteration and continue to the next.

Code: **Output:**

```
 7 for (int i=0; i<=360; i++) {               0
 8     if (i % 90 != 0) {                      90
 9         continue;                           180
10     }                                       270
11     print ( i );                            360
12 }
```

In the preceding code, any time that i%90 != 0 (that is, i/90 has a remainder other than 0), the continue will cause the for loop to move on to the next iteration, skipping the print (i); line. The continue statement can also be used in while, do...while, and foreach loops.

> ## MODULUS OPERATOR
>
> Line 8 of the code listing for the `continue` jump statement is the first instance in this book of the *modulus* operator (`%`). Modulus (or mod) returns the remainder of dividing one number by another. For example, `12%10` would return a value of 2 because the remainder of 12/10 is 2.
>
> Mod can also be used with floats, so `12.4f%1f` would return 0.4f, the remainder when 12.4 is divided by 1.

Summary

Understanding loops is one of the key elements of becoming a good programmer. However, it's fine if not all of this makes perfect sense right now. Once you start using loops in the development of some actual game prototypes, they will become clearer to you. Just make sure that you are actually typing each code example into Unity and running it to help with your understanding of the material.

Also remember that in my coding, I most commonly use `for` and `foreach` and rarely or never use `while` and `do...while` because of the danger of infinite loops.

In the next chapter, you will learn about arrays and Lists, two forms of enumerable, ordered collections of similar items, and you will see how loops are used to iterate over these collections.

CHAPTER 22

LISTS AND ARRAYS

This chapter covers two important types of collections available to you in C#. These collections enable you to act on several things as a group. For example, you could loop over a List of GameObjects each frame to update all of their positions and states.

By the end of this chapter, you will understand how these collection types work and which to use in various situations.

C# Collections

A collection is a group of objects that are referenced by a single variable. In regular life, collections would be things like a group of people, a pride of lions, a parliament of rooks, or a murder of crows. In C#, there are two important types of collections for you to understand:

- **Array:** Arrays are the most primitive but fastest collection type. Arrays can only hold data of a single type, and their length must be set when they are defined. It is possible to make both multidimensional arrays and jagged arrays (arrays of arrays), both of which are covered later in this chapter. The word *array* will only be capitalized when referring to the C# class Array, which is different from primitive arrays of data.

- **List:** Lists are more flexible than arrays but are still strongly typed (meaning that they can only hold one type of data). Lists are flexible in length, making them useful when you don't know exactly how many objects will be in the collection. In this book, List will be capitalized when referring to the C# type to help distinguish it from the common usage of "list."

Because Lists are more flexible, we'll start with them and then cover arrays. We'll also discuss converting from one type to another, and I'll provide a handy guide as to which collection type is best suited to any given situation.

SET UP A PROJECT FOR THIS CHAPTER

Following the standard project setup procedure, create a new project in Unity. If you need a refresher on the standard project setup procedure, see Appendix A, "Standard Project Setup Procedure."

- **Project name:** Collections Project
- **Scene name:** Scene_Collections
- **C# script names:** ListEx and ArrayEx

Attach both C# scripts to the Main Camera in Scene_Collections.

List

The first `using` line at the top of each C# script gives the script knowledge of standard Unity objects (see line 1 in the following code listing). The second line, `using System.Collections`, gives the script knowledge of ArrayLists (a third collection type without strong typing) and how to use them; however, the List collection type is not actually part of the standard `using` lines we have included in previous scripts. List and other *generic collections* are part of the `System.Collections.Generic` library that is included in line 3 of the following code listing. A generic collection is one that is strongly typed to hold a collection of a single specific data type that is defined using angle brackets. Examples of this include:

- `public List<string> sList;` — This declares a List of strings
- `public List<GameObject> goList;` — This declares a List of GameObjects

`System.Collections.Generic` also defines other generic data types, but they beyond the scope of this chapter. These include `Dictionary` and the generic versions of `Queue` and `Stack`. Unlike arrays, which are locked to a specified length, all generic collection types can adjust their length dynamically.

Double-click the ListEx C# script in the Project pane to open it in MonoDevelop and add the following bolded code (you do not need to add the `//` `#` comments on the far-right side of the code listing; these are references to explanations listed after the code):

```
1 using UnityEngine;                                              // 1
2 using System.Collections;                                       // 2
3 using System.Collections.Generic;                               // 3
4
5 public class ListEx : MonoBehaviour {
6     public List<string>          sList;                          // 4
7
8     void Start () {
9         sList = new List<string>();                              // 5
10        sList.Add( "Experience" );                               // 6
11        sList.Add( "is" );
12        sList.Add( "what" );
13        sList.Add( "you" );
14        sList.Add( "get" );
15        sList.Add( "when" );
16        sList.Add( "you" );
17        sList.Add( "didn't" );
18        sList.Add( "get" );
19        sList.Add( "what" );
20        sList.Add( "you" );
21        sList.Add( "wanted." );
22        // This quote is from my professor, Dr. Randy Pausch (1960-2008)
23
24        print( "sList Count = "+sList.Count );                   // 7
25        print( "The 0th element is: "+sList[0] );                // 8
26        print( "The 1st element is: "+sList[1] );
27        print( "The 3rd element is: "+sList[3] );
28        print( "The 8th element is: "+sList[8] );
29
30        string str = "";
31        foreach (string sTemp in sList) {                        // 9
32            str += sTemp+" ";
33        }
34        print( str );
35    }
36 }
```

The numbers in the list below refer to lines in the preceding code that are marked with // # to the right of the line.

1. The UnityEngine library enables all of the classes and types that are specific to Unity (e.g., GameObject, Renderer, Mesh). It is mandatory that it be included in any Unity C# script.

2. The System.Collections library that is at the beginning of all C# scripts enables the ArrayList type (among others). ArrayList is another type of C# collection that is similar to List except that ArrayLists are not limited to a single type of data. This enables more flexibility, but I have found it to have more detriments than benefits when compared to Lists (including a significant performance penalty).

3. The List collection type is part of the System.Collections.Generic C# library, so that library must be imported to enable the use of Lists. System.Collections.Generic enables a whole slew of generic collection types beyond just List. You can learn more about them online by searching "C# System.Collections.Generic" on the Internet.

4. This declares the `List<string>` `sList`. All generic collection data types have their name followed by angle brackets `< >` surrounding a specified data type. In this case, the List is a List of strings. However, the strength of generics is that they can be used for any data type. You could just as easily create a `List<int>`, `List<GameObject>`, `List<Transform>`, `List<Vector3>`, and so on. The type of the List must be assigned at the time of declaration.

5. The declaration of `sList` on line 6 makes `sList` a variable name that can hold a List of strings, but the value of `sList` is `null` (that is, it has no value) until `sList` is defined on line 9. Before this definition, any attempt to add elements to `sList` would have caused an error. The List definition must repeat the type of the List in the `new` statement. A newly defined List initially contains no elements and has a `Count` of zero.

6. A List's `Add()` function adds an element to the List. This will insert the string literal `"Experience"` into the 0th (pronounced "zeroth") element of the List. See the "Lists and Arrays are Zero-Indexed" sidebar for information about zero-indexed Lists.

7. A List's `Count` property returns an `int` representing the number of elements in the List.

8. Lines 25–28 demonstrate the use of *bracket access* (e.g., `sList[0]`). Bracket access uses brackets `[]` and an integer to reference a specific element in a List or array. The integer between the brackets is known as the "index."

9. `foreach` (introduced in the previous chapter) is often used with Lists and other collections. Just as a string is a collection of chars, `List<string>` `sList` is a collection of strings. The string `sTemp` variable is scoped to the `foreach` statement, so it will cease to exist once the `foreach` loop has completed. Because Lists are strongly typed (that is, C# knows that `sList` is a `List<string>`) the elements of `sList` can be assigned to string `sTemp` without requiring any kind of conversion. This is one of the major advantages of the List collection over the nontyped ArrayList type.

The console output of the preceding code will be the following lines:

```
sList Count = 12
The 0th element is: Experience
The 1st element is: is
The 3rd element is: you
The 8th element is: get
Experience is what you get when you didn't get what you wanted.
```

LISTS AND ARRAYS ARE ZERO-INDEXED

List and array collection types are zero-indexed, meaning that what you might think of as the "first" element is actually element [0]. Throughout the book, I will refer to this element as the 0th or "zeroth" element.

For these examples, we'll consider the pseudocode collection `coll`. "Pseudocode" is code that is not from any specific programming language but is used to illustrate a conceptual point more easily.

```
coll = [ "A", "B", "C", "D", "E" ]
```

The *count* or *length* of `coll` is 5, and the valid indices for the elements would be from 0 to `coll.Count-1` (that is, 0, 1, 2, 3, and 4)

```
print( coll.Count );   // 5

print( coll[0] );      // A
print( coll[1] );      // B
print( coll[2] );      // C
print( coll[3] );      // D
print( coll[4] );      // E

print( coll[5] );      // Index Out of Range Error!!!
```

If you try to use bracket access to access an index that is not in range, you will see the following runtime error:

```
IndexOutOfRangeException: Array index is out of range.
```

It is important to keep this in mind as you're working with any collection in C#.

As always, remember to save your script in MonoDevelop when you're done editing. Then, switch back to Unity and select the Main Camera in the Hierarchy pane. You will see that `List<string> sList` appears in the ListEx (Script) component of the Inspector pane. If you play the Unity scene, you can click the disclosure triangle next to `sList` in the Inspector and actually see the values that populate it. (Another drawback of ArrayLists is that they do not appear in the Inspector collection.)

IMPORTANT LIST PROPERTIES AND METHODS

There are many, many properties and methods available for Lists, but these are the most often used. All of these method examples refer to the following `List<string>` `sL` and are noncumulative. In other words, each example starts with the List `sL` as it is defined in the following three lines, unmodified by the other examples.

```
List<string> sL = new List<string>();
sL.Add( "A" );  sL.Add( "B" );  sL.Add( "C" );  sL.Add( "D" );
// Resulting in the List: [ "A", "B", "C", "D" ]
```

Properties

- `sL[2]` (Bracket access): Returns the element of the array at the index specified by the parameter (2). Because C is the second element of `sL`, this returns: C.

- `sL.Count`: Returns the number of elements currently in the List. Because the length of a List can vary over time, `Count` is very important. The last valid index in a List is always `Count-1`. The value of `sL.Count` is 4, so the last valid index is 3.

Methods

- `sL.Add("Hello")`: Adds the parameter "Hello" to the end of `sL`. In this case, `sL` becomes: ["A", "B", "C", "D", "Hello"].

- `sL.Clear()`: Removes all existing elements from `sL` returning it to an empty state. `sL` becomes empty: [ ].

- `sL.IndexOf("A")`: Finds the first instance in `sL` of the parameter "A" and returns the index of that element. Because "A" is the 0th element of `sL`, this call returns 0. If the variable does not exist in the List, a -1 is returned. This is a safe and fast method to determine whether a List contains an element.

- `sL.Insert(2, "B.5")`: Inserts the second parameter ("B.5") into `sL` at the index specified by the first parameter (2). This shifts the subsequent elements of the List forward. In this case, this would cause `sL` to become ["A", "B", "B.5", "C", "D"]. Valid index values for the first parameter are 0 through `sL.Count`. Any value outside this range will cause a runtime error.

- `sL.Remove("C")`: Removes the specified element from the List. If there happened to be two "C"s in the List, only the first would be removed. `sL` becomes ["A", "B", "D"].

- `sL.RemoveAt(0)`: Removes the element at the specified index from the List. Because "A" is the 0th element of the List, `sL` becomes ["B", "C", "D"].

Converting a List to an array

- `sL.ToArray()`: Generates an array that has all the elements of `sL`. The new array will be of the same type as the List. Returns a new string array with the elements ["A", "B", "C", "D"].

To move on to learning about arrays, make sure that Unity playback is stopped and then uncheck the check box next to the name of the *ListEx (Script)* component in the Inspector pane to make the ListEx script inactive (as is shown in Figure 22.1).

Figure 22.1 Clicking the check box to deactivate the ListEx Script component

Array

An array is the simplest collection type, which also makes it the fastest. Arrays do not require any libraries to be imported (via the `using` command) to work because they are built into core C#. In addition, arrays have multidimensional and jagged forms that can be very useful.

Basic Array Creation

Arrays are of a fixed length that must be determined when the array is defined. Double-click the ArrayEx C# script in the Project pane to open it in MonoDevelop and enter the following code:

```
1 using UnityEngine;
2 using System.Collections;
3
4 public class ArrayEx : MonoBehaviour {
5     public string[]       sArray;                              // 1
6
7     void Start () {
8         sArray = new string[10];                               // 2
9
10        sArray[0] = "These";                                   // 3
11        sArray[1] = "are";
12        sArray[2] = "some";
13        sArray[3] = "words";
14
15        print( "The length of sArray is: "+sArray.Length );    // 4
16
17        string str = "";
18        foreach (string sTemp in sArray) {                     // 5
19            str += "|"+sTemp;
20        }
21        print( str );
22    }
23
24 }
```

1. Unlike a list, an array in C# isn't actually a separate data type; rather, it's a collection formed from any existing data type by adding brackets after the type name. The type of `sArray` in the preceding code is not declared as `string`; it is `string[]`, a collection of multiple `strings`. Note that while `sArray` is declared as an array here, its length is not yet defined.

2. Here, `sArray` is defined as a `string[]` with a length of 10. When an array is defined, its length is filled with elements of the default value for that data type. For `int[]` or `float[]`, the default would be 0. For `string[]` and other complex data types like `GameObject[]`, each element of the array is filled with `null` (which indicates no that value has been assigned).

3. Rather than using the `Add()` method like Lists, standard arrays use bracket access for assignment of value as well as retrieval of value from the array.

4. Rather than using `Count` like other C# collections, arrays use the property `Length`. It is important to note (as you can see from the preceding code output) that `Length` returns the entire length of the array, including both defined elements (for example, `sArray[0]` through `sArray[3]` in the preceding code) and elements that are empty (that is, still their default, undefined value as are `sArray[4]` through `sArray[9]` in the previous code).

5. `foreach` works for arrays just as it does for other C# collections. The only difference is that the array may have empty or null elements, and `foreach` will iterate over them.

When you run the code, be sure to have Main Camera selected in the Hierarchy pane. This will enable you to open the disclosure triangle next to `sArray` in the *ArrayEx (Script)* component of the Inspector pane and see the elements of `sArray`.

The code output looks like this:

```
The length of sArray is: 10
|These|are|some|words||||||
```

Empty Elements in the Middle of an Array

One thing allowed by arrays that is not possible in Lists is an empty element in the middle of the collection. This would be useful in a game if you had something like a scoring track where each player had a marker on the track but it was possible to have empty spaces in between the markers.

Modify the previous code as follows:

```
10      sArray[0] = "These";
11      sArray[1] = "are";
12      sArray[3] = "some";
13      sArray[6] = "words";
```

The code output would look like this: `|These|are||some|||words|||`

As you can see from the output, `sArray` now has empty elements at indices 2, 4, 5, 7, 8, and 9. As long as the index (for example, 0, 1, 3, and 6 here) of the assignment is within the valid range for the array, you can use bracket access to place a value anywhere in the array, and the `foreach` loop will handle it gracefully.

Attempting to assign a value to an index that is outside of the defined range for the array (for example, `sArray[10] = "oops!";` or `sArray[99] = "error!";`) will lead to this runtime error:

```
IndexOutOfRangeException: Array index is out of range.
```

Return the code back to its original state:

```
10        sArray[0] = "These";
11        sArray[1] = "are";
12        sArray[2] = "some";
13        sArray[3] = "words";
```

Empty Array Elements and `foreach`

Play the project again and look at the output, which has returned to its previous state:

```
|These|are|some|words||||||
```

The `str += "|"+sTemp;` statement concatenates (that is, adds) a pipe (`|`) onto `str` before each element of the array. Even though `sArray[4]` through `sArray[9]` are still the default value of `null`, they are counted by `foreach` and iterated over. This is a good opportunity to use a `break` jump statement. Modify the code as follows:

```
18        foreach (string sTemp in sArray) {
19            str += "|"+sTemp;
20            if (sTemp == null) break;
21        }
```

The new code output is as follows: `|These|are|some|words|`

When C# iterates over `sArray[4]`, it will still concatenate `"|"+null` onto the end of `str` but will then check `sArray[4]`, see that it is `null`, and break out of the foreach loop before iterating over `sArray[5]` through `sArray[9]`. As an exercise, think about how you could use the jump statement `continue` to skip empty elements in the middle of the array but not completely break out of the `foreach` loop.

IMPORTANT ARRAY PROPERTIES AND METHODS

There are also many properties and methods available for arrays. These are the most often used. All of these refer to the following array and are noncumulative.

```
string[] sA = new string[] { "A", "B", "C", "D" };
// Resulting in the Array: [ "A", "B", "C", "D" ]
```

Here you see the array initialization expression that allows the declaration, definition, and population of an array in a single line. Note that when using the array initialization expression, the `Length` of the array is implied by the number of elements between the braces and does not need to be specified; in fact, if you use braces to define an array, you cannot use the brackets in the array declaration to specify a length that is different from the number of elements between the braces.

Properties

- `sA[2]` (bracket access): Returns the element of the array at the index specified by the parameter (2). Because `"C"` is the second element of `sA`, this returns: `"C"`.

  If the index parameter is outside of the valid range of the array (which for `sA` is 0 to 3), it will generate a runtime error.

- `sA[1] = "Bravo"` (bracket access used for assignment): Assigns the value on the right side of the = assignment operator to the specified position in the array, replacing the previous value. `sA` would become `[ "A", "Bravo", "C", "D" ]`.

  If the index parameter is outside of the valid range of the array, it will generate a runtime error.

- `sA.Length`: Returns the total capacity of the array. Elements will be counted regardless of whether they have been assigned or are still default values. Returns 4.

Static Methods

The static methods here are of the System.Array class and can act on arrays to give them some of the abilities of Lists.

- `System.Array.IndexOf( sA, "C" )`: Finds the first instance in `sA` of the element `"C"` and returns the index of that element. Because `"C"` is the second element of `sA`, this returns 2.

  If the variable does not exist in the Array, a -1 is returned. This is often used to determine whether an array contains a specific element.

- `System.Array.Resize( ref sA, 6 )`: This is a C# method that adjusts the length of an array. The first parameter is a reference to the array instance (which is why the `ref` keyword is required), and the second parameter is the new length. `sA` would become `[ "A", "B", "C", "D", null, null ]`.

  If the second parameter specifies a Length that is shorter than the original array, the extra elements will be culled. `System.Array.Resize( ref sA, 2 )` would cause `sA` to become `[ "A", "B" ]`. `System.Array.Resize()` does not work for multidimensional arrays.

Converting an array to a List

- `List<string> sL = new List<string>( sA )`: This line will create a List `sL` that duplicates all the elements of `sA`.

It is also possible to use the array initialization expression to declare, define, and populate a List in one line, but it's a little convoluted:

```
List<string> sL = new List<string>( new string[] { "A", "B", "C" } );
```

This declares, defines, and populates an anonymous new `string[]` array that is immediately passed into the `new List<string>()` function.

To prepare for the next example, deactivate the ArrayEx script by clicking the check box next to its name in the Inspector pane for Main Camera.

Multidimensional Arrays

It is possible—and often useful—to create multidimensional arrays that have two or more indices. This means that instead of just one index number in the brackets, the array could use two or more. This would be useful for creating a two-dimensional grid that could hold one item in each grid square.

Create a new C# script named *Array2dEx* and attach it to Main Camera. Open Array2dEx in MonoDevelop and enter the following code:

```
1 using UnityEngine;
2 using System.Collections;
3
4 public class Array2dEx : MonoBehaviour {
5
6     public string[,]        sArray2d;
7
8     void Start () {
9         sArray2d = new string[4,4];
10
11        sArray2d[0,0] = "A";
12        sArray2d[0,3] = "B";
13        sArray2d[1,2] = "C";
14        sArray2d[3,1] = "D";
15
16        print( "The Length of sArray2d is: "+sArray2d.Length );
17    }
18 }
```

The code will yield the following output: `The Length of sArray2d is: 16`

As you can see, `Length` is still only a single int, even though this is a multidimensional array. `Length` here is now just the total number of elements in the array, so it is the coder's responsibility to keep track of each separate dimension of the array.

Now, let's create a nicely formatted output of the values in sArray2d. When we're done, it should look something like this:

```
|A| | |B|
| | |C| |
| | | | |
| |D| | |
```

As you can see, the A is in the 0th row, 0th column ([0,0]), the B is in the 0th row, 3rd column ([0,3]) and so on. To implement this, add the following bolded lines to the code:

```
16          print( "The Length of sArray2d is: "+sArray2d.Length );
17
18          string str = "";
19          for ( int i=0; i<4; i++ ) {                      // 1
20              for ( int j=0; j<4; j++ ) {
21                  if (sArray2d[i,j] != null) {             // 2
22                      str += "|"+sArray2d[i,j];
23                  } else {
24                      str += "|_";
25                  }
26              }
27              str += "|"+"\n";                             // 3
28          }
29          print( str );
30      }
31 }
```

1. Lines 19 and 20 demonstrate the use of two nested `for` loops to iterate over a multidimensional array. When nested in this manner, the code will:

   1. Start with `i=0`
   2. Iterate over all `j` values from 0 to 3
   3. Increment to `i=1`
   4. Iterate over all `j` values from 0 to 3
   5. Increment to `i=2`
   6. Iterate over all `j` values from 0 to 3
   7. Increment to `i=3`
   8. Iterate over all `j` values from 0 to 3

   This will guarantee that the code moves through the multidimensional array in an orderly manner. Keeping the grid example, it will move through all the elements in a row (by incrementing `j` from 0 to 3) and then advance to the next row by incrementing `i` to the next value.

2. Lines 21–25 check to see whether the string at sArray[i,j] has a value other than null. If so, it concatenates a pipe and sArray2d[i,j] onto str. If the value is null, a pipe and one space are concatenated onto str. The pipe character is found on the keyboard above the Return (or Enter) key. It is usually shift–backslash (\ ).

3. This line occurs after all of the iterations of the j for loop but before the next iteration of the i for loop. The effect of it is to concatenate a trailing pipe and carriage return (i.e., line break) onto str, giving the output the nice formatting of a line for each iteration of the i for loop. The backslash-n (\n) is a *new line* character.

The code produces the following output, though you will only see the first couple of lines in the Unity Console pane.

```
The Length of sArray2d is: 16

|A|  |B|
|  |  |C|  |
|  |  |  |  |
|  |D|  |  |
```

Just looking at the output in the Console pane of Unity, you will only see the top two lines of the sArray2d grid array listed in the output. However, if you click that line in the Console pane, you will see that more data is revealed in the bottom half of the Console pane (see Figure 22.2).

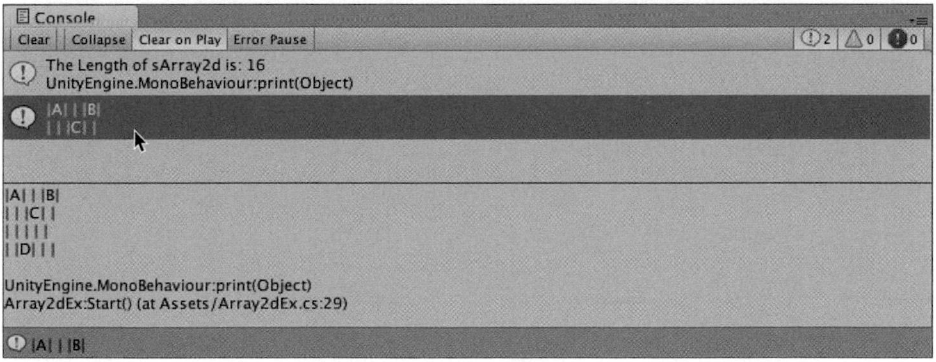

Figure 22.2 Clicking an output message in the Console causes an expanded view to appear below. Note that the first line of the most recent Console message is also shown in the lower-left corner of the Unity window.

As you can see in the figure, the fancy text formatting that we did doesn't line up as well in the Console pane because it uses a non-monospaced font (that is, a font where an *i* has a different width than an *m;* in monospaced fonts, i and m have the same width). You can click any line in the Console pane and choose *Edit > Copy* from the menu bar to copy that data and then paste it into another program. This is something that I do often, and I most commonly paste into a text editor. (I prefer TextWrangler[1] on the Mac or EditPad Pro[2] on the PC, both of which are quite powerful.)

You should also be aware that the Unity Inspector pane does not display multidimensional arrays. In fact, if the Inspector does not know how to properly display a variable, it will completely ignore it, so not even the name of a public multidimensional array will appear in the Inspector pane.

Stop Unity's execution by clicking the Play button again (so that it is not blue) and then use the Main Camera Inspector to disable the *Array2dEx (Script)* component.

Jagged Arrays

A jagged array is an array of arrays. This is similar to the multidimensional array, but it allows the subarrays to be different lengths. We'll create a jagged array that holds the following data:

```
| A | B | C | D |
| E | F | G |
| H | I |
| J |   |   | K |
```

As you can see, the 0th and 3rd rows each contain four elements, while rows 1 and 2 contain three and two elements respectively. Note that null elements are allowed as is shown in the 3rd row. In fact, it is also possible for an entire row to be null (though that would cause an error on line 32 in the following code listing because that code is not designed to handle null rows).

Create a new C# script named *JaggedArrayEx* and attach it to Main Camera. Open JaggedArrayEx in MonoDevelop and enter the following code:

```
1 using UnityEngine;
2 using System.Collections;
3
4 public class JaggedArrayEx : MonoBehaviour {
5     public string[][]        jArray;                        // 1
6
7     void Start () {
8         jArray = new string[4][];                           // 2
9
10        jArray[0] = new string[4];                          // 3
11        jArray[0][0] = "A";
12        jArray[0][1] = "B";
```

---

[1] TextWrangler is available for free from BareBones Software: http://www.barebones.com.

[2] EditPad Pro has a free trial available from Just Great Software: http://editpadpro.com.

```
13              jArray[0][2] = "C";
14              jArray[0][3] = "D";
15
16              // The following lines use single-line Array initialization    // 4
17              jArray[1] = new string[] { "E", "F", "G" };
18              jArray[2] = new string[] { "H", "I" };
19
20              jArray[3] = new string[4];                                      // 5
21              jArray[3][0] = "J";
22              jArray[3][3] = "K";
23
24              print( "The Length of jArray is: "+jArray.Length );            // 6
25              // Outputs: The Length of jArray is: 4
26
27              print( "The Length of jArray[1] is: "+jArray[1].Length );      // 7
28              // Outputs: The Length of jArray[1] is: 3
29
30              string str = "";
31              foreach (string[] sArray in jArray) {                          // 8
32                  foreach( string sTemp in sArray ) {
33                      if (sTemp != null) {
34                          str += " | "+sTemp;                                // 9
35                      } else {
36                          str += " |   ";                                   //10
37                      }
38                  }
39                  str += " | \n";
40              }
41
42              print( str );
43          }
44 }
```

1. Line 5 declares `jArray` as a jagged array (that is, an array of arrays). Where a `string[]` is a collection of strings, a `string[][]` is a collection of string arrays (or `string[]`s).

2. Line 8 defines `jArray` as a jagged array with a length of 4. Note that the second set of brackets is still empty, denoting that the subarrays can be of any length.

3. Line 10 defines the 0th element of `jArray` to be an array of strings with a length of 4.

4. Lines 17 and 18 use the single-line form of array definition. Because the elements of the array are defined between the braces, the length of the array does not need to be explicitly stated (hence the empty brackets in `new string[]`).

5. Lines 20–22 define the 3rd element of `jArray` to be a `string[]` with a length of 4 and then fill only the 0th and 3rd elements of that `string[]`, leaving elements 1 and 2 null.

6. Line 24 outputs `"The Length of jArray is: 4"`. Because `jArray` is an array of arrays (rather than a multidimensional array), `jArray.Length` counts only the number of elements that can be accessed via the first set of brackets.

7. Line 27 outputs `"The Length of jArray[1] is: 3"`. Because `jArray` is an array of arrays, subarray `Length` can also now be easily determined.

8. In jagged arrays, `foreach` works separately on the array and sub-arrays. `foreach` on `jArray` will iterate through the four `string[]` (string array) elements of `jArray`, and `foreach` on any of those `string[]`s will iterate over the strings within. Note that `sArray` is a `string[]` (string array) and that `sTemp` is a string.

   As was mentioned previously, line 32 would throw a *null reference error* if one of the rows of `jArray` were null. In that case, `sArray` would be null, and trying to run the `foreach` statement in line 32 on a null variable would lead to a *null reference*, the attempt to reference an element of something that is null. The `foreach` statement would be attempting to access data of `sArray` like `sArray.Length` and `sArray[0]`. Because null data have no elements or value, accessing things like `null.Length` throws an error.

9. On a keyboard, the string literal in line 34 is typed: space pipe space.

10. On a keyboard, the string literal in line 36 is typed: space pipe space space.

The code outputs the following to the Console pane:

```
The Length of jArray is: 4
The Length of jArray[1] is: 3
 | A | B | C | D |
 | E | F | G |
 | H | I |
 | J |   |   | K |
```

Using `for` Loops Instead of `foreach` for Jagged Arrays

It is also possible to use `for` loops based on the `Length` of the array and subarrays. The preceding `foreach` loop could be replaced with this code:

```
31          string str = "";
32          for (int i=0; i<jArray.Length; i++) {
33              for (int j=0; j<jArray[i].Length; j++) {
34                  str += " | "+jArray[i][j];
35              }
36              str += " | \n";
37          }
```

This code produces the exact same output as the `foreach` loops shown earlier. Whether you choose to use `for` or `foreach` will depend on the situation.

Jagged Lists

As a final note on jagged collections, it is also possible to create jagged Lists. A jagged two-dimensional list of strings would be declared `List<List<string>> jaggedStringList`. Just as with jagged arrays, the subLists would initially be null, so you would have to initialize them as you added them, as is shown in the following code. Just like all Lists, jagged Lists do *not* allow empty elements. Create a new C# script named *JaggedListTest*, attach it to Main Camera, and enter this code:

```
1 using UnityEngine;
2 using System.Collections.Generic;                            // 1
3
4 public class JaggedListTest : MonoBehaviour {
5
6     public List<List<string>> jaggedList;
7
8     // Use this for initialization
9     void Start () {
10        jaggedList = new List<List<string>>();
11
12        // Add a couple List<string>s to jaggedList
13        jaggedList.Add( new List<string>() );
14        jaggedList.Add( new List<string>() );
15
16        // Add two strings to jaggedList[0]
17        jaggedList[0].Add ("Hello");
18        jaggedList[0].Add ("World");
19
20        // Add a third List<string> to jaggedList, including data
21        jaggedList.Add ( new List<string>( new string[] {"complex",
              ➥"initialization"} ) );                          // 2
22
23        string str = "";
24        foreach (List<string> sL in jaggedList) {
25            foreach (string sTemp in sL) {
26                if (sTemp != null) {
27                    str += " | "+sTemp;
28                } else {
29                    str += " |   ";
30                }
31            }
32            str += " | \n";
33        }
34        print( str );
35    }
36
37 }
```

1. Though using `System.Collections;` is included in all Unity C# scripts by default, it's not actually necessary (though `System.Collections.Generic` is required for Lists).

2. This is one of the first instances in this book of the ➥ code continuation character. This is used throughout the book when a single line is longer than can fit the width of the page. You should not try to type the ➥ character, rather it is there to let you know to continue

typing the single line as if there were no line break. With no leading tabs, line 21 would appear as follows:

```
jaggedList.Add( new List<string>( new string[] {"complex","initialization"} ) );
```

The code outputs the following to the Console pane:

```
| Hello | World |
|
| complex | initialization |
```

Whether to Use Array or List

The primary differences between the array and List collections types are as follows:

- List has flexible length, whereas array length is more difficult to change.
- Array is slightly faster, though it's too little to notice most of the time.
- Array allows multidimensional indices.
- Array allows empty elements in the middle of the collection.

Because they are simpler to implement and take less forethought (due to their flexible length), I personally tend to use Lists much more often than arrays. This is especially true when prototyping games, since prototyping requires a lot of flexibility.

Summary

Now that you have a handle on Lists and arrays, it will be possible for you to work easily with large numbers of objects in your games. For example, you could return to the Hello World project from Chapter 18, "Hello World: Your First Program," and add a List<GameObject> to the CubeSpawner code that had every new cube added to it at the time the cube was instantiated. This would give you a reference to each cube, allowing you to manipulate the cube after it was created.

Summary Exercise

In this exercise, we return to the Hello World project from Chapter 18 and write a script that will add each new cube created to a List<GameObject> named gameObjectList. Every frame that a cube exists, it will be scaled down to 95% of the size it was in the previous frame. Once a cube has shrunk to a scale of 0.1 or less, it will be deleted from the scene and gameObjectList.

However, if we delete an element from gameObjectList while the foreach loop is iterating over it, this will cause an error. To avoid this, the cubes that need to be deleted will be temporarily stored in another List named removeList, and then the List will be iterated over to remove them from gameObjectList. (You'll see what I mean in the code.)

Open your Hello World project and create a new scene (*File* > *Scene* from the menu bar). Save the scene as *_Scene_3*. Create a new script named *CubeSpawner3* and attach it to the Main Camera in the scene. Then, open CubeSpawner3 in MonoDevelop and enter the following code:

```
 1 using UnityEngine;
 2 using System.Collections;
 3 using System.Collections.Generic;
 4
 5 public class CubeSpawner3 : MonoBehaviour {
 6     public GameObject         cubePrefabVar;
 7     public List<GameObject>   gameObjectList; // Will hold all the  Cubes
 8     public float              scalingFactor = 0.95f;
 9     // ^ Amount that each cube will shrink each frame
10     public int                numCubes = 0; // Total # of Cubes instantiated
11
12     // Use this for initialization
13     void Start() {
14         // This initializes the List<GameObject>
15         gameObjectList = new List<GameObject>();
16     }
17
18     // Update is called once per frame
19     void Update () {
20         numCubes++; // Add to the number of Cubes                         // 1
21
22         GameObject gObj = Instantiate( cubePrefabVar ) as GameObject;     // 2
23
24         // These lines set some values on the new Cube
25         gObj.name = "Cube "+numCubes;                                     // 3
26         Color c = new Color(Random.value, Random.value, Random.value);   // 4
27         gObj.renderer.material.color = c;
28         // ^ Gives the Cube a random color
29         gObj.transform.position = Random.insideUnitSphere;               // 5
30
31         gameObjectList.Add (gObj); // Add gObj to the List of Cubes
32
33         List<GameObject> removeList = new List<GameObject>();            // 6
34         // ^ This removeList will store information on Cubes that should be
35         //     removed from gameObjectList
36
37         // Iterate through each Cube in gameObjectList
38         foreach (GameObject goTemp in gameObjectList) {                  // 7
39
40             // Get the scale of the Cube
41             float scale = goTemp.transform.localScale.x;                 // 8
42             scale *= scalingFactor; // Shrink it by the scalingFactor
43             goTemp.transform.localScale = Vector3.one * scale;
44
```

```
45              if (scale <= 0.1f) { // If the scale is less than 0.1f...      // 9
46                  removeList.Add (goTemp); // ...then add it to the removeList
47              }
48          }
49
50          foreach (GameObject goTemp in removeList) {                         // 7
51              gameObjectList.Remove (goTemp);                                 //10
52              // ^ Remove the Cube from gameObjectList
53              Destroy (goTemp);  // Destroy the Cube's GameObject
54          }
55
56      }
57 }
```

1. The increment operator (++) is used to increase the `numCubes` count of the total number of cubes that have been created.

2. An instance of `cubePrefabVar` is instantiated. The words `"as GameObject"` are necessary because `Instantiate()` can be used on any kind of object (meaning that C# has no way of knowing what kind of data `Instantiate()` will return). The `"as GameObject"` tells C# that this object should be treated as a GameObject.

3. The `numCubes` variable is used to give unique names to each cube. The first cube will be named *Cube 1*, the second *Cube 2*, and so on.

4. Lines 26 and 27 assign a random color to each cube. Colors are accessed through the material attached to the GameObject's Renderer, as is demonstrated on line 27.

5. `Random.insideUnitSphere` returns a random location that is inside a sphere with a radius of 1 (centered on the point [0,0,0]). This code makes the cubes spawn at a random location near [0,0,0] rather than all at exactly the same point.

6. As is stated in the code comments, `removeList` will be used to store cubes that need to be removed from `gameObjectList`. This is necessary because C# does not allow you to remove elements from a List in the middle of a `foreach` loop that is iterating over the List. (That is, it is not possible to call `gameObjectList.Remove()` anywhere within the `foreach` loop on lines 38–48 that iterates over `gameObjectList`.)

7. This `foreach` loop iterates over all of the cubes in `gameObjectList`. Note that the temporary variable created for the `foreach` is `goTemp`. `goTemp` is also used in the `foreach` loop on line 50, so `goTemp` is declared on both lines 38 and 50. Because `goTemp` is locally scoped to the `foreach` loop in each case, there is no conflict caused by declaring the variable twice in the same `Update()` function. See "Variable Scope" in Appendix B, "Useful Concepts," for more information.

8. Lines 41–43 get the current scale of a cube (by getting the x dimension of its `transform.localScale`), multiply that scale by 95%, and then set the `transform.localScale` to this new value. Multiplying a Vector3 by a float (as is done on line 43) multiplies each individual dimension by that same number, so [2,4,6] * 0.5f would yield [1,2,3].

9. As mentioned in the code comments, if the newly reduced scale is less than 0.1f, the cube will be added to `removeList`.

10. The `foreach` loop from lines 50–54 iterates over `removeList` and removes any cube that is in `removeList` from `gameObjectList`. Because the `foreach` is iterating over `removeList`, it's perfectly fine to remove elements from `gameObjectList`. The removed cube GameObject still exists on screen until the `Destroy()` command is used to destroy it. Even then, it still exists in the computer's memory because it is still an element of `removeList`. However, because `removeList` is a local variable scoped to the `Update()` function, once the `Update()` function is complete, `removeList` will cease to exist, and then any objects that are exclusively stored in `removeList` will also be deleted from memory.

Save your script and then switch back to Unity. You must assign *Cube Prefab* from the Project pane to the `cubePrefabVar` variable in the Main Camera:CubeSpawner3 (Script) component of the Main Camera Inspector if you want to actually instantiate any cubes.

After you have done this, press Play in Unity, and you should see that a number of cubes spawn in as they did in previous versions of Hello World. However, they spawn in different colors, they shrink over time, and they are eventually destroyed (instead of existing indefinitely as they did in earlier versions).

Because the CubeSpawner3 code keeps track of each cube through the `gameObjectList`, it is able to modify each cube's scale every frame and then destroy each cube once it's smaller than a scale of 0.1f. At a `scalingFactor` of 0.95f, it takes each cube 45 frames to shrink to a scale <= 0.1f, so what would be the 0th cube in `gameObjectList` is always removed and destroyed for being too small, and the `Count` of `gameObjectList` stays at 45.

Moving Forward

In the next chapter, you learn how to create and name functions other than `Start()` and `Update()`.

CHAPTER 23

FUNCTIONS AND PARAMETERS

In this chapter, you learn to take advantage of the immense power of functions. You write your own custom functions which can take any kind of variables as input arguments and can return a single variable as the function's result. We also explore some special cases of parameters for function input like function overloading, optional parameters, and the `params` keyword modifier, all of which will help you to write more effective, modular, reusable, and flexible code.

Set Up the Function Examples Project

In Appendix A, "Standard Project Setup Procedure," detailed instructions show you how to set up Unity projects for the chapters in this book. At the start of each project, you will also see a sidebar like the one here. Please follow the directions in the sidebar to create the project for this chapter.

SET UP THE PROJECT FOR THIS CHAPTER

Following the standard project setup procedure, create a new project in Unity. For information on the standard project setup procedure, see Appendix A.

- **Project name:** Function Examples
- **Scene name:** _Scene_Functions
- **C# Script names:** CodeExample

Attach the script CodeExample to the Main Camera in the scene.

Definition of a Function

You've actually been writing functions since your first Hello World program, but up until now, you've been adding content to built-in Unity MonoBehaviour functions like `Awake()`, `Start()`, and `Update()`. From now on, you'll also be writing custom functions.

The best way to think about a function is as a chunk of code that does something. For instance, to count the number of times that `Update()` has been called, you can create a new C# script with the following code (you will need to add the bold lines):

```
1  using UnityEngine;
2  using System.Collections;
3
4  public class CodeExample : MonoBehaviour {
5
6      public int        numTimesCalled = 0;                        // 1
7
8      void Update() {
9          numTimesCalled++;                                       // 2
10         CountUpdates();                                         // 3
11     }
12
13     void CountUpdates() {                                       // 4
14         string outputMessage = "Updates: "+numTimesCalled;     // 5
```

```
15          print( outputMessage ); // Output example: "Updates: 1"  // 6
16      }
17
18 }
```

1. Declares the public variable `numTimesCalled` and defines it to initially have the value 0. Because `numTimesCalled` is declared as a public variable inside the class `CodeExample` but outside of any function, it is scoped to the `CodeExample` class and is available to be accessed by any of the functions within the `CodeExample` class.

2. `numTimesCalled` is incremented (1 is added to it).

3. Line 10 *calls* the function `CountUpdates()`. When your code calls a function, it causes the function to be executed. This will be described in more detail soon.

4. Lines 13 *declares* the function `CountUpdates()`. Declaring a function is similar to declaring a variable. `void` is the return type of the function (as will be covered later in the chapter). Lines 13–16 *define* the function. All lines of code between the opening brace { on line 13 and the closing brace } on line 16 are part of the definition of `CountUpdates()`.

   Note that it the order in which your functions are declared in the class doesn't matter. Whether `CountUpdates()` or `Update()` is declared first is irrelevant as long as they are both within the braces of the class `CodeExample`. C# will look through all the declarations in a class before running any code. It's perfectly fine for `CountUpdates()` to be called on line 10 and declared on line 13 because both `CountUpdates()` and `Update()` are functions declared in the class `CodeExample`.

5. Line 14 defines a *local* string variable named `outputMessage`. Because `outputMessage` is defined within the function `CountUpdate()` its *scope* is limited to `CountUpdate()`, meaning that `outputMessage` has no value outside of the function `CountUpdate()`. For more information about variable scope, see the "Variable Scope" section of Appendix B, "Useful Concepts."

   Line 14 also defines `outputMessage` to be the concatenation of `"Updates:  "` and `numTimesCalled`.

6. The Unity function `print()` is called with the single *argument* `outputMessage`. This prints the value of `outputMessage` to the Unity Console. Function arguments are covered later in this chapter.

In practice, `CountUpdate()` would not be a terribly useful function, but it does showcase two of the important concepts covered in this chapter.

- **Functions encapsulate actions:** A function can be thought of as a named collection of several lines of code. Every time the function is called, those lines of code are executed. This was demonstrated by both `CountUpdate()` and the `BuySomeMilk()` example from Chapter 17, "Introducing Our Language: C#."

- **Functions contain their own scope:** As you can read in the "Variable Scope" section of Appendix B, variables declared within a function have their scope limited to that function. Therefore, the variable `outputMessage` (declared on line 14) has a scope limited to just the function `CountUpdates()`. This can either be stated as "`outputMessage` is scoped to `CountUpdates()`" or "`outputMessage` is *local to* `CountUpdates()`."

Contrast the scope of `outputMessage` with that of the public variable `numTimesCalled`, which has a scope of the entire `CodeExample` class and can be used by any function in `CodeExample`.

If you run this code in Unity, you will see that `numTimesCalled` is incremented every frame, and `CountUpdate()` is called every frame (which outputs the value of `numTimesCalled` to the Console pane). Calling a function causes it to execute, and when the function is done, execution then returns to the point from where it was called. So, in the class `CodeExample`, the following happens every frame:

1. Every frame, the Unity engine calls the `Update()` function (line 8).

2. Then, line 9 increments `numTimesCalled`.

3. Line 10 calls `CountUpdate()`.

4. Execution then jumps to the beginning of the `CountUpdate()` function on line 13.

5. Lines 14 and 15 are executed.

6. When Unity reaches the closing brace of `CountUpdate()` on line 16, execution returns to line 10 (the line from which it was called).

7. Execution continues to line 11.

The remainder of this chapter covers both simple and complex uses of functions, and it's an introduction to some pretty complex concepts. As you continue into the tutorials later in this book, you'll get a much better understanding of how functions work and get more ideas for your own functions, so if there's anything that doesn't make sense the first time through this chapter, that's okay. You can return to it once you've read a bit more of the book.

USING CODE FROM THIS CHAPTER IN UNITY

Though the first code listing in this chapter includes all of the lines of the `CodeExample` class, later code examples do not. If you want to actually run the rest of the code from this chapter in Unity, you will need to wrap it inside of a class. Classes are covered in detail in Chapter 25, "Classes," but for now, you can accomplish this by adding the bolded lines that follow around any of the code listed in this chapter:

```
1 using UnityEngine;
2 using System.Collections;
3
4 public class CodeExample : MonoBehaviour {
5
      // The code listing would replace this comment
16
17 }
```

For example, without the bold lines here, the first code listing in this chapter would have looked like this:

```
 6 public int          numTimesCalled = 0;
 7
 8 void Update() {
 9     CountUpdates();
10 }
11
12 void CountUpdates() {
13     numTimesCalled++;
14     print( "Updates: "+numTimesCalled );   // e.g., "Updates: 5"
15 }
```

If you wanted to try this listing of lines 6–15, you would need to add the bold lines from the previous listing around them. The final version of code in MonoDevelop would be identical to the first code listing in this chapter.

The remainder of the code listings in this chapter will arbitrarily start line numbers at 6 to indicate that other lines would need to precede and follow them in a full C# script.

Function Parameters and Arguments

Some functions are called with empty parentheses following them (for example, CountUpdates() in the first code listing). Other functions can be passed information in between the parentheses (for example, Say("Hello") in the following listing). When a function is designed to receive outside information via the parentheses like this, the type of information is specified by one or more *parameters* that create a local function variable (with a specific type) to hold the information. In line 10 of the following code listing, void Say(string sayThis) declares a parameter named sayThis that is of the string type. sayThis can then be used as a local variable within the Say() function.

When information is sent to a function via its parameters, it is referred to as *passing* information to the function. The information passed is called an *argument*. In line 7 of the following listing, the function Say() is called with the argument "Hello". Another way to say this is that "Hello" is passed to the function Say(). The argument passed to a function must match the parameters of the function, or it will cause an error.

```
 6 void Awake() {
 7     Say("Hello");                                   // 2
 8 }
 9
10 void Say( string sayThis ) {                        // 1
11     print(sayThis);
12 }
```

1. The string `sayThis` is declared as a parameter variable of the function `Say()`.

2. When `Say()` is called by line 7, the string literal `"Hello"` is passed into the function `Say()` as an argument, and line 10 then sets the value of `sayThis` to `"Hello"`.

In the function `Say()` in the previous listing, we've added a single parameter named `sayThis`. Just as with any other variable declaration, the first word is the variable type (`string`) and the second is the name of the variable (`sayThis`).

Just like other local function variables, the parameter variables of a function disappear from memory as soon as the function is complete; if the parameter `sayThis` were used anywhere in the `Awake()` function, it would cause a compiler error due to `sayThis` being undefined outside of the scope of the function `Say()`.

In line 7 of the previous code listing, the argument passed into the function is the string literal `"Hello"`, but any kind of variable or literal can be passed into a function as an argument as long as it matches the parameter(s) of the function (for example, line 7 of the following code listing, passes `this.gameObject` as an argument to the function `PrintGameObjectName()`). If a function has multiple parameters, arguments passed to it should be separated by commas (see line 8 in the following code listing).

```
 6 void Awake() {
 7     PrintGameObjectName( this.gameObject );
 8     SetColor( Color.red, this.gameObject );
 9 }
10
11 void PrintGameObjectName( GameObject go ) {
12     print( go.name );
13 }
14
15 void SetColor( Color c, GameObject go ) {
16     Renderer r = go.renderer;
17     r.material.color = c;
18 }
```

Returning Values

In addition to receiving values as parameters, functions can also return back a single value, known as the *result* of the function as shown on line 13 of the following code listing.

```
 6 void Awake() {
 7     int num = Add( 2, 5 );
 8     print( num ); // Prints the number 7 to the Console
 9 }
10
11 int Add( int numA, int numB ) {
12     int sum = numA + numB;
13     return( sum );
14 }
```

In this example, the function `Add()` has two parameters, the integers `numA` and `numB`. When called, it will sum the two integer arguments that were passed in and then return the result. The `int` at the beginning of the function definition declares that `Add()` will be returning an integer as its result. Just as you must declare the type of any variable for it to be useful, you must also declare the return type of a function for it to be used elsewhere in code.

Returning `void`

Most of the functions that we've written so far have had a return type of `void`, which means no value can be returned. Though these functions don't return a specific value, there are still times that you might want to call `return` within them.

Any time `return` is used within a function, it stops execution of the function and returns execution back to the line from which the function was called. (For example, the `return` on line 16 of the following code listing returns execution back to line 9.)

It is sometimes useful to return from a function to avoid the remainder of the function. For example, if you had a list of over 100,000 GameObjects (e.g., `reallyLongList` in the following code listing), and you wanted to move the GameObject named "Phil" to the origin (Vector3. zero), but didn't care about doing anything else, you could write this function:

```
 6 public List<GameObject> reallyLongList; // Defined in the Unity Editor    // 1
 7
 8 void Awake() {
 9     MoveToOrigin("Phil");                                                   // 2
10 }
11
12 void MoveToOrigin(string theName) {                                         // 3
13     foreach (GameObject go in reallyLongList) {
14         if (go.name == theName) {                                           // 4
15             go.transform.position = Vector3.zero;                           // 5
16             return;                                                         // 6
17         }
18     }
19 }
```

1. `List<GameObject> reallyLongList` is a very long list of GameObjects that we are imagining has been predefined in the Unity Inspector. Because we must imagine this predefined List for this example, entering this code into Unity would not work unless you defined `reallyLongList` yourself.
2. The function `MoveToOrigin()` is called with the string literal `"Phil"` as its argument.
3. The `foreach` statement iterates over `reallyLongList`.
4. If a GameObject with the name "Phil" is found...
5. ...then it is moved to the *origin*, which is the position [0,0,0].
6. Line 16 returns execution to line 9. This avoids iterating over the rest of the List.

In `MoveToOrigin()`, you really don't care about checking the other GameObjects after you've found the one named Phil, so it is better to short circuit the function and return before wasting computing power on doing so. If Phil is the last GameObject in the list, you haven't saved any time, however, if Phil is the first GameObject, you have saved a lot.

Note that when `return` is used in a function with the `void` return type, it does not require parentheses.

Proper Function Names

As you'll recall, variable names should be sufficiently descriptive, start with a lowercase letter, and use camel caps (uppercase letters at each word break). For example:

```
int        numEnemies;
float      radiusOfPlanet;
Color      colorAlert;
string     playerName;
```

Function names are similar; however, function names should all start with a capital letter so that they are easy to differentiate from the variables in your code. Here are some good function names:

```
void ColorAGameObject( GameObject go, Color c ) {...}
void AlignX( GameObject go0, GameObject go1, GameObject go2 ) {...}
void AlignListX( List<GameObject> goList ) {...}
void SetX( GameObject go, float eX ) {...}
```

When Should You Use Functions?

Functions are a perfect method for encapsulating code and functionality in a reusable form. Generally, any time that you would write the same lines of code more than a couple of times, it's good style to define a function to do so instead. Let's start with a code listing that has some repeated code in it.

The function `AlignX()` in the following code listing takes three GameObjects as parameters, averages their position in the X direction, and sets them all to that average X position:

```
 6 void AlignX( GameObject go0, GameObject go1, GameObject go2 ) {
 7     float avgX = go0.transform.position.x;
 8     avgX += go1.transform.position.x;
 9     avgX += go2.transform.position.x;
10     avgX = avgX/3.0f;
11     Vector3 tempPos;
12     tempPos = go0.transform.position;                              // 1
13     tempPos.x = avgX;                                              // 1
14     go0.transform.position = tempPos;                             // 1
15     tempPos = go1.transform.position;
```

```
16    tempPos.x = avgX;
17    go1.transform.position = tempPos;
18    tempPos = go2.transform.position;
19    tempPos.x = avgX;
20    go2.transform.position = tempPos;
21 }
```

1. In lines 12–14, you can see how we handle Unity's restriction that does not allow you to directly set the position.x of a transform. Instead, you must first assign the current position to another variable (for example, `Vector3 tempPos`), then change the x value of that variable, and finally copy the whole Vector3 back onto `transform.position`. This is very tedious to write repeatedly (as demonstrated on lines 12-20), which is why it should be replaced by the `SetX()` function shown in the next code listing. The `SetX()` function in that listing enables you to set the x position of a transform in a single step (e.g., `SetX( this.gameObject, 25.0f )`).

Because of the limitations on directly setting an x, y, or z value of the `transform.position`, there is a lot of repeated code on lines 12 through 20 of the `AlignX()` function. Typing that can be very tedious, and if anything needs to be changed later, it would necessitate repeating the same change three times. This is one of the main reasons for writing functions. In the following code listing, the repetitive lines have been replaced by calls to a new function, `SetX()`. The bold lines have been altered from the previous code listing.

```
6 void AlignX( GameObject go0, GameObject go1, GameObject go2 ) {
7     float avgX = go0.transform.position.x;
8     avgX += go1.transform.position.x;
9     avgX += go2.transform.position.x;
10    avgX = avgX/3.0f;
11    SetX ( go0, avgX );
12    SetX ( go1, avgX );
13    SetX ( go2, avgX );
14 }
15
16 void SetX( GameObject go, float eX ) {
17    Vector3 tempPos = go.transform.position;
18    tempPos.x = eX;
19    go.transform.position = tempPos;
20 }
```

In this improved code listing, the ten lines from 11 to 20 in the previous code have been replaced by the definition of a new function `SetX()` (lines 16–20) and three calls to it (lines 11–13). If anything needed to change about how we were setting the x value, it would only require making a change once to `SetX()` rather than making the change three times in the prior code listing. Though this is a simple example, I hope it serves to demonstrate the power that functions allow us as programmers.

The remainder of this chapter covers some more complex and interesting ways to write functions in C#.

Function Overloading

Function overloading is a fancy term for the capability of functions in C# to act differently based upon the type and number of parameters that are passed into them. The bold sections of the following code demonstrate function overloading.

```
6     void Awake() {
7         print( Add( 1.0f, 2.5f ) );
8         // ^ Prints: "3.5"
9         print( Add( new Vector3(1, 0, 0), new Vector3(0, 1, 0) ) );
10        // ^ Prints "(1.0, 1.0, 0.0)"
11        Color colorA = new Color( 0.5f,  1,     0, 1);
12        Color colorB = new Color( 0.25f, 0.33f, 0, 1);
13        print( Add( colorA, colorB ) );
14        // ^ Prints "RGBA(0.750, 1.000, 0.000, 1.000)"
15    }
16
17    float Add( float f0, float f1 ) {                          // 1
18        return( f0 + f1 );
19    }
20
21    Vector3 Add( Vector3 v0, Vector3 v1 ) {                    // 1
22        return( v0 + v1 );
23    }
24
25    Color Add( Color c0, Color c1 ) {                         // 1
26        float r, g, b, a;
27        r = Mathf.Min( c0.r + c1.r, 1.0f );                   // 2
28        g = Mathf.Min( c0.g + c1.g, 1.0f );                   // 2
29        b = Mathf.Min( c0.b + c1.b, 1.0f );                   // 2
30        a = Mathf.Min( c0.a + c1.a, 1.0f );                   // 2
31        return( new Color( r, g, b, a ) );
32    }
```

1. There are three different Add() functions in this listing, and each is called based on the parameters passed in by various lines of the Awake() function. When two floating-point numbers are passed in, the float version of Add() is used; when two Vector3s are passed in, the Vector3 version is used; and when two Colors are passed in, the Color version is used.

2. In the Color version of Add(), care is taken to not allow r, g, b, or a to exceed 1 because the red, green, blue, and alpha channels of a color are limited to values between 0 and 1. This is done through the use of the Mathf.Min() function. Mathf.Min() takes any number of arguments as parameters and returns the one with the minimum value. In the previous listing, if the summed reds are equal to 0.75f, then 0.75f will be returned in the red channel; however, if the greens were to sum to any number greater than 1.0f, a green value of 1.0f will be returned instead.

Optional Parameters

There are times when you want a function to have optional parameters that may either be passed in or omitted:

```
6      void Awake() {
7          SetX( this.gameObject, 25 );                                        // 2
8          print( this.gameObject.transform.position.x ); // Outputs: "25"
9          SetX( this.gameObject );                                           // 3
10         print( this.gameObject.transform.position.x ); // Outputs: "0"
11     }
12
13     void SetX( GameObject go, float eX=0.0f ) {                            // 1
14         Vector3 tempPos = go.transform.position;
15         tempPos.x = eX;
16         go.transform.position = tempPos;
17     }
```

1. The float eX is defined as an optional parameter with a default value of 0.0f.

2. Because a float can hold any integer value,[1] it is perfectly fine to pass an int into a float. (For example, the integer literal 25 on line 7 is passed into the float eX on line 13.)

3. Because the float eX parameter is optional, it is not required, as is shown on line 9.

In this version of the SetX() function, float eX is an optional parameter. If you give a parameter a default value in the definition of the function, the compiler will interpret that parameter as optional (for example, line 13 in the code listing where the float eX is given a default value of 0.0f).

The first time it's called from Awake(), the eX parameter is set to 25.0f, which overrides the default of 0.0f. However, the second time it's called, the eX parameter is omitted, leaving eX to default to a value of 0.0f.

Optional parameters must come after any required parameters in the function definition.

The `params` Keyword

The `params` keyword can be used to make a function accept any number of parameters of the same type. These parameters are converted into an array of that type.

---

[1] To be more precise, a float can hold *most* int values. As was described in Chapter 19, "Variables and Components," floats get somewhat inaccurate for very big and very small numbers, so a very large int might be rounded to the nearest number that a float can represent. Based on an experiment I ran in Unity, a float seems to be able to represent every whole number up to 16,777,217 after which it will lose accuracy.

```
 6      void Awake() {
 7          print( Add( 1 ) );          // Outputs: "1"
 8          print( Add( 1, 2 ) );       // Outputs: "3"
 9          print( Add( 1, 2, 3 ) );    // Outputs: "6"
10          print( Add( 1, 2, 3, 4 ) ); // Outputs: "10"
11      }
12
13      int Add( params int[] ints ) {
14          int sum = 0;
15          foreach (int i in ints) {
16              sum += i;
17          }
18          return( sum );
19      }
```

Add() can now accept any number of integers and return their sum. As with optional parameters, the params list needs to come after any other parameters in your function definition (meaning that you can have other required parameters before the params list).

This also allows us to rewrite the AlignX() function from before to take any number of possible GameObjects as is demonstrated in the following code listing.

```
 6 void AlignX( params GameObject[] goArray ) {                      // 1
 7      float sumX = 0;
 8      foreach (GameObject go in goArray) {                         // 2
 9          sumX += go.transform.position.x;                         // 3
10      }
11      float avgX = sumX / goArray.Length;                          // 4
12
13      foreach (GameObject go in goArray) {                         // 5
14          SetX ( go, avgX );
15      }
16 }
17
18 void SetX( GameObject go, float eX ) {
19      Vector3 tempPos = go.transform.position;
20      tempPos.x = eX;
21      go.transform.position = tempPos;
22 }
```

1. The params keyword creates an array of GameObjects from any GameObjects passed in.

2. foreach can iterate over every GameObject in goArray. The GameObject go variable is scoped to the foreach loop, so it does not conflict with the GameObject go variable in the foreach loop on lines 13–15.

3. The X position of the current GameObject is added to sumX.

4. The average X position is found by dividing the sum of all X positions by the number of GameObjects.

5. Another `foreach` loop iterates over all the GameObjects in `goArray` and calls `SetX()` with each GameObject as a parameter.

Recursive Functions

Sometimes a function is designed to call itself repeatedly, this is known as a recursive function. One simple example of this is calculating the factorial of a number.

In math, 5! (5 factorial) is the multiplication of that number and every other natural number below it. (Natural numbers are the integers greater than 0.)

5! = 5 * 4 * 3 * 2 * 1 = 120

It is a special case that 0!=1, and the factorial of a negative number will be 0 for our purposes:

0! = 1

We can write a recursive function to calculate the factorial of any integer:

```
6     void Awake() {
7         print( Fac(-1) );    // Outputs: "0"
8         print( Fac(0)  );    // Outputs: "1"
9         print( Fac(5)  );    // Outputs: "120"
10    }
11
12    int Fac( int n ) {
13        if (n < 0) {     // This handles the case if n<0
14            return( 0 );
15        }
16        if (n == 0) {    // This is the "terminal case"
17            return( 1 );
18        }
19        int result = n * Fac( n-1 );
20        return( result );
21    }
```

When `Fac(5)` is called (line 9), and the code reaches the 19th line, `Fac()` is called again with a parameter of `n-1` (which is 4) in a process called recursion. This recursion continues with `Fac()` called four more times until it reaches the case where `Fac(0)` is called. Because n is equal to 0, this hits the terminal case on line 16, which returns 1. The 1 is passed back up to line 19 of the previous recursion and multiplied by n, the result of which is passed back up again until all the recursions of `Fac()` have finished, and it eventually returns the value 120 to line 9 (where it is printed). The chain of all these recursive `Fac()` calls works something like this:

```
Fac(5)
5 * Fac(4)
5 * 4 * Fac(3)
5 * 4 * 3 * Fac(2)
5 * 4 * 3 * 2 * Fac(1)
5 * 4 * 3 * 2 * 1 * Fac(0)
5 * 4 * 3 * 2 * 1 * 1
5 * 4 * 3 * 2 * 1
5 * 4 * 3 * 2
5 * 4 * 6
5 * 24
120
```

The best way to really understand what's happening in this recursive function is to explore it using the debugger, a feature in MonoDevelop that enables you to watch each step of the execution of your programs and see how different variables are affected by your code. The process of debugging is the topic of the next chapter.

Summary

In this chapter, you have seen the power of functions and many different ways that you can use them. Functions are a cornerstone of any modern programming language, and the more programming you do, the more you will see how powerful and necessary they are.

Chapter 24, "Debugging," shows you how to use the debugging tools in Unity. These tools are meant to help you find problems with your code, but they are also very useful for understanding how your code works. After you have learned about debugging from the next chapter, I recommend returning to this chapter and examining the Fac() function in more detail. And, of course, feel free to use the debugger to explore and better understand any of the functions in this chapter or others.

CHAPTER 24

DEBUGGING

To the uninitiated, debugging can seem somewhat like a black art. On the contrary, it's actually one of the best skills you can have as a developer, though it's rarely taught to novice coders, which I think is a tragic missed opportunity. All beginning coders make mistakes, and knowing about debugging will enable you to find and correct those mistakes much faster than just staring at the code and hoping the bug will reveal itself.

By the end of this chapter, you'll understand the difference between a compile-time error and a runtime error, you'll know how to set breakpoints in your code, and you'll know how to step through the lines of your program one at a time to help you root out hard-to-find bugs.

Getting Started with Debugging

Before we can start finding bugs, we need to make some. For this chapter, we'll start from the project you created for Chapter 18, "Hello World: Your First Program." If you don't have that project on hand, you can always download it from this book's website:

> http://book.prototools.net/

On the website, find this Chapter 24, "Debugging" and click to download the project for the beginning of the chapter.

Throughout this chapter, I instruct you to make a number of bugs on purpose. This might seem like a strange way to do things, but my goal in doing so is to give you some experience with tracking down and fixing several different kinds of bugs and other errors you will almost certainly encounter while working with Unity. Each of these example bugs will introduce you to a different kind of potential future problem and help you understand how to go about finding and fixing bugs when you encounter them.

> **note**
>
> Throughout this chapter, I refer to errors occurring on specific line numbers. Sometimes this will be the exact same line number that you get for the error, and sometimes it may be shifted up or down by a couple of lines. Don't worry if you don't have exactly the same line numbers as I do, just look for the content that I'm discussing *near* the line numbers that I reference.

Compile-Time Bugs

A compile-time bug (or error) is a problem that can be discovered by Unity when it is compiling C# code (that is, attempting to interpret the C# code and turn it into the Common Intermediate Language that is then converted to machine language that can run on your computer). After you have opened the Hello World project in Unity, follow these instructions to intentionally cause a compile-time error and explore how they work:

1. Duplicate the existing _Scene_1. To do so, click _Scene_1 in the Project pane to select it and choose *Edit > Duplicate* from the menu bar. Unity is pretty good at counting things, so it will automatically increment the name of the scene and call this new scene _Scene_2.

2. Double-click _Scene_2 to open it in the Hierarchy and Scene panes. Once it's open, the title of your Unity window should be *_Scene_2.unity - Hello World - PC, Mac, & Linux Standalone*. If you press Play, you should see everything behaving just as it did in _Scene_1.

3. Now we should make a second version of the CubeSpawner class so that we don't end up damaging the one from _Scene_1. Click the CubeSpawner script in the Project pane to select it and then choose *Edit > Duplicate* from the menu bar. A script named

CubeSpawner1 will be created and an error will immediately appear in the Console pane
(see Figure 24.1). Click the error to get more information.

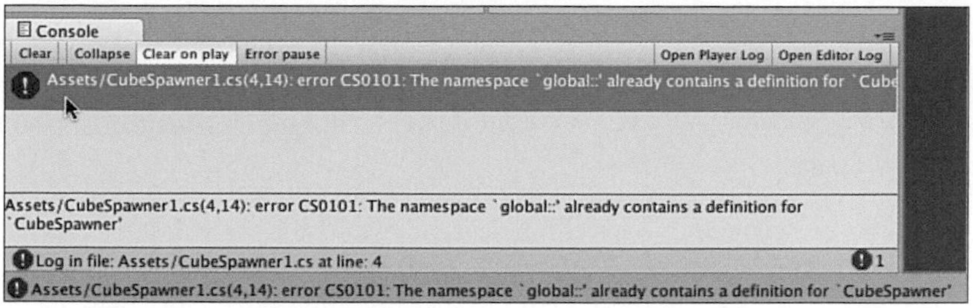

Figure 24.1 Your first bug: a compile-time error caught by Unity

There's a ton of useful information in this error message, so let's go through it bit by bit.

Assets/CubeSpawner1.cs(4,14):

Every error you encounter will include information about where Unity encountered it. This tells
us that the error was in the CubeSpawner1.cs script inside the Assets folder of our project and
that it happened on line 4, character 14.

error CS0101:

The second chunk of the message tells us what kind of error we've encountered. If you encounter an error that you don't understand, you can do a web search for the words "Unity error" and
the error code. (In this example, our web search would be for "Unity error CS0101.") A search
like this will almost always find a forum post or something similar that describes the problem
you're having. In my experience, you will generally get good results from http://forum.unity3d.
com and http://answers.unity3d.com, and some of the best answers to issues come from http://
stackoverflow.com.

The namespace 'global::' already contains a definition for 'CubeSpawner'

The final chunk of the error message attempts to put the error into plain English. In this case, it's
telling us that the term *CubeSpawner* is already defined somewhere else in our code, which it
is. At this time, the scripts CubeSpawner and CubeSpawner1 are both attempting to define the
class CubeSpawner.

Let's get to work fixing this:

1. Double-click *CubeSpawner1* to open MonoDevelop. (Alternatively, you can double-click the
   error message in the Console pane, which will open the script to the line that produced the
   error.)

2. Within the CubeSpawner1 script, change line 4 (the line that declares CubeSpawner) to read:

```
public class CubeSpawner2 : MonoBehaviour {
```

The CubeSpawner2 class name is intentionally different from the name of the script so that we can see another error in a moment.

3. Save your file and return to Unity, where you'll see that the error message disappears from the Console pane.

Whenever you save a script, Unity detects the save and recompiles the script to make sure that there are no errors. If it does run into a bug, you'll get a compile-time error message like the one we just fixed. These are the easiest bugs to fix because Unity knows exactly where the problem took place and passes this information on to you. Now that the CubeSpawner script is defining the class CubeSpawner and the CubeSpawner1 script is defining the class CubeSpawner2, the compile-time error is gone.

Compile-Time Errors Caused by a Missing Semicolon

Delete the semicolon (;) at the end of line 14, which is the line that reads:

```
14          Instantiate( cubePrefabVar );
```

This will cause another one of these compile-time error messages.

> Assets/CubeSpawner1.cs(15,9): error CS1525: Unexpected symbol '}'

You'll notice that it doesn't say "Hey, you forgot a semicolon," but it does tell you where it ran into trouble compiling the script (character 9 of line 15). It also tells you that it encountered the closing brace (}) in an unexpected place. Given this information, you should be able to look around that area of the code and discover the missing semicolon.

Add the semicolon back on to the end of line 14 and save, and Unity should stop complaining. A compile-time error will almost always be detected either on the line that has the problem or on a later line. In this example, the missing semicolon was on line 14, but the problem was discovered on line 15.

Attaching and Removing Scripts

Switch back to Unity and try dragging the CubeSpawner1 script onto Main Camera in the hierarchy. This time, you'll get the error shown in Figure 24.2.

Unity is complaining because the name of our script, CubeSpawner1, doesn't match the name of the class that we're defining in the script: CubeSpawner2. In Unity, when you create a class that extends MonoBehavior (for example, CubeSpawner2 : Monobehaviour), the name of the class must match the name of the file in which it is defined.

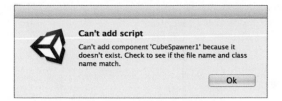

Figure 24.2   Some errors are only caught when you try to attach a script to a GameObject.

To fix this, just make sure that the two names match. Click once on CubeSpawner1 in the Project pane to select it and then click a second time on the name to rename it. (You can also press the Return key on Mac or the F2 key on Windows to rename the script.) Change the name to *CubeSpawner2* and try attaching it to the Main Camera again. This time, it should go with no problems.

Click *Main Camera* in the Hierarchy. In the Inspector, you should now see that Main Camera has both a CubeSpawner and a CubeSpawner2 script attached. Click the small gear icon to the right of the name *Cube Spawner (Script)* in the Inspector and choose *Remove Component* from the drop-down menu, as shown in Figure 24.3.

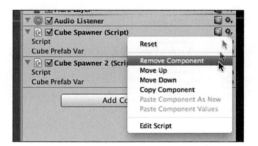

Figure 24.3   Removing the extra CubeSpawner Script component

This way, we won't have two different scripts trying to spawn cubes at the same time. For the next several chapters, we'll only attach a single script component to each GameObject.

Runtime Errors

Now, click Play, and you'll encounter another kind of error (see Figure 24.4). Click the Pause button to pause playback (the button with two vertical bars next to the Play button), and we'll take a look at this error.

This is a *runtime error*, which means it's an error that only occurs when Unity is actually trying to play the project. Runtime errors occur when you've typed everything correctly, as far as the compiler can determine, yet something is not right when the code actually runs.

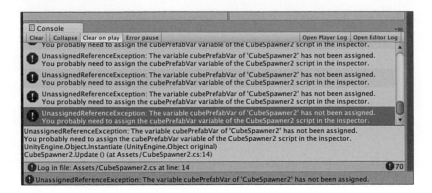

Figure 24.4   Many repetitions of the same runtime error

You'll see that this error looks a little different from the others you've seen so far. For one thing, the beginning of the error message doesn't include information about where the error occurred, however if you click one of the error messages, you'll see that additional information pops up in the bottom half of the Console. With runtime errors, the last line tells you the point at which Unity realized that an error had occurred. This sometimes happens on the line with the bug, and it sometimes happens on the next line. The error message here tells us to look at or near line 14 of CubeSpawner2.cs for the error.

> CubeSpawner2.Update () (at Assets/CubeSpawner2.cs:14)

Looking at line 14 of CubeSpawner2, we see that it's the line where we instantiate an instance of `cubePrefabVar`. (Note that your line number may be slightly different; if so, that's okay.)

```
14          Instantiate( cubePrefabVar );
```

Just as the compiler thought, this line looks fine. Let's delve into the error message further:

> UnassignedReferenceException: The variable cubePrefabVar of 'CubeSpawner2' has not been assigned. You probably need to assign the cubePrefabVar variable of the Cube-Spawner2 script in the inspector. UnityEngine.Object.Instantiate (UnityEngine.Object original) CubeSpawner2.Update () (at Assets/CubeSpawner2.cs:14)

This tells us that the variable `cubePrefabVar` has not been assigned, and if you look at the *CubeSpawner2 (Script)* component of Main Camera in the Inspector (click Main Camera in the Hierarchy to do so), you'll see that this is correct. So, just as we did in the previous chapter, click the circular target next to cubePrefabVar in the Inspector and choose *Cube Prefab* from the list of assets. You should now see it assigned to cubePrefabVar in the Inspector.

Click the Pause button again to resume simulation, and you'll see that the cubes start spawning happily.

Click the Play button to stop the simulation. Now, click Play once more to start it up again.

What happened?!? We just got the same error again! Click the Play button once more to stop the simulation again.

> ### warning
>
> **CHANGES MADE WHILE PLAYING DON'T STICK!**   This is an issue that you will encounter many times. There are good reasons for making Unity work this way, but it's sometimes confusing to new users. Any changes you make while Unity is playing or paused (like the change you just made to `cubePrefabVar`) are reset back to their previous values when playback is stopped. If you want a change to stick, make sure that Unity is not playing when you make the change.

Now that Unity is stopped again, use the Main Camera Inspector to assign Cube Prefab to the field cubePrefabVar again, and this time, it should stick. Press Play, and everything should work out fine.

Stepping Through Code with the Debugger

In addition to the automatic code checking tools that we've already explored in this chapter, Unity and MonoDevelop also enable you to step through code one line at a time, which can be very helpful for understanding what's happening in your code. Add the bolded lines in the following code listing (that is, lines 13 and 16–26) to your CubeSpawner2 script. If you need to make room in the script, just press Return (Enter on Windows keyboards to add new lines). The code is also shown in Figure 24.5:

```
1 using UnityEngine;
2 using System.Collections;
3
4 public class CubeSpawner2 : MonoBehaviour {
5     public GameObject         cubePrefabVar;
6
7     // Use this for initialization
8     void Start () {
9     }
10
11     // Update is called once per frame
12     void Update () {
13         SpellItOut();                              // 1
14         Instantiate( cubePrefabVar );
15     }
16
17     public void SpellItOut () {                    // 2
18         string sA = "Hello World!";
```

```
19          string sB = "";
20
21          for (int i=0; i<sA.Length; i++) {          // 3
22              sB += sA[i];                           // 4
23          }
24
25          print(sB);
26      }
27 }
```

1. Line 13 calls the `SpellItOut()` function.

2. Lines 17–26 declare and define the function `SpellItOut()`. This function will copy the contents of string `sA` to string `sB` one character at a time.

3. This `for` loop iterates over the length of `sA`. Because `"Hello World"` consists of 11 chars, the loop will iterate 11 times.

4. Line 22 pulls the ith character from `sA` and concatenates it onto the end of `sB`.

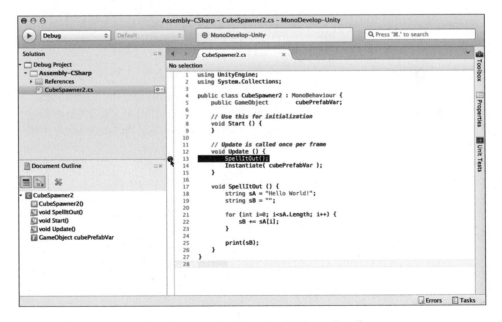

Figure 24.5   The `SpellItOut()` function showing a breakpoint on line 13.

Here, we've created a function called `SpellItOut()` that will copy the string `sA` to the string `sB` letter by letter. This is a horribly inefficient way to copy a string, but it will work very well to demonstrate how the debugger works.

Once you've typed in all the code and double-checked it, click in the gutter to the left of line 13 (as shown in Figure 24.5). This will create a breakpoint on line 13, which appears as a red circle.

When a breakpoint is set and MonoDevelop is debugging Unity, Unity will pause execution every time it hits that breakpoint. Let's check it out.

Attaching the Debugger to Unity

> ## warning
>
> **ATTACHING THE DEBUGGER BEFORE STARTING YOUR UNITY PROJECT WILL SOMETIMES CRASH UNITY ON OS X!**   As of the time of writing this book, Unity and MonoDevelop on OS X still have a sporadic issue with pressing Play in Unity with the MonoDevelop debugger already attached. Unity is aware of the issue, so hopefully it will be resolved by the time you read this book, but in case it is not, the instructions in this section about how to attach the debugger to Unity will direct you to attach it once Unity is already playing and to detach and reattach it any time you want to stop and restart playback. If you are on a PC (or if you're on OS X and you're feeling lucky), you can attach the debugger to Unity before pressing Play in Unity, and everything should work fine. This shouldn't be a problem on OS X for the small projects in this section of the book, but it has happened to me sporadically on large projects.
>
> If you encounter this bug, Unity will freeze when you start playback without MonoDevelop having any reaction. Both Unity and MonoDevelop will become unresponsive. To solve this, you will need to force quit Unity, as explained in the "How to Force Quit an Application" sidebar.

HOW TO FORCE QUIT AN APPLICATION

On an OS X Computer

Implement a force quit by doing the following:

1. Press Command-Option-Esc on the keyboard. This will bring up the Force Quit window.

2. Find the application that is misbehaving. Its name will often be followed by "(not responding)" in the applications list.

3. Click that application, and then click Force Quit.

On a Windows Computer

Implement a force quit by doing the following:

1. Press Shift+Ctrl+Esc on the keyboard. This will bring up the Windows Task Manager.

> 2. Find the application that is misbehaving.
>
> 3. Click that application, and then click End Task.
>
> If you have to force quit Unity while it's running, you will lose any work that you've done since your last save. Because you must constantly save C# scripts, they shouldn't be an issue, but you might have to redo unsaved changes made to your scene.

For MonoDevelop to be able to debug what's happening in Unity when it plays, you need to attach it to the Unity process. Once the MonoDevelop debugger is attached to Unity, it will be able to peer into the depths of what's happening in your C# code and can pause execution of the code at breakpoints (like the one you set on line 13).

Because of the potential Unity/MonoDevelop bug mentioned in the warning, it is best to first start Unity playing and then attach the debugger. To do so, follow these steps:

1. Click the Pause button in Unity (next to the Play button at the top of the Unity window).

2. Click the Play button. Pressing the Pause button before play ensures that Unity goes through the setup to play but only plays the first frame of your application before pausing. Now both the Play and Pause buttons should be colored blue.

3. Switch to the MonoDevelop application and either click the Play button in the top-left corner of the MonoDevelop window (as shown in Figure 24.6) or choose *Run > Attach to Process* from the MonoDevelop menu bar.

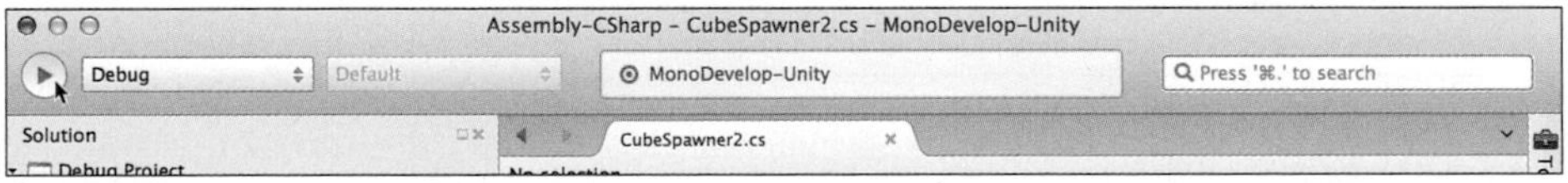

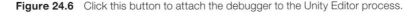

Figure 24.6   Click this button to attach the debugger to the Unity Editor process.

This will pop up a window (see Figure 24.7) that enables you to choose a process to debug (on Windows machines, the *null (mono)* process usually does not appear). The processes listed are applications running on your machine that MonoDevelop can connect to and debug. Unity and MonoDevelop are separate programs (that is, processes), and through this interface, Unity allows MonoDevelop to attach to it and control its execution.

4. Click the *Unity Editor (Unity)* process to select it, and then click the *Attach* button. This will cause MonoDevelop to switch into its debug mode and will set us up for debugging. It can take a few seconds for this to happen, so don't worry if things seem to freeze for a bit. When the switch is complete, you'll notice that the MonoDevelop window has changed (see Figure 24.8). The Play button in the top left has become a Stop button, a couple of panes have appeared at the bottom of the MonoDevelop window, and a number of buttons to control the debugger have appeared at the top of MonoDevelop window (see Figure 24.9).

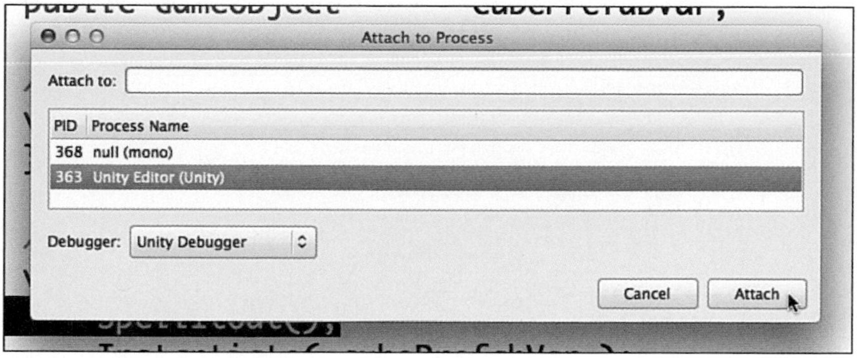

Figure 24.7   Selecting the Unity Editor process for debugging

> **note**
>
> **MY MONODEVELOP MAY LOOK A BIT DIFFERENT**   In MonoDevelop, you can move window panes (or panels) around just as you can in Unity. I've moved mine to make it easier for you to see what I'm doing in these book examples, but that will probably mean that it looks a little different from what you're seeing on your screen. You should have all the same panes, they will just be arranged slightly differently.

5. Now that we have the debugger ready and attached, switch to Unity and click the Pause button to unpause Unity. Almost immediately, Unity will freeze, and MonoDevelop should pop up. Sometimes, on Windows, MonoDevelop won't automatically pop up, but Unity will look frozen. Just switch to the MonoDevelop task manually, and you should see what is shown in Figure 24.8.

Execution of the `Update()` function has paused on line 13 where we placed the breakpoint. The yellow arrow in the gutter shows the current line of execution. While execution is stopped in the debugger, the Unity process is completely frozen. That means that we can't switch back to Unity through any normal means until it is running again.

In debug mode, some of the buttons at the top of the toolbar have changed (see Figure 24.9).

The following steps show you how the various debugger control buttons work. Before following these steps, I recommend reading the "Watching Variables in the Debugger" sidebar.

1. Click the debugger's *Run* button in MonoDevelop (shown in Figure 24.9). This will cause Unity to continue the execution of the script. When Unity is stopped at a breakpoint like the one on line 13, everything about Unity is frozen until you tell it to continue.

    When you click the Run button, Unity starts running again and does so until it hits another breakpoint. When you clicked Run, Unity passed through the game loop, started a new frame, and then stopped on line 13 again (when `Update()` was called).

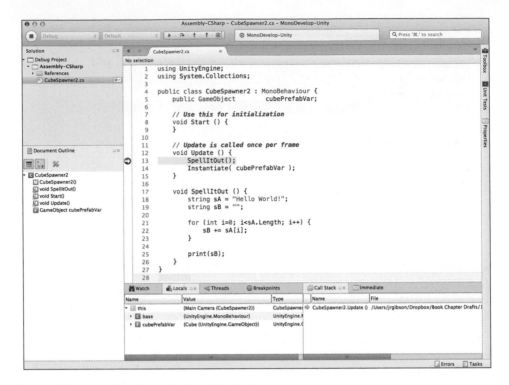

Figure 24.8   Execution stopped at line 13 in the debugger.

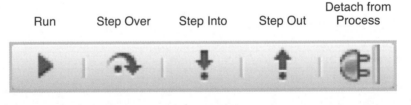

Figure 24.9   The debugger control buttons

note

Depending on the type of computer you have, you may need to switch back to the Unity process (that is, application) for Unity to actually move on to the next frame. On some machines, Unity will continue on to the next frame while you are using MonoDevelop, and on some it won't. If the yellow arrow doesn't return to the breakpoint in the debugger after you've clicked run, switch to the Unity process, and it should start the next frame and then stop on the breakpoint again.

As mentioned previously, while the code is stopped in the debugger (that is, when you can see the yellow arrow shown in Figure 24.8), you cannot switch to the Unity process. This is normal and occurs because Unity is completely frozen while it is waiting for you to look at code in the debugger. Unity will resume normal function once you're no longer debugging.

2. Once the yellow execution arrow has stopped on the line 13 breakpoint again, click the *Step Over* button. The yellow arrow will move on to line 14 without stepping into the function `SpellItOut()`. The `SpellItOut()` function is still called and still runs, but the debugger passes over it. Step Over is useful if you don't want to see the inner working of a function that is called.

3. Click Run again. Unity will advance to the next frame, and the yellow execution arrow will again stop on the line 13 breakpoint.

4. This third time around, click *Step Into*. You'll see that the yellow arrow jumps from line 13 into line 18 of the function `SpellItOut()`. Any time you click Step Into, the debugger will enter into any functions called, whereas Step Over will jump over them.

5. Now that you are inside the `SpellItOut()` function, click Step Over several times to walk through the execution of the `SpellItOut()` function.

6. As you continue to click Step Over, you can watch `sA` and `sB` change through the course of this function (see the sidebar "Watching Variables in the Debugger"). Each pass through the `for` loop on lines 21–23 adds a character from `sA` to the string `sB`. You can see the values of the variables change in the *Locals* debugger panel.

WATCHING VARIABLES IN THE DEBUGGER

One of the great strengths of any debugger is the ability to look at the value of an individual variable at almost any time. There are three possible ways to do so in MonoDevelop's debugger. Before trying any of these, be sure that you've followed the directions in this chapter to start the debugging process and that the yellow execution arrow is currently paused on a line of code in the debugger.

The first and simplest method is to just hover your mouse pointer over any variable in the MonoDevelop code pane. If you position the mouse pointer over a variable name and keep it still for about 1 second, a tool tip will appear telling you the value of that variable. However, it is very important to note that the value shown is the current value of the variable based on the position of the yellow arrow, not the position of that variable in the code. For example, the variable `sB` of the function `SpellItOut()` is repeated several times throughout the code, and holding the mouse over any of them will show the current value of `sB` regardless of which `sB` you hover over.

The second method is to find the variable in the Locals pane of the debugger. To view this pane, choose *View > Debug Windows > Locals* from the MonoDevelop menu bar. This will bring the Locals variable watching pane to the front. Here, you will see a list of all local variables that are available to the debugger at the current time. If you step into the `SpellItOut()` function as instructed in this chapter, you will see three local variables listed: `this`, `sA`, and `sB`. The variables `sA` and `sB` are initially set to null, but their value appears in the Locals pane once it has been defined on lines 18 and 19, respectively. When you have used Step Over a few times and reached line 21 in the debugger, you will see that the integer `i` is both declared and defined on that line. The variable `this` refers to the current instance of the CubeSpawner2 script. Click the disclosure triangle next to `this` to reveal the public field `cubePrefabVar` inside `this` as well as a variable named `base`. Opening the disclosure triangle next to `base` reveals all of the variables associated with the base class of CubeSpawner2, which is MonoBehaviour. Base classes like MonoBehaviour (a.k.a. superclasses or parent classes) are covered in Chapter 25, "Classes."

The third way that you can watch a variable is to enter it explicitly into the Watch pane. To bring the pane to the front, choose *View > Debug Windows > Watch* from the menu bar. In the Watch pane, click a blank line to add a watched variable. (Click in the field with the text "Click here to add a new watch.") In this field, type the name of a variable, and MonoDevelop will try to show you its value. For example, enter the variable `this.gameObject.name` and press Return, and it will show you "Main Camera," the name of the GameObject to which this script is attached. If the value is ever too large to fit in the Watch pane, you can click the magnifying glass next to the value to read the whole thing; this sometimes happens when you're working with large strings of text.

7. If the yellow execution arrow is still within `SpellItOut()` continue to Step 8, but if you clicked Step Over enough times to exit the function `SpellItOut()`, click Run, and then click Step Into to return execution to the inside of `SpellItOut()`.

8. While still inside the `SpellItOut()` function, click *Step Out*. This will cause the debugger to exit the `SpellItOut()` function and then continue to line 14 (the line immediately after `SpellItOut()` was called). This is different from a `return` statement because the rest of the `SpellItOut()` function is still executed, you just don't witness it in the debugger. This is useful when you want to exit the current function yet don't want to completely return to full-speed execution by clicking Run.

Finally, the *Detach from Process* button shown in Figure 24.9 will detach the MonoDevelop debugger from the Unity process, stop debugging, and return Unity to normal execution.[1]

---

[1] If you do encounter the crash on debug start issue mentioned in the warning at the beginning of this section, you need to detach and reattach the MonoDevelop debugger after each time you stop your game in Unity. Otherwise, if the debugger is still attached, you may get the crash the next time you press Play in Unity.

You can also press the large Stop button in the top-left corner of the MonoDevelop window to detach from the Unity process and stop debugging.

I highly recommend using the debugger to examine the execution of the recursive `Fac()` function that is featured at the end of Chapter 23, "Functions and Parameters." That function is an excellent example of how the debugger can help you better understand code.

Summary

That's it for your introduction to debugging. Although in this case we did not use the debugger to discover a bug, you can see how it can help you better understand code. Remember this: Whenever something is confusing in your code, you can always step through it using the debugger.

Though it may have seemed a bit frustrating for me to instruct you to generate so many bugs, my sincere hope is that helping you to experience and understand these bugs and how to investigate and fix them will give you a leg up later when you encounter real bugs on your own. Remember that you can always search the Internet for the text of the bug (or at least the error number) to find clues for fixing it. As I wrote at the beginning of the chapter, good debugging skills are one of the major things that can help you to become both a competent and confident programmer.

CHAPTER 25

CLASSES

By the end of this chapter, you will understand how to use classes. A class is a collection of both variables and functions in a single C# object. Classes are an essential building block in modern games and, more widely, in object-oriented programming.

Understanding Classes

Classes combine functionality and data. Another way to put this is that classes are composed of both functions and variables, which are called *methods* and *fields* respectively, when they are used within a class. Classes are often used to represent objects in the world of your game project. For example, consider a character in a standard roleplaying game. There are several fields (or variables) that she might have:

```
string      name;          // The character's name
float       health;        // The amount of health she has
float       healthMax;     // The maximum amount of health she could have
List<Item>  inventory;     // A List of all Items in her inventory
List<Item>  equipped;      // A List of Items that she currently has equipped
```

All of these fields are applicable to any character in a roleplaying game (RPG), because all characters have health, equipment, and a name. There are also several methods (functions) that could be used by or on that character. (The ellipses [...] in the following code listing show where code would need to be added to make the functions work.)

```
void Move(Vector3 newLocation) {...}       // Allows the character to move
void Attack(Character target) {...}         // Attacks target Character
void TakeDamage(float damageAmt) {...}      // Causes this character to lose health
void Equip(Item newItem) {...}              // Adds an Item to the equipped List
```

Obviously, you would want a character in an actual game to have many more fields and methods than are described here, but the core idea is that all characters in your RPG would need to have these variables and functions on them.

> tip
>
> You're already using classes! In fact, though it wasn't explicitly stated until now, every bit of code you've written so far in this book has been part of a class, and in general, you can think of each C# file that you create as being its own class.

The Anatomy of a Class (and of a C# Script)

Several important elements of many classes are illustrated in Figure 25.1. Not all of them are necessary in every class, but they are extremely common.

■ **Includes** make it possible for your C# scripts to make use of various classes that have been created by others. Includes are enabled by using statements, and the includes shown here enable all of the standard elements of Unity as well as generic collections like Lists. These should be the first part of your script.

- The **class declaration** names your class and determines what other classes it extends (see the discussion on class inheritance later in this chapter). In this case, `Enemy` extends `MonoBehaviour`.

- **Fields** are variables that are local to your class, meaning that any function in the class can access them by name. In addition, variables labeled "public" can be accessed by any other entity that can see the class (see the "Variable Scope" section of Appendix B, "Useful Concepts").

- **Methods** are functions contained within a class. They can access any of the fields in the class, and they can also have local variables (for example, the Vector3 `tempPos` in `Move()` that only exist within each function. Methods are what enable classes to do things. Virtual functions are a special type of method that is covered in the "Class Inheritance" section later in this chapter.

- **Properties** can be thought of as methods masquerading as fields through use of the `get` and `set` accessors. These are discussed later in this chapter.

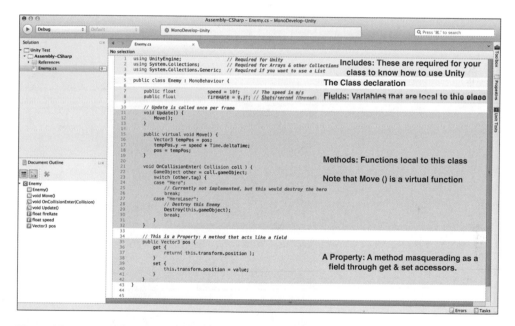

Figure 25.1   Diagram showing some important elements of a class

Before getting into this too much more, set up a project in which you can use this code.

Setting Up the Enemy Class Sample Project

Appendix A, "Standard Project Setup Procedure," contains information about how to create a new Unity project for the examples in this chapter. Please follow the instructions in the appendix using the information contained in the sidebar.

SET UP THE PROJECT FOR THIS CHAPTER

Following the standard project setup procedure, create a new project in Unity. Information on the standard project setup procedure is contained in Appendix A.

- **Project name:** Enemy Class Sample Project

- **Scene name:** _Scene_0 (The underscore at the beginning of the scene name will keep it sorted at the top of the Project pane.)

- **C# script names:** None at this time

You do not need to attach a script to the Main Camera. There is no Main Camera script in this project.

After following the Appendix A instructions to create a new project and saving your new scene as _Scene_0, use the Create menu in the Hierarchy pane to create a new sphere by selecting *Create > Sphere*, as shown in Figure 25.2.

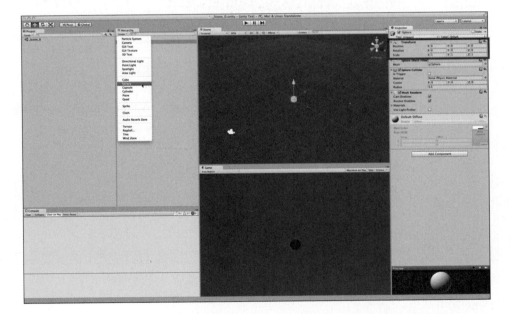

Figure 25.2   Creating a sphere in _Scene_0

Select Sphere by clicking its name in the Hierarchy pane. Then set the position of the sphere to the origin [0, 0, 0] (that is, x=0, y=0, z=0) using the Transform component (highlighted with a red box in Figure 25.2).

In the Project pane, choose *Create > C# Script* and name the script *Enemy*. Double-click the script to open it in MonoDevelop, and enter the following code (identical to Figure 25.1). Lines that you need to add are bolded in the code listing.

```csharp
1 using UnityEngine;                    // Required for Unity
2 using System.Collections;            // Automatically included by Unity
3 using System.Collections.Generic;    // Required if you want to use a List
4
5 public class Enemy : MonoBehaviour {
6
7     public float            speed = 10f;     // The speed in m/s
8     public float            fireRate = 0.3f; // Shots/second (Unused)
9
10    // Update is called once per frame
11    void Update() {
12        Move();
13    }
14
15    public virtual void Move() {
16        Vector3 tempPos = pos;
17        tempPos.y -= speed * Time.deltaTime;
18        pos = tempPos;
19    }
20
21    void OnCollisionEnter( Collision coll ) {
22        GameObject other = coll.gameObject;
23        switch (other.tag) {
24        case "Hero":
25            // Currently not implemented, but this would destroy the hero
26            break;
27        case "HeroLaser":
28            // Destroy this Enemy
29            Destroy(this.gameObject);
30            break;
31        }
32    }
33
34    // This is a Property: A method that acts like a field
35    public Vector3 pos {
36        get {
37            return( this.transform.position );
38        }
39        set {
40            this.transform.position = value;
41        }
42    }
43 }
```

Most of this should look pretty straightforward and familiar to you except for the property and the virtual function. Both are covered in this chapter.

Properties

You can see in the previous code listing that the property pos is treated as if it were a variable in both lines 16 and 18 of Move(). This is accomplished through the use of the get{} and set{} *accessor* clauses, which enable you to run code each time you read or set a property. Every time the pos property is read, the code within the get{} accessor is run, and the get{} accessor must return a value of the same type as the property (that is, Vector3). Code within set{} is run every time the pos property is assigned a value, and the value keyword is used as an *implicit variable* that holds the value assigned. In other words, in line 18, pos is assigned the value of tempPos; then in line 40, the value of tempPos is held by the variable value and assigned to this.transform.position. An implicit variable is one that exists without you, the programmer, explicitly declaring it. All set{} clauses in properties have the implicit variable value. It is possible to create a property with only a get{} accessor (or only a set{} accessor) to make the property read-only (or write-only).

In the pos property example, pos is used simply to access the field this.transform.position with less typing. However, the following code listing holds a more interesting example. Create a new C# script named *CountItHigher*, attach it to the sphere in the scene, and enter the following code:

```
 1 using UnityEngine;
 2 using System.Collections;
 3
 4 class CountItHigher : MonoBehaviour {
 5     [SerializeField]
 6     private int       _num = 0;                                // 1
 7
 8     void Update() {
 9         print( nextNum );
10     }
11
12     public int nextNum {                                       // 2
13         get {
14             _num++;          // Increase the value of _num by 1
15             return( _num );  // Return the new value of _num
16         }
17     }
18
19     public int currentNum {                                    // 3
20         get { return( _num ); }                                // 4
21         set { _num = value;   }                                // 4
22     }
23
24 }
```

1. The integer _num is private, so it can only be accessed by this instance of the CountItHigher class. Other classes and class instances can't see it at all. The [SerializeField] attribute on the previous line allows this private variable to be seen and edited in the Inspector.

2. nextNum is a property that is read-only. Because there is no set{} clause, it can only be read (e.g., int x = nextNum;) and cannot be set (e.g., nextNum = 5; would cause an error).

3. currentNum is a property that can either be read or set. Both int x = currentNum; and currentNum = 5; would work.

4. The get{} and set{} clauses can alternatively be written on a single line. Note that when in the single-line format, the semicolon ending the statement (;) comes before the closing brace (}) as shown on line 21.

When you press Play, you will see that as the Update() function is called by Unity each frame, the output of the print(nextNum); statement increments every frame. The output from the first five frames is as follows:

```
1
2
3
4
5
```

Each time that the property nextNum is read (by print(nextNum);), it increments the private field _num and then returns the new value (lines 14 and 15 of the code listing). Though this is a small example, it's possible to use a get or set accessor to do anything that a regular method can do, even call another method or function.

Similarly, currentNum is a property that enables you to either read or set the value of _num. Because _num is a private field, it is helpful to have the property currentNum publicly available.

Class Instances are GameObject Components

As you've seen in previous chapters, when you drag a C# script onto a GameObject, it becomes a component of that GameObject just as Transform, Rigidbody, and other elements that you see in the Unity Inspector are GameObject components. This means that you can get a reference to any class that is attached to a GameObject via GameObject.GetComponent<>() with the type of the class placed between the angle brackets (see line 7 of the following code listing).

Create a new C# script named *MoveAlong* and attach it to the same Sphere GameObject as CountItHigher. Enter the following code into the MoveAlong script:

```
1 using UnityEngine;
2 using System.Collections;
3
4 class MoveAlong : MonoBehaviour {
```

```
 5
 6      void LateUpdate() {                                                        // 1
 7          CountItHigher cih=this.gameObject.GetComponent<CountItHigher>();  // 2
 8          if ( cih != null ) {                                                  // 3
 9              float tX = cih.currentNum/10f;                                    // 4
10              Vector3 tempLoc = pos;                                            // 5
11              tempLoc.x = tX;
12              pos = tempLoc;
13          }
14      }
15
16      public Vector3 pos {                                                      // 6
17          get { return( this.transform.position ); }
18          set { this.transform.position = value;   }
19      }
20
21  }
```

1. `LateUpdate()` is another built-in function call that Unity makes every frame. Each frame, Unity first calls `Update()` on all classes that are attached to GameObjects and then, once all the `Update()`s are complete, Unity calls `LateUpdate()` on all objects. Using `LateUpdate()` here ensures that `Update()` in the `CountItHigher` class is called before `LateUpdate()` in the `MoveAlong` class.

2. `cih` is a local variable of the type `CountItHigher`, meaning that it can hold a reference to the instance of `CountItHigher` that is a component attached to the Sphere GameObject. The `GetComponent<CountItHigher>()` call finds the *CountItHigher (Script)* component attached to the same Sphere GameObject as this *MoveAlong (Script)* component.

3. If you use the `GetComponent<>()` method, and the type of component you ask for is *not* attached to the GameObject, `GetComponent<>()` will return `null` (a value that means nothing is there). It is important to check for this before trying to use `cih`.

4. Although `cih.currentNum` is an int, when it is used in a mathematical operation with a float (e.g., `cih.currentNum/10f`) or assigned to a float (which also occurs on line 9), it is automatically treated as a float.

5. Line 10 and 12 use the `pos` property that is defined in lines 16–19.

6. This is effectively the same as the `pos` property of the `Enemy` class, but it uses a single line to define each of the `get{}` and `set{}` clauses.

Every `LateUpdate`, this code will find the `CountItHigher` script component of this GameObject and then pull the `currentNum` from it. The script then divides `currentNum` by 10 and sets the x position of the GameObject to the resultant value (using the `pos` property). As `CountItHigher._num` increases every frame, the GameObject will also move along the X axis. Press Play in Unity to see this happen. Save your scene (from the menu bar, choose *File > Save Scene*) before continuing in the chapter.

> ### warning
>
> **WATCH OUT FOR RACE CONDITIONS!** A race condition occurs any time two things rely on each other, but you're not certain which one will happen first. This is why `LateUpdate()` is used in the preceding example. Had `Update()` been used in `MoveAlong`, it would be uncertain whether the `Update()` in `CountItHigher` or `MoveAlong` would be called by Unity first, so the GameObject could possibly be moved either before or after `_num` was incremented, depending on which was called first. By using `LateUpdate()` we are assured that all `Update()`s in the scene will be called first, followed by all `LateUpdate()`s.

Class Inheritance

Classes extend (or are based on) the contents of other classes. In the first code listing of the chapter, `Enemy` extends `MonoBehaviour`, as do all the classes you've seen so far in this book. Implement the following instructions to get Enemy working in your game, and then we'll discuss this further.

Implementing the `Enemy` Class Sample Project

Complete the following steps:

1. Create a new scene (*File > New Scene* from the menu bar). Immediately save it as *_Scene_1*. Create a new sphere in the scene (*GameObject > Create Other > Sphere*) and rename it *EnemyGO* (the GO stands for GameObject). This new sphere is not connected in any way to the Sphere in _Scene_0. (For example, it doesn't have the two script components attached.)

2. Set the transform.position of EnemyGO to [0,4,0] using the Transform component in the Inspector.

3. Drag the Enemy script you wrote earlier from the Project pane onto EnemyGO in the Hierarchy pane of _Scene_1. You should now see *Enemy (Script)* appear as a component of the EnemyGO GameObject.

4. Drag EnemyGO from the Hierarchy pane into the Project pane to create a prefab named EnemyGO. As described in previous chapters, you'll know that the prefab was created successfully because an item named EnemyGO with a blue box icon will appear in the Project pane, and the name of the EnemyGO GameObject in the Hierarchy pane will turn blue, indicating that it's an instance of the EnemyGO prefab.

5. Add a directional light to the scene by choosing *Create > Directional Light* from the Hierarchy pane.

6. Select the Main Camera in the Hierarchy and set its position and camera settings to those highlighted by green boxes in Figure 25.3:

   ■ Set the transform position to [0,-15,-10].

   ■ Set the camera projection to Orthographic.

   ■ Set the camera size to 20.

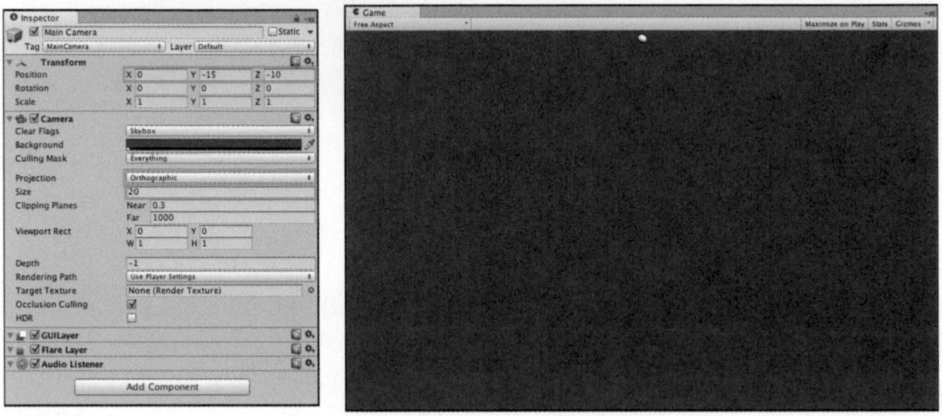

Figure 25.3 Camera settings for _Scene_1 and the resultant Game pane

The Game pane shown at the right of Figure 25.3 should approximate what you now see through the camera.

Press Play. You should see the Enemy instance move down the screen at a constant rate.

Superclasses and Subclasses

Superclass and *subclass* describe the relationship between two classes where one *inherits* from the other. In our example, the Enemy class inherits from MonoBehaviour, which means that the Enemy class is composed of not only the fields and methods of the Enemy C# script but also of all the fields and methods of its superclass, MonoBehaviour, and all the classes from which MonoBehaviour inherits. This is why any C# script that we write in Unity already knows about fields such as gameObject, transform, and rigidbody and methods such as GetComponent<>().

It is also possible to create subclasses that extend Enemy.

1. Create a new C# script in the Project pane and name it *EnemyZig*. Then open the script and change the superclass from MonoBehaviour to Enemy.

```
1 using UnityEngine;
2 using System.Collections;
3
```

```
4 public class EnemyZig : Enemy {
5
6 }
```

2. Now, choose *Create > Cube* in the Hierarchy pane. Set the cube's position to the origin
   (0,0,0), and rename it to *EnemyZigGO*. Drag the EnemyZig Script onto the EnemyZigGO
   GameObject in the Hierarchy, and then drag the EnemyZigGO from the Hierarchy pane to
   the Project pane, creating a prefab of EnemyZigGO.

3. Set the position of the instance of EnemyZigGO in the Hierarchy pane to (-4, 0, 0) and press
   Play. See how the EnemyZigGO box falls at exactly the same rate as the EnemyGO sphere?
   That's because EnemyZig has inherited all the behaviors of Enemy! Now try adding this
   code to EnemyZig to change that; new lines are bolded:

```
1 using UnityEngine;
2 using System.Collections;
3
4 public class EnemyZig : Enemy {
5
6     public override void Move () {
7         Vector3 tempPos = pos;
8         tempPos.x = Mathf.Sin(Time.time * Mathf.PI*2) * 4;
9         pos = tempPos;      // Uses the pos property of the superclass
10        base.Move();        // Calls Move() on the superclass
11     }
12
13 }
```

In this code, we've *overridden* the *virtual function* Move() from the superclass Enemy and
replaced it with a new one in EnemyZig. Move() must be declared as a virtual function in the
superclass (as it is on line 15 of the Enemy class script) for it to be able to be overridden in a
subclass.

This new Move() function causes the box to zigzag right and left following a sine wave. Sine
and cosine are often useful for cyclical behavior like this. In this code, the x component of the
position of the GameObject is set to the sine of the current time (the number of seconds since
the Play button was pressed) times 2π, which causes a full cycle of the sine wave to occur every
second. This value is then multiplied by 4 to cause the x position to range from x=-4 to x=4.

The base.Move() function call tells EnemyZig to also call the version of Move() that is part of
the superclass (or "base" class). Therefore, EnemyZig.Move() handles the left and right motion,
while Enemy.Move() causes the box to fall at the same rate as the Sphere.

The GameObjects in this example are called *enemies* because a similar class hierarchy system
will be used for the various enemies in Chapter 30, "Prototype 3: Space SHMUP."

Summary

A class's ability to combine data with functionality enables developers to use the object-oriented approach that is presented in the next chapter. Object-oriented programming enables programmers to think of their classes as objects that can move and think on their own, and this approach combines very well with the GameObject-based structure of Unity and will help us make games more easily and rapidly.

CHAPTER 26

OBJECT-ORIENTED THINKING

This chapter covers how to think in terms of object-oriented programming (OOP), the logical extension of the classes discussed in the preceding chapter.

By the end of this chapter, you'll understand not only how to think in terms of OOP but also how to specifically structure projects in the manner that is best for the Unity development environment.

The Object-Oriented Metaphor

The easiest way to describe object orientation is through a metaphor. Think about all of the birds in a flock. Flocks can consist of hundreds or even thousands of individual birds, each of which must avoid obstacles and other birds while still moving along with the flock. Flocks of birds exhibit brilliantly coordinated behaviors that for many years defied simulation.

Simulating a Flock of Birds in a Monolithic Way

Before the advent of object-oriented programming (OOP), a program was basically a single large function that did everything.[1] That single function controlled all data, moved every object, and handled everything from keyboard input to game logic to graphic display. This is now referred to as *monolithic programming,* the attempt to do everything with a single, gigantic function.

To attempt to simulate a flock of birds in a monolithic way, it would make sense to store a large array of the birds and then create a program that would consider every bird in the flock and attempt to generate swarming-style behavior for them. This program would individually move each bird from its position in one frame to its position in the next, and it would maintain all data about the birds in the array.

A monolithic program like this would be very large, unwieldy, and difficult to debug. Thankfully, there is a better way.

OOP takes a different approach by attempting to simulate each individual bird and its perceptions and actions (all local to itself). This is exactly what was shown in the example of the two `Enemy` classes in the previous chapter. By contrast, this is what the code would have looked like if done in a monolithic way:

```
1  using UnityEngine;
2  using System.Collections;
3  using System.Collections.Generic;
4
5  public class MonolithicEnemyController : MonoBehaviour {
6      // The List of all enemies. This is populated in the Unity inspector
7      public List<GameObject>        enemies;                              // 1
8      public float                   speed = 10f;
9
10     void Update () {
11         Vector3 tempPos;
12
13         foreach ( GameObject enemy in enemies ) {                        // 2
14             tempPos = enemy.transform.position;
15
16             switch ( enemy.name ) {                                      // 3
```

---

[1] This is, of course, a drastic simplification, but it serves to make the point.

```
17              case "EnemyGO":
18                  tempPos.y -= speed * Time.deltaTime;
19                  break;
20              case "EnemyZigGO":
21                  tempPos.x = 4 * Mathf.Sin(Time.time * Mathf.PI*2);
22                  tempPos.y -= speed * Time.deltaTime;
23                  break;
24              }
25
26              enemy.transform.position = tempPos;
27          }
28      }
29 }
```

1. This list of GameObjects holds all of the enemies. None of the enemies have any code attached to them.

2. The `foreach` loop on line 13 iterates over each GameObject in the list enemies.

3. Because the enemies don't have any code on them, this `switch` statement is required to store all information about all kinds of movement available to the enemies.

In this simple example, this code is rather short and isn't really very "monolithic," but it does lack the elegance and extensibility of the code from Chapter 25, "Classes." If one were to create a game with 20 such enemies using this monolithic method, this single Update() function would easily grow to several hundred lines. However, adding 20 additional enemies using the object-oriented subclassing method from Chapter 25 would instead generate 20 small classes (like EnemyZig), each of which would be short and easy to both understand and debug.

Simulating a Flock of Birds Using OOP and Boids

Prior to 1987, several attempts had been made at simulating the flocking behavior of birds and the schooling behavior of fish via monolithic programming practices. It was generally thought that to generate the complex coordinated behavior of a swarm, a single function would need to manage all the data in the simulation.

This preconception was shattered with the publication of the paper "Flocks, Herds, and Schools: A Distributed Behavioral Model" by Craig W. Reynolds in 1987.[2] In this paper, Reynolds described an incredibly simple, object-oriented approach to simulating swarm-like behavior, which he called Boids. At its most basic level, Boids uses only three simple rules:

- **Collision avoidance:** Avoid collisions with nearby flockmates
- **Velocity matching:** Attempt to match velocity and direction with nearby flockmates
- **Flock centering:** Attempt to stay near the average location of nearby flockmates

---

[2] C. W. Reynolds, "Flocks, Herds, and Schools: A Distributed Behavioral Model," *Computer Graphics, 21*(4), July 1987 (acm SIGGRAPH '87 Proceedings), 25–34.

An Object-Oriented Boids Implementation

In this tutorial, you'll build an implementation of Reynold's Boids that shows the power of simple object-oriented code to create complex, emergent behavior. First, create a new project following the instructions in the sidebar.

SET UP THE BOIDS PROJECT

Following the standard project setup procedure, create a new project in Unity. If you need a refresher on the standard project setup procedure, see Appendix A, "Standard Project Setup Procedure."

- **Project Name:** Boids

- **Scene Name:** _Scene_0

Everything else will be created through the course of the chapter.

Making a Simple Boid Model

To make a visual representation of the Boids, we'll build something from a combination of stretched cubes. When finished, the Boid GameObject prefab will be similar to that shown in Figure 26.4.

1. Select *GameObject > Create Empty* from the menu bar.

2. Rename the GameObject to *Boid*.

3. Select *GameObject > Create Empty* from the menu bar. Rename this GameObject *Fuselage* and drag it onto Boid in the Hierarchy pane as shown in the top image of Figure 26.1. This will make Fuselage a child of Boid. You will see a new disclosure triangle appear next to Boid that you can click to show Boid's children. When you click the disclosure triangle, your Hierarchy should look like the bottom-right image in Figure 26.1.

4. Select *GameObject > Create Other > Cube* from the menu bar. Drag Cube under Fuselage (making it a child of Fuselage). Set the transforms of the Fuselage and Cube to match those shown in Figure 26.2. The combination of scaling and rotation of the parent Fuselage will cause the child Cube to skew into a sleek shape.

5. Select the Cube under Fuselage. Right-click the component name *Box Collider* in the Inspector pane and choose *Remove Component* from the pop-up menu. This will remove the Box Collider from Cube, which will allow other objects to move through it. Another reason for removing the collider is that colliders don't stretch the same way that cubes do, so the physical boundaries of the collider would not match the visual dimensions of the cube.

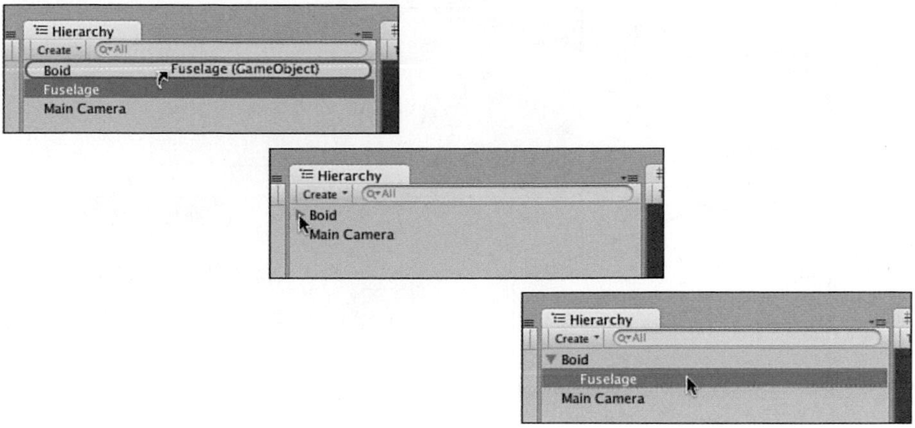

Figure 26.1 Nesting GameObjects in the hierarchy

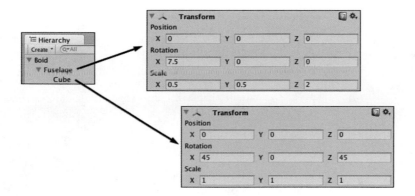

Figure 26.2 Transform settings for Fuselage its child Cube

6. Select Fuselage and select *Edit > Duplicate* from the menu bar. A second Fuselage should appear under Boid in the Hierarchy. Rename this second Fuselage to *Wing*. Set the transform for the Wing and the Main Camera to match those in Figure 26.3. This will give the Main Camera a top-down view.

7. Click Boid in the Hierarchy pane to highlight it. Select *Component > Effects > Trail Renderer* from the menu bar. This will add a Trail Renderer component to the Boid.

8. In the Trail Renderer component of the Inspector pane, click the disclosure triangle next to *Materials* to open it. Click the small circle to the right of *Element 0 None (Material)* and choose *Default-Particle (Material)* from the list of materials that appears. Set the *Time* of the Trail Renderer to 0.5 and the *End Width* to 0.25.

9. Now, using the Move tool to move the Boid in the Scene window should leave a trail.

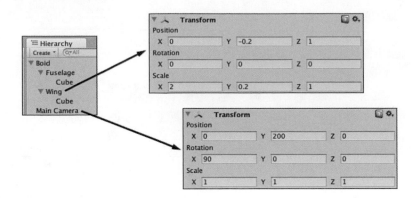

Figure 26.3   Transform settings for Wing and Main Camera

10. Drag Boid from the Hierarchy pane to the Project pane, which will make a prefab named Boid. Your finished Boid model should look like the one in Figure 26.4.

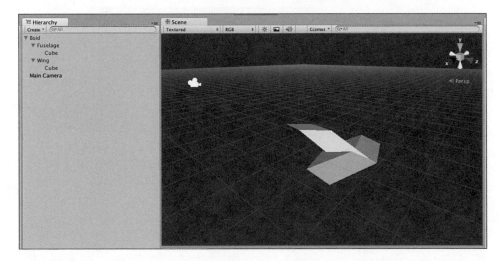

Figure 26.4   The finished Boid model

11. Rename the Main Camera to _MainCamera. This will keep it at the top of the Hierarchy pane once the program starts.

12. Select *GameObject > Create Empty* from the menu bar. Rename this new GameObject to *Boids*. This empty Boids GameObject will act as a parent for all of the Boid instances that are added to the scene, keeping the Hierarchy pane as clean as possible.

13. Select *GameObject > Create Other > Directional Light* from the menu bar. This will add some light to the scene.

14. Finally, delete the blue Boid instance from the Hierarchy pane. Now that there is a Boid prefab, the Boid in the Hierarchy is no longer necessary.

The C# Scripts

In this program, there will be two different C# scripts. The BoidSpawner script will be attached to _MainCamera. It will store the fields (variables) that are shared by all Boids and will instantiate all the instances of the Boid prefab.

The Boid script[3] will be attached to the Boid prefab, and it will handle the movement of each individual Boid. Because this is an object-oriented program, each Boid will think for itself and will react to its own individual understanding of the world.

Now that there is a model to work with, it's time to get into the code. Select *Assets > Create > C# script* from the menu bar and rename the NewBehaviour script to *BoidSpawner*. Double-click the BoidSpawner C# script to open it in MonoDevelop and input the code in Listing 26.1. Lines you need to add are bolded.

Listing 26.1   BoidSpawner C# Script

```
 1 using UnityEngine;
 2 using System.Collections;
 3
 4 public class BoidSpawner : MonoBehaviour {
 5
 6     // This is a Singleton of the BoidSpawner. There is only one instance
 7     //   of BoidSpawner, so we can store it in a static variable named S.
 8     static public BoidSpawner    S;                                    // 1
 9
10     // These fields allow you to adjust the behavior of the Boids as a group
11     public int              numBoids = 100;
12     public GameObject        boidPrefab;                                // 2
13     public float             spawnRadius = 100f;
14     public float             spawnVelocity = 10f;
15     public float             minVelocity = 0f;
16     public float             maxVelocity = 30f;
17     public float             nearDist = 30f;
18     public float             collisionDist = 5f;
19     public float             velocityMatchingAmt = 0.01f;
20     public float             flockCenteringAmt = 0.15f;
21     public float             collisionAvoidanceAmt = -0.5f;
22     public float             mouseAttractionAmt = 0.01f;
23     public float             mouseAvoidanceAmt = 0.75f;
24     public float             mouseAvoidanceDist = 15f;
25     public float             velocityLerpAmt = 0.25f;
26
27     public bool _____;                                      // 3
28
```

---

[3] The Boid script in this chapter is based on pseudocode for Boids by Conrad Parker. Conrad Parker, "Boids Pseudocode," http://www.vergenet.net/~conrad/boids/pseudocode.html, accessed March 1, 2014.

```
29    public Vector3              mousePos;
30
31    void Start () {
32        // Set the Singleton S to be this instance of BoidSpawner
33        S = this;                                                    // 4
34        // Instantiate numBoids (currently 100) Boids
35        for (int i=0; i<numBoids; i++) {
36            Instantiate(boidPrefab);
37        }
38    }
39
40    void LateUpdate() {                                              // 5
41        // Track the mouse position. This keeps it the same for all Boids.
42        Vector3 mousePos2d = new Vector3( Input.mousePosition.x,
            ➥Input.mousePosition.y, this.transform.position.y );       // 6
43        mousePos = this.camera.ScreenToWorldPoint( mousePos2d );
44    }
45
46 }
```

1. The field S is a *singleton*. You can read more about them in the "Software Design Patterns" section of Appendix B, "Useful Concepts." A singleton is used when there will only ever be one instance of a particular class. Because there will only ever be one instance of the class BoidSpawner, it can be stored in the *static* field S. When a field is static, it is scoped to the class itself rather than any instance of the class. Therefore, anywhere in code, we can use BoidSpawner.S to refer to this singleton instance.

2. The Boid prefab will need to be assigned to the field boidPrefab using the Unity Inspector for this script to work.

3. This bool with the name "_____" is used to draw a line in the Inspector pane between fields that you should change in the Inspector and fields that will be adjusted by Unity once the game is playing. In this script, the Vector3 mousePos is the only variable that will be set dynamically by Unity while the game is playing.

4. On line 33, this instance of BoidSpawner is assigned to the singleton S.

5. The LateUpdate() function is called by Unity every frame. It differs from Update() because it is called after all Update()s have been called on all GameObjects. If you want to make sure that all other objects have updated before something happens, use LateUpdate().

6. Note that line 42 is a single line with a code continuation character (➥). Don't type the code continuation character when entering this line.

Drag the finished BoidSpawner C# script onto _MainCamera. After you have done this, you also need to set the boidPrefab variable in the Inspector pane for _MainCamera. To do so, select _MainCamera in the Hierarchy pane. Then look for the *boidPrefab* variable in the BoidSpawner (Script) component of the Inspector. Click the circular target to the right of the *boidPrefab* variable and then select *Boid* from the Assets tab.

The Boids themselves are a bit more complicated, and this will be the longest script you've written thus far, but the script is still relatively short when compared with the complexity of the behavior it generates. Select *Assets > Create > C# script* from the menu bar and rename the script to *Boid*. Double-click the Boid C# script to open it in MonoDevelop and input the code in Listing 26.2.

Listing 26.2 Boid C# Script

```
1 using UnityEngine;
2 using System.Collections;
3 using System.Collections.Generic;  // Necessary to use generic Lists
4
5 public class Boid : MonoBehaviour {
6   // This static List holds all Boid instances & is shared amongst them
7     static public List<Boid>    boids;
8
9     // Note:This code does NOT use a Rigidbody. It handles velocity directly
10    public Vector3    velocity;       // The current velocity
11    public Vector3    newVelocity;    // The velocity for next frame
12    public Vector3    newPosition;    // The position for next frame
13
14    public List<Boid> neighbors;      // All nearby Boids
15    public List<Boid> collisionRisks; // All Boids that are too close
16    public Boid       closest;        // The single closest Boid
17
18    // Initialize this Boid on Awake()
19    void Awake () {                                           // 1
20        // Define the boids List if it is still null
21        if (boids == null) {                                 // 2
22            boids = new List<Boid>();
23        }
24        // Add this Boid to boids
25        boids.Add(this);
26
27        // Give this Boid instance a random position and velocity
28        Vector3 randPos = Random.insideUnitSphere *
                ➥BoidSpawner.S.spawnRadius;
29        randPos.y = 0;     // Flatten the Boid to only move in the XZ plane
30        this.transform.position = randPos;
31        velocity = Random.onUnitSphere;
32        velocity *= BoidSpawner.S.spawnVelocity;
33
34        // Initialize the two Lists
35        neighbors = new List<Boid>();                        // 3
36        collisionRisks = new List<Boid>();
37
38        // Make this.transform a child of the Boids GameObject
```

```
39          this.transform.parent = GameObject.Find("Boids").transform;     // 4
40
41          // Give the Boid a random color, but make sure it's not too dark
42          Color randColor = Color.black;
43          while ( randColor.r + randColor.g + randColor.b < 1.0f ) {
44             randColor = new Color(Random.value, Random.value, Random.value);
45          }
46          Renderer[] rends = gameObject.GetComponentsInChildren<Renderer>();
47          foreach ( Renderer r in rends ) {
48             r.material.color = randColor;
49          }
50
51       }
52
53       // Update is called once per frame
54       void Update () {                                                     // 5
55
56          // Get the list of nearby Boids (this Boid's neighbors)
57          List<Boid> neighbors = GetNeighbors(this);                       // 6
58
59          // Initialize newVelocity and newPosition to the current values
60          newVelocity = velocity;
61          newPosition = this.transform.position;
62
63          // Velocity Matching: This sets the velocity of the boid to be
64          //   similar to that of its neighbors
65          Vector3 neighborVel = GetAverageVelocity( neighbors );
66          // Utilizes the fields set on the BoidSpawner.S Singleton
67          newVelocity += neighborVel * BoidSpawner.S.velocityMatchingAmt;
68
69          // Flock Centering: Move toward middle of neighbors
70          Vector3 neighborCenterOffset = GetAveragePosition( neighbors ) -
                ➥this.transform.position;
71       newVelocity += neighborCenterOffset*BoidSpawner.S.flockCenteringAmt;
72
73          // Collision Avoidance: Avoid running into Boids that are too close
74          Vector3 dist;
75          if (collisionRisks.Count > 0) {
76             Vector3 collisionAveragePos=GetAveragePosition(collisionRisks);
77             dist = collisionAveragePos - this.transform.position;
78             newVelocity += dist * BoidSpawner.S.collisionAvoidanceAmt;
79          }
80
81          // Mouse Attraction - Move toward the mouse no matter how far away
82          dist = BoidSpawner.S.mousePos - this.transform.position;
83          if (dist.magnitude > BoidSpawner.S.mouseAvoidanceDist) {
84             newVelocity += dist * BoidSpawner.S.mouseAttractionAmt;
85          } else {
86             // If the mouse is too close, move away quickly!
```

```
87              newVelocity -= dist.normalized*BoidSpawner.S.mouseAvoidanceDist
                   ➥*BoidSpawner.S.mouseAvoidanceAmt;
88          }
89
90          // newVelocity & newPosition are ready, but wait until LateUpdate()
91          //   to set them so that this Boid doesn't move before others have
92          //   had a chance to calculate their new values.
93      }
94
95      // By allowing all Boids to Update() themselves before any Boids
96      //   move, we avoid race conditions that could be caused by some Boids
97      //   moving before others have decided where to go.
98      void LateUpdate() {                                              // 7
99          // Adjust the current velocity based on newVelocity using a linear
100         //   interpolation (see Appendix B, "Useful Concepts")
101         velocity = (1-BoidSpawner.S.velocityLerpAmt)*velocity +
                   ➥BoidSpawner.S.velocityLerpAmt*newVelocity;
104
105         // Make sure the velocity is within min and max limits
106         if (velocity.magnitude > BoidSpawner.S.maxVelocity) {
107             velocity = velocity.normalized * BoidSpawner.S.maxVelocity;
108         }
109         if (velocity.magnitude < BoidSpawner.S.minVelocity) {
110             velocity = velocity.normalized * BoidSpawner.S.minVelocity;
111         }
112
113         // Decide on the newPosition
114         newPosition = this.transform.position + velocity * Time.deltaTime;
115         // Keep everything in the XZ plane
116         newPosition.y = 0;
117         // Look from the old position at the newPosition to orient the model
118         this.transform.LookAt(newPosition);
119         // Actually move to the newPosition
120         this.transform.position = newPosition;
121     }
122
123     // Find which Boids are near enough to be considered neighbors
124     //   boi is BoidOfInterest, the Boid on which we're focusing
125     public List<Boid> GetNeighbors(Boid boi) {                       // 8
126         float closestDist = float.MaxValue;    // Max value a float can hold
127         Vector3 delta;
128         float dist;
129         neighbors.Clear();
130         collisionRisks.Clear();
131
132         foreach ( Boid b in boids ) {
133             if (b == boi) continue;
134             delta = b.transform.position - boi.transform.position;
135             dist = delta.magnitude;
```

```
136                  if ( dist < closestDist ) {
137                       closestDist = dist;
138                       closest = b;
139                  }
140                  if ( dist < BoidSpawner.S.nearDist ) {
141                       neighbors.Add( b );
142                  }
143                  if ( dist < BoidSpawner.S.collisionDist ) {
144                       collisionRisks.Add( b );
145                  }
146              }
147              if (neighbors.Count == 0) {
148                   neighbors.Add( closest );
149              }
150              return( neighbors );
151      }
152
153      // Get the average position of the Boids in a List<Boid>
154      public Vector3 GetAveragePosition( List<Boid> someBoids ) {          // 9
155          Vector3 sum = Vector3.zero;
156          foreach (Boid b in someBoids) {
157              sum += b.transform.position;
158          }
159          Vector3 center = sum / someBoids.Count;
160          return( center );
161      }
162
163      // Get the average velocity of the Boids in a List<Boid>
164      public Vector3 GetAverageVelocity( List<Boid> someBoids ) {{        // 10
165          Vector3 sum = Vector3.zero;
166          foreach (Boid b in someBoids) {
167              sum += b.velocity;
168          }
169          Vector3 avg = sum / someBoids.Count;
170          return( avg );
171      }
172 }
```

1. The Awake() function is called by Unity at the moment that this GameObject is instantiated. This means that it is called before Start().

2. All instances of the Boid class can access the shared static List<Boid> Boid. The first Boid to be created will initialize a new List<Boid>, and then the others will just add themselves to the list.

3. Each Boid maintains its own list of neighbors and collision risks. The neighbors are other Boids that are within BoidSpawner.S.nearDist (which is 30f by default) of this Boid. The collision risks are those that are within BoidSpawner.S.collisionDist (default: 5f).

4. MakIng all the Boids children of the same GameObject will help keep the Hierarchy pane organized. It places them all underneath a single parent GameObject named Boids. If you want to see them all listed in the hierarchy, you just need to click the disclosure triangle next to the parent object Boids.

5. Every `Update()`, each Boid needs to find its neighbors and react to their locations using collision avoidance, velocity matching, and flock centering.

6. The `GetNeighbors()` function is defined later in the code. It finds other Boids that are nearby.

7. `LateUpdate()` is called after `Update()` has been called on every object.

8. `GetNeighbors()` will find other Boids that are near the `boi`.

9. `GetAveragePosition()` will return the average position of a group of Boids.

10. `GetAverageVelocity()` will return the average velocity Vector3 of a group of Boids.

Drag the finished Boid C# script onto the Boid prefab in the Project pane.

Press Play. Use the mouse to play with the Boids and enjoy the complex behavior that they exhibit.

Summary

In this chapter, you learned about object-orientation, a concept that will be exhibited throughout the rest of the book. Because of its structure of GameObjects with components, Unity is perfectly designed for an OOP mindset.

Another interesting element of OOP is the concept of *modularity*. In many ways, modular code is the opposite of monolithic code. Modular coding focuses on making small, reusable functions and classes that do one thing really well. Because modular classes and functions are small (that is, fewer than about 500 lines), they are easier to debug and understand. Modular code is also designed to be reusable. As you progress into the tutorial chapters in Part III of this book, you will start to see code that is reused from one project to the next in the form of a Utils class.

The next chapter takes a bit of a departure from the coding that we've been doing in the rest of Part II. In Chapter 27, "The Agile Mentality," you learn about a method of managing small development projects that I have found works very well for individuals and small teams. It may seem a little dry for a book about game design and development, but I have seen it be a tremendous help to small teams looking to develop games on schedule.

THE AGILE MENTALITY

In this chapter, you learn how to think about projects as an agile prototyper and how to weigh your options when beginning to tackle a project. You are introduced to the Agile development mindset and Scrum methodology. We also look extensively at burndown charts, which I recommend using on all your future projects.

After this chapter, you'll have a better understanding of how to approach your own game projects, how to break them down into sprints that can be tackled in a specific amount of time, and how to prioritize tasks within those sprints.

The Manifesto for Agile Software Development

For many years, a large number of software titles, including games, tended to be developed using what was commonly known as the "waterfall" method of development. Using the waterfall method, a small preproduction team would define the entire project via a massive game design document that was expected to be followed to the letter by the production team as they developed the game. Sticking to waterfall too strictly often led to games that were not tested until they neared completion, and members of these production teams could feel more like cogs in a massive machine than actual game developers.

With the experience you've now gained through paper and digital prototyping in this book, I'm sure you can immediately see some issues with this approach. In 2001, the developers who formed the Agile Alliance saw these issues as well, leading to their Manifesto for Agile Software Development,[1] which reads as follows:

> We are uncovering better ways of developing software by doing it and helping others do it. Through this work we have come to value:
>
> - **Individuals and interactions** over processes and tools
> - **Working software** over comprehensive documentation
> - **Customer collaboration** over contract negotiation
> - **Responding to change** over following a plan
>
> That is, while there is value in the items on the right, we value the items on the left more.

Embedded in these four core values, you can see many of the principles that I've tried to impress upon you throughout this book:

- Following your individual design sense, continually asking questions, and developing an understanding of procedural thinking is more important than following predefined rules or using a specific development framework.
- Making a simple prototype that works and iterating on it until it's fun is more successful than waiting for months until you have the perfect game idea or solution to your problem.
- Bouncing your ideas off of other creative people in a positive, collaborative environment is more important than worrying about who owns specific intellectual property.[2]
- Listening to and reacting to playtesters' feedback about your game is much, much more important than following your original design vision. You must let your game evolve.

---

[1] Kent Beck, et al. "Manifesto for Agile Software Development," Agile Alliance (2001).

[2] You do, of course, want to respect other people's ownership of their IP. My point here is that it's more important to make something than to argue over who should own what percentage of it.

Prior to my introduction of Agile development methodologies into my classes, students often got drastically behind schedule when developing their games. In fact, they even had trouble understanding how behind they were because they lacked the tools to manage their development process. This also meant that it was difficult to playtest student work until very late in the project.

After my introduction of Agile and its associated tools and methodologies to my classes, I found that several things occurred:

- Students had a much better understanding of their progress on projects and were better able to stick to their schedule.

- The games being produced by students showed a marked improvement, largely because the students' focus on constantly having a playable build allowed them to playtest the games earlier and more frequently.

- Student understanding of both C# and Unity increased as did their confidence in their technical skills.

Of those three points, the first two were expected. The third initially took me by surprise, but I have found it to be the case in every class that I have taught using Agile methodologies. As a result, I have continued to use Agile in all of my classes, in my own personal game development practice, and even while writing this book. I hope that you will too.[3]

Scrum Methodology

In the years since 2001, many people have developed tools and methodologies to help teams easily adapt to the Agile mentality. One of my favorites is Scrum.

Scrum actually started several years before the Agile Manifesto and was developed by various people, but its relationship to Agile was solidified in the 2001 book *Agile Software Development with Scrum* by Ken Schwaber and Mike Beedle.[4] In it, they describe many of the common elements of the Scrum methodology that have remained popular in the years since their publication.

The goal of Scrum, like most Agile methodologies, is to get to a working product or game as quickly as possible while allowing for the design to flexibly adapt to feedback from playtesters and members of the design team. The remainder of this chapter will introduce you to some of the terminology and practices used in the Scrum methodology and show you how to use a spreadsheet-based burndown chart that I have developed for my classes and this book.

---

[3] Many thanks to Tom Frisina, my colleague at USC, the MDM, and Electronic Arts, for introducing me to Agile and Scrum.

[4] Ken Schwaber and Mike Beedle, *Agile Software Development with Scrum*, (Upper Saddle River, NJ: Prentice Hall, 2002).

The Scrum Team

A Scrum team for game prototyping is composed of one *product owner,* one *scrum master,* and an interdisciplinary *development team* consisting of up to ten other people who are skilled in various fields, including programming, game design, modeling, texturing, audio, etc.

- **Product owner:** The voice of the client or the voice of the future players of your game. The product owner wants to make sure that all the cool features make it into the game, and she is responsible for understanding the gestalt vision of the game.

- **Scrum master:** The voice of reason. The Scrum master runs the daily Scrum meeting and wants to make sure that everyone is on-task without being overworked. The Scrum master acts as a foil for the product owner by keeping a realistic eye on how much work remains on the project and how quickly the members of the development team are completing the tasks assigned to them. If the project is behind schedule or certain features need to be cut, it's the Scrum master's responsibility to make sure it happens.

- **Development team:** The people in the trenches. The development team is composed of everyone working on the project and can include the product owner and Scrum master who often work as standard members of the team outside of the Scrum meeting. Individuals on the development team are assigned tasks at the daily Scrum meeting and are relied upon to accomplish those tasks by the next meeting. In Scrum, individual team members are given far more agency than in other development methods, but that agency comes coupled with the accountability of daily check-ins with the rest of the team.

Product Backlog / Feature List

A Scrum project starts with a *product backlog* (a.k.a. *feature list*), which is a list of all the features, mechanics, art, and so on that the team expects to implement for the final game. Some of these start out pretty vague and must be broken down into more specific sub-features as development progresses.

Releases and Sprints

A product is broken down into *releases* and *sprints*. You can think of a release as a known time when you will be showing the game to others (for example, a meeting with investors, a public beta, or a formal playtest round) whereas a sprint is a step along the way to a release. At the beginning of a sprint, a *sprint backlog* list is created that contains of all the features that will be completed by the end of the sprint. A sprint usually takes between 1 and 4 weeks, and you need to make sure that regardless of what you choose to work on during the sprint, you have a game (or part of a game) that can be played by the end of the sprint. In fact, in the best case, from the moment when you have your first playable prototype, you should strive to never have a day that ends with the game in an unplayable state (though that's sometimes a pretty difficult task).

The Scrum Meeting

A *Scrum meeting* is a daily 15-minute stand-up meeting (literally, everyone stands throughout the meeting) that keeps the whole team on-track. The meeting is run by the Scrum master, and in the meeting, each person answers three questions:

1. What did you accomplish since yesterday?
2. What do you plan to accomplish today?
3. What obstacles might get in your way?

That's it. The Scrum meeting is meant to get everyone on the same page quickly. Questions 1 and 2 are checked against the *burndown chart* to see how the project is progressing. Any issues that arise as part of question 3 are marked for discussion after the meeting. When acting as a Scrum master, if an obstacle is brought up during the meeting, I ask for a volunteer to help the person with the potential obstacle but restrict further discussion of the obstacle until after the Scrum meeting is over. You want to keep the Scrum meeting as short as possible so that the creative people on your team are wasting as little time as possible in full-group meetings.

Burndown Chart

I have found the burndown chart to be one of the most useful tools in my game development process and my classes. A burndown chart starts with a list of tasks to be performed during a sprint (the sprint backlog) and estimates the amount of time it will take to complete each task (in hours, days, weeks, and so on). Throughout the project, the burndown chart tracks each team member's progress on the goals that have been assigned to her and converts it into a chart that not only tracks the total number of hours of work remaining on the project but also the team's *burndown velocity* (that is, the average number of hours of work that are being completed each day). When the burndown velocity is paired with the number of hours of work remaining, team members can quickly and easily see whether or not they are on target to complete the work on time.

There is a burndown chart template in the OpenOffice Calc spreadsheet (.ods) format at the website for this book that you can use to create charts for your own project. Go to http://book.prototools.net and look under Chapter 27, "The Agile Mentality."

OpenOffice is the open source, free alternative to the Microsoft Office suite that was featured in Chapter 11, "Math and Game Balance." If you have not yet downloaded it, you can acquire it at http://openoffice.org. I've found the OpenOffice Calc program to be very comparable to Microsoft Excel, but there are some differences. See Chapter 11 for more information.

Explaining the spreadsheet formulae used in this burndown chart is beyond the scope of this book, but if you have not yet read it, you can learn the basics of spreadsheets and how to use them to balance games from Chapter 11.

Burndown Chart Example

A *Burndown Chart Example* spreadsheet is available at the website for this book: http://book.
prototools.net. This chart is referenced several times on the following pages, so please download it now. For consistency with the images in this chapter, I recommend downloading the
version that is available for OpenOffice.

Burndown Chart: Setup Worksheet

Modern spreadsheets are broken into several worksheets, which can be selected by choosing
from among the tabs at the bottom of the window (labeled *Setup* and *Data* in Figure 27.1). Once
you've downloaded the *Burndown Chart Example* spreadsheet and opened it, click the leftmost
worksheet tab (labeled Setup).

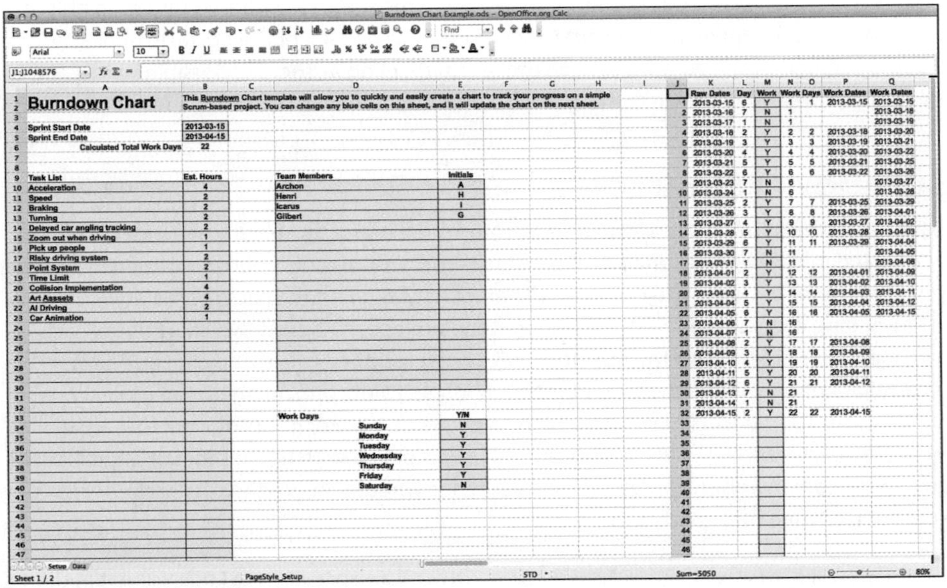

Figure 27.1 The Setup worksheet

This Setup worksheet allows you to input several important pieces of data, all of which should
be put into cells with a blue background. At the top left, you can input the start and end dates
for your sprint. The example project is set to start one week before today and end 31 calendar
days later. Depending on what day of the week it is when you open the example document,
that will give the example team between 21 and 23 working days on this sprint (because the
example team plans to not work on weekends). In your real sprints, of course, you'll have fixed
start and end dates, but I wanted the example to show you some flexibility.

Below the start and end dates, the total number of working days is calculated, and below that
is the task list (also known as the sprint backlog). Here you can see a list of the example tasks

for this sprint as well as the number of hours that the team estimated each task would take to complete.

> **tip**
>
> **ESTIMATING HOURS**   One of the toughest tasks for programmers and other creative workers is estimating the number of hours that it will take to finish a task. Things will almost always take longer than you expect, except for that one thing that you expect will take 20 hours but is somehow complete in only 2. For now, you need to just make the best guess that you can while following some simple estimation rules, all based on the fact that as the size of a task increases, the accuracy of your estimate will necessarily decrease. If you estimate that a task will take somewhere between 4 and 8 hours, just round it up to 8.
>
> - If you're estimating in hours, stick to values of 1, 2, 4, or 8 hours.
>
> - In days: 1, 2, 3, or 5 days.
>
> - In weeks: 1, 2, 4 or 8 weeks.
>
> However, if you're estimating anything in weeks for a sprint, you need to break it down into much smaller tasks!

To the right of the tasks is a list of the team members on this sprint as well as one- or two-letter identifying initials for them, which will be used to assign them tasks on the next worksheet. Below this are a list of the days of the week and information on whether each day should be considered a work day (Y) or a day off (N).

Off to the right (columns J and beyond), you will see calculations that are done to figure out which days of the month will be work days based on the weekly work days that are selected. If you set cell E39 to N (making Friday a day off), you'll see that this is instantly reflected to the right, and it will lower the total number of work days that you have between the start and end dates of the sprint (shown in cell B6). You can also set work days directly in column M if, for instance, you have a holiday in the middle of your sprint and need to make a specific Monday a holiday where all the other ones should be work days.

Please set E39 back to Y, and continue to the Data worksheet by clicking the *Data* worksheet tab at the bottom of the window.

Example Burndown Chart: Data Worksheet

This is where daily progress on all of the tasks from the Setup worksheet is tracked. This spreadsheet can handle up to 100 tasks in the sprint backlog as well as 100 work days in a sprint. An actual sprint should be far shorter than this, as a standard sprint lasts about 2 to 3 weeks. If you're dealing with a project that won't fit on this spreadsheet, you should really consider commercial sprint tracking software.

Cell D5, which is highlighted in Figure 27.2, shows the most important element of information provided by this chart. The positive 2.4 there (in white text on a red background) tells us that at the current rate of work, there will be 2.4 hours of work remaining unfinished at the end of the sprint. In your actual work, you want this number to be negative, indicating that the sprint should be done ahead of time.

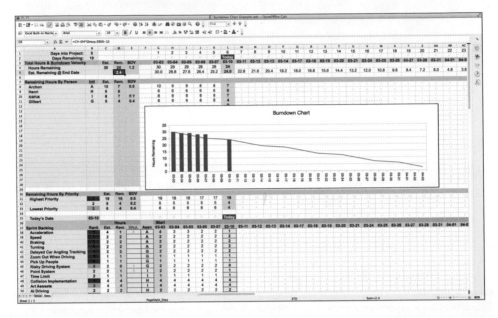

Figure 27.2   The Data worksheet

On this worksheet, as with the last, you want to edit only cells that are highlighted in blue. This includes:

- **Assn (F38:F138 [the column from cell F38 to cell F138]):** This is where you can assign tasks to individuals on your team by entering their initials as defined in the Setup worksheet.

- **Hours Rem. (L38:L138):** This shows the hours remaining in each task as of the current day. As you proceed through the project, the Today label and the blue column will progress to the right. By editing the number of hours remaining on a task in the blue column, you will always be editing the correct day.

- **Hours Wkd. (E38:E138):** This optional column allows you to accumulate the number of actual hours worked on a task, though it is just used to provide postmortem project information and is not included in any calculations.

Estimated Hours Versus Real Hours

One of the most important concepts in a burndown chart is the difference between estimated hours and real hours. After you have estimated the number of hours for a task, the time you spend working on that task is counted not in actual hours worked but instead in terms of the percent of the task that is complete. For an example, take a look at the *Acceleration* task in the spreadsheet (see Figure 27.3).

Today's Date	03-23										**Today**	
			Hours			Start						
Sprint Backlog	Rnk	Est.	Rem.	Wkd.	Assn	03-18	03-19	03-20	03-21	03-22	03-25	0
Acceleration		4	1	5	A	4	3	3	2	2	1	
Speed		2	2		A	2	2	2	2	2	2	
Braking		2	2		A	2	2	2	2	2	2	
Turning		2	2		A	2	2	2	2	2	2	
Delayed Car Angling Tracking		2	2		G	2	2	2	2	2	2	
Zoom Out When Driving		1	1		G	1	1	1	1	1	1	
Pick Up People		1	1		G	1	1	1	1	1	1	
Risky Driving System	3	2	0	1	G	2	2	2	2	2	0	
Point System	2	2	1	1	I	2	2	2	2	2	1	
Time Limit												

Figure 27.3   Close up of the Data worksheet showing progression of task work for the first 5 days of the project

The initial estimate of hours for the Acceleration task was 4; this comes from the Setup worksheet:

- **03-19 (March 19th):** Archon (A) worked on Acceleration for 2 hours but only accomplished about 25% of the task. This left 75% of the work remaining on the task, so he entered a 3 into the spreadsheet (cell H38) for 03-19 because 3 is 75% of the original 4-hour estimate. He also placed a 2 into the Wkd. column to track his actual hours worked.

- **03-21:** He worked another 2 hours, bringing the task to 50% complete and leaving 2 hours of the original 4-hour estimate remaining. So, he entered a 2 into the column for 03-21 (J38) and increased the hours in the Wkd. column to 4.

- **03-25 (Today):** One hour of work burned down another 25% of the task (he's working a bit faster now), and now, as of today, he has 25% or 1-hour remaining of the Acceleration task. He places a 1 in the 03-25 column (L38) and increases the Wkd. cell to 5.

As you can see, the most important data is the percent of the task remaining as represented by the number of hours remaining of the original estimate. However, Archon has also recorded the 5 hours he has put in on the Acceleration task in the Wkd. column (E) to help him improve his task estimation in the future.

In Figure 27.3, you can also see that Gilbert (G) estimated 2 hours of work for the *Risky Driving System* yet was able to complete 100% of the task in only 1 hour on 03-25. Icarus (I) has completed 50% of the *Point System* task in 1 hour as expected (also on 03-25).

Burndown Velocity and the Burndown Chart

The upper part of the Data worksheet shows the actual burndown information (see Figure 27.4).

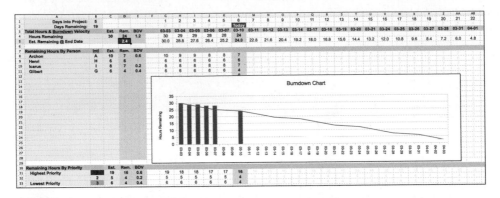

Figure 27.4   Burndown velocity (BDV) and the actual burndown chart in the Data worksheet

Here, Today is shown in orange, and the number of hours remaining on each task is used to determine the *burndown velocity* (BDV), which is the average rate at which work is accomplished on the project. In cell D4 of the example, you can see that, as of today, 24 hours of work remain of the initial 30-hour estimate for the sprint. Dividing the 6 hours of work completed by the 5 days that this team has spent so far on the project gives a burndown velocity of 1.2 hours/day (shown in cell E4), meaning that each day that the team works on the project, it is expected they will burn down (that is, complete) 1.2 hours of estimated work. If this BDV were maintained across the total 23 workdays of the project, 27.6 hours of work would be completed, leaving a deficit of 2.4 hours remaining (as shown in cell D5). This is a big problem for the team because it means that they will not complete the sprint on time. As mentioned earlier in the chapter, this is the key piece of knowledge that a burndown chart will give you. Your team can quickly see whether they are behind schedule and decide how to intelligently deal with the problem before it's too late.

This information can also be seen in the burndown chart in the middle of the worksheet. The blue columns represent a daily tally of the number of work hours required to complete the tasks in the sprint, and the red line shows the anticipated progress for future days based on the history of the project so far. The red line and the blue bar will always match up for Today, and for the remainder of the project, the red line will estimate the rate at which work will be done.

Just above the burndown chart, you can also see individual burndown velocity reports for each member of the team based on their individual progress on the tasks that have been assigned to them.

Prioritizing and Assigning Tasks

The Rnk column of the Data worksheet (starting at cell B38) holds task priority information. Tasks are ranked with the numbers 1, 2, or 3, with 1 being the highest rank. This assigns a color (red, yellow, and green, respectively). It also causes the task to be tracked in the *Remaining Hours By Priority* section of the worksheet (rows 30–33). This section tracks hours remaining and burndown velocity for each rank of tasks. In general, you will want to burn down all of the rank 1 tasks before spending too much time on tasks that are rank 2 or 3.

The Assn column of the Data worksheet (starting at cell F38) holds information about which team member has been assigned to each task. Tasks are assigned using the initials for each person as defined in the Setup worksheet. (The example uses a single letter, but any number of letters can be used for initials.) Once a task has been assigned to a specific person, it contributes to the *Remaining Hours By Person* section of the Data worksheet (rows 8–28). This way, each team member's progress can be tracked, and workload can be balanced if one team member has been assigned too much or too little work.

A Potential Burndown Velocity Pitfall

As mentioned before, I have found burndown charts to be invaluable to me in my work over the last several years; however, I have also encountered two specific situations in which the burndown chart can give you somewhat misleading information, as shown in Figure 27.5.

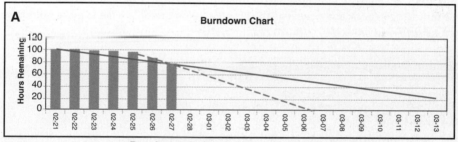

Burndown velocity predicts a false late delivery

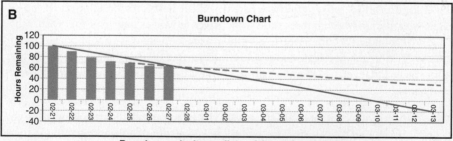

Burndown velocity predicts a false ontime delivery

Figure 27.5   Two niche situations where burndown velocity can be misleading

In image A of Figure 27.5, the team initially had a terribly slow burndown velocity (BDV), but over the last three days, they have drastically improved their progress. Because the BDV is calculated based on total work / total time since the beginning of the project, the BDV doesn't update to show the increased rate at which the team is now working, and so the burndown chart predicts a late finish even though (as the dashed line shows), the team will be early if they continue with the current faster rate of progress.

Image B of Figure 27.5 shows a much more serious issue. In image B, the team was initially working very quickly but has slowed drastically over the last three days. Now, the BDV still reflects the initial work, so it looks like the team is still on schedule to finish on time. However, if they continue their actual shown rate of work over the last three days, the project will be late (as shown by the dashed line)!

Either of these two niche cases will only occur if the work rate of the team changes drastically over the course of the project, but it is important to be aware that they can happen, and you need to consider not only the BDV since the beginning of the project but also the rate of work over the last few days. On most projects with a professional team, these two rates would be very close to each other because the team wouldn't have drastic changes in productivity.

Creating Your Own Burndown Charts

Now that you're familiar with the features of the Burndown Chart Example, you can return to the website for this book and download the burndown chart template file to make burndown charts for your own projects:

> http://book.prototools.net

Summary

As you move on to designing and developing your own games, it can be very difficult to keep your development process on track. In my years as a developer and professor, I have found that the Agile mindset and Scrum methodology are two of the best tools for doing so. Of course, I can't tell you for sure whether these tools work as well for you as they have for my students and me, but I strongly encourage you to give them a try. In the end, it's not important whether Scrum and Agile are the perfect tools for you. The important thing is that you find tools that do work for you and that you use them to help you stay motivated and productive when working on your games.

In the next chapter, the content of this book will make a radical shift. From now on, each chapter is a self-contained tutorial for a game prototype. I do recommend working through them in numeric order because they are meant to build upon one another, but that's up to you. Each of these tutorials should get you thinking about how a certain genre of game is built and will give you a starting point from which you can build your own games.

PART III

GAME PROTOTYPE EXAMPLES AND TUTORIALS

CHAPTER 28

PROTOTYPE 1: APPLE PICKER

Here it is. Today, you make your first digital game prototype.

Because this is your first prototype, it is rather simple. As you continue through the prototyping chapters, the projects get more complex and use more of the features of Unity.

By the end of this chapter, you will have a working prototype of a simple arcade game.

The Purpose of a Digital Prototype

Before we start making the prototype of Apple Picker, now's probably a good time to think again about the purpose of a digital prototype. In the first part of the book, there was considerable discussion of paper prototypes and why they are useful. Paper game prototypes help you do the following:

- Test, reject, and/or refine game mechanics and rules quickly
- Explore the dynamic behavior of your game and understand the emergent possibilities created by the rules
- Ascertain whether rules and gameplay elements are easily understood by players
- Understand the emotional response that players have to your game

Digital prototypes also add the fantastic ability to see how the game *feels*; in fact, that is their primary purpose. Although it is possible for you to spend hours describing game mechanics to someone in detail, it is much more efficient (and interesting) for them to just play the game and see how it feels. This is discussed at length in the book *Game Feel* by Steve Swink.[1]

In this chapter, you create a working game, and the end result will be something that you can show to friends and colleagues. After letting them play it for a while, you can ask whether the difficulty feels too easy, too difficult, or just right. Use that information to tweak the variables in the game and custom craft a specific difficulty for each of them.

Let's get started making Apple Picker.

SET UP THE PROJECT FOR THIS CHAPTER

Following the standard project setup procedure, create a new project in Unity. If you need a refresher on the standard project setup procedure, see Appendix A, "Standard Project Setup Procedure."

- **Project name:** Apple Picker Prototype
- **Scene name:** _Scene_0 (The underscore at the beginning of the scene name will keep it sorted at the top of the Project pane.)
- **C# script names:** ApplePicker, Apple, AppleTree, and Basket

Attach the ApplePicker C# script to the Main Camera in _Scene_0. Do not attach the C# scripts Apple, AppleTree, or Basket to anything.

---

[1] Steve Swink, *Game Feel: A Game Designer's Guide to Virtual Sensation* (Boston: Elsevier, 2009).

Preparing

Happily, you've already done a lot of the preparation for this prototype in Chapter 15, "Thinking in Digital Systems," when we analyzed Apple Picker and the classic game *Kaboom!* As mentioned in that chapter, Apple Picker will have the same game mechanics as *Kaboom!* It's very useful for you as a designer to understand classic games and how they worked, and this is a nice easy one to start with.

Take a moment to look back at Chapter 15 and make sure that you understand the flow charts for each element: the AppleTree, the Apples, and the Baskets.

Getting Started: Art Assets

As a prototype, this game doesn't need fantastic art; it needs to work. The kind of art that we'll create throughout this book is commonly known as *programmer art,* which is the placeholder art made by programmers that will eventually be replaced by the actual game art created by artists. As with nearly everything in a prototype, the purpose of this art is to get you from a concept to a playable prototype as quickly as possible. If your programmer art doesn't look terrible, that's nice, but it's certainly not necessary.

AppleTree

From the menu bar, choose *GameObject > Create Other > Cylinder.* This will be the trunk of our tree. Set the name of the Cylinder to *Trunk* by selecting it in the Hierarchy and clicking its name at the top of the Inspector. Set the Transform component of Trunk to match the settings of the Transform component shown in Figure 28.1.

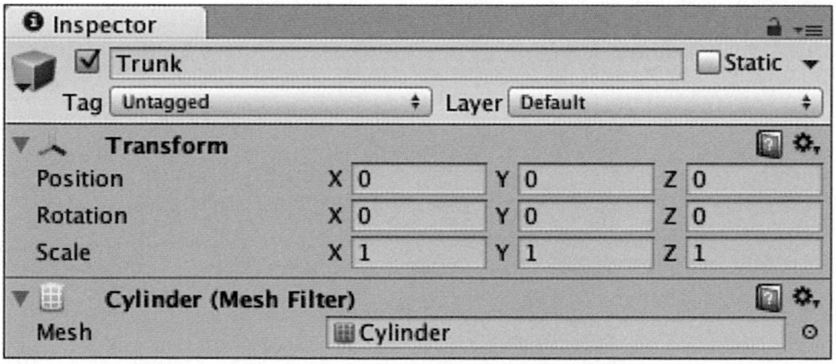

Figure 28.1 The Transform component for the cylinder named Trunk

Throughout the tutorials in this book, I use the following format to give you settings for GameObject transform components:

Trunk (Cylinder)　　　P:[0,0,0]　R:[0,0,0]　S:[1,1,1]

The preceding line instructs you to set the transform of the GameObject named Trunk to a position of x=0, y=0, and z=0; a rotation of x=0, y=0, and z=0; and a scale of x=1, y=1, and z=1. The word *Cylinder* in parentheses tells you the type of GameObject that it is. You will also sometimes see this format listed in the middle of a paragraph as P:[0,0,0] R:[0,0,0] S:[1,1,1].

Now choose *GameObject > Create Other > Sphere*. Set its transform as follows:

> Sphere (Sphere)   P:[0,0.5,0]   R:[0,0,0]   S:[3,2,3]

This sphere and the cylinder together should look (a bit) like a tree, but they are currently two separate objects. You need to create an empty GameObject to contain the two of them in a single object.

From the menu bar, choose *GameObject > Create Empty*. This should create an empty GameObject. Make sure that its transform is set to the following:

> GameObject (Empty)   P:[0,0,0]   R:[0,0,0]   S:[1,1,1]

An empty GameObject only includes a Transform component, and it is therefore a simple, useful container for other GameObjects.

In the Hierarchy pane, first change the name of GameObject to *AppleTree*. This can be done by clicking the name GameObject to highlight it, waiting for a second, and either pressing Return on the keyboard (F2 on PC) or clicking it a second time. Next, individually drag the Trunk and Sphere GameObjects onto AppleTree (similar to how you attach a C# script to a GameObject), and they will be placed under AppleTree in the Hierarchy. You can click the new disclosure triangle next to the word *AppleTree* to see them. When you're done, your AppleTree should look like the one shown in Figure 28.2.

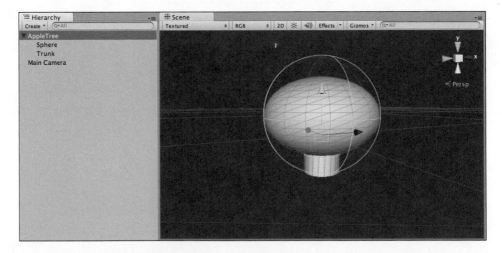

Figure 28.2   The AppleTree shown in both the Hierarchy and Scene panes

Now that Trunk and Sphere GameObjects are parented to AppleTree, if you move, scale, or rotate AppleTree, both Trunk and Sphere will move, rotate, and scale alongside it. Give it a try by manipulating the Transform component of AppleTree. After you're done playing with this, set the transform of AppleTree to the following:

> AppleTree   P:[0,0,0]   R:[0,0,0]   S:[2,2,2]

These settings move the AppleTree to the origin and make it twice as large as it was initially.

Simple Materials for AppleTree

Though this is all programmer art, that doesn't mean that it has to be just flat shaded white objects. Let's add a little color to the scene.

From the menu bar, choose *Assets > Create > Material*. This will make a new material in the Project pane. Rename this material to *Mat_Wood*. Set the main color in the Inspector for Mat_Wood to a brown of your liking. Then, drag the Mat_Wood material onto Trunk in your Scene or Hierarchy pane.

Do the same to create a material named *Mat_Leaves*, color it green, and drag it onto Sphere in your Hierarchy or Scene pane.

Once this is done, drag AppleTree from the Hierarchy pane over to the Project pane to make a prefab from it. As you saw in previous chapters, this creates an AppleTree prefab in the Project pane and turns the name of AppleTree in the Hierarchy blue.

Add some light to the scene by choosing *GameObject > Create Other > Directional Light* from the menu bar. Set the position, rotation, and scale of the directional light to the following:

> Directional Light   P:[0,10,0]   R:[50,-30,0]   S:[1,1,1]

This should put a nice diagonal light across the scene. It's worth noting here that the position of a directional light is unimportant—directional lights shine in the same direction regardless of position—but I've given you the position of [0,10,0] to move it out of the middle of the scene view since its *gizmo* (that is, icon) would be in the middle of the Scene pane otherwise.

Now, move the AppleTree up and out of the way a bit. Select the AppleTree in the Hierarchy and change its position to:

> AppleTree   P:[0,4,0]   R:[0,0,0]   S:[2,2,2]

This may move it out of the view of the Scene pane, but you can zoom out to see it by scrolling your mouse wheel while the mouse cursor is over the Scene pane.

Apple

Now that you have the AppleTree, you need to make the Apple GameObject prefab that it will drop. From the menu bar, choose *GameObject > Create Other > Sphere*. Rename this sphere to *Apple*, and set its transform as follows:

Apple (Sphere) P:[0,0,0] R:[0,0,0] S:[1,1,1]

Create a new material named *Mat_Apple*, color it red (or light green, if you prefer green apples), and attach it to Apple.

Adding Physics to the Apple

Select Apple in the Hierarchy pane. From the menu bar, choose *Component > Physics > Rigidbody*. As you may remember from Chapter 16, "Introducing Our Development Environment: Unity," the Rigidbody component enables an object to react to physics (e.g., fall, collide with other objects). If you click the Play button now, you will see Apple fall off screen due to gravity.

Giving Apples the Tag "Apple"

Eventually you will want to quickly get an array of all the Apple GameObjects on screen, and giving the Apples a specific tag can help with this. With Apple selected in the Hierarchy, choose *Add Tag* from the pop-up menu next to *Tag* in the Inspector, as shown in the left half of Figure 28.3. This will bring up Unity's *Tag and Layers Manager* in the Inspector. Click the disclosure triangle next to Tags and type *Apple* into the Element 0 field, as shown in the right half of Figure 28.3.

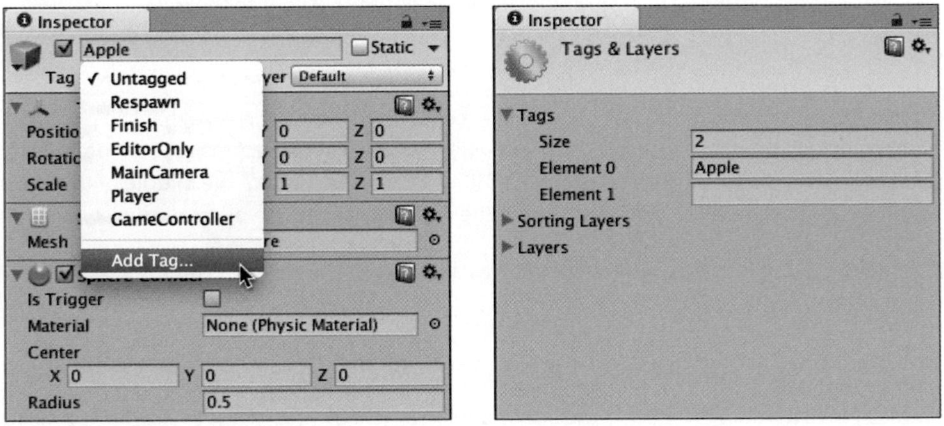

Figure 28.3 Adding the Apple tag to the list of tags

Now, click Apple in the Hierarchy again to return to the Inspector for Apple. Clicking the Tags pop-up menu once more will now give you Apple as a tag option. Choose *Apple* from the list of tags. All apples will now have the tag *Apple*, which will make them easier to identify and select.

Making the Apple Prefab

Finally, drag Apple from the Hierarchy pane to the Project pane to make it a prefab. Once you're sure that there is an Apple prefab in the Project pane, click the Apple instance in the Hierarchy pane and delete it (by choosing Delete from the right-click menu or by pressing Command-Delete [just Delete for Windows] on your keyboard). Because the apples in our game will be instantiated from the Apple prefab in the Project pane, we don't need to start with one in the scene.

Basket

Like the other art assets, the basket will be very simple. Choose *GameObject > Create Other > Cube* from the menu bar. Rename Cube to *Basket* and set its transform to the following:

> Basket (Cube)   P:[0,0,0]   R:[0,0,0]   S:[4,1,4]

This should give you a flat, wide rectangular solid. Now create a new material named *Mat_Basket*, color it a light, desaturated yellow (like straw), and apply it to Basket. Drag Basket from the Hierarchy pane to the Project pane to make it into a prefab and delete the remaining instance of Basket from the Hierarchy. Be sure to save your scene.

Your Project and Hierarchy panes should now look like Figure 28.4.

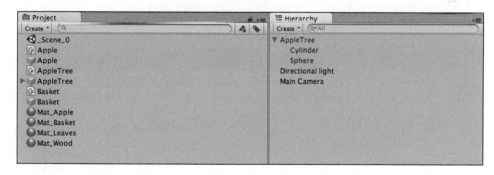

Figure 28.4   The Project and Hierarchy panes at this point in the prototype

Camera Setup

One of the most important things to get right in your games is the position of the camera. For Apple Picker, we want a camera that will show a decent-sized play area. Because the gameplay in this game is entirely two dimensional, we also want an orthographic camera instead of a perspective one. See the sidebar for more information on the two types of camera projections.

ORTHOGRAPHIC VERSUS PERSPECTIVE CAMERAS

Orthographic and *perspective* are two types of virtual 3D cameras in games and can be seen in Figure 28.5.

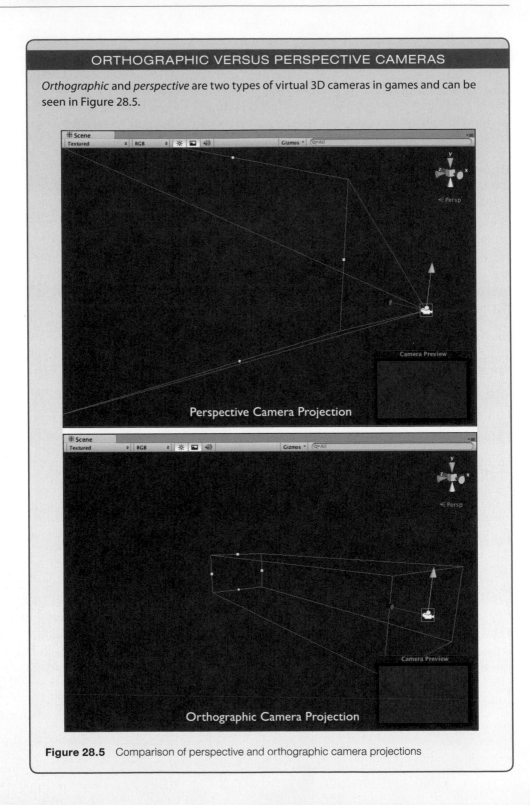

Figure 28.5 Comparison of perspective and orthographic camera projections

A *perspective* camera works like the human eye; because light comes in through a lens, objects that are close to the camera appear larger, and objects that are farther away appear smaller. This gives a perspective camera a field of view (a.k.a. projection) shaped like a square frustum (or more simply, like a square pyramid with the top cut off). To see this, click Main Camera in your hierarchy, and then zoom out in the Scene pane. The pyramidal wireframe shape extending out from the camera is the *view frustum* and shows everything that the camera will see.

Through an *orthogonal* camera, an object will appear to be the same size regardless of how far it is from the camera. The projection for an orthogonal camera is rectangular rather than frustum shaped. To see this, select Main Camera in the Hierarchy pane. Find the Camera component in the Inspector and change the projection from Perspective to Orthogonal. Now, the gray view frustum represents a 3D rectangle rather than a pyramid.

It is also sometimes useful to set the Scene pane to be orthogonal rather than perspective. To do this, click the word *<Persp* under the axes gizmo in the upper-right corner of the Scene pane (see each of the images in Figure 28.5). Clicking the *<Persp* under the axes gizmo will switch between perspective and *isometric* (abbreviated =*Iso*) scene views (isometric being another word for orthographic).

Camera Settings for Apple Picker

Select Main Camera in the Hierarchy pane. In the Inspector, set the Camera component's projection to *Orthographic*. Now, set the *size* to 16. This makes the AppleTree appear to be a good size and leaves room for the apples to fall and be caught by the player. Often, you will make a good first guess at things like camera settings and then will refine them once you've had a chance to play the game. Just like everything else in game development, there is an iterative process to finding the right settings for the camera. For now, I recommend the following:

> Main Camera (Camera)   P:[0,0,-10]   R:[0,0,0]   S:[1,1,1]

This position will move the camera viewpoint down 1 meter (a unit in Unity is the equivalent of 1m in length) to be at a height of exactly 0. Because Unity units are equivalent to meters, I sometimes abbreviate "1 unit" as 1m in this book. Your final Main Camera Inspector should now look like what is shown in Figure 28.6.

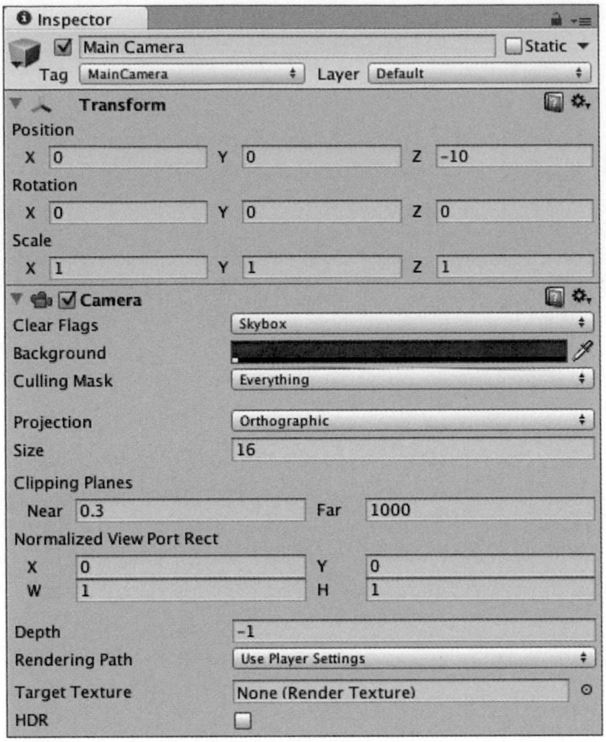

Figure 28.6   Main Camera Inspector settings

Coding the Apple Picker Prototype

Now it's time to make the code of this game prototype actually work. Figure 28.7 presents the flow chart of the AppleTree's actions from Chapter 15.

The actions we will need to code for the AppleTree are as follows:

1. Move at a certain speed every frame.
2. Change directions upon hitting the edge of the play area.
3. Change directions based on random chance.
4. Drop an Apple every second.

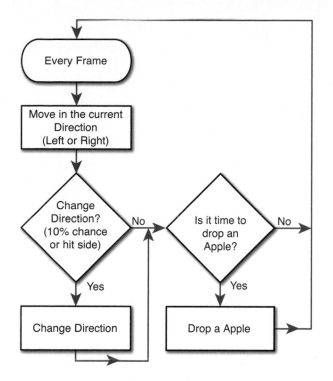

Figure 28.7   AppleTree flow chart

That's it! Let's start coding. Double-click the AppleTree C# script in the Project pane to open it. We will need some configuration variables, so alter the `AppleTree` class to look like this:

```
using UnityEngine;
using System.Collections;

public class AppleTree : MonoBehaviour {

    // Prefab for instantiating apples
    public GameObject    applePrefab;

    // Speed at which the AppleTree moves in meters/second
    public float         speed = 1f;

    // Distance where AppleTree turns around
    public float         leftAndRightEdge = 10f;

    // Chance that the AppleTree will change directions
    public float         chanceToChangeDirections = 0.1f;

    // Rate at which Apples will be instantiated
    public float         secondsBetweenAppleDrops = 1f;
```

```
    void Start () {
        // Dropping apples every second
    }

    void Update () {
        // Basic Movement
        // Changing Direction
    }
}
```

You may have noticed that the preceding code does not include the line numbers that were present in prior chapters. The code listings in this part of the book will generally not have line numbers because I needed every character possible to fit the code on the page.

To see this code actually do something, you need to attach it to the AppleTree GameObject. Drag the AppleTree C# script from the Project pane onto the AppleTree prefab that is also in the Project pane. Then, click the AppleTree instance in the Hierarchy pane, and you'll see that the script has been added not only to the AppleTree prefab but also to its instance in the Hierarchy.

With the AppleTree selected in the Hierarchy, you should see all of the variables you just typed appear in the Inspector under the *AppleTree (Script)* component.

Try moving the AppleTree around in the scene by adjusting the X and Y coordinates in the Transform Inspector to find a good height (position.y) for the AppleTree and a good limit for left and right movement. On my machine, 12 looks like a good position.y, and it looks like the tree can move from -20 to 20 in position.x and still be on screen. Set the position of AppleTree to [0,12,0] and set the `leftAndRightEdge` float in the AppleTree (Script) component Inspector to 20.

THE UNITY ENGINE SCRIPTING REFERENCE

Before you get too far into this project, it's extremely important that you remember to look at the Unity Scripting Reference if you have any questions at all about the code you see here. There are two ways to get into the Script Reference:

1. Choose *Help > Scripting Reference* from the menu bar in Unity. This brings up the Scripting Reference that is saved locally on your machine, meaning that it will work even without a connection to the Internet. You can type any function or class name into the search field on the left to find out more about it.

   Enter *MonoBehaviour* into the search field and press Return. Then click the first result to see all the methods built in to every MonoBehaviour script (and by extension, built in to every class script you will attach to a GameObject in Unity). For readers from the United States, note the European spelling of *Behaviour*.

2. When working in MonoDevelop, select any text you would like to learn more about and then choose *Help > Unity API Reference* from the menu bar. This will

launch an online version of the Unity Scripting Reference, so it won't work properly without Internet access, but it has the exact same information as the local reference that you can reach through the first method.

Unfortunately, all the code examples in the Scripting Reference default to JavaScript, but there is either a pop-up menu or a C# button (depending on the version of the documentation) that allows you to switch nearly all code examples to C#. Trust me; this is a small price to pay for using a vastly superior language.

Basic Movement

Right now, rather than include code that actually moves the AppleTree, this script only includes code comments (preceded by //) that describe the actions that will be added to the code. I often find it useful to list these actions in code comments first and then add functionality progressively. This can help you organize your thoughts and is similar to writing an outline for a paper.

Now, make these bolded changes to the Update method in the AppleTree script:

```
void Update () {
    // Basic Movement
    Vector3 pos = transform.position;
    pos.x += speed * Time.deltaTime;
    transform.position = pos;
    // Changing Direction
}
```

The first bold line in this code defines the Vector3 pos to be the current position of the AppleTree. Then, the x component of pos is increased by the speed times Time.deltaTime (which is a measure of the number of seconds since the last frame). This makes the movement of the AppleTree *time-based*, which is a very important concept in game programming (see the sidebar "Making Your Games Time-Based"). The third line assigns this modified pos back to transform.position (which moves AppleTree to a new position).

MAKING YOUR GAMES TIME-BASED

When movement in a game is *time-based*, it happens at the same speed regardless of the framerate at which the game is running. Time.deltaTime enables this because it tells us the number of seconds that have passed since the last frame. Time.deltaTime is usually very small. For a game running at 25 fps (frames per second), Time.deltaTime is 0.04f, meaning that each frame takes 4/100ths of a second to display. If this line of code were run at 25 fps, the result would resolve like this:

```
pos.x += speed * Time.deltaTime;
pos.x += 1.0f * 0.04f;
pos.x += 0.04f;
```

So, in 1/25th of a second, `pos.x` would increase by 0.04m per frame. Over the course of a full second, `pos.x` would increase by 0.04m per frame * 25 frames, for a total of 1 meter in 1 second. This equals the 1m/s that `speed` is set to.

If instead the game were running at 100 fps, it would resolve as follows:

```
pos.x += speed * Time.deltaTime;
pos.x += 1.0f * 0.01f;
pos.x += 0.01f;
```

So, in 1/100th of a second, `pos.x` would increase by 0.01m per frame. Over the course of a full second, `pos.x` would increase by 0.01m per frame * 100 frames, for a total of 1 meter in 1 second.

Time-based movement ensures that regardless of framerate, the elements in your game will move at a consistent speed, and it is this consistency that will enable you to make games that are enjoyable for both players using the latest hardware and those using older machines. Time-based coding is also very important to consider when programming for mobile devices because the speed and power of mobile devices is changing very quickly.

You might be wondering why this was three lines instead of just one. Why couldn't the code just be this:

```
transform.position.x += speed * Time.deltaTime;
```

The answer is that `transform.position` is a *property*, a method that is masquerading as a field through the use of `get{}` and `set{}` accessors (see Chapter 25, "Classes"). Although it is possible to read the value of a property's subcomponent, it is not possible to set a subcomponent of a property. In other words, `transform.position.x` can be read, but it cannot be set directly. This necessitates the creation of the intermediate Vector3 `pos` that can be modified and then assigned back to `transform.position`.

When you press the Play button, you'll notice that the AppleTree is moving very slowly. Try some different values for `speed` in the Inspector and see what feels good to you. I personally set it to 10, which makes it move at 10m/s (10 meters per second or 10 Unity units per second).

Changing Direction

Now that the AppleTree is moving at a decent rate, it will run off of the screen pretty quickly. Let's make it change directions when it hits the `leftAndRightEdge` value. Modify the AppleTree script as follows:

```
void Update () {
    // Basic Movement
    Vector3 pos = transform.position;
    pos.x += speed * Time.deltaTime;
    transform.position = pos;
    // Changing Direction
    if ( pos.x < -leftAndRightEdge ) {
        speed = Mathf.Abs(speed);   // Move right
    } else if ( pos.x > leftAndRightEdge ) {
        speed = -Mathf.Abs(speed); // Move left
    }
}
```

Press Play and see what happens. The first line under `//Changing Direction` checks to see whether the new `pos.x` that was just set in the previous lines is less than the side-to-side limit that is set by `leftAndRightEdge`. If `pos.x` is too small, `speed` is set to `Mathf.Abs(speed)`, which takes the absolute value of `speed`, guaranteeing that the resulting value will be positive, which translates into movement to the right. If `pos.x` is greater than `leftAndRightEdge`, then `speed` is set to the negative of `Mathf.Abs(speed)`, ensuring that the AppleTree will move to the left.

Changing Direction Randomly

Add the bolded lines shown here to introduce random changes in direction as well:

```
// Changing Direction
if ( pos.x < -leftAndRightEdge ) {
    speed = Mathf.Abs(speed);   // Move right
} else if ( pos.x > leftAndRightEdge ) {
    speed = -Mathf.Abs(speed); // Move left
} else if ( Random.value < chanceToChangeDirections ) {
    speed *= -1;   // Change direction
}
```

`Random.value` is a static property of the class Random that returns a random float value between 0 and 1 (non-inclusive, which means that the results can get very close to 1, but `Random.value` will never actually return 1 itself). If this random number is less than `chanceToChangeDirections`, the AppleTree will change directions by setting `speed` to the negative of itself. If you press Play, you'll see that this happens far too often at a `chanceToChangeDirections` of `0.1f`. In the Inspector, change the value of `chanceToChangeDirections` to `0.02`, and it should feel a lot better. Note that you do not add the `f` at the end when typing a float value into the Inspector.

To continue the discussion of time-based games, this chance to change directions is actually not time based. Every frame, there is a 2% chance that the AppleTree will change directions. On a very fast computer, that chance could happen 200 times per second (yielding an average of 4 directions changes per second), whereas on a slow computer, it could happen as few as 30 times per second (for an average of 0.6 direction changes per second). To fix this, move the direction change code out of `Update()` (which is called as fast as the computer can render frames) into `FixedUpdate()` (which is called exactly 50 times per second, regardless of the computer on which it's running).

```
void Update () {
    // Basic Movement
    Vector3 pos = transform.position;
    pos.x += speed * Time.deltaTime;
    transform.position = pos;
    // Changing Direction
    if ( pos.x < -leftAndRightEdge ) {
        speed = Mathf.Abs(speed);  // Move right
    } else if ( pos.x > leftAndRightEdge ) {
        speed = -Mathf.Abs(speed); // Move left
    }
}

void FixedUpdate() {
    // Changing Direction Randomly
    if ( Random.value < chanceToChangeDirections ) {
        speed *= -1;  // Change direction
    }
}
```

This will cause the AppleTree to randomly change directions an average of 1 time every second (50 `FixedUpdates` per second * a random chance of 0.02 = 1 time per second). You should also note that the code for the AppleTree class still lists the value for `chanceToChangeDirections` as `0.1f`. However, because `chanceToChangeDirections` is a public field, it is /serialized/ by Unity, which allows it to be seen in the Inspector and allows the value of `0.02` in the Inspector to override the value in the script. If you were to change the value of this field in the script, you would not see any change in the behavior of the game because the Inspector value will always override the value in the script for any serialized field.

Dropping Apples

Select AppleTree in the Hierarchy and look at the *Apple Tree (Script)* component in its Inspector. Currently, the value of the field `applePrefab` is *None (Game Object)*, meaning that it has not yet been set (the *GameObject* in parentheses is there to let you know that the type of the `applePrefab` field is GameObject). This value needs to be set to the Apple GameObject prefab in the Project pane. You can do this either by clicking the tiny target to the right of *Apple Prefab None (Game Object)* in the Inspector and selecting Apple from the Assets tab or by dragging the Apple GameObject prefab from the Project pane onto the `applePrefab` value in the Inspector pane.

Return to MonoDevelop and add the following bolded code to the `AppleTree` class:

```
void Start () {
    // Dropping apples every second
    InvokeRepeating( "DropApple", 2f, secondsBetweenAppleDrops );
}
```

```
void DropApple() {
    GameObject apple = Instantiate( applePrefab ) as GameObject;
    apple.transform.position = transform.position;
}
```

The `InvokeRepeating` function will call another named function on a repeating basis. In this case, the first argument tells it to call the new function `DropApple()`. The second argument, `2f`, tells `InvokeRepeating` to wait 2 seconds before the first time that it calls `DropApple()`. The third argument tells it to then call `DropApple()` again every `secondsBetweenAppleDrops` seconds thereafter (in this case, every 1 second based on the settings in the Inspector). Press Play and see what happens.

Did you expect the Apples to fly off to the sides? Remember the Hello World example that we did with all the cubes flying all over the place? The same thing is happening here. The Apples are colliding with the AppleTree, and that causes them to fly off to the left and right rather than falling straight down. To fix this, you need to put them in a *layer* that doesn't collide with the AppleTree. Layers are groups of objects that can either collide with or ignore each other. If the AppleTree and Apple GameObjects are placed in two different physics layers, and those layers are set to ignore each other in the Physics Manager, then the AppleTree and Apples will cease colliding with each other.

Setting GameObject Layers

First, you will need to make some new layers. Click the AppleTree in the Hierarchy and then choose *Add Layer* from the pop-up menu next to Layer. This will open up the *Tags and Layers Manager* in the Inspector, which allows you to set the names of layers under the *Layers* label (make sure you're not editing *Tags* or *Sorting Layers*). You can see that Builtin Layers 0 through 7 are grayed out, but you are able to edit User Layers 8 through 31. Name User Layer 8 *AppleTree*, User Layer 9 *Apple*, and User Layer 10 *Basket*. It should look like Figure 28.8.

Figure 28.8   The steps required to make new physics layers and assign them

From the menu bar, now choose *Edit > Project Settings > Physics*. This will set the Inspector to the *Physics Manager*. The *Layer Collision Matrix* grid of check boxes at the bottom of the Physics Manager sets which layers will collide with each other (and whether GameObjects in the same layer will collide with each other as well). You want the Apple to collide with neither the

AppleTree nor other Apples, but to still collide with the Basket, so your Layer Collision Matrix grid should look like what is shown in Figure 28.9.

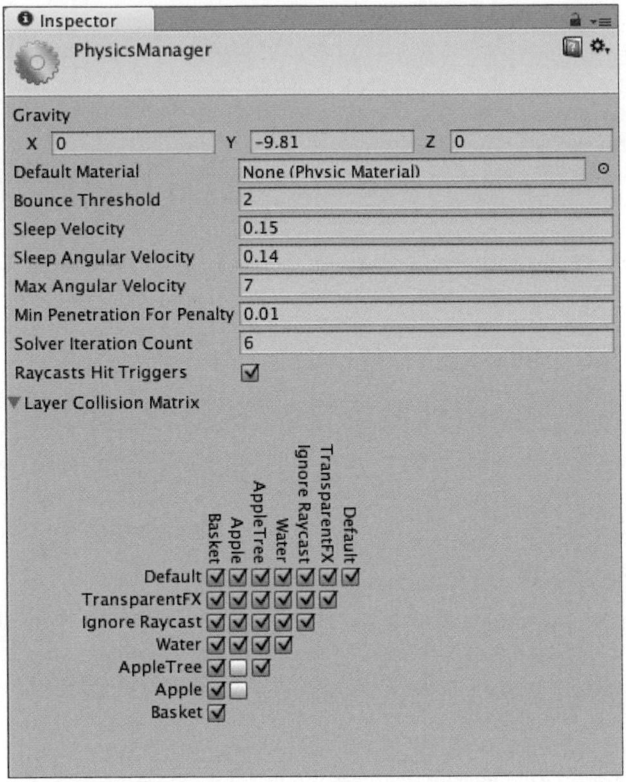

Figure 28.9 The required Layer Collision Matrix settings in the Physics Manager

Now that the Layer Collision Matrix is set properly, it's time to assign layers to the important GameObjects in the game. Click Apple in the Project pane. Then, at the top of the Inspector, select the Apple layer from the pop-up menu next to Layer at the top of the Inspector pane. Select the Basket in the Project pane and set its Layer to Basket. Then select the AppleTree in the Project pane and set its Layer to AppleTree. When you choose the layer for AppleTree, Unity will ask you if you want to change the layer for just AppleTree or for both AppleTree and its children. You definitely want to choose *Yes* because you need the cylinder and sphere that make up the trunk and the leaves of the tree to also be in the AppleTree physics layer. This change will also trickle forward to the AppleTree instance in the scene. You can click AppleTree in the Hierarchy pane to confirm this.

Now if you press Play, you should see the apples dropping properly from the tree.

Stopping Apples If They Fall Too Far

If you leave the current version of the game running for a while, you'll notice that there are *a lot* of Apples in the Hierarchy. That's because the code is creating a new Apple every second but never deleting any Apples. Open the Apple C# script and add the following code to kill each Apple once it reaches a depth of `transform.position.y == -20` (which is comfortably off-screen). Here's the code:

```csharp
using UnityEngine;
using System.Collections;

public class Apple : MonoBehaviour {
    public static float     bottomY = -20f;

    void Update () {
        if ( transform.position.y < bottomY ) {
            Destroy( this.gameObject );
        }
    }
}
```

You will need to attach the Apple C# script to the Apple GameObject prefab in the Project pane for this code to function in the game. To do so, drag the script onto the prefab and release. Now, if you press Play in Unity and zoom out in the scene, you can see that Apples drop for a ways, but once they reach a y position of -20, they disappear.

The bolded `public static float` line declares and defines a static variable named `bottomY`. As was mentioned in Chapter 25, static variables are shared by all instances of a class, so every instance of Apple will have the same value for `bottomY`. If `bottomY` is ever changed for one instance, it will simultaneously change for all instances. However, it's also important to point out that static fields like `bottomY` do *not* appear in the Inspector.

The `Destroy()` function removes things that are passed into it from the game, and it can be used to destroy both components and GameObjects. `Destroy(this.gameObject)` must be used in this case because `Destroy(this)` would just remove the Apple (Script) component from the Apple GameObject instance. In any script, `this` refers to the current instance of the C# class in which it is called (the Apple class in this instance), not to the entire GameObject. Any time you want to destroy an entire GameObject from within an attached component class, you must call `Destroy( this.gameObject )`.

This is all we need to do for the Apple GameObject.

Instantiating the Baskets

To make the Basket GameObjects work, we're going to introduce a concept that will recur throughout these prototype tutorials. While object-oriented thinking encourages us to create an independent class for each GameObject (as we have just done for AppleTree and Apple), it is often very useful to also have a script that runs the game as a whole. From the menu bar, choose *Assets > Create > C# Script* and name the script *ApplePicker*. Attach the ApplePicker script to the Main Camera in the Hierarchy. I often attach these game management scripts to the Main Camera because I am guaranteed that there is a Main Camera in every scene. Open the ApplePicker script in MonoDevelop and type the following code:

```
using UnityEngine;
using System.Collections;

public class ApplePicker : MonoBehaviour {

    public GameObject        basketPrefab;
    public int               numBaskets = 3;
    public float             basketBottomY = -14f;
    public float             basketSpacingY = 2f;

    void Start () {
        for (int i=0; i<numBaskets; i++) {
            GameObject tBasketGO = Instantiate( basketPrefab ) as GameObject;
            Vector3 pos = Vector3.zero;
            pos.y = basketBottomY + ( basketSpacingY * i );
            tBasketGO.transform.position = pos;
        }
    }
}
```

Click Main Camera in the Hierarchy pane and set the `basketPrefab` in the Inspector to be the Basket GameObject prefab that was made earlier, and then click Play. You'll see that this code creates three baskets at the bottom of the screen.

Moving the Baskets with the Mouse

Open the Basket C# script in MonoDevelop and enter this code:

```
using UnityEngine;
using System.Collections;

public class Basket : MonoBehaviour {

    void Update () {
        // Get the current screen position of the mouse from Input
        Vector3 mousePos2D = Input.mousePosition;                           // 1

        // The Camera's z position sets the how far to push the mouse into 3D
        mousePos2D.z = -Camera.main.transform.position.z;                   // 2

        // Convert the point from 2D screen space into 3D game world space
        Vector3 mousePos3D = Camera.main.ScreenToWorldPoint( mousePos2D );  // 3
```

```
            // Move the x position of this Basket to the x position of the Mouse
            Vector3 pos = this.transform.position;
            pos.x = mousePos3D.x;
            this.transform.position = pos;
        }
    }
```

1. `Input.mousePosition` gets assigned to `mousePos2D`. This value is in screen coordinates, meaning that it measures how many pixels the mouse is from the top-left corner of the screen. The z position of `Input.mousePositon` will always start at 0 because it is essentially a two-dimensional measurement.

2. This line sets the z coordinate of `mousePos2D` to the negative of the Main Camera's z position. In our game, the Main Camera is at a z of -10, so `mousePos2D.z` is set to 10. This tells the upcoming `ScreenToWorldPoint` function how far to push the `mousePos3D` into the 3D space.

3. `ScreenToWorldPoint()` converts `mousePoint2D` into a point in 3D space inside the scene. If `mousePos2D.z` were 0, the resulting `mousePos3D` point would be at a z of -10 (the same as the Main Camera). By setting `mousePos2D.z` to 10, `mousePos3D` is projected into the 3D space 10 meters away from the Main Camera position, resulting in a `mousePos3D.z` of 0. This doesn't change the resultant x or y position in games with an orthographic camera projection, but it matters significantly in games with a perspective camera projection. If this is at all confusing, I recommend looking at `Camera.ScreenToWorldPoint` in the Unity Scripting Reference.

Now that the Baskets are moving, you can use them to collide with Apples, though the Apples aren't really being caught yet; instead, they're just landing on the Baskets.

Catching Apples

Add the following bold lines to the Basket C# script:

```
public class Basket : MonoBehaviour {

    void Update () {
        ...                                                           // 1
    }

    void OnCollisionEnter( Collision coll ) {                         // 2
        // Find out what hit this basket
        GameObject collidedWith = coll.gameObject;                   // 3
        if ( collidedWith.tag == "Apple" ) {                         // 4
            Destroy( collidedWith );
        }
    }
}
```

1. Throughout the tutorial chapters of this book, I use ellipses (...) to indicate parts of the code that I am skipping in the code listing. Without these, the code listings would be ridiculously long in some of the later chapters. When you see ellipses like these, you shouldn't change anything about the code where they are; just leave it alone and focus on the new code (which is bolded for clarity). This code listing requires no changes to the `Update()` function, so I have used ellipses to skip it.

2. The `OnCollisionEnter` method is called whenever another GameObject collides with this Basket, and a `Collision` argument is passed in with information about the collision, including a reference to the GameObject that hit this Basket's Collider.

3. This line assigns this colliding GameObject to the temporary variable `collidedWith`.

4. Check to see whether `collidedWith` is an Apple by looking for the `"Apple"` tag that was assigned to all Apple GameObjects. If `collidedWith` is an Apple, it is destroyed. Now, if an Apple hits this Basket, it will be destroyed.

At this point, the game functions very similarly to our inspiration *Kaboom!*, though it doesn't yet have any *graphical user interface* (GUI) elements like a score or a representation of how many lives the player has remaining. However, even without these elements, Apple Picker would be a successful prototype in its current state. As is, this prototype will allow you to tweak several aspects of the game to give it the right level of difficulty.

Save your scene. Then click the _Scene_0 in the Project pane to select it. Press Command-D on the keyboard (Control+D on Windows) to duplicate the scene. This will create a new scene named _Scene_1. Double-click _Scene_1 to open it. As an exact duplicate of _Scene_0, the game in this new scene will work as well. This gives you a chance to tweak variables in the scene without changing any of them in _Scene_0 because each scene will store different Inspector values for serialized public fields in C# script components. Try making the game more difficult by increasing the speed of the AppleTree, increasing the random chance of the AppleTree changing direction, dropping apples more frequently, and so on. After you have the game balanced for a harder difficulty level in _Scene_1, save it and reopen _Scene_0. If you're ever concerned about which scene you have open, just look at the title at the top of the Unity window. It will always include the scene name.

GUI and Game Management

The final things to add to our game are the GUI and *game management* that will make it feel like more of a real game. The GUI element we'll add is a score counter, and the game management elements we'll add are rounds and the ability for the game to restart when the player has run out of Baskets.

Score Counter

The score counter will help players get a sense of their level of achievement in the game.

Open _Scene_0 by double-clicking it in the Project pane. Then go to the menu bar and choose *GameObject > Create Other > GUI Text*. This will place a GUIText in the middle of the screen with the words *Gui Text* in it. Rename GUI Text to *ScoreCounter*. Try changing the x and y position of ScoreCounter. You'll notice that the coordinates for GUITexts differ completely from those for other GameObjects. This is because GUITexts are positioned relative to the screen rather than being positioned in world space. An x value of 0 is the far-left edge of the screen, and an x value of 1 is the right edge. A y value of 0 is the bottom of the screen, and a y value of 1 is the top. (Note that this also differs from the screen coordinates of Input.mousePosition, for which a y value of 0 is the top of the screen.)

Set the Transform and GUIText components of ScoreCounter as shown in the left half of Figure 28.10.

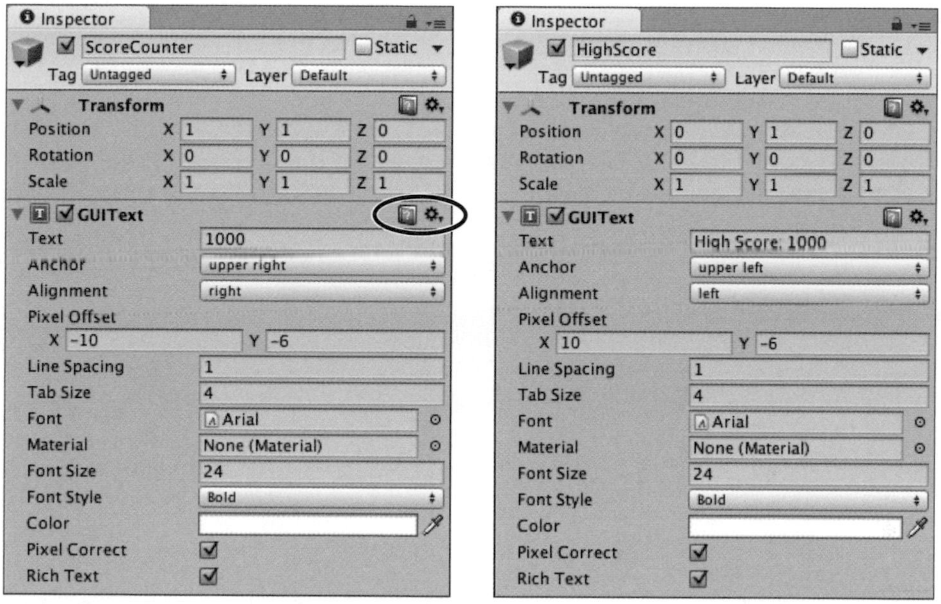

Figure 28.10 Transform and GUIText component settings for ScoreCounter and HighScore

For more information on the GUIText component, click the help icon in the top-right corner of the GUIText component (circled in black in Figure 28.10). You can use these help icons to learn more about any component.

Add Points for Each Caught Apple

There are two scripts that are notified when a collision occurs between an Apple and a Basket: the Apple and Basket scripts. In this game, there is already an `OnCollisionEnter()` method on the Basket C# script, so we'll modify this to give the player points for each Apple that is caught. 100 points per Apple seems like a reasonable number (though I've personally always thought it was a little ridiculous to have those extra zeroes at the end of scores). Open the Basket script in MonoDevelop and add the bolded lines shown here:

```
using UnityEngine;
using System.Collections;

public class Basket : MonoBehaviour {

    public GUIText        scoreGT;                                    // 1

    void Update () {
        …
    }

    void Start() {
        // Find a reference to the ScoreCounter GameObject
        GameObject scoreGO = GameObject.Find("ScoreCounter");        // 2
        // Get the GUIText Component of that GameObject
        scoreGT = scoreGO.GetComponent<GUIText>();                   // 3
        // Set the starting number of points to 0
        scoreGT.text = "0";
    }

    void OnCollisionEnter( Collision coll ) {
        // Find out what hit this Basket
        GameObject collidedWith = coll.gameObject;
        if ( collidedWith.tag == "Apple" ) {
            Destroy( collidedWith );
        }

        // Parse the text of the scoreGT into an int
        int score = int.Parse( scoreGT.text );                       // 4
        // Add points for catching the apple
        score += 100;
        // Convert the score back to a string and display it
        scoreGT.text = score.ToString();
    }
}
```

1. Be sure you don't neglect to enter this line. It's in an earlier part of the code than the others.
2. `GameObject.Find("ScoreCounter")` searches through all the GameObjects in the scene for one named `"ScoreCounter"` and assigns it to the local variable `scoreGO`.
3. `scoreGO.Getcomponent<GUIText>()` searches for a GUIText component on the `scoreGO` GameObject, and this is assigned to the public field `scoreGT`. The starting score is then set to zero on the next line.
4. `int.Parse( scoreGT.text )` takes the text shown in ScoreCounter and converts it to an integer. 100 points are added to the int `score`, and it is then assigned back to the text of `scoreGT` after being parsed from an int to a string by `score.ToString()`.

Notifying Apple Picker That an Apple Was Dropped

Another aspect of making Apple Picker feel more like a game is ending the round and deleting a Basket if an Apple is dropped. At this point, Apples manage their own destruction, which is fine, but the Apple needs to somehow notify the AplePicker script of this event so that Apple Picker can end the round and destroy the rest of the Apples. This will involve one script calling a function on another. Start by making these modifications to the Apple C# script:

```
using UnityEngine;
using System.Collections;

public class Apple : MonoBehaviour {
    public static float     bottomY = -20f;

    void Update () {
        if ( transform.position.y < bottomY ) {
            Destroy( this.gameObject );

            // Get a reference to the ApplePicker component of Main Camera
            ApplePicker apScript = Camera.main.GetComponent<ApplePicker>(); // 1
            // Call the public AppleDestroyed() method of apScript
            apScript.AppleDestroyed();                                      // 2
        }
    }
}
```

1. Grabs a reference to the ApplePicker script component on the Main Camera. Because the Camera class has a built-in static variable Camera.main that references the Main Camera, it is not necessary to use GameObject.Find("Main Camera") to obtain a reference to Main Camera. Getcomponent<ApplePicker>() is then used to grab a reference to the *ApplePicker (Script)* component on Main Camera and assign it to apScript. After this is done, it is possible to access public variables and methods of the ApplePicker instance that is attached to Main Camera.

2. This calls a non-existant AppleDestroyed() method of the ApplePicker instance.

There is currently no public AppleDestroyed() method in the ApplePicker script, so you will need to open the ApplePicker C# script in MonoDevelop and make the following bolded changes:

```
using UnityEngine;
using System.Collections;

public class ApplePicker : MonoBehaviour {

    public GameObject       basketPrefab;
    ...                                                                     // 1
    public float            basketSpacingY = 2f;
```

```
    void Start () {
        ...
    }

    public void AppleDestroyed() {                                          // 2
        //// Destroy all of the falling Apples
        GameObject[] tAppleArray=GameObject.FindGameObjectsWithTag("Apple");// 3
        foreach ( GameObject tGO in tAppleArray ) {
            Destroy( tGO );
        }
    }
}
```

1. This is another way that ellipses (...) are used to shorten code listings. Here, lines have been omitted between the lines above and below the ellipses. Again, this is an indication that you don't need to modify any code between the lines.

2. The `AppleDestroyed()` method must be declared `public` for other classes (like Apple) to be able to call it. By default, methods are all *private* and unable to be called (or even seen) by other classes.

3. `GameObject.FindGameObjectsWithTag("Apple")` will return an array of all existing Apple GameObjects. The subsequent `foreach` loop iterates through each of these and destroys them.

Destroying a Basket When an Apple Is Dropped

The final bit of code for this scene will manage the deletion of one of the Baskets each time an Apple is dropped and stop the game when all the Baskets have been destroyed. Make the following changes to the ApplePicker C# script:

```
using UnityEngine;
using System.Collections;
using System.Collections.Generic;                                          // 1

public class ApplePicker : MonoBehaviour {

    ...                                                                     // 2
    public float            basketSpacingY = 2f;
    public List<GameObject> basketList;

    void Start () {
        basketList = new List<GameObject>();
        for (int i=0; i<numBaskets; i++) {
            GameObject tBasketGO = Instantiate( basketPrefab ) as GameObject;
            Vector3 pos = Vector3.zero;
            pos.y = basketBottomY + ( basketSpacingY * i );
            tBasketGO.transform.position = pos;
            basketList.Add( tBasketGO );                                    // 3
        }
    }
```

```
public void AppleDestroyed() {
    //// Destroy all of the falling Apples
    GameObject[] tAppleArray = GameObject.FindGameObjectsWithTag( "Apple" );
    foreach ( GameObject tGO in tAppleArray ) {
        Destroy( tGO );
    }

    //// Destroy one of the Baskets
    // Get the index of the last Basket in basketList
    int basketIndex = basketList.Count-1;
    // Get a reference to that Basket GameObject
    GameObject tBasketGO = basketList[basketIndex];
    // Remove the Basket from the List and destroy the GameObject
    basketList.RemoveAt( basketIndex );
    Destroy( tBasketGO );
}

}
```

1. We will be storing the Basket GameObjects in a List, so it is necessary to use the `System.Collections.Generic` code library. (For more information about Lists, see Chapter 22, "Lists and Arrays.") The `public List<GameObject> basketList` is declared at the beginning of the class, and it is defined and initialized in the first line of `Start()`.

2. Here, the ellipses omit all the lines before `public float basketSpacingY = 2f;`.

3. A new line is added to the end of the for loop that `Adds` the baskets to `basketList`. The baskets are added in the order they are created, which means that they are added bottom to top.

In the method `AppleDestroyed()` a new section has been added to destroy one of the Baskets. Because the Baskets are added from bottom to top, it's important that the last Basket in the List is destroyed first (to destroy the Baskets top to bottom).

Adding a High Score

Create a new GUIText in the scene just as you did for the ScoreCounter and name it *HighScore*. Give its Transform and GUIText components the settings shown in the right side of Figure 28.10.

Next, create a new C# script named *HighScore*, attach it to the HighScore GameObject in the Hierarchy pane, and give it the following code:

```
using UnityEngine;
using System.Collections;

public class HighScore : MonoBehaviour {
    static public int    score = 1000;
```

```
    void Update () {
        GUIText gt = this.GetComponent<GUIText>();
        gt.text = "High Score: "+score;
    }
}
```

The lines in `Update()` simply display the value of `score` in the GUIText component. It is not necessary to call `ToString()` on the `score` in this instance because when the + operator is used to concatenate a string with another data type (the int `score` in this case), `ToString()` is called implicitly (that is, automatically).

Making the int `score` not only public but also static gives us the ability to access it from any other script by simply typing `HighScore.score`. This is one of the powers of static variables that we will use throughout the prototypes in this book. Open the Basket C# script and add the following lines to see how this is used:

```
void OnCollisionEnter( Collision coll ) {
    ...
    // Convert the score back to a string and display it
    scoreGT.text = score.ToString();

    // Track the high score
    if (score > HighScore.score) {
        HighScore.score = score;
    }
}
```

Now `HighScore.score` is set any time the current score exceeds it.

Finally, open the ApplePicker C# script and add the following lines to reset the game whenever a player runs out of Baskets:

```
public void AppleDestroyed() {
    ...

    //// Destroy one of the Baskets
    ...
    basketList.RemoveAt( basketIndex );
    Destroy( tBasketGO );

    // Restart the game, which doesn't affect HighScore.Score
    if ( basketList.Count == 0 ) {
        Application.LoadLevel( "_Scene_0" );
    }
}
```

`Application.LoadLevel( "_Scene_0" )` will reload _Scene_0. This effectively resets the game to its beginning state. However, because `HighScore.score` is a static variable, it is not reset along with the rest of the game. This means that high scores will remain from one round to the next. However, whenever you press the Play button again to stop the game, HighScore. score will reset. It is possible to fix this through the use of Unity's PlayerPrefs. PlayerPrefs store information from Unity scripts on the computer so that the information can be recalled later and isn't destroyed when playback stops. Add the following bolded changes to the HighScore C# script:

```csharp
using UnityEngine;
using System.Collections;

public class HighScore : MonoBehaviour {
    static public int    score = 1000;

    void Awake() {                                                    // 1
        // If the ApplePickerHighScore already exists, read it
        if (PlayerPrefs.HasKey("ApplePickerHighScore")) {            // 2
            score = PlayerPrefs.GetInt("ApplePickerHighScore");
        }
        // Assign the high score to ApplePickerHighScore
        PlayerPrefs.SetInt("ApplePickerHighScore", score);          // 3
    }

    void Update () {
        GUIText qt = this.GetComponent<GUIText>();
        gt.text = "High Score: "+score;
        // Update ApplePickerHighScore in PlayerPrefs if necessary
        if (score > PlayerPrefs.GetInt("ApplePickerHighScore")) {   // 4
            PlayerPrefs.SetInt("ApplePickerHighScore", score);
        }
    }
}
```

1. Awake() is a built-in Unity method (like Start() or Update()) that happens when the instance of HighScore is first created (so Awake() always occurs before Start()).

2. PlayerPrefs is a dictionary of values that are referenced through keys (that is, unique strings). In this case, we're referencing the key *ApplePickerHighScore*. Here, the first line checks to see whether an *ApplePickerHighScore* already exists in PlayerPrefs and reads it in if it does exist.

3. The last line of Awake() assigns the current value of score to the ApplePickerHighScore PlayerPrefs key. If an ApplePickerHighScore already exists, this will rewrite the value back to PlayerPrefs; if the key does not already exist, however, this ensures that an ApplePicker-HighScore key is created.

4. With the added lines, Update() now checks every frame to see whether the current High-Score.score is higher than the one stored in PlayerPrefs and updates PlayerPrefs if that is the case.

This usage of PlayerPrefs enables the Apple Picker high score to be remembered on this machine, and the high score will survive stopping playback, quitting Unity, and even restarting your computer.

Summary

Now you have a game prototype that plays very similarly to the original Activision game *Kaboom!* Although this game still lacks elements like steadily increasing difficulty and an opening and closing screen, these are things that you can add yourself once you gain more experience.

Next Steps

Here is some further explanation of the elements that you could add to the prototype in the future:

- **Start screen:** A start screen could be added. You could build it in its own scene and give it a splash image and a *Start* button. The Start button could then call `Application.Load-Level("_Scene_0")` to start the game.

- **Game Over screen:** Another scene could be created as a Game Over screen. The Game Over screen could display the final score that the player achieved and could let the player know if she exceeded the previous high score. It should have a button labeled *Play Again* that calls `Application.LoadLevel("_Scene_0")`.

- **Increasing difficulty:** Varying difficulty levels are discussed in later prototypes, but if you wanted to add them here, it would make sense to store an array or List for each of the values on AppleTree, such as speed, chanceToChangeDirections, and secondsBetweenApple-Drops. Each element in the list could be a different level of difficulty, with the 0th element being the easiest and the last element being the most difficult. As the player played the game, a level counter could increase over time and be used as the index for these lists; so at level=0, the 0th element of each variable would be used.

CHAPTER 29

PROTOTYPE 2: MISSION DEMOLITION

Physics games are some of the most popular around, making games like *Angry Birds* household names. In this chapter, you make your own physics game that is inspired by *Angry Birds* and all the physics games, such as the board game *Crossbows and Catapults*, that came before it.

This chapter covers the following: physics, collision, mouse interaction, levels, and game state management.

Getting Started: Prototype 2

Because this is the second prototype and you now have some experience under your belt, this chapter is going to move a bit faster than the last on things that you already know. However, new topics will still be covered in detail.

SET UP THE PROJECT FOR THIS CHAPTER

Following the standard project setup procedure, create a new project in Unity. If you need a refresher on the standard project setup procedure, see Appendix A, "Standard Project Setup Procedure."

- **Project name:** Mission Demolition Prototype
- **Scene name:** _Scene_0
- **C# script names:** None yet

Game Prototype Concept

In this game, the player will be using a slingshot to fire projectiles at a castle, hoping to demolish it. Each castle will have a goal area that must be touched by the projectile to continue to the next level.

This is the sequence of events we want:

1. When the player's mouse pointer is in range of the slingshot, the slingshot should glow.
2. If the player presses the left mouse button (numbered button 0 in Unity) down while the slingshot is glowing, a projectile will instantiate at the location of the mouse pointer.
3. As the player moves and drags the mouse around with the button held down, the projectile follows it, yet will remain within the limits of the Sphere Collider on the slingshot.
4. A white line will stretch from each arm of the slingshot around the projectile to make it look more like an actual slingshot.
5. When the player releases mouse button 0, the projectile will be fired from the slingshot.
6. A castle will be set up several meters away; the player's goal will be to knock down the castle to hit a target area inside.
7. The player can fire as many shots as she likes to hit the goal. Each shot will leave a trail so that the player may better judge her next shot.

Many of these events relate to mechanics, but one is exclusively aesthetics: Step 4. All of the other elements that mention art use that art for the purpose of game mechanics, but Step 4 is just to make the game look nicer, so it's less critical to the prototype. When you're writing down your concepts for games, this is an important thing to keep in mind. That isn't to say that you shouldn't implement things that are entirely aesthetics in a prototype; you just need to be aware of and prioritize the elements that will have the most direct impact on the game mechanics. For the sake of time and space, this prototype will focus on the other elements, and we'll leave the implementation of Step 4 for you to tackle later.

Art Assets

You should create several art assets now to prepare the project for coding.

Ground

To create the ground, follow these steps:

1. Open _Scene_0 and create a cube (*GameObject > Create Other > Cube* from the menu bar). Rename the cube to *Ground*. To make a rectangular solid that is very wide in the x direction, set the transform of Ground to the following:

   Ground (Cube)   P:[0,-10,0]   R[0,0,0]   S[100,1,1]

2. Create a new material (*Assets > Create > Material*) and name it *Mat_Ground*. Give it a brown color and attach it to the Ground GameObject in the Hierarchy. (These actions are described in detail in the preceding chapter.)

3. Save your scene.

Directional Light

Next you want to drop a simple directional light into the scene, as follows:

1. From the menu bar, select *GameObject > Create Other > Directional Light*. One of the features of directional lights is that their position doesn't matter to the scene; only the rotation of a directional light is taken into consideration. That being the case, move it out of the way by setting its transform to the following:

   Directional Light   P:[-10,0,0]   R:[50,-30,0]   S:[1,1,1].

2. Save your scene.

Camera Settings

Camera settings are next:

1. Select the Main Camera in the Hierarchy and rename it to _*Main Camera* to keep it sorted at the top of the Hierarchy pane. Then set its transform to the following:

   _Main Camera   P:[0,0,-10]   R:[0,0,0]   S:[1,1,1].

2. Now set _Main Camera's *Projection* to Orthographic and its *Size* to 10. Then choose a brighter background color to look more like a blue sky. The final settings should look like Figure 29.1.

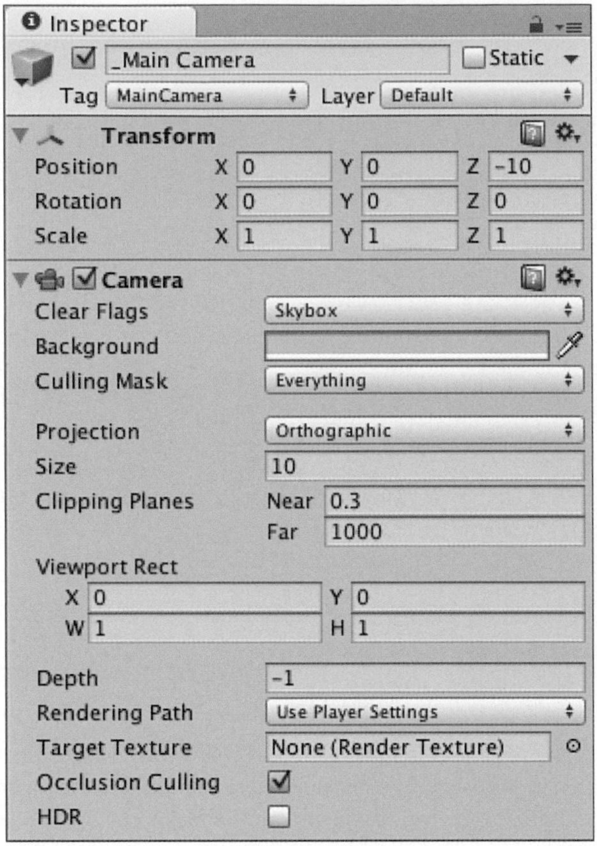

Figure 29.1 _Main Camera settings for Transform and Camera components

3. Though you have used orthographic cameras before, the meaning of the Size setting was never really discussed. In an orthographic projection, Size sets the distance from the center to the bottom of the camera view, so Size is half the height of what the camera is able to see. You can see that illustrated now in the Game pane. Ground is at a y position of -10, and it is perfectly bisected by the bottom of the Game window. Try changing the aspect ratio of the Game pane via the pop-up menu highlighted in Figure 29.2. You will see that no matter what aspect ratio you select, the center of the Ground cube is still positioned perfectly at the bottom of the Game pane. After you've explored this for a while, choose an aspect ratio of 16:9, as shown the figure.

4. Save your scene. Always save your scene.

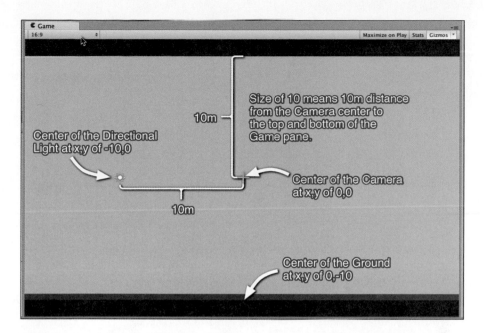

Figure 29.2 Demonstration of the meaning of an orthographic camera size of 10

The Slingshot

We'll make a simple slingshot out of three cylinders:

1. Start by creating an empty GameObject (*GameObject > Create Empty*). Change the GameObject's name to *Slingshot* and set its transform to the following:

   Slingshot (Empty)   P:[0,0,0]   R:[0,0,0]   S:[1,1,1]

2. Create a new cylinder (*GameObject > Create Other > Cylinder*) and change its name to *Base*. Drag it under Slingshot in the Hierarchy, making Slingshot its parent. Click the disclosure triangle next to Slingshot and select Base again. Set Base's transform to the following:

   Base (Cylinder)   P:[0,1,0]   R:[0,0,0]   S:[0.5,1,0.5]

   When modifying the transform of a GameObject like Base that is the child of another GameObject, you're working in *local coordinates*, meaning that the position you're setting is the position of Base *relative to* its parent Slingshot, not the position of Base in global, world coordinates.

3. With Base selected, click the gear icon next to the Capsule Collider component in the Inspector and select *Remove Component* (see Figure 29.3). This will remove the Collider component from Base.

4. Create a new Material named *Mat_Slingshot* and color it a light yellow (or whatever color you want). Drag Mat_Slingshot onto Base to apply the material to the GameObject.

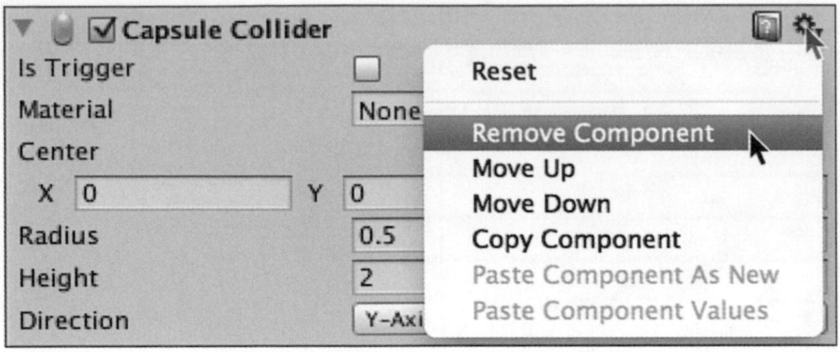

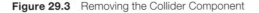

Figure 29.3   Removing the Collider Component

5. Select Base in the Hierarchy pane and duplicate it by pressing Command-D on your key-board (Control+D on Windows machines). By duplicating, you ensure that the new dupli-cate is also a child of Slingshot and retains the Mat_Slingshot material. Change the name of the new duplicate from Base to *LeftArm*. Set the transform of LeftArm to the following:

   LeftArm (Cylinder)   P:[0,3,1]   R:[45,0,0]   S:[0.5,1.414,0.5]

   This makes one of the arms of the slingshot.

6. Select LeftArm in the Hierarchy and duplicate it (Command-D). Rename this instance *RightArm*. Set the transform of RightArm to the following:

   RightArm (Cylinder   P:[0,3,-1]   R:[-45,0,0]   S[0.5,1.414,0.5]

7. Select Slingshot in the Hierarchy. Add a Sphere Collider component to Slingshot (*Component > Physics > Sphere Collider*). Set the Sphere Collider component to the settings shown in Figure 29.4.

8. Make sure to set *Is Trigger* to true (checked). As you might expect, a collider with *Is Trigger = true* is known as a *trigger*. Triggers are part of the physics simulation in Unity and send noti-fications when other colliders or triggers pass through them. However, other objects don't bounce off of triggers as they do normal colliders. We'll use this large spherical trigger to handle the mouse interaction with Slingshot.

9. Set the transform of Slingshot to the following:

   Slingshot (Empty)   P:[-9,-10,0]   R:[0,15,0]   S:[1,1,1]

   This will ground it on the left side of the screen, and the 15° y rotation will give it a bit of dimensionality, even through an orthographic camera.

10. Finally, you need to add a launch point to the slingshot that will give it a specific location from which to shoot the projectiles. Create an empty GameObject (*GameObject > Create Empty*) and name it *LaunchPoint*. Drag LaunchPoint onto Slingshot in the Hierarchy to make Slingshot its parent. Set the transform of LaunchPoint to the following:

   LaunchPoint (Empty)   P:[0,4,0]   R:[0,-15,0]   S:[1,1,1]

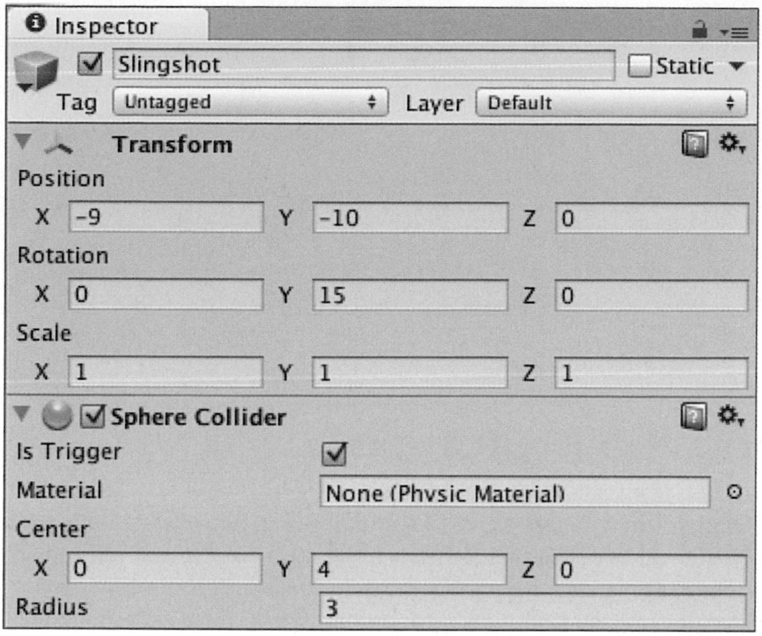

Figure 29.4 Settings for the Sphere Collider component of Slingshot

The -15° y rotation of LaunchPoint in local coordinates causes LaunchPoint to be aligned with the xyz axes in world coordinates. (That is, it removes the 15° rotation that was added to Slingshot.)

11. Save your scene.

Projectile

Next comes the projectile.

1. Create a sphere and name it *Projectile*. Select Projectile in the Hierarchy and attach a Rigidbody component (*Component > Physics > Rigidbody*). This Rigidbody component will allow the projectile to be physically simulated, similar to the Apples in Apple Picker.

2. Create a new material and name it *Mat_Projectile*. Make Mat_Projectile a dark gray color and apply it to Projectile.

3. Drag Projectile from the Hierarchy pane to the Project pane to make it a prefab. Then delete the Projectile instance that remains in the Hierarchy pane.

    Your final Project and Hierarchy panes should look like those shown in Figure 29.5.

4. Save your scene.

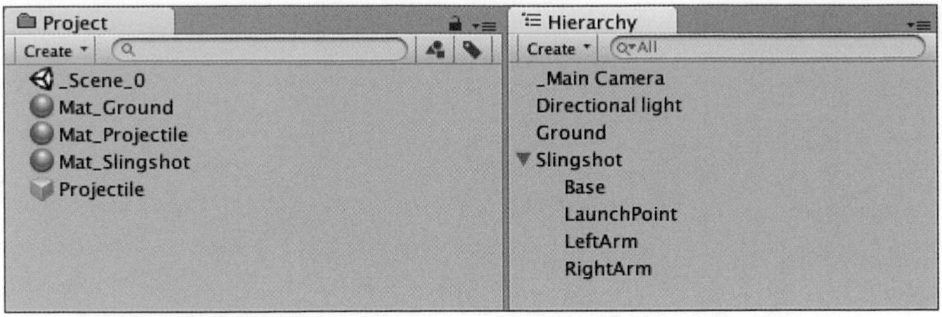

Figure 29.5   Project and Hierarchy panes prior to coding

Coding the Prototype

With the art assets in place, it's time to start adding code to this project. The first script we'll add is one for Slingshot that will cause it to react to mouse input, instantiate a Projectile, and fire that Projectile. This script will be approached in an iterative manner with you adding only small sections of code at a time, testing the code, and then adding a little more. When you start creating your own scripts, this is a fantastic way to approach them: Implement something small and easy to code, test it, implement another small thing, repeat.

Slingshot

Follow these steps to create the Slingshot class:

1. Create a new C# script and name it *Slingshot* (*Assets > Create > C# Script*). Attach it to the Slingshot in the Hierarchy and open the Slingshot C# script in MonoDevelop. Enter the following code:

```
using UnityEngine;
using System.Collections;

public class Slingshot : MonoBehaviour {

    void OnMouseEnter() {
        print("Slingshot:OnMouseEnter()");
    }

    void OnMouseExit() {
        print("Slingshot:OnMouseExit()");
    }

}
```

2. Press Play, and pass the mouse pointer over Slingshot in the Game pane. You'll see that when the mouse enters the Sphere Collider of Slingshot, "Slingshot:OnMouseEnter()"

is output to the Console pane. When the mouse exits the Sphere Collider, "Slingshot:OnMouseExit()" is output. `OnMouseEnter()` and `OnMouseExit()` are functions that work on any collider or trigger.

This is just the first step of the script we'll write to launch Projectiles, but it's important to start with small steps and build progressively.

3. Save your scene.

Showing When the Slingshot Is Active
Next, let's add a highlight to show the player that the slingshot is active:

1. Select LaunchPoint in the Hierarchy. Then add a Halo component to LaunchPoint (*Component > Effects > Halo*). Set the *Size* of the halo to 1 and make the *Color* a light gray to make sure that it's visible (my settings are [r:191,g:191,b:191,a:255]).

2. Now add the following code to the Slingshot C# script. As you can see, this is also a good time to comment out the `print()` statements from the last test:

```csharp
public class Slingshot : MonoBehaviour {
    public GameObject          launchPoint;

    void Awake() {
        Transform launchPointTrans = transform.Find("LaunchPoint");
        launchPoint = launchPointTrans.gameObject;
        launchPoint.SetActive( false );
    }

    void OnMouseEnter() {
        //print("Slingshot:OnMouseEnter()");
        launchPoint.SetActive( true );
    }

    void OnMouseExit() {
        //print("Slingshot:OnMouseExit()");
        launchPoint.SetActive( false );
    }

}
```

Now when you press Play, you'll see that the halo turns on and off, indicating that the player can interact with the slingshot.

The `SetActive()` method on GameObjects like launchPoint tells the game whether or not to ignore them. If a GameObject has active set to false, it will not render on screen, and it will not receive any calls to functions like `Update()` or `OnCollisionEnter()`. This does not destroy the GameObject; it just removes it from being an active part of the game. In the Inspector for a GameObject, the check box at the top of the Inspector just to the left of the GameObject's name indicates whether the GameObject is active (see Figure 29.6).

Components have a similar check box. This sets whether a component is enabled. For most components (for example, Renderer and Collider) this can also be set in code (e.g., `Renderer.enabled = false`), but for some reason, Halo is not an accessible component in Unity, meaning that we can't affect a Halo component from C#. Every once in a while, you will encounter an inconsistency like this, and you need to find a workaround. In this case, we can't disable the halo, so instead we deactivate the GameObject that contains it.

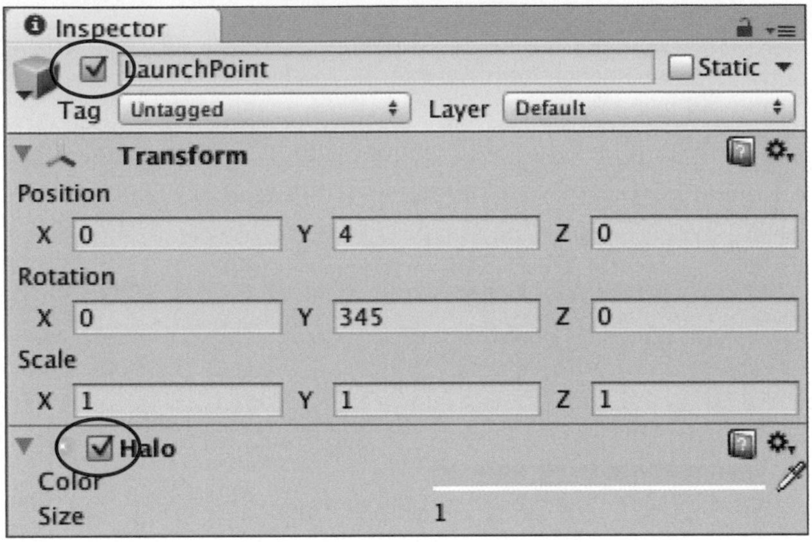

Figure 29.6   The GameObject active check box and the component enabled check box.

3. Save your scene.

Instantiating a Projectile
The next step is to instantiate the Projectile when mouse button 0 is pressed.

> ## warning
>
> **DON'T CHANGE ONMOUSEENTER() OR ONMOUSEEXIT()!!!**   This was mentioned in the previous chapter, but is repeated here just in case.
>
> In the following code listing for Slingshot, `OnMouseEnter()` and `OnMouseExit()` contain an ellipsis between braces: {...}. As we write more and more complicated games, the scripts are going to get longer and longer. Whenever you see the name of a preexisting function followed by {...}, this indicates that all the code from the previous listing is to remain unchanged between those braces. In this example, `OnMouseEnter()` and `OnMouseExit()` should still remain:

```
void OnMouseEnter() {
    //print("Slingshot:OnMouseEnter()");
    launchPoint.SetActive( true );
}

void OnMouseExit() {
    //print("Slingshot:OnMouseExit()");
    launchPoint.SetActive( false );
}
```

Be sure to watch for these. Anywhere that you see ellipses in code, it means that I've used them to help shorten the code listings in this book and eliminate things you've already typed. {...} is **not** actual C# code.

1. Add the following code to Slingshot:

```
public class Slingshot : MonoBehaviour {
    // fields set in the Unity Inspector pane
    public GameObject        prefabProjectile;
    public bool                                    _____;
    // fields set dynamically
    public GameObject        launchPoint;
    public Vector3           launchPos;
    public GameObject        projectile;
    public bool              aimingMode;


    void Awake() {
        Transform launchPointTrans = transform.FindChild("LaunchPoint");
        launchPoint = launchPointTrans.gameObject;
        launchPoint.SetActive( false );
        launchPos = launchPointTrans.position;
    }

    void OnMouseEnter() {...}    // Do not change OnMouseEnter()

    void OnMouseExit() {...}     // Do not change OnMouseExit()

    void OnMouseDown() {
        // The player has pressed the mouse button while over Slingshot
        aimingMode = true;
        // Instantiate a Projectile
        projectile = Instantiate( prefabProjectile ) as GameObject;
        // Start it at the launchPoint
```

```
        projectile.transform.position = launchPos;
        // Set it to isKinematic for now
        projectile.rigidbody.isKinematic = true;
    }
}
```

The first thing to note here are all the additional fields (that is, variables) at the top of the Slingshot class. One public bool has a name that looks particularly strange: _____. This is a variable that is to be used for a very specific purpose: the division of the Slingshot script component in the Inspector into fields that are meant to be set in the Inspector and fields that will be set dynamically by your code once the game is running. In this example, prefabProjectile (a reference to the prefab for all the Projectiles) must be set in the Unity Inspector before running the game, whereas all the other variables are meant to be set dynamically. Because the Unity Inspector sorts serialized public fields by the order in which they're declared, the underline bool variable will appear in the Inspector as a divider between these preset and dynamic public variables.

The other new fields are much more self-explanatory: launchPos stores the 3D world position of launchPoint, and projectile is a reference to the new Projectile instance that is created. mouseActive is normally false, but is set to true when mouse button 0 has been pressed down over Slingshot. This is a state variable that lets the rest of the code know how to behave. In the next section, we'll be writing code for Slingshot's Update() that only runs when mouseActive == true.

In Awake(), we've added a single line to set launchPos.

The OnMouseDown() method contains the bulk of changes for this listing. OnMouseDown() will only be called when the player presses the mouse button down over the Collider component of the Slingshot GameObject, so this method can only be called if the mouse is in a valid start position. An instance of prefabProjectile is created and assigned to projectile. Then projectile is placed at the launchPos location. Finally, isKinematic on Projectile's Rigidbody is set to true. When a Rigidbody is kinematic, it is not moved automatically by physics but is still part of the simulation (meaning that a kinematic Rigidbody will not move as a result of a collision or gravity but can still cause other nonkinematic Rigidbodies to move).

2. Before you press Play, select Slingshot in the Hierarchy pane and set *prefabProjectile* to be the Projectile prefab in the Project pane (either by clicking the target to the right of prefab-Projectile in the Inspector or by dragging the Projectile prefab from the Project pane onto the prefabProjectile in the Inspector).

3. Press Play, move your mouse pointer inside the active area for the Slingshot, and click. You will see the Projectile field instance appear.

4. Now let's make it do more. Add the following field and Update() method to the class Slingshot:

```
public GameObject       prefabProjectile;
public float            velocityMult = 4f;
public bool             _____;
```

…   // As you see from the ellipses, some lines are skipped here

```
void Update() {
    // If Slingshot is not in aimingMode, don't run this code
    if (!aimingMode) return;
    // Get the current mouse position in 2D screen coordinates
    Vector3 mousePos2D = Input.mousePosition;
    // Convert the mouse position to 3D world coordinates
    mousePos2D.z = -Camera.main.transform.position.z;
    Vector3 mousePos3D = Camera.main.ScreenToWorldPoint( mousePos2D );
    // Find the delta from the launchPos to the mousePos3D
    Vector3 mouseDelta = mousePos3D-launchPos;
    // Limit mouseDelta to the radius of the Slingshot SphereCollider
    float maxMagnitude = this.GetComponent<SphereCollider>().radius;
    if (mouseDelta.magnitude > maxMagnitude) {
        mouseDelta.Normalize();
        mouseDelta *= maxMagnitude;
    }
    // Move the projectile to this new position
    Vector3 projPos = launchPos + mouseDelta;
    projectile.transform.position = projPos;

    if ( Input.GetMouseButtonUp(0) ) {
        // The mouse has been released
        aimingMode = false;
        projectile.rigidbody.isKinematic = false;
        projectile.rigidbody.velocity = -mouseDelta * velocityMult;
        projectile = null;
    }
}
```

Most of this is explained in the in-line comments; however, a little vector math bears closer examination (see Figure 29.7).

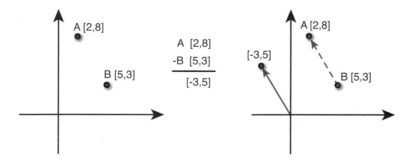

Figure 29.7 Two-dimensional vector subtraction

As you can see in Figure 29.7, vectors are added and subtracted one component at a time. The figure is two dimensional, but the same methods work for 3D. The x components of the vectors A and B are subtracted as are the y components, making a new Vector2 defined as Vector2(2-5, 8-3), which becomes Vector2(-3, 5). The figure illustrates that A-B gives us the vector distance between A and B, which is also the distance and direction that one must move to get from point B to point A. A mnemonic to remember which one the vector will point at is AMBLAA, "A Minus B Looks At A."

This is important in the `Update()` method because Projectile needs to be positioned along the vector from `launchPos` to the current `mousePos3D`, and this vector is named `mouseDelta`. However, the distance that the Projectile can move along `mouseDelta` is limited to `maxMagnitude`, which is the radius of the SphereCollider on Slingshot (currently set to 3m in the Inspector for the Collider component).

If `mouseDelta` is longer than `maxMagnitude`, its magnitude is clamped to `max Magnitude`. This is accomplished by first calling `mouseDelta.Normalize()` (which sets the length of `mouseDelta` to 1 but keeps it pointing in the same direction) and then multiplying `mouseDelta` by `maxMagnitude`.

`projectile` is moved to this new position, and if you play the game, you will see that the Projectile moves with the mouse but is limited to a specific radius.

`Input.GetMouseButtonUp(0)` will return true only on the *first frame* that the left mouse button has been released. That means that the `if` statement at the end of `Update()` is executed on the frame that the mouse button is released. On this frame, `aimingMode` is set to false. `projectile`'s Rigidbody is set to nonkinematic, allowing it to once again respond to gravity. `projectile` is given a velocity that is proportional to the distance that it is from `launchPos`. Finally, `projectile` is set back to `null`. This doesn't delete the Projectile instance that was created, it just opens the field `projectile` to be filled by another instance when the slingshot is fired again.

5.   Press Play and see how the Slingshot feels. Is the Projectile instance launching at a good velocity? Try adjusting `velocityMult` in the Inspector to see what value feels right to you. I ended up with a value of 10.

   As it is now, the Projectile instance flies off screen very quickly. Let's make a follow camera to chase after the Projectile as it flies.

6.   Save your scene.

Making a Follow Camera

We need _Main Camera to follow the Projectile when launched, but the behavior is a little more complicated than that. The full behavior should be as follows:

1.   The camera sits at an initial position and doesn't move during Slingshot's aimingMode.

2.   Once a Projectile is launched, the camera follows it (with a little easing to make it feel smoother).

3.   As the camera moves up into the air, increase the Camera.orthographicSize to keep Ground in view.

4. When the Projectile comes to rest, the camera stops following it and returns to the initial position.

Follow these steps:

1. Start by creating a new C# script and naming it *FollowCam* (*Assets > Create > C# Script*). Drag the FollowCam Script onto _Main Camera in the Inspector to make it a component of _Main Camera.

2. Now double-click the FollowCam script to open it and input the following code:

```csharp
using UnityEngine;
using System.Collections;

public class FollowCam : MonoBehaviour {
    static public FollowCam  S; // a FollowCam Singleton

    // fields set in the Unity Inspector pane
    public bool            _____;

    // fields set dynamically
    public GameObject      poi; // The point of interest
    public float           camZ; // The desired Z pos of the camera

    void Awake() {
        S = this;
        camZ = this.transform.position.z;
    }

    void Update () {
        // if there's only one line following an if, it doesn't need braces
        if (poi == null) return; // return if there is no poi

        // Get the position of the poi
        Vector3 destination = poi.transform.position;
        // Retain a destination.z of camZ
        destination.z = camZ;
        // Set the camera to the destination
        transform.position = destination;
    }
}
```

The first thing you'll notice at the top of the code listing is the `FollowCam` singleton `S`. As covered in the "Software Design Patterns" section of Appendix B, "Useful Concepts," a *singleton* is a design pattern that is used when there will be only one instance of a specific class in the game. Because there is only a single camera in Mission Demolition, it is a good candidate for a singleton. As a public static variable, the singleton `S` can be accessed anywhere in the code of the game as `FollowCam.S`, allowing us to set the public `poi` field from anywhere by setting `FollowCam.S.poi`.

The next thing that you'll notice is that there are no fields in this class that are meant to be set in the Inspector. That will change shortly.

The remaining two fields are `poi`, which holds the GameObject that the camera will follow, and `camZ`, which holds the initial z position of the camera.

In `Update()`, the camera is moved to the position of the poi except for the z coordinate, which is set to `camZ` every frame. (This prevents the camera from being so close to `poi` that `poi` becomes invisible.)

3. Open the Slingshot C# script and add the single bold line from the following code listing between the other two lines near the end of `Update()`:

```
projectile.rigidbody.velocity = -mouseDelta * velocityMult;
FollowCam.S.poi = projectile;
projectile = null;
```

This line uses the `FollowCam.S` singleton to set the value of `poi` for the camera. The new `poi` will be the newly fired Projectile. Try pressing Play and see how it looks.

You should notice a few issues:

A. If you zoom out the Scene pane view enough, you'll see that the Projectile actually flies past the end of Ground.

B. If you fire at Ground, you'll see that the Projectile neither bounces nor stops once it has hit Ground. If you pause right after firing, select the Projectile in the Hierarchy, and then unpause, you'll see that it rolls upon hitting Ground and never stops rolling.

C. When the Projectile is first launched, the camera jumps to the position of the Projectile, which is visually jarring.

D Once the Projectile is at a certain height, all you see is sky, so it's difficult to tell how high up the Projectile is.

Each of these issues will be fixed in order by taking the following steps (which are generally ordered from the easiest fix to the most difficult).

1. First, fix issue A by setting the transform of Ground to P:[100,-10,0] R:[0,0,0] S:[400,1,1]. This will make Ground extend much farther to the right.

2. To fix issue B, both Rigidbody constraints and a *Physic Material* need to be added to Projectile. Select the Projectile prefab in the Project pane. In the Rigidbody component, click the disclosure triangle next to Constraints and check *Freeze Position* z and *Freeze Rotation* x, y, & z. Freeze Position z will keep the projectile from moving toward or away from the camera (basically keeping it in the same z depth as both the ground and the castle that will be added later). Freeze Rotation x, y, & z will keep it from rolling around.

   While here, you should also set the pop-up menu for *Collision Detection* to Continuous. For information about the types of collision detection, click the help icon in the top-right corner of the Rigidbody component. In short, *continuous* collision detection takes more processor power than *discrete*, but it is more accurate for fast-moving objects like the Projectiles. Press Play and try launching a Projectile again.

3. These Rigidbody settings keep the Projectile from rolling endlessly, but it still doesn't feel right. You've spent your whole life experiencing physics, and that gives you an intuitive feel for the kinds of behaviors that feel like natural, real-world physics. This is true for your players as well, which means that even though physics is a complex system that requires a lot of math to model, if you make your game physics feel like the physics that players are used to, you won't have to explain that math to them.

    Adding a Physic Material can make your physically simulated objects feel a lot more realistic. From the menu bar, choose *Assets > Create > Physic Material*. Name this Physic material *PMat_Projectile*. Click PMat_Projectile and set the *bounciness* to 1 in the Inspector. Then drag PMat_Projectile in the Project pane onto the Projectile prefab (also in the Project pane) to apply it to Projectile.SphereCollider. Selecting Projectile should reveal that PMat_Projectile has been assigned as the *material* of the Sphere Collider in the Inspector. Now when you press Play, you'll see that the projectile bounces to a stop instead of just gliding along the ground.

4. Issue C will be fixed via two means: easing through interpolation and limits on the camera's location. To start with easing, add the following bolded lines to FollowCam:

```
// fields set in the Unity Inspector pane
public float            easing = 0.05f;
public bool             _____;
...
    Vector3 destination = poi.transform.position;
    // Interpolate from the current Camera position toward destination
    destination = Vector3.Lerp(transform.position, destination, easing);
    // Retain a destination.z of camZ
```

    The `Vector3.Lerp()` method interpolates between two points, returning a weighted average of the two. If `easing` is 0, `Lerp()` will return the first point (`transform.position`); if `easing` is 1, `Lerp()` will return the second point (`destination`). If `easing` is any value in between 0 and 1, it will return a point between the two (with an easing of 0.5 returning the midpoint between the two). By setting `easing = 0.05`, we are telling Unity to move the camera about 5% of the way from its current location to the location of the `poi` every frame. Because the `poi` is constantly moving, this gives us a nice smooth camera follow movement. Try playing with the value of easing to see how it affects the camera movement. This kind of use of `Lerp` is a very simplistic, non-time-based form of linear interpolation. For more information on linear interpolation, you can read about it in Appendix B.

5. You might now notice a little glitching and jerkiness in the movement of the camera even with this easing. That is happening because the physics simulation is updating at a rate of 50fps while `Update()` is being called at the highest framerate possible. On a fast machine, this means that the camera will update many more times per second than the physics, causing the camera to catch up to the Projectile over several `Updates()` before the Projectile has a chance to move. To fix this, change the name of the `Update()` method to `FixedUpdate()`. Unlike an `Update()`, which happens every frame, a `FixedUpdate()` happens every frame of the physics simulation (or exactly 50fps) regardless of computer speed. Making this change should smooth out the jerkiness in FollowCam.

6. Now, add some limits to the FollowCam position:

```
// fields set in the Unity Inspector pane
public float           easing = 0.05f;
public Vector2         minXY;
public bool                                          ;
...
    Vector3 destination = poi.transform.position;
    // Limit the X & Y to minimum values
    destination.x = Mathf.Max( minXY.x, destination.x );
    destination.y = Mathf.Max( minXY.y, destination.y );
    // Interpolate from the current Camera position toward destination
```

The default value of Vector2 `minXY` is [0,0], which works perfectly for our needs. The `Mathf.Max()` chooses the maximum value of the two passed in. When the projectile is initially launched, its x and y coordinates are both negative, so the `Mathf.Max()` ensures that the camera never moves into negative territory along either the x or y axes. This also keeps the camera from dipping below the ground when the projectile lands.

7. Issue D is fixed by dynamically adjusting the `orthographicSize` of the camera. Add the following bolded lines to the FollowCam script:

```
    transform.position = destination;
    // Set the orthographicSize of the Camera to keep Ground in view
    this.camera.orthographicSize = destination.y + 10;
}
```

This works because we know that the destination.y will never be allowed to be less than 0. So, the minimum `orthographicSize` is 10, and the camera's `orthographicSize` will expand as needed to always keep the ground in view. Double-click Ground in the Hierarchy to zoom out and show the whole thing in the Scene pane. Then select _Main Camera, press Play, and launch a Projectile. In the Scene pane, you will see the field of view of the camera expand smoothly as the Projectile flies.

8. Save your scene.

Vection and a Sense of Speed

The FollowCam moves pretty well now, but it's still difficult to tell how fast the Projectile is moving, especially when it's high in the air. To fix this issue, we're going to take advantage of the concept of *vection*. Vection is the sensation of movement that you get from seeing other things passing by quickly, and it is the concept that led to *parallax scrolling* in 2D video games. Parallax scrolling causes foreground objects to pass by quickly while background objects move more slowly relative to the movement of the main camera in a 2D game. While a full paral-lax system is beyond the scope of this tutorial, it is possible to at least get a simple feeling of vection by creating a lot of clouds and distributing them randomly through the sky. As the Projectile passes by them, the player will have more of a feeling of movement.

Making Cloud Art

To make this work, you're going to need to make some simple clouds:

1. Start by creating a new sphere (*GameObject > Create Other > Sphere*). Hover your mouse over the name of the Sphere Collider component in the Inspector for the sphere. Right-click and choose *Remove Component* from the pop-up menu. Set the Transform.Position of the Sphere to [0,0,0] so that it is visible in the Game pane as well as the Scene pane. Rename Sphere to *CloudSphere*.

2. Create a new material and name it *Mat_Cloud* (*Assets > Create > Material*). Drag Mat_Cloud onto CloudSphere and then select Mat_Cloud in the Project pane. From the pop-up menu next to *Shader* in the Inspector, choose *Self-Illumin > Diffuse*. This shader is self-illuminating (it generates its own light), and it also responds to the directional light in the scene. Click the color swatch next to *Main Color* in the Inspector for Mat_Cloud and set it to a gray of 65% (or RGBA of [166,166,166,255] in the Unity color picker). This should give CloudSphere just a little gray on the bottom-left side in the Game pane, which looks a bit like a cloud in the sun.

3. Drag CloudSphere to the Project pane to make it a prefab, and then drag several instances of CloudSphere into the Hierarchy pane and position and scale them to make an object the looks a bit like a cloud. Create an empty GameObject (*GameObject > Create Empty*), rename it *Cloud_0*, and set its transform to P:[0,0,0], R:[0,0,0], S:[1,1,1]. Make Cloud_0 the parent of the CloudSphere group (by dragging them all underneath it in the Hierarchy). Try to make sure that the CloudSpheres are grouped around the Cloud_0 parent. Each CloudSphere's position in the Inspector should be between -2 and 2 in each dimension (x, y, & z). Drag Cloud_0 to the Project pane to make a prefab. Then delete the remaining Cloud_0 instance from the Hierarchy.

4. Click on Cloud_0 in the Project pane and duplicate it by pressing Command-D (Control+D on Windows). The duplicate will automatically be named *Cloud_1*. Drag Cloud_1 into the Hierarchy to place an instance of it into the Scene pane. Choose each of the CloudSpheres in Cloud_1 and scale and reposition them as you wish to make a different-looking cloud. When you're satisfied, select Cloud_1 in the Hierarchy, click the *Apply* button (to the right of the word *Prefab* at the top of the Inspector for Cloud_1). This will apply the changes you made back to the Cloud_1 prefab.

5. Repeat this duplication, modification, and application process to create a total of five different clouds named Cloud_0 through Cloud_4. You can make as many clouds as you would like, but five will be sufficient for our purposes. When finished, if you add an instance of each cloud to the Hierarchy, it should look something like Figure 29.8.

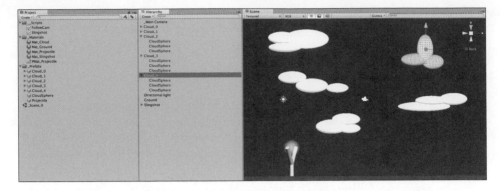

Figure 29.8 An example image of the hierarchical Cloud_#s composed of CloudSpheres

6. You can also see in Figure 29.8 that I've added folders to organize my Project pane. I usually do this at the very beginning of a project but have waited this time so that you could experience how much better the project feels once it's organized. Create a folder by choosing *Assets > Create > Folder* from the menu bar. The folders I've created are named *__Scripts*, *_Materials*, and *_Prefabs*. The underscores in their names help sort them above any non-foldered assets, and the double-underscore of the *__Scripts* folder ensures that it is the top folder in the Project pane. After you have created these folders, drag the proper assets into them in the Project pane. This will simultaneously create folders on your hard drive inside the Assets folder for your project, so not only your Project pane but also your Assets folder will be organized.

7. Now, delete the instances of Cloud_#s in the Hierarchy pane. Create a new empty GameObject named *CloudAnchor* (*GameObject > Create Empty*). This will give us a GameObject to act as the parent for all Cloud_#s, which will keep the Hierarchy tidy while the game is running.

8. Create a new C# script titled *CloudCrafter*. Drag CloudCrafter into the *__Scripts* folder and also drag it onto *_Main Camera*. This will add a second Script component to _Main Camera, which is perfectly fine in Unity so long as the two scripts don't conflict with each other (e.g., so long as they don't both try to set the position of the GameObject each frame). Because FollowCam is moving the camera, and CloudCrafter will just be placing Cloud_#s in the air, they shouldn't conflict at all. Enter the following code into CloudCrafter:

```
using UnityEngine;
using System.Collections;

public class CloudCrafter : MonoBehaviour {
    // fields set in the Unity Inspector pane
    public int          numClouds = 40;       // The # of clouds to make
    public GameObject[] cloudPrefabs;         // The prefabs for the clouds
    public Vector3      cloudPosMin;          // Min position of each cloud
    public Vector3      cloudPosMax;          // Max position of each cloud
    public float        cloudScaleMin = 1;    // Min scale of each cloud
```

```csharp
public float          cloudScaleMax = 5;      // Max scale of each cloud
public float          cloudSpeedMult = 0.5f; // Adjusts speed of clouds

public bool           _____;

// fields set dynamically
public GameObject[]    cloudInstances;

void Awake() {
    // Make an array large enough to hold all the Cloud_ instances
    cloudInstances = new GameObject[numClouds];
    // Find the CloudAnchor parent GameObject
    GameObject anchor = GameObject.Find("CloudAnchor");
    // Iterate through and make Cloud_s
    GameObject cloud;
    for (int i=0; i<numClouds; i++) {
        // Pick an int between 0 and cloudPrefabs.Length-1
        // Random.Range will not ever pick as high as the top number
        int prefabNum = Random.Range(0,cloudPrefabs.Length);
        // Make an instance
        cloud = Instantiate( cloudPrefabs[prefabNum] ) as GameObject;
        // Position cloud
        Vector3 cPos = Vector3.zero;
        cPos.x = Random.Range( cloudPosMin.x, cloudPosMax.x );
        cPos.y = Random.Range( cloudPosMin.y, cloudPosMax.y );
        // Scale cloud
        float scaleU = Random.value;
        float scaleVal = Mathf.Lerp( cloudScaleMin, cloudScaleMax, scaleU );
        // Smaller clouds (with smaller scaleU) should be nearer the ground)
        cPos.y = Mathf.Lerp( cloudPosMin.y, cPos.y, scaleU );
        // Smaller clouds should be further away
        cPos.z = 100 - 90*scaleU;
        // Apply these transforms to the cloud
        cloud.transform.position = cPos;
        cloud.transform.localScale = Vector3.one * scaleVal;
        // Make cloud a child of the anchor
        cloud.transform.parent = anchor.transform;
        // Add the cloud to cloudInstances
        cloudInstances[i] = cloud;
    }
}

void Update() {
    // Iterate over each cloud that was created
    foreach (GameObject cloud in cloudInstances) {
        // Get the cloud scale and position
```

```
        float scaleVal = cloud.transform.localScale.x;
        Vector3 cPos = cloud.transform.position;
        // Move larger clouds faster
        cPos.x -= scaleVal * Time.deltaTime * cloudSpeedMult;
        // If a cloud has moved too far to the left…
        if (cPos.x <= cloudPosMin.x) {
            // Move it to the far right
            cPos.x = cloudPosMax.x;
        }
        // Apply the new position to cloud
        cloud.transform.position = cPos;
    }
  }
}
```

There are several fields here that must be set in the Inspector. They should be set to the values shown in Figure 29.9. To set `cloudPrefabs`, click the disclosure triangle next to the variable name *Cloud Prefabs* and enter 5 for the *Size*. Then drag each numbered Cloud_ prefab from the Project pane into the five *Element* slots of `cloudPrefabs`.

9. Save your scene.

In the CloudCrafter class, the `Awake()` method creates all the clouds and positions them. The `Update()` method moves each cloud a little to the left every frame. When a cloud moves to the left past cloudPosMin.x, it is moved to cloudPosMax.x on the far right. Zoom out in the Scene pane and watch the clouds blow by. Now when you launch a Projectile, the vection of the clouds passing by should make it feel much more like the projectile is actually moving.

Building the Castle

Mission Demolition needs something to demolish, so let's build a castle to serve that purpose. Figure 29.11 shows what the final castle should look like.

1. Adjust the Scene pane so that you are viewing the scene from the back in isometric view by clicking the arrow on the axes gizmo opposite the z-axis (see Figure 29.10).

2. Now, double click _Main Camera in the Hierarchy to zoom the Scene pane to a good view from which to build the castle.

3. Create an empty GameObject to be the root node of the castle (*GameObject > Create Empty*). Name it *Castle* and set its transform to P:[0,-9.5,0] R:[0,0,0] S:[1,1,1]. This will position it well for construction and put its base resting exactly on top of Ground.

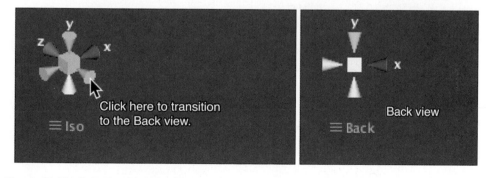

▼ G ✓ **Cloud Crafter (Script)**		□ ✿,
Script	G CloudCrafter	⊙
Num Clouds	40	
▼ Cloud Prefabs		
Size	5	
Element 0	Cloud_0	⊙
Element 1	Cloud_1	⊙
Element 2	Cloud_2	⊙
Element 3	Cloud_3	⊙
Element 4	Cloud_4	⊙
▼ Cloud Pos Min		
X	−50	
Y	−5	
Z	10	
▼ Cloud Pos Max		
X	150	
Y	100	
Z	10	
Cloud Scale Min	1	
Cloud Scale Max	5	
Cloud Speed Mult	0.5	
-------------------------	□	
▶ Cloud Instances		

Figure 29.9 The settings for the CloudCrafter Script component

Figure 29.10 Selecting the Back view

4. Make the vertical walls of the castle:

   4.1. Create a new cube (*GameObject > Create Other > Cube*) and rename it *Wall_Stone*.

   4.2. Drag it onto Castle in the Hierarchy to make it a child of Castle.

4.3. Add a Rigidbody component to Wall_Stone (*Component > Physics > Rigidbody*). Use the Inspector to constrain the z position of the Wall_Stone by setting Rigidbody.FreezePosition.z to true. Set the Rigidbody.mass to 4.

4.4. Set the Wall_Stone Transform to P:[-2,2,0] R:[0,0,0] S:[1,4,1].

4.5. Drag Wall_Stone to the Project pane to make it a prefab (be sure to put it in the _Prefabs folder).

4.6. Make three duplicates of Wall_Stone in the Hierarchy and set their x positions to -6, 2, and 6. This will form the 4 vertical walls of the first floor of the castle.

5. Make the horizontal walls that form the ceiling of the first floor.

5.1. Create another cube and name it *Wall_Stone_H* (for "Horizontal").

5.2. Make Wall_Stone_H a child of Castle and set its transform to P:[0,4.25,0] R:[0,0,0] S:[4,0.5,1].

5.3. Add a Rigidbody component to Wall_Stone_H (*Component > Physics > Rigidbody*). Constrain the z position of the Wall_Stone_H by setting Rigidbody.FreezePosition.z to true. Set the Rigidbody.mass to 4.

5.4. Make Wall_Stone_H a prefab and place it in the _Prefabs folder.

5.5. Make two duplicates of Wall_Stone_H in the Hierarchy with x positions of -4 and 4.

6. To make the second floor of the castle, use your mouse to select three adjacent Wall_Stones of the first floor and the two Wall_Stone_Hs above them. Duplicate them (Command-D or Control+D) and move them to be resting above the others. You will need to tweak their positions, and the final positions for the new Walls should be as follows:

Wall_Stone	P:[-4,6.5,0]
Wall_Stone	P:[0,6.5,0]
Wall_Stone	P:[4,6.5,0]
Wall_Stone_H	P:[-2,8.75,0]
Wall_Stone_H	P:[2,8.75,0]

7. Continue the duplication trick to make the third floor by adding three more vertical walls and one more horizontal wall:

Wall_Stone	P:[-2,11,0]
Wall_Stone	P:[2,11,0]
Wall_Stone	P:[0,15.5,0]
Wall_Stone_H	P:[0,13.25,0]

8. The final GameObject to add to Castle is a goal for the player to hit with the Projectile.

8.1. Create a cube, name it *Goal*, make it a child of Castle, and set its transform to P:[0,2,0] R:[0,0,0] S:[3,4,4].

8.2. Create a new material named *Mat_Goal*. Drag Mat_Goal onto Goal to apply it. Select Mat_Goal in the Project pane and choose the *Transparent > Diffuse* shader. Then set the color to a bright green with an opacity of 25% (an RGBA in the Unity color picker of [0,255,0,64]).

8.3. Select Goal in the Hierarchy and set BoxCollider.isTrigger to true.

8.4. Drag Goal into the _Prefabs folder in the Project pane to make it a prefab.

9. One of the major advantages of building a castle out of prefabs like this is that we can easily make changes to every Wall_Stone_H if we want. Select the Wall_Stone_H prefab in the Project pane and set its scale.x to 3.5 in the Transform Inspector. Every Wall_Stone_H in your castle should reflect this change. Your finished castle should look like Figure 29.11.

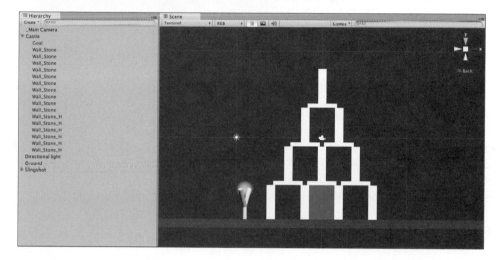

Figure 29.11 The finished castle

10. Set the position of Castle to P:[50,-9.5,0]. And press Play. You may have to try and restart a couple times, but you should be able to hit Castle with a Projectile.

If you want, you can also add a material to the walls to make them something other than just solid white.

11. Save your scene.

Returning for Another Shot

Now that there's a castle to knock down, it's time to add a little more game logic. Once the Projectile has settled, the camera should move back to focus on Slingshot again:

1. Before doing anything else, you should add a tag of *Projectile* to the Projectile prefab. Select the Projectile prefab in the Project pane. In the Inspector, click the pop-up menu next to Tag and choose *Add Tag*. Click the disclosure triangle next to Tags and enter *Projectile* into *Element 0*. Click Projectile in the Project pane again. Give it a tag by selecting *Projectile* from the updated list of tags in the Inspector.

2. Open the FollowCam C# script in MonoDevelop and modify the following lines:

```
void FixedUpdate () {
    Vector3 destination;
    // If there is no poi, return to P:[0,0,0]
    if (poi == null) {
        destination = Vector3.zero;
    } else {
        // Get the position of the poi
        destination = poi.transform.position;
        // If poi is a Projectile, check to see if it's at rest
        if (poi.tag == "Projectile") {
            // if it is sleeping (that is, not moving)
            if ( poi.rigidbody.IsSleeping() ) {
                // return to default view
                poi = null;
                // in the next update
                return;
            }
        }
    }
    // Limit the X & Y to minimum values
    …
    this.camera.orthographicSize = destination.y + 10;
}
```

Now, once a Projectile has stopped moving (which makes `Rigidbody.IsSleeping()` true), the FollowCam will nullify its `poi`, resetting the camera back to its default position.

3. Save your scene.

Adding a Projectile Trail

While Unity does have a built-in Trail Renderer effect, it won't really serve our purpose because we need more control over the trail than it allows. Instead, we'll make use of the Line Renderer Component upon which the Trail Renderer is built:

1. Start by creating an empty GameObject (*GameObject > Create Empty*) and naming it *ProjectileLine*. Add a Line Renderer component (*Components > Effects > Line Renderer*). In the Line Renderer Inspector for ProjectileLine, expand the disclosure triangles for *Materials* and *Parameters*. Set them to the settings shown in Figure 29.12.

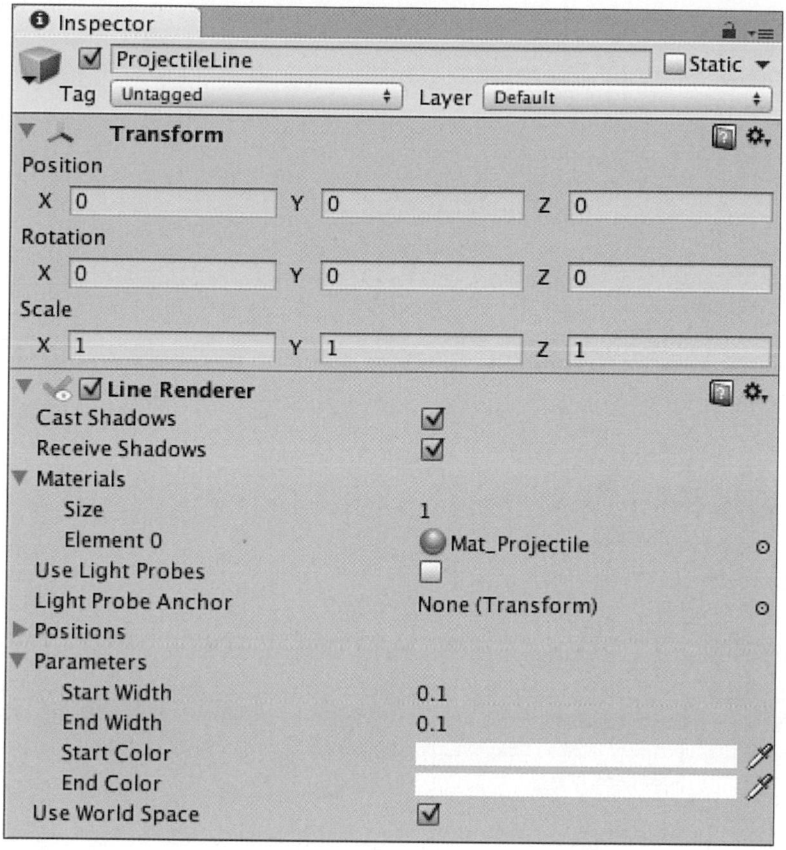

Figure 29.12   Settings for ProjectLine

2. Create a C# script (*Asset > Create > C# Script*), name it *ProjectileLine*, and attach it to the
   ProjectileLine GameObject. Open the ProjectileLine script in MonoDevelop and write the
   following code:

```
using UnityEngine;
using System.Collections;
// Remember, the following line is needed to use Lists
using System.Collections.Generic;

public class ProjectileLine : MonoBehaviour {
    static public ProjectileLine S; // Singleton

    // fields set in the Unity Inspector pane
    public float          minDist = 0.1f;
    public bool                                           ;
```

```
// fields set dynamically
public LineRenderer     line;
private GameObject      _poi;
public List<Vector3>    points;

void Awake() {
    S = this; // Set the singleton
    // Get a reference to the LineRenderer
    line = GetComponent<LineRenderer>();
    // Disable the LineRenderer until it's needed
    line.enabled = false;
    // Initialize the points List
    points = new List<Vector3>();
}

// This is a property (that is, a method masquerading as a field)
public GameObject poi {
    get {
        return( _poi );
    }
    set {
        _poi = value;
        if ( _poi != null ) {
            // When _poi is set to something new, it resets everything
            line.enabled = false;
            points = new List<Vector3>();
            AddPoint();
        }
    }
}

// This can be used to clear the line directly
public void Clear() {
    _poi = null;
    line.enabled = false;
    points = new List<Vector3>();
}

public void AddPoint() {
    // This is called to add a point to the line
    Vector3 pt = _poi.transform.position;
    if ( points.Count > 0 && (pt - lastPoint).magnitude < minDist ) {
        // If the point isn't far enough from the last point, it returns
        return;
    }
```

```
        if ( points.Count == 0 ) {
            // If this is the launch point…
            Vector3 launchPos = Slingshot.S.launchPoint.transform.position;
            Vector3 launchPosDiff = pt - launchPos;
            // …it adds an extra bit of line to aid aiming later
            points.Add( pt + launchPosDiff );
            points.Add(pt);
            line.SetVertexCount(2);
            // Sets the first two points
            line.SetPosition(0, points[0] );
            line.SetPosition(1, points[1] );
            // Enables the LineRenderer
            line.enabled = true;
        } else {
            // Normal behavior of adding a point
            points.Add( pt );
            line.SetVertexCount( points.Count );
            line.SetPosition( points.Count-1, lastPoint );
            line.enabled = true;
        }
    }


    // Returns the location of the most recently added point
    public Vector3 lastPoint {
        get {
            if (points == null) {
                // If there are no points, returns Vector3.zero
                return( Vector3.zero );
            }
            return( points[points.Count-1] );
        }
    }


    void FixedUpdate () {
        if ( poi == null ) {
            // If there is no poi, search for one
            if (FollowCam.S.poi != null) {
                if (FollowCam.S.poi.tag == "Projectile") {
                    poi = FollowCam.S.poi;
                } else {
                    return; // Return if we didn't find a poi
                }
            } else {
                return; // Return if we didn't find a poi
            }
        }
```

```
            // If there is a poi, it's loc is added every FixedUpdate
            AddPoint();
            if ( poi.rigidbody.IsSleeping() ) {
                // Once the poi is sleeping, it is cleared
                poi = null;
            }
        }
    }
}
```

3. You will also need to add a singleton to the Slingshot C# script. This will allow `AddPoint()` to reference the location of Slingshot's launchPoint:

```
public class Slingshot : MonoBehaviour {
    static public Slingshot    S;

    // fields set in the Unity Inspector pane
    ...
    void Awake() {
        // Set the Slingshot singleton S
        S = this;

        Transform launchPointTrans = transform.FindChild("LaunchPoint");
```

Now when you play the game, you should get a nice gray line that traces the path of the Projectile as it moves. The line is replaced with each subsequent shot.

4. Save your scene.

Hitting the Goal

The goal of the castle needs to react when hit by the projectile:

1. Create a new C# script named *Goal* and attach it to the Goal prefab. Enter the following code into the Goal script.

```
using UnityEngine;
using System.Collections;

public class Goal : MonoBehaviour {
    // A static field accessible by code anywhere
    static public bool        goalMet = false;

    void OnTriggerEnter( Collider other ) {
        // When the trigger is hit by something
        // Check to see if it's a Projectile
        if ( other.gameObject.tag == "Projectile" ) {
            // If so, set goalMet to true
            Goal.goalMet = true;
            // Also set the alpha of the color to higher opacity
```

```
            Color c = renderer.material.color;
            c.a = 1;
            renderer.material.color = c;

        }
    }
}
```

Now when you fire, if you can hit the goal, it will turn bright green.

2. Save your scene.

Adding More Levels and Game Logic

The single castle as served us well so far, but let's add a few more.

1. Rename Castle to *Castle_0* and make it a prefab by dragging it into the Project pane.

2. Make a duplicate of Castle_0 (which will name itself Castle_1).

3. Drop Castle_1 into the Scene pane, and change its layout. It's very likely that you will "lose the prefab" if you delete one of the walls. That is completely fine. Just structure Castle_1 however you like, and then delete the Castle_1 Prefab in the Project pane and drag the new Castle_1 in from the Hierarchy.

4. Repeat this process to make a few different castles. Figure 29.13 shows a few that I made.

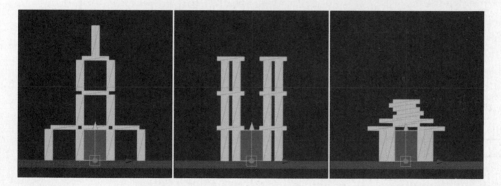

Figure 29.13 More castles

5. Save your scene.

6. Add a GUIText to your scene (*GameObject > Create Other > GUIText*) and name it *GT_Level*. Create a second GUIText and name it *GT_Shots*. Give each the settings shown in Figure 29.14.

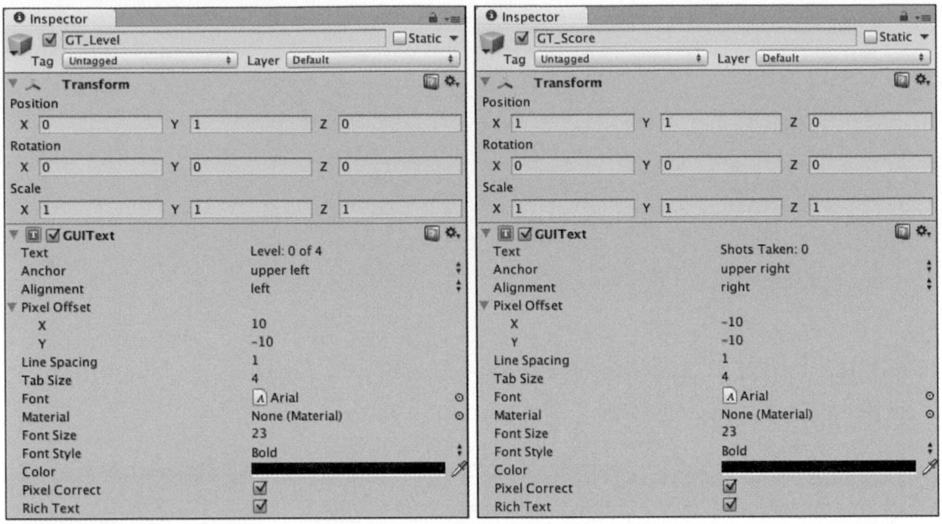

Figure 29.14 Settings for GT_Level and GT_Score

7. Create a new empty GameObject (*GameObject > Create Empty*) and name it *ViewBoth*. Set the transform of ViewBoth to P:[25,25,0] R:[0,0,0] S:[1,1,1]. This will serve as the `poi` for the camera when we want to view both the Castle and the Slingshot.

8. Create a new C# script named *MissionDemolition* and attach it to _Main Camera. This will serve as the game state manager for the game. Open it and write the following code:

```
using UnityEngine;
using System.Collections;

public enum GameMode {
    idle,
    playing,
    levelEnd
}

public class MissionDemolition : MonoBehaviour {
    static public MissionDemolition    S; // a Singleton

    // fields set in the Unity Inspector pane
    public GameObject[]       castles;   // An array of the castles
    public GUIText            gtLevel;   // The GT_Level GUIText
    public GUIText            gtScore;   // The GT_Score GUIText
    public Vector3            castlePos; // The place to put castles

    public bool                                           ;

    // fields set dynamically
```

```csharp
public int               level;    // The current level
public int               levelMax; // The number of levels
public int               shotsTaken;
public GameObject        castle;   // The current castle
public GameMode          mode = GameMode.idle;
public string            showing = "Slingshot"; // FollowCam mode

void Start() {
    S = this; // Define the Singleton

    level = 0;
    levelMax = castles.Length;
    StartLevel();
}

void StartLevel() {
    // Get rid of the old castle if one exists
    if (castle != null) {
        Destroy( castle );
    }

    // Destroy old projectiles if they exist
    GameObject[] gos = GameObject.FindGameObjectsWithTag("Projectile");
    foreach (GameObject pTemp in gos) {
        Destroy( pTemp );
    }

    // Instantiate the new castle
    castle = Instantiate( castles[level] ) as GameObject;
    castle.transform.position = castlePos;
    shotsTaken = 0;

    // Reset the camera
    SwitchView("Both");
    ProjectileLine.S.Clear();

    // Reset the goal
    Goal.goalMet = false;

    ShowGT();

    mode = GameMode.playing;
}

void ShowGT() {
    // Show the data in the GUITexts
    gtLevel.text = "Level: "+(level+1)+" of "+levelMax;
    gtScore.text = "Shots Taken: "+shotsTaken;
}
```

```csharp
void Update() {
    ShowGT();

    // Check for level end
    if (mode == GameMode.playing && Goal.goalMet) {
        // Change mode to stop checking for level end
        mode = GameMode.levelEnd;
        // Zoom out
        SwitchView("Both");
        // Start the next level in 2 seconds
        Invoke("NextLevel", 2f);
    }
}

void NextLevel() {
    level++;
    if (level == levelMax) {
        level = 0;
    }
    StartLevel();
}

void OnGUI() {
    // Draw the GUI button for view switching at the top of the screen
    Rect buttonRect = new Rect( (Screen.width/2)-50, 10, 100, 24 );

    switch(showing) {
    case "Slingshot":
        if ( GUI.Button( buttonRect, "Show Castle" ) ) {
            SwitchView("Castle");
        }
        break;

    case "Castle":
        if ( GUI.Button( buttonRect, "Show Both" ) ) {
            SwitchView("Both");
        }
        break;

    case "Both":
        if ( GUI.Button( buttonRect, "Show Slingshot" ) ) {
            SwitchView( "Slingshot" );
        }
        break;

    }
}
```

```
    // Static method that allows code anywhere to request a view change
    static public void SwitchView( string eView ) {
        S.showing = eView;
        switch (S.showing) {
        case "Slingshot":
            FollowCam.S.poi = null;
            break;

        case "Castle":
            FollowCam.S.poi = S.castle;
            break;

        case "Both":
            FollowCam.S.poi = GameObject.Find("ViewBoth");
            break;

        }
    }

    // Static method that allows code anywhere to increment shotsTaken
    public static void ShotFired() {
        S.shotsTaken++;
    }

}
```

9. Now that there is a static `ShotFired()` method on the `MissionDemolition` class, it's possible to call it from the Slingshot class. Add the following bold line to the Slingshot C# script:

```
public class Slingshot : MonoBehaviour {
    …
    void Update() {
        …
        if ( Input.GetMouseButtonUp(0) ) {
            …
            projectile = null;
            MissionDemolition.ShotFired();
        }
    }
}
```

Because the `ShotFired()` method on MissionDemolition is static, it can be accessed through the `MissionDemolition` class itself rather than requiring you to access it via a specific instance of MissionDemolition. When Slingshot calls `MissionDemolition.Shot-Fired()`, it causes `MissionDemolition.S.shotsTaken` to increment.

10. Switch back to Unity and select _Main Camera in the Hierarchy. In the *MissionDemolition* (Script) component Inspector, you will need to set a few variables.

   10.1. First, set `castlePos` to [50,-9.5,0], which will place the castles a nice distance from your Slingshot.

   10.2. To set `gtLevel`, click the target in the Inspector to the right of gtLevel and select GT_Level from the Scene tab in the pop-up dialog box.

   10.3. Click the target next to `gtScore` in the Inspector and choose GT_Score from the Scene tab.

   10.4. Next, click the disclosure triangle next to `castles` and set its length to the number of castles you made previously. (In the example in Figure 29.15, I made four castles.)

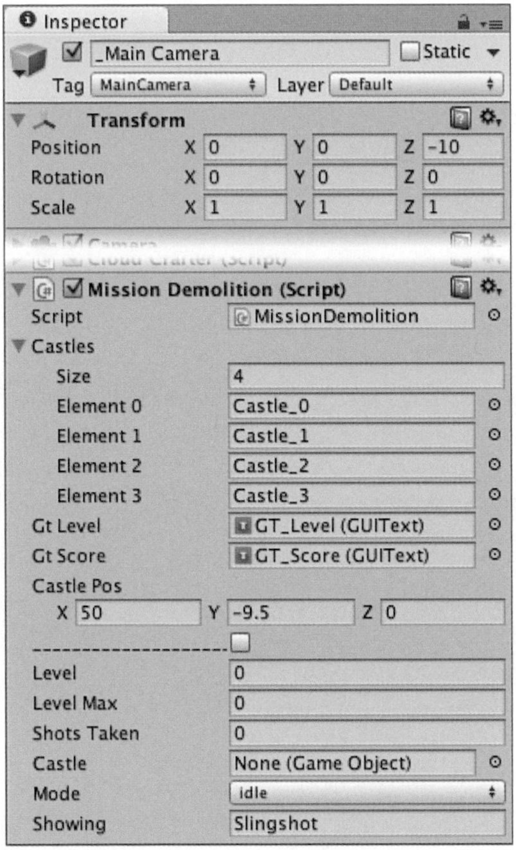

Figure 29.15 Final settings (with Castles array) for _Main Camera:MissionDemolition

10.5. Drag each of the numbered Castle prefabs you made into an element of the `castles` array to set the levels for your game. Try to order them from easiest to most difficult.

10.6. Save your scene and press Play. Now the game will play through various levels and keep track of how many shots you've fired.

Summary

That's it for the Mission Demolition prototype. In just one chapter, you've made a physics-based game like *Angry Birds* that you can continue to improve and expand on your own. This and all of the following tutorials are really meant to be frameworks on top of which you can build whatever game you want, and there are a ton of additional features you could add, some of which include the following:

1. Use PlayerPrefs to store the best score on each level as was done in Apple Picker.

2. Make the castle parts out of various materials, some of which would have more or less mass. Some materials could even break if struck hard enough.

3. Show lines for multiple previous paths rather than just the most recent one.

4. Use a Line Renderer to draw the rubber band of the slingshot.

5. Implement actual parallax scrolling on the background clouds, and add more background elements like mountains or buildings.

6. Limit the number of shots so that the player loses the level if she doesn't hit the goal in only 3 shots. Adding risk like this increases the tension and excitement in the game.

7. Anything else that you want!

Next Steps

After you've worked your way through the other prototypes, come back to this one and think about what you could add to it. Create your own designs, show them to people, and iterate to make the game better. Remember that design is always an iterative process. If you make a change you don't like, don't let it discourage you; just chalk it up to experience and try something else.

CHAPTER 30

PROTOTYPE 3: SPACE SHMUP

The SHMUP (or shoot 'em up) game genre includes such classic games as *Galaga* and *Galaxian* from the 1980s and the modern masterpiece Ikaruga.

In this chapter, you create a SHMUP using several programming techniques that will serve you well throughout your programming and prototyping careers, including class inheritance, enums, static fields and methods, and the singleton pattern. Though you've seen many of these techniques before, they will be used more extensively in this prototype.

Getting Started: Prototype 3

In this project, you make a prototype for a classic space-based SHMUP. Figure 30.1 shows two images of what the finished prototype will look like. In both images, the player has powered-up her weapons and already taken out some enemy ships (which left behind the power-up cubes marked B, O, and S). In the left image, she is using the blaster weapon, and in the right, she is using the spread weapon.

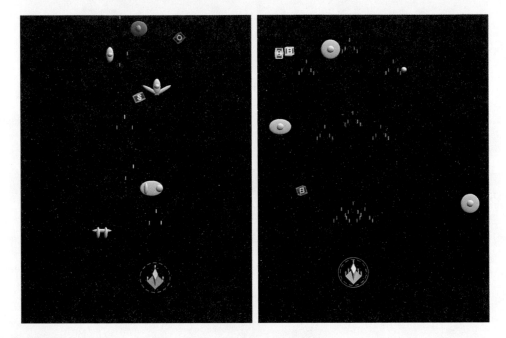

Figure 30.1   Two views of the Space SHMUP game prototype

Importing a Unity Asset Package

One new thing in the setup for this prototype is that you will be asked to download and import a custom Unity asset package. The creation of complex art and imagery for games is beyond the scope of this book, but I've created a package of some simple assets for you that will allow you to create all the visual effects required for this game. Of course, as mentioned several times throughout this book, when you're making a prototype, how it plays and feels are much more important than how it looks, but it's still important to have an understanding of how to work with art assets.

SET UP THE PROJECT FOR THIS CHAPTER

Following the standard project setup procedure, create a new project in Unity. If you need a refresher on this procedure, see Appendix A, "Standard Project Setup Procedure."

- **Project name:** Space SHMUP Prototype
- **Scene name:** __Scene_0
- **Project folders:** __Scripts, _Materials, _Prefabs
- **Download and import package:** Find Chapter 30 at http://book.prototools.net
- **C# script names:** (none yet)
- **Rename:** Change Main Camera to _MainCamera

To download and install the package mentioned in the sidebar "Set Up the Project for This Chapter," first follow the URL listed (http://book.prototools.net) and search for this chapter. Download *Chapter30.unitypackage* to your machine, which will usually place it in your Downloads folder. Open your project in Unity and select *Assets > Import Package > Custom Package* from the menu bar. Navigate to and select *Chapter30.unitypackage* from your Downloads folder. This will open the import dialog box shown in Figure 30.2.

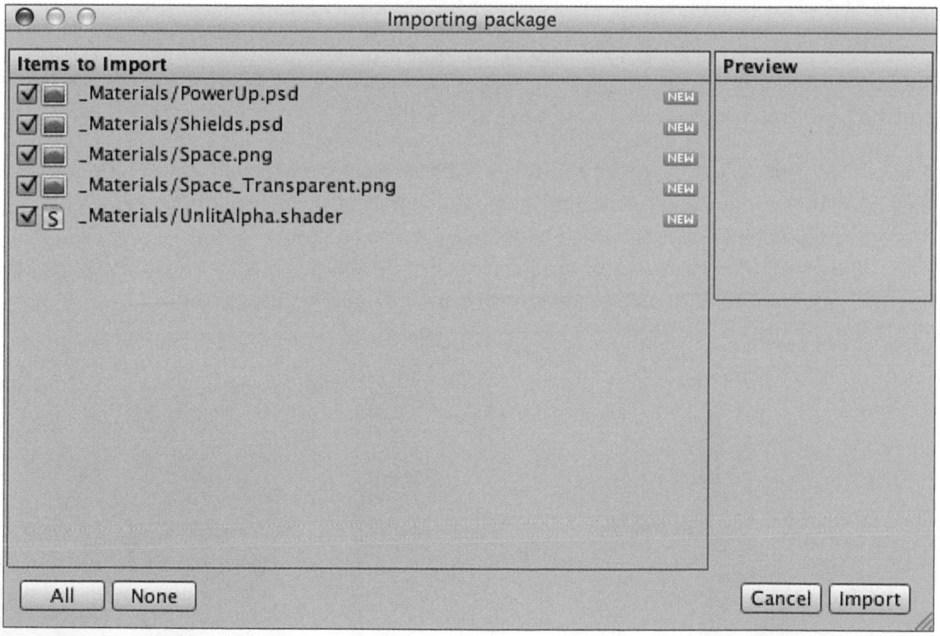

Figure 30.2   The .unitypackage import dialog box

Select all the files as shown in Figure 30.2, and click *Import*. This will place four new textures and one new shader into the _Materials folder. The creation of textures is beyond the scope of this book, but many books and online tutorials cover texture creation. Adobe Photoshop is probably the most commonly used image editing tool, but it's very expensive. A common open source alternative is Gimp (http://www.gimp.org).

The creation of shaders is also far beyond the scope of this book. Shaders are programs that tell your computer how to render a texture on a GameObject. They can make a scene look realistic, cartoony, or however else you like, and they are an important part of the graphics of any modern game. Unity uses its own unique shader language called ShaderLab. If you want to learn more about it, a good place to start is the Unity Shader Reference documentation (http://docs.unity3d.com/Documentation/Components/SL-Reference.html).

The included shader is a simple one that bypasses most of the things a shader can do to simply render a colored, unlit shape on the screen. For on-screen elements that you want to be a specific bright color, the imported UnlitAlpha.shader is perfect. UnlitAlpha also allows for alpha blending and transparency, which will be very useful for the power-up cubes in this game.

Setting the Scene

Add a directional light to the scene (*GameObject > Create Other > Directional Light* from the menu bar). Set its transform to P:[0,20,0] R:[50,330,0] S:[1,1,1].

Select _MainCamera and set its transform to P:[0,0,-10] R:[0,0,0] S:[1,1,1]. In the Camera component, set the *Background color* to black. Set *Projection* to Orthographic and *Size* to 40. Set the *Near* and *Far Clipping Planes* to 0.3 and 100, respectively.

Because this game will be a vertical, top-down shooter, we need to set an aspect ratio for the Game pane that is in portrait orientation. In the Game pane, click the pop-up menu list of aspect ratios directly underneath the tab for the pane. At the bottom of the list, you will see a + symbol. Click this to add a new aspect ratio preset. Set the values to those shown in Figure 30.3, and then click *Add OK*. Set the Game pane to this new *Portrait (3:4)* aspect ratio.

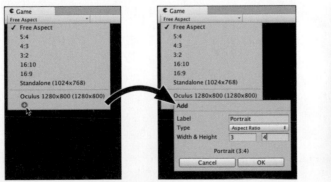

Figure 30.3   Adding a new aspect ratio preset to the Game pane

Making the Hero Ship

In this chapter, we interleave the construction of artwork and code rather than building all the art first. To make the player's spaceship, complete these steps:

1. Create an empty GameObject and name it _Hero (GameObject > Create Empty). Set its transform to P:[0,0,0] R:[0,0,0] S:[1,1,1].

2. Create a cube (GameObject > Create Other > Cube) and drag it onto _Hero in the Hierarchy, making it a child of _Hero. Name the cube Wing and set its transform to P:[0,-1,0] R:[0,0,45] S:[3,3,0.5].

3. Create an empty GameObject, name it Cockpit, and make it a child of _Hero.

4. Create a cube and make it a child of Cockpit. Set the Cube's transform to P:[0,0,0] R:[315,0,45] S:[1,1,1].

5. Make Cockpit's transform P:[0,0,0] R:[0,0,180] S:[1,3,1]. This uses the same trick as in Chapter 26, "Object-Oriented Thinking," to make a quick, angular ship.

6. Create a new C# script and name it Hero (Assets > Create > C# Script from the menu bar). Be sure to place this script into the __Scripts folder. Drag the Hero script onto the _Hero GameObject to attach it.

7. Add a Rigidbody component to _Hero by selecting _Hero in the Hierarchy and then choosing Component > Physics > Rigidbody from the menu bar. Set Use Gravity to false and isKinematic to true. Open the disclosure triangle for Constraints and freeze z position and x, y, and z rotation.

You'll add more to _Hero later, but this will suffice for now.

Save your scene! Remember that you should be saving your scene every time you make a change to it. I'll quiz you later.

Hero.Update()

In the code listing that follows, the Update() method first reads the horizontal and vertical axes from the InputManager (see the "Input.GetAxis() and The InputManager" sidebar), placing values between –1 and 1 into the floats xAxis and yAxis. The second chunk of Update() code moves the ship in a time-based way, taking into account the speed setting.

The last line (marked // 2) rotates the ship based on the input. Although we earlier froze rotation in the Rigidbody component, it is still possible for us to manually set the rotation on a Rigidbody with isKinematic set to true. (As discussed in an earlier chapter, isKinematic=true means that the Rigidbody will be tracked by the physics system but that it will not move automatically due to Rigidbody.velocity.) This rotation will make the movement of the ship feel more dynamic and expressive, or "juicy."[1]

---

[1] *Juiciness,* as a term that relates to gameplay, was coined in 2005 by Kyle Gabler and the other members of the Experimental Gameplay Project at Carnegie Mellon University's Entertainment Technology Center. To them, a juicy element had "constant and bountiful user feedback." You can read about it more in their Gamasutra article "How to Prototype a Game in Under 7 Days." http://www.gamasutra.com/view/feature/130848/how_to_prototype_a_game_in_under_7_php.

Open the Hero C# script in MonoDevelop and enter the following code:

```csharp
using UnityEngine;
using System.Collections;

public class Hero : MonoBehaviour {
    static public Hero      S; // Singleton

    // These fields control the movement of the ship
    public float            speed = 30;
    public float            rollMult = -45;
    public float            pitchMult = 30;

    // Ship status information
    public float            shieldLevel = 1;

    public bool _____;

    void Awake() {
        S = this;  // Set the Singleton
    }

    void Update () {
        // Pull in information from the Input class
        float xAxis = Input.GetAxis("Horizontal");          // 1
        float yAxis = Input.GetAxis("Vertical");            // 1

        // Change transform.position based on the axes
        Vector3 pos = transform.position;
        pos.x += xAxis * speed * Time.deltaTime;
        pos.y += yAxis * speed * Time.deltaTime;
        transform.position = pos;

        // Rotate the ship to make it feel more dynamic         // 2
        transform.rotation = Quaternion.Euler(yAxis*pitchMult,xAxis*rollMult,0);
    }
}
```

1. These two lines use Unity's `Input` class to pull information from the Unity InputManager. See the sidebar for more information.

2. The `transform.rotation`... line below this comment is used to give the ship a bit of rotation based on the speed at which it is moving, which can make the ship feel more reactive and juicy.

INPUT.GETAXIS() AND THE INPUTMANAGER

Much of the code in the `Hero.Update()` code listing should look familiar to you, though this is the first time in the book that we've used the `Input.GetAxis()` method. Various axes are configured in Unity's InputManager, and `Input.GetAxis()` allows them to be read. To view the default Input axes, choose *Edit > Project Settings > Input* from the menu bar.

One thing to note about the settings in Figure 30.4 is that there are several that are listed twice (for example, Horizontal, Vertical, Jump). As you can see in the expanded view of the horizontal axes in the figure, this allows the horizontal axis to be controlled by either presses on the keyboard (shown in the left image of Figure 30.4) or a joystick axis (shown in the right image). This is one of the great strengths of the input axes; several different types of input can control a single axis. As a result, your games only need one line to read the value of an axis rather than a line to handle joystick input, a line for each arrow key, and a line each for the A and D keys.

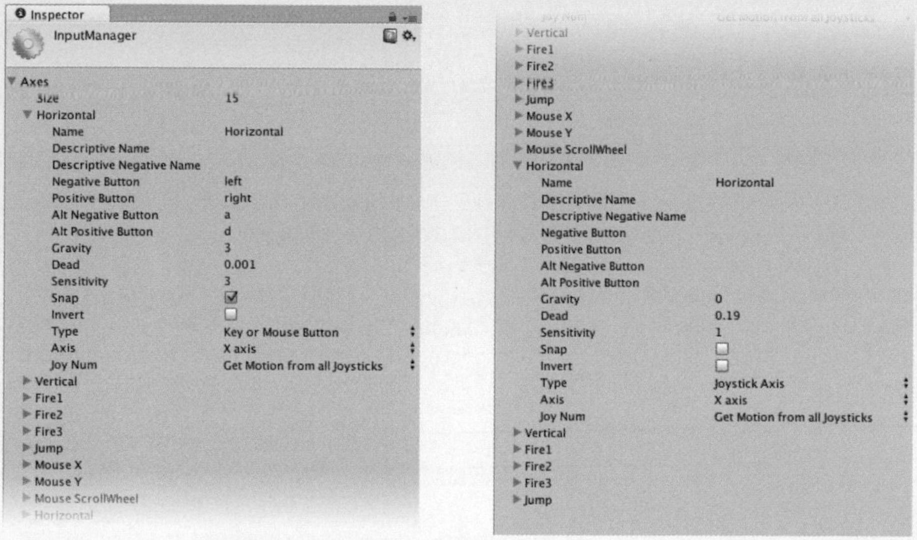

Figure 30.4 Unity's InputManager showing default settings (shown in two halves)

Every call to `Input.GetAxis()` will return a float betweevn -1 and 1 in value (with a default of 0). Each axis in the InputManager also includes values for *Sensitivity* and *Gravity*, though these are only used for *Key or Mouse Button* input (see the left image of Figure 30.4). Sensitivity and gravity cause the axis value to interpolate smoothly when a key is pressed or released. (That is, instead of immediately jumping to the final value, the axis value will blend from the original value to the final value over time.) In the horizontal axis shown, a sensitivity of 3 means that when the right-arrow key is pressed, it will take 1/3 of a second for the value to interpolate from 0 to 1. A gravity of 3 means that when

> the right-arrow key is released, it will take 1/3 of a second for the axis value to interpolate back to 0. The higher the sensitivity or gravity, the faster the interpolation will take place.
>
> As with almost anything in Unity, you can find out a lot more about the InputManager by clicking the Help button (that looks like a blue book with a question mark and is between the name InputManager and the gear at the top of the Inspector).

Try playing the game and see how the ship feels to you. The settings for `speed`, `rollMult`, and `pitchMult` work for me, but this is your game, and you should have settings that feel right to you. Make changes as necessary in the Inspector for _Hero.

Part of what makes this feel nice is the apparent inertia that the ship carries. When you release the movement key, it takes the ship a little while to slow down. Similarly, upon pressing a movement key, it takes the ship a little while to get up to speed. This apparent movement inertia is caused by the *sensitivity* and *gravity* axis settings that are described in the sidebar. Changing these settings in the InputManager will affect the movement and maneuverability of _Hero.

The Hero Shield

The shield for _Hero will be a combination of a transparent, textured quad (to provide the visuals) and a Sphere Collider (for collision handling).

Create a new quad (*GameObject > Create Other > Quad*). Rename the quad *Shield* and make it a child of _Hero. Set the transform of Shield to P:[0,0,0] R:[0,0,0], S:[8,8,8].

Select Shield in the Hierarchy and add a Sphere Collider component (*Component > Physics > Sphere Collider*). Then delete the existing Mesh Collider component by clicking the tiny gear to the right of the Mesh Collider name in the Inspector and choosing *Remove Component* from the pop-up menu.

Create a new material (*Assets > Create > Material*), name it *Mat Shield*, and place it in the _Materials folder in the Project pane. Drag Mat Shield onto Shield (under _Hero in the Hierarchy) to assign it to the Shield quad.

Select Shield in the Hierarchy, and you will now see Mat Shield in the Inspector for Shield. Set the *Shader* of Mat Shield to *ProtoTools > UnlitAlpha*. Below the shader selection pop-up for Mat Shield, there should be an area that allows you to choose the main color for the material as well as the texture. (If you don't see this, click once on the name *Mat Shield* in the Inspector, and it should appear.) Click *Select* in the bottom-right corner of the texture square and select the texture named *Shields*. Click the color swatch next to *Main Color* and choose a bright green (RGBA:[0,255,0,255]). Then set the *Tiling.x* to 0.2 and the *Offset.x* to 0.4. The x Tiling of 0.2 causes Mat Shield to only use 1/5 of the total Shield texture in the x direction, and the x Offset chooses which fifth. Try x Offsets of 0, 0.2, 0.4, 0.6, and 0.8 to see the different levels of shield strength.

Tiling.y should remain 1.0, and Offset.y should remain 0. This is because the texture was designed to be split into five sections horizontally but only one vertically.

Create a new C# script named *Shield* (*Asset > Create > C# Script*). Drop it into the __Scripts folder in the Project pane and then drag it onto Shield in the Hierarchy to assign it as a component of the Shield GameObject. Open the Shield script in MonoDevelop and enter the following code:

```
using UnityEngine;
using System.Collections;

public class Shield : MonoBehaviour {
    public float    rotationsPerSecond = 0.1f;
    public bool     _____;
    public int      levelShown = 0;

    void Update () {
        // Read the current shield level from the Hero Singleton
        int currLevel = Mathf.FloorToInt( Hero.S.shieldLevel );        // 1
        // If this is different from levelShown…
        if (levelShown != currLevel) {
            levelShown = currLevel;
            Material mat = this.renderer.material;
            // Adjust the texture offset to show different shield level
            mat.mainTextureOffset = new Vector2( 0.2f*levelShown, 0 );  // 2
        }
        // Rotate the shield a bit every second
        float rZ = (rotationsPerSecond*Time.time*360) % 360f;          // 3
        transform.rotation = Quaternion.Euler( 0, 0, rZ );
    }

}
```

1. `currLevel` is set to the floor of the current `Hero.S.shieldLevel` float. By flooring the `shieldLevel`, we make sure that the shield jumps to the new x Offset rather than showing an Offset between two shield icons.
2. This line adjusts the x Offset of Mat Shield to show the proper shield level.
3. This line and the next cause the Shield GameObject to rotate slowly around the z axis every frame.

Keeping _Hero On Screen

The motion of your _Hero ship should feel pretty good now, and the rotating shield looks pretty nice, but at this point, you can easily drive the ship off the screen. This is going to be a bit more complex than some of the other things we've done, but you're now going to write some reusable code to keep the ship constrained to the screen.

Bounds

Both renderers and colliders have a `bounds` field that is of the type Bounds. Bounds are defined by a center and a size, each of which are Vector3s. In Figure 30.5, this is explained in two dimensions; just remember that there is also a z dimension when working in Unity.

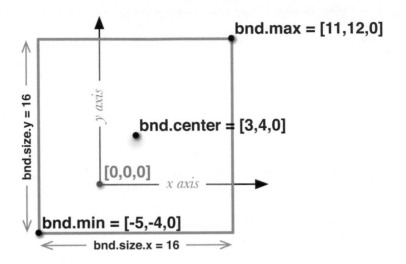

Figure 30.5   Diagram showing the various fields of Bounds bnd, defined as

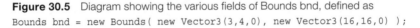

```
Bounds bnd = new Bounds ( new Vector3(3,4,0), new Vector3(16,16,0) );
```

Compositing the Bounds of a Complex GameObject

_Hero is a complex GameObject with several children, however _Hero itself has no colliders. To find the collision bounds of _Hero, it is necessary to find the bounds of each of the children of _Hero and then to create a Bounds variable that encompasses all of them. Unity doesn't include any function for expanding Bounds to envelope other Bounds, so we'll need to write one called `BoundsUnion` (named so because it returns the mathematical union of the two Bounds). This seems like something that might also be useful in later games, so we'll make this part of a new *Utils* C# class that we will fill with reusable game code. The Utils class is going to be almost entirely composed of static functions so that the functions can easily be called from anywhere in your code.

Create a new C# script named *Utils* and place it in the __Scripts folder. Open Utils in MonoDevelop and enter the following code:

```
using UnityEngine;
using System.Collections;
using System.Collections.Generic;

public class Utils : MonoBehaviour {
```

```
//============================ Bounds Functions ============================\\

    // Creates bounds that encapsulate the two Bounds passed in.
    public static Bounds BoundsUnion( Bounds b0, Bounds b1 ) {
        // If the size of one of the bounds is Vector3.zero, ignore that one
        if ( b0.size == Vector3.zero && b1.size != Vector3.zero ) {        // 1
            return( b1 );
        } else if ( b0.size != Vector3.zero && b1.size == Vector3.zero ) {
            return( b0 );
        } else if ( b0.size == Vector3.zero && b1.size == Vector3.zero ) {
            return( b0 );
        }
        // Stretch b0 to include the b1.min and b1.max
        b0.Encapsulate(b1.min);                                           // 2
        b0.Encapsulate(b1.max);
        return( b0 );
    }
}
```

1. This `if` clause ensures that neither of the bounds have a size of 0. If the size of one is Vector3.zero, then the other is returned. If both have a size of zero, `b0` is returned.

2. Though the Unity Bounds class doesn't include a function to expand to encompass other Bounds, it does have one to encompass a Vector3. `b0.Encapsulate(b1.min)` will expand Bounds `b0` to include the Vector3 `b1.min`, and if both `b1.min` and `b1.max` are inside the newly expanded `b0`, then `b0` has expanded to surround `b1` as well.

Add the following bold code to the `Utils` class after `BoundsUnion()`:

```
public class Utils : MonoBehaviour {

//============================ Bounds Functions ============================\\

    // Creates bounds that encapsulate of the two Bounds passed in.
    public static Bounds BoundsUnion( Bounds b0, Bounds b1 ) {
        …
    }

    public static Bounds CombineBoundsOfChildren(GameObject go) {
        // Create an empty Bounds b
        Bounds b = new Bounds(Vector3.zero, Vector3.zero);
        // If this GameObject has a Renderer Component…
        if (go.renderer != null) {
            // Expand b to contain the Renderer's Bounds
            b = BoundsUnion(b, go.renderer.bounds);
        }
        // If this GameObject has a Collider Component…
        if (go.collider != null) {
            // Expand b to contain the Collider's Bounds
            b = BoundsUnion(b, go.collider.bounds);
```

```
        }
        // Recursively iterate through each child of this gameObject.transform
        foreach( Transform t in go.transform ) {                          // 1
            // Expand b to contain their Bounds as well
            b = BoundsUnion( b, CombineBoundsOfChildren( t.gameObject ) );  // 2
        }

        return( b );
    }

}
```

1. The Transform class supports enumerators (by implementing the IEnumerable interface), which makes it possible to loop over each child of a Transform using a `foreach` loop.

2. Because `CombineBoundsOfChildren()` calls itself (actually another instance of itself), this is also another example of a recursive function. (Recursive functions were first covered in Chapter 23, "Functions and Parameters.")

Now it's possible to get the combined bounds of any GameObject and its children by passing it into the `CombineBoundsOfChildren()` method. Open the Hero C# script and add the following bold lines of code to get the combined bounds of _Hero:

```
public bool _____;

public Bounds            bounds;

void Awake() {
    S = this;  // Set the Singleton
    bounds = Utils.CombineBoundsOfChildren(this.gameObject);
}
```

Making `CombineBoundsOfChildren()` a static method of Utils makes it very easy to call from anywhere in your code. The call to `Utils.CombineBoundsOfChildren()` has the potential to take a good amount of processing power and time if it's called on a GameObject with many children, so it's called only once. Later, we'll update the center of the bounds every frame to keep it up-to-date as the ship moves across the screen.

Finding the Bounds of the Camera

To keep _Hero on screen, it's also necessary to know the bounds of the camera's field of view. With a perspective camera, this would be pretty tricky, but orthographic cameras are much easier as long as the orthographic camera is not rotated. To find the bounds of the camera, we'll create two Vector3s (`boundTLN` and `boundBRF` for top-left near and bottom-right far, respectively). These will be defined by passing the top-left and bottom-right coordinates of the screen into `Camera.ScreenToWorldPoint` and replacing the z value of the resultant Vector3s with the z plane of the near and far settings of the camera.

Open Utils in MonoDevelop and add the following bold code after the static method
`CombineBoundsOfChildren()`:

```
public class Utils : MonoBehaviour {

//============================ Bounds Functions ============================\\

    // Creates bounds that encapsulate of the two Bounds passed in.
    public static Bounds BoundsUnion( Bounds b0, Bounds b1 ) {
        …
    }

    public static Bounds CombineBoundsOfChildren(GameObject go) {
        …
    }

    // Make a static read-only public property camBounds
    static public Bounds camBounds {                                    // 1
        get {
            // if _camBounds hasn't been set yet
            if (_camBounds.size == Vector3.zero) {
                // SetCameraBounds using the default Camera
                SetCameraBounds();
            }
            return( _camBounds );
        }
    }
    // This is the private static field that camBounds uses
    static private Bounds _camBounds;                                   // 2

    // This function is used by camBounds to set _camBounds and can also be
    //  called directly.
    public static void SetCameraBounds(Camera cam=null) {              // 3
        // If no Camera was passed in, use the main Camera
        if (cam == null) cam = Camera.main;
        // This makes a couple of important assumptions about the camera!:
        //   1. The camera is Orthographic
        //   2. The camera is at a rotation of R:[0,0,0]

        // Make Vector3s at the topLeft and bottomRight of the Screen coords
        Vector3 topLeft = new Vector3( 0, 0, 0 );
        Vector3 bottomRight = new Vector3( Screen.width, Screen.height, 0 );

        // Convert these to world coordinates
        Vector3 boundTLN = cam.ScreenToWorldPoint( topLeft );
        Vector3 boundBRF = cam.ScreenToWorldPoint( bottomRight );
```

```
        // Adjust their zs to be at the near and far Camera clipping planes
        boundTLN.z += cam.nearClipPlane;
        boundBRF.z += cam.farClipPlane;

        // Find the center of the Bounds
        Vector3 center = (boundTLN + boundBRF)/2f;
        _camBounds = new Bounds( center, Vector3.zero );
        // Expand _camBounds to encapsulate the extents.
        _camBounds.Encapsulate( boundTLN );
        _camBounds.Encapsulate( boundBRF );
    }

}
```

1. `Utils.camBounds` is a public static read-only property. As a property, it runs the code in the `get{}` clause whenever it is accessed. If the private static field `_camBounds` has not yet been set, the `get{}` clause will call `Utils.SetCameraBounds()` to set `_camBounds` before returning. This technique is used to make sure that `_camBounds` is set just in time to be read by `camBounds` and to make sure that `Utils.SetCameraBounds()` is called only once.

2. Note that the order in which `camBounds` and `_camBounds` are declared does not matter to C#. The compiler reads everything that is declared in the Utils class before interpreting any code.

3. The static public `SetCameraBounds()` method has a default `Camera cam` value of `null`. If nothing is passed into `SetCameraBounds()` as an argument, it will replace the `null` value in `cam` with `Camera.main` (the main camera of the scene, or _MainCamera in this scene). If a programmer wishes to use a camera other than _MainCamera for `_camBounds`, she can call `Utils.SetCameraBounds()` directly instead.

Testing and Responding to the Overlap of Two Bounds

The last component we will need to keep _Hero on screen is the ability to test whether two Bounds overlap. The following code will make use of an *enum*, which you can learn more about in the "Enum" sidebar.

Start by adding the bold code in the following listing *before* the declaration of the `Utils` class in the Utils C# script:

```
using UnityEngine;
using System.Collections;
using System.Collections.Generic;

// This is actually OUTSIDE of the Utils Class
public enum BoundsTest {
    center,      // Is the center of the GameObject on screen?
    onScreen,    // Are the bounds entirely on screen?
    offScreen    // Are the bounds entirely off screen?
}
```

```
public class Utils : MonoBehaviour {
    …
}
```

Now, add the following bold methods as part of the `Utils` class. Note how the `BoundsTest` enum is used in the `switch` statement. In the code that follows, there are a few uses of the code continuation character (➡). Remember that this character represents the continuation of the previous line (which was too long to fit the width of the pages in this book).

```
public class Utils : MonoBehaviour {

//============================ Bounds Functions ============================\\

    …

    public static void SetCameraBounds(Camera cam=null) {
        …
    }

    // Checks to see whether the Bounds bnd are within the camBounds
    public static Vector3 ScreenBoundsCheck(Bounds bnd, BoundsTest test =
➡BoundsTest.center) {
        return( BoundsInBoundsCheck( camBounds, bnd, test ) );
    }
```

```
   // Checks to see whether Bounds lilB are within Bounds bigB
   public static Vector3 BoundsInBoundsCheck( Bounds bigB, Bounds lilB,
➥BoundsTest test = BoundsTest.onScreen ) {

       // The behavior of this function is different based on the BoundsTest
       //  that has been selected.

       // Get the center of lilB
       Vector3 pos = lilB.center;

       // Initialize the offset at [0,0,0]
       Vector3 off = Vector3.zero;

       switch (test) {
       // The center test determines what off (offset) would have to be applied
       //  to lilB to move its center back inside bigB
       case BoundsTest.center:
           if ( bigB.Contains( pos ) ) {
               return( Vector3.zero );
           }

           if (pos.x > bigB.max.x) {
               off.x = pos.x - bigB.max.x;
           } else  if (pos.x < bigB.min.x) {
               off.x = pos.x - bigB.min.x;
           }
           if (pos.y > bigB.max.y) {
               off.y = pos.y - bigB.max.y;
           } else  if (pos.y < bigB.min.y) {
               off.y = pos.y - bigB.min.y;
           }
           if (pos.z > bigB.max.z) {
               off.z = pos.z - bigB.max.z;
           } else  if (pos.z < bigB.min.z) {
               off.z = pos.z - bigB.min.z;
           }
           return( off );

       // The onScreen test determines what off would have to be applied to
       //  keep all of lilB inside bigB
       case BoundsTest.onScreen:
           if ( bigB.Contains( lilB.min ) && bigB.Contains( lilB.max ) ) {
               return( Vector3.zero );
           }

           if (lilB.max.x > bigB.max.x) {
               off.x = lilB.max.x - bigB.max.x;
           } else  if (lilB.min.x < bigB.min.x) {
               off.x = lilB.min.x - bigB.min.x;
```

```
        }
        if (lilB.max.y > bigB.max.y) {
            off.y = lilB.max.y - bigB.max.y;
        } else  if (lilB.min.y < bigB.min.y) {
            off.y = lilB.min.y - bigB.min.y;
        }
        if (lilB.max.z > bigB.max.z) {
            off.z = lilB.max.z - bigB.max.z;
        } else  if (lilB.min.z < bigB.min.z) {
            off.z = lilB.min.z - bigB.min.z;
        }
        return( off );

    // The offScreen test determines what off would need to be applied to
    //  move any tiny part of lilB inside of bigB
    case BoundsTest.offScreen:
        bool cMin = bigB.Contains( lilB.min );
        bool cMax = bigB.Contains( lilB.max );
        if ( cMin || cMax ) {
            return( Vector3.zero );
        }

        if (lilB.min.x > bigB.max.x) {
            off.x = lilB.min.x - bigB.max.x;
        } else  if (lilB.max.x < bigB.min.x) {
            off.x = lilB.max.x - bigB.min.x;
        }
        if (lilB.min.y > bigB.max.y) {
            off.y = lilB.min.y - bigB.max.y;
        } else  if (lilB.max.y < bigB.min.y) {
            off.y = lilB.max.y - bigB.min.y;
        }
        if (lilB.min.z > bigB.max.z) {
            off.z = lilB.min.z - bigB.max.z;
        } else  if (lilB.max.z < bigB.min.z) {
            off.z = lilB.max.z - bigB.min.z;
        }
        return( off );

    }

    return( Vector3.zero );
    }

}
```

These two functions will return a Vector3 value that represents how far the lilB bounds are
outside of the bigB bounds (or the camera bounds) according to the type of test passed into
`BoundsTest test`.

Add the bold lines that follow to the `Hero` class to see how this works:

```
public class Hero : MonoBehaviour {
    …

    void Update () {
        …
        transform.position = pos;

        bounds.center = transform.position;                              // 1

        // Keep the ship constrained to the screen bounds
        Vector3 off = Utils.ScreenBoundsCheck(bounds, BoundsTest.onScreen); // 2
        if ( off != Vector3.zero ) {                                      // 3
            pos -= off;
            transform.position = pos;
        }

        // Rotate the ship to make it feel more dynamic
        transform.rotation = Quaternion.Euler(yAxis*pitchMult,xAxis*rollMult,0);
    }
}
```

1. This line moves the center of bounds to line up with the position of _Hero after it's been moved by the existing code in the `Update()` method.

2. This line uses `Utils.ScreenBoundsCheck()` to determine whether the ship is off screen.

3. If the `off` ship offset value is not zero, then move the _Hero back on screen.

Try altering the line labeled `// 2` to use the other BoundsTest options (BoundsTest.center and BoundsTest.offScreen) and see how they change the behavior of the `ScreenBoundsCheck()`. With BoundsTest.center, the ship should stop halfway off screen. With BoundsTest.offScreen, you should see that just a tiny sliver of the shield remains on screen.

Adding Some Enemies

The enemies for a game like this were covered a bit in Chapter 25, "Classes." There you learned about setting up a superclass for all enemies that can be extended by subclasses. For this game, we extend that further, but first, let's create the artwork.

Enemy Artwork

Because the hero ship has such an angular aesthetic, all the enemies will be constructed of spheres as shown in Figure 30.6.

Figure 30.6   Each of the five enemy ship types

Enemy_0

Create an empty GameObject and name it *Enemy_0*. Create a sphere named *Cockpit*, make it a child of Enemy_0, and set its transform to P:[0,0,0] R:[0,0,0] S:[2,2,1]. Create a second sphere named *Wing*, make it a child of Enemy_0, and set its transform to P:[0,0,0] R:[0,0,0] S:[5,5,0.5]. Another way of writing this would be:

Enemy_0 (Empty)	P:[0,0,0]	R:[0,0,0]	S:[1,1,1]
Cockpit (Sphere)	P:[0,0,0]	R:[0,0,0]	S:[2,2,1]
Wing (Sphere)	P:[0,0,0]	R:[0,0,0]	S:[5,5,0.5]

Follow this formatting to make the remaining four enemies. When finished, they should look like the enemies in Figure 30.6.

Enemy_1

Enemy_1 (Empty)	P:[0,0,0]	R:[0,0,0]	S:[1,1,1]
Cockpit (Sphere)	P:[0,0,0]	R:[0,0,0]	S:[2,2,1]
Wing (Sphere)	P:[0,0,0]	R:[0,0,0]	S:[6,4,0.5]

Enemy_2

Enemy_2 (Empty)	P:[0,0,0]	R:[0,0,0]	S:[1,1,1]
Cockpit (Sphere)	P:[-1.5,0,0]	R:[0,0,0]	S:[1,3,1]
Sphere	P:[2,0,0]	R:[0,0,0]	S:[2,2,1]
Wing (Sphere)	P:[0,0,0]	R:[0,0,0]	S:[6,4,0.5]

Enemy_3

Enemy_3 (Empty)	P:[0,0,0]	R:[0,0,0]	S:[1,1,1]
CockpitL (Sphere)	P:[-1,0,0]	R:[0,0,0]	S:[1,3,1]
CockpitR (Sphere)	P:[1,0,0]	R:[0,0,0]	S:[1,3,1]
Wing (Sphere)	P:[0,0.5,0]	R:[0,0,0]	S:[5,1,0.5]

Enemy_4

Enemy_4 (Empty)	P:[0,0,0]	R:[0,0,0]	S:[1,1,1]
Cockpit (Sphere)	P:[0,1,0]	R:[0,0,0]	S:[1.5,1.5,1.5]
Fuselage (Sphere)	P:[0,1,0]	R:[0,0,0]	S:[2,4,1]
Wing_L (Sphere)	P:[-1.5,0,0]	R:[0,0,-30]	S:[5,1,0.5]
Wing_R (Sphere)	P:[1.5,0,0]	R:[0,0,30]	S:[5,1,0.5]

You must add a Rigidbody component to each of the enemy GameObjects (that is, Enemy_0, Enemy_1, Enemy_2, Enemy_3, and Enemy_4). To add a Rigidbody, complete these steps:

1. Select each enemy in the Hierarchy and choose *Component > Physics > Rigidbody* from the menu bar to add the Rigidbody component.
2. In the Rigidbody component for the enemy, set *Use Gravity* to false.
3. Set *isKinematic* to true.
4. Open the disclosure triangle for *Constraints* and freeze z position and x, y, and z rotation.

Be sure to do this for all five enemies. If a moving GameObject doesn't have a Rigidbody component, the GameObject's collider location will not move with the GameObject, but if a moving GameObject does have a Rigidbody, the colliders of both it and all of its children are updated every frame (which is one of the reasons that you don't need to add a Rigidbody component to any of the children of the enemies).

Drag each of these enemies to the _Prefabs folder of the Project pane to create a prefab for each, and then delete all of the enemy instances from the Hierarchy except for Enemy_0.

The Enemy C# Script

Create a new C# script named *Enemy*. Drag the Enemy script onto Enemy_0 in the Project pane. When you click on Enemy_0 in either the Project or Hierarchy panes, you should see the *Enemy (Script)* component attached. Open the Enemy script in MonoDevelop and enter the following code:

```csharp
using UnityEngine;              // Required for Unity
using System.Collections;       // Required for Arrays & other Collections

public class Enemy : MonoBehaviour {
    public float      speed = 10f;      // The speed in m/s
    public float      fireRate = 0.3f; // Seconds/shot (Unused)
    public float      health = 10;
    public int        score = 100; // Points earned for destroying this

    public bool _____;

    public Bounds     bounds; // The Bounds of this and its children
    public Vector3    boundsCenterOffset; // Dist of bounds.center from position

    // Update is called once per frame
    void Update() {
        Move();
    }

    public virtual void Move() {
        Vector3 tempPos = pos;
        tempPos.y -= speed * Time.deltaTime;
        pos = tempPos;
    }

    // This is a Property: A method that acts like a field
    public Vector3 pos {
        get {
            return( this.transform.position );
        }
        set {
            this.transform.position = value;
        }
    }

}
```

Press Play, and the instance of Enemy_0 in the scene should move toward the bottom of the screen. However, as it is, this instance will continue off screen and exist until you stop your game. We need to have the enemy destroy itself once it has moved entirely off screen. This is another place where we'll use Utils.ScreenBoundsTest().

In the following code listing, the single line in the Awake() method creates a repeated call to the CheckOffscreen() method. InvokeRepeating() is a built-in Unity function that is used to schedule repeated calls to the same function. The first parameter is the name of the function as a string, the second parameter is the delay (in seconds) before the named function is called the first time, and the last parameter is the delay between each subsequent call. In the Awake() function, CheckOffscreen() will first be called immediately (0 seconds) after the enemy is instantiated, and then it will be called again every 2 seconds until the object is destroyed.

The `CheckOffscreen()` method first checks to see whether `bounds.size` is [0,0,0]. Because Bounds is a value type (not a reference type), it is initially a default value of center:[0,0,0] size:[0,0,0] rather than null. (Value types can never be set to null.) To check to see whether it has been set, we check to see whether the size is something other than the default. If the bounds really haven't yet been set, `Utils.CombineBoundsOfChildren()` is called to do so. Unlike _Hero, it's very possible that the center of the bounds of one of the Enemy ships could be offset from the actual center of the GameObject, so Vector3 boundsCenterOffset is set to the value of this offset (with the enemy ships defined previously, this is necessary for Enemy_4).

Add the following bold code to the Enemy script:

```
public class Enemy : MonoBehaviour {
    …
    public Vector3    boundsCenterOffset; // Dist of bounds.center from position

    void Awake() {
        InvokeRepeating( "CheckOffscreen", 0f, 2f );
    }

    …

    // This is a Property: A method that acts like a field
    public Vector3 pos {
        …
    }

    void CheckOffscreen() {
        // If bounds are still their default value…
        if (bounds.size == Vector3.zero) {
            // then set them
            bounds = Utils.CombineBoundsOfChildren(this.gameObject);
            // Also find the diff between bounds.center & transform.position
            boundsCenterOffset = bounds.center - transform.position;
        }

        // Every time, update the bounds to the current position
        bounds.center = transform.position + boundsCenterOffset;
        // Check to see whether the bounds are completely offscreen
        Vector3 off = Utils.ScreenBoundsCheck( bounds, BoundsTest.offScreen );
        if ( off != Vector3.zero ) {
            // If this enemy has gone off the bottom edge of the screen
            if (off.y < 0) {
                // then destroy it
                Destroy( this.gameObject );
            }
        }
    }
}
```

Now, when you play the scene, you should see that the Enemy_0 ship moves down the screen, then off screen, and within a couple of seconds of moving off screen, it is destroyed.

Spawning Enemies at Random

With all of this in place, it's now possible to instantiate a number of Enemy_0s randomly. Create a new C# script called *Main* and attach it to _MainCamera. Enter the following code:

```csharp
using UnityEngine;                    // Required for Unity
using System.Collections;             // Required for Arrays & other Collections
using System.Collections.Generic;     // Required to use Lists or Dictionaries

public class Main : MonoBehaviour {
    static public Main S;

    public GameObject[]        prefabEnemies;
    public float               enemySpawnPerSecond = 0.5f; // # Enemies/second
    public float               enemySpawnPadding = 1.5f; // Padding for position

    public bool            _____;

    public float               enemySpawnRate; // Delay between Enemy spawns

    void Awake() {
        S = this;
        // Set Utils.camBounds
        Utils.SetCameraBounds(this.camera);
        // 0.5 enemies/second = enemySpawnRate of 2
        enemySpawnRate = 1f/enemySpawnPerSecond;                  // 1
        // Invoke call SpawnEnemy() once after a 2 second delay
        Invoke( "SpawnEnemy", enemySpawnRate );                  // 2
    }

    public void SpawnEnemy() {
        // Pick a random Enemy prefab to instantiate
        int ndx = Random.Range(0, prefabEnemies.Length);
        GameObject go = Instantiate( prefabEnemies[ ndx ] ) as GameObject;
        // Position the Enemy above the screen with a random x position
        Vector3 pos = Vector3.zero;
        float xMin = Utils.camBounds.min.x+enemySpawnPadding;
        float xMax = Utils.camBounds.max.x-enemySpawnPadding;
        pos.x = Random.Range( xMin, xMax );
        pos.y = Utils.camBounds.max.y + enemySpawnPadding;
        go.transform.position = pos;
        // Call SpawnEnemy() again in a couple of seconds
```

```
        Invoke( "SpawnEnemy", enemySpawnRate );                    // 3
    }
}
```

1. The public field to set the spawn rate of enemies is `enemySpawnPerSecond`, storing the number of enemies that will spawn every second. By default, it is set to 0.5f (or half an enemy every second). The line here converts this into the number of seconds of delay between each enemy spawn (2 seconds in this case) and assigns that value to `enemySpawnRate`.

2. The `Invoke()` function works much like `InvokeRepeating()`, except that it only calls the invoked function once.

3. The reason that `Invoke()` is used instead of `InvokeRepeating()` is that we want to be able to dynamically adjust the amount of time between each enemy spawn. Once `InvokeRepeating()` is called, the invoked function is always called at the rate specified. Adding an `Invoke()` call at the end of `SpawnEnemy()` allows the game to adjust `enemySpawnRate` on the fly and have it affect how frequently `SpawnEnemy()` is called.

Once you've typed this code and saved the file, switch back to Unity and follow these instructions:

1. Delete the instance of Enemy_0 from the Hierarchy (leaving the prefab in the Project pane alone, of course).

2. Select _MainCamera in the Hierarchy.

3. Open the disclosure triangle next to `prefabEnemies` in the *Main (Script)* component of _MainCamera and set the *Size* of `prefabEnemies` to 1.

4. Drag Enemy_0 from the Project pane into *Element 0* of the `prefabEnemies` array.

5. *Save your scene!* Have you been remembering? If you didn't save your scene after creating all of those enemies, you really should have. There are all sorts of things beyond your control that could cause Unity to crash, and you really don't want to have to redo work. Getting into a habit of saving your scene frequently can save you a ton of wasted time and sorrow as a developer.

Play your scene. You should now see an Enemy_0 spawn about once every 2 seconds, travel down to the bottom of the screen, and then disappear within a few seconds of exiting the bottom of the screen.

However, right now, when the _Hero collides with an enemy, nothing happens. This needs to be fixed, and to do so, we're going to have to look at layers.

Setting Tags, Layers, and Physics

As was presented in Chapter 28, "Prototype 1: Apple Picker," one of the things that layers control in Unity is which objects may or may not collide with each other. First, let's think about the

Space SHMUP prototype. In this game, several different types of GameObjects could be placed on different layers and interact with each other in different ways:

- **Hero:** The _Hero ship should collide with enemies, enemy projectiles, and power-ups but should not collide with hero projectiles.
- **ProjectileHero:** Projectiles fired by _Hero should only collide with enemies.
- **Enemy:** Enemies should collide with _Hero and hero projectiles but not with power-ups.
- **ProjectileEnemy:** Projectiles fired by enemies should only collide with _Hero.
- **PowerUp:** Power-ups should only collide with _Hero.

To create these five layers, complete these steps:

1. Open the Tags and Layers Manager in the Inspector pane (*Edit > Project Settings > Tags and Layers*). Tags and layers are different from each other, but both are set in the Tags and Layers Manager.

2. Open the disclosure triangle next to Tags. Set the *Size* of Tags to 7 and enter the tags shown in the left image of Figure 30.7. Note that in the middle of your typing the name of *Tags Element 5*, PowerUpBox, you may receive a console message ("Default GameObject Tag: PowerUp already registered"), which you can safely ignore.

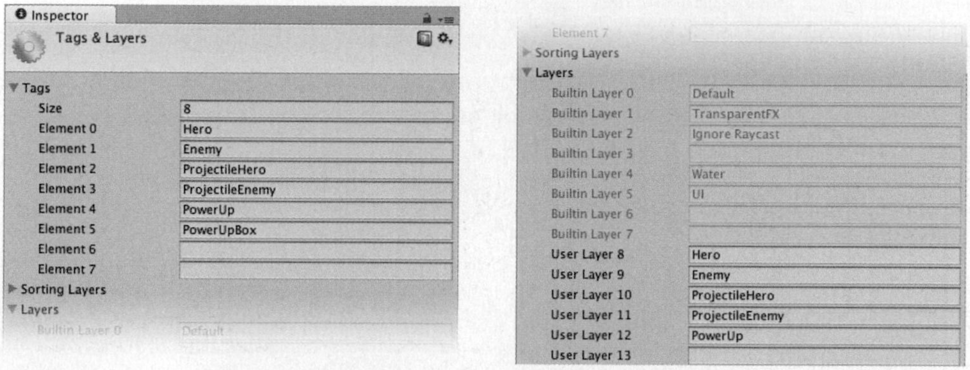

Figure 30.7   TagManager showing tags and layer names for this prototype

3. Open the disclosure triangle next to *Layers*. Starting with *User Layer 8*, enter the layer names shown in the right image of Figure 30.7. *Builtin Layers 0–7* are reserved by Unity, but you can set the names of *User Layers 8–31*.

4. Open the PhysicsManager (*Edit > Project Settings > Physics*) and set it as shown in Figure 30.8.

> **note**
> As of Unity 4.3, there are settings for both Physics and Physics2D. In this chapter, you should be setting Physics (the standard 3D PhysX physics library), not Physics2D.

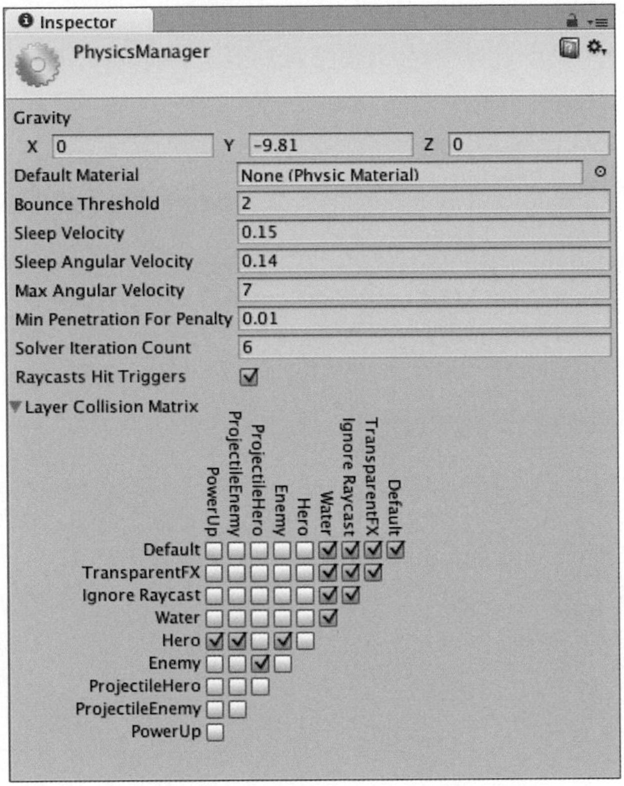

Figure 30.8   PhysicsManager with proper settings for this prototype

The grid at the bottom of the PhysicsManager sets which layers collide with each other. If there is a check, objects in the two layers are able to collide, if there is no check, they won't. Removing checks can speed the execution of your game because it will test fewer objects versus each other for collision. As you can see in Figure 30.8, the layers and collision we've chosen achieve the collision behavior we specified earlier.

Assign the Proper Layers to GameObjects

Now that the layers have been defined, you must assign the GameObjects you've created to the correct layer, as follows:

1. Select _Hero in the Hierarchy and choose *Hero* from the Layer pop-up menu in the Inspector. When Unity asks if you'd like to also assign the children of _Hero to this new layer, choose *Yes, change children*.

2. Set the tag of _Hero to *Hero* using the Tag pop-up menu in the Inspector. You do not need to change the tags of the children of _Hero.

3. Select each of the Enemy prefabs in the Project pane and set each to the *Enemy* layer. When asked, elect to change the layer of their children as well.

4. Also set the tag of each Enemy prefab to *Enemy*. You do not need to set the tags of the children of each enemy.

Making the Enemies Damage the Player

Now that the enemies and hero have colliding layers, we need to make them react to the collisions.

Open the disclosure triangle next to _Hero in the Hierarchy and select its child Shield. In the Inspector, set the Sphere Collider of Shield to be a trigger (check the box next to *Is Trigger*). We don't need things to bounce off of Shield; we just need to know when they've hit.

Add the following bolded method to the end of the Hero C# script:

```
public class Hero : MonoBehaviour {
    …
    void Update() {
        …
    }

    void OnTriggerEnter(Collider other) {
        print("Triggered: "+other.gameObject.name);
    }
}
```

Play the scene and try running into some enemies. You will see that you get a trigger event for the children GameObjects of the Enemy (for example, Cockpit and Wing) but not for the Enemy itself. Add this pair of methods to the `Utils` class to enable you to move up the transform.parent tree to find the parent with a tag (in this case, Enemy):

```
public class Utils : MonoBehaviour {

//============================ Bounds Functions ============================\\

    ...

    // Checks to see whether Bounds lilB are within Bounds bigB
    public static Vector3 BoundsInBoundsCheck( Bounds bigB, Bounds lilB,
➥BoundsTest test = BoundsTest.onScreen ) {
        ...
    }


//============================ Transform Functions ============================\\

    // This function will iteratively climb up the transform.parent tree
    //   until it either finds a parent with a tag != "Untagged" or no parent
    public static GameObject FindTaggedParent(GameObject go) {          // 1
        // If this gameObject has a tag
        if (go.tag != "Untagged") {                                     // 2
            // then return this gameObject
            return(go);
        }
        // If there is no parent of this Transform
        if (go.transform.parent == null) {                              // 3
            // We've reached the top of the hierarchy with no interesting tag
            // So return null
            return( null );
        }
        // Otherwise, recursively climb up the tree
        return( FindTaggedParent( go.transform.parent.gameObject ) );   // 4
    }
    // This version of the function handles things if a Transform is passed in
    public static GameObject FindTaggedParent(Transform t) {            // 5
        return( FindTaggedParent( t.gameObject ) );
    }

}
```

1. FindTaggedParent() searches for a GameObject that is in the transform hierarchy above GameObject go and is tagged (that is, it has a tag other than the default tag Untagged).

2. If GameObject go has a tag, go is returned.

3. If go.transform.parent is null, then GameObject go has no parent. This means that neither the original GameObject nor any of its parents had a tag, so null is returned.

4. Because go.transform.parent is not null, Utils.FindTaggedParent() is called recursively with the parent GameObject of go.

5. This is an overload of the function `FindTaggedParent()` that takes a Transform as its initial argument rather than the GameObject required by the other version of `FindTaggedParent()`.

Next, modify the `OnTriggerEnter()` method in the `Hero` class as follows to take advantage of the `Utils.FindTaggedParent()` method:

```
public class Hero : MonoBehaviour {
    …
    void Update() {
        …
    }

    void OnTriggerEnter(Collider other) {
        // Find the tag of other.gameObject or its parent GameObjects
        GameObject go = Utils.FindTaggedParent(other.gameObject);
        // If there is a parent with a tag
        if (go != null) {
            // Announce it
            print("Triggered: "+go.name);
        } else {
            // Otherwise announce the original other.gameObject
            print("Triggered: "+other.gameObject.name); // Move this line here!
        }
    }
}
```

Now when you play the scene and run the ship into enemies, you should see that `OnTriggerEnter()` announces it has hit *Enemy_0(Clone)*, an instance of Enemy_0.

> ## tip
>
> **ITERATIVE CODE DEVELOPMENT**   When prototyping on your own, this kind of announcement test is something that you will do often to test whether the code you've written is working properly. I find that it is much better to do small tests along the way like this than to work on code for hours only to find at the end that something is causing a bug. Testing incrementally makes things *a lot* easier to debug because you know that you've only made slight changes since the last test that worked, so it's easier to find the place where you added a bug.
>
> Another key element of this approach is using the debugger. Throughout the authoring of this book, any time I ran into something that worked a little differently than I expected, I used the debugger to understand what was happening. If you don't remember how to use the MonoDevelop debugger, I highly recommend rereading Chapter 24, "Debugging."

> Using the debugger effectively is often the difference between solving your code problems and just staring at pages of code blankly for several hours. Try putting a debug breakpoint into the `OnTriggerEnter()` method you just modified and watching how code is called and variables change. The recursive calling of `Utils.FindTaggedParent()` in particular should be interesting.
>
> Iterative code development has the same strengths as the iterative process of design, and it is the key to the agile development methodology discussed in Chapter 27, "The Agile Mentality."

Next, modify the `OnTriggerEnter()` method of the `Hero` class to make a collision with an enemy decrease the player's shield by 1 and destroy the Enemy that was hit. It's also very important to make sure that the same parent GameObject doesn't trigger the Shield collider twice (which could happen with very fast-moving objects if two child colliders of one object hit the Shield trigger in the same frame).

```
public class Hero : MonoBehaviour {
    …
    void Update() {
        …
    }

    // This variable holds a reference to the last triggering GameObject
    public GameObject lastTriggerGo = null;                           // 1

    void OnTriggerEnter(Collider other) {
        …
        if (go != null) {
            // Make sure it's not the same triggering go as last time
            if (go == lastTriggerGo) {                                // 2
                return;
            }
            lastTriggerGo = go;                                       // 3

            if (go.tag == "Enemy") {
                // If the shield was triggered by an enemy
                // Decrease the level of the shield by 1
                shieldLevel--;
                // Destroy the enemy
                Destroy(go);                                          // 4
            } else {
                print("Triggered: "+go.name);         // Move this line here!
            }
        } else {
            …
        }
    }
```

1. This field holds a reference to the last GameObject that triggered Shield collider. It is initially set to null. Though we usually declare fields at the top of the class, they can actually be declared anywhere throughout the class, as we have done with this line.

2. If `lastTriggerGo` is the same as `go` (the current triggering GameObject), this collision is ignored as a duplicate, which can happen if two children GameObjects of the same Enemy trigger the Shield collider at the same time (that is, in the same single frame).

3. Assign `go` to `lastTriggerGo` so that it is updated the next time `OnTriggerEnter()` is called.

4. `go`, the enemy GameObject, is destroyed by hitting the shield. Because the actual GameObject `go` that we're testing is the Enemy GameObject found by `Utils. FindTaggedParent()`, this will delete the entire Enemy (and by extension, all of its children), and not just one of the Enemy's child GameObjects.

Play the scene and try running into some ships. After running into more than a few, you may notice a strange shield behavior. The shield will loop back around to full strength after being completely drained. What do you think is causing this? Try selecting _Hero in the Hierarchy while playing the scene to see what's happening to the `shieldLevel` field.

Because there is no bottom limit to `shieldLevel`, it continues past 0 into negative territory. The Shield C# script then translates this into negative x offset values for Mat Shield, and because the material's texture is set to loop, it looks like the shield is returning to full strength.

To fix this, we will convert `shieldLevel` to a property that insulates and limits a new private field named `_shieldLevel`. The `shieldLevel` property will watch the value of the `_shieldLevel` field and make sure that `_shieldLevel` never gets above 4 and that the ship is destroyed if `_shieldLevel` ever drops below 0. An insulated field like `_shieldLevel` should be set to private because it does not need to be accessed by other classes; however, in Unity, private fields are not viewable in the Inspector. To remedy this, the line `[SerializeField]` is added above the declaration of `_shieldLevel` to instruct Unity to show it in the Inspector even though it is a private field. Properties are never visible in the Inspector, even if they're public.

First, change the name of the public variable `shieldLevel` to `_shieldLevel` near the top of the `Hero` class, set it to private, and add the `[SerializeField]` line:

```
// Ship status information
[SerializeField]
private float          _shieldLevel = 1;              // Add the underscore!
```

Next, add the `shieldLevel` property to the end of the `Hero` class.

```
public class Hero : MonoBehaviour {

    ...

    void OnTriggerEnter(Collider other) {
        ...
    }
```

```
public float shieldLevel {
    get {
        return( _shieldLevel );                              // 1
    }
    set {
        _shieldLevel = Mathf.Min( value, 4 );                // 2
        // If the shield is going to be set to less than zero
        if (value < 0) {                                     // 3
            Destroy(this.gameObject);
        }
    }
}
}
```

1. The `get` clause just returns the value of `_shieldLevel`.
2. `Mathf.Min()` ensures that `_shieldLevel` is never set to a number higher than 4.
3. If the value passed into the set clause is less than 0, _Hero is destroyed.

Restarting the Game

From your testing, you can see that the game gets exceedingly boring once _Hero has been destroyed. We'll now modify both the `Hero` and `Main` classes to call a method when _Hero is destroyed that waits for 2 seconds and then restarts the game.

Add a gameRestartDelay field to the top of the `Hero` class:

```
static public Hero       S; // Singleton

public float             gameRestartDelay = 2f;

// These fields control the movement of the ship
```

Then add the following lines to the `shieldLevel` property definition in the `Hero` class:

```
if (value < 0) {
    Destroy(this.gameObject);
    // Tell Main.S to restart the game after a delay
    Main.S.DelayedRestart( gameRestartDelay );
}
```

Finally, add the following methods to the `Main` class to make this work.

```
public class Main : MonoBehaviour {
    …

    public void SpawnEnemy() {
        …
    }
```

```
public void DelayedRestart( float delay ) {
        // Invoke the Restart() method in delay seconds
        Invoke("Restart", delay);
}

public void Restart() {
        // Reload _Scene_0 to restart the game
        Application.LoadLevel("_Scene_0");
}

}
```

Now, once the player ship has been destroyed, the game waits a couple of seconds and then restarts by reloading the scene.

Shooting (Finally)

Now that the enemy ships can hurt the player, it's time to give _Hero a way to fight back.

Artwork

Create an empty GameObject, name it *Weapon*, and give it the following structure and children:

Weapon (Empty)	P:[0,0,0]	R:[0,0,0]	S:[1,1,1]
Barrel (Cube)	P:[0,0.5,0]	R:[0,0,0]	S:[0.25,1,0.1]
Collar (Cube)	P:[0,1,0]	R:[0,0,0]	S:[0.375,0.5,0.2]

Remove the Collider component from both Barrel and Collar by selecting them individually and then right-clicking on the name of the Box Collider component and choosing *Remove Component* from the pop-up menu. You can also click the gear to the right of the Box Collider name to get the same menu.

Now, create a new material named *Mat Collar*. Drag this material on to Collar to assign it. In the Inspector, choose *ProtoTools > UnlitAlpha* from the Shader pop-up menu. The Collar should now be a bright white (see Figure 30.9).

Now, create a new C# script named *Weapon* and drag it onto the Weapon GameObject in the Hierarchy. Then drag the Weapon GameObject into the _Prefabs folder in the Project pane to make it a prefab. Make the Weapon instance in the Hierarchy a child of _Hero and set its position to [0,2,0]. This should place the Weapon on the nose of the _Hero ship, as is shown in Figure 30.9.

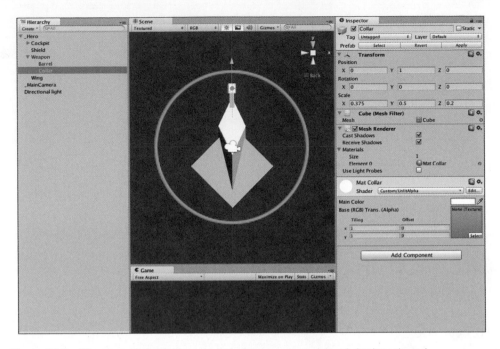

Figure 30.9 Weapon with the Collar selected and proper material and shader selected

Save your scene! Are you remembering to save constantly?

Next, create a cube named *ProjectileHero* in the Hierarchy as follows:

ProjectileHero (Cube)   P:[10,0,0]   R:[0,0,0]   S:[0.25,1,0.5]

Set both the tag and layer of ProjectileHero to *ProjectileHero*. Create a new material named *Mat Projectile*, give it the *ProtoTools > UnlitAlpha* shader, and assign it to the ProjectileHero GameObject. Add a Rigidbody component to the ProjectileHero GameObject with the settings shown in Figure 30.10. (The transform.position of ProjectileHero doesn't actually matter because it will be a prefab that is positioned via code.) Create a new C# script named *Projectile* and drag it onto ProjectileHero. We'll edit the script later.

In the Box Collider component of the ProjectileHero GameObject, set Size.z to 10. This will make sure that the projectile is able to hit anything that is slightly off of the z=0 plane.

Save your scene.

Drag ProjectileHero into the _Prefabs folder in the Project pane to make it a prefab and delete the instance remaining in the Hierarchy.

Save your scene. As I've said, you want to save as often as you can.

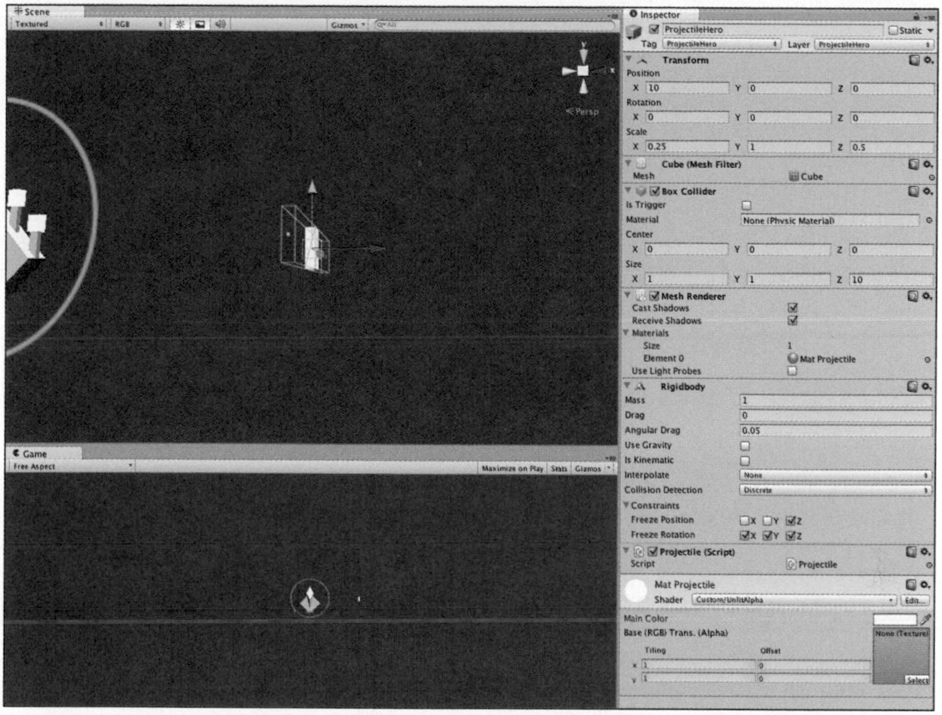

Figure 30.10   ProjectileHero with the proper settings showing the large Size.z of the Box Collider

The Serializable `WeaponDefinition` Class

Open the Weapon script in MonoDevelop and enter the following code:

```
using UnityEngine;
using System.Collections;


// This is an enum of the various possible weapon types
// It also includes a "shield" type to allow a shield power-up
// Items marked [NI] below are Not Implemented in this book
public enum WeaponType {
    none,       // The default / no weapon
    blaster,    // A simple blaster
    spread,     // Two shots simultaneously
    phaser,     // Shots that move in waves [NI]
    missile,    // Homing missiles [NI]
    laser,      // Damage over time [NI]
    shield      // Raise shieldLevel
}


// The WeaponDefinition class allows you to set the properties
//   of a specific weapon in the Inspector. Main has an array
```

```
//   of WeaponDefinitions that makes this possible.
// [System.Serializable] tells Unity to try to view WeaponDefinition
//   in the Inspector pane. It doesn't work for everything, but it
//   will work for simple classes like this!
[System.Serializable]
public class WeaponDefinition {
    public WeaponType    type = WeaponType.none;
    public string        letter;              // The letter to show on the power-up
    public Color         color = Color.white;        // Color of Collar & power-up
    public GameObject    projectilePrefab;           // Prefab for projectiles
    public Color         projectileColor = Color.white;
    public float         damageOnHit = 0;            // Amount of damage caused
    public float         continuousDamage = 0;       // Damage per second (Laser)
    public float         delayBetweenShots = 0;
    public float         velocity = 20;              // Speed of projectiles
}

// Note: Weapon prefabs, colors, and so on. are set in the class Main.

public class Weapon : MonoBehaviour {
    // The Weapon class will be filled in later.
}
```

As described in the code comments, the enum WeaponType defines all the possible weapon types and power-up types. WeaponDefinition is a class that combines a WeaponType with several other fields that will be useful for defining each weapon. Add the following code to the Main class:

```
public class Main : MonoBehaviour {
    …
    public float                enemySpawnPadding = 1.5f; // Padding for position
    public WeaponDefinition[]    weaponDefinitions;

    public bool _____;

    public WeaponType[]          activeWeaponTypes;
    public float                 enemySpawnRate; // Delay between Enemies

    void Awake() {…}

    void Start() {
        activeWeaponTypes = new WeaponType[weaponDefinitions.Length];
        for ( int i=0; i<weaponDefinitions.Length; i++ ) {
            activeWeaponTypes[i] = weaponDefinitions[i].type;
        }
    }
    …
}
```

Save this and then select _MainCamera in the Hierarchy. You should now see a `weaponDefinitions` array in the Main (Script) component Inspector. Click the disclosure triangle next to it and set the *Size* of the array to 3. Enter settings for the three WeaponDefinitions as shown in Figure 30.11. The colors don't have to be exactly right, but it is important that the alpha value of each color is set to fully opaque (which appears as a white bar beneath the color swatch).

> ## warning
>
> **COLORS SOMETIMES DEFAULT TO AN INVISIBLE ALPHA**   When you create a serializable class like `WeaponDefinition` that includes color fields, the alpha values of those colors will default to 0 (i.e., invisible). To fix this, make sure that the white bar under each of your color definitions is actually white (and not black). If you click on the color itself, you will be presented with four values to set (R, G, B, and A). Make sure that A is set to 255 (i.e., fully opaque) or your shots will be invisible.
>
> If you are using OS X and have chosen to use the OS X color picker in Unity instead of the default one, the A value is set by the Opacity slider at the bottom of the color picker window (which should be set to 100% for these colors).

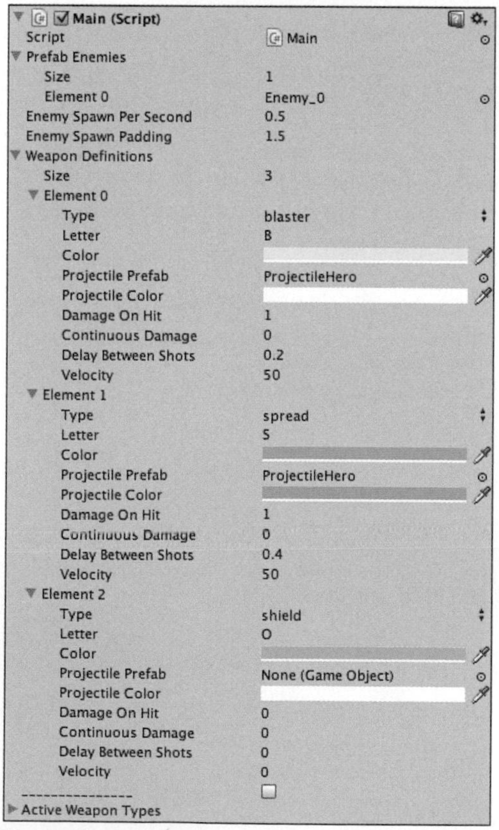

Figure 30.11 Settings for the WeaponDefinitions of blaster, spread, and shield on Main

A Generic Dictionary for WeaponDefinitions

Now, open the Main script in MonoDevelop and enter the following bold code. This code uses a *Dictionary*, which is another type of generic collection like List. Dictionaries have a *key* type and *value* type, and the key is used to retrieve the value. Here, the Dictionary has the enum WeaponType as the key and the class WeaponDefinition as the value. We will create the static public W_DEFS dictionary to hold the WeaponDefinition information that we just entered into the array in the Main (Script) Inspector. Unfortunately, Dictionaries do not appear in the Inspector, or we would have just used one from the start. Instead, the W_DEFS Dictionary is defined in the Awake() method of Main and then used by the static function Main. GetWeaponDefinition().

```
public class Main : MonoBehaviour {
    static public Main S;
    static public Dictionary<WeaponType, WeaponDefinition> W_DEFS;
    …
    void Awake() {
        …
        Invoke( "SpawnEnemy", enemySpawnRate );

        // A generic Dictionary with WeaponType as the key
        W_DEFS = new Dictionary<WeaponType, WeaponDefinition>();
        foreach( WeaponDefinition def in weaponDefinitions ) {
            W_DEFS[def.type] = def;
        }
    }

    static public WeaponDefinition GetWeaponDefinition( WeaponType wt ) {
        // Check to make sure that the key exists in the Dictionary
        // Attempting to retrieve a key that didn't exist, would throw an error,
        //    so the following if statement is important.
        if (W_DEFS.ContainsKey(wt)) {
            return( W_DEFS[wt]);
        }
        // This will return a definition for WeaponType.none,
        //    which means it has failed to find the WeaponDefinition
        return( new WeaponDefinition() );
    }

    void Start() {…}
}
```

Now, open the Projectile class in MonoDevelop and enter this code:

```
using UnityEngine;
using System.Collections;

public class Projectile : MonoBehaviour {
    [SerializeField]
    private WeaponType    _type;
```

```
    // This public property masks the field _type & takes action when it is set
    public WeaponType    type {
        get {
            return( _type );
        }
        set {
            SetType( value );
        }
    }

    void Awake() {
        // Test to see whether this has passed off screen every 2 seconds
        InvokeRepeating( "CheckOffscreen", 2f, 2f );
    }

    public void SetType( WeaponType eType ) {
        // Set the _type
        _type = eType;
        WeaponDefinition def = Main.GetWeaponDefinition( _type );
        renderer.material.color = def.projectileColor;
    }

    void CheckOffscreen() {
        if ( Utils.ScreenBoundsCheck( collider.bounds, BoundsTest.offScreen ) !=
➥Vector3.zero ) {
            Destroy( this.gameObject );
        }
    }

}
```

Whenever the type property of this Projectile is set, SetType() will be called, and the Projectile will automatically set its own color based on the WeaponDefinitions in Main.

Using a Function Delegate to Fire

Before continuing, read the "Function Delegates" section of Appendix B.

In this game prototype, the Hero class will have a function delegate fireDelegate that is called to fire all weapons, and each Weapon attached to it will add its individual Fire() target method to fireDelegate.

Add the following bold code to the Hero class:

```
public class Hero : MonoBehaviour {
    …
    public Bounds           bounds;
```

```
// Declare a new delegate type WeaponFireDelegate
public delegate void WeaponFireDelegate();
// Create a WeaponFireDelegate field named fireDelegate.
public WeaponFireDelegate fireDelegate;

void Awake() {
    …
}

void Update () {
    …
    // Rotate the ship to make it feel more dynamic
    transform.rotation = Quaternion.Euler(yAxis*pitchMult,xAxis*rollMult,0);

    // Use the fireDelegate to fire Weapons
    // First, make sure the Axis("Jump") button is pressed
    // Then ensure that fireDelegate isn't null to avoid an error
    if (Input.GetAxis("Jump") == 1 && fireDelegate != null) {          // 1
        fireDelegate();
    }
}
…
}
```

1. If `fireDelegate` is called when it has no methods assigned to it, it will throw an error. To avoid this, `fireDelegate != null` is tested to see whether it is null before calling it.

Open the Weapon C# script in MonoDevelop and add the following code:

```
public class Weapon : MonoBehaviour {
    static public Transform    PROJECTILE_ANCHOR;

    public bool _____;
    [SerializeField]
    private WeaponType    _type = WeaponType.blaster;
    public WeaponDefinition    def;
    public GameObject    collar;
    public float    lastShot; // Time last shot was fired

    void Start() {
        collar = transform.Find("Collar").gameObject;
        // Call SetType() properly for the default _type
        SetType( _type );

        if (PROJECTILE_ANCHOR == null) {
            GameObject go = new GameObject("_Projectile_Anchor");
            PROJECTILE_ANCHOR = go.transform;
        }
        // Find the fireDelegate of the parent
```

```
        GameObject parentGO = transform.parent.gameObject;
        if (parentGO.tag == "Hero") {
            Hero.S.fireDelegate += Fire;
        }
    }

    public WeaponType type {
        get {    return( _type );    }
        set {    SetType( value );    }
    }

    public void SetType( WeaponType wt ) {
        _type = wt;
        if (type == WeaponType.none) {
            this.gameObject.SetActive(false);
            return;
        } else {
            this.gameObject.SetActive(true);
        }
        def = Main.GetWeaponDefinition(_type);
        collar.renderer.material.color = def.color;
        lastShot = 0; // You can always fire immediately after _type is set.
    }

    public void Fire() {
        // If this.gameObject is inactive, return
        if (!gameObject.activeInHierarchy) return;
        // If it hasn't been enough time between shots, return
        if (Time.time - lastShot < def.delayBetweenShots) {
            return;
        }
        Projectile p;
        switch (type) {
        case WeaponType.blaster:
            p = MakeProjectile();
            p.rigidbody.velocity = Vector3.up * def.velocity;
            break;

        case WeaponType.spread:
            p = MakeProjectile();
            p.rigidbody.velocity = Vector3.up * def.velocity;
            p = MakeProjectile();
            p.rigidbody.velocity = new Vector3( -.2f, 0.9f, 0 ) * def.velocity;
            p = MakeProjectile();
            p.rigidbody.velocity = new Vector3(  .2f, 0.9f, 0 ) * def.velocity;
            break;

        }
    }
}
```

```
    public Projectile MakeProjectile() {
        GameObject go = Instantiate( def.projectilePrefab ) as GameObject;
        if ( transform.parent.gameObject.tag == "Hero" ) {
            go.tag = "ProjectileHero";
            go.layer = LayerMask.NameToLayer("ProjectileHero");
        } else {
            go.tag = "ProjectileEnemy";
            go.layer = LayerMask.NameToLayer("ProjectileEnemy");
        }
        go.transform.position = collar.transform.position;
        go.transform.parent = PROJECTILE_ANCHOR;
        Projectile p = go.GetComponent<Projectile>();
        p.type = type;
        lastShot = Time.time;
        return( p );

    }
}
```

Most of this code should make sense to you. Note that the various kinds of projectiles and weapons are handled with a switch statement inside of the `Fire()` method.

Now, it's important to make projectiles actually damage enemies. Open the Enemy C# script in MonoDevelop and add the following `OnCollisionEnter()` method:

```
public class Enemy : MonoBehaviour {
    …
    void CheckOffscreen() {

        …

    }


    void OnCollisionEnter( Collision coll ) {
        GameObject other = coll.gameObject;
        switch (other.tag) {
        case "ProjectileHero":
            Projectile p = other.GetComponent<Projectile>();
            // Enemies don't take damage unless they're onscreen
            // This stops the player from shooting them before they are visible
            bounds.center = transform.position + boundsCenterOffset;
            if (bounds.extents == Vector3.zero ||
➥Utils.ScreenBoundsCheck(bounds, BoundsTest.offScreen) != Vector3.zero) {
                Destroy(other);
                break;
            }
            // Hurt this Enemy
            // Get the damage amount from the Projectile.type & Main.W_DEFS
            health -= Main.W_DEFS[p.type].damageOnHit;
            if (health <= 0) {
```

```
                // Destroy this Enemy
                Destroy(this.gameObject);
            }
            Destroy(other);
            break;
        }
    }
}
```

Now when you play the scene, it is possible to destroy an Enemy, but each one takes 10 shots to take down, and it's difficult to tell that they're being damaged. We will add code that makes an Enemy blink red for a couple of frames every time it is hit, but to do so, we're going to need to have access to all the materials of all the children of each Enemy. This sounds like something that may be useful in later prototypes, so we will add it to the Utils script. Open the Utils script in MonoDevelop and add the following static method to achieve this:

```
public class Utils : MonoBehaviour {

//========================== Bounds Functions ===========================\\
    …

//========================== Transform Functions ==========================\\

    …

    public static GameObject FindTaggedParent(Transform t) {
        return( FindTaggedParent( t.gameObject ) );
    }

}


//========================== Materials Functions =========================\\

    // Returns a list of all Materials on this GameObject or its children
    static public Material[] GetAllMaterials( GameObject go ) {
        List<Material> mats = new List<Material>();
        if (go.renderer != null) {
            mats.Add(go.renderer.material);
        }
        foreach( Transform t in go.transform ) {
            mats.AddRange( GetAllMaterials( t.gameObject ) );
        }
        return( mats.ToArray() );
    }
}
```

Now, add the following bold code to the Enemy class:

```
public class Enemy : MonoBehaviour {
    …
    public int            score = 100; // Points earned for destroying this

    public int            showDamageForFrames = 2; // # frames to show damage

    public bool _____;

    public Color[]        originalColors;
    public Material[]     materials;// All the Materials of this & its children
    public int            remainingDamageFrames = 0; // Damage frames left

    public Bounds    bounds; // The Bounds of this and its children


    void Awake() {
        materials = Utils.GetAllMaterials( gameObject );
        originalColors = new Color[materials.Length];
        for (int i=0; i<materials.Length; i++) {
            originalColors[i] = materials[i].color;
        }
        InvokeRepeating( "CheckOffscreen", 0f, 2f );
    }

    // Update is called once per frame
    void Update() {
        Move();
        if (remainingDamageFrames>0) {
            remainingDamageFrames--;
            if (remainingDamageFrames == 0) {
                UnShowDamage();
            }
        }
    }

    void OnCollisionEnter( Collision coll ) {
        GameObject other = coll.gameObject;
        switch (other.tag) {
        case "ProjectileHero":
            …
            // Hurt this Enemy
            ShowDamage();
            // Get the damage amount from the Projectile.type & Main.W_DEFS
```

```
            ...
            break;
        }
    }

    void ShowDamage() {
        foreach (Material m in materials) {
            m.color = Color.red;
        }
        remainingDamageFrames = showDamageForFrames;
    }
    void UnShowDamage() {
        for ( int i=0; i<materials.Length; i++ ) {
            materials[i].color = originalColors[i];
        }
    }
}

}
```

Now, when an Enemy is struck by a projectile from the _Hero, it will turn entirely red for `showDamageForFrames` frames by setting the color of all materials to red and setting `remainingDamageFrames` to `showDamageForFrames`. Each update, if `remainingDamageFrames` is greater than 0, it is decremented until it reaches 0, at which time, the enemy ship and children revert to their original colors.

Now it's possible to see that the player is damaging the ship, but it still takes many hits to destroy one. Let's make some power-ups that will increase the power and number of the player's weapons.

Adding Power-Ups

At this point, there will be three power-ups in the game:

- **blaster [B]:** If the player weapon type is not blaster, switches to blaster and resets to 1 gun. If the player weapon type is already blaster, increases the number of guns.
- **spread [S]:** If the player weapon type is not spread, switches to spread and resets to 1 gun. If the player weapon type is already spread, increases the number of guns.
- **shield [O]:** Increases the player's shieldLevel by 1.

Artwork for Power-Ups

The power-ups will be made of a letter rendered as 3D text with a spinning cube behind it. (You can see some of them in Figure 30.1 at the beginning of the chapter.) To make the power-ups, complete these steps:

1. Create a new 3D text (*GameObject > Create Other > 3D Text* from the menu bar). Name it *PowerUp* and give it the following settings:

PowerUp (3D Text)	P:[10,0,0]	R:[0,0,0]	S:[1,1,1]
Cube (Cube)	P:[0,0,0]	R:[0,0,0]	S:[2,2,2]

2. Create a cube that is a child of PowerUp as described in the preceding settings.
3. Select the PowerUp.
4. Set the *Text Mesh* component properties of PowerUp to those shown in Figure 30.12.
5. Add a *Rigidbody* component to PowerUp (*Component > Physics > Rigidbody*) and set it as shown in Figure 30.12.
6. Set both the tag and the layer of PowerUp to *PowerUp*. When asked, click *Yes, change children*.

Next, you will create a custom material for the PowerUp cube, as follows:

1. Create a new Material named *Mat PowerUp*.
2. Drag it on to the cube that is a child of PowerUp.
3. Select the cube that is a child of PowerUp.
4. Set the Shader of Mat PowerUp to *ProtoTools > UnlitAlpha*.
5. Click the *Select* button at the bottom right of the texture for Mat PowerUp and choose the texture named *PowerUp* from the Assets tab.
6. Set the main color of Mat PowerUp to cyan (a light blue that is RGBA:[0,255,255,255]), and you can see how the PowerUp will look when colored.
7. Set the *Box Collider* of cube to be a trigger (check the box next to *Is Trigger*).

Double-check that all the settings for PowerUp and its child Cube match those in Figure 30.12 and save your scene.

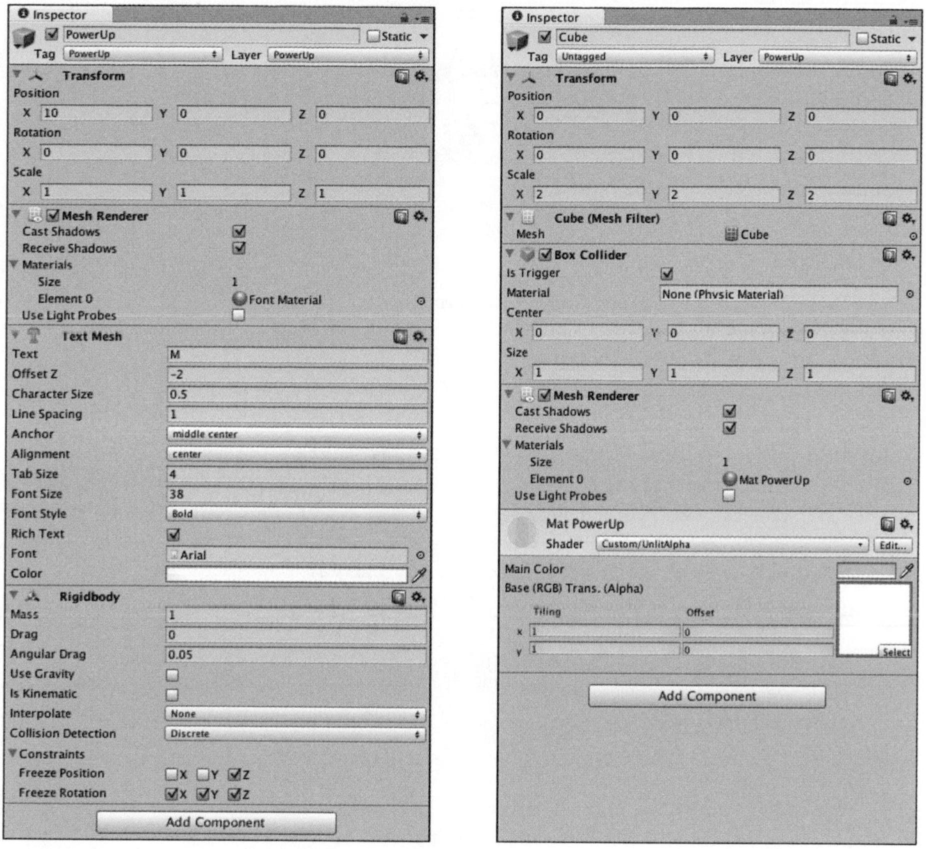

Figure 30.12 Settings for PowerUp and its child Cube prior to attaching any scripts

PowerUp Code

Now create a new C# script named *PowerUp* and assign it to the PowerUp GameObject in the Hierarchy. Open the PowerUp script in MonoDevelop and enter the following code:

```csharp
using UnityEngine;
using System.Collections;

public class PowerUp : MonoBehaviour {
    // This is an unusual but handy use of Vector2s. x holds a min value
    //   and y a max value for a Random.Range() that will be called later
    public Vector2          rotMinMax = new Vector2(15,90);
    public Vector2          driftMinMax = new Vector2(.25f,2);
    public float            lifeTime = 6f; // Seconds the PowerUp exists
```

```csharp
public float              fadeTime = 4f; // Seconds it will then fade
public bool _____;
public WeaponType         type; // The type of the PowerUp
public GameObject         cube; // Reference to the Cube child
public TextMesh           letter; // Reference to the TextMesh
public Vector3            rotPerSecond; // Euler rotation speed
public float              birthTime;

void Awake() {
    // Find the Cube reference
    cube = transform.Find("Cube").gameObject;
    // Find the TextMesh
    letter = GetComponent<TextMesh>();

    // Set a random velocity
    Vector3 vel = Random.onUnitSphere; // Get Random XYZ velocity
    // Random.onUnitSphere gives you a vector point that is somewhere on
    //   the surface of the sphere with a radius of 1m around the origin
    vel.z = 0; // Flatten the vel to the XY plane
    vel.Normalize(); // Make the length of the vel 1
    // Normalizing a Vector3 makes it length 1m
    vel *= Random.Range(driftMinMax.x, driftMinMax.y);
    // Above sets the velocity length to something between the x and y
    //   values of driftMinMax
    rigidbody.velocity = vel;

    // Set the rotation of this GameObject to R:[0,0,0]
    transform.rotation = Quaternion.identity;
    // Quaternion.identity is equal to no rotation.

    // Set up the rotPerSecond for the Cube child using rotMinMax x & y
    rotPerSecond = new Vector3( Random.Range(rotMinMax.x,rotMinMax.y),
                               Random.Range(rotMinMax.x,rotMinMax.y),
                               Random.Range(rotMinMax.x,rotMinMax.y) );

    // CheckOffscreen() every 2 seconds
    InvokeRepeating( "CheckOffscreen", 2f, 2f );

    birthTime = Time.time;
}

void Update () {
    // Manually rotate the Cube child every Update()
    // Multiplying it by Time.time causes the rotation to be time-based
    cube.transform.rotation = Quaternion.Euler( rotPerSecond*Time.time );

    // Fade out the PowerUp over time
    // Given the default values, a PowerUp will exist for 10 seconds
```

```
    //   and then fade out over 4 seconds.
    float u = (Time.time - (birthTime+lifeTime)) / fadeTime;
    // For lifeTime seconds, u will be <= 0. Then it will transition to 1
    //   over fadeTime seconds.
    // If u >= 1, destroy this PowerUp
    if (u >= 1) {
        Destroy( this.gameObject );
        return;
    }
    // Use u to determine the alpha value of the Cube & Letter
    if (u>0) {
        Color c = cube.renderer.material.color;
        c.a = 1f-u;
        cube.renderer.material.color = c;
        // Fade the Letter too, just not as much
        c = letter.color;
        c.a = 1f - (u*0.5f);
        letter.color = c;
    }
}


    // This SetType() differs from those on Weapon and Projectile
public void SetType( WeaponType wt ) {
    // Grab the WeaponDefinition from Main
    WeaponDefinition def = Main.GetWeaponDefinition( wt );
    // Set the color of the Cube child
    cube.renderer.material.color = def.color;
    //letter.color = def.color; // We could colorize the letter too
    letter.text = def.letter; // Set the letter that is shown
    type = wt; // Finally actually set the type
}


public void AbsorbedBy( GameObject target ) {
    // This function is called by the Hero class when a PowerUp is collected
    // We could tween into the target and shrink in size,
    //   but for now, just destroy this.gameObject
    Destroy( this.gameObject );
}


void CheckOffscreen() {
    // If the PowerUp has drifted entirely off screen…
    if ( Utils.ScreenBoundsCheck( cube.collider.bounds, BoundsTest.offScreen
➥ ) != Vector3.zero ) {
        // …then destroy this GameObject
        Destroy( this.gameObject );
    }
}
}
```

When you press Play, you should see the power-up drifting and rotating. If you fly _Hero into the power-up, you will get the console message "Triggered: Cube," letting you know that the Trigger Collider on the PowerUp cube is working properly.

Drag the PowerUp GameObject from the Hierarchy into the _Prefabs folder in the Project pane to make it into a prefab. Delete the remaining PowerUp instance from the Hierarchy.

Now, make the following changes to the Hero C# script to enable the Hero to collide with and collect power-ups:

```csharp
public class Hero : MonoBehaviour {
    …
    private float             _shieldLevel = 1;

    // Weapon fields
    public Weapon[]           weapons;

    public bool _____;

    void Awake() {
        S = this;  // Set the Singleton
        bounds = Utils.CombineBoundsOfChildren(this.gameObject);

        // Reset the weapons to start _Hero with 1 blaster
        ClearWeapons();
        weapons[0].SetType(WeaponType.blaster);
    }

    void OnTriggerEnter(Collider other) {
        …
        if (go != null) {
            …

            if (go.tag == "Enemy") {
                // If the shield was triggered by an enemy
                // Decrease the level of the shield by 1
                shieldLevel--;
                // Destroy the enemy
                Destroy(go);
            } else if (go.tag == "PowerUp") {
                // If the shield was triggerd by a PowerUp
                AbsorbPowerUp(go);
            } else {
                print("Triggered: "+go.name);          // Move this line here!
            }
        }
        …
    }
```

```
    public void AbsorbPowerUp( GameObject go ) {
        PowerUp pu = go.GetComponent<PowerUp>();
        switch (pu.type) {
        case WeaponType.shield: // If it's the shield
            shieldLevel++;
            break;

        default: // If it's any Weapon PowerUp
            // Check the current weapon type
            if (pu.type == weapons[0].type) {
                // then increase the number of weapons of this type
                Weapon w = GetEmptyWeaponSlot(); // Find an available weapon
                if (w != null) {
                    // Set it to pu.type
                    w.SetType(pu.type);
                }
            } else {
                // If this is a different weapon
                ClearWeapons();
                weapons[0].SetType(pu.type);
            }
            break;
        }
        pu.AbsorbedBy( this.gameObject );
    }

Weapon GetEmptyWeaponSlot() {
    for (int i=0; i<weapons.Length; i++) {
        if ( weapons[i].type == WeaponType.none ) {
            return( weapons[i] );
        }
    }
    return( null );
}

void ClearWeapons() {
    foreach (Weapon w in weapons) {
        w.SetType(WeaponType.none);
    }
}
}
```

Now that the code is set up, you need to make a couple of changes to _Hero in Unity. Open the disclosure triangle next to the GameObject _Hero in the Hierarchy. Select the Weapon child of _Hero. Press Command-D (or Control+D on Windows) four times to make four duplicates of Weapon. These should all still be children of _Hero. Rename the five weapons *Weapon_0* through *Weapon_4* and configure their transforms as follows:

_Hero		P:[0,0,0]	R:[0,0,0]	S:[1,1,1]
	Weapon_0	P:[0,2,0]	R:[0,0,0]	S:[1,1,1]
	Weapon_1	P:[-2,-1,0]	R:[0,0,0]	S:[1,1,1]
	Weapon_2	P:[2,-1,0]	R:[0,0,0]	S:[1,1,1]
	Weapon_3	P:[-1.25,-0.25,0]	R:[0,0,0]	S:[1,1,1]
	Weapon_4	P:[1.25,-0.25,0]	R:[0,0,0]	S:[1,1,1]

Next, select _Hero and open the disclosure triangle for the weapons field in the Hero (Script) component Inspector. Set the *Size* of weapons to 5 and assign Weapon_0 through Weapon_4 to the five Weapon slots in order (either by dragging them in from the Hierarchy or by clicking the target to the right of the Weapon slot and selecting each Weapon_# from the Scene tab). Figure 30.13 shows the final setup.

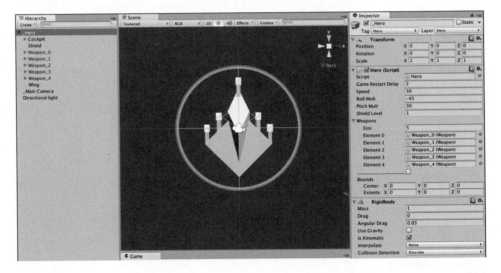

Figure 30.13   The _Hero ship showing five Weapons as children and assigned to the weapons field

Resolving Race Conditions in Code

Now, when you try to play the scene as we've created it, you may encounter an error message in the Console pane. It's also possible that you will not get this error. In this code, I've tried to intentionally create a *race condition* to show you how to resolve them. A race condition occurs when one piece of code must be executed before another piece of code, but it's possible that they will execute in the wrong order. The two pieces of code end up racing against each other.

The thing about race conditions is that they're unpredictable, so you might not get the error that I tried to create. Regardless, please read this section. Race conditions are an important kind of error that you should understand. The error you may encounter is as follows:

> `NullReferenceException`: Object reference not set to an instance of an object Main.GetWeaponDefinition (WeaponType wt) (at Assets/__Scripts/Main.cs:38) Weapon.SetType (WeaponType wt) (at Assets/__Scripts/Weapon.cs:77) Hero.Awake () (at Assets/__Scripts/Hero.cs:35)

If you double-click the error message, it should take you to line 38 of Main.cs. (Your line number might differ slightly.) Line 38 is:

```
if (W_DEFS.ContainsKey(wt)) {
```

Let's use the debugger to learn more about what's causing the error. (Please do this even if you're not getting the error.) Add a breakpoint next to this line in Main.cs and attach the debugger to Unity (by clicking the Play icon in the top-left corner of the MonoDevelop window or selecting *Run > Attach to Process* from the MonoDevelop menu bar). If you need a refresher on the debugger, reread Chapter 24. Unfortunately, in this case, you will need to have the debugger attached when the scene first starts playing, so the trick described in Chapter 24 where you start the game paused and then attach the debugger later won't work for these bugs.

When you run the project (in Unity) with the debugger attached, it will freeze on your line 38 breakpoint immediately before executing that line. We know that something's wrong with this line, and as a `NullReferenceException`, we know that the code is trying to access some variable that isn't yet defined. Let's look at each variable and see what's happening.

1. Open the Watch panel in MonoDevelop (*View > Debug Windows > Watch* from the menu bar; there should be already a check mark next to it, and selecting it again will bring the Watch panel to the front).

2. The two variables used in this line are `W_DEFS` (a static variable of the Main class) and `wt` (a local variable of the method `GetWeaponDefinition()`).

3. Type each of these into a line of the Watch window, and you'll be able to see their individual values.

4. As expected, `W_DEFS` isn't defined (its value is null). (That is, if you're experiencing the race condition error on your machine.) But we know that `W_DEFS` is properly defined in `Main.Awake()`. You can see the code that does so just a few lines above. The only way that `W_DEFS` could not be defined is if `Main.Awake()` hasn't run yet.

This is the race condition. `Main.Awake()` defines `W_DEF`, and `Hero.Awake()` is trying to use that value. We know that `Awake()` is called on each GameObject as it comes into being, but it is unclear in what order they are called. I believe that it probably happens in the order that the objects are listed in the Hierarchy, but I'm not certain of that. It's possible that your `Awake()` methods may be called in a different order than mine.

This is the major problem with race conditions. The two `Awake()` functions are racing against each other. When one is called first, your code works fine, but when the other is called first, everything breaks. Regardless of whether your code happens to be working, this is an issue that you need to resolve, because even on the same computer, the two `Awake()` functions could be called in different orders from one time to the next..

This is one reason that there are both `Awake()` and `Start()` methods in Unity. `Awake()` is called immediately when a GameObject is instantiated, while `Start()` is called immediately before the first `Update()` that the GameObject ever receives. This can be a difference of several milliseconds, which for a computer program is a very long time. If you have a number of objects in your scene, you can be guaranteed that `Awake()` will be called on all of them before `Start()` is called on any of them. `Awake()` will always happen before `Start()`.

Knowing this, take a look back at the original error. If you look at the Call Stack pane in Mono Develop (*View > Debug Windows > Call Stack* from the menu bar), it looks like `Hero.Awake()` on line 35 called `Weapon.SetType()`, which in turn called `Main.GetWeaponDefinition()`. To start fixing this issue, we will choose to delay the call from `Hero.Awake()` by moving it into `Hero.Start()`. Make the following changes to the Hero C# script. You should click the Stop sign in the MonoDevelop debugger (or select *Run > Stop* from the menu bar) as well as stop playback in Unity before changing the Hero script code:

```
public class Hero : MonoBehaviour {
    …

    void Awake() {
        S = this;  // Set the Singleton
        bounds = Utils.CombineBoundsOfChildren(this.gameObject);
    }

    void Start() {
        // Reset the weapons to start _Hero with 1 blaster
        ClearWeapons();
        weapons[0].SetType(WeaponType.blaster);
    }

    …

}
```

However after doing so, playing the project will expose yet another race condition error!

> `UnassignedReferenceException`: The variable collar of Weapon has not been assigned. You probably need to assign the collar variable of the Weapon script in the Inspector. Weapon.SetType (WeaponType wt) (at Assets/__Scripts/Weapon.cs:78) Hero.Start () (at Assets/__Scripts/Hero.cs:38)

Attach the MonoDevelop debugger to the Unity process again to get more information on this error. Place a breakpoint on line 78 of Weapon.cs and then press Play in Unity. Because the `Start()` functions are called at different times, I sometimes saw the code first stop on line 38 of

Hero.cs (where the breakpoint still remains from the previous debug) and sometimes saw it first stop on line 78 of Weapon. This is happening because both `Hero.Start()` and `Weapon.Start()` call `Weapon.SetType()`. If `Weapon.Start()` happens to be called before `Hero.Start()`, this is fine, but if `Hero.Start()` is called first, we get an error due to the race condition. The issue here is that all Weapons need to define `Weapon.collar` before `Hero.Start()` is run. To resolve this, move the definition of collar from the `Start()` method to an `Awake()` method in the the Weapon C# script.

```
void Awake() {
    collar = transform.Find("Collar").gameObject;
}

void Start() {
    // Call SetType() properly for the default _type
    SetType( _type );

    ...

}
```

Now, the race conditions should finally be resolved. `Weapon.Awake()` will define collar before either `Weapon.Start()` or `Hero.Start()` are called. Also, `Main.Awake()` will set the value of `Main.W_DEFS` before `Hero.Start()` is called. Race conditions are a common error for new game developers to step into, and it's important to be able to recognize when you may be encountering one. This is why I have lead you into this one and shown you how to discover and resolve the problem.

Making Enemies Drop Power-Ups

Getting back to the power-ups. Let's make enemies have the potential to drop a random power-up when they are destroyed. This gives the player a lot more incentive to try to destroy enemies rather than just avoid them, and it gives the player a path to improving her ship.

Add the following code to the Enemy and Main C# scripts:

```
public class Enemy : MonoBehaviour {
    ...
    public int            showDamageForFrames = 2; // # frames to show damage
    public float          powerUpDropChance = 1f;  // Chance to drop a power-up

    public bool _____;
    ...
    void OnCollisionEnter( Collision coll ) {
        ...
        case "ProjectileHero":
            ...
            if (health <= 0) {
                // Tell the Main singleton that this ship has been destroyed
```

```
                    Main.S.ShipDestroyed( this );
                    // Destroy this Enemy
                    Destroy(this.gameObject);
                }
            ...
        }
    }
    ...
}


public class Main : MonoBehaviour {
    ...
    public WeaponDefinition[]   weaponDefinitions;
    public GameObject           prefabPowerUp;
    public WeaponType[]         powerUpFrequency = new WeaponType[] {
                                    WeaponType.blaster, WeaponType.blaster,
                                    WeaponType.spread,
                                    WeaponType.shield               };

    public bool _____;
    ...

    public void ShipDestroyed( Enemy e ) {
        // Potentially generate a PowerUp
        if (Random.value <= e.powerUpDropChance) {
            // Random.value generates a value between 0 & 1 (though never == 1)
            // If the e.powerUpDropChance is 0.50f, a PowerUp will be generated
            //   50% of the time. For testing, it's now set to 1f.

            // Choose which PowerUp to pick
            // Pick one from the possibilities in powerUpFrequency
            int ndx = Random.Range(0,powerUpFrequency.Length);
            WeaponType puType = powerUpFrequency[ndx];

            // Spawn a PowerUp
            GameObject go = Instantiate( prefabPowerUp ) as GameObject;
            PowerUp pu = go.GetComponent<PowerUp>();
            // Set it to the proper WeaponType
            pu.SetType( puType );

            // Set it to the position of the destroyed ship
            pu.transform.position = e.transform.position;
        }
    }

}
```

Before this code will work, you need to select _MainCamera in the Unity Hierarchy and set the `prefabPowerUp` field of the Main Script component to be the PowerUp prefab in the _Prefabs folder of the Project pane. `powerUpFrequency` should already be set in the Inspector, but just in case, Figure 30.14 shows the correct settings. Note that enums appear in the Unity Inspector as pop-up menus.

Prefab Power Up	PowerUp	⊙
▼ Power Up Frequency		
Size	4	
Element 0	blaster	‡
Element 1	blaster	‡
Element 2	spread	‡
Element 3	shield	‡
	☐	

Figure 30.14   prefabPowerUp and powerUpFrequency on the Main (Script) component of _MainCamera

Now play the scene and destroy some enemies. They should drop power-ups that will now improve your ship!

You should notice over time that the blaster [B] power-up is more common than spread [S] or shield [O]. This is because there are two occurrences of blaster in `powerUpFrequency` and only one each of spread and shield. By adjusting the relative numbers of occurrences of each of these in `powerUpFrequency`, you can determine the chance that each will be chosen relative to the others. This same trick could also be used to set the frequency of different types of enemies spawning by assigning some enemies to the `prefabEnemies` array more times than other enemy types.

Programming Other Enemies

Now that the core elements of the game are each working, it's time to expand the different offerings of enemies. Create new C# scripts named *Enemy_1*, *Enemy_2*, *Enemy_3*, and *Enemy_4* and assign them each to their respective Enemy_# prefab in the Project pane.

Enemy_1

Open Enemy_1 scripts in MonoDevelop and enter the following code:

```csharp
using UnityEngine;
using System.Collections;

// Enemy_1 extends the Enemy class
public class Enemy_1 : Enemy {
    // Because Enemy_1 extends Enemy, the _____ bool won't work      // 1
    //   the same way in the Inspector pane. :/

    // # seconds for a full sine wave
    public float    waveFrequency = 2;
    // sine wave width in meters
    public float    waveWidth = 4;
    public float    waveRotY = 45;

    private float    x0 = -12345; // The initial x value of pos
    private float    birthTime;

    void Start() {
        // Set x0 to the initial x position of Enemy_1
        // This works fine because the position will have already
        //   been set by Main.SpawnEnemy() before Start() runs
        //   (though Awake() would have been too early!).
        // This is also good because there is no Start() method
        //   on Enemy.
        x0 = pos.x;

        birthTime = Time.time;
    }

    // Override the Move function on Enemy
    public override void Move() {                                    // 2
        // Because pos is a property, you can't directly set pos.x
        //   so get the pos as an editable Vector3
        Vector3 tempPos = pos;
        // theta adjusts based on time
        float age = Time.time - birthTime;
        float theta = Mathf.PI * 2 * age / waveFrequency;
        float sin = Mathf.Sin(theta);
        tempPos.x = x0 + waveWidth * sin;
        pos = tempPos;

        // rotate a bit about y
        Vector3 rot = new Vector3(0, sin*waveRotY, 0);
        this.transform.rotation = Quaternion.Euler(rot);
```

```
        // base.Move() still handles the movement down in y
        base.Move();                                             // 3
    }

}
```

1. The bool _____ that is used to divide the elements you should set in the Inspector from those you should not won't work that way in these subclasses of `Enemy` because when the Inspector sees a subclass like this, it will first list all the public fields of the superclass and then all the public fields of the subclass. This will place `wave Frequency`, `waveWidth`, and `waveRotY` below the line, even though you should feel free to manipulate them in the Inspector.

2. Because the method `Move()` is marked as a virtual method in the `Enemy` superclass, we are able to override it here and replace it with another function.

3. `base.Move()` calls the `Move()` function on the superclass `Enemy`.

Back in Unity, select _MainCamera in the Hierarchy and change *Element 0* of `prefab Enemies` from Enemy_0 to Enemy_1 (which is the Enemy_1 prefab in the Project pane) in the *Main (Script)* component. Now, when you press Play, the Enemy_1 ship will appear instead of Enemy_0, and it will move in a wave.

> **tip**
>
> **SPHERE COLLIDERS ONLY SCALE UNIFORMLY**   You might have noticed that the collision with Enemy_1 actually occurs before the projectile reaches the wing. If you select Enemy_1 in the Project pane and drag an instance into the scene, you will see that the green collider spheres around Enemy_1 don't scale to match the flat ellipse of the wing. This isn't a huge problem, but it is something to be aware of. A Sphere Collider will scale with the largest single component of scale in the transform. (In this case, because wing has a Scale.x of 6, the Sphere Collider scales up to that.)
>
> If you want, you can try other types of colliders to see whether one of them will scale to match the wing more accurately. A Box Collider will scale nonuniformly. You can also approximate one direction being much longer than the others with a Capsule Collider. A Mesh Collider will match the scaling most exactly, but Mesh Colliders are much slower than other types. This shouldn't be a problem on a modern high-performance PC, but Mesh Colliders are often too slow for mobile platforms like iOS or Android.
>
> If you choose to give Enemy_1 a Box Collider or Mesh Collider, then when it rotates about the y axis, it will move the edges of the wing out of the XY (that is, z=0) plane. This is why the ProjectileHero prefab has a Box Collider Size.z of 10 (to make sure that it can hit the wingtips Enemy_1 even if they are not in the XY plane).

Preparing for the Other Enemies

The remaining enemies make use of *linear interpolation*, an important development concept that is described in Appendix B. You saw a very simple interpolation in Chapter 29, "Prototype 2: Mission Demolition," but these will be a bit more interesting. Take a moment to read the "Interpolation" section of Appendix B, before tackling the remaining enemies.

Enemy_2

Enemy_2 will move via a linear interpolation that is heavily eased by a sine wave. It will rush in from the side of the screen, slow, reverse direction for a bit, slow, and then fly off the screen along its initial velocity. Only two points will be used in this interpolation, but the u value will be drastically curved by a sine wave. The easing function for the u value of Enemy_2 will be along the lines of

$$u = u + 0.6 * Sin(2\pi * u)$$

This is one of the easing functions depicted in the "Interpolation" section of Appendix B.

Open the Enemy_2 C# script and enter the following code. After you have the code working, you're welcome to adjust the easing curve and see how it affects the motion.

```csharp
using UnityEngine;
using System.Collections;

public class Enemy_2 : Enemy {
    // Enemy_2 uses a Sin wave to modify a 2-point linear interpolation
    public Vector3[]        points;
    public float            birthTime;
    public float            lifeTime = 10;
    // Determines how much the Sine wave will affect movement
    public float            sinEccentricity = 0.6f;

    void Start () {
        // Initialize the points
        points = new Vector3[2];

        // Find Utils.camBounds
        Vector3 cbMin = Utils.camBounds.min;
        Vector3 cbMax = Utils.camBounds.max;

        Vector3 v = Vector3.zero;
        // Pick any point on the left side of the screen
        v.x = cbMin.x - Main.S.enemySpawnPadding;
        v.y = Random.Range( cbMin.y, cbMax.y );
        points[0] = v;

        // Pick any point on the right side of the screen
        v = Vector3.zero;
```

```
        v.x = cbMax.x + Main.S.enemySpawnPadding;
        v.y = Random.Range( cbMin.y, cbMax.y );
        points[1] = v;

        // Possibly swap sides
        if (Random.value < 0.5f) {
            // Setting the .x of each point to its negative will move it to the
            //   other side of the screen
            points[0].x *= -1;
            points[1].x *= -1;
        }

        // Set the birthTime to the current time
        birthTime = Time.time;
    }

    public override void Move() {
        // Bézier curves work based on a u value between 0 & 1
        float u = (Time.time - birthTime) / lifeTime;

        // If u>1, then it has been longer than lifeTime since birthTime
        if (u > 1) {
            // This Enemy_2 has finished its life
            Destroy( this.gameObject );
            return;
        }

        // Adjust u by adding an easing curve based on a Sine wave
        u = u + sinEccentricity*(Mathf.Sin(u*Mathf.PI*2));

        // Interpolate the two linear interpolation points
        pos = (1-u)*points[0] + u*points[1];
    }
}
```

Swap the Enemy_2 prefab into the Element 0 slot of Main.S.prefabEnemies using the _MainCamera Inspector and press Play. As you can see the easing function causes each Enemy_2 to have very smooth movement that waves between the points it has selected on either side of the screen.

Enemy_3

Enemy_3 will use a Bézier curve to swoop down from above, slow, and fly back up off the top of the screen. For this example, we will use a simple version of the three-point Bézier curve function. In the "Interpolation" section of Appendix B you can find a recursive version of the Bézier curve function that can use any number of points (not just three).

Open the Enemy_3 script and enter the following code:

```
using UnityEngine;
using System.Collections;

// Enemy_3 extends Enemy
public class Enemy_3 : Enemy {

    // Enemy_3 will move following a Bezier curve, which is a linear
    //   interpolation between more than two points.
    public Vector3[]        points;
    public float            birthTime;
    public float            lifeTime = 10;

    // Again, Start works well because it is not used by Enemy
    void Start () {
        points = new Vector3[3]; // Initialize points

        // The start position has already been set by Main.SpawnEnemy()
        points[0] = pos;

        // Set xMin and xMax the same way that Main.SpawnEnemy() does
        float xMin = Utils.camBounds.min.x+Main.S.enemySpawnPadding;
        float xMax = Utils.camBounds.max.x-Main.S.enemySpawnPadding;

        Vector3 v;
        // Pick a random middle position in the bottom half of the screen
        v = Vector3.zero;
        v.x = Random.Range( xMin, xMax );
        v.y = Random.Range( Utils.camBounds.min.y, 0 );
        points[1] = v;

        // Pick a random final position above the top of the screen
        v = Vector3.zero;
        v.y = pos.y;
        v.x = Random.Range( xMin, xMax );
        points[2] = v;

        // Set the birthTime to the current time
        birthTime = Time.time;
    }

    public override void Move() {
        // Bezier curves work based on a u value between 0 & 1
        float u = (Time.time - birthTime) / lifeTime;
```

```
    if (u > 1) {
        // This Enemy_3 has finished its life
        Destroy( this.gameObject );
        return;
    }

    // Interpolate the three Bezier curve points
    Vector3 p01, p12;
    p01 = (1-u)*points[0] + u*points[1];
    p12 = (1-u)*points[1] + u*points[2];
    pos = (1-u)*p01 + u*p12;

    }
}
```

Now try swapping Enemy_3 into the Element 0 of `prefabEnemies` on _MainCamera. These have a very different movement than the previous enemies. After playing for a bit, you'll notice a couple of things about Bézier curves:

1. Even though the midpoint is at or below the bottom of the screen, no Enemy_3 ever gets that far down. That is because a Bézier curve touches both the start and end points but is only influenced by the midpoint.

2. Enemy_3 slows down a lot in the middle of the curve. This is also a feature of Bézier curves. If you want, you can correct this by adding the following bold line to the Enemy_3 `Move()` method just before the curve points are interpolated. This will add easing to the Enemy_3 movement that will speed up the middle of the curve to make the movement feel more consistent:

```
Vector3 p01, p12;
u = u - 0.2f*Mathf.Sin(u*Mathf.PI*2);
p01 = (1-u)*points[0] + u*points[1];
```

Enemy_4

As somewhat of a boss type, Enemy_4 will have more health than other Enemy types and will have destructible parts (rather than all the parts being destroyed at the same time). It will also stay on screen, moving from one position to another, until the player destroys it completely.

Collider Modifications

Before getting into code issues, you need to make a few adjustments to the colliders of Enemy_4. First, drag an instance of Enemy_4 into the Hierarchy and make sure that it's positioned away from other GameObjects in the scene.

Open the disclosure triangle next to Enemy_4 in the Hierarchy and select Enemy_4.Fuselage. Replace the Sphere Collider with a Capsule Collider by selecting *Component > Physics > Capsule Collider* from the menu bar. If Unity asks you, choose to replace the Sphere Collider with the Capsule Collider, if it doesn't ask you, you will need to manually remove the Sphere Collider. Set the Capsule Collider as follows in the Fuselage Inspector:

Center	[0,0,0]
Radius	0.5
Height	1
Direction	Y-Axis

Feel free to play with the values somewhat to see how they affect things. As you can see, the Capsule Collider is a much better approximation of Fuselage than the Sphere Collider was.

Now, select Wing_L in the Hierarchy and replace its Sphere Collider with a Capsule Collider as well. The settings for this collider are as follows:

Center	[0,0,0]
Radius	0.1
Height	5
Direction	X-Axis

The Direction setting chooses which is the long axis of the capsule. This is determined in local coordinates, so the Capsule Collider height of 5 along the X-axis matches the Transform scale of 5 in the X dimension. The radius of 0.1 states that the radius should be 1/10th of the height (5 * 1/10th = 0.5, which is the Z Scale dimension). You can see that the capsule does not perfectly match the wing, but it is a much better approximation than a sphere.

Select Wing_R, replace its collider with a Capsule Collider, and give that collider the same settings as used on Wing_L. Once these changes have been made, click the *Prefab > Apply* button at the top of the Inspector pane to commit these changes to the Enemy_4 prefab in the Project pane. To double-check that this worked successfully, drag a second instance of the Enemy_4 prefab into the Hierarchy pane and check to make sure that the colliders all look correct. Once this is done, delete both instances of Enemy_4 from the Hierarchy pane.

This same Capsule Collider strategy could also be applied to Enemy_3 if you want.

Movement of Enemy_4

Enemy_4 will start in the standard position off the top of the screen, pick a random point on screen, and move to it over time using a linear interpolation. Each time Enemy_4 reaches the end of an interpolation, it will pick a new point and start moving toward it. Open the Enemy_4 script and input this code:

```
using UnityEngine;
using System.Collections;

public class Enemy_4 : Enemy {
    // Enemy_4 will start offscreen and then pick a random point on screen to
    //   move to. Once it has arrived, it will pick another random point and
    //   continue until the player has shot it down.
```

```
public Vector3[]        points;  // Stores the p0 & p1 for interpolation
public float            timeStart;  // Birth time for this Enemy_4
public float            duration = 4;  // Duration of movement

void Start () {
    points = new Vector3[2];
    // There is already an initial position chosen by Main.SpawnEnemy()
    //   so add it to points as the initial p0 & p1
    points[0] = pos;
    points[1] = pos;

    InitMovement();
}

void InitMovement() {
    // Pick a new point to move to that is on screen
    Vector3 p1 = Vector3.zero;
    float esp = Main.S.enemySpawnPadding;
    Bounds cBounds = Utils.camBounds;
    p1.x = Random.Range(cBounds.min.x + esp, cBounds.max.x - esp);
    p1.y = Random.Range(cBounds.min.y + esp, cBounds.max.y - esp);

    points[0] = points[1];  // Shift points[1] to points[0]
    points[1] = p1;         // Add p1 as points[1]

    // Reset the time
    timeStart = Time.time;
}

public override void Move () {
    // This completely overrides Enemy.Move() with a linear interpolation

    float u = (Time.time-timeStart)/duration;
    if (u>=1) {  // if u >=1…
        InitMovement();  // …then initialize movement to a new point
        u=0;
    }

    u = 1 - Mathf.Pow( 1-u, 2 );          // Apply Ease Out easing to u

    pos = (1-u)*points[0] + u*points[1]; // Simple linear interpolation
}
}
```

Swap the Enemy_4 prefab into the Element 0 slot of Main.S.prefabEnemies using the _Main-Camera Inspector and save your scene. Did you remember to save after altering the colliders?

Press Play. You can see that the spawned Enemy_4s stay on screen until you destroy them. However, they're currently just as simple to take down as any of the other enemies. Now we'll break the Enemy_4 ship into four different parts with the central Cockpit protected by the others.

Open the Enemy_4 C# script and start by adding a new serializable class named `Part` to the top of Enemy_4.cs. Also be sure to add a `Part[]` array to the Enemy_4 class named `parts`.

```
using UnityEngine;
using System.Collections;

// Part is another serializable data storage class just like WeaponDefinition
[System.Serializable]
public class Part {
    // These three fields need to be defined in the Inspector pane
    public string      name;        // The name of this part
    public float       health;      // The amount of health this part has
    public string[]    protectedBy; // The other parts that protect this

    // These two fields are set automatically in Start().
    // Caching like this makes it faster and easier to find these later
    public GameObject   go;          // The GameObject of this part
    public Material     mat;         // The Material to show damage
}

public class Enemy_4 : Enemy {
    ...
    public float            duration = 4;  // Duration of movement

    public Part[]           parts;   // The array of ship Parts

    void Start() {
        ...
    }
    ...
}
```

The `Part` class will store individual information about the four `parts` of Enemy_4: Cockpit, Fuselage, Wing_L, and Wing_R.

Switch back to Unity and do the following:

1. Select the Enemy_4 prefab in the Project pane.
2. Expand the disclosure triangle next to parts in the *Inspector > Enemy_4 (Script)*.
3. Enter the settings shown in Figure 30.15. The GameObject `go` and Material `mat` of each Part will be set automatically by code.

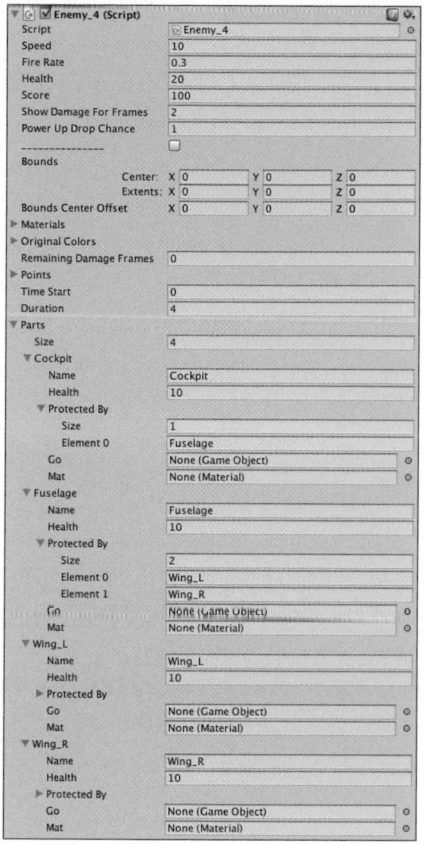

Figure 30.15 The settings for the `Parts` array of Enemy_4

As you can see in Figure 30.15, each part has 10 health, and there is a tree of protection. Cockpit is protected by Fuselage, and Fuselage is protected by both Wing_L and Wing_R. Now, switch back to MonoDevelop and make the following additions to the Enemy_4 class to make this protection work:

```
public class Enemy_4 : Enemy {
    …
    void Start () {
        …
        InitMovement();

        // Cache GameObject & Material of each Part in parts
        Transform t;
        foreach(Part prt in parts) {
            t = transform.Find(prt.name);
            if (t != null) {
                prt.go = t.gameObject;
```

```
                prt.mat = prt.go.renderer.material;
            }
        }
    }

    …

public override void Move() {
    …
}

// This will override the OnCollisionEnter that is part of Enemy.cs
// Because of the way that MonoBehaviour declares common Unity functions
//    like OnCollisionEnter(), the override keyword is not necessary.
void OnCollisionEnter( Collision coll ) {
    GameObject other = coll.gameObject;
    switch (other.tag) {
    case "ProjectileHero":
        Projectile p = other.GetComponent<Projectile>();
        // Enemies don't take damage unless they're on screen
        // This stops the player from shooting them before they are visible
        bounds.center = transform.position + boundsCenterOffset;
        if (bounds.extents == Vector3.zero || Utils.ScreenBoundsCheck(
➥bounds, BoundsTest.offScreen) != Vector3.zero) {
            Destroy(other);
            break;
        }

        // Hurt this Enemy
        // Find the GameObject that was hit
        // The Collision coll has contacts[], an array of ContactPoints
        // Because there was a collision, we're guaranteed that there is at
        //    least a contacts[0], and ContactPoints have a reference to
        //    thisCollider, which will be the collider for the part of the
        //    Enemy_4 that was hit.
        GameObject goHit = coll.contacts[0].thisCollider.gameObject;
        Part prtHit = FindPart(goHit);
        if (prtHit == null) { // If prtHit wasn't found
            //    …then it's usually because, very rarely, thisCollider on
            //    contacts[0] will be the ProjectileHero instead of the ship
            //    part. If so, just look for otherCollider instead
            goHit = coll.contacts[0].otherCollider.gameObject;
            prtHit = FindPart(goHit);
        }
        // Check whether this part is still protected
        if (prtHit.protectedBy != null) {
            foreach( string s in prtHit.protectedBy ) {
                // If one of the protecting parts hasn't been destroyed…
                if (!Destroyed(s)) {
```

```
                            // ...then don't damage this part yet
                            Destroy(other);   // Destroy the ProjectileHero
                            return; // return before causing damage
                        }
                    }
                }
                // It's not protected, so make it take damage
                // Get the damage amount from the Projectile.type & Main.W_DEFS
                prtHit.health -= Main.W_DEFS[p.type].damageOnHit;
                // Show damage on the part
                ShowLocalizedDamage(prtHit.mat);
                if (prtHit.health <= 0) {
                    // Instead of Destroying this enemy, disable the damaged part
                    prtHit.go.SetActive(false);
                }
                // Check to see if the whole ship is destroyed
                bool allDestroyed = true; // Assume it is destroyed
                foreach( Part prt in parts ) {
                    if (!Destroyed(prt)) { // If a part still exists
                        allDestroyed = false; // ...change allDestroyed to false
                        break;                 // and break out of the foreach loop
                    }
                }
                if (allDestroyed) { // If it IS completely destroyed
                    // Tell the Main singleton that this ship has been destroyed
                    Main.S.ShipDestroyed( this );
                    // Destroy this Enemy
                    Destroy(this.gameObject);
                }
                Destroy(other);   // Destroy the ProjectileHero
                break;
            }
    }
}

// These two functions find a Part in this.parts by name or GameObject
Part FindPart(string n) {
    foreach( Part prt in parts ) {
        if (prt.name == n) {
            return( prt );
        }
    }
    return( null );
}
Part FindPart(GameObject go) {
    foreach( Part prt in parts ) {
        if (prt.go == go) {
            return( prt );
        }
    }
```

```
        return( null );
    }

    // These functions return true if the Part has been destroyed
    bool Destroyed(GameObject go) {
        return( Destroyed( FindPart(go) ) );
    }
    bool Destroyed(string n) {
        return( Destroyed( FindPart(n) ) );
    }
    bool Destroyed(Part prt) {
        if (prt == null) { // If no real Part was passed in
            return(true); // Return true (meaning yes, it was destroyed)
        }
        // Returns the result of the comparison: prt.health <= 0
        // If prt.health is 0 or less, returns true (yes, it was destroyed)
        return (prt.health <= 0);
    }

    // This changes the color of just one Part to red instead of the whole ship
    void ShowLocalizedDamage(Material m) {
        m.color = Color.red;
        remainingDamageFrames = showDamageForFrames;
    }
}
```

Now when you play the scene, you should be overwhelmed by many Enemy_4s, each of which has two wings that protect the fuselage and a fuselage that protects the cockpit. If you want more of a chance against these, you can change the value of *Main (Script).enemySpawn PerSecond* on the _MainCamera to something lower, which will give you more time between Enemy_4 spawns (though it will also delay the initial spawn).

Adding Particle Effects and Background

After all of that coding, here are a couple of things you can do just for fun to make the game look a little better.

Starfield Background

Create a two-layer starfield background to make things look more like outer space.

Create a quad in the Hierarchy (*GameObject > Create Other > Quad*). Name it *StarfieldBG*.

StarfieldBG (Quad)   P:[0,0,10]   R:[0,0,0]   S:[80,80,1]

This will place StarfieldBG in the center of the camera's view and fill the view entirely. Now, create a new material named *Mat Starfield* and set its shader to *ProtoTools > UnlitAlpha*. Set the texture of Mat Starfield to the *Space Texture2D* that you imported at the beginning of this tutorial. Now drag Mat Starfield onto StarfieldBG, and you should see a starfield behind your _Hero ship.

Select Mat Starfield in the Project pane and duplicate it (Command-D on Mac or Control+D on PC). Name the new material *Mat Starfield Transparent*. Select *Space_Transparent* as the texture for this new material.

Select StarfieldBG in the Hierarchy and duplicate it. Name the duplicate *StarfieldFG_0*. Drag the Mat Starfield Transparent material onto StarfieldFG_0 and set its transform.

StarfieldFG_0	P:[0,0,5]	R:[0,0,0]	S:[160,160,1]

Now if you drag StarfieldFG_0 around a bit, you'll see that it moves some stars in the foreground past stars in the background, creating a nifty parallax scrolling effect. Now duplicate Starfield_FG_0 and name the duplicate *Starfield_FG_1*. You will need two copies of the foreground for the scrolling trick that we're going to employ.

Create a new C# script named *Parallax* and edit it in MonoDevelop.

```csharp
using UnityEngine;
using System.Collections;

public class Parallax : MonoBehaviour {

    public GameObject      poi; // The player ship
    public GameObject[]    panels; // The scrolling foregrounds
    public float           scrollSpeed = -30f;
    // motionMult controls how much panels react to player movement
    public float           motionMult = 0.25f;

    private float panelHt; // Height of each panel
    private float depth;   // Depth of panels (that is, pos.z)

    // Use this for initialization
    void Start () {
        panelHt = panels[0].transform.localScale.y;
        depth = panels[0].transform.position.z;

        // Set initial positions of panels
        panels[0].transform.position = new Vector3(0,0,depth);
        panels[1].transform.position = new Vector3(0,panelHt,depth);
    }
```

```
    // Update is called once per frame
    void Update () {
        float tY, tX=0;
        tY= Time.time * scrollSpeed % panelHt + (panelHt*0.5f);

        if (poi != null) {
            tX = -poi.transform.position.x * motionMult;
        }

        // Position panels[0]
        panels[0].transform.position = new Vector3(tX, tY, depth);
        // Then position panels[1] where needed to make a continuous starfield
        if (tY >= 0) {
            panels[1].transform.position = new Vector3(tX, tY-panelHt, depth);
        } else {
            panels[1].transform.position = new Vector3(tX, tY+panelHt, depth);
        }
    }
}
```

Save the script, return to Unity, and assign the script to _MainCamera. Select _MainCamera in the Hierarchy and find the *Parallax (Script)* component in the Inspector. There, set the poi to _Hero and add StarfieldFG_0 and StarfieldFG_1 to the panels array. Now press Play, and you should see the starfield moving in response to the player.

And of course, remember to save your scene.

Summary

This was a long chapter, but it introduced a lot of important concepts that I hope will help you with your own game projects in the future. Over the years, I have made extensive use of linear interpolation and Bézier curves to make the motion in my games and other projects smooth and refined. Just a simple easing function can make the movement of an object look graceful, excited, or lethargic, which is a powerful when you're trying to balance and tune the feel of a game.

In the next chapter, we move on to a very different kind of game: a solitaire card game (actually, my favorite solitaire card game). The next chapter demonstrates how to read information from an XML file to construct an entire deck of cards out of just a few art assets and also how to use XML to lay out the game itself. And, at the end, you'll have a fun digital card game to play.

Next Steps

From your experience in the previous tutorials, you already understand how to do many of the things listed in this section. These are just some recommendations on what you can do if you want to keep going with this prototype.

Tune Variables

As you have learned in both paper and digital games, tuning of numbers is critically important and has a significant effect on experience. The following is a list of variables you should consider tuning to change the feel of the game:

- _Hero: Change how movement feels
  - Adjust the `speed`.
  - Modify the gravity and sensitivity of the horizontal and vertical axes in the InputManager.
- Weapons: Differentiate weapons more
  - Spread: The spread gun could shoot five projectiles instead of just three but have a much longer `delayBetweenShots`.
  - Blaster: The blaster could fire more rapidly (smaller `delayBetweenShots`) but do less damage with each shot (reduced `damageOnHit`).
- Power-ups: Adjust drop rate
  - Each `Enemy` class has a `powerUpDropChance` field that can be set to any number between 0 (never drop a power-up) to 1 (always drop a power-up). These were set to 1 for testing, but you can adjust them to whatever you want.
  - It's also possible now for multiple Projectiles to hit an Enemy on the same turn that the Enemy's health drops to 0. This will cause multiple PowerUps to be spawned. Try to change the code to stop this from happening.

Add Additional Elements

While this prototype has so far shown five kinds of enemies and two kinds of weapons, there are infinite possibilities for either open to you:

- **Weapons:** Add additional weapons
  - Phaser: Shoots two projectiles that move in a sine wave pattern (similar to the movement of Enemy_1).
  - Laser: Instead of doing all of its damage at once, the laser does continuous damage over time.
  - Missiles: Missiles could have a lock-on mechanic and have a very slow fire-rate but would track enemies and always hit. Perhaps missiles could be a different kind of weapon with limited ammunition that were fired using a different button (that is, not the space bar).
  - Swivel Gun: Like the blaster but actually shoots at the nearest enemy. However, the gun is very weak.
- **Enemies:** Add additional enemies. There are countless kinds of enemies that could be created for this game.

- Add additional enemy abilities
  - Allow some enemies to shoot.
  - Some enemies could track and follow the player, possibly acting like missiles homing in on the player.
- Add level progression
  - Make specific, timed waves instead of the randomized infinite attack in the existing prototype. This could be accomplished using a `[System.Serializable]` Wave class as defined here:

```
[System.Serializable]
public class Wave {
    float      delayBeforeWave=1; // secs to delay after the prev wave
    GameObject[] ships;              // array of ships in this wave
    // Delay the next wave until this wave is completely killed?
    bool       delayNextWaveUntilThisWaveIsDead=false;
}
```

- Add a `Level` class to contain the `Wave[]` array:

```
[System.Serializable]
public class Level {
    Wave[]     waves;  // Holder for waves
    float      timeLimit=-1; // If -1, there is no time limit
    string     name = ""; // If the name is left blank (i.e., ""),
                          //  the name could appear as "Level #1"
}
```

However, this will cause issues because even if `Level` is serializable, the `Wave[]` array won't appear properly because the Unity Inspector won't allow nested serializable classes. This means that you should probably try something like an XML document to define levels and waves which can then be read into `Level` and `Wave` classes. XML is covered in the "XML" section of Appendix B and is used in the next prototype, Prospector Solitaire.

- Add more game structure and GUI (graphical user interface) elements:
  - Give the player a score and a specific number of lives (both of these were covered in Chapter 29).
  - Add difficulty settings.
  - Track high scores (as covered in the Apple Picker and Mission Demolition prototypes).
  - Create a title screen scene that welcomes the player to the game and allows her to choose the difficulty setting. This could also show high scores.

CHAPTER 31

PROTOTYPE 4: PROSPECTOR SOLITAIRE

In this chapter, you make your first digital card game. The game you create is a version of the popular *Tri-Peaks Solitaire* game that has been updated for the digital age.

This chapter includes several new techniques, including using XML configuration files, designing for mobile devices, and your first look at the 2D sprite tools that are included in Unity 4.3 and above.

By the end of the chapter, you'll have not only a working card game but also a great framework for future card games you wish to create.

Getting Started: Prototype 4

As with Prototype 3, this starts with you being asked to download and import a unitypackage of assets for this game. The art assets we'll be using are constructed from parts of the publicly available Vectorized Playing Cards 1.3 by Chris Aguilar.[1]

It's also important to note that this project will work only with Unity 4.3 and later. In this chapter, we make extensive use of the Unity 2D tools that were introduced in version 4.3.

SET UP THE PROJECT FOR THIS CHAPTER

Following the standard project setup procedure, create a new project in Unity. If you need a refresher on the standard project setup procedure, see Appendix A, "Standard Project Setup Procedure." When you are creating the project, you will be asked if you want to set up defaults for 2D or 3D. Choose 2D for this project.

- **Project name:** Prospector.
- **Scene name:** _Prospector_Scene_0.
- **Project folders:** __Scripts, _Prefabs, _Sprites.
- **Download and import package:** Go to Chapter 31 at http://book.prototools.net
- **C# script names:** (none yet).
- **Rename:** Change Main Camera to _MainCamera.

Importing the unitypackage should set _MainCamera correctly, but just in case, here are the settings:

_MainCamera (Camera)	P:[0,0,-40]	R:[0,0,0]	S:[1,1,1]
	Projection: Orthographic		
	Size: 10		

Note that this unitypackage includes a version of the Utils script that has additional functions beyond what you wrote in the previous chapter.

Build Settings

This will be the first project designed to be able to be compiled on mobile devices. As an example, I'll be using settings for the Apple iPad, but it's perfectly fine to use Android, BlackBerry,

---

[1] Chris Aguilar, "Vectorized Playing Cards 1.3," http://code.google.com/p/vectorized-playing-cards. Copyright 2011—Chris Aguilar. Licensed under LGPL 3—www.gnu.org/copyleft/lesser.html.

Windows 8 Phone, or even a Web Player build instead if you prefer. This project is designed for the 4:3 aspect ratio screen of an iPad in portrait mode. Though this project is designed to be able to be compiled for a mobile device, the actual build process for mobile devices is beyond the scope of this book (and would differ widely based on which device you own), but you can find a lot of information about doing so on Unity's website. The link for iOS development is http://docs.unity3d.com/Documentation/Manual/iphone-GettingStarted.html. There is also more information about compiling for mobile at the end of this chapter

1. Double-click the __Prospector_Scene_0 scene in the Project pane to open it.

2. From the menu bar choose *File > Build Settings*, which will bring up the window shown in Figure 31.1.

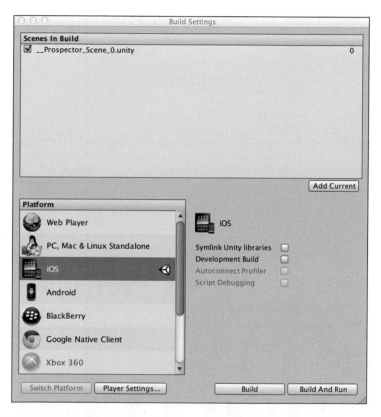

Figure 31.1   The Build Settings window

3. Click *Add Current* to add __Prospector_Scene_0 to the list of scenes for this build.

4. Select iOS from the list of platforms and click *Switch Platform*. Unity will reimport all of your images to match the default iOS settings. The *Switch Platform* button will turn gray once the switch is complete. Once your Build Settings look like the image in Figure 31.1, you can close this window. (Don't click Build yet; that would happen after actually making the game.)

Importing Images as Sprites

Next, we'll need to properly import the images we're using as *sprites*. A sprite is a 2D image that can be moved around the screen and rotated, and they are very common in 2D games:

1. Open the _Sprites folder in your Project pane and select all the images therein. (Click the top image and then Shift-click the bottom image in the _Sprites folder.) Looking at the Preview in the Inspector pane, you can see that all of them are currently imported as square images with no transparency. We're going to change that and make them usable sprites.

2. In the *21 Texture 2Ds Import Settings* section of the Inspector pane, set the *Texture Type* to *Sprite*. Then click *Apply*, and Unity will reimport all the images at their proper aspect ratio; however, you will see a warning in the console that "Only square textures can be compressed to PVRTC format." Now change the *Format* in the Inspector from Compressed to *TrueColor* and click Apply. This will eliminate that warning, and your images should now be ready to be used as sprites. Figure 31.2 shows the final import settings.

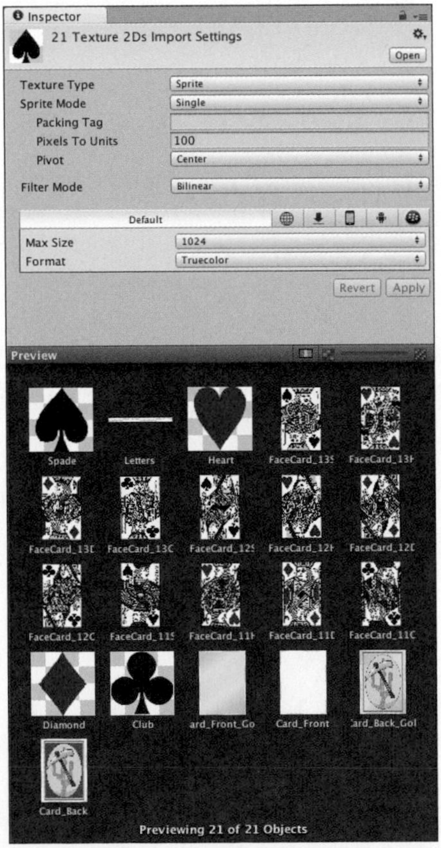

Figure 31.2   Import settings for the Texture 2Ds that will become sprites

3. Looking at the Project pane, you will see that each of the images now has a disclosure triangle next to it. If you open the disclosure triangle, you'll find a sprite with the same name as the image under each image.

4. Select the Letters image in the Project pane. For most of the images that were imported, a Sprite Mode of Single is appropriate because each image becomes a single sprite. However, the Letters image is actually a sprite atlas (a series of sprites saved as a single image), so it requires different settings. In *Letters Import Settings* in the Inspector pane, change the Sprite Mode to *Multiple* and click Apply. This will add a new *Sprite Editor* button under the *Pixels to Units* field. Click this button to open the *Sprite Editor*. You'll see the Letters image there with a single blue box around it defining the bounds of the Letters sprite. Click the small icon with either a rainbow or a letter *A* on it in the Sprite Editor (circled in Figure 31.3) to switch between viewing the actual image and the alpha channel of the image. Because Letters is an image of white letters over a transparent background, it may be easier to see what's happening if you look at the alpha channel.

5. Now, click the *Slice* pop-up menu in the top-left corner of the Sprite Editor and change the *Type* from Automatic to Grid (see Figure 31.3). Set the *Pixel size* to X:32 Y:32 and click the *Slice* button. This will chop Letters horizontally into 16 sprites that are each 32x32 pixels in size. Click Apply (in the top-right corner of the Sprite Editor) to generate these sprites in the Project pane. Now instead of one Letters sprite, there are 16 sprites named Letters_0 to Letters_15. In this game, you will use Letters_1 to Letters_13 for each of the 13 ranks of cards (Ace through King). Now all the sprites are set up and ready to be used.

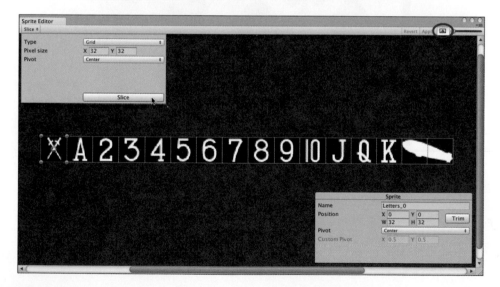

Figure 31.3 The Sprite Editor showing the correct settings for the grid slicing of Letters. The button circled in the top right switches between viewing the color channels and the alpha channel of Letters.

6. Save your scene. You haven't actually altered the scene yet, but it's good practice to save your scene all the time, so you should be in the habit of saving your scene any time you change anything.

Constructing Cards from Sprites

One of the most important aspects of this project is that we're going to procedurally construct an entire deck of cards from the 21 images that were imported. This will make the final build for mobile smaller and will give you a chance to see how XML works.

The image in Figure 31.4 shows an example of how this will be done. The 10 of Spades in the image is constructed from Card_Front, 12 copies of Spade, and 2 copies of the Letters_10 sprite.

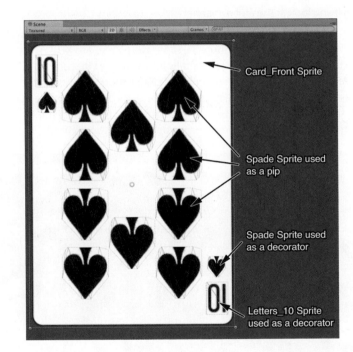

Figure 31.4   The 10 of Spades showing autogenerated borders around each of the sprites from which it is made. The visible part of this card is composed of 15 different sprites (12 Spades, 2 Letter_10s, and 1 Card_Front).

This is defined through the use of an XML file. Read the "XML" section of Appendix B, "Useful Concepts," now to learn more about XML and how it can be read using the PT_XMLReader that was part of the imported unitypackage. The structure of the DeckXML.xml file used in this project is also shown in that section of Appendix B.

Making Use of XML Through Code

For the first part of this project, create three C# files named *Card*, *Deck*, and *Prospector*.

- Card: The class for each individual card in the deck. Card will also contain the CardDefinition class (which holds information about where sprites are to be positioned on each rank of card) and the Decorator class (which holds information about the decorators and pips described in the XML document).

- Deck: The Deck class interprets the information in DeckXML.xml and uses that information to create an entire deck of cards.

- Prospector: The Prospector class manages the overall game. While Deck handles the creation of cards, Prospector turns those cards into a game. Prospector collects the cards into various piles (like the draw pile and discard pile) and manages game logic.

1. Start by creating the Card C# script and opening it in MonoDevelop. Enter the following code:

```csharp
using UnityEngine;
using System.Collections;
using System.Collections.Generic;

public class Card : MonoBehaviour {
    // This will be defined later
}


[System.Serializable]
public class Decorator {
// This class stores information about each decorator or pip from DeckXML
    public string    type; // For card pips, type = "pip"
    public Vector3   loc;  // The location of the Sprite on the Card
    public bool      flip = false;  // Whether to flip the Sprite vertically
    public float     scale = 1f;    // The scale of the Sprite
}


[System.Serializable]
public class CardDefinition {
// This class stores information for each rank of card
    public string            face; // Sprite to use for each face card
    public int               rank; // The rank (1-13) of this card
    public List<Decorator>   pips = new List<Decorator>();  // Pips used
    // Because decorators (from the XML) are used the same way on every card
in
    //   the deck, pips only stores information about the pips on numbered
cards
}
```

2. These small classes in Card.cs will store the information created when Deck reads the XML file. Open the Deck C# script in MonoDevelop and enter the following code:

```
using UnityEngine;
using System.Collections;
using System.Collections.Generic;

public class Deck : MonoBehaviour {

    public bool _____;

    public PT_XMLReader          xmlr;

    // InitDeck is called by Prospector when it is ready
    public void InitDeck(string deckXMLText) {
        ReadDeck(deckXMLText);
    }

    // ReadDeck parses the XML file passed to it into CardDefinitions
    public void ReadDeck(string deckXMLText) {
        xmlr = new PT_XMLReader(); // Create a new PT_XMLReader
        xmlr.Parse(deckXMLText);   // Use that PT_XMLReader to parse DeckXML

        // This prints a test line to show you how xmlr can be used.
        // For more information read about XML in the Useful Concepts Appendix
        string s = "xml[0] decorator[0] ";
        s += "type="+xmlr.xml["xml"][0]["decorator"][0].att("type");
        s += " x="+xmlr.xml["xml"][0]["decorator"][0].att("x");
        s += " y="+xmlr.xml["xml"][0]["decorator"][0].att("y");
        s += " scale="+xmlr.xml["xml"][0]["decorator"][0].att("scale");
        print(s);

    }
}
```

The lines that grab data from the parsed XML may look a little strange at first. xmlr is the PT_XMLReader instance, and xmlr.xml is the parsed XML. Bracket access is then used to delve into the XML in a nested way. xmlr.xml["xml"] grabs a collection of all the <xml> elements at the top level of the XML file, and xmlr.xml["xml"][0] gets the 0th element of that collection. This continues, digging down into the various elements of the XML file to get the attributes (e.g., att("type")) of the decorators.

3. Now open the Prospector class and enter this code:

```
using UnityEngine;
using System.Collections;
using System.Collections.Generic;

public class Prospector : MonoBehaviour {
    static public Prospector    S;
```

```
    public Deck                    deck;
    public TextAsset               deckXML;

    void Awake() {
        S = this; // Set up a Singleton for Prospector
    }

    void Start () {
        deck = GetComponent<Deck>(); // Get the Deck
        deck.InitDeck(deckXML.text); // Pass DeckXML to it
    }
}
```

4. Now that the code is ready, go back to Unity and attach both the `Prospector` and `Deck` classes to _MainCamera. (Drag each script from the Project pane onto _MainCamera in the Hierarchy pane.) Then select _MainCamera in the Hierarchy. You should see both scripts attached as Script components. Drag DeckXML from the Resources folder in the Project pane into the `deckXML` TextAsset variable in the Inspector for the Prospector (Script) component.

5. Save your scene and click Play. You should see the following output in the console:

```
xml[0] decorator[0] type=letter x=-1.05 y=1.42 scale=1.25
```

This line comes from the test code in `Deck:ReadDeck()` and shows that `ReadDeck()` is properly reading the type, x, y, and scale attributes from the 0th decorator of the 0th xml in the XML file, as shown in the following lines from DeckXML.xml. (You can double-click the DeckXML file in the Resources folder to open it in MonoDevelop and view the entire thing.)

```
<xml>
    <decorator type="letter" x="-1.05" y="1.42" z="0" flip="0" scale="1.25"/>
    ...
</xml>
```

Now, let's actually do something with this information.

1. Make the following bolded changes to the `Deck` class:

```
public class Deck : MonoBehaviour {

    public bool _____;

    public PT_XMLReader                xmlr;
    public List<string>                cardNames;
    public List<Card>                  cards;
    public List<Decorator>             decorators;
    public List<CardDefinition>        cardDefs;
    public Transform                   deckAnchor;
    public Dictionary<string,Sprite>   dictSuits;
```

```
// InitDeck is called by Prospector when it is ready
public void InitDeck(string deckXMLText) {
    ReadDeck(deckXMLText);
}

// ReadDeck parses the XML file passed to it into CardDefinitions
public void ReadDeck(string deckXMLText) {
    xmlr = new PT_XMLReader(); // Create a new PT_XMLReader
    xmlr.Parse(deckXMLText);   // Use that PT_XMLReader to parse DeckXML

    // This prints a test line to show you how xmlr can be used.
    // For more information read about XML in the Useful Concepts Appendix
    string s = "xml[0] decorator[0] ";
    s += "type="+xmlr.xml["xml"][0]["decorator"][0].att("type");
    s += " x="+xmlr.xml["xml"][0]["decorator"][0].att("x");
    s += " y="+xmlr.xml["xml"][0]["decorator"][0].att("y");
    s += " scale="+xmlr.xml["xml"][0]["decorator"][0].att("scale");
    //print(s); // Comment out this line, since we're done with the test

    // Read decorators for all Cards
    decorators = new List<Decorator>(); // Init the List of Decorators
    // Grab a PT_XMLHashList of all <decorator>s in the XML file
    PT_XMLHashList xDecos = xmlr.xml["xml"][0]["decorator"];
    Decorator deco;
    for (int i=0; i<xDecos.Count; i++) {
        // For each <decorator> in the XML
        deco = new Decorator(); // Make a new Decorator
        // Copy the attributes of the <decorator> to the Decorator
        deco.type = xDecos[i].att("type");
        // Set the bool flip based on whether the text of the attribute is
        //   "1" or something else. This is an atypical but perfectly fine
        //   use of the == comparison operator. It will return a true or
        //   false, which will be assigned to deco.flip.
        deco.flip = ( xDecos[i].att("flip") == "1" );
        // floats need to be parsed from the attribute strings
        deco.scale = float.Parse( xDecos[i].att("scale") );
        // Vector3 loc initializes to [0,0,0], so we just need to modify it
        deco.loc.x = float.Parse( xDecos[i].att("x") );
        deco.loc.y = float.Parse( xDecos[i].att("y") );
        deco.loc.z = float.Parse( xDecos[i].att("z") );
        // Add the temporary deco to the List decorators
        decorators.Add (deco);
    }

    // Read pip locations for each card number
    cardDefs = new List<CardDefinition>(); // Init the List of Cards
    // Grab a PT_XMLHashList of all the <card>s in the XML file
    PT_XMLHashList xCardDefs = xmlr.xml["xml"][0]["card"];
```

```
for (int i=0; i<xCardDefs.Count; i++) {
    // For each of the <card>s
    // Create a new CardDefinition
    CardDefinition cDef = new CardDefinition();
    // Parse the attribute values and add them to cDef
    cDef.rank = int.Parse( xCardDefs[i].att ("rank") );
    // Grab a PT_XMLHashList of all the <pip>s on this <card>
    PT_XMLHashList xPips = xCardDefs[i]["pip"];
    if (xPips != null) {
        for (int j=0; j<xPips.Count; j++) {
            // Iterate through all the <pip>s
            deco = new Decorator();
            // <pip>s on the <card> are handled via the Decorator Class
            deco.type = "pip";
            deco.flip = ( xPips[j].att ("flip") == "1" );
            deco.loc.x = float.Parse( xPips[j].att ("x") );
            deco.loc.y = float.Parse( xPips[j].att ("y") );
            deco.loc.z = float.Parse( xPips[j].att ("z") );
            if ( xPips[j].HasAtt("scale") ) {
                deco.scale = float.Parse( xPips[j].att ("scale") );
            }
            cDef.pips.Add(deco);
        }
    }
    // Face cards (Jack, Queen, & King) have a face attribute
    // cDef.face is the base name of the face card Sprite
    // e.g., FaceCard_11 is the base name for the Jack face Sprites
    // the Jack of Clubs is FaceCard_11C, hearts is FaceCard_11H, etc.
    if (xCardDefs[i].HasAtt("face")) {
        cDef.face = xCardDefs[i].att ("face");
    }
    cardDefs.Add(cDef);
}

    }

}
```

2. Now, the `ReadDeck()` method will parse the XML and turn it into a list of Decorators (the suit and rank in the corners of the card) and CardDefinitions (a class containing information about each of the ranks of card (Ace through King). Switch back to Unity and press Play. Then click on the _MainCamera and look at the Inspector for the Deck (Script) component. Because both Decorator and CardDefinition were set to [System.Serializable], they appear properly in the Unity Inspector, as shown in Figure 31.5. (Note that this is due to an improvement in the Inspector for Unity 4.3.)

3. Stop playback and *save your scene*.

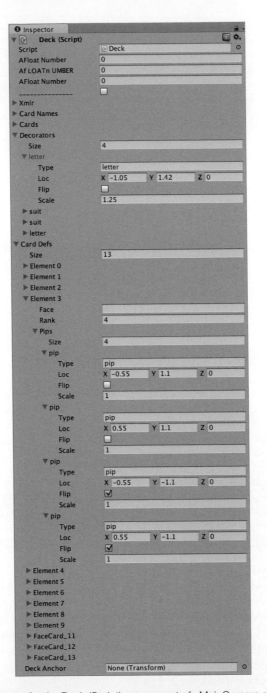

Figure 31.5 The Inspector for the Deck (Script) component of _MainCamera showing Decorators and Card Defs that have been read from the DecXML.xml file

Assigning the Sprites That Become Cards

Now that the XML has been properly read and parsed into usable Lists, it's time to make some cards. The first step in doing so is to get references to all of those sprites that we made earlier in the chapter:

1. Add the following variables to the top of the `Deck` class to hold these sprites:

```
public class Deck : MonoBehaviour {
    // Suits
    public Sprite              suitClub;
    public Sprite              suitDiamond;
    public Sprite              suitHeart;
    public Sprite              suitSpade;

    public Sprite[]            faceSprites;
    public Sprite[]            rankSprites;

    public Sprite              cardBack;
    public Sprite              cardBackGold;
    public Sprite              cardFront;
    public Sprite              cardFrontGold;

    // Prefabs
    public GameObject          prefabSprite;
    public GameObject          prefabCard;

    public bool _____;
```

When you switch back to Unity, there will now be many new public variables that need to be defined in the Deck (Sprite) Inspector.

2. Drag the Club, Diamond, Heart, and Spade textures from the _Sprites folder in the Project pane into their respective variables under Deck (`suitClub`, `suitDiamond`, `suitHeart`, and `suitSpade`). Unity will automatically assign the sprite to the variable (as opposed to attempting to assign the Texture2D to a sprite variable).

3. The next bit is a touch trickier. Lock the Inspector on _MainCamera by selecting _MainCamera in the Hierarchy pane and then clicking the tiny lock icon at the top of the Inspector pane (circled in red in the Figure 31.6). Locking the Inspector pane ensures that it won't change which object is displayed when you select something new.

4. Disclose the triangle next to the variable `faceSprites` in the Inspector for Deck (Script) and set its Size to 12. Now, drag each of the Texture2Ds with names that start with *Face-Card_* into an element of `faceSprites`. The order doesn't matter as long as there is exactly one of each when you're done (see Figure 31.6).

5. Open the disclosure triangle next to Letters in the Project pane. Select Letters_0 and then Shift-click Letters_15. You should now have all 16 sprites under Letters selected. Drag this group of sprites onto the `rankSprites` variable in Deck (Script). You should see a plus icon appear next to the word *<multiple>* when hovering over the variable name `rankSprites` (on PC, you may only see the + icon). Release the mouse button, and if done correctly,

the rankSprites list should now be full of 16 Letters sprites named Letters_0 through Letters_15. Double-check to make sure that they're in the correct order with Letters_0 in Element 0 and Letters_15 in Element 15; if not, you may have to add them one at a time.

6. Drag the sprites Card_Back, Card_Back_Gold, Card_Front, and Card_Front_Gold from the Project pane to their respective variable slots in the Deck (Script) Inspector.

7. Unlock the Inspector pane by clicking the tiny lock icon again (circled in red in Figure 31.6). Your Inspector for Deck (Script) should now look like what is shown in the figure.

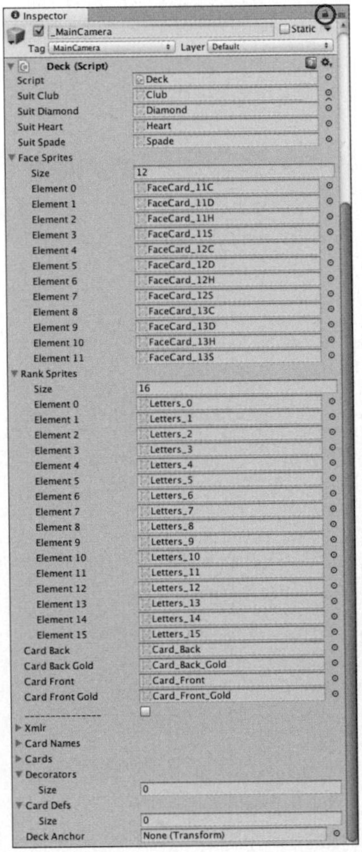

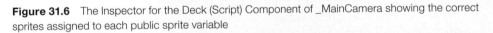

Figure 31.6　The Inspector for the Deck (Script) Component of _MainCamera showing the correct sprites assigned to each public sprite variable

Creating Prefab GameObjects for Sprites and Cards

Just like anything else on screen, sprites need to be enclosed in GameObjects. For this project, you will need two prefabs: a generic *PrefabSprite* that will be used for all decorators and pips, and a *PrefabCard* that will form the basis of all the cards in the deck.

PrefabSprite

To create PrefabSprite, do the following:

1. From the menu bar, choose *GameObject > Create Other > Sprite*.

2. Name this GameObject *PrefabSprite* and drag it into the _Prefabs folder of the Project pane to make it a prefab.

3. Delete the remaining PrefabSprite instance from the Hierarchy.

PrefabCard

To create PrefabCard, do the following:

1. From the menu bar, choose *GameObject > Create Other > Sprite*. Name this GameObject *PrefabCard*.

2. Drag Card_Front from the Project pane into the sprite variable of the Sprite Renderer in the PrefabCard Inspector. Now you should see the Card_Front sprite in the Scene pane.

3. Drag the Card script from the Project pane onto PrefabCard in the Hierarchy. This will assign the Card script to PrefabCard (and the Card (Script) component will now appear in the Inspector for PrefabCard).

4. In the Inspector for PrefabCard, click the *Add Component* button. Choose *Physics > Box Collider* from the menu that appears. (This is the same as choosing *Component > Physics > Box Collider* from the menu bar.) The Size of the Box Collider should automatically set itself to [2.56, 3.56, 0.2], but if not, set the Size to those values.

5. Drag PrefabCard from the Hierarchy into the _Prefabs folder to make a prefab from it. Delete the remaining instance of PrefabCard from the Hierarchy.

Now, you need to assign these two prefabs to their respective public variables in the Inspector for the Deck (Script) Component on _MainCamera.

1. Select _MainCamera in the hierarchy, and drag PrefabCard and PrefabSprite from the Project pane into their respective variables in the Deck (Script) Inspector.

2. Save your scene.

Building the Cards in Code

Before actually adding the method to the Deck class to make the cards, we need to add variables to Card, as follows:

1. Add the following code to the Card C# script:

```
public class Card : MonoBehaviour {
    public string        suit; // Suit of the Card (C,D,H, or S)
    public int           rank; // Rank of the Card (1-14)
    public Color         color = Color.black; // Color to tint pips
    public string        colS = "Black"; // or "Red". Name of the Color
```

```
            // This List holds all of the Decorator GameObjects
            public List<GameObject> decoGOs = new List<GameObject>();
            // This List holds all of the Pip GameObjects
            public List<GameObject> pipGOs  = new List<GameObject>();

            public GameObject        back; // The GameObject of the back of the card

            public CardDefinition    def; // Parsed from DeckXML.xml
    }
```

2. And now, add this code to `Deck`:

```
public class Deck : MonoBehaviour {
    …

        // InitDeck is called by Prospector when it is ready
        public void InitDeck(string deckXMLText) {
            // This creates an anchor for all the Card GameObjects in the Hierarchy
            if (GameObject.Find("_Deck") == null) {
                GameObject anchorGO = new GameObject("_Deck");
                deckAnchor = anchorGO.transform;
            }

            // Initialize the Dictionary of SuitSprites with necessary Sprites
            dictSuits = new Dictionary<string, Sprite>() {
                { "C", suitClub },
                { "D", suitDiamond },
                { "H", suitHeart },
                { "S", suitSpade }
            };

            ReadDeck(deckXMLText);
            MakeCards();
        }

        // ReadDeck parses the XML file passed to it into CardDefinitions
        public void ReadDeck(string deckXMLText) {
            …
        }

        // Get the proper CardDefinition based on Rank (1 to 14 is Ace to King)
        public CardDefinition GetCardDefinitionByRank(int rnk) {
            // Search through all of the CardDefinitions
            foreach (CardDefinition cd in cardDefs) {
                // If the rank is correct, return this definition
                if (cd.rank == rnk) {
                    return( cd );
                }
            }
```

```csharp
        return( null );
}



// Make the Card GameObjects
public void MakeCards() {
    // cardNames will be the names of cards to build
    // Each suit goes from 1 to 13 (e.g., C1 to C13 for Clubs)
    cardNames = new List<string>();
    string[] letters = new string[] {"C","D","H","S"};
    foreach (string s in letters) {
        for (int i=0; i<13; i++) {
            cardNames.Add(s+(i+1));
        }
    }

    // Make a List to hold all the cards
    cards = new List<Card>();
    // Several variables that will be reused several times
    Sprite tS = null;
    GameObject tGO = null;
    SpriteRenderer tSR = null;

    // Iterate through all of the card names that were just made
    for (int i=0; i<cardNames.Count; i++) {
        // Create a new Card GameObject
        GameObject cgo = Instantiate(prefabCard) as GameObject;
        // Set the transform.parent of the new card to the anchor.
        cgo.transform.parent = deckAnchor;
        Card card = cgo.GetComponent<Card>(); // Get the Card Component

        // This just stacks the cards so that they're all in nice rows
        cgo.transform.localPosition = new Vector3( (i%13)*3, i/13*4, 0 );

        // Assign basic values to the Card
        card.name = cardNames[i];
        card.suit = card.name[0].ToString();
        card.rank = int.Parse( card.name.Substring(1) );
        if (card.suit == "D" || card.suit == "H") {
            card.colS = "Red";
            card.color = Color.red;
        }
        // Pull the CardDefinition for this card
        card.def = GetCardDefinitionByRank(card.rank);

        // Add Decorators
        foreach( Decorator deco in decorators ) {
            if (deco.type == "suit") {
```

```
                    // Instantiate a Sprite GameObject
                    tGO = Instantiate( prefabSprite ) as GameObject;
                    // Get the SpriteRenderer Component
                    tSR = tGO.GetComponent<SpriteRenderer>();
                    // Set the Sprite to the proper suit
                    tSR.sprite = dictSuits[card.suit];
                } else {                    //if it's not a suit, it's a rank deco
                    tGO = Instantiate( prefabSprite ) as GameObject;
                    tSR = tGO.GetComponent<SpriteRenderer>();
                    // Get the proper Sprite to show this rank
                    tS = rankSprites[ card.rank ];
                    // Assign this rank Sprite to the SpriteRenderer
                    tSR.sprite = tS;
                    // Set the color of the rank to match the suit
                    tSR.color = card.color;
                }
                // Make the deco Sprites render above the Card
                tSR.sortingOrder = 1;
                // Make the decorator Sprite a child of the Card
                tGO.transform.parent = cgo.transform;
                // Set the localPosition based on the location from DeckXML
                tGO.transform.localPosition = deco.loc;
                // Flip the decorator if needed
                if (deco.flip) {
                    // An Euler rotation of 180° around the Z-axis will flip it
                    tGO.transform.rotation = Quaternion.Euler(0,0,180);
                }
                // Set the scale to keep decos from being too big
                if (deco.scale != 1) {
                    tGO.transform.localScale = Vector3.one * deco.scale;
                }
                // Name this GameObject so it's easy to find
                tGO.name = deco.type;
                // Add this deco GameObject to the List card.decoGOs
                card.decoGOs.Add(tGO);

            }

            // Add the card to the deck
            cards.Add (card);
        }
    }
}
```

3. Press Play. You should see 52 cards lined up. They don't yet have pips, but they do appear, and the correct decorators and coloring are on them. Now let's add the code for pips and faces. Add the following to the `MakeCards()` method of the `Deck` class:

```csharp
// Make the Card GameObjects
public void MakeCards() {
    …
    // Iterate through all of the card names that were just made
    for (int i=0; i<cardNames.Count; i++) {
        …

        // Add Decorators
        foreach( Decorator deco in decorators ) {
            …
        }

        // Add Pips
        // For each of the pips in the definition
        foreach( Decorator pip in card.def.pips ) {
            // Instantiate a Sprite GameObject
            tGO = Instantiate( prefabSprite ) as GameObject;
            // Set the parent to be the card GameObject
            tGO.transform.parent = cgo.transform;
            // Set the position to that specified in the XML
            tGO.transform.localPosition = pip.loc;
            // Flip it if necessary
            if (pip.flip) {
                tGO.transform.rotation = Quaternion.Euler(0,0,180);
            }
            // Scale it if necessary (only for the Ace)
            if (pip.scale != 1) {
                tGO.transform.localScale = Vector3.one * pip.scale;
            }
            // Give this GameObject a name
            tGO.name = "pip";
            // Get the SpriteRenderer Component
            tSR = tGO.GetComponent<SpriteRenderer>();
            // Set the Sprite to the proper suit
            tSR.sprite = dictSuits[card.suit];
            // Set sortingOrder so the pip is rendered above the Card_Front
            tSR.sortingOrder = 1;
            // Add this to the Card's list of pips
            card.pipGOs.Add(tGO);
        }

        // Handle Face Cards
        if (card.def.face != "") { // If this has a face in card.def
            tGO = Instantiate( prefabSprite ) as GameObject;
            tSR = tGO.GetComponent<SpriteRenderer>();
            // Generate the right name and pass it to GetFace()
            tS = GetFace( card.def.face+card.suit );
            tSR.sprite = tS;        // Assign this Sprite to tSR
```

```
            tSR.sortingOrder = 1; // Set the sortingOrder
            tGO.transform.parent = card.transform;
            tGO.transform.localPosition = Vector3.zero;
            tGO.name = "face";
        }


        // Add the card to the deck
        cards.Add (card);


    }
} // This is the closing brace for MakeCards()

// Find the proper face card Sprite
public Sprite GetFace(string faceS) {
    foreach (Sprite tS in faceSprites) {
        // If this Sprite has the right name…
        if (tS.name == faceS) {
            // …then return the Sprite
            return( tS );
        }
    }
    // If nothing can be found, return null
    return( null );
}
```

4. Pressing Play now, you should see all 52 cards laid out properly with pips and faces for face
    cards. The next thing to do is add a back to the cards. The back will have a higher sorting
    order than anything else on the card, and it will be visible when the card is face-down and
    invisible when the card is face-up.

    To accomplish this visibility toggle, add the following `faceUp` property to the `Card` class. As
    a property, `faceUp` is actually two functions (a get and a set) masquerading as a single field:

```
public class Card : MonoBehaviour {
    …
    public CardDefinition   def; // Parsed from DeckXML.xml

    public bool faceUp {
        get {
            return( !back.activeSelf );
        }
        set {
            back.SetActive(!value);
        }
    }
}
```

5. Now, the back can be added to the card in `MakeCards()`. Add the following lines to the `MakeCards()` method of the `Deck` class:

```
// Make the Card GameObjects
public void MakeCards() {
    …

    // Iterate through all of the card names that were just made
    for (int i=0; i<cardNames.Count; i++) {
        …
        // Handle Face Cards
        if (card.def.face != "") { // If this has a face in card.def
            …
        }

        // Add Card Back
        // The Card_Back will be able to cover everything else on the Card
        tGO = Instantiate( prefabSprite ) as GameObject;
        tSR = tGO.GetComponent<SpriteRenderer>();
        tSR.sprite = cardBack;
        tGO.transform.parent = card.transform;
        tGO.transform.localPosition = Vector3.zero;
        // This is a higher sortingOrder than anything else
        tSR.sortingOrder = 2;
        tGO.name = "back";
        card.back = tGO;

        // Default to face-up
        card.faceUp = false; // Use the property faceUp of Card

        // Add the card to the deck
        cards.Add (card);

    }
}
```

6. Press Play, and you'll see that all the cards are now flipped face-down. If you change the last added line to `card.faceUp = true;`, all of them will be face-up.

Shuffling the Cards

Now that cards can be built and displayed on screen, the last generic thing that we will need from the `Deck` class is the ability to shuffle cards.

1. Add the following `Shuffle()` method to end of the `Deck` class:

```
public class Deck : MonoBehaviour {
    …

    // Shuffle the Cards in Deck.cards
```

```
static public void Shuffle(ref List<Card> oCards) {                    // 1
    // Create a temporary List to hold the new shuffle order
    List<Card> tCards = new List<Card>();

    int ndx; // This will hold the index of the card to be moved
    tCards = new List<Card>(); // Initialize the temporary List
    // Repeat as long as there are cards in the original List
    while (oCards.Count > 0) {
        // Pick the index of a random card
        ndx = Random.Range(0,oCards.Count);
        // Add that card to the temporary List
        tCards.Add (oCards[ndx]);
        // And remove that card from the original List
        oCards.RemoveAt(ndx);
    }
    // Replace the original List with the temporary List
    oCards = tCards;
    // Because oCards is a reference variable, the original that was
    //   passed in is changed as well.
}
}
```

At the line marked by `// 1` in the preceding code listing, the `ref` keyword is used to make sure that the `List<Card>` that is passed to `List<Card> oCards` is passed as a reference rather than copied into `oCards`. This means that anything that happens to `oCards` is actually happening to the variable that is passed in. In other words, if the cards of a `Deck` are passed in via reference, those cards will be shuffled without requiring a return variable.

2. Make the following change to the Prospector script to see this work:

```
public class Prospector : MonoBehaviour {
    static public Prospector    S;

    public Deck                 deck;
    public TextAsset            deckXML;

    void Awake() {
        S = this; // Set up a Singleton for Prospector
    }

    void Start () {
        deck = GetComponent<Deck>();        // Get the Deck
        deck.InitDeck(deckXML.text);        // Pass DeckXML to it
        Deck.Shuffle(ref deck.cards);       // This shuffles the deck
        // The ref keyword passes a reference to deck.cards, which allows
        //   deck.cards to be modified by Deck.Shuffle()
    }
}
```

3. If you play the scene now, you can select _MainCamera in the scene Hierarchy and look at the Deck.cards variable to see a shuffled deck of cards.

Now that the Deck class can shuffle any list of cards, you have the basic tools to create *any* card game. The game you will make in this prototype is called Prospector.

The Prospector Game

The code up till now has given you the basic tools to make any card game. Now let's talk about the specific game we're going to make.

Prospector is based on the classic solitaire card game *Tri-Peaks*. The rules of both are the same, except for two things:

1. The premise of *Prospector* is that they player is digging down for gold, whereas the premise of *Tri-Peaks* is that they player is trying to climb three mountains.

2. The objective of *Tri-Peaks* is just to clear all of the cards. The objective of *Prospector* is to earn points by having long runs of cards played without having to draw a card from the draw pile, and each gold card in the run doubles the value of the whole run

Prospector Rules

To try this out, grab a normal deck of playing cards (like a physical, real deck, not the virtual one we just made). Remove the Jokers and shuffle the remaining 52 cards:

1. Lay out 28 of the cards as shown in the Figure 31.7. The bottom three rows of cards should be face-down, and the top row is face-up. The card edges don't need to be touching, but the lower cards do need to be covered by the upper cards. This sets up the initial tableau of cards for the "mine" that our prospector will be excavating.

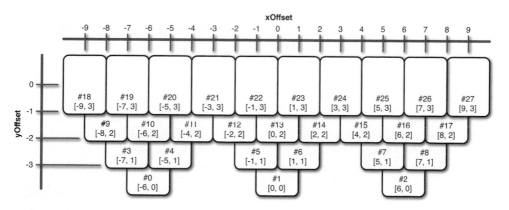

Figure 31.7 The initial tableau layout for the mine in Prospector

2. The rest of the deck forms a draw pile. Place it above the top row of cards face-down.

3. Draw the top card from the draw deck and place it face-up and centered above the top row of cards. This is the target card.

4. Any card that is either exactly one rank above or below the target card may be moved from the tableau onto the target card, making it the new target. Aces and Kings wrap around, so an Ace can be played on a King and vice versa.

5. If a face-down card is no longer covered by a card from a higher row, it can be turned face-up.

6. If none of the face-up cards can be played on the target card, draw a new target card from the draw pile.

7. If the tableau is emptied before the draw pile, you win! (Scoring and gold cards will be saved for the digital version of the game.)

Example of Play

The image in Figure 31.8 shows an example initial layout for Prospector. In the situation shown, the player can initially play either the 9C (9 of Clubs) or the 7S (7 of Spades) onto the 8H.

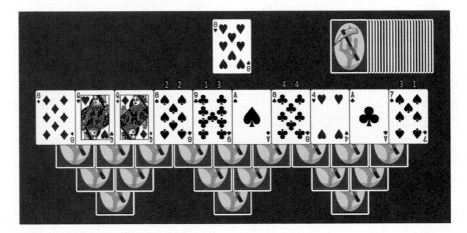

Figure 31.8   An example initial layout for Prospector

The amber and green numbers show two possible four-card runs. In the amber run, the 9C is played, becoming the new target card. This allows the play of 8S, 8D, or 8C. The player chooses 8S because it will then reveal the card that was hidden by 9C and 8S. Then the amber run continues with 7S and finally 8C. This results in the layout shown in Figure 31.9.

Now, because there are no more valid face-up cards to play from the tableau, the player must draw a card from the draw pile to become the next target card. This ends the first run of the game.

Try playing the game a few times to get a feel for it.

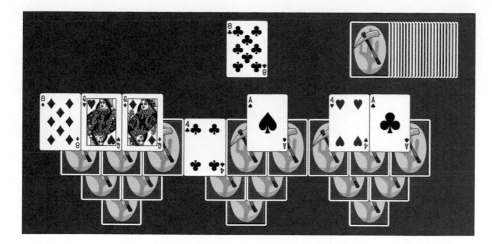

Figure 31.9 The Prospector example game after the first run

Implementing Prospector in Code

As you have seen from playing, Prospector is a pretty simple game, but it's also pretty fun. We can add to that fun later with some nice visuals and scoring tweaks, but for now, let's just get the basic game working.

Laying Out the Mine Tableau

We'll need to implement the same tableau layout for the mine cards in the digital version of Prospector as we did with the paper prototype you just played. To do this, we'll generate some XML code from the layout diagram in Figure 31.7.

1. In Unity, open the LayoutXML.xml file in the Resources folder, and you'll see this layout information:

```
<xml>
    <!-- This file holds info for laying out the Prospector card game. -->

    <!-- The multiplier is multiplied by the x and y attributes below. -->
    <!-- This determines how loose or tight the layout is. -->
    <multiplier x="1.25" y="1.5" />

    <!-- In the XML below, id is the number of the card -->
    <!-- x and y set position -->
    <!-- faceup is 1 if the card is face-up -->
    <!-- layer sets the depth layer so cards overlap properly -->
    <!-- hiddenby is the ids of cards that keep a card face-down -->

    <!-- Layer0, the deepest cards. -->
    <slot id="0" x="-6" y="-5" faceup="0" layer="0" hiddenby="3,4" />
```

```
<slot id="1" x="0"  y="-5" faceup="0" layer="0" hiddenby="5,6" />
<slot id="2" x="6"  y="-5" faceup="0" layer="0" hiddenby="7,8" />

<!-- Layer1, the next level. -->
<slot id="3" x="-7" y="-4" faceup="0" layer="1" hiddenby="9,10" />
<slot id="4" x="-5" y="-4" faceup="0" layer="1" hiddenby="10,11" />
<slot id="5" x="-1" y="-4" faceup="0" layer="1" hiddenby="12,13" />
<slot id="6" x="1"  y="-4" faceup="0" layer="1" hiddenby="13,14" />
<slot id="7" x="5"  y="-4" faceup="0" layer="1" hiddenby="15,16" />
<slot id="8" x="7"  y="-4" faceup="0" layer="1" hiddenby="16,17" />

<!-- Layer2, the next level. -->
<slot id="9"  x="-8" y="-3" faceup="0" layer="2" hiddenby="18,19" />
<slot id="10" x="-6" y="-3" faceup="0" layer="2" hiddenby="19,20" />
<slot id="11" x="-4" y="-3" faceup="0" layer="2" hiddenby="20,21" />
<slot id="12" x="-2" y="-3" faceup="0" layer="2" hiddenby="21,22" />
<slot id="13" x="0"  y="-3" faceup="0" layer="2" hiddenby="22,23" />
<slot id="14" x="2"  y="-3" faceup="0" layer="2" hiddenby="23,24" />
<slot id="15" x="4"  y="-3" faceup="0" layer="2" hiddenby="24,25" />
<slot id="16" x="6"  y="-3" faceup="0" layer="2" hiddenby="25,26" />
<slot id="17" x="8"  y="-3" faceup="0" layer="2" hiddenby="26,27" />

<!-- Layer3, the top level. -->
<slot id="18" x="-9" y="-2" faceup="1" layer="3" />
<slot id="19" x="-7" y="-2" faceup="1" layer="3" />
<slot id="20" x="-5" y="-2" faceup="1" layer="3" />
<slot id="21" x="-3" y="-2" faceup="1" layer="3" />
<slot id="22" x="-1" y="-2" faceup="1" layer="3" />
<slot id="23" x="1"  y="-2" faceup="1" layer="3" />
<slot id="24" x="3"  y="-2" faceup="1" layer="3" />
<slot id="25" x="5"  y="-2" faceup="1" layer="3" />
<slot id="26" x="7"  y="-2" faceup="1" layer="3" />
<slot id="27" x="9"  y="-2" faceup="1" layer="3" />

<!-- This positions the draw pile and staggers it -->
<slot type="drawpile" x="6" y="5" xstagger="0.15" layer="4"/>

<!-- This positions the discard pile and target card -->
<slot type="discardpile" x="0" y="1" layer="5"/>

</xml>
```

As you can see, this has layout information for each of the cards in the tableau (which is formed of `<slot>`s without a `type` attribute) as well as two special slots (that do have `type` attributes), the `drawpile` and `discardpile`.

2. Now, let's write some code to parse this LayoutXML into useful information. Create a new class named `Layout` and enter the following code:

```csharp
using UnityEngine;
using System.Collections;
using System.Collections.Generic;


// The SlotDef class is not a subclass of MonoBehaviour, so it doesn't need a
//  separate C# file.
[System.Serializable] // This makes SlotDefs visible in the Unity Inspector pane
public class SlotDef {
    public float        x;
    public float        y;
    public bool         faceUp=false;
    public string       layerName="Default";
    public int          layerID = 0;
    public int          id;
    public List<int>    hiddenBy = new List<int>();
    public string       type="slot";
    public Vector2      stagger;
}

public class Layout : MonoBehaviour {
    public PT_XMLReader     xmlr;  // Just like Deck, this has a PT_XMLReader
    public PT_XMLHashtable  xml;   // This variable is for easier xml access
    public Vector2          multiplier;  // Sets the spacing of the tableau
    // SlotDef references
    public List<SlotDef>    slotDefs; // All the SlotDefs for Row0-Row3
    public SlotDef          drawPile;
    public SlotDef          discardPile;
    // This holds all of the possible names for the layers set by layerID
    public string[]         sortingLayerNames = new string[] { "Row0", "Row1",
➥"Row2", "Row3", "Discard", "Draw" };

    // This function is called to read in the LayoutXML.xml file
    public void ReadLayout(string xmlText) {
        xmlr = new PT_XMLReader();
        xmlr.Parse(xmlText);       // The XML is parsed
        xml = xmlr.xml["xml"][0]; // And xml is set as a shortcut to the XML

        // Read in the multiplier, which sets card spacing
        multiplier.x = float.Parse(xml["multiplier"][0].att("x"));
        multiplier.y = float.Parse(xml["multiplier"][0].att("y"));

        // Read in the slots
        SlotDef tSD;
        // slotsX is used as a shortcut to all the <slot>s
        PT_XMLHashList slotsX = xml["slot"];

        for (int i=0; i<slotsX.Count; i++) {
            tSD = new SlotDef();  // Create a new SlotDef instance
```

```
        if (slotsX[i].HasAtt("type")) {
            // If this <slot> has a type attribute parse it
            tSD.type = slotsX[i].att("type");
        } else {
            // If not, set its type to "slot"; it's a tableau card
            tSD.type = "slot";
        }
        // Various attributes are parsed into numerical values
        tSD.x = float.Parse( slotsX[i].att("x") );
        tSD.y = float.Parse( slotsX[i].att("y") );
        tSD.layerID = int.Parse( slotsX[i].att("layer") );
        // This converts the number of the layerID into a text layerName
        tSD.layerName = sortingLayerNames[ tSD.layerID ];
        // The layers are used to make sure that the correct cards are
        //   on top of the others. In Unity 2D, all of our assets are
        //   effectively at the same Z depth, so the layer is used
        //   to differentiate between them.

        switch (tSD.type) {
            // pull additional attributes based on the type of this <slot>
        case "slot":
            tSD.faceUp = (slotsX[i].att("faceup") == "1");
            tSD.id = int.Parse( slotsX[i].att("id") );
            if (slotsX[i].HasAtt("hiddenby")) {
                string[] hiding = slotsX[i].att("hiddenby").Split(',');
                foreach( string s in hiding ) {
                    tSD.hiddenBy.Add ( int.Parse(s) );
                }
            }
            slotDefs.Add(tSD);
            break;

        case "drawpile":
            tSD.stagger.x = float.Parse( slotsX[i].att("xstagger") );
            drawPile = tSD;
            break;
        case "discardpile":
            discardPile = tSD;
            break;
        }
    }
  }
}
```

At this point, most of the preceding syntax should look familiar to you. The SlotDef class is created to store information read in from the XML <slot>s in a more accessible way. Then, the Layout class is defined, and the ReadLayout() method is created, which will take an XML-formatted string as input and turn it into a series of SlotDefs.

3. Open the `Prospector` class and add the following bolded lines:

```
public class Prospector : MonoBehaviour {
    static public Prospector     S;

    public Deck               deck;
    public TextAsset          deckXML;

    public Layout             layout;
    public TextAsset          layoutXML;

    void Awake() {
        S = this; // Set up a Singleton for Prospector
    }

    void Start () {
        deck = GetComponent<Deck>();        // Get the Deck
        deck.InitDeck(deckXML.text);        // Pass DeckXML to it
        Deck.Shuffle(ref deck.cards);       // This shuffles the deck
        // The ref keyword passes a reference to deck.cards, which allows
        //   deck.cards to be modified by Deck.Shuffle()

        layout = GetComponent<Layout>();    // Get the Layout
        layout.ReadLayout(layoutXML.text); // Pass LayoutXML to it
    }
}
```

4. Once this is done, you will need to set up a couple of things in Unity. Switch to Unity and select _MainCamera in the Hierarchy. From the menu bar, choose *Component > Scripts > Layout* to attach a Layout script to _MainCamera (this is just another different way to attach a script to a GameObject). You should now be able to scroll down in the Inspector pane and see the *Layout (Script)* component at the bottom.

5. Find the *Prospector (Script)* component of _MainCamera. You'll see that the public fields `layout` and `layoutXML` have appeared there. Click the target next to `layoutXML` and choose *LayoutXML* from the Assets tab. (You may need to click the Assets button at the top of the window that appeared.)

6. *Save your scene.*

7. Now, press Play. If you select _MainCamera in the Hierarchy and scroll down to the *Layout (Script)* component, you should be able to open the disclosure triangle next to `slots` and see that all of the `<slot>`s have been parsed from the XML.

Working with `CardProspector`, a Subclass of Card

Before we can position the cards in the tableau, it will be necessary to add some features to the Card class that are specific to the Prospector game. Because `Card` and `Deck` are intended to be reused on other card games, we will choose to create a `CardProspector` class as a subclass of Card rather than modifying `Card` directly. Create a new C# script named *CardProspector* and enter this code:

```csharp
using UnityEngine;
using System.Collections;
using System.Collections.Generic;

// This is an enum, which defines a type of variable that only has a few
// possible named values. The CardState variable type has one of four values:
// drawpile, tableau, target, & discard
public enum CardState {
    drawpile,
    tableau,
    target,
    discard
}


public class CardProspector : Card { // Make sure CardProspector extends Card
    // This is how you use the enum CardState
    public CardState            state = CardState.drawpile;
    // The hiddenBy list stores which other cards will keep this one face down
    public List<CardProspector>  hiddenBy = new List<CardProspector>();
    // LayoutID matches this card to a Layout XML id if it's a tableau card
    public int                  layoutID;
    // The SlotDef class stores information pulled in from the LayoutXML <slot>
    public SlotDef              slotDef;
}
```

These extensions to Card will handle things like the four types of places that the card can be in the tableau (drawpile, tableau [one of the initial 28 cards in the mine], discard, or target [the active card on top of the discard pile]), the storage of layout information (slotDef), and the information that determines when a card should be face-up or face-down (hiddenBy and layoutID).

Now that this subclass is available, it'll be necessary to convert the cards in the deck from Cards to CardProspectors. This will be done by adding the following code to the Prospector class:

```csharp
public class Prospector : MonoBehaviour {
    …

    public List<CardProspector>    drawPile;

    void Start () {
        deck = GetComponent<Deck>(); // Get the Deck
        deck.InitDeck(deckXML.text); // Pass DeckXML to it

        layout = GetComponent<Layout>();   // Get the Layout
        layout.ReadLayout(layoutXML.text); // Pass LayoutXML to it
```

```
        drawPile = ConvertListCardsToListCardProspectors( deck.cards ),
    }

    List<CardProspector> ConvertListCardsToListCardProspectors(List<Card> lCD) {
        List<CardProspector> lCP = new List<CardProspector>();
        CardProspector tCP;
        foreach( Card tCD in lCD ) {
            tCP = tCD as CardProspector;                              // 1
            lCP.Add( tCP );
        }
        return( lCP );
    }
}
```

Once this code is in, try running it and then look at the drawPile in the Inspector pane. You'll notice that all the cards in the drawPile are null. (You can also see this happen by placing a break point on the line marked // 1 in the preceding code.) When we try to treat the Card tCD as a CardProspector, the as returns null instead of a converted Card. This is because of how object-oriented coding works in C# (see the "On Superclasses and Subclasses" sidebar).

ON SUPERCLASSES AND SUBCLASSES

You're familiar, of course, with superclasses and subclasses from Chapter 25, "Classes." However, you might wonder why attempting to cast a superclass to a subclass doesn't work.

In Prospector, Card is the superclass, and the subclass is CardProspector. You could just as easily think of this as a superclass Animal and a subclass Scorpion. All Scorpions are Animals, but not all Animals are Scorpions. You can always refer to a Scorpion as "that Animal", but you can't refer to any Animal as a Scorpion. Along the same lines, a Scorpion might have a Sting() function, but a Cow would not. This is why it's not possible to treat any Animal as a Scorpion, because trying to call Sting() on any other Animal might cause an error.

In Prospector, we want to use a bunch of cards that are created by the Deck script as if they were CardProspectors. This is akin to having a bunch of Animals that we want to treat like Scorpions (but we've already decided this is impossible). However, it's always possible to refer to a Scorpion as an Animal, so the solution that we use in Prospector is to make PrefabCard have a *CardProspector (Script)* component instead of just a *Card (Script)* component. If we just create Scorpions from the beginning, and then treat them as Animals through several functions (which we can do because Scorpion is a subclass of Animal), when we choose to call Scorpion s = Animal as Scorpion; later, that will work perfectly because the Animal was always secretly a Scorpion.

The solution in this case is to make sure that the CardProspector was always a CardProspector and was just masquerading as a Card for all of the code in the Deck class. To do this, select PrefabCard in the Project pane, and you'll see that it appears in the Inspector with a *Card (Script)* component. If you click the target next to the *Script* variable (that is currently set to Card), you can choose a different script for this component. Select CardProspector, and the PrefabCard will now have a *CardProspector (Script)* component instead of just a Card. If you select _MainCamera from the Hierarchy and play the scene now, you will see that all of the entries in drawPile are now full of CardProspectors instead of null.

When the Deck script instantiates PrefabCard and gets the Card component of it, this will still work perfectly fine because a CardPrefab can always be referred to as a Card. Then, when the ConvertListCardsToListCardProspectors() function attemps to call tCP = tCD as CardProspector;, it works just fine.

Save your scene.

Positioning Cards in the Tableau

Now that everything is ready, it's time to add some code to the Prospector class to actually lay out the game:

```
public class Prospector : MonoBehaviour {
    ...
    public Layout              layout;
    public TextAsset           layoutXML;
    public Vector3             layoutCenter;
    public float               xOffset = 3;
    public float               yOffset = -2.5f;
    public Transform           layoutAnchor;

    public CardProspector       target;
    public List<CardProspector>  tableau;
    public List<CardProspector>  discardPile;

    public List<CardProspector>  drawPile;

    void Start () {
        ...
        drawPile = ConvertListCardsToListCardProspectors( deck.cards );
        LayoutGame();
    }

    // The Draw function will pull a single card from the drawPile and return it
    CardProspector Draw() {
```

```
        CardProspector cd = drawPile[0]; // Pull the 0th CardProspector
        drawPile.RemoveAt(0);            // Then remove it from List<> drawPile
        return(cd);                      // And return it
    }


    // LayoutGame() positions the initial tableau of cards, a.k.a. the "mine"
    void LayoutGame() {
        // Create an empty GameObject to serve as an anchor for the tableau //1
        if (layoutAnchor == null) {
            GameObject tGO = new GameObject("_LayoutAnchor");
            // ^ Create an empty GameObject named _LayoutAnchor in the Hierarchy
            layoutAnchor = tGO.transform;               // Grab its Transform
            layoutAnchor.transform.position = layoutCenter;    // Position it
        }

        CardProspector cp;
        // Follow the layout
        foreach (SlotDef tSD in layout.slotDefs) {
            // ^ Iterate through all the SlotDefs in the layout.slotDefs as tSD
            cp = Draw(); // Pull a card from the top (beginning) of the drawPile
            cp.faceUp = tSD.faceUp;    // Set its faceUp to the value in SlotDef
            cp.transform.parent = layoutAnchor;  // Make its parent layoutAnchor
            // This replaces the previous parent: deck.deckAnchor, which appears
            //   as _Deck in the Hierarchy when the scene is playing.
            cp.transform.localPosition = new Vector3(
                layout.multiplier.x * tSD.x,
                layout.multiplier.y * tSD.y,
                -tSD.layerID );
            // ^ Set the localPosition of the card based on slotDef
            cp.layoutID = tSD.id;
            cp.slotDef = tSD;
            cp.state = CardState.tableau;
            // CardProspectors in the tableau have the state CardState.tableau

            tableau.Add(cp); // Add this CardProspector to the List<> tableau
        }
    }
}
```

When you play this, you will see that the cards are indeed laid out in the mine tableau layout described in LayoutXML.xml, and the right ones are face-up and face-down, but there are some serious issues with sorting layers (see Figure 31.10).

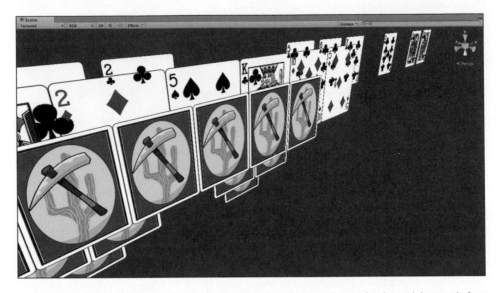

Figure 31.10   Cards are laid out, but there are several sorting layer issues (and remaining cards from the initial grid layout that existed previously)

Hold the Option/Alt key down and use the left mouse button in the Scene window to look around, and you will see that when using Unity's 2D tools, the distance of the 2D object to the camera has nothing to do with the depth sorting of the objects (that is, which objects are rendered on top of each other). We actually got a little lucky with the construction of the cards because we built them from back to front so that all the pips and decorators showed up on top of the card face. However, here we're actually going to have to be more careful about it for the layout of the game to avoid the problems you can see in Figure 31.10.

Unity 2D has two methods of dealing with depth sorting:

- **Sorting Layers:** Sorting layers are used to group 2D objects. Everything in a lower sorting layer is rendered behind everything in a higher sorting layer. Each SpriteRenderer component has a `sortingLayerName` string variable that can be set to the name of a sorting layer.

- **Sorting Order:** Each SpriteRenderer component also has a `sortingOrder` variable that can be set. This is used to position elements within each sorting layer relative to each other.

In the absence of sorting layers and sortingOrder, sprites are often rendered from back to front in the order that they were created, but this is not at all reliable.

Setting Up Sorting Layers

From the menu bar, choose *Edit > Project Settings > Tags and Layers*. You've used tags and layers for physics layers and tags before, but we haven't yet touched sorting layers. Open the disclosure triangle next to *Sorting Layers*, and enter the layers as shown in Figure 31.11. You will need to click the + button at the bottom-right of the list to add new sorting layers.

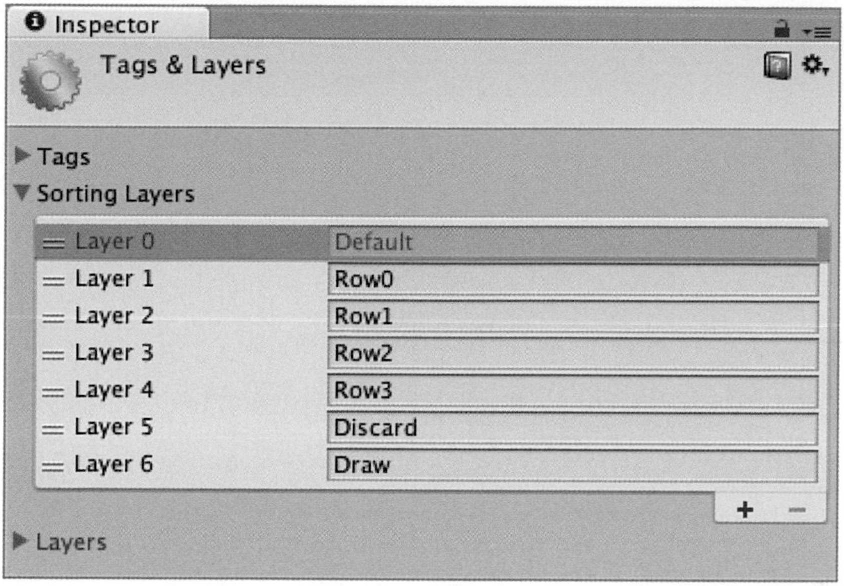

Figure 31.11   The sorting layers required for Prospector

Because SpriteRenderers and depth sorting are something that will be necessary for any card game built using our code base, the code to deal with depth sorting should be added to the Card class. Open the Card script and add the following code:

```
public class Card : MonoBehaviour {
    …
    public CardDefinition   def; // Parsed from DeckXML.xml

    // List of the SpriteRenderer Components of this GameObject and its children
    public SpriteRenderer[]        spriteRenderers;

    void Start() {
        SetSortOrder(0);   // Ensures that the card starts properly depth sorted
    }

    public bool faceUp {
        …
    }

    // If spriteRenderers is not yet defined, this function defines it
    public void PopulateSpriteRenderers() {
        // If spriteRenderers is null or empty
        if (spriteRenderers == null || spriteRenderers.Length == 0) {
            // Get SpriteRenderer Components of this GameObject and its children
```

```
            spriteRenderers = GetComponentsInChildren<SpriteRenderer>();
        }
    }

    // Sets the sortingLayerName on all SpriteRenderer Components
    public void SetSortingLayerName(string tSLN) {
        PopulateSpriteRenderers();

        foreach (SpriteRenderer tSR in spriteRenderers) {
            tSR.sortingLayerName = tSLN;
        }
    }

    // Sets the sortingOrder of all SpriteRenderer Components
    public void SetSortOrder(int sOrd) {
        PopulateSpriteRenderers();

        // The white background of the card is on bottom (sOrd)
        // On top of that are all the pips, decorators, face, etc. (sOrd+1)
        // The back is on top so that when visisble, it covers the rest (sOrd+2)

        // Iterate through all the spriteRenderers as tSR
        foreach (SpriteRenderer tSR in spriteRenderers) {
            if (tSR.gameObject == this.gameObject) {
                // If the gameObject is this.gameObject, it's the background
                tSR.sortingOrder = sOrd;  // Set its order to sOrd
                continue;  // And continue to the next iteration of the loop

            }
            // Each of the children of this GameObject are named
            // switch based on the names
            switch (tSR.gameObject.name) {
            case "back": // if the name is "back"
                tSR.sortingOrder = sOrd+2;
                // ^ Set it to the highest layer to cover everything else
                break;
            case "face": // if the name is "face"
            default:     // or if it's anything else
                tSR.sortingOrder = sOrd+1;
                // ^ Set it to the middle layer to be above the background
                break;
            }
        }
    }
}
```

Now, Prospector needs one line added to make sure that the cards in the initial mine layout are placed in the proper sorting layer. Add this line near the end of `Prospector.LayoutGame()`:

```
public class Prospector : MonoBehaviour {
    ...
    // LayoutGame() positions the initial tableau of cards, the "mine"
    void LayoutGame() {
        ...
        foreach (SlotDef tSD in layout.slotDefs) {
            ...
            cp.state = CardState.tableau;
            // CardProspectors in the tableau have the state CardState.tableau

            cp.SetSortingLayerName(tSD.layerName); // Set the sorting layers

            tableau.Add(cp); // Add this CardProspector to the List<> tableau
        }
    }
}
```

Now, when you run the scene, you'll see that the cards stack properly on top of each other in the mine.

Implementing Draw, Discard, and Game Logic

Before we move cards into place for the draw pile, let's start by delineating the possible actions that can happen in the game:

1. If the target card is replaced by any other card, the replaced target card then moves to the discard pile.
2. A card can move from the drawPile to become the target card.
3. A card in the mine tableau that is one higher or one lower in rank than the target card can move to become the target card.
4. If a face-down card has no more cards hiding it, it becomes face-up.
5. The game is over when either the mine is empty (win) or the draw pile is empty and there are no more possible plays (loss).

Actions number 2 and 3 here are the possible move actions, where a card is physically moved, and numbers 1, 4, and 5 are passive actions that happen as a result of either number 2 or 3.

Making Cards Clickable

Because all of these actions are instigated by a click on one of the cards, we first need to make the cards clickable. This is something that will be needed for every card game, so add the following method to the Card class:

```
public class Card : MonoBehaviour {
    ...

    // Virtual methods can be overridden by subclass methods with the same name
    virtual public void OnMouseUpAsButton() {
```

```
        print (name);   // When clicked, this outputs the card name
    }
}
```

Now, when you press Play, you can click any card in the scene, and it will output its name. However, in Prospector, we need card clicks to do more than that, so add the following method to the end of the `CardProspector` class:

```
public class CardProspector : Card {
    …

    // This allows the card to react to being clicked
    override public void OnMouseUpAsButton() {
        // Call the CardClicked method on the Prospector singleton
        Prospector.S.CardClicked(this);
        // Also call the base class (Card.cs) version of this method
        base.OnMouseUpAsButton();
    }
}
```

Now, the `CardClicked` method must be written in the Prospector script. For now, let's just tackle moving a card from the drawPile to the target (number 2 from the action list):

```
public class Prospector : MonoBehaviour {
    …

    // CardClicked is called any time a card in the game is clicked
    public void CardClicked(CardProspector cd) {
        // The reaction is determined by the state of the clicked card
        switch (cd.state) {
        case CardState.target:
            // Clicking the target card does nothing
            break;
        case CardState.drawpile:
            // Clicking any card in the drawPile will draw the next card
            MoveToDiscard(target); // Moves the target to the discardPile
            MoveToTarget(Draw());  // Moves the next drawn card to the target
            UpdateDrawPile();      // Restacks the drawPile
            break;
        case CardState.tableau:
            // Clicking a card in the tableau will check if it's a valid play
            break;
        }
    }
}
```

Of course, you also will need to add the `MoveToDiscard()`, `MoveToTarget()`, and `UpdateDraw-Pile()` methods to the `Prospector` class, as well as bits to the end of `Prospector.Layout-Game()` to draw the initial target card and arrange the drawPile:

```
public class Prospector : MonoBehaviour {
    …

    // LayoutGame() positions the initial tableau of cards, the "mine"
    void LayoutGame() {
        …
        foreach (SlotDef tSD in layout.slotDefs) {
            …
        }

        // Set up the initial target card
        MoveToTarget(Draw ());

        // Set up the Draw pile
        UpdateDrawPile();
    }

    // CardClicked is called any time a card in the game is clicked
    public void CardClicked(CardProspector cd) {
        …
    }

    // Moves the current target to the discardPile
    void MoveToDiscard(CardProspector cd) {
        // Set the state of the card to discard
        cd.state = CardState.discard;
        discardPile.Add(cd);   // Add it to the discardPile List<>
        cd.transform.parent = layoutAnchor; // Update its transform parent
        cd.transform.localPosition = new Vector3(
            layout.multiplier.x * layout.discardPile.x,
            layout.multiplier.y * layout.discardPile.y,
            -layout.discardPile.layerID+0.5f );
        // ^ Position it on the discardPile
        cd.faceUp = true;
        // Place it on top of the pile for depth sorting
        cd.SetSortingLayerName(layout.discardPile.layerName);
        cd.SetSortOrder(-100+discardPile.Count);
    }

    // Make cd the new target card
    void MoveToTarget(CardProspector cd) {
        // If there is currently a target card, move it to discardPile
        if (target != null) MoveToDiscard(target);
        target = cd; // cd is the new target
        cd.state = CardState.target;
        cd.transform.parent = layoutAnchor;
        // Move to the target position
        cd.transform.localPosition = new Vector3(
            layout.multiplier.x * layout.discardPile.x,
```

```
                layout.multiplier.y * layout.discardPile.y,
                -layout.discardPile.layerID );
        cd.faceUp = true; // Make it face-up
        // Set the depth sorting
        cd.SetSortingLayerName(layout.discardPile.layerName);
        cd.SetSortOrder(0);
    }


    // Arranges all the cards of the drawPile to show how many are left
    void UpdateDrawPile() {
        CardProspector cd;
        // Go through all the cards of the drawPile
        for (int i=0; i<drawPile.Count; i++) {
            cd = drawPile[i];
            cd.transform.parent = layoutAnchor;
            // Position it correctly with the layout.drawPile.stagger
            Vector2 dpStagger = layout.drawPile.stagger;
            cd.transform.localPosition = new Vector3(
                layout.multiplier.x * (layout.drawPile.x + i*dpStagger.x),
                layout.multiplier.y * (layout.drawPile.y + i*dpStagger.y),
                -layout.drawPile.layerID+0.1f*i );
            cd.faceUp = false; // Make them all face-down
            cd.state = CardState.drawpile;
            // Set depth sorting
            cd.SetSortingLayerName(layout.drawPile.layerName);
            cd.SetSortOrder(-10*i);
        }
    }


}
```

Now, when you play the scene, you will see that you can click on the drawPile to draw a new target card. We're getting close to having a game now!

Matching Cards from the Mine

To make the card in the mine work, we need to have a little code that checks to make sure that the clicked card is either one higher or one lower than the target card (and, of course, also handles A-to-King wraparound). Add these bolded lines to the Prospector script:

```
public class Prospector : MonoBehaviour {
    …

    // CardClicked is called any time a card in the game is clicked
    public void CardClicked(CardProspector cd) {
        // The reaction is determined by the state of the clicked card
        switch (cd.state) {
            …
```

```
        case CardState.tableau:
            // Clicking a card in the tableau will check if it's a valid play
            bool validMatch = true;
            if (!cd.faceUp) {
                // If the card is face-down, it's not valid
                validMatch = false;
            }
            if (!AdjacentRank(cd, target)) {
                // If it's not an adjacent rank, it's not valid
                validMatch = false;
            }
            if (!validMatch) return; // return if not valid
            // Yay! It's a valid card.
            tableau.Remove(cd); // Remove it from the tableau List
            MoveToTarget(cd);   // Make it the target card
            break;
        }
    }

    ...


    // Return true if the two cards are adjacent in rank (A & K wrap around)
    public bool AdjacentRank(CardProspector c0, CardProspector c1) {
        // If either card is face-down, it's not adjacent.
        if (!c0.faceUp || !c1.faceUp) return(false);

        // If they are 1 apart, they are adjacent
        if (Mathf.Abs(c0.rank - c1.rank) == 1) {
            return(true);
        }
        // If one is A and the other King, they're adjacent
        if (c0.rank ==  1 && c1.rank == 13) return(true);
        if (c0.rank == 13 && c1.rank ==  1) return(true);

        // Otherwise, return false
        return(false);
    }
}
```

Now, you can play the game and actually play the top row correctly. However, as you play more, you'll notice that the face-down cards are never flipping to face-up. This is what the List<CardProspector> CardProspector.hiddenBy field is for. We have the information about which cards hide others in List<int> SlotDef.hiddenBy, but we need to be able to convert from the integer IDs in SlotDef.hiddenBy to the actual CardProspectors that have that ID. Add this code to Prospector to do so:

```
public class Prospector : MonoBehaviour {
    …

    CardProspector Draw() {
        …
    }

    // Convert from the layoutID int to the CardProspector with that ID
    CardProspector FindCardByLayoutID(int layoutID) {
        foreach (CardProspector tCP in tableau) {
            // Search through all cards in the tableau List<>
            if (tCP.layoutID == layoutID) {
                // If the card has the same ID, return it
                return( tCP );
            }
        }
        // If it's not found, return null
        return( null );
    }

    // LayoutGame() positions the initial tableau of cards, the "mine"
    void LayoutGame() {
        …
        // Follow the layout
        foreach (SlotDef tSD in layout.slotDefs) {
            …
        }

        // Set which cards are hiding others
        foreach (CardProspector tCP in tableau) {
            foreach( int hid in tCP.slotDef.hiddenBy ) {
                cp = FindCardByLayoutID(hid);
                tCP.hiddenBy.Add(cp);
            }
        }

        // Set up the target card
        MoveToTarget(Draw ());
        …
    }

    // CardClicked is called any time a card in the game is clicked
    public void CardClicked(CardProspector cd) {
        // The reaction is determined by the state of the clicked card
        switch (cd.state) {
        …
        case CardState.tableau:
            …
            MoveToTarget(cd);    // Make it the target card
```

```
            SetTableauFaces();   // Update tableau card face-ups
            break;
        }
    }

    ...

    // This turns cards in the Mine face-up or face-down
    void SetTableauFaces() {
        foreach( CardProspector cd in tableau ) {
            bool fup = true; // Assume the card will be face-up
            foreach( CardProspector cover in cd.hiddenBy ) {
                // If either of the covering cards are in the tableau
                if (cover.state == CardState.tableau) {
                    fup = false; // then this card is face-down
                }
            }
            cd.faceUp = fup; // Set the value on the card
        }
    }
}
```

Now, an entire round of the game is playable! Next up is making the game know when it's over. This only needs to be checked once after each time the player has clicked a card, so the check will be called from the end of `Prospector.CardClicked()`. Add the following to the `Prospector` class:

```
public class Prospector : MonoBehaviour {
    ...

    // CardClicked is called any time a card in the game is clicked
    public void CardClicked(CardProspector cd) {
        // The reaction is determined by the state of the clicked card
        switch (cd.state) {
            ...
        }
        // Check to see whether the game is over or not
        CheckForGameOver();
    }

    ...

    // Test whether the game is over
    void CheckForGameOver() {
        // If the tableau is empty, the game is over
        if (tableau.Count==0) {
            // Call GameOver() with a win
            GameOver(true);
            return;
        }
```

```
        // If there are still cards in the draw pile, the game's not over
        if (drawPile.Count>0) {
            return;
        }
        // Check for remaining valid plays
        foreach ( CardProspector cd in tableau ) {
            if (AdjacentRank(cd, target)) {
                // If there is a valid play, the game's not over
                return;
            }
        }
        // Since there are no valid plays, the game is over
        // Call GameOver with a loss
        GameOver (false);
    }

    // Called when the game is over. Simple for now, but expandable
    void GameOver(bool won) {
        if (won) {
            print ("Game Over. You won! :)");
        } else {
            print ("Game Over. You Lost. :(");
        }
        // Reload the scene, resetting the game
        Application.LoadLevel("__Prospector_Scene_0");
    }
}
```

Now the game is playable and repeatable, and it knows when it has won or lost. Next up, it's time to add some scoring.

Adding Scoring to Prospector

The original card game of *Prospector* (or *Tri-Peaks*, on which it was based) had no scoring mechanism beyond the player winning or losing. But as a digital game, it's really helpful to have scores and a high score so that players have a reason to keep playing (to beat their high score).

Ways to Earn Points in the Game

We will implement several ways to earn points in Prospector:

1. Moving a card from the mine to the target card earns 1 point.

2. Every subsequent card removed from the mine without drawing from the draw pile increases the points awarded per card by 1, so a *run* of five cards removed without a draw would be worth 1, 2, 3, 4, and 5 points, respectively, for a total of 15 points for the run $(1 + 2 + 3 + 4 + 5 = 15)$.

3. If the player wins the round, she carries her score on to the next round. Whenever a round is lost, her score for all rounds is totaled and checked against the high score list.

4. The number of points earned for a run will double for each special gold card in the run. If two of the cards in the example run from #2 were gold, then the run would be worth 60 points (15 x 2 x 2 = 60).

The scoring will be handled by the `Prospector` class because it is aware of all the conditions that could contribute to the score. We will also create a script named *Scoreboard* to handle all the visual elements of showing the score to the player.

We'll implement numbers 1 through 3 in this chapter, and I'll leave number 4 for you to implement on your own later.

Making the Run Scoring Work

For now, let's just make some changes to Prospector to track the score. Because we're enabling runs and eventually will add run score doubling via gold cards, it makes sense to store the score for the run separately and then apply that to the total score for the round once the run has been ended (by drawing a card from the drawPile). Add the following code to Prospector to implement this:

```
using UnityEngine;
using System.Collections;
using System.Collections.Generic;

// An enum to handle all the possible scoring events
public enum ScoreEvent {
    draw,
    mine,
    mineGold,
    gameWin,
    gameLoss
}

public class Prospector : MonoBehaviour {
    static public Prospector     S;
    static public int            SCORE_FROM_PREV_ROUND = 0;
    static public int            HIGH_SCORE = 0;

    ...
    public List<CardProspector>  drawPile;

    // Fields to track score info
    public int                   chain = 0; // of cards in this run
    public int                   scoreRun = 0;
    public int                   score = 0;
```

```
void Awake() {
    S = this; // Set up a Singleton for Prospector
    // Check for a high score in PlayerPrefs
    if (PlayerPrefs.HasKey ("ProspectorHighScore")) {
        HIGH_SCORE = PlayerPrefs.GetInt("ProspectorHighScore");
    }
    // Add the score from last round, which will be >0 if it was a win
    score += SCORE_FROM_PREV_ROUND;
    // And reset the SCORE_FROM_PREV_ROUND
    SCORE_FROM_PREV_ROUND = 0;
}

…

// CardClicked is called any time a card in the game is clicked
public void CardClicked(CardProspector cd) {
    // The reaction is determined by the state of the clicked card
    switch (cd.state) {
    …
    case CardState.drawpile:
        …
        ScoreManager(ScoreEvent.draw);
        break;
    case CardState.tableau:
        …
        ScoreManager(ScoreEvent.mine);
        break;
    }
    …
}

…

// Called when the game is over. Simple for now, but expandable
void GameOver(bool won) {
    if (won) {
        ScoreManager(ScoreEvent.gameWin);      // This replaces the old line
    } else {
        ScoreManager(ScoreEvent.gameLoss);     // This replaces the old line
    }
    // Reload the scene, resetting the game
    Application.LoadLevel("__Prospector_Scene_0");
}

// ScoreManager handles all of the scoring
void ScoreManager(ScoreEvent sEvt) {
    switch (sEvt) {
    // Same things need to happen whether it's a draw, a win, or a loss
    case ScoreEvent.draw: // Drawing a card
```

```
case ScoreEvent.gameWin:  // Won the round
case ScoreEvent.gameLoss:  // Lost the round
    chain = 0;          // resets the score chain
    score += scoreRun;  // add scoreRun to total score
    scoreRun = 0;       // reset scoreRun
    break;
case ScoreEvent.mine:  // Remove a mine card
    chain++;            // increase the score chain
    scoreRun += chain;  // add score for this card to run
    break;
}


// This second switch statement handles round wins and losses
switch (sEvt) {
case ScoreEvent.gameWin:
    // If it's a win, add the score to the next round
    // static fields are NOT reset by Application.LoadLevel()
    Prospector.SCORE_FROM_PREV_ROUND = score;
    print ("You won this round! Round score: "+score);
    break;
case ScoreEvent.gameLoss:
    // If it's a loss, check against the high score
    if (Prospector.HIGH_SCORE <= score) {
        print("You got the high score! High score: "+score);
        Prospector.HIGH_SCORE = score;
        PlayerPrefs.SetInt("ProspectorHighScore", score);
    } else {
        print ("Your final score for the game was: "+score);
    }
    break;
default:
    print ("score: "+score+"  scoreRun:"+scoreRun+"  chain:"+chain);
    break;
}
    }
}
```

Now, as you play the game, you'll see little notes in the Console pane that tell you your score. This works fine for testing, but let's make things look a little better for our players.

Showing the Score to the Players

For this game, we'll make a couple of reusable components that can show the score. One will be a `Scoreboard` class that will manage all of the score display. The other will be FloatingScore, which will be an on-screen number that can move around the screen on its own. We'll also make use of Unity's `SendMessage()` feature, which can call a method by name with one parameter on any GameObject:

1. Create a new C# script named *FloatingScore* and enter the following code:

```csharp
using UnityEngine;
using System.Collections;
using System.Collections.Generic;

// An enum to track the possible states of a FloatingScore
public enum FSState {
    idle,
    pre,
    active,
    post
}

// FloatingScore can move itself on screen following a Bézier curve
public class FloatingScore : MonoBehaviour {
    public FSState        state = FSState.idle;
    [Serialize Field]
    private int           _score = 0; // The score field
    public string         scoreString;

    // The score property also sets scoreString when set
    public int score {
        get {
            return(_score);
        }
        set {
            _score = value;
            scoreString = Utils.AddCommasToNumber(_score);
            GetComponent<GUIText>().text = scoreString;
        }
    }

    public List<Vector3>  bezierPts; // Bezier points for movement
    public List<float>    fontSizes; // Bezier points for font scaling
    public float          timeStart = -1f;
    public float          timeDuration = 1f;
    public string         easingCuve = Easing.InOut; // Uses Easing in Utils.cs

    // The GameObject that will receive the SendMessage when this is done moving
    public GameObject     reportFinishTo = null;

    // Set up the FloatingScore and movement
    // Note the use of parameter defaults for eTimeS & eTimeD
    public void Init(List<Vector3> ePts, float eTimeS = 0, float eTimeD = 1) {
        bezierPts = new List<Vector3>(ePts);

        if (ePts.Count == 1) { // If there's only one point
            // …then just go there.
            transform.position = ePts[0];
```

```
            return;
        }


        // If eTimeS is the default, just start at the current time
        if (eTimeS == 0) eTimeS = Time.time;
        timeStart = eTimeS;
        timeDuration = eTimeD;


        state = FSState.pre; // Set it to the pre state, ready to start moving
    }

    public void FSCallback(FloatingScore fs) {
        // When this callback is called by SendMessage,
        //  add the score from the calling FloatingScore
        score += fs.score;
    }


    // Update is called once per frame
    void Update () {
        // If this is not moving, just return
        if (state == FSState.idle) return;

        // Get u from the current time and duration
        // u ranges from 0 to 1 (usually)
        float u = (Time.time - timeStart)/timeDuration;
        // Use Easing class from Utils to curve the u value
        float uC = Easing.Ease (u, easingCurve);
        if (u<0) { // If u<0, then we shouldn't move yet.
            state = FSState.pre;
            // Move to the initial point
            transform.position = bezierPts[0];
        } else {
            if (u>=1) { // If u>=1, we're done moving
                uC = 1; // Set uC=1 so we don't overshoot
                state = FSState.post;
                if (reportFinishTo != null) { //If there's a callback GameObject
                    // Use SendMessage to call the FSCallback method
                    //  with this as the parameter.
                    reportFinishTo.SendMessage("FSCallback", this);
                    // Now that the message has been sent,
                    //  Destroy this gameObject
                    Destroy (gameObject);
                } else { // If there is nothing to callback
                    // …then don't destroy this. Just let it stay still.
                    state = FSState.idle;
                }
            } else {
                // 0<=u<1, which means that this is active and moving
                state = FSState.active;
```

```
        }
        // Use Bezier curve to move this to the right point
        Vector3 pos = Utils.Bezier(uC, bezierPts);
        transform.position = pos;
        if (fontSizes != null && fontSizes.Count>0) {
            // If fontSizes has values in it
            // ...then adjust the fontSize of this GUIText
            int size = Mathf.RoundToInt( Utils.Bezier(uC, fontSizes) );
            GetComponent<GUIText>().fontSize = size;
        }
    }
}
```

2. Create a new C# script named *Scoreboard* and enter this code into it:

```
using UnityEngine;
using System.Collections;
using System.Collections.Generic;

// The Scoreboard class manages showing the score to the player
public class Scoreboard : MonoBehaviour {
    public static Scoreboard S; // The singleton for Scoreboard

    public GameObject     prefabFloatingScore;

    public bool _____;
    [Serialize Field]
    private int          _score = 0;
    public string        _scoreString;

    // The score property also sets the scoreString
    public int score {
        get {
            return(_score);
        }
        set {
            _score = value;
            scoreString = Utils.AddCommasToNumber(_score);
        }
    }

    // The scoreString property also sets the GUIText.text
    public string scoreString {
        get {
            return(_scoreString);
        }
```

```
        set {
            _scoreString = value;
            GetComponent<GUIText>().text = _scoreString;
        }
    }

    void Awake() {
        S = this;
    }

    // When called by SendMessage, this adds the fs.score to this.score
    public void FSCallback(FloatingScore fs) {
        score += fs.score;
    }

    // This will Instantiate a new FloatingScore GameObject and initialize it.
    // It also returns a pointer to the FloatingScore created so that the
    //  calling function can do more with it (like set fontSizes, etc.)
    public FloatingScore CreateFloatingScore(int amt, List<Vector3> pts) {
        GameObject go = Instantiate(prefabFloatingScore) as GameObject;
        FloatingScore fs = go.GetComponent<FloatingScore>();
        fs.score = amt;
        fs.reportFinishTo = this.gameObject; // Set fs to call back to this
        fs.Init(pts);
        return(fs);
    }
}

}
```

3. Now, you need to make the GameObjects for both the Scoreboard and the FloatingScore. In Unity, from the menu bar, choose *GameObject > Create Other > GUIText*. Rename the GUIText to *PrefabFloatingScore* and give it the settings shown in Figure 31.12.

4. Now attach the script FloatingScore to the GameObject PrefabFloatingScore (by dragging the script onto FloatingScore in the Hierarchy). Then convert PrefabFloatingScore to a prefab by dragging it from the Hierarchy into the _Prefabs folder in the Project pane. Finally, delete the instance of PrefabFloatingScore that remains in the Hierarchy pane.

5. To make the scoreboard, create another GUIText GameObject in the scene (*GameObject > Create Other > GUIText*). Rename this GUIText GameObject to *_Scoreboard*. (The underscore at the beginning of the name will keep it sorted to the top of the Hierarchy pane.) Attach the Scoreboard C# script to the _Scoreboard GameObject and give _Scoreboard the settings shown in Figure 31.13. This includes dragging the PrefabFloatingScore prefab into the public `prefabFloatingScore` field of the *Scoreboard (Script)* component.

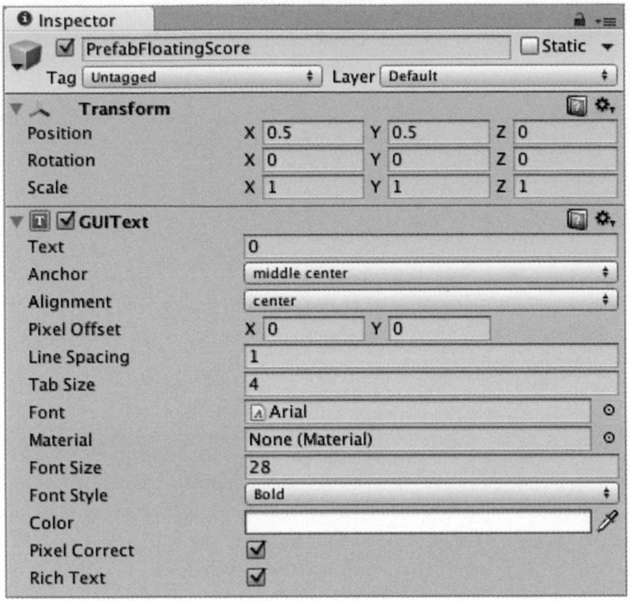

Figure 31.12 The settings for PrefabFloatingScore

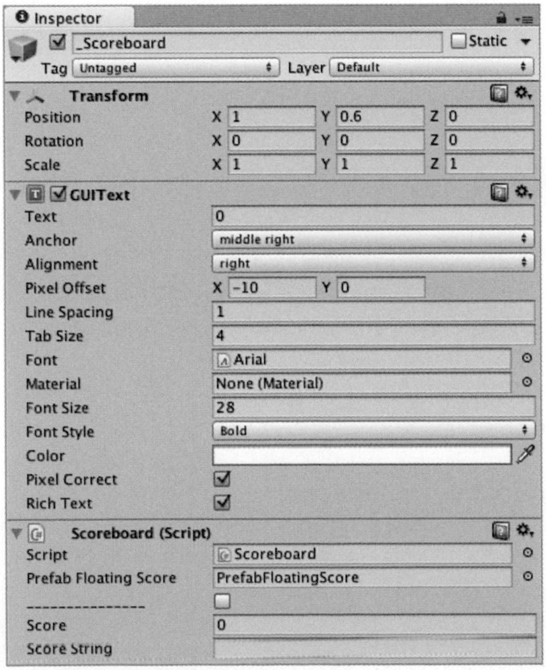

Figure 31.13 The settings for _Scoreboard

6. Now, all you need to do is make a few changes to the `Prospector` class to incorporate the new code and GameObjects. Add the following bolded code to the `Prospector` class:

```
public class Prospector : MonoBehaviour {
    …
    static public int          HIGH_SCORE = 0;

    public Vector3             fsPosMid  = new Vector3(0.5f, 0.90f, 0);
    public Vector3             fsPosRun  = new Vector3(0.5f, 0.75f, 0);
    public Vector3             fsPosMid2 = new Vector3(0.5f, 0.5f,  0);
    public Vector3             fsPosEnd  = new Vector3(1.0f, 0.65f, 0);

    public Deck                deck;
    …
    // Fields to track score info
    public int                 chain = 0;
    public int                 scoreRun = 0;
    public int                 score = 0;
    public FloatingScore        fsRun;

    void Start () {
        Scoreboard.S.score = score;

        deck = GetComponent<Deck>();      // Get the Deck
        …
    }

    …

    // ScoreManager handles all of the scoring
    void ScoreManager(ScoreEvent sEvt) {
        List<Vector3> fsPts;
        switch (sEvt) {
        case ScoreEvent.draw:      // Drawing a card
        case ScoreEvent.gameWin:   // Won the round
        case ScoreEvent.gameLoss:  // Lost the round
        // The same things need to happen whether it's a draw, win, or loss
            chain = 0;          // resets the score chain
            score += scoreRun;  // add scoreRun to total score
            scoreRun = 0;       // reset scoreRun
            // Add fsRun to the _Scoreboard score
            if (fsRun != null) {
                // Create points for the Bezier curve
                fsPts = new List<Vector3>();
                fsPts.Add( fsPosRun );
                fsPts.Add( fsPosMid2 );
                fsPts.Add( fsPosEnd );
                fsRun.reportFinishTo = Scoreboard.S.gameObject;
                fsRun.Init(fsPts, 0, 1);
                // Also adjust the fontSize
```

```
                fsRun.fontSizes = new List<float>(new float[] {28,36,4});
                fsRun = null; // Clear fsRun so it's created again
            }
            break;
        case ScoreEvent.mine: // Remove a mine card
            chain++;              // increase the score chain
            scoreRun += chain; // add score for this card to run
            // Create a FloatingScore for this score
            FloatingScore fs;
            // Move it from the mousePosition to fsPosRun
            Vector3 p0 = Input.mousePosition;
            p0.x /= Screen.width;
            p0.y /= Screen.height;
            fsPts = new List<Vector3>();
            fsPts.Add( p0 );
            fsPts.Add( fsPosMid );
            fsPts.Add( fsPosRun );
            fs = Scoreboard.S.CreateFloatingScore(chain,fsPts);
            fs.fontSizes = new List<float>(new float[] {4,50,28});
            if (fsRun == null) {
                fsRun = fs;
                fsRun.reportFinishTo = null;
            } else {
                fs.reportFinishTo = fsRun.gameObject;
            }
            break;
    }
    …
  }
}
```

Now when you play the game, you should see the score flying around. This is actually pretty important because it helps your players understand where the score is coming from and helps reveal the mechanics of the game to them through play (rather than requiring them to read instructions).

Adding Some Art to the Game

Let's add some theming to the game by adding a background. In the _Sprites folder with the various card elements are a PNG named *ProspectorBackground* and a material named *ProspectorBackground Mat*. These are already set up for you, since you already learned how to do so in previous chapters.

In Unity, add a quad to the scene (*GameObject > Create Other > Quad*). Drag the *ProspectorBackground Mat* onto the quad. Rename the quad *ProspectorBackground* and set its transform as follows:

ProspectorBackground (Quad)   P:[0,0,0]   R:[0,0,0]   S:[26.667,20,1]

Because _MainCamera's orthographic size is 10, that means that it is 10 units between the center of the screen and the nearest edge (which in this case is the top and bottom), for a total height of 20 units visible on screen. The ProspectorBackground quad is 20 units high (y-scale) because of this. And, because the screen is at a 4:3 aspect ratio, 20 / 3 * 4 = 26.667 is the width (x-scale) that we need to set the background to.

When you play the game now, it should look something like Figure 31.14.

Figure 31.14 The Prospector game with a background

Announcing the Beginning and End of Rounds

I'm sure you've noticed that the rounds of the game end rather abruptly. Let's do something about that. First off, we'll delay the actual reloading of the level using an Invoke() function. Add the following bolded code to Prospector:

```
public class Prospector : MonoBehaviour {
    static public Prospector   S;
    static public int          SCORE_FROM_PREV_ROUND = 0;
    static public int          HIGH_SCORE = 0;

    public float               reloadDelay = 1f; // The delay between rounds

    public Vector3             fsPosMid  = new Vector3(0.50f, 0.90f, 0);
    …

    // Called when the game is over. Simple for now, but expandable
    void GameOver(bool won) {
        if (won) {
            ScoreManager(ScoreEvent.gameWin);
        } else {
            ScoreManager(ScoreEvent.gameLoss);
        }
        // Reload the scene in reloadDelay seconds
        // This will give the score a moment to travel
        Invoke ("ReloadLevel", reloadDelay);                          //1
        // Application.LoadLevel("__Prospector_Scene_0"); // Now commented out
    }

    void ReloadLevel() {
        // Reload the scene, resetting the game
        Application.LoadLevel("__Prospector_Scene_0");
    }
    …
}
```

1. The Invoke() at //1 works by calling a function named `ReloadLevel` in `reloadDelay` seconds. This is similar to how `SendMessage()` works, but it does so with a delay. Now when you play the game, it will wait for the score for the final run to move all the way to the _Scoreboard before the game reloads.

Giving the Player Feedback on Her Score

We also want to tell the player how she did at the end of each round. Add two new GUITexts to the scene and name them *GameOver* and *RoundResult*. Give them the settings shown in Figure 31.15.

At this time, you should also add another GUIText named *HighScore* to display the high score information to the player. Give HighScore the settings shown in Figure 31.16.

The numbers in these settings were determined by trial and error, and you should feel free to adjust them as you see fit.

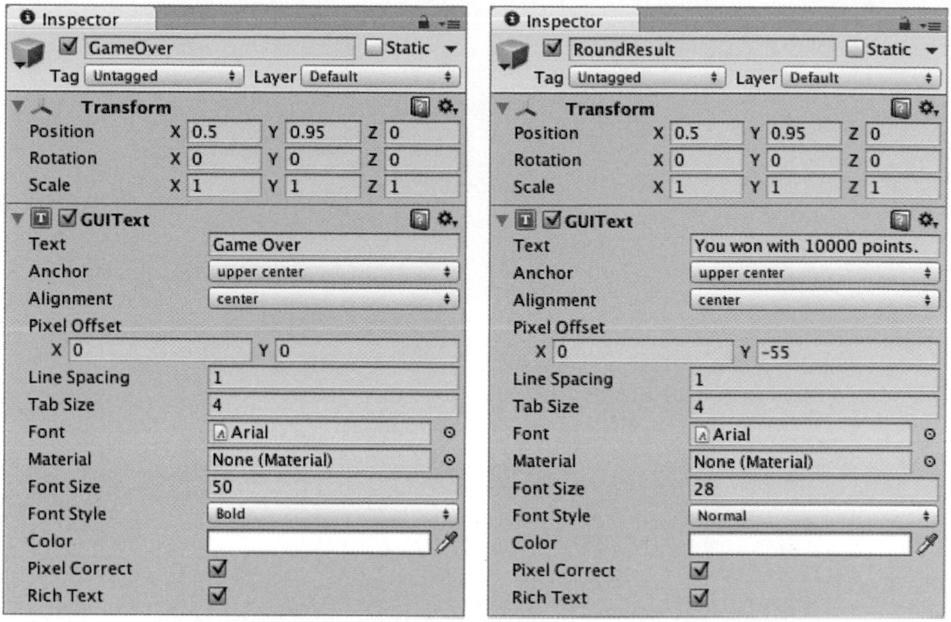

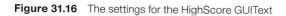

Figure 31.15   The settings for the GameOver and RoundResult GUITexts

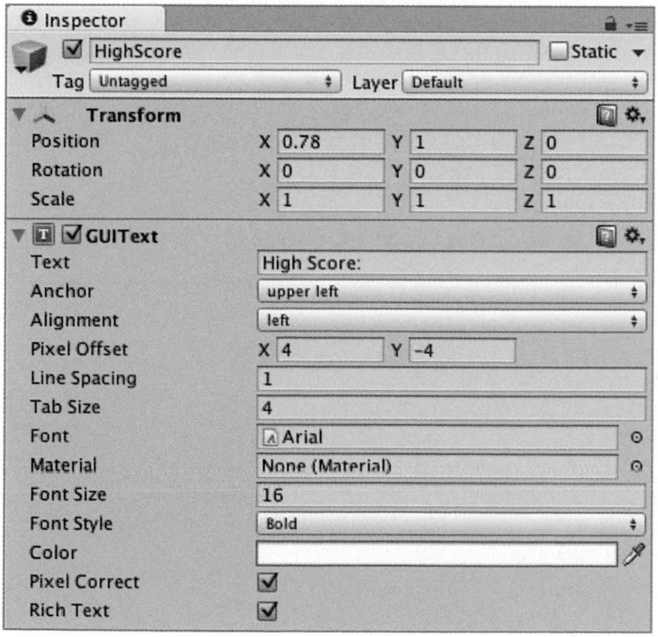

Figure 31.16   The settings for the HighScore GUIText

To make these GUITexts functional, add the following bolded code to the `Prospector` class:

```
public class Prospector : MonoBehaviour {
    …
    public FloatingScore        fsRun;

    public GUIText                  GTGameOver;
    public GUIText                  GTRoundResult;

    void Awake() {
        …

        // Set up the GUITexts that show at the end of the round
        // Get the GUIText Components
        GameObject go = GameObject.Find ("GameOver");
        if (go != null) {
            GTGameOver = go.GetComponent<GUIText>();
        }
        go = GameObject.Find ("RoundResult");
        if (go != null) {
            GTRoundResult = go.GetComponent<GUIText>();
        }
        // Make them invisible
        ShowResultGTs(false);

        go = GameObject.Find("HighScore");
        string hScore = "High Score: "+Utils.AddCommasToNumber(HIGH_SCORE);
        go.GetComponent<GUIText>().text = hScore;
    }

    void ShowResultGTs(bool show) {
        GTGameOver.gameObject.SetActive(show);
        GTRoundResult.gameObject.SetActive(show);
    }

    …

    // ScoreManager handles all of the scoring
    void ScoreManager(ScoreEvent sEvt) {
        …

        // This second switch statement handles round wins and losses
        switch (sEvt) {
        case ScoreEvent.gameWin:
            GTGameOver.text = "Round Over";
            // If it's a win, add the score to the next round
            // static fields are NOT reset by Application.LoadLevel()
            Prospector.SCORE_FROM_PREV_ROUND = score;
            print ("You won this round! Round score: "+score);
```

```
            GTRoundResult.text = "You won this round!\nRound Score: "+score;
            ShowResultGTs(true);
            break;
        case ScoreEvent.gameLoss:
            GTGameOver.text = "Game Over";
            // If it's a loss, check against the high score
                if (Prospector.HIGH_SCORE <= score) {
                print("You got the high score! High score: "+score);
                string sRR = "You got the high score!\nHigh score: "+score;
                GTRoundResult.text = sRR;
                Prospector.HIGH_SCORE = score;
                PlayerPrefs.SetInt("ProspectorHighScore", score);
            } else {
                print ("Your final score for the game was: "+score);
                GTRoundResult.text = "Your final score was: "+score;
            }
            ShowResultGTs(true);
            break;
        ...
        }
    }
}
```

Now, when you finish a round or game, you should see messages like those in Figure 31.17.

Figure 31.17 Example game over messages

Summary

In this chapter, you created a complete card game that constructs itself from XML files and that contains scoring, background images, and theming. One of the purposes of the tutorials in this book is to give you a framework on which to build your own games. In the next chapter, we do just that. I'll guide you through building the *Bartok* game from the first chapter of the book based on this project.

Next Steps

The following are some possible directions that you can take this game yourself.

Gold Cards

We mentioned this as number 4 in the list of ways to add scoring to the game, but gold cards were not implemented in the chapter. There are graphics in the package you imported for gold cards (both Card_Back_Gold and Card_Front_Gold). The purpose of the gold cards is to double the value of any run that they are part of. Gold cards can only start in the mine, and any card in the mine has a 10% chance of being a gold card. Try implementing the gold cards on your own.

Compile This Game on a Mobile Device

Though the build settings in this game were designed for an iPad, it's not within the scope of this book to instruct you on actual compilation for a mobile device. Unity has several pages that document this; however, and I recommend that you look at the proper one for the device that you own. In order to keep the information here as current as possible, my best recommendation for you is to do a web search for *Unity getting started* and the name of the mobile platform on which you want to develop (e.g., *Unity getting started iOS*). Right now, that could be *iOS*, *Android*, *BlackBerry*, or *Windows Phone*. The Unity documentation includes "getting started" pages for all of these platforms.

In my personal experience, I have found compilation on Android devices to be the easiest. Including the time to install and configure the additional software to do so, compiling this game for iOS took about two hours (most of which was spent setting up and paying for my Apple iOS developer account and provisioning profile), and compiling this game for Android took about 20 minutes.

I also highly recommend looking into some of the tools out there that can help you with mobile development. Test Flight (http://testflightapp.com) is a tool that helps you to distribute test builds of your game to iOS devices easily over the Internet, and there are many developers who use it. A newer service, Tsugi (http://tsugi.co) takes this a step further by also managing and automating the Unity build process for both iOS and Android through a cloud service. As different members of your team make changes to the game, Tsugi will automatically build it and distribute it to all team members.

CHAPTER 32

PROTOTYPE 5: BARTOK

This chapter differs somewhat from the other prototypes because instead of creating an entirely new project, this one shows you how you can build a different game on top of the prototype projects that you've developed while reading this book.

Before starting this project, you should have first completed Chapter 31, "Prototype 4: *Prospector Solitaire*" so that you understand the inner workings of the card game framework developed in that chapter.

Bartok is the game you first encountered in Chapter 1, "Thinking Like a Designer." Now you'll build it yourself.

Getting Started: Prototype 5

This time, instead of downloading a unitypackage as you did before, just make a duplicate of your entire project folder for Prospector (or you can download it from http://book.prototools.net under Chapter 32). Again, the art assets we'll be using are constructed from parts of the Vectorized Playing Cards 1.3 by Chris Aguilar.[1]

Note that *this project will only work with Unity version 4.3 and later.*

Understanding Bartok

For a description of *Bartok* and how to play, see Chapter 1, where it is used extensively as a design exercise. In short, *Bartok* is very similar to the commercial game *Uno*, except that it is played with a standard deck of cards, and in the traditional Bartok card game, the winner of each round is able to add a rule to the game. In the Chapter 1 example, we also included three variations of the rules, but those will not be created in this chapter; I'll leave that to you to accomplish later.

To play an online version of the Bartok game, visit http://book.prototools.net and look under Chapter 1.

Making a New Scene

As with much of this project, the scene we will use will be based on the scene from *Prospector*. Click __Prospector_Scene_0 in the Project pane and then choose *Edit > Duplicate* from the menu bar. This will make a new Scene named __Prospector_Scene_1. Rename this to *__Bartok_Scene_0* and double-click it to open it. You can tell that it has opened because the title bar of the Unity window will change to reflect the new scene name.

Cleaning the Scene

Let's get rid of some of the things we don't need. Select _Scoreboard and HighScore in the Hierarchy pane and delete them (*Edit > Delete* from the menu bar). This game won't be scored, so we don't need either of those.

Similarly, you can delete both GameOver and RoundResult from this scene. We'll be making use of them later but can always grab copies from __Prospector_Scene_0 when we need them.

Select _MainCamera and remove the *Prospector (Script)* and *Layout (Script)* components (right-click the name of each [or click the gear to the right of the name of each] and choose *Remove Component*). You should be left with a _MainCamera that has all the proper settings for Transform and Camera and also still has a *Deck (Script)* component.

Lastly, let's change the background. Start by selecting the ProspectorBackground GameObject in the Hierarchy pane (not the Texture2D ProjectPane) and renaming it *BartokBackground*. Then

---

[1] Chris Aguilar, "Vectorized Playing Cards 1.3," http://code.google.com/p/vectorized-playing-cards/
    ©2011–Chris Aguilar. Licensed under LGPL 3–www.gnu.org/copyleft/lesser.html

create a new Material in the _Sprites folder (*Assets > Create > Material* from the menu bar) and name it *BartokBackground Mat*. Drag this new material on to BartokBackground. You'll notice in the Game pane that this made things very dark. (This is because the new material has a Diffuse shader while the previous material used the UnlitAlpha shader.) To remedy this, add a directional light to the scene (*GameObject > Create Other > Directional Light*). The transform for the BartokBackground and directional light should be as follows:

BartokBackground (Quad)	P:[0,0,1]	R:[0,0,0]	S:[26.667,20,1]
Directional Light	P:[0,0,0]	R:[50,-30,0]	S:[1,1,1]

This should set the scene properly.

The Importance of Adding Card Animation

This will be a game for a single human player, but the game of Bartok works best with four players, so three of the players will be AIs (artificial intelligences). Because Bartok is such a simple game, they won't have to be good AIs; they just need to act. The other thing that will need to happen is that we will have to let the player know whose turn it is and what the other players are doing. For this to work, we're going to make the cards animate from place to place in this game. This wasn't necessary in Prospector because the player was taking all of the actions herself, and it was obvious to her what the result should be. Because the player of Bartok is presented with three other hands that will be face-down to her, the animation can be used as an important way to message what actions are being taken by the AI players.

Much of the challenge in designing this tutorial was in creating good animations and in making sure that the game waited properly for each animation to end before moving on to the next thing. Because of that, you will see use of `SendMessage()` and `Invoke()` in this project as well as the use of more specific callback messages than `SendMessage()` allows. Instead, we will be passing a C# class instance to an object to and then call a *callback function* on the instance when the object is done moving, which is less flexible than `SendMessage()` but faster and more specific and can also be used for C# classes that don't extend `MonoBehaviour`.

Build Settings

Whereas the last project was designed as a mobile app, this will be a standalone application for Mac or PC, so the build settings will need to change. From the menu bar, choose *File > Build Settings*, which will bring up the window shown in Figure 32.1.

You'll see that __Prospector_Scene_0 is currently in the list of *Scenes In Build*, but __Bartok_Scene_0 is not. Click the *Add Current* button to add __Bartok_Scene_0 to the list of scenes for this build. Then, uncheck the box next to __Prospector_Scene_0 to remove it from the list of scenes. Next, select *PC, Mac & Linux Standalone* from the list of platforms and click *Switch Platform*. The *Switch Platform* button will turn gray once the switch is complete. This may take a second, but it should be pretty fast. When you've done this, double-check to make sure that your target platform is set to the type for your machine (for example, *Mac OS X* if you're working on an OS X and *Windows* if you're working on a PC). All the other settings should be fine as they are.

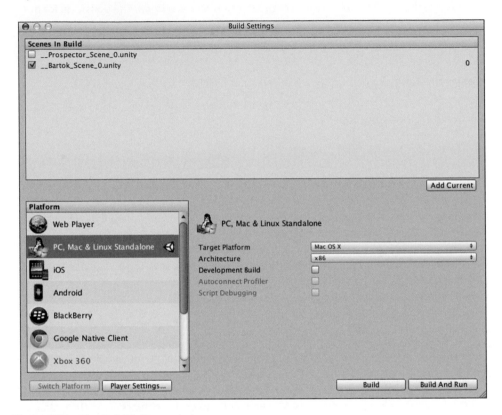

Figure 32.1 The Build Settings window

Once your build settings look like the image in Figure 32.1, you can close this window. (Don't click Build yet; that will happen after actually making the game.)

Once you've closed the window, look at the pop-up menu under the title of the Game pane. From that list of aspect ratios, change it to *Standalone (1024x768)*. This will ensure that your game aspect ratio looks the same as the examples that you'll see throughout this tutorial.

Coding Bartok

Just as we had a `Prospector` class to manage the game and a `CardProspector:Card` class to extend `Card` and add game-specific capabilities, we will need a `Bartok` and `CardBartok` class in this game. Create both a *Bartok* and a *CardBartok* C# script in the __Scripts folder of the Project pane (*Assets > Create > C# Script*). Drag Bartok on to _MainCamera in the Hierarchy (or assign it some other way; you should know what you're doing by now). Double-click CardBartok to open it in MonoDevelop and enter the following code. (If you want, you can copy some of this from CardProspector.)

```csharp
using UnityEngine;
using System.Collections;
using System.Collections.Generic;

// CBState includes both states for the game and to___ states for movement
public enum CBState {
    drawpile,
    toHand,
    hand,
    toTarget,
    target,
    discard,
    to,
    idle
}


// CardBartok extends Card just as CardProspector did.
public class CardBartok : Card {
    // These static fields are used to set values that will be the same
    //  for all instances of CardBartok
    static public float     MOVE_DURATION = 0.5f;
    static public string    MOVE_EASING = Easing.InOut;
    static public float     CARD_HEIGHT = 3.5f;
    static public float     CARD_WIDTH = 2f;

    public CBState          state = CBState.drawpile;

    // Fields to store info the card will use to move and rotate
    public List<Vector3>    bezierPts;
    public List<Quaternion> bezierRots;
    public float            timeStart, timeDuration; // declares 2 fields

    // When the card is done moving, it will call reportFinishTo.SendMessage()
    public GameObject       reportFinishTo = null;

    // MoveTo tells the card to interpolate to a new position and rotation
    public void MoveTo(Vector3 ePos, Quaternion eRot) {
        // Make new interpolation lists for the card.
        // Position and Rotation will each have only two points.
        bezierPts = new List<Vector3>();
        bezierPts.Add ( transform.localPosition );  // Current position
        bezierPts.Add ( ePos );                     // New position
        bezierRots = new List<Quaternion>();
```

```
        bezierRots.Add ( transform.rotation );    // Current rotation
        bezierRots.Add ( eRot );                  // New rotation

        // If timeStart is 0, then it's set to start immediately,
        //   otherwise, it starts at timeStart. This way, if timeStart is
        //   already set, it won't be overwritten.
        if (timeStart == 0) {
            timeStart = Time.time;
        }
        // timeDuration always starts the same but can be altered later
        timeDuration = MOVE_DURATION;

        // Setting state to either toHand or toTarget will be handled by the
        //   calling method
        state  = CBState.to;
    }
    // This overload of MoveTo doesn't require a rotation argument
    public void MoveTo(Vector3 ePos) {
        MoveTo(ePos, Quaternion.identity);
    }


    void Update() {
        switch (state) {
        // All the to___ states are ones where the card is interpolating
        case CBState.toHand:
        case CBState.toTarget:
        case CBState.to:
            // Get u from the current time and duration
            // u ranges from 0 to 1 (usually)
            float u = (Time.time - timeStart)/timeDuration;

            // Use Easing class from Utils to curve the u value
            float uC = Easing.Ease (u, MOVE_EASING);

            if (u<0) { // If u<0, then we shouldn't move yet.
                // Stay at the initial position
                transform.localPosition = bezierPts[0];
                transform.rotation = bezierRots[0];
                return;
            } else if (u>=1) { // If u>=1, we're finished moving
                uC = 1; // Set uC=1 so we don't overshoot
                // Move from the to___ state to the following state
                if (state == CBState.toHand)   state = CBState.hand;
                if (state == CBState.toTarget) state = CBState.toTarget;
                if (state == CBState.to)       state = CBState.idle;
                // Move to the final position
```

```
            transform.localPosition = bezierPts[bezierPts.Count-1];
            transform.rotation = bezierRots[bezierPts.Count-1];
            // Reset timeStart to 0 so it gets overwritten next time
            timeStart = 0;

            if (reportFinishTo != null) { //If there's a callback GameObject
                // … then use SendMessage to call the CBCallback method
                //   with this as the parameter.
                reportFinishTo.SendMessage("CBCallback", this);
                // After calling SendMessage(), reportFinishTo must be set
                //   to null so that it the card doesn't continue to report
                //   to the same GameObject every subsequent time it moves.
                reportFinishTo = null;
            } else { // If there is nothing to callback
                // Do nothing
            }
        } else { // 0<=u<1, which means that this is interpolating now
            // Use Bezier curve to move this to the right point
            Vector3 pos = Utils.Bezier(uC, bezierPts);
            transform.localPosition = pos;
            Quaternion rotQ = Utils.Bezier(uC, bezierRots);
            transform.rotation = rotQ;

        }
        break;

    }
    }
}
```

A lot of this is an adaptation and expansion on the code that you saw in the preceding chapter for the `FloatingScore` class. The CardBartok version of interpolation also interpolates Quaternions (a class that handles rotations), which will be important because we want the cards in Bartok to fan as if they were being held by a player.

Now, open the `Bartok` class and enter this code. The first thing we want to do is to make sure that the `Deck` class is working properly to create all 52 cards:

```
using UnityEngine;
using System.Collections;
using System.Collections.Generic;

public class Bartok : MonoBehaviour {
    static public Bartok S;
```

```
public TextAsset            deckXML;
public TextAsset            layoutXML;
public Vector3              layoutCenter = Vector3.zero;

public bool _____;

public Deck                 deck;
public List<CardBartok>     drawPile;
public List<CardBartok>     discardPile;


void Awake() {
    S = this;

}

void Start () {
    deck = GetComponent<Deck>();       // Get the Deck
    deck.InitDeck(deckXML.text);       // Pass DeckXML to it
    Deck.Shuffle(ref deck.cards);      // This shuffles the deck
    // The ref keyword passes a reference to deck.cards, which allows
    //   deck.cards to be modified by Deck.Shuffle()

}

}
```

As you can see, most of this is the same as what you saw in Prospector, except that you're now dealing with the `CardBartok` class for cards rather than the `CardProspector` class. At this time, you should also adjust other aspects of PrefabCard in the Inspector. Select PrefabCard in the _Prefabs folder of the Project pane and follow these instructions:

1. Set the Box Collider component's *Is Trigger* field to true.

2. Set the Size.z of the Box Collider component to 0.1.

3. Add a Rigidbody component to PrefabCard (*Component > Physics > Rigidbody*).

4. Set the Rigidbody's *Use Gravity* field to false.

5. Set the Rigidbody's *Is Kinematic* field to true.

When finished, the Box Collider and Rigidbody components on PrefabCard should look like those shown in Figure 32.2.

You will also need to make some changes inside the Unity editor before the code you just wrote will work. In the Hierarchy pane, select _MainCamera. The attached Bartok (Script) component is at the bottom of the inspector. (If you want to move it up, you can click the gear next to its name and choose Move Up.) Set the `DeckXML` field of Bartok (Script) to the DeckXML file that is in the Resources folder of the Project pane. (Because the deck remains unchanged [still 13 cards of 4 suits], this is the same file that was used by Prospector.)

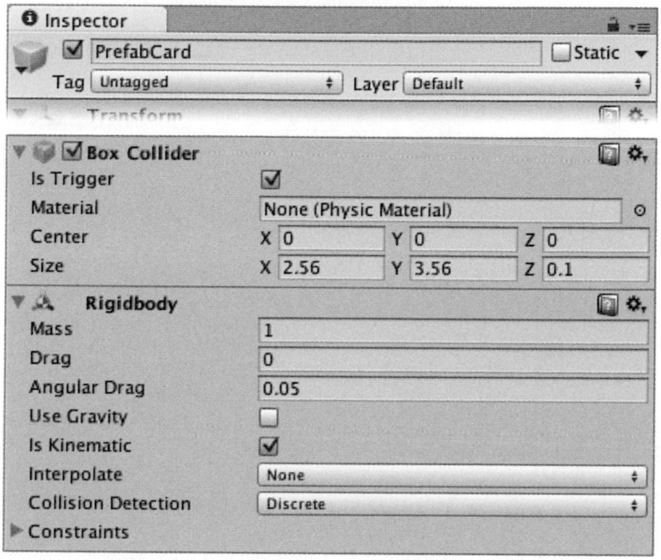

Figure 32.2   Box Collider and Rigidbody settings for PrefabCard

Now select PrefabCard in the _Prefabs folder of the Project pane. You're going to need to swap a new *CardBartok (Script)* component for the existing CardProspector one. Next to the `Script` variable in the *CardProspector (Script)* component, click the Target button and choose CardBartok to replace it. Alternatively, you could just attach the CardBartok script to PrefabCard and then remove the *CardProspector (Script)* component.

Now when you press Play, you should see a grid of cards just as you saw in the early stages of Prospector.

The Game Layout

The layout for Bartok differs significantly from Prospector. In Bartok, there will be a draw pile and discard pile in the middle of the screen as well as four hands of cards distributed to the top, left, bottom, and right sides of the screen. The hands should be fanned as if they were being held by a player (see Figure 32.3).

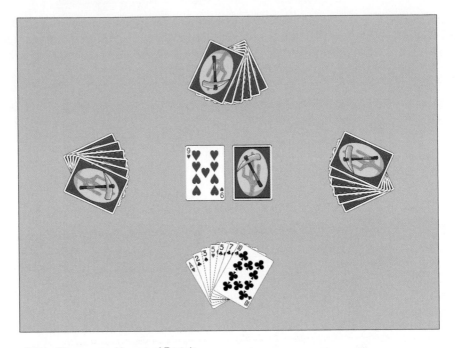

Figure 32.3 The eventual layout of Bartok

This will require a somewhat different layout XML document than was used for Prospector. Select LayoutXML in the Resources folder of the Project pane and duplicate it (*Edit > Duplicate*). Name the duplicate *BartokLayoutXML* and enter the following text. (Bold text differs from the original LayoutXML text.)

```
<xml>
    <!-- This file includes info for laying out the Bartok card game. -->

    <!-- The multiplier is multiplied by the x and y attributes below. -->
    <!-- This determines how loose or tight the layout is. -->
    <multiplier x="1" y="1" />

    <!-- This positions the draw pile and staggers it -->
    <slot type="drawpile" x="1.5" y="0" xstagger="0.05" layer="1"/>

    <!-- This positions the discard pile -->
    <slot type="discardpile" x="-1.5" y="0" layer="2"/>

    <!-- This positions the target card -->
    <slot type="target" x="-1.5" y="0" layer="4"/>

    <!-- These slots are for the four hands held by the four players -->
    <slot type="hand" x="0"   y="-8" rot="0"   player="1" layer="3"/>
    <slot type="hand" x="-10" y="0"  rot="270" player="2" layer="3"/>
```

```
<slot type="hand" x="0"    y="8"   rot="180" player="3" layer="3"/>
<slot type="hand" x="10"   y="0"   rot="90"  player="4" layer="3"/>
```

```
</xml>
```

Now, the class that does the layout must also be rewritten to both fan the cards properly and to take advantage of the new ability to interpolate cards. Create a new C# script named *BartokLayout* and enter this code:

```csharp
using UnityEngine;
using System.Collections;
using System.Collections.Generic;


// SlotDef class is not based on MonoBehaviour, so it doesn't need its own file.
[System.Serializable] // Makes SlotDef able to be seen in the Unity Inspector
public class SlotDef {
    public float       x;
    public float       y;
    public bool        faceUp=false;
    public string      layerName="Default";
    public int         layerID = 0;
    public int         id;
    public List<int>   hiddenBy = new List<int>(); // Unused in Bartok
    public float       rot;         // rotation of hands
    public string      type="slot";
    public Vector2     stagger;
    public int         player;      // player number of a hand
    public Vector3     pos;         // pos derived from x, y, & multiplier
}


public class BartokLayout : MonoBehaviour {
    ...
}
```

Save this code and return to Unity. You'll notice that this causes an error in the console:

"error CS0101: The namespace 'global::' already contains a definition for 'SlotDef'."

This is because the public class `SlotDef` in the Layout script (from Prospector) is conflicting with the public class `SlotDef` in the new BartokLayout script. Either delete the Layout script entirely or open the Layout script in MonoDevelop and comment out the section defining `SlotDef`. To comment out a large chunk of code, just place a /* before the code and a */ after the code you wish to comment. You can also comment out a large section by selecting the lines of code in MonoDevelop and choosing *Edit > Format > Toggle Line Comment(s)* from the menu bar, which will place a single line comment (//) before each line you have selected. After you have eliminated the `SlotDef` class from the Layout script, return to the BartokLayout script and continue editing it by adding the bolded lines in the following code listing:

```
public class BartokLayout : MonoBehaviour {
    public PT_XMLReader       xmlr;  // Just like Deck, this has an PT_XMLReader
    public PT_XMLHashtable    xml;   // This variable is for faster xml access
    public Vector2            multiplier;  // Sets the spacing of the tableau
    // SlotDef references
    public List<SlotDef>      slotDefs; // The SlotDefs hands
    public SlotDef            drawPile;
    public SlotDef            discardPile;
    public SlotDef            target;

    // This function is called to read in the LayoutXML.xml file
    public void ReadLayout(string xmlText) {
        xmlr = new PT_XMLReader();
        xmlr.Parse(xmlText);          // The XML is parsed
        xml = xmlr.xml["xml"][0]; // And xml is set as a shortcut to the XML

        // Read in the multiplier, which sets card spacing
        multiplier.x = float.Parse(xml["multiplier"][0].att("x"));
        multiplier.y = float.Parse(xml["multiplier"][0].att("y"));

        // Read in the slots
        SlotDef tSD;
        // slotsX is used as a shortcut to all the <slot>s
        PT_XMLHashList slotsX = xml["slot"];

        for (int i=0; i<slotsX.Count; i++) {
            tSD = new SlotDef();  // Create a new SlotDef instance
            if (slotsX[i].HasAtt("type")) {
                // If this <slot> has a type attribute parse it
                tSD.type = slotsX[i].att("type");
            } else {
                // If not, set its type to "slot"
                tSD.type = "slot";
            }

            // Various attributes are parsed into numerical values
            tSD.x = float.Parse( slotsX[i].att("x") );
            tSD.y = float.Parse( slotsX[i].att("y") );
            tSD.pos = new Vector3( tSD.x*multiplier.x, tSD.y*multiplier.y, 0 );

            // Sorting Layers
            tSD.layerID = int.Parse( slotsX[i].att("layer") );
            // In this game, the Sorting Layers are named 1, 2, 3, ...through 10
            // This converts the number of the layerID into a text layerName
            tSD.layerName = tSD.layerID.ToString();
            // The layers are used to make sure that the correct cards are
            //    on top of the others. In Unity 2D, all of our assets are
            //    effectively at the same Z depth, so sorting layers are used
            //    to differentiate between them.
```

```
        // pull additional attributes based on the type of each <slot>
        switch (tSD.type) {
        case "slot":
            // ignore slots that are just of the "slot" type
            break;

        case "drawpile":
            // The drawPile xstagger is read but not actually used in Bartok
            tSD.stagger.x = float.Parse( slotsX[i].att("xstagger") );
            drawPile = tSD;
            break;

        case "discardpile":
            discardPile = tSD;
            break;

        case "target":
            // The target card has a different layer from discardPile
            target = tSD;
            break;

        case "hand":
            // Information for each player's hand
            tSD.player = int.Parse( slotsX[i].att("player") );
            tSD.rot = float.Parse( slotsX[i].att("rot") );
            slotDefs.Add (tSD);
            break;

        }
    }
  }
}
```

To use this code, you'll need to attach the BartokLayout script to _MainCamera. (Drag the BartokLayout script from the Project pane onto _MainCamera in the Hierarchy pane.) You will also need to assign the BartokLayoutXML to the `layoutXML` field of the *Bartok (Script)* component on _MainCamera.

Now, add the following bolded code to the Bartok script to make use of BartokLayout:

```
public class Bartok : MonoBehaviour {
    static public Bartok S;
    …

    public List<CardBartok>     discardPile;

    public BartokLayout         layout;
    public Transform            layoutAnchor;
```

```
    ...

    void Start () {
        deck = GetComponent<Deck>();         // Get the Deck
        deck.InitDeck(deckXML.text);         // Pass DeckXML to it
        Deck.Shuffle(ref deck.cards);        // This shuffles the deck
        // The ref keyword passes a reference to deck.cards, which allows
        //   deck.cards to be modified by Deck.Shuffle()

        layout = GetComponent<BartokLayout>();    // Get the Layout
        layout.ReadLayout(layoutXML.text); // Pass LayoutXML to it

        drawPile = UpgradeCardsList( deck.cards );

    }


    // UpgradeCardsList casts the Cards in lCD to be CardBartoks
    // Of course, they were all along, but this lets Unity know it
    List<CardBartok> UpgradeCardsList(List<Card> lCD) {
        List<CardBartok> lCB = new List<CardBartok>();
        foreach( Card tCD in lCD ) {
            lCB.Add ( tCD as CardBartok );
        }
        return( lCB );
    }


}
```

When you run the project now, you should be able to select _MainCamera from the Hierarchy pane and expand the variables in the *BartokLayout (Script)* component to see that they're being read in correctly. You should also look at the `drawPile` field of *Bartok (Script)* to see that it is properly filled with 52 shuffled CardBartok instances.

The Player Class

Because this game has four players, I've chosen to create a class to represent players that can do things like gather cards into a hand and eventually choose what to play using simple artificial intelligence. One thing that is unique about the `Player` class relative to others that you've written is that the `Player` class does *not* extend `MonoBehaviour` (or any other class). This means that it doesn't receive calls from `Awake()`, `Start()`, or `Update()` and that you can't call some functions like `print()` from within it or attach it to a GameObject as a component. However, none of that is necessary for the `Player` class, so it is actually easier in this case to work without it.

Create a new C# script named Player and enter this code:

```
using UnityEngine;
using System.Collections;
using System.Collections.Generic;
using System.Linq; // Enables LINQ queries, which will be explained soon
```

```csharp
// The player can either be human or an ai
public enum PlayerType {
    human,
    ai
}


// The individual player of the game
// Note: Player does NOT extend MonoBehaviour (or any other class)

[System.Serializable] // Make the Player class visible in the Inspector pane
public class Player {

    public PlayerType        type = PlayerType.ai;
    public int               playerNum;

    public List<CardBartok>  hand; // The cards in this player's hand

    public SlotDef           handSlotDef;

    // Add a card to the hand
    public CardBartok AddCard(CardBartok eCB) {
        if (hand == null) hand = new List<CardBartok>();

        // Add the card to the hand
        hand.Add (eCB);

        return( eCB );
    }

    // Remove a card from the hand
    public CardBartok RemoveCard(CardBartok cb) {
        hand.Remove(cb);
        return(cb);
    }

}


}
```

Now, add the following code to Bartok to make use of the Player:

```csharp
public class Bartok : MonoBehaviour {
    ...
    public Vector3            layoutCenter = Vector3.zero;

    // The number of degrees to fan each card in a hand
    public float             handFanDegrees = 10f;
    public bool _____;
    ...
    public Transform          layoutAnchor;
```

```
public List<Player>          players;
public CardBartok            targetCard;

...

void Start () {
    ...
    drawPile = UpgradeCardsList( deck.cards );
    LayoutGame();

}

List<CardBartok> UpgradeCardsList(List<Card> lCD) {
    ...
}

// Position all the cards in the drawPile properly
public void ArrangeDrawPile() {
    CardBartok tCB;

    for (int i=0; i<drawPile.Count; i++) {
        tCB = drawPile[i];
        tCB.transform.parent = layoutAnchor;
        tCB.transform.localPosition = layout.drawPile.pos;
        // Rotation should start at 0
        tCB.faceUp = false;
        tCB.SetSortingLayerName(layout.drawPile.layerName);
        tCB.SetSortOrder(-i*4); // Order them front-to-back
        tCB.state = CBState.drawpile;
    }

}

// Perform the initial game layout
void LayoutGame() {
    // Create an empty GameObject to serve as an anchor for the tableau
    if (layoutAnchor == null) {
        GameObject tGO = new GameObject("_LayoutAnchor");
        // ^ Create an empty GameObject named _LayoutAnchor in the Hierarchy
        layoutAnchor = tGO.transform;                       // Grab its Transform
        layoutAnchor.transform.position = layoutCenter;     // Position it
    }

    // Position the drawPile cards
    ArrangeDrawPile();

    // Set up the players
    Player pl;
    players = new List<Player>();
```

```
    foreach (SlotDef tSD in layout.slotDefs) {
        pl = new Player();
        pl.handSlotDef = tSD;
        players.Add(pl);
        pl.playerNum = players.Count;
    }
    players[0].type = PlayerType.human; // Make the 0th player human

}


// The Draw function will pull a single card from the drawPile and return it
public CardBartok Draw() {
    CardBartok cd = drawPile[0];      // Pull the 0th CardProspector
    drawPile.RemoveAt(0);             // Then remove it from List<> drawPile
    return(cd);                        // And return it
}



// This Update method is used to test adding cards to players' hands
void Update() {
    if (Input.GetKeyDown(KeyCode.Alpha1)) {
        players[0].AddCard(Draw ());
    }
    if (Input.GetKeyDown(KeyCode.Alpha2)) {
        players[1].AddCard(Draw ());
    }
    if (Input.GetKeyDown(KeyCode.Alpha3)) {
        players[2].AddCard(Draw ());
    }
    if (Input.GetKeyDown(KeyCode.Alpha4)) {
        players[3].AddCard(Draw ());
    }
}
}
```

Now run the game again. Select _MainCamera in the Hierarchy and find the `Players` field on the Bartok (Script) component. Open the disclosure triangle for `Players`, and you'll see four elements, one for each player. Open those disclosure triangles, as well, and then open up the disclosure triangles for each hand. Because of the test code in the new `Update()` method, if you click in the Game pane (which gives the game focus and allows it to react to keyboard input), you can press the number keys 1 to 4 on your keyboard (across the top of the keyboard, not the keypad) and watch cards be added to the players' hands. The Inspector for the Bartok (Script) component should show cards being added to hands as shown in Figure 32.4.

This `Update()` method of course won't be used in the final version of the game, but it is often useful to build little functions like this that allow you to test features before other aspects of the game are ready. In this case, we needed a way to test whether the `Player.AddCard()` method worked properly, and this was a quick way to do so.

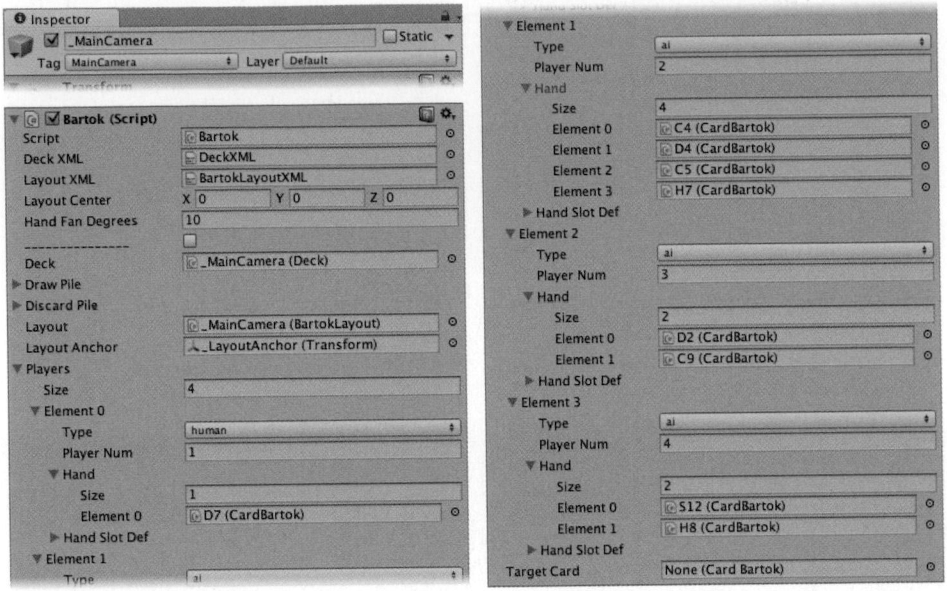

Figure 32.4   Bartok (Script) component showing players and their hands

Fanning the Hands

Now that cards are being moved from the drawPile into players' hands, it's time to graphically represent them there. Add the following code to Player to make this happen:

```
public class Player {
    …

    public CardBartok AddCard(CardBartok eCB) {
        if (hand == null) hand = new List<CardBartok>();

        // Add the card to the hand
        hand.Add (eCB);
        FanHand();
        return( eCB );
    }

    public CardBartok RemoveCard(CardBartok cb) {
        hand.Remove(cb);
        FanHand();
        return(cb);
    }

    public void FanHand() {
        // startRot is the rotation about Z of the first card
        float startRot = 0;
```

```
        startRot = handSlotDef.rot;
        if (hand.Count > 1) {
            startRot += Bartok.S.handFanDegrees * (hand.Count-1) / 2;
        }
        // Then each card is rotated handFanDegrees from that to fan the cards

        // Move all the cards to their new positions
        Vector3 pos;
        float rot;
        Quaternion rotQ;
        for (int i=0; i<hand.Count; i++) {
            rot = startRot - Bartok.S.handFanDegrees*i; // Rot about the z axis
            // ^ Also adds the rotations of the different players' hands
            rotQ = Quaternion.Euler( 0, 0, rot );
            // ^ Quaternion representing the same rotation as rot

            // pos is a V3 half a card height above [0,0,0] (i.e., [0,1.75,0])
            pos = Vector3.up * CardBartok.CARD_HEIGHT / 2f;

            // Multiplying a Quaternion by a Vector3 rotates that Vector3 by
            //  the rotation stored in the Quaternion. The result gives us a
            //  vector above [0,0,0] that has been rotated by rot degrees
            pos = rotQ * pos;

            // Add the base position of the player's hand (which will be at the
            //  bottom-center of the fan of the cards)
            pos += handSlotDef.pos;
            // This staggers the cards in the z direction, which isn't visible
            //  but which does keep their colliders from overlapping
            pos.z = -0.5f*i;

            // Set the localPosition and rotation of the ith card in the hand
            hand[i].transform.localPosition = pos;
            hand[i].transform.rotation = rotQ;
            hand[i].state = CBState.hand;

            // This uses a comparison operator to return a true or false bool
            // So, if (type == PlayerType.human), hand[i].faceUp is set to true
            hand[i].faceUp = (type == PlayerType.human);

            // Set the SortOrder of the cards so that they overlap properly
            hand[i].SetSortOrder(i*4);
        }

    }

}
```

Now if you play the scene and press the numbers 1, 2, 3, and 4 on your keyboard, you should see cards jumping into the players' hands and being fanned correctly. However, you probably noticed that the cards aren't sorted by rank in the human player's hand and look kind of sloppy. Luckily, we can do something about that.

A Tiny Introduction to LINQ

LINQ, which stands for Language INtegrated Query, is a fantastic extension to C# that has had many books written about it. Fully 24 pages of Joseph and Ben Albahari's fantastic *C# 5.0 Pocket Reference*[2] are devoted to LINQ (wherein they only devote 4 pages to arrays). Most of LINQ is far beyond the scope of this book, but it's important that you know that it exists and what it can do.

LINQ has the capability to do database-like queries within a single line of C#, allowing you to select and order specific elements in an array. This is how we will sort the cards in the human player's hand. Add the following bolded lines to `Player.AddCard()`:

```
public class Player {
    …

    public CardBartok AddCard(CardBartok eCB) {
        if (hand == null) hand = new List<CardBartok>();

        // Add the card to the hand
        hand.Add (eCB);

        // Sort the cards by rank using LINQ if this is a human
        if (type == PlayerType.human) {
            CardBartok[] cards = hand.ToArray(); // Copy hand to a new array

            // Below is the LINQ call that works on the array of CardBartoks.
            //  It is similar to doing a foreach(CardBartok cd in cards)
            //  and sorting them by rank. It then returns a sorted array
            cards = cards.OrderBy( cd => cd.rank ).ToArray();

            // Convert the array CardBartok[] back to a List<CardBartok>
            hand = new List<CardBartok>(cards);
            // Note: LINQ operations can be a bit slow (like it could take a
            //  couple of milliseconds), but since we're only doing it once
            //  every turn, it isn't a problem.
        }
```

---

[2] Joseph Albahari and Ben Albahari, *C# 5.0 Pocket Reference: Instant Help for C# 5.0 Programmers* (Beijing: O'Reilly Media, Inc., 2012).

```
        FanHand();
        return( eCB );
    }

    ...
}
```

As you can see, in very few lines, we were able to sort the list. LINQ has tremendous capabilities that are beyond the scope of this book, but I highly recommend you look them up if you need to do sorting or other query-like operations on elements in an array (for example, if you had an array of people and needed to find all of them between the ages of 18 and 25).

Play the scene now, and you'll see that the cards in the human player's hand are always in order by rank.

The cards are going to need to animate into position for the game to be intelligible to the player, so it's time to make the cards move.

Making Cards Move!

Now comes the fun part where we make the cards actually interpolate from one position and rotation to the next. This will make the card game look much more like it's actually being played, and as you'll see, it makes it easier for the player to understand what is happening in the game.

A lot of the interpolation that we'll do here is based on that which was done for FloatingScore in Prospector. Just like FloatingScore, we'll start an interpolation that will be handled by the card itself, and when the card is done moving, it will send a callback message to notify the game that it's done.

Let's start by moving the cards smoothly into the players' hands. CardBartok already has a lot of the movement code written, so let's take advantage of it. Modify the following bolded code of the `Player.FanHand()` method:

```
public class Player {
    ...
    public void FanHand() {
        ...
        for (int i=0; i<hand.Count; i++) {
            ...

            // Set the localPosition and rotation of the ith card in the hand
            hand[i].MoveTo(pos, rotQ); // Tell CardBartok to interpolate
            hand[i].state = CBState.toHand;
            // ^ After the move, CardBartok will set the state to CBState.hand

            /* <= This "/*" begins a multiline comment                    // 1
            hand[i].transform.localPosition = pos;
```

```
            hand[i].transform.rotation = rotQ;
            hand[i].state = CBState.hand;
            */                                                       // 1

            ...
        }
    }
}
```

1. The /* begins a multiline comment, so all lines of code between it and the following */ are considered to be commented out (and are ignored by C#). This is the same way that you could have commented out the SlotDef class in the Layout script at the beginning of this chapter.

Now, when you play the scene and press the number keys (1, 2, 3, 4), you will see the cards actually move into place! Because most of the heavy lifting is done by CardBartok, this took very little code to implement. This is one of the great advantages of object-oriented code. We trust that CardBartok knows how to move on its own so we can just call MoveTo() with a position and rotation, and CardBartok will do the rest.

Managing the Initial Card Deal

In the beginning of a round of Bartok, seven cards are dealt to each player, and then a single card is turned up from the drawPile to become the first target card. Add the following code to Bartok to make this happen:

```
public class Bartok : MonoBehaviour {
    ...
    public float            handFanDegrees = 10f;
    public int              numStartingCards = 7;
    public float            drawTimeStagger = 0.1f;
    ...

    void LayoutGame() {
        ...
        players[0].type = PlayerType.human; // Make the 0th player human

        CardBartok tCB;
        // Deal 7 cards to each player
        for (int i=0; i<numStartingCards; i++) {
            for (int j=0; j<4; j++) { // There are always 4 players
                tCB = Draw (); // Draw a card
                // Stagger the draw time a bit. Remember order of operations.
                tCB.timeStart = Time.time + drawTimeStagger * ( i*4 + j );
                // ^ By setting the timeStart before calling AddCard, we
                //   override the automatic setting of timeStart in
                //   CardBartok.MoveTo().
```

```
                // Add the card to the player's hand. The modulus (%4)
                //  results in a number from 0 to 3
                players[ (j+1)%4 ].AddCard(tCB);
            }
        }

        // Call Bartok.DrawFirstTarget() when the hand cards have been drawn.
        Invoke("DrawFirstTarget", drawTimeStagger * (numStartingCards*4+4) );
    }

    public void DrawFirstTarget() {
        // Flip up the first target card from the drawPile
        CardBartok tCB = MoveToTarget( Draw () );
    }

    // This makes a new card the target
    public CardBartok MoveToTarget(CardBartok tCB) {
        tCB.timeStart = 0;
        tCB.MoveTo(layout.discardPile.pos+Vector3.back);
        tCB.state = CBState.toTarget;
        tCB.faceUp = true;

        targetCard = tCB;

        return(tCB);
    }
    …
}
```

Upon playing the scene, you will see that the distribution of the seven cards and the draw of the first target happen properly on schedule; however, the human player's cards are overlapping each other in strange ways. Just as we did with Prospector, we need to very carefully manage both the `sortingLayerName` and the `sortingOrder` of each element of the cards.

Managing 2D Depth-Sorting Order

In addition to the standard issue of depth-sorting 2D objects, we now have to deal with the fact that the cards are moving, and there will be some times that we want them in one sort order at the beginning of the move and a different sort order when they arrive. To enable that, we will add fields for an `eventualSortLayer` and `eventualSortOrder` to CardBartok. This way, when a card is moving, it will switch to the `eventualSortLayer` and `eventualSortOrder` partway through the move.

The first thing you need to do is rename all of the sorting layers. Open the Tags & Layers manager by choosing *Edit > Project Settings > Tags & Layers* from the menu bar. Then set the names of Sorting Layers 1 through 10 to *1* through *10*, as shown in Figure 32.5.

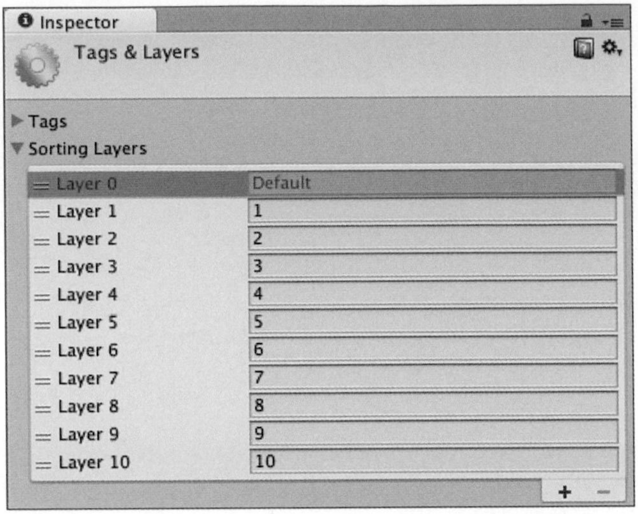

Figure 32.5   Simply named sorting layers for Bartok

Once this is done, add the following bolded code to CardBartok:

```
public class CardBartok : Card {
    …
    public float            timeStart, timeDuration;

    public int              eventualSortOrder;
    public string           eventualSortLayer;
    …

    void Update() {
        switch (state) {
        // All the to… states are ones where the card is interpolating
        case CBState.toHand:
        case CBState.toTarget:
        case CBState.to:
            …
            } else { // 0<=u<1, which means that this is interpolating now
                …
                transform.rotation = rotQ;

                if (u>0.5f && spriteRenderers[0].sortingOrder !=
➥eventualSortOrder) {
                    // Jump to the proper sort order
                    SetSortOrder(eventualSortOrder);
                }
                if (u>0.75f && spriteRenderers[0].sortingLayerName !=
➥eventualSortLayer) {
```

```
                // Jump to the proper sort layer
                SetSortingLayerName(eventualSortLayer);
            }

        }
        break;
    }
}
```

Now that the `eventualSortOrder` and `eventualSortLayer` fields exist, we need to use them throughout the code that has already been written. In Bartok, we'll make this change and also add a `MoveToDiscard()` function that moves the target card into the discardPile:

```
public class Bartok : MonoBehaviour {
    …

    public CardBartok MoveToTarget(CardBartok tCB) {
        tCB.timeStart = 0;
        tCB.MoveTo(layout.discardPile.pos+Vector3.back);
        tCB.state = CBState.toTarget;
        tCB.faceUp = true;
        tCB.SetSortingLayerName("10");//layout.target.layerName);
        tCB.eventualSortLayer = layout.target.layerName;
        if (targetCard != null) {
            MoveToDiscard(targetCard);
        }
        targetCard = tCB;

        return(tCB);
    }

    public CardBartok MoveToDiscard(CardBartok tCB) {
        tCB.state = CBState.discard;
        discardPile.Add ( tCB );
        tCB.SetSortingLayerName(layout.discardPile.layerName);
        tCB.SetSortOrder( discardPile.Count*4 );
        tCB.transform.localPosition = layout.discardPile.pos + Vector3.back/2;

        return(tCB);
    }
    …
}
```

And there are a couple of changes to be made in Player as well:

```
public class Player {
    …
    public CardBartok AddCard(CardBartok eCB) {
```

```
    …
    // Sort the cards by rank using LINQ if this is a human
    if (type == PlayerType.human) {
        …
    }

    eCB.SetSortingLayerName("10"); // This sorts the moving card to the top
    eCB.eventualSortLayer = handSlotDef.layerName;

    FanHand();
    return( eCB );
    }

…

public void FanHand() {
    …
    for (int i=0; i<hand.Count; i++) {
        …

        // Set the SortOrder of the cards so that they overlap properly
        hand[i].eventualSortOrder = i*4;
        //hand[i].SetSortOrder(i*4);
    }
}
}
```

Handling Turns

In this game, players will need to take turns, and the human player will have to know whose turn it is. We will accomplish this by highlighting the background behind the current player with a light.

In Unity, choose *GameObject > Create Other > Point Light* from the menu bar. Name the new light *TurnLight* and set its transform to the following:

TurnLight (Point Light)   P:[0,0,-5]   R:[0,0,0]   S:[1,1,1]

As you can see, this casts a nice, obvious light on the background. We also need to add code to manage the light and the turns. Open the Bartok script and add the bolded code shown here:

```
using UnityEngine;
using System.Collections;
using System.Collections.Generic;

// This enum contains the different phases of a game turn
public enum TurnPhase {
```

```csharp
    idle,
    pre,
    waiting,
    post,
    gameOver
}

public class Bartok : MonoBehaviour {
    static public Bartok S;
    // This field is static to enforce that there is only 1 current player
    static public Player CURRENT_PLAYER;
    …

    public CardBartok          targetCard;

    public TurnPhase           phase = TurnPhase.idle;
    public GameObject          turnLight;

    void Awake() {
        S = this;

        // Find the TurnLight by name
        turnLight = GameObject.Find ("TurnLight");
    }

    …

    public void DrawFirstTarget() {
        // Flip up the target card in the middle
        CardBartok tCB = MoveToTarget( Draw () );
        // Set the CardBartok to call CBCallback on this Bartok when it is done
        tCB.reportFinishTo = this.gameObject;
    }

    // This callback is used by the last card to be dealt at the beginning
    // It is only used once per game.
    public void CBCallback(CardBartok cb) {
        // You sometimes want to have reporting of method calls like this    // 1
        Utils.tr(Utils.RoundToPlaces(Time.time),"Bartok.CBCallback()",cb.name);

        StartGame(); // Start the Game
    }

    public void StartGame() {
        // Pick the player to the left of the human to go first.
        // (players[0] is the human)
        PassTurn(1);
    }
```

```
public void PassTurn(int num=-1) {
    // If no number was passed in, pick the next player
    if (num == -1) {
        int ndx = players.IndexOf(CURRENT_PLAYER);
        num = (ndx+1)%4;
    }
    int lastPlayerNum = -1;
    if (CURRENT_PLAYER != null) {
        lastPlayerNum = CURRENT_PLAYER.playerNum;
    }
    CURRENT_PLAYER = players[num];
    phase = TurnPhase.pre;

    CURRENT_PLAYER.TakeTurn();

    // Move the TurnLight to shine on the new CURRENT_PLAYER
    Vector3 lPos = CURRENT_PLAYER.handSlotDef.pos + Vector3.back*5;
    turnLight.transform.position = lPos;

    // Report the turn passing
    Utils.tr(Utils.RoundToPlaces(Time.time), "Bartok.PassTurn()",
      ➥"Old: "+lastPlayerNum,"New: "+CURRENT_PLAYER.playerNum);
}

// ValidPlay verifies that the card chosen can be played on the discard pile
public bool ValidPlay(CardBartok cb) {
    // It's a valid play if the rank is the same
    if (cb.rank == targetCard.rank) return(true);

    // It's a valid play if the suit is the same
    if (cb.suit == targetCard.suit) {
        return(true);
    }

    // Otherwise, return false
    return(false);
}

...

/* Now is a good time to comment out this testing code        // 2
// This Update method is used to test passing cards to players
void Update() {
    if (Input.GetKeyDown(KeyCode.Alpha1)) {
        players[0].AddCard(Draw ());
    }
    if (Input.GetKeyDown(KeyCode.Alpha2)) {
        players[1].AddCard(Draw ());
    }
```

```
        if (Input.GetKeyDown(KeyCode.Alpha3)) {
            players[2].AddCard(Draw ());
        }
        if (Input.GetKeyDown(KeyCode.Alpha4)) {
            players[3].AddCard(Draw ());
        }
    }
    */                                                      // 2
}
```

1. The line following the `// 1` is the first use of the static public `Utils.tr()` method (`tr` is short for "trace", another term for outputting to the console). This method takes any number of arguments (via the params keyword), concatenates them, and outputs them to the Console pane. It is one of the elements that was added to the Utils class in the version contained in the unitypackage that you imported into Prospector.

2. Make sure that you add both the opening and closing lines of this multiline comment.

Press Play, and you will see the scene deal out the cards and then move the TurnLight to hover over the left player, signifying that it is that player's turn. Now, let's make the AI players able to take turns. Open the Player script and add the bolded code:

```
public class Player {
    …

    public void FanHand() {
        …
        for (int i=0; i<hand.Count; i++) {
            …
            pos.z = -0.5f*i;

            // The line below makes sure that the card starts moving immediately
            //  if it's not the initial deal at the beginning of the game.
            if (Bartok.S.phase != TurnPhase.idle) {
                hand[i].timeStart = 0;
            }

            // Set the localPosition and rotation of the ith card in the hand
            …
        }

    }

    // The TakeTurn() function enables the AI of the computer Players
    public void TakeTurn() {
        Utils.tr (Utils.RoundToPlaces(Time.time), "Player.TakeTurn");

        // Don't need to do anything if this is the human player.
        if (type == PlayerType.human) return;
```

```
        Bartok.S.phase = TurnPhase.waiting;

        CardBartok cb;

        // If this is an AI player, need to make a choice about what to play
        // Find valid plays
        List<CardBartok> validCards = new List<CardBartok>();
        foreach (CardBartok tCB in hand) {
            if (Bartok.S.ValidPlay(tCB)) {
                validCards.Add ( tCB );
            }
        }
        // If there are no valid cards
        if (validCards.Count == 0) {
            // …then draw a card
            cb = AddCard( Bartok.S.Draw () );
            cb.callbackPlayer = this;
            return;
        }

        // Otherwise, if there is a card or more to play, pick one
        cb = validCards[ Random.Range (0,validCards.Count) ];
        RemoveCard(cb);
        Bartok.S.MoveToTarget(cb);
        cb.callbackPlayer  = this;

    }

    public void CBCallback(CardBartok tCB) {
        Utils.tr (Utils.RoundToPlaces(Time.time),
          ➥"Player.CBCallback()",tCB.name,"Player "+playerNum);
        // The card is done moving, so pass the turn
        Bartok.S.PassTurn();
    }

}
```

The last method you just added is a CBCallback function that a CardBartok should call when it's done moving; however, because Player does not extend MonoBehaviour, we need to use a method other than SendMessage() to do so. Instead, we'll pass the CardBartok a reference to this Player, and then the CardBartok can call CBCallback directly on the Player instance when it's done moving. This Player reference will be stored on CardBartok as the field callbackPlayer. Open CardBartok and add this code:

```
public class CardBartok : Card {
    …
    // When the card is done moving, it will call reportFinishTo.SendMessage()
    public GameObject        reportFinishTo = null;
    public Player            callbackPlayer = null;
```

```
void Awake() {
    callbackPlayer = null; // Just to be sure.
}

// MoveTo tells the card to interpolate to a new position and rotation
…

void Update() {
    switch (state) {
        // All the to… states are ones where the card is interpolating
    case CBState.toHand:
    case CBState.toTarget:
    case CBState.to:
        …
        } else if (u>=1) { // If u>=1, we're finished moving
            uC = 1; // Set uC=1 so we don't overshoot
            …

            if (reportFinishTo != null) { //If there's a callback GameObject
                // … then use SendMessage to call the CBCallback method
                //   with this as the parameter.
                reportFinishTo.SendMessage("CBCallback", this);
                // After calling SendMessage(), reportFinishTo must be set
                //   to null so that it the card doesn't continue to report
                //   to the same GameObject every subsequent time it moves.
                reportFinishTo = null;
            } else if (callbackPlayer != null) {
                // If there's a callback Player
                // then call CBCallback directly on the Player
                callbackPlayer.CBCallback(this);
                callbackPlayer = null;
            } else { // If there is nothing to callback
                // Just let it stay still.
            }
        } else {
            …
        }
        break;
    }
}
```

Now, you'll see that when you play the scene, the other three players each play. It's time to make the human able to play too by making the cards clickable.

Add the `OnMouseUpAsButton()` method to the end of CardBartok:

```
public class CardBartok : Card {
    …
    void update() {…}

    // This allows the card to react to being clicked
    override public void OnMouseUpAsButton() {
        // Call the CardClicked method on the Bartok singleton
        Bartok.S.CardClicked(this);
        // Also call the base class (Card.cs) version of this method
        base.OnMouseUpAsButton();
    }
}
```

And now add the `CardClicked()` method to the end of the Bartok script:

```
public class Bartok : MonoBehaviour {
    …

    public void CardClicked(CardBartok tCB) {
        // If it's not the human's turn, don't respond
        if (CURRENT_PLAYER.type != PlayerType.human) return;
        // If the game is waiting on a card to move, don't respond
        if (phase == TurnPhase.waiting) return;

        // Act differently based on whether it was a card in hand
        //  or on the drawPile that was clicked
        switch (tCB.state) {
        case CBState.drawpile:
            // Draw the top card, not necessarily the one clicked.
            CardBartok cb = CURRENT_PLAYER.AddCard( Draw() );
            cb.callbackPlayer = CURRENT_PLAYER;
            Utils.tr (Utils.RoundToPlaces(Time.time),
              ➥"Bartok.CardClicked()","Draw",cb.name);
            phase = TurnPhase.waiting;
            break;
        case CBState.hand:
            // Check to see whether the card is valid
            if (ValidPlay(tCB)) {
                CURRENT_PLAYER.RemoveCard(tCB);
                MoveToTarget(tCB);
                tCB.callbackPlayer = CURRENT_PLAYER;
                Utils.tr(Utils.RoundToPlaces(Time.time), "Bartok.CardClicked()",
                  ➥"Play",tCB.name,targetCard.name+" is target");
                phase = TurnPhase.waiting;
            } else {
                // Just ignore it
                Utils.tr(Utils.RoundToPlaces(Time.time), "Bartok.CardClicked()",
                  ➥"Attempted to Play",tCB.name,targetCard.name+" is target");
```

```
        }
      break;

    }
  }
}
```

Now, you can play as well, and the game works fine. But right now there is no logic to end the game when it's over. Just a few more additions, and this prototype will be playable!

Adding Game Logic

Just as with Prospector, we want to message the player when she finishes the game. Create two new GUITexts and name them *GTGameOver* and *GTRoundResult*. Their settings should be those shown in Figure 32.6.

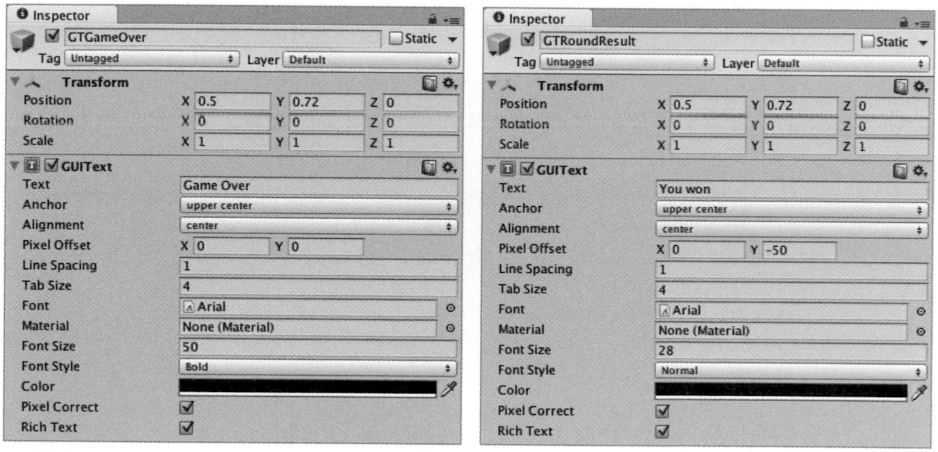

Figure 32.6   Settings for GTGameOver and GTRoundResult

Once you have these, add the following code to Bartok to both manage these GUITexts and to test whether the game is over and restart it after one second if it is:

```
public class Bartok : MonoBehaviour {
    ...
    public GameObject         turnLight;

    public GameObject         GTGameOver;
    public GameObject         GTRoundResult;

    void Awake() {
        S = this;
```

```
        // Find the TurnLight by name
        turnLight = GameObject.Find ("TurnLight");
        GTGameOver = GameObject.Find("GTGameOver");
        GTRoundResult = GameObject.Find("GTRoundResult");
        GTGameOver.SetActive(false);
        GTRoundResult.SetActive(false);
    }

    …

    public void PassTurn(int num=-1) {
        …
        if (CURRENT_PLAYER != null) {
            lastPlayerNum = CURRENT_PLAYER.playerNum;
            // Check for Game Over and need to reshuffle discards
            if ( CheckGameOver() ) {
                return;
            }
        }
        …
    }

    …

    public bool CheckGameOver() {
        // See if we need to reshuffle the discard pile into the draw pile
        if (drawPile.Count == 0) {
            List<Card> cards = new List<Card>();
            foreach (CardBartok cb in discardPile) {
                cards.Add (cb);
            }
            discardPile.Clear();
            Deck.Shuffle( ref cards );
            drawPile = UpgradeCardsList(cards);
            ArrangeDrawPile();
        }

        // Check to see if the current player has won
        if (CURRENT_PLAYER.hand.Count == 0) {
            // The current player has won!
            if (CURRENT_PLAYER.type == PlayerType.human) {
                GTGameOver.guiText.text = "You Won!";
                GTRoundResult.guiText.text = "";
            } else {
                GTGameOver.guiText.text = "Game Over";
                GTRoundResult.guiText.text = "Player "+CURRENT_PLAYER.playerNum
                   ➥+ " won";
            }
            GTGameOver.SetActive(true);
```

```
        GTRoundResult.SetActive(true);
        phase = TurnPhase.gameOver;
        Invoke("RestartGame", 1);
        return(true);
    }

    return(false);
}

public void RestartGame() {
    CURRENT_PLAYER = null;
    Application.LoadLevel("__Bartok_Scene_0");
}

}
```

Now the game will play properly, it will end when it's over, and it will restart properly as well.

Summary

The goal of this chapter was to demonstrate how possible it is to take the digital prototypes that you make in this book and adapt them to your own games. Once you finish all the tutorial chapters, you will have the framework for a classic arcade game (*Apple Picker*), a physics-based casual game (*Mission Demolition*), a space shooter (*Space SHMUP*), a card game (*Prospector* and *Bartok*), a word game (*Word Game*), a first-person shooter (*Quick Snap*), and a third-person adventure game (*Omega Mage*). As prototypes, none of these are finished games, but any of them could serve as a foundation on which to build your own games.

Next Steps

The classic paper version of the Bartok card game included the ability for the winner of any round to add additional rules to the game. While it's not possible to allow the player to just make up rules for this digital game, it is certainly possible to add your own optional rules through code just as I did for the version you played with in Chapter 1.

If you visit the http://book.prototools.net website, you can look under Chapter 32 for the Unity project of the expanded version of Bartok that includes all the optional rules you were able to play with in Chapter 1. That should be a good starting point for you to use to add your own rules to the game.

CHAPTER 33

PROTOTYPE 6: WORD GAME

In this chapter, you learn how to create a simple word game. This game uses several concepts that you have already learned, and it introduces the concept of *coroutines*, methods that can yield during execution to allow the processor to handle other methods.

By the end of this chapter, you'll have a simple word game that you can expand yourself.

Getting Started: Word Game Prototype

As usual, you'll import a unitypackage to start this chapter. This package contains a few art assets and some C# Scripts that you created in previous chapters.

SET UP THE PROJECT FOR THIS CHAPTER

Following the standard project setup procedure, create a new project in Unity. If you need a refresher on the standard project setup procedure, see Appendix A, "Standard Project Setup Procedure." When you are creating the project, you will be asked if you want to set up defaults for 2D or 3D. Choose 3D for this project.

For this project, we will import the main scene from the unitypackage, so you do not need to set up the _MainCamera.

- **Project name:** Word Game
- **Download and import package:** See Chapter 33 at http://book.prototools.net
- **Scene name:** __WordGame_Scene_0 (imported in unitypackage)
- **Project folders:** __Scripts, _Prefabs, Materials & Textures, Resources
- **C# script names:** Just the imported scripts in the ProtoTools folder

---

Open the scene __WordGame_Scene_0, and you will find a _MainCamera that is already set up for an orthographic game. You'll also notice that some of the reusable C# scripts that were created in previous chapters have been moved into a ProtoTools folder to keep them separate from the new scripts you'll create for this project. I find this is useful because it enables me to just place a copy of the ProtoTools folder into the __Scripts folder of any new project and have all that functionality ready to go.

In your Build Settings, make sure that this one is set to *PC, Mac, & Linux Standalone*. Set the aspect ratio of the Game pane to *Standalone (1024 x 768)*.

About the Word Game

This game is a classic form of word game. Commercial examples of this game include *Word Whomp* by Pogo.com, *Jumbline 2* by Branium, *Pressed for Words* by Words and Maps, and many others. The player will be presented with six letters that spell at least one six-letter word, and she is tasked with finding all of the words that can be created with those six letters. Our version of the game will include some slick animations (using Bézier interpolations) and a scoring paradigm that encourages the player to find long words before short ones. Figure 33.1 shows an image of the game you'll create in this chapter. As you can see in the image, this game can handle words up to 8 letters in length, though 6 is the standard for this kind of game.

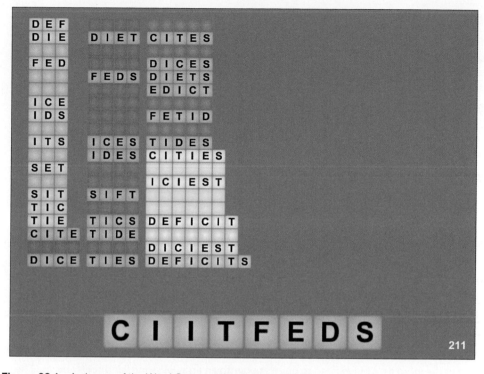

Figure 33.1   An image of the Word Game created in this chapter

In this image, you can see that each of the words are divided into individual letters, and there are two sizes of letters. For the sake of object orientation, we'll create a `Letter` class that handles each letter and a `Word` class to collect them into words. We'll also create a `WordList` class to read the large dictionary of possible words that we have and turn it into usable data for the game. The game will be controlled by a `WordGame` class, and the `Scoreboard` and `FloatingScore` classes from previous prototypes will be used to show the score to the player. In addition, the `Utils` class will be used for interpolation and easing. The `PT_XMLReader` class is imported with this project, but is unused. I left this script in the unitypackage because I want to encourage you to start building your own collection of useful scripts that you can import into any project to help you get started (just as the ProtoTools folder is for the projects in this book). Feel free to add any useful scripts that you create to this collection, and think about importing it as the first thing you do for each new game prototype that you start.

Parsing the Word List

This game uses a modified form of the 2of12inf word list created by Alan Beale.[1] I've removed some offensive words and attempted to correct others. You are more than welcome to use this word list however you wish in the future, as long as you follow the copyright wishes of both Alan Beale and Kevin Atkinson (as listed in the footnote). I also modified the list by shifting all of the letters to uppercase and by changing the line ending from \r\n (a carriage return and a line feed, which is the standard Windows text file format) to \n (just a line feed, the standard Macintosh text format). This was done because it makes it easier to split the file into individual words based on line feed, and it will work on Windows just as well as Mac.

The decision to remove offensive words was based on the kind of game this is. In a game like *Scrabble* or *Letterpress*, the player is given a series of letter tiles, and she is able to choose which words she wishes to spell with those tiles. If this game were of that ilk, I would not have removed any words from the word list. However, in this game, the player is forced to spell every word in the list that can be made from the collection of letters that she is given. This means that the game could force players to spell some terms that would be very offensive to them. In this game, the decision of which words are chosen has shifted from the player to the computer, and I did not feel comfortable forcing players to spell offensive words. However, in the over 75,000 words in the list, there are probably some words that I missed, so if you find any words in the game that you feel I should omit (or ones I should add), please let me know by sending me a message via the website http://book.prototools.net. Thanks.

To read the word list file, we need to pull its text into an array of strings and split it by \n. The following code listing includes the first instance of a *coroutine* in this book. Coroutines are functions that can execute progressively with yields in between to allow other functions to run. You can learn more about them in Appendix B, "Useful Concepts." Create a new C# script named *WordList* and enter the following code:

```csharp
using UnityEngine;
using System.Collections;
using System.Collections.Generic;

public class WordList : MonoBehaviour {
    public static WordList      S;

    public TextAsset            wordListText;
    public int                  numToParseBeforeYield = 10000;
    public int                  wordLengthMin = 3;
    public int                  wordLengthMax = 7;
```

---

[1] Alan Beale has released all of his word lists into the public domain apart from the aspects of the 2of12inf list that were based on the AGID word list, Copyright 2000 by Kevin Atkinson. Permission to use, copy, modify, distribute and sell this [the AGID] database, the associated scripts, the output created from the scripts and its documentation for any purpose is hereby granted [by Atkinson] without fee, provided that the above copyright notice appears in all copies and that both that copyright notice and this permission notice appear in supporting documentation. Kevin Atkinson makes no representations about the suitability of this array for any purpose. It is provided "as is" without express or implied warranty.

```
public bool      _____;

public int            currLine = 0;
public int            totalLines;
public int            longWordCount;
public int            wordCount;

// Some variables below are private to keep them from appearing in the
//  Inspector. Because these variables will be so long, it can drastically
//  slow playback if the Inspector is trying to display them. Private
//  variables are restricted so that only this instance of the WordList
//  class can see them.
private string[]      lines;                                        // 1
private List<string>  longWords;
private List<string>  words;

void Awake() {
    S = this;  // Set up the singleton
}

void Start () {
    // Split the text of wordListText on line feeds, which creates a large,
    //  populated string[] with all the words from the list
    lines = wordListText.text.Split('\n');
    totalLines = lines.Length;

    // This starts the coroutine ParseLines(). Coroutines can be paused in
    //  the middle to allow other code to execute.
    StartCoroutine( ParseLines() );                                // 2
}

// All coroutines have IEnumerator as their return type.
public IEnumerator ParseLines() {                                  // 3
    string word;
    // Init the Lists to hold the longest words and all valid words
    longWords = new List<string>();
    words = new List<string>();

    for (currLine = 0; currLine < totalLines; currLine++) {
        word = lines[currLine];

        // If the word is as long as wordLengthMax
        if (word.Length == wordLengthMax) {
            // …then store it in longWords
            longWords.Add(word);
        }
        // If it's between wordLengthMin and wordLengthMax in length
        if ( word.Length>=wordLengthMin && word.Length<=wordLengthMax ) {
```

```
                    // ...then add it to the list of all valid words
                    words.Add(word);
            }

            // Determine whether the coroutine should yield
            // This uses a modulus (%) function to yield every 10,000th record
            //   (or whatever you have numToParseBeforeYield set to)
            if (currLine % numToParseBeforeYield == 0) {
                // Count the words in each list to show that the parsing is
                //   progressing
                longWordCount = longWords.Count;
                wordCount = words.Count;
                // This yields execution until the next frame
                yield return null;                                             // 4

                // The yield will cause the execution of this method to wait
                //   here while other code executes and then continue from this
                //   point.
            }
        }
    }

    // These methods allow other classes to access the private List<string>s
    public List<string> GetWords() {
        return(words);
    }

    public string GetWord(int ndx) {
        return( words[ndx] );
    }

    public List<string> GetLongWords() {
        return( longWords );
    }

    public string GetLongWord(int ndx) {
        return( longWords[ndx] );
    }
}
```

1. Another way to hide variables from the Inspector without making them private is to use the *attribute* [System.NonSerialized]. An attribute sends an instruction to Unity about how to treat the next line in the code. If you were to make a variable public and then place [System.NonSerialized] on the line preceding it, then the public variable would not appear in the Inspector. Private variables were used in this code to show how methods like GetWord() can be used to access them, but if all you really need to do is hide a variable from the Inspector, [System.NonSerialized] may be a better way to go.

2. This starts the *coroutine* ParseLines(). Coroutines can be *yielded* in the middle to allow other code to execute. When a coroutine yields, it transfers execution back to other code

and then continues the coroutine after a certain amount of time has passed. So, if a corou-tine had a yield in the middle of an infinite `while` loop, other code could still execute even though the loop never exited.

3. All coroutines have `IEnumerator` as their return type. This enables them to yield their exe-cution and allow other methods to run before returning to the coroutine. This is extremely important for processes like loading large files or like parsing a large amount of data (as we're doing in this case).

4. This is the yield statement. When a coroutine yields, it effectively pauses on the `yield` line until a certain amount of time has passed and then continues from there. The coroutine and yield statements are necessary in this code because the `for` loop will be iterating more than 75,000 times to interpret all 75,000+ lines of WordList. On a slower computer, this could make it appear that the program had frozen, so the coroutine allows us to keep Unity updating and interactive while in the middle of a time-consuming process.

   In this code, we want to have the coroutine yield for as little time as possible (a single frame), so the yield statement returns null. It is possible to have coroutines yield for a specific amount of time by entering code like `yield return new WaitForSeconds(5);`, which would cause the coroutine to yield for about 5 seconds (coroutine yield times are not exact). See the "Using Coroutines" sidebar for more information.

Once the code is written and saved, switch back to Unity and attach the WordList C# script to _MainCamera. Then, select _MainCamera in the Hierarchy and set the `wordListText` variable of the *WordList (Script)* component in the Inspector to be the file *2of12inf*, which you can find in the Resources folder of the Project pane. Once this is set, press Play. You will see that the `currLine`, `longWordCount`, and `wordCount` will count up progressively. This is happening because the numbers are allowed to update every time the coroutine `ParseLines()` yields.

If you use the Inspector to change `numToParseBeforeYield` to 100, you will see that these numbers build much more slowly because the coroutine is yielding every 100 words. How-ever, if you change it to something like 100000, these numbers will update only once because there are fewer than 100 thousand words in the word list. If you're interested in seeing how much time each pass through the `ParseLines()` coroutine is taking, try using the profiler, as described in the sidebar titled "The Unity Profiler."

USING COROUTINES

While the coroutine in this chapter probably isn't strictly necessary as long as you have a fast computer, this kind of thing becomes much more important when you're develop-ing for mobile devices (or other devices with slower processors). Parsing this same word list on an older iPhone can take as much as 10 to 20 seconds, so it's important to include breaks in the parsing where the app can handle other tasks and not appear frozen.

An important thing to note about the required `StartCoroutine()` method is that it can only be called within a class that extends MonoBehaviour.

You can learn more about coroutines in the Unity documentation or Appendix B.

THE UNITY PROFILER

The Unity profiler is one of the most powerful tools for optimizing the performance of your games, though sadly, it's only available in Unity Pro. For every frame of your game, the profiler maintains stats on the amount of time spent on each C# function, calls to the graphics engine, handling user input, and so on. You can see a great example of how this works by running the profiler on this project.

First, make sure that the WordList code from the preceding pages is working properly. Next, we'll add a Profiler pane to the same group as the Scene pane. That will ensure that you can see both the Game pane and the Profiler pane simultaneously. To add the Profiler pane, click the pop-up menu button at the top right of the current Scene pane and choose *Add Tab > Profiler* (as shown in Figure 33.2).

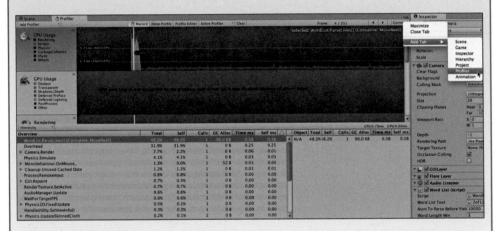

Figure 33.2   The Profiler pane

To see the profiler in action, first click the Pause button at the top of the Unity window and then click Play. This will cause Unity to prepare itself to run your game but to be paused before the first frame. If you click Pause again, you will see a graph start to appear in the profiler. Pause the game again before the graph completely reaches the left side of the screen.

With the game paused, the profiler should stop graphing yet maintain the graph of the frames that have already passed. Each of the colors in the graph next to CPU Usage covers a different aspect of things for which the CPU (the main processor in your computer) is used. In the later frames, if you're on a fast computer, you should see that most of the chart is yellow; the yellow represents the time Unity spends on VSync (that is, waiting for the screen to be ready to display another frame). This is blocking our view of how much time is taken by the scripts (which are light blue), so we'll hide it from the graph. The little colored boxes below CPU Usage on the left side of the profiler each represent a different kind of process that runs on the CPU. You want to turn all of them off except for the

Scripts box (which is blue). To do this, click the colored box next to everything except for Scripts. This should leave you with a blue graph like the one shown in Figure 33.2.

Now, click and drag the mouse along the blue graph, and you should see a white line following the mouse. This white line represents a single frame in the graph. As you move, the text in the bottom half of the profiler will update to show how much processing time was taken by each function or background process during that frame. The function we're interested in is the `WordList.ParseLines()` coroutine. This only runs in the first few frames, so you won't see it on the right side of the graph; however, you should see a spike of script activity at the beginning of the graph (as shown in Figure 33.2), which is the time taken by the `ParseLines()` coroutine. Move the white line to that part of the graph and click `WordList.ParseLines()` in the Overview column. This will highlight the graph contribution of that one routine and dim the others. If you use the left and right arrows at the top-right corner of the Profiler pane, you can step one frame back or forward (respectively) and see the CPU resources used by `ParseLines()` in each frame. In my profiling, I found that for the first several frames, `ParseLines()` took up nearly 50% of the CPU time spent on each frame (although your numbers may vary due to computer type and processing speed).

In addition to script profiling, the profiler can also help you find what aspects of rendering or physics simulation are taking the most time in your game. If you ever run into frame rate issues in one of your games, try checking the profiler to see what's happening. (You'll want to be sure to turn all of the other types of CPU profiling back on when you do [that is, re-check all the boxes that we unchecked to isolate scripts]).

To see a very different profiler graph, you can try running the profiler on the Hello World project from Chapter 18, "Hello World: Your First Program." You'll see that in Hello World, much more time is spent on physics than scripts. (You may need to turn the VSync element of the graph off again to see this clearly.)

You can learn more about the profiler in the Unity documentation.

Setting Up the Game

We're going to create a WordGame class to manage the game, but before we do so, we need to make a couple of changes to WordList. First, we need to make it not start parsing the words on `Start()` but instead wait until an `Init()` method is called by another class. Second, we need to make WordList notify the upcoming WordGame script when the parsing is complete. To do this, we will have the WordList send a message to the _MainCamera GameObject using the `SendMessage()` command. This message will be interpreted by WordGame as you'll soon see. Change the name of the `void Start()` method in WordList to `public void Init()` and add the following bold code to the end of the `ParseLines` method in WordList:

```csharp
public class WordList : MonoBehaviour {
    ...

    void Awake() {
        S = this;  // Set up the singleton
    }

    public void Init() { // This line replaces "void Start()"
        // Split the text of wordListText on line feeds, which creates a large,
        //  populated string[] with all the words from the list
        lines = wordListText.text.Split('\n');
        totalLines = lines.Length;

        // This starts a coroutine of ParseLines. Coroutines can be paused in
        //  the middle to allow other code to execute.
        StartCoroutine( ParseLines() );
    }

    ...

    public IEnumerator ParseLines() {
        ...
        for (currLine = 0; currLine < totalLines; currLine++) {
            ...
        }

        // Send a message to this gameObject to let it know the parse is done
        gameObject.SendMessage("WordListParseComplete");
    }
}
```

The `SendMessage()` command is executed on the GameObject _MainCamera (because WordList is a Script Component of _MainCamera). This command will call a `WordListParseComplete()` method on any script that is attached to the GameObject on which it is called (that is, _MainCamera).

Now, create a *WordGame* C# script and attach it to _MainCamera as a Script component. Then enter the following code to take advantage of the changes just made to WordList:

```csharp
using UnityEngine;
using System.Collections;
using System.Collections.Generic;   // We'll be using List<> & Dictionary<>
using System.Linq;                  // We'll be using LINQ

public enum GameMode {
    preGame,     // Before the game starts
    loading,     // The word list is loading and being parsed
    makeLevel,   // The individual WordLevel is being created
    levelPrep,   // The level visuals are Instantiated
```

```
        inLevel      // The level is in progress
}

public class WordGame : MonoBehaviour {
    static public WordGame      S; // Singleton

    public bool _____;

    public GameMode          mode = GameMode.preGame;

    void Awake() {
        S = this; // Assign the singleton
    }

    void Start () {
        mode = GameMode.loading;
        // Tells WordList.S to start parsing all the words
        WordList.S.Init();
    }

    // Called by the SendMessage() command from WordList
    public void WordListParseComplete() {
        mode = GameMode.makeLevel;
    }

}
```

Select _MainCamera in the Hierarchy pane, and look at the *WordGame (Script)* component in the Inspector. When you press Play, you'll see the value of the mode field initially move from preGame to loading. Then, after all the words have been parsed, it will change from loading to makeLevel. This shows us that everything is working as we had hoped.

Now, it's time to take the words in the WordList and make a level from them. The Level class will include the following:

- The long word on which the level is based. (If maxWordLength is 6, this is the six-letter word whose letters will be reshuffled into the other words.)
- The index number of that word in longWords.
- The level number as the int levelNum. In this chapter, every time the game starts, we'll choose a random word, but later you could use a pseudo-random function to ensure that the eighth level would always be the same word.
- A Dictionary<,> of each character in the word and how many times it is used. Dictionaries are part of System.Collections.Generic along with Lists.
- A List<> of all the other words that can be formed from the characters in the Dictionary above.

A `Dictionary<,>` is a generic collection type that holds a series of key value pairs. In each level, the `Dictionary<,>` will use char keys and int values to hold information about how many times each char is used in the long word. For example, this is how the long word MISSISSIPPI would look:

```
Dictionary<char,int> charDict = new Dictionary<char,int>();
charDict.Add('M',1); // MISSISSIPPI has 1 M
charDict.Add('I',4); // MISSISSIPPI has 4 Is
charDict.Add('S',4); // MISSISSIPPI has 4 Ss
charDict.Add('P',2); // MISSISSIPPI has 2 Ps
```

WordLevel will also contain two useful static methods:

- `MakeCharDict()`: Creates a charDict like the one in the preceding code from any string
- `CheckWordInLevel()`: Checks to see whether a word can be spelled using the chars in a WordLevel's charDict

Create a new C# script named *WordLevel* and enter the following code. Note that WordLevel does not extend MonoBehaviour, so it is not a class that can be attached to a GameObject as a Script component, and it cannot have `StartCoroutine()` called within it.

```
using UnityEngine;
using System.Collections;
using System.Collections.Generic;

[System.Serializable] // WordLevels can be viewed in the Inspector
public class WordLevel { // WordLevel does NOT extend MonoBehaviour
    public int              levelNum;
    public int              longWordIndex;
    public string           word;
    // A Dictionary<,> of all the letters in word
    public Dictionary<char,int>   charDict;
    // All the words that can be spelled with the letters in charDict
    public List<string>          subWords;

    // A static function that counts the instances of chars in a string and
    //  returns a Dictionary<char,int> that contains this information
    static public Dictionary<char,int> MakeCharDict(string w) {
        Dictionary<char,int> dict = new Dictionary<char, int>();
        char c;
        for (int i=0; i<w.Length; i++) {
            c = w[i];
            if (dict.ContainsKey(c)) {
                dict[c]++;
            } else {
                dict.Add (c,1);
            }
        }
```

```
        }
        return(dict);
    }


    // This static method checks to see whether the word can be spelled with the
    //  chars in level.charDict
    public static bool CheckWordInLevel(string str, WordLevel level) {
        Dictionary<char,int> counts = new Dictionary<char, int>();
        for (int i=0; i<str.Length; i++) {
            char c = str[i];
            // If the charDict contains char c
            if (level.charDict.ContainsKey(c)) {
                // If counts doesn't already have char c as a key
                if (!counts.ContainsKey(c)) {
                    // …then add a new key with a value of 1
                    counts.Add (c,1);
                } else {
                    // Otherwise, add 1 to the current value
                    counts[c]++;
                }
                // If this means that there are more instances of char c in str
                //  than are available in level.charDict
                if (counts[c] > level.charDict[c]) {
                    // … then return false
                    return(false);
                }
            } else {
                // The char c isn't in level.word, so return false
                return(false);
            }
        }
        return(true);
    }
}
```

Now, to make use of this, make the following bolded changes to WordGame:

```
public class WordGame : MonoBehaviour {
    …

    public GameMode          mode = GameMode.preGame;
    public WordLevel         currLevel;

    …

    // Called by the SendMessage() command from WordList
    public void WordListParseComplete() {
        mode = GameMode.makeLevel;
        // Make a level and assign it to currLevel, the current WordLevel
```

```
        currLevel = MakeWordLevel();
}


// With the default value of -1, this method will generate a level from
//   a random word.
public WordLevel MakeWordLevel(int levelNum = -1) {
    WordLevel level = new WordLevel();
    if (levelNum == -1) {
        // Pick a random level
        level.longWordIndex = Random.Range(0,WordList.S.longWordCount);
    } else {
        // This can be added later
    }
    level.levelNum = levelNum;
    level.word = WordList.S.GetLongWord(level.longWordIndex);
    level.charDict = WordLevel.MakeCharDict(level.word);

    // Call a coroutine to check all the words in the WordList and see
    // whether each word can be spelled by the chars in level.charDict
    StartCoroutine( FindSubWordsCoroutine(level) );

    // This returns the level before the coroutine finishes, so
    //   SubWordSearchComplete() is called when the coroutine is done
    return( level );
}


// A coroutine that finds words that can be spelled in this level
public IEnumerator FindSubWordsCoroutine(WordLevel level) {
    level.subWords = new List<string>();
    string str;

    List<string> words = WordList.S.GetWords();
    // ^ This is very fast because List<string> is passed by reference

    // Iterate through all the words in the WordList
    for (int i=0; i<WordList.S.wordCount; i++) {
        str = words[i];
        // Check whether each one can be spelled using level.charDict
        if (WordLevel.CheckWordInLevel(str, level)) {
            level.subWords.Add(str);
        }
        // Yield if we've parsed a lot of words this frame
        if (i%WordList.S.numToParseBeforeYield == 0) {
            // yield until the next frame
            yield return null;
        }
    }
```

```
        // List<string>.Sort() sorts alphabetically by default
        level.subWords.Sort ();
        // Now sort by length to have words grouped by number of letters
        level.subWords = SortWordsByLength(level.subWords).ToList();

        // The coroutine is complete, so call SubWordSearchComplete()
        SubWordSearchComplete();
    }

    public static IEnumerable<string> SortWordsByLength(IEnumerable<string> e)
    {
        // Use LINQ to sort the array received and return a copy
        // The LINQ syntax is different from regular C# and is beyond
        //   the scope of this book                                    // 1
        var sorted = from s in e
            orderby s.Length ascending
                select s;
        return sorted;
    }

    public void SubWordSearchComplete() {
        mode = GameMode.levelPrep;

    }

}
```

1. There is a good explanation of LINQ at the Unity Gems website. This link is from the Internet Archive to ensure that it remains valid. https://web.archive.org/web/20140209060811/http://unitygems.com/linq-1-time-linq/

This code creates the level, chooses a goal word, and populates it with subWords that can be spelled using the characters in the goal word. When you press Play, you should now see the currLevel field populate in the _MainCamera Inspector.

Save your scene! If you haven't been saving your scene all along—and this served as a reminder to do so—you need to be reminding yourself to save more often.

Laying Out the Screen

Now that the level has been created, it's time to generate on-screen visuals to represent both the big letters that can be used to spell words and the regular letters of the words. To start, you need to create a PrefabLetter to be instantiated for each letter.

Making PrefabLetter

Follow these steps to make PrefabLetter:

1. From the menu bar, choose *GameObject > Create Other > Quad*. Rename the quad to *PrefabLetter*.

2. From the menu bar, choose *Assets > Create > Material*. Name the material *LetterMat* and place it in the Materials & Textures folder.

3. Drag LetterMat onto PrefabLetter to assign it. Click on PrefabLetter, and set the *shader* of LetterMat to *ProtoTools > UnlitAlpha*. Then select *Rounded Rect 256* as the texture for the LetterMat material.

4. If you double-click PrefabLetter in the Hierarchy, you should now see a nice rounded rectangle there. If you can't see it, you may need to orbit the camera around to the other side. (Backface culling makes quads visible only from one side and invisible from the other.)

5. From the menu bar, choose *GameObject > Create Other > 3D Text* and rename it *3D Text*. Drag the 3D Text onto PrefabLetter in the Hierarchy to make it a child of PrefabLetter. Then select 3D Text in the Hierarchy and set it to the settings shown in Figure 33.3.

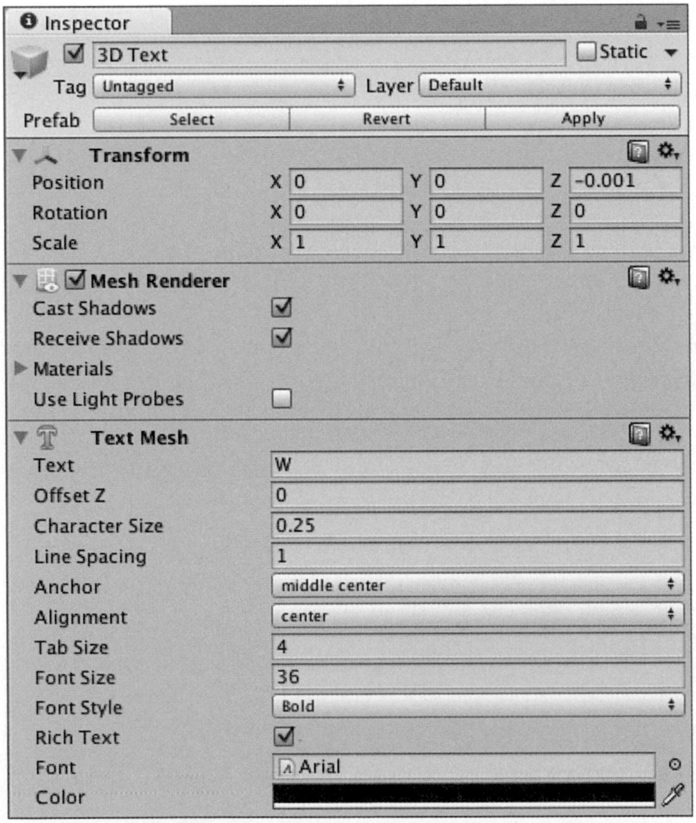

Figure 33.3   The Inspector settings for 3D Text, a child of PrefabLetter

6. Once PrefabLetter is ready, drag it into the _Prefabs folder in the Project pane and delete the remaining instance from the Hierarchy.

The Letter C# Script

PrefabLetter will have its own C# script to handle setting the character it shows, its color, and various other things. Create a new C# script named *Letter* and attach it to PrefabLetter. Then open it in MonoDevelop and enter the following code:

```csharp
using UnityEngine;
using System.Collections;
using System.Collections.Generic;

public class Letter : MonoBehaviour {

    private char            _c;     // The char shown on this Letter
    public TextMesh         tMesh;  // The TextMesh shows the char
    public Renderer         tRend;  // The Renderer of 3D Text. This will
                                    //  determine whether the char is visible
    public bool             big = false; // Big letters act differently

    void Awake() {
        tMesh = GetComponentInChildren<TextMesh>();
        tRend = tMesh.renderer;
        visible = false;
    }

    // Used to get or set _c and the letter shown by 3D Text
    public char             c {
        get {
            return( _c );
        }
        set {
            _c = value;
            tMesh.text = _c.ToString();
        }
    }

    // Gets or sets _c as a string
    public string str {
        get {
            return( _c.ToString() );
        }
        set {
            c = value[0];
        }
    }
}
```

```
// Enables or disables the renderer for 3D Text, which causes the char to be
//  visible or invisible respectively.
public bool visible {
    get {
        return( tRend.enabled );
    }
    set {
        tRend.enabled = value;
    }
}


// Gets or sets the color of the rounded rectangle
public Color color {
    get {
        return(renderer.material.color);
    }
    set {
        renderer.material.color = value;
    }
}


// Sets the position of the Letter's gameObject
public Vector3 pos {
    set {
        transform.position = value;
    }
}
}
```

This class makes use of several properties (faux fields with get{} and set{}) to perform various actions when variables are set. This enables, for instance, WordGame to set the char c of a Letter without worrying about how that gets converted to a string and then shown by 3D Text. This kind of encapsulation of functionality within a class is central to object-oriented programming.

The Wyrd Class: A Collection of Letters

Create a new C# script named *Wyrd*. The Wyrd class will act as a collection of Letters, and its name is spelled with a *y* to differentiate it from the other instances of the word *word* throughout the code and the text of this book. Wyrd is another class that does not extend MonoBehaviour and cannot be attached to a GameObject, but it can still contain List<>s of classes that are attached to GameObjects.

Enter the following code:

```csharp
using UnityEngine;
using System.Collections;
using System.Collections.Generic;

public class Wyrd {
    public string       str; // A string representation of the word
    public List<Letter> letters = new List<Letter>();
    public bool         found = false; // True if the player has found this word

    // A property to set visibility of the 3D Text of each Letter
    public bool visible {
        get {
            if (letters.Count == 0) return(false);
            return(letters[0].visible);
        }
        set {
            foreach( Letter lett in letters) {
                lett.visible = value;
            }
        }
    }

    // A property to set the rounded rectangle color of each Letter
    public Color color {
        get {
            if (letters.Count == 0) return(Color.black);
            return(letters[0].color);
        }
        set {
            foreach( Letter lett in letters) {
                lett.color = value;
            }
        }
    }

    // Adds a Letter to letters
    public void Add(Letter lett) {
        letters.Add(lett);
        str += lett.c.ToString();
    }

}
```

WordGame Layout

The Layout() function will generate Wyrds and Letters for the game as well as big Letters that the player can use to spell words (shown as large gray letters in the screenshot at the beginning of this chapter). We'll start with the small letters, and for this phase of the prototype, we'll make the letters visible to begin with (rather than hiding them as we'll do in the final version). Add the following code to WordGame:

```csharp
public class WordGame : MonoBehaviour {
    static public WordGame    S; // Singleton

    public GameObject         prefabLetter;
    public Rect               wordArea = new Rect(-24,19,48,28);
    public float              letterSize = 1.5f;
    public bool               showAllWyrds = true;
    public float              bigLetterSize = 4f;

    public bool   _____;

    public GameMode           mode = GameMode.preGame;
    public WordLevel          currLevel;
    public List<Wyrd>         wyrds;

    …

    public void SubWordSearchComplete() {
        mode = GameMode.levelPrep;
        Layout(); // Call the Layout() function after SubWordSearch
    }

    void Layout() {
        // Place the letters for each subword of currLevel on screen
        wyrds = new List<Wyrd>();

        // Declare a lot of variables that will be used in this method
        GameObject go;
        Letter lett;
        string word;
        Vector3 pos;
        float left = 0;
        float columnWidth = 3;
        char c;
        Color col;
        Wyrd wyrd;
```

```
        // Determine how many rows of Letters will fit on screen
        int numRows = Mathf.RoundToInt(wordArea.height/letterSize);

        // Make a Wyrd of each level.subWord
        for (int i=0; i<currLevel.subWords.Count; i++) {
            wyrd = new Wyrd();
            word = currLevel.subWords[i];

            // if the word is longer than columnWidth, expand it
            columnWidth = Mathf.Max( columnWidth, word.Length );

            // Instantiate a PrefabLetter for each letter of the word
            for (int j=0; j<word.Length; j++) {
                c = word[j]; // Grab the jth char of the word
                go = Instantiate(prefabLetter) as GameObject;
                lett = go.GetComponent<Letter>();
                lett.c = c; // Set the c of the Letter
                // Position the Letter
                pos = new Vector3(wordArea.x+left+j*letterSize, wordArea.y, 0);
                // The % here makes multiple columns line up
                pos.y -= (i%numRows)*letterSize;
                lett.pos = pos;
                go.transform.localScale = Vector3.one*letterSize;
                wyrd.Add(lett);
            }

            if (showAllWyrds) wyrd.visible = true; // This line is for testing

            wyrds.Add(wyrd);

            // If we've gotten to the numRows(th) row, start a new column
            if (i%numRows == numRows-1) {
                left += (columnWidth+0.5f)*letterSize;
            }
        }

    }
}
```

Before pressing Play, you need to assign the PrefabLetter prefab from the Project pane to the prefabLetter field of the *WordGame (Script)* component of   MainCamera. After doing so, press Play, and you should see a list of words pop up on screen, as shown in Figure 33.4.

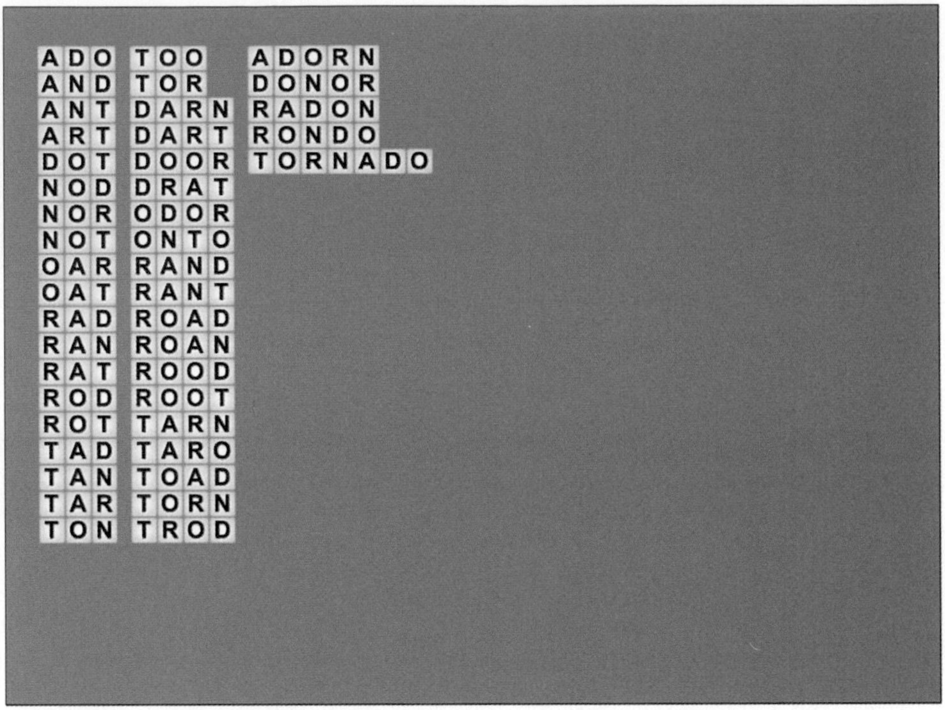

Figure 33.4 An example of the current state of the game: the level for the word TORNADO

Adding the Big Letters at the Bottom

The next step in Layout() is to place the large letters at the bottom of the screen. Add the following code to do so:

```
public class WordGame : MonoBehaviour {
    …

    public float          bigLetterSize = 4f;
    public Color          bigColorDim = new Color(0.8f, 0.8f, 0.8f);
    public Color          bigColorSelected = Color.white;
    public Vector3        bigLetterCenter = new Vector3(0, -16, 0);

    public bool _____;

    public GameMode       mode = GameMode.preGame;
    public WordLevel      currLevel;
    public List<Wyrd>     wyrds;
    public List<Letter>   bigLetters;
    public List<Letter>   bigLettersActive;
```

...

```csharp
void Layout() {
    ...

    // Make a Wyrd of each level.subWord
    for (int i=0; i<currLevel.subWords.Count; i++) {
        ...
    }

    // Place the big letters
    // Initialize the List<>s for big Letters
    bigLetters = new List<Letter>();
    bigLettersActive = new List<Letter>();

    // Create a big Letter for each letter in the target word
    for (int i=0; i<currLevel.word.Length; i++) {
        // This is similar to the process for a normal Letter
        c = currLevel.word[i];
        go = Instantiate(prefabLetter) as GameObject;
        lett = go.GetComponent<Letter>();
        lett.c = c;
        go.transform.localScale = Vector3.one*bigLetterSize;

        // Set the initial position of the big Letters below screen
        pos = new Vector3( 0, -100, 0 );
        lett.pos = pos;

        col = bigColorDim;
        lett.color = col;
        lett.visible = true; // This is always true for big letters
        lett.big = true;
        bigLetters.Add(lett);
    }
    // Shuffle the big letters
    bigLetters = ShuffleLetters(bigLetters);
    // Arrange them on screen
    ArrangeBigLetters();

    // Set the mode to be in-game
    mode = GameMode.inLevel;
}

// This shuffles a List<Letter> randomly and returns the result
List<Letter> ShuffleLetters(List<Letter> letts) {
    List<Letter> newL = new List<Letter>();
    int ndx;
    while(letts.Count > 0) {
        ndx = Random.Range(0,letts.Count);
```

```
            newL.Add(letts[ndx]);
            letts.RemoveAt(ndx);
        }
        return(newL);
    }


    // This arranges the big Letters on screen
    void ArrangeBigLetters() {
        // The halfWidth allows the big Letters to be centered
        float halfWidth = ( (float) bigLetters.Count )/2f-0.5f;
        Vector3 pos;
        for (int i=0; i<bigLetters.Count; i++) {
            pos = bigLetterCenter;
            pos.x += (i-halfWidth)*bigLetterSize;
            bigLetters[i].pos = pos;
        }
        // bigLettersActive
        halfWidth = ( (float) bigLettersActive.Count )/2f-0.5f;
        for (int i=0; i<bigLettersActive.Count; i++) {
            pos = bigLetterCenter;
            pos.x += (i-halfWidth)*bigLetterSize;
            pos.y += bigLetterSize*1.25f;
            bigLettersActive[i].pos = pos;
        }
    }


}
```

Now, in addition to the Letters up top, you should also see big Letters below, the shuffled form of the goal word. It's time to add some interactivity.

Adding Interactivity

For this game, we want the player to be able to type words from the available big Letters on her keyboard and press Return/Enter to submit them. She can also press Backspace/Delete to remove a letter from the end of what she has typed and press the space bar to shuffle the remaining unselected letters.

When she presses Enter, the word she typed will be compared with the possible words in the WordLevel. If the word she typed is in the WordLevel, she will get a point for each letter in the word. In addition, if the word she typed contains any smaller words that are in the WordLevel, she will also get points for those plus a multiplier for each word. Looking at the TORNADO example earlier, if a player typed TORNADO as her first word and hit Return, she would get 36 total points as follows:

TORNADO	7 x 1 points	1 point for each letter x 1 for first word
TORN	4 x 2 points	1 point per letter x 2 for second word = 8 points
TOR	3 x 3 points	1 point per letter x 3 = 9 points
ADO	+ 3 x 4 points	1 point per letter x 4 = 12 points
	36 total points	

All of this interactivity will be handled by the `Update()` function and will be based on `Input.inputString`, a string of all the keyboard input that occurred this frame. Add the following `Update()` method and supporting methods to WordGame:

```
public class WordGame : MonoBehaviour {
    …

    public List<Letter>        bigLettersActive;
    public string              testWord;
    private string             upperCase = "ABCDEFGHIJKLMNOPQRSTUVWXYZ";

    …

    void Update() {
        // Declare a couple of useful local variables
        Letter lett;
        char c;

        switch (mode) {
        case GameMode.inLevel:
            // Iterate through each char input by the player this frame
            foreach (char cIt in Input.inputString) {
                // Shift cIt to UPPERCASE
                c = System.Char.ToUpperInvariant(cIt);

                // Check to see if it's an uppercase letter
                if (upperCase.Contains(c)) { // Any uppercase letter
                    // Find an available Letter in bigLetters with this char
                    lett = FindNextLetterByChar(c);
                    // If a Letter was returned
                    if (lett != null) {
                        // … then add this char to the testWord and move the
                        //  returned big Letter to bigLettersActive
                        testWord += c.ToString();
                        // Move it from the inactive to the active List<>
                        bigLettersActive.Add(lett);
                        bigLetters.Remove(lett);
                        lett.color = bigColorSelected; // Make it the active
                          ➥color
                        ArrangeBigLetters();        // Rearrange the big Letters
                    }
                }
            }
        }
```

```
            if (c == '\b') { // Backspace
                // Remove the last Letter in bigLettersActive
                if (bigLettersActive.Count == 0) return;
                if (testWord.Length > 1) {
                    // Clear the last char of testWord
                    testWord = testWord.Substring(0,testWord.Length-1);
                } else {
                    testWord = "";
                }

                lett = bigLettersActive[bigLettersActive.Count-1];
                    // Move it from the active to the inactive List<>
                bigLettersActive.Remove(lett);
                bigLetters.Add (lett);
                lett.color = bigColorDim;       // Make it the inactive color
                ArrangeBigLetters();            // Rearrange the big Letters
            }

            if (c == '\n' || c == '\r') { // Return/Enter
                // Test the testWord against the words in WordLevel
                CheckWord();
            }

            if (c == ' ') { // Space
                // Shuffle the bigLetters
                bigLetters = ShuffleLetters(bigLetters);
                ArrangeBigLetters();
            }
        }

        break;
    }

}


// This finds an available Letter with the char c in bigLetters.
// If there isn't one available, it returns null.
Letter FindNextLetterByChar(char c) {
    // Search through each Letter in bigLetters
    foreach (Letter l in bigLetters) {
        // If one has the same char as c
        if (l.c == c) {
            // …then return it
            return(l);
        }
    }
    // Otherwise, return null
    return( null );
}
```

```csharp
public void CheckWord() {
    // Test testWord against the level.subWords
    string subWord;
    bool foundTestWord = false;

    // Create a List<int> to hold the indices of other subWords that are
    //   contained within testWord
    List<int> containedWords = new List<int>();

    // Iterate through each word in currLevel.subWords
    for (int i=0; i<currLevel.subWords.Count; i++) {

        // If the ith Wyrd on screen has already been found
        if (wyrds[i].found) {
            // …then continue & skip the rest of this iteration
            continue;
            // This works because the Wyrds on screen and the words in the
            //   subWords List<> are in the same order
        }

        subWord = currLevel.subWords[i];
        // if this subWord is the testWord
        if (string.Equals(testWord, subWord)) {
            // …then highlight the subWord
            HighlightWyrd(i);
            foundTestWord = true;
        } else if (testWord.Contains(subWord)) {
        // ^else if testWord contains this subWord (e.g., SAND contains AND)
            // …then add it to the list of containedWords
            containedWords.Add(i);
        }
    }

    // If the test word was found in subWords
    if (foundTestWord) {
        // …then highlight the other words contained in testWord
        int numContained = containedWords.Count;
        int ndx;
        // Highlight the words in reverse order
        for (int i=0; i<containedWords.Count; i++) {
            ndx = numContained-i-1;
            HighlightWyrd( containedWords[ndx] );
        }
    }

    // Clear the active big Letters regardless of whether testWord was valid
    ClearBigLettersActive();

}
```

```
    // Highlight a Wyrd
    void HighlightWyrd(int ndx) {
        // Activate the subWord
        wyrds[ndx].found = true;    // Let it know it's been found
        // Lighten its color
        wyrds[ndx].color = (wyrds[ndx].color+Color.white)/2f;
        wyrds[ndx].visible = true; // Make its 3D Text visible
    }

    // Remove all the Letters from bigLettersActive
    void ClearBigLettersActive() {
        testWord = "";              // Clear the testWord
        foreach (Letter l in bigLettersActive) {
            bigLetters.Add(l);      // Add each Letter to bigLetters
            l.color = bigColorDim; // Set it to the inactive color
        }
        bigLettersActive.Clear();  // Clear the List<>
        ArrangeBigLetters();        // Rearrange the Letters on screen
    }

}
```

After you've entered all this, you will also need to set `showAllWyrds` to false in the Inspector for the *WordGame (Script)* component of _MainCamera. Then, press Play.

You should be presented with a working version of the game and a random level.

Adding Scoring

Because of the Scoreboard and FloatingScore code that we've already written and imported into this project, adding scoring to this game should be very easy. Start by dragging Scoreboard from the _Prefab folder in the Project pane into the Hierarchy pane. Both the Scoreboard instance now in the Hierarchy and the PrefabFloatingScore should be preset for this game. (If you want to learn more about how they work, refer to Chapter 31, "Prototype 4: Prospector Solitaire.")

Now, you must add scoring code to the WordGame C# script by making the following edits:

```
public class WordGame : MonoBehaviour {
    ...
    public Vector3          bigLetterCenter = new Vector3(0, -16, 0);
    public List<float>      scoreFontSizes = new List<float> { 24, 36, 36, 1 };
    public Vector3          scoreMidPoint = new Vector3(1,1,0);
    public float            scoreComboDelay = 0.5f;

    ...
```

```
public void CheckWord() {
    …
    // Iterate through each word in currLevel.subWords
    for (int i=0; i<currLevel.subWords.Count; i++) {

        …

        // if this subWord is the testWord
        if (string.Equals(testWord, subWord)) {
            // …then highlight the subWord
            HighlightWyrd(i);
            Score( wyrds[i], 1 ); // Score the testWord
            foundTestWord = true;
        }
        …
    }


    // If the test word was found in subWords
    if (foundTestWord) {
        …
        // Highlight the words in reverse order
        for (int i=0; i<containedWords.Count; i++) {
            ndx = numContained-i-1;
            HighlightWyrd( containedWords[ndx] );
            Score( wyrds[ containedWords[ndx] ], i+2 ); // Score other words
            // The second parameter (i+2) is the # of this word in the combo
        }
    }
    …

}


…


// Add to the score for this word
// int combo is the number of this word in a combo
void Score(Wyrd wyrd, int combo) {
    // Get the position of the first Letter in the wyrd
    Vector3 pt = wyrd.letters[0].transform.position;
    // Create a List<> of Bezier points for the FloatingScore
    List<Vector3> pts = new List<Vector3>();

    // Convert the pt to a ViewportPoint. ViewportPoints range from 0 to 1
    //  across the screen and are used for GUI coordinates
    pt = Camera.main.WorldToViewportPoint(pt);
    pt.z = 0;

    // Make pt the first Bezier point
    pts.Add(pt);
```

```
          // Add a second Bezier point
          pts.Add( scoreMidPoint );

          // Make the Scoreboard the last Bezier point
          pts.Add(Scoreboard.S.transform.position);

          // Set the value of the Floating Score
          int value = wyrd.letters.Count * combo;
          FloatingScore fs = Scoreboard.S.CreateFloatingScore(value, pts);

          fs.timeDuration = 2f;
          fs.fontSizes = scoreFontSizes;

          // Double the InOut Easing effect
          fs.easingCurve = Easing.InOut+Easing.InOut;

          // Make the text of the FloatingScore something like "3 x 2"
          string txt = wyrd.letters.Count.ToString();
          if (combo > 1) {
              txt += " x "+combo;
          }
          fs.guiText.text = txt;
      }

  }
```

After you've entered this code and run the game, you'll see that you get a score for each correct word you enter, and you get a multiplier for each additional valid word contained in the word you type. However, all the scores happen at the same time. Happily, this is something else that we can use coroutines to fix. Make the following changes to make the CheckWord() function into a coroutine that pauses for 0.5 seconds between each word in the combo:

```
public class WordGame : MonoBehaviour {
    ...

    void Update() {
        ...
        switch (mode) {
        case GameMode.inLevel:
            ...
            // Iterate through each char input by the player this frame
            foreach (char cIt in Input.inputString) {
                ...
                if (c == '\n') { // Return/Enter
                    // Test the testWord against the words in WordLevel
                    StartCoroutine( CheckWord() );
                }
                ...
            }
```

```
            break;
        }
    }

    …

    public IEnumerator CheckWord() {
        …

        // If the test word was found in subWords
        if (foundTestWord) {
            // …then highlight the other words contained in testWord
            int numContained = containedWords.Count;
            int ndx;
            // Highlight the words in reverse order
            for (int i=0; i<containedWords.Count; i++) {

                // yield for a bit before highlighting each word
                yield return( new WaitForSeconds(scoreComboDelay) );

                ndx = numContained-i-1;
                HighlightWyrd( containedWords[ndx] );
                Score( wyrds[ containedWords[ndx] ], i+2 ); // Score other words
                // The second parameter (i+2) is the # of this word in the combo
            }
        }
        …
    }
    …
}
```

Now, the scores will fly and the words will show with a separation of about 0.5 seconds.

Adding Animation

In a similar manner to scoring, we can very easily add smooth animation of Letters by taking advantage of the interpolation functions that we imported in the Utils script.

Add the following code to the Letter C# script:

```
public class Letter : MonoBehaviour {
    …
    public bool             big = false; // Big letters are a little different
    // Linear interpolation fields
    public List<Vector3>    pts = null;
    public float            timeDuration = 0.5f;
    public float            timeStart = -1;
    public string           easingCuve = Easing.InOut; // Easing from Utils.cs
```

...

```
// Now set up a Bezier curve to move to the new position
public Vector3 pos {
    set {
        // transform.position = value; // This line is now commented out

        // Find a midpoint that is a random distance from the actual
        //  midpoint between the current position and the value passed in
        Vector3 mid = (transform.position + value)/2f;
        // The random distance will be within 1/4 of the magnitude of the
        //  line from the actual midpoint
        float mag = (transform.position - value).magnitude;
        mid += Random.insideUnitSphere * mag*0.25f;
        // Create a List<Vector3> of Bezier points
        pts = new List<Vector3>() { transform.position, mid, value };
        // If timeStart is at the default -1, then set it
        if (timeStart == -1 ) timeStart = Time.time;
    }
}

// Moves immediately to the new position
public Vector3 position {
    set {
        transform.position = value;
    }
}

// Interpolation code
void Update() {
    if (timeStart == -1) return;

    // Standard linear interpolation code
    float u = (Time.time-timeStart)/timeDuration;
    u = Mathf.Clamp01(u);
    float u1 = Easing.Ease(u,easingCurve);
    Vector3 v = Utils.Bezier(u1, pts);
    transform.position = v;

    // If the interpolation is done, set timeStart back to -1
    if (u == 1) timeStart = -1;
}
}
```

Now, if you play the scene, you'll see the Letters all interpolate to their new positions. However, it looks a little strange for all the Letters to move at the same time and start from the center of the screen. Let's add some small changes to `WordGame.Layout()` to improve this:

```csharp
public class WordGame : MonoBehaviour {
    …

    void Layout() {
        …

        // Make a Wyrd of each level.subWord
        for (int i=0; i<currLevel.subWords.Count; i++) {
            …

            // Instantiate a PrefabLetter for each letter of the word
            for (int j=0; j<word.Length; j++) {
                …
                // The % here makes multiple columns line up
                pos.y -= (i%numRows)*letterSize;

                // Move the lett immediately to a position above the screen
                lett.position = pos+Vector3.up*(20+i%numRows);
                // Then set the pos for it to interpolate to
                lett.pos = pos;
                // Increment lett.timeStart to move wyrds at different times
                lett.timeStart = Time.time + i*0.05f;

                go.transform.localScale = Vector3.one*letterSize;
                wyrd.Add(lett);
            }
            …
        }

        …
        // Create a big Letter for each letter in the target word
        for (int i=0; i<currLevel.word.Length; i++) {
            …
            go.transform.localScale = Vector3.one*bigLetterSize;

            // Set the initial position of the big Letters below screen
            pos = new Vector3( 0, -100, 0 );
            lett.pos = pos;

            // Increment lett.timeStart to have big Letters come in last
            lett.timeStart = Time.time + currLevel.subWords.Count*0.05f;
            lett.easingCuve = Easing.Sin+"-0.18"; // Bouncy easing

            col = bigColorDim;
            lett.color = col;
```

```
            ...
        }
        ...
    }
    ...
}
```

With this code, the game should now layout with nice smooth motions.

Adding Color

Now that the game moves well, it's time to add a little color:

1. Add the following code to WordGame to color the wyrds based on their length:

```
public class WordGame : MonoBehaviour {
    ...
    public float            scoreComboDelay = 0.5f;
    public Color[]          wyrdPalette;

    public bool _____;
    ...

    void Layout() {
        ...
        // Make a Wyrd of each level.subWord
        for (int i=0; i<currLevel.subWords.Count; i++) {
            ...
            // Instantiate a PrefabLetter for each letter of the word
            for (int j=0; j<word.Length; j++) {
                ...
                wyrd.Add(lett);
            }

            if (showAllWyrds) wyrd.visible = true; // This line is for testing

            // Color the wyrd based on length
            wyrd.color = wyrdPalette[word.Length-WordList.S.wordLengthMin];

            wyrds.Add(wyrd);
            ...
        }
        ...
    }
}
```

These last few code changes have been so simple because we already had supporting code in place (for example, the Wyrd.color and Letter.color properties as well as the Easing code in the `Utils` class).

2. Now, you need to set about eight colors for wyrdPalette. To do this, we'll use the Color Palette image included in the import at the beginning of the project. We're going to be using the eye dropper to set color, which may leave you wondering how to see both the Color Palette image and the _MainCamera Inspector at the same time. To do this, we'll take advantage of Unity's capability to have more than one Inspector window open at the same time.

3. As shown in Figure 33.5, click the pane options button (circled in red) and choose *Add Tab > Inspector* to add an Inspector to the Game tab. Then select the Color Palette image in the Project pane. It will appear in both Inspectors. (You might need to drag the edge of the image preview part of the Inspector to make it look like the Figure 33.6.) Click the lock icon on one inspector (circled in red in the Figure 33.6), and then select _MainCamera in the Hierarchy pane. You'll see that the unlocked Inspector changes to _MainCamera, but the locked one is still showing Color Palette.

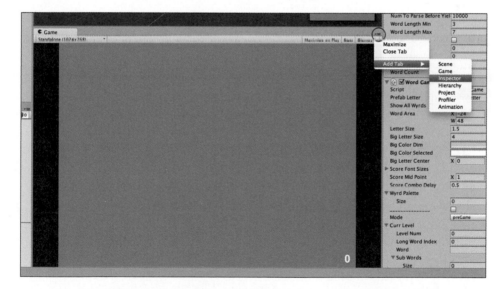

Figure 33.5 Using the pane options button to add an Inspector to the Game pane

4. Expand the disclosure triangle next to `wyrdPalette` in the _MainCamera Inspector and set its size to 8. Click the eye dropper next to each `wyrdPalette` element (circled in light blue in Figure 33.6), and then click one of the colors in the Color Palette image. Doing this for each element of `wyrdPalette` will give you the eight different colors of the Color Palette image, but they will all default to having an alpha of 0 (and therefore being invisible). Click each color bar in the `wyrdPalette` array and set each one's alpha (or A) to 255 to make it fully opaque, as indicated by the white bar below the color swatch.

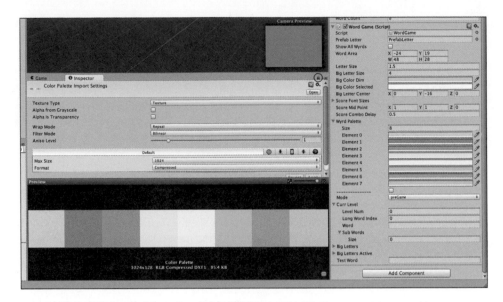

Figure 33.6   The lock icon on one Inspector (circled in red) and the eye dropper in the other inspector (circled in light blue)

Now when you play the scene, you should see something that looks like the screen shot from the beginning of the chapter.

Summary

In this chapter, you created a simple word game and added a little flair to it with some nice interpolated movement. If you've been following these tutorials in order, you may have realized that the process of making them is getting a little bit easier. With the expanded understanding of Unity that you now have and the capabilities of readymade utility scripts like Scoreboard, FloatingScore, and Utils, you're able to focus more of the coding effort on the things that are new and different in each game and less on reinventing the wheel.

Next Steps

In the previous prototypes, you saw examples of how to set up a series of game states to handle the different phases of the game and transition from one level to the next. Right now, this prototype doesn't have any of that. On your own, you should add that kind of control structure to this game.

Here are some things to think about as you do so:

- When should the player be able to move on to the next level? Must she guess every single word, or can she move on once she has either reached a specific point total or has guessed the target word.

- How will you handle levels? Will you just pick a completely random word as we are now, or will you modify the randomness to make sure that level 5 is always the same word (therefore making it fair for players to compare their scores on level 5)? Here's a hint if you decide to try for a modified randomness:

```
int PickNthRandom(int n, int range) {
    // If 0 is passed in, 0 is returned.

    int seed = Random.seed; // Store the current Random.seed

    // The Random.seed sets the starting point for the Random function.
    // With the same Random.seed, Random.value will generate the same
    //  results, in the same order, every time.

    Random.seed = 0; // Set a new Random.seed

    // Get the nth random number between 0 and range-1
    int j=0;
    for (int i=0; i<n; i++) {
        j = Random.Range(0,range);
    }

    Random.seed = seed; // Restore the original Random.seed

    return(j);
}
```

- How do you want to handle levels with too many or too few subWords? Some collections of seven letters have so many words that they extend off the screen to the right, whereas others have so few that there's only one column. Do you want to make the game ask for the next word in this case? If so, how do you then instruct something like the PickNthRandom function to skip certain numbers?

You should have enough knowledge of programming and prototyping now that you can take these questions and make this into a real game. You've got the skills, now go for it!

CHAPTER 34

PROTOTYPE 7: QUICKSNAP

In this chapter, you make a puzzle game based on first-person shooter (FPS) movement and control. The player is shown a complex environment and tasked with taking specific photos.

Although this book certainly could have included a more traditional FPS (first-person shooter), you could probably already make one yourself using the skills you've learned from previous chapters. Instead, this prototype focuses on a different style of gameplay and enables me to present some concepts such as XML creation and light baking.

Getting Started: QuickSnap Prototype

You'll be importing a much larger unitypackage for this project than you have in the past. This is because the game will be built inside a modified version of the environment that Unity Technologies created for their *Stealth* game prototype. It's an environment that contains a number of interesting objects and complex lighting, so it will look much better than any of our earlier prototypes.

You have two choices for the unitypackage to import. One contains high-resolution graphics and is about 200 MB in size, whereas the other uses lower-resolution graphics and is only about 88 MB. However, both will work equally well for the development of the prototype, and you shouldn't notice any real difference between the two unless you play at very high resolution and are looking for it. Baking lightmaps will probably take longer on the 200 MB version, but it will also be a little bit prettier.

SET UP THE PROJECT FOR THIS CHAPTER

Following the standard project setup procedure, create a new project in Unity. If you need a refresher on the standard project setup procedure, see Appendix A, "Standard Project Setup." When you are creating the project, you will be asked if you want to set up defaults for 2D or 3D. Choose 3D for this project.

- **Project name** QuickSnap.
- **unitypackage:** Find and download one of the two packages for Chapter 34 at http://book.prototools.net. Check your build settings *before* importing the package.
- **Scene name:** __QuickSnap_Scene_0.
- **Project folders:** These are all imported from the unitypackage.
- **C# script names:** Just the imported scripts in the ProtoTools folder.

Build and Aspect Ratio Settings

If you have recently completed one of the other projects in the book, your build settings and the aspect ratio of your Game pane may need to be updated.

Build Settings

Open the Build Settings window in Unity (*File > Build Settings* from the menu bar) and make sure that the Platform is set to *PC, Mac & Linux Standalone*. If it is not, click that selection in the Platforms list and then click the *Switch Platform* button. The *Switch Platform* button will turn gray once the switch is complete. Close the Build Settings window.

Aspect Ratio

In the Game pane, choose *16:9* from the pop-up menu of aspect ratio choices (located directly beneath the heading tab of the Game pane).

Importing the unitypackage

Choose which package you want to import and do so. The package import might take a while—especially if you chose the high-res version—because Unity needs to import and compress all the image files for the environment.

Building the Scene

Once the import is done, drag *environment* from the _Prefabs folder into the Hierarchy pane. You'll see that this is a very complex environment, and it may even render somewhat slowly on your machine. If so, click the button that looks like a sun at the top of the Scene pane; this will toggle lighting calculations. The darker-looking scene is actually lit, whereas the brighter rendering of the scene is just the raw textures and should render faster.

Adding a First-Person Controller

Unity Technologies has built a couple of character controller scripts that they include with every install of Unity. To import them, choose *Assets > Import Package > Character Controller* from the menu bar. This will pop up a list of all the assets in the package. Go ahead and import them all.

The import will create a new folder in the Project pane called *Standard Assets*. Open the disclosure triangle next to *Standard Assets* and then the one next to *Character Controllers*, and you'll find two character controller prefabs. Drag the *First Person Controller* into the Hierarchy pane, click it, and change the name of the instance to *_FPC*. _FPC should have a Transform of:

_FPC (GameObject)   P:[-2,1,0]   R:[0,-90,0]   S:[1,1,1]

Opening the disclosure triangle next to _FPC, you'll see that there are two GameObjects: *Graphics* and *Main Camera*. Graphics holds the white capsule that you can see in the Scene pane, and Main Camera holds the camera that's attached to _FPC. Because there is a Camera on _FPC, we no longer need the original Main Camera that came with the scene. Select the black *Main Camera* at the top level of the Hierarchy and delete it (Command-Delete on Mac or just Delete on PC). Next, select the child of _FPC named *Graphics* and disable it by clicking the check box in the top left of the Inspector pane. This will keep the white capsule from appearing in the Game or Scene panes.

Press Play, and you should be able to move around the space using standard First-Person Shooter (FPS) controls (WASD or arrows for movement, Space to jump, and mouse movement to look around). You should notice a couple of things while walking around: The eye point of the camera seems a bit high, and the scene is pretty dull and dark.

The first of these issues is easy to fix. Select _FPC in the Hierarchy and change the `Height` value within the *Character Controller* component of the Inspector from 2 to 1. Now, the camera will be at a lower height that is more fitting for the environment.

The second is going to take more work, and it's going to take some time.

Lightmapping in Unity

Lightmapping is the process in Unity of creating textures for objects that have complicated lighting calculations *baked* into them. This means that rather than having the same texture repeat across an entire wall, a lightmap texture is made that also includes the effects of various lights on the wall. Unity 4 lightmapping works through an included piece of software called Autodesk Beast, while Unity 5 uses Geomerics Enlighten engine. Because of the differences in interface and settings between these lightmapping solutions, if you are using Unity 5 you should download the Unity 5 version of this chapter from http://book.prototools.net that covers the Enlighten engine instead of Beast.

Beast calculates information about all of the lights in your scene and where they would hit various objects that are marked as *static* (that is, they will never move during the course of the game). If you open the disclosure triangle next to *environment* in the Hierarchy and select the child *env_stealth_static*, you'll see that *Static* is checked in the top-right corner of the Inspector for both *env_stealth_static* and all of its children. Clicking the downward triangle pop-up menu in the Inspector next to *Static* will also reveal that it is set to static for all types of lighting calculations.

At high quality levels, lightmapping can create beautiful shadows and even handles reflections of light so that, for instance, the area around a shiny red object would be tinted red by the light bouncing off of it. All of this information is collected and baked into the textures for static objects in the scene, meaning that the original texture for an object is replaced by a texture that includes the additional lighting information.

However, lightmapping is one of the few areas of difference between Unity Free and Unity Pro. Pro allows you to take advantage of deferred rendering and dual lightmaps, both of which improve the visuals that Unity is able to produce in real time. Take a look at Figure 34.1.

The three series of images in Figure 34.1 show the same scene rendered first with forward rendering and no lightmapping. The second shows the scene with forward rendering and single lightmaps. The third column shows deferred rendering and directional lightmaps. The changes between the first two columns are most obvious, but there are subtle differences in the third column that make it look even better. As you can see in the top and middle rows of images, the deferred rendering of the third column enables images and light to be correctly mapped to the floor (the blue glow beneath the large, floating security card in the corner of the room in the top row, and the shadows cast by the barrel in the second row). In addition, in the third column, you can see that the walls are casting subtle shadows on the ground that are missing in the middle column. Though deferred rendering and directional lightmaps are not available in Unity

Free, the good news is that you can still get all of the benefits from lightmap baking that are shown in the second column.

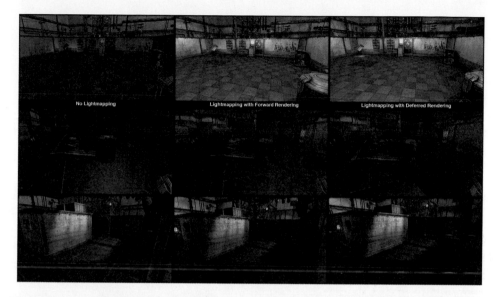

Figure 34.1   Various levels of lightmapping and rendering in Unity

Light Probes

One of the limitations of lightmapping is that it can only be used on static objects, so a character or other object that moves through the scene cannot be lightmapped. However, with Unity Pro, it is possible to fake lightmapping on a dynamic (that is, nonstatic) object through the use of *light probes*. Light probes are a way for Unity to map what the light would look like in the open spaces of a scene, as is shown in Figure 34.2. Each spherical light probe stores information about the lighting at a certain location in the scene (though they are, of course, invisible when the scene is playing). If a dynamic object is set to use light probes, the shading on that object will be interpolated based on its position relative to the position of the light probes. For more information, search for "light probes" in the Unity Manual.

Baking Lightmaps

As you can see in the preceding figures, lightmapping can create incredibly realistic scenes that will still render at real-time speeds. Unfortunately for you as the developer, this means that all the processing savings seen by the player are passed back to you. Therefore, lightmapping can take hours to complete on a complex scene, and the baking for the small scene in this prototype could take you from 30 minutes to a few hours, during which you can still work in Unity, but you can't quit, and you can't play the scene. Please make sure that you have sufficient time for your computer to do the baking before starting the process.

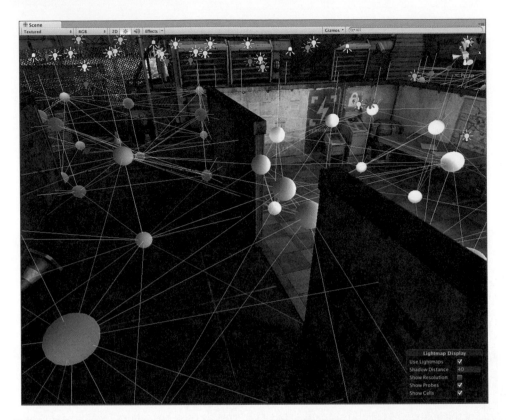

Figure 34.2   Network of light probes in the scene (Unity Pro feature)

To implement lightmapping in your prototype, choose *Window > Lightmapping* from the menu bar and click the *Bake* button at the top. The settings you choose will be different for Unity Pro and Unity Free, as shown in Figure 34.3. You can choose to use the Unity Free settings in Unity Pro to speed the baking process (at the expense of better visuals).

In both cases, you have two options to choose from for the quality of your lightmaps: low quality will generate shadows that have obvious jagged edges, but it will bake much faster; whereas high quality will produce better shadows and lighting but will take much longer to bake. I highly recommend setting the Quality pop-up menu to *Low* for your first bake. That will let you know how long it will take, and you can multiply that by at least four when you're estimating the time for the high-quality bake. Enter the rest of the settings shown in Figure 34.3 based on whether you want to use single lightmaps or the directional lightmaps available in Unity Pro.

After you've entered these settings, you can click the *Bake Scene* button at the bottom of the Lightmapping pane (if you don't see *Bake Scene* on that button, you may need to choose it from the attached pop-up menu triangle) and get a coffee or maybe get yourself a snowcone; you may be waiting for a while. Otherwise, you can choose to continue working on this prototype and just bake the scene when you take a break. I tend to bake scenes overnight when I can, but if you have a fast machine, it may only take 10 to 20 minutes for single lightmaps on low quality. When the baking is processing, a progress bar will appear in the bottom-right corner of the Unity window and the Bake Scene button will be replaced by a Cancel button. As mentioned before, you can still work in Unity while the scene is baking, but some of the things you can do are limited.

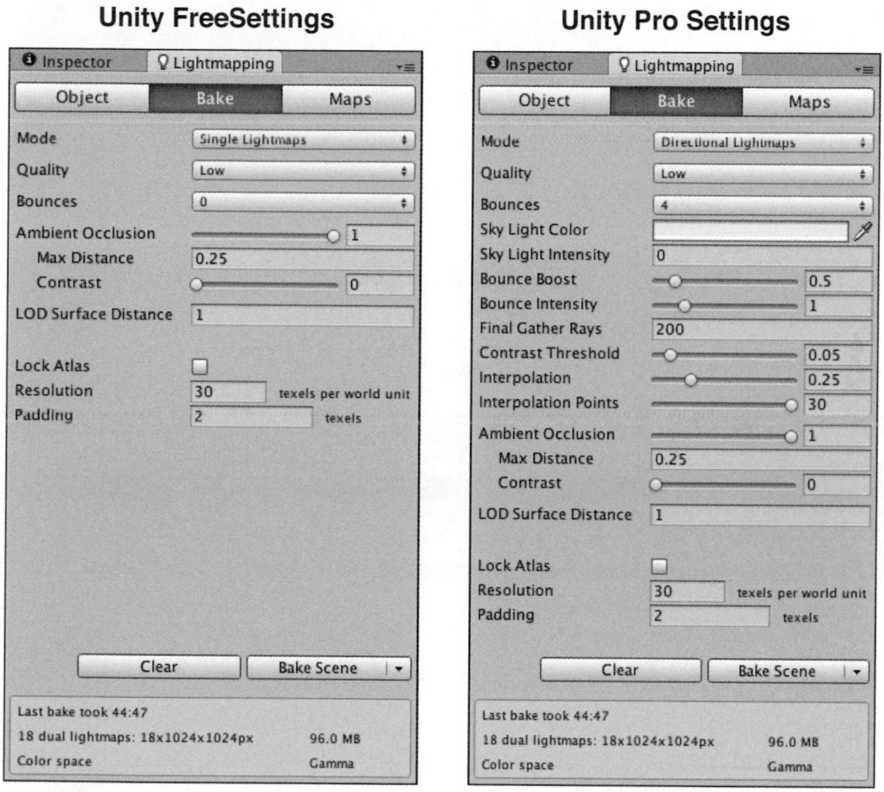

Figure 34.3 Lightmapping settings for Beast in Unity Free and Unity Pro

Quality Settings

The kind of tricks we're using to improve the look of the game are highly dependent on the Unity quality settings that are chosen by the player, but as a developer, you can choose the default quality settings for your games. From the Unity menu bar, choose *Edit > Project Settings > Quality*. This will open the *QualitySettings* pane in the Inspector. By default, there are six quality levels listed, with *Good* selected (as is shown by the darker highlighting of the Good row). When a quality level is selected, the bottom half of the Inspector shows the values for that quality level. Underneath the list of quality levels are pop-up triangles that allow you to set the default quality level on a specific platform. For now, the only platform we care about is *PC, Mac & Linux Standalone*, which is represented by the second column. Click the default setting triangle (circled in black in Figure 34.4) at the bottom of the second column, and choose *Fantastic*. This will change the color of the check box for Fantastic in the second column to green, as is shown in Figure 34.4.

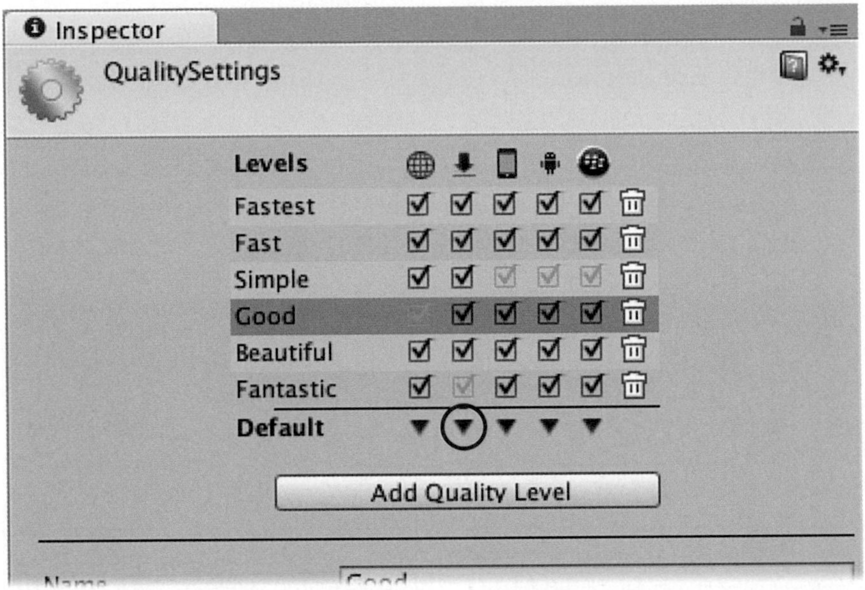

Figure 34.4   Quality settings in the Inspector with Fantastic as the default for standalone builds

Creating the _TargetCamera

In this game, we'll use a _TargetCamera to show the player the shot that she's trying to mimic. Before doing so, let's change the name of the *Main Camera* inside of _FPC for clarity's sake. Open the disclosure triangle next to _FPC and rename Main Camera to *FPCamera*. If you're using Unity Pro, look in the FPCamera Inspector under the Camera component and set the *Rendering Path* to *Deferred Lighting*. (If you're using Unity Free, leave the *Rendering Path* set to *Use Player Settings*.)

Next, choose *GameObject > Create Other > Camera* from the menu bar. Rename this new camera to *_TargetCamera* and select it in the Hierarchy. In the _TargetCamera Inspector pane, click the gear for the *Audio Listener* component and choose *Remove Component*. (Unity only allows one Audio Listener in the scene, and FPCamera already has one.) Set the _TargetCamera transform to the following:

    _TargetCamera (Camera)   P:[0,1,0]   R:[0,0,0]   S:[1,1,1]

Right now, the images from the two cameras in the scene are directly on top of each other in the Game pane. In the *Camera* component of the _TargetCamera Inspector, set the *Depth* to 1. This will layer the image from _TargetCamera above that from FPCamera. Then, set the *Viewport Rect* to [x:0, y:0.8, w:0.2, h:0.2], which will shrink the image from _TargetCamera to the top-left corner of the screen. If you are using Unity Pro, set the *Rendering Path* of _TargetCamera to *Deferred Lighting* as you did for FPCamera (or *Use Player Settings* in Unity Free).

GUIs, Layers, and Cameras (Oh My!)

The layers you've used before for physics calculations can also be used to cause various objects to render exclusively to one camera or the other.

1. First, we'll make a GUI component to demonstrate this. Inside the Textures folder in the Project pane you'll find a texture named _Crosshairs. Select it and choose *GameObject > Create Other > GUI Texture* from the menu bar. (Selecting _Crosshairs ahead of time causes the new GUI Texture to be made from it.) Set the *Color* of _Crosshairs to [r:64, g:64, b:64, a:128].

   Notice that the _Crosshairs appear in both cameras, and their size on screen is not scaled to the display size of the camera. This is where layers come in.

2. From the menu bar, choose *Edit > Project Settings > Tags and Layers*. The list of Layers should already be disclosed, but if not, click the triangle next to it. Type *FPCamera* into User Layer 8 and *_TargetCamera* into User Layer 9.

3. We want the _Crosshairs to only appear on the FPCamera, so select _Crosshairs in the Hierarchy and use the Inspector to set its layer to FPCamera.

4. Now, select _TargetCamera in the Hierarchy. The pop-up menu for *Culling Mask* in the Camera component of _TargetCamera is used to exclude certain layers from being rendered to the camera. Click the pop-up menu (that currently says *Everything*) and select *FPCamera* to toggle the check mark (turning it off). The text on the pop-up menu will change to *Mixed...* to show that some layers are disabled, and the _Crosshairs image will disappear from _TargetCamera.

5. Select FPCamera and disable the layer _TargetCamera in its culling mask. This will make the _TargetCamera layer work in the opposite manner.

When you finish, the camera FPCamera should not show the layer _TargetCamera, and the camera _TargetCamera should not show the layer FPCamera.

Additional GUI Elements

As you can see in Figure 34.5, we want to have several GUI elements in the scene.

There are two GUITexts that need to be added to the scene. Create two GUI Texts (*GameObject > Create Other > GUI Text* from the menu bar). Name one *ShotCounter* and the other *ShotRating*. In each, set the values shown in Figure 34.6. Be sure to set the *Layer* as well.

Figure 34.5   Scene showing various GUI elements

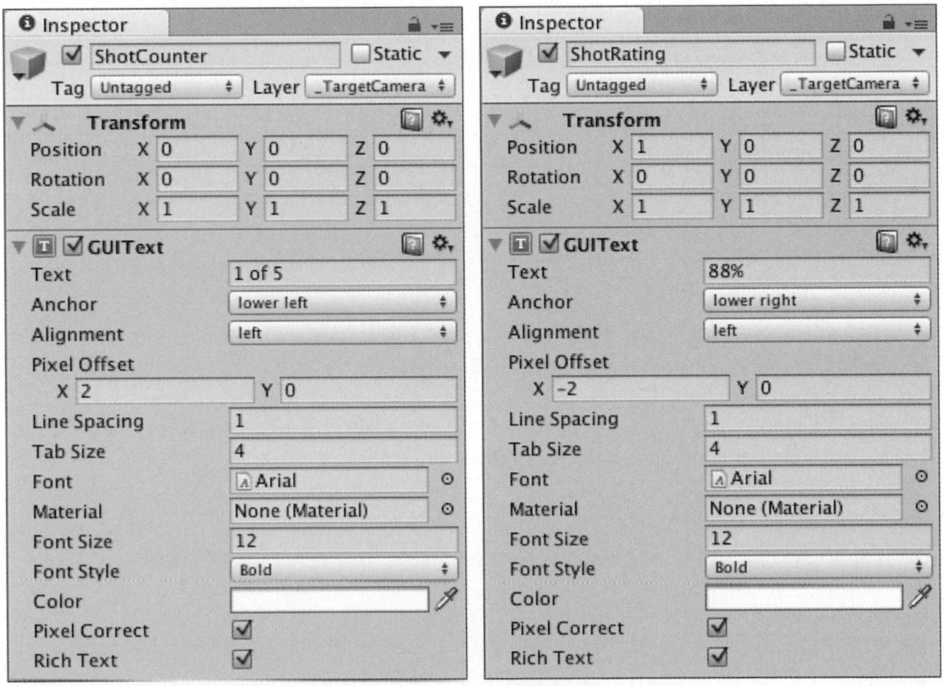

Figure 34.6   GUIText settings for ShotCounter and ShotRating

This should place two bits of text in the left and right bottom corners of the _TargetCamera image in the Game pane (as shown in Figure 34.5).

In the Textures folder of the Project pane, you'll find the following textures. Select each in turn and then make a new GUI Texture from it (*GameObject > Create Other > GUI Texture*):

_Check_64

_Crosshairs_12

_White

Once these are in the Hierarchy, give them the settings in Figure 34.7.

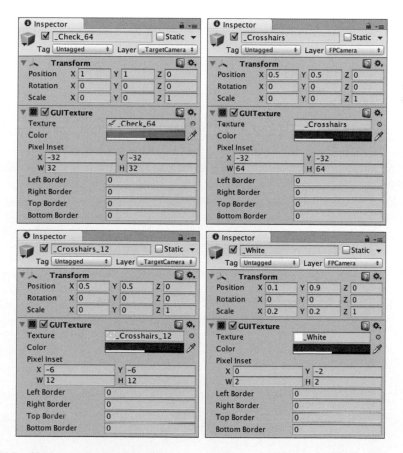

Figure 34.7   GUITexture settings for _Check_64, _Crosshairs, _Crosshairs_12, and _White

Again, be sure to set the *Layer* properly. Also, set the color of _Crosshairs_12 to [r:64, g:64, b:64, a:128] like _Crosshairs. Your Game window should now look like that shown in Figure 34.5.

Coding the Game

With the experience you now have, coding this game will actually seem pretty simple, but like the others, you'll learn things here that can serve as a foundation for further projects.

1. Create a new C# script named *Shot* in the __Scripts folder. Open it and replace all the default text in the Shot class with the following code:

```
using UnityEngine;
using System.Collections;
using System.Collections.Generic;


[System.Serializable] // Make this visible in the Inspector
public class Shot { // Shot does not extend MonoBehaviour

    public Vector3        position; // Position of the Camera
    public Quaternion     rotation; // Rotation of the Camera
    public Vector3        target;   // Where the Camera is pointed

}
```

This `Shots` class will keep track of the information about the photographic shots taken in the game. Because we want the game to be able to work with Unity Free, we can't record the images from a camera to an image (which is a Unity Pro-only feature), but we can still record the position and orientation of the camera (and the position of its target as well). Shot will handle this for us.

2. Create a second new C# script named *TargetCamera*, place it in the __Scripts folder, and attach it to _TargetCamera in the Hierarchy. The TargetCamera class will be responsible for both creating the list of shots to be taken (in an edit mode) and checking the player's shots against the target shots in play mode. Enter the following code:

```
using UnityEngine;
using System.Collections;
using System.Collections.Generic;

public class TargetCamera : MonoBehaviour {

    public GameObject          fpCamera; // First-person Camera

    public bool                _____;

    void Update () {
        Shot sh;

        // Mouse Input
        if (Input.GetMouseButtonDown(0)) { // Left mouse button
            sh = new Shot();
            // Grab the position and rotation of fpCamera
            sh.position = fpCamera.transform.position;
            sh.rotation = fpCamera.transform.rotation;
```

```
            // Shoot a ray from the camera and see what it hits
            Ray ray = new Ray(sh.position, fpCamera.transform.forward);
            RaycastHit hit;
            if ( Physics.Raycast(ray, out hit) ) {
                sh.target = hit.point;
            }

            // Position _TargetCamera with the Shot
            ShowShot(sh);
        }
    }

    public void ShowShot(Shot sh) {
        // Position _TargetCamera with the Shot
        transform.position = sh.position;
        transform.rotation = sh.rotation;
    }
}
```

3. Assign the FPCamera child of _FPC in the Hierarchy to the `fpCamera` field of TargetCamera in the Inspector for _TargetCamera.

4. Save your scene!

Press Play, and you should see that when you click the left mouse button, the _TargetCamera image shifts to show the shot you took when you clicked. Now that we know this works, we need a way to store the shots from one play session to the next.

Using PlayerPrefs to Store Shots

As we saw in the *Apple Picker* prototype, PlayerPrefs is a great place to store things long term; however, it can only store floats, ints, and strings. To handle this, we'll convert the Shot into XML and then we can read it back in using the PT_XMLReader (that was used in the card game prototypes of Chapter 31, "Prototype 4: Prospector Solitaire," and Chapter 32, "Prototype 5: Bartok") when we start the game the next time:

1. The first step in doing so is converting each Shot into XML. Add the following code to Shot:

```
public class Shot { // Shot does not extend MonoBehaviour

    public Vector3       position; // Position of the Camera
    public Quaternion    rotation; // Rotation of the Camera
    public Vector3       target;   // Where the Camera is pointed

    // Generates a single-line <shot> entry for an XML document
    public string ToXML() {
        string ss = "<shot ";
        ss +=   "x=\""+position.x+"\" ";                          // 1
        ss +=   "y=\""+position.y+"\" ";
        ss +=   "z=\""+position.z+"\" ";
```

```
        ss += "qx=\""+rotation.x+"\" ";
        ss += "qy=\""+rotation.y+"\" ";
        ss += "qz=\""+rotation.z+"\" ";
        ss += "qw=\""+rotation.w+"\" ";
        ss += "tx=\""+target.x+"\" ";
        ss += "ty=\""+target.y+"\" ";
        ss += "tz=\""+target.z+"\" ";
        ss += " />";

        return(ss);
    }

}
```

1.1. In this line and those that follow, you see `\"` inside of the double quotes that define a string literal (for example, `"x=\""`). The backslash (`\`) is used as an *escape character* in this situation, and as such, it causes the character that immediately follows it to be interpreted as part of the string literal, regardless of what character it is. Normally, a double quote would end the string literal, but with the backslash before it, a double quote is added to the string literal instead.

2. And add a line to TargetCamera to test it:

```
public class TargetCamera : MonoBehaviour {
    …
    void Update () {
        …
        if (Input.GetMouseButtonDown(0)) { // Left mouse button
            …
            ShowShot( sh );

            Utils.tr( sh.ToXML() );
        }
    }
    …
}
```

3. Press Play and take some shots. You should see output in the Console window that is formatted like the following:

```
<shot x="-9.014837" y="1.457083" z="24.45312" qx="0.02179807" qy="0.0392502"
qz="-0.0008564426" qw="0.9989913" tx="-7.948404" ty="0.8636315" tz="38.00353"  />
```

This lets you know that it's working properly.

4. Now, expand this further by adding a static public `List<Shot>` to Shot so that it can keep track of multiple shots at a time. We'll also add the ability to read and write XML to Player-Prefs now. Add the following to Shot:

```
public class Shot { // Shot does not extend MonoBehaviour
    static public List<Shot>    shots = new List<Shot>(); // List of all shots
    static public string        prefsName = "QuickSnap_Shots";
```

```
public Vector3        position; // Position of the Camera

...

public string ToXML() {
    ...
}

// Takes a PT_XMLHashtable from PT_XMLReader of a <shot> entry in XML and
//   parses it into a Shot
static public Shot ParseShotXML( PT_XMLHashtable xHT ) {
    Shot sh = new Shot();

    sh.position.x = float.Parse(xHT.att("x"));
    sh.position.y = float.Parse(xHT.att("y"));
    sh.position.z = float.Parse(xHT.att("z"));
    sh.rotation.x = float.Parse(xHT.att("qx"));
    sh.rotation.y = float.Parse(xHT.att("qy"));
    sh.rotation.z = float.Parse(xHT.att("qz"));
    sh.rotation.w = float.Parse(xHT.att("qw"));
    sh.target.x   = float.Parse(xHT.att("tx"));
    sh.target.y   = float.Parse(xHT.att("ty"));
    sh.target.z   = float.Parse(xHT.att("tz"));

    return( sh );
}

// Loads all of the Shots from PlayerPrefs
static public void LoadShots() {
    // Empty the shots List<Shot>
    shots = new List<Shot>();

    if (!PlayerPrefs.HasKey(prefsName)) {
        // If there are no shots, return
        return;
    }

    // Get the full XML and parse it
    string shotsXML = PlayerPrefs.GetString(prefsName);
    PT_XMLReader xmlr = new PT_XMLReader();
    xmlr.Parse(shotsXML);

    // Pull the PT_XMLHashList of all <shot>s
    PT_XMLHashList hl = xmlr.xml["xml"][0]["shot"];
    for (int i=0; i<hl.Count; i++) {
        // Parse each <shot> in the PT_XMLHashlist into a Shot
        PT_XMLHashtable ht = hl[i];
        Shot sh = ParseShotXML(ht);
        // Add it to the List<shot> shots
```

```
            shots.Add(sh);
        }
    }

    // Save List<Shot> shots to PlayerPrefs
    static public void SaveShots() {
        string xs = Shot.XML;

        Utils.tr(xs); // Trace all the XML to the Console

        // Set the PlayerPrefs
        PlayerPrefs.SetString(prefsName, xs);

        Utils.tr("PlayerPrefs."+prefsName+" has been set.");
    }

    // Convert all Shot.shots to XML
    static public string XML {
        get {
            // Start an XML string
            string xs = "<xml>\n";
            // Add each of the Shots as a <shot> in XML
            foreach( Shot sh in shots ) {
                xs += sh.ToXML()+"\n";
            }
            // Add the closing XML tag
            xs += "</xml>";
            return(xs);
        }
    }
}
```

5. Next, you need to add some code to the TargetCamera class to take advantage of this:

```
public class TargetCamera : MonoBehaviour {
    public bool              editMode = true;
    public GameObject        fpCamera; // First-person Camera

    public bool              _____;

    public int               shotNum;
    public GUIText           shotCounter, shotRating;
    public GUITexture        checkMark;

    void Start() {
        // Find the GUI components
        GameObject go = GameObject.Find("ShotCounter");
        shotCounter = go.GetComponent<GUIText>();
```

```csharp
    go = GameObject.Find("ShotRating");
    shotRating = go.GetComponent<GUIText>();
    go = GameObject.Find("_Check_64");
    checkMark = go.GetComponent<GUITexture>();
    // Hide the checkMark
    checkMark.enabled = false;

    // Load all the shots from PlayerPrefs
    Shot.LoadShots();
    // If there were shots stored in PlayerPrefs
    if (Shot.shots.Count>0) {
        shotNum = 0;
        ShowShot(Shot.shots[shotNum]);
    }

    // Hide the cursor (Note: this doesn't work in the Unity Editor unless
    //   the Game pane is set to Maximize on Play.)
    Screen.showCursor = false;
}

void Update () {
    …
    if (Input.GetMouseButtonDown(0)) { // Left mouse button

        …
        Utils.tr( sh.ToXML() );

        // Record a new shot
        Shot.shots.Add(sh);
        shotNum = Shot.shots.Count-1;

    }


    // Keyboard Input
    // Use Q and E to cycle Shots
    // Note: Either of these will throw an error if Shot.shots is empty.
    if (Input.GetKeyDown(KeyCode.Q)) {
        shotNum--;
        if (shotNum < 0) shotNum = Shot.shots.Count-1;
        ShowShot(Shot.shots[shotNum]);
    }
    if (Input.GetKeyDown(KeyCode.E)) {
        shotNum++;
        if (shotNum >= Shot.shots.Count) shotNum = 0;
        ShowShot(Shot.shots[shotNum]);
    }
    // If in editMode & Left Shift is held down…
    if (editMode && Input.GetKey(KeyCode.LeftShift)) {
```

```
            // Use Shift-S to Save
            if (Input.GetKeyDown(KeyCode.S)) {
                Shot.SaveShots();
            }
            // Use Shift-X to output XML to Console
            if (Input.GetKeyDown(KeyCode.X)) {
                Utils.tr(Shot.XML);
            }
        }

        // Update the GUITexts
        shotCounter.text = (shotNum+1).ToString()+" of "+Shot.shots.Count;
        if (Shot.shots.Count == 0) shotCounter.text = "No shots exist";
        // ^ Shot.shots.Count doesn't require .ToString() because it is assumed
        //   when the left side of the + operator is a string
        shotRating.text = ""; // This line will be replaced later
    }
    …
}
```

6. Now, upon pressing Play, you will see that no shots yet exist. Walk around the scene and use the left mouse button to take about eight interesting shots. You can switch between shots by tapping the *Q* and *E* keys.

    Players will find the shots easier to match if you give them a specific object to focus on and if you give them some hints about framing (like objects that line up with the sides or corners of the image). After you have some shots that you like, press Shift+S (using the left Shift key), and the Console window should tell you that you have saved the shots to PlayerPrefs. Press the Play button to stop playback, and then press it again to start the game anew. You'll see that this second time it properly loads all of the shots from Player Prefs.

    Figure 34.8 shows the eight shots that I took.

Figure 34.8   Eight shots from around the scene

7. Save your Scene. Remember, *always* save your scene.

Two Uses of `OnDrawGizmos()`

Gizmos are the various on-screen icons and tools that you see in Unity's Scene pane. These include the axes gizmo (that shows the orientation of the Scene view) and all of the icons for lights and such. Gizmos can also be used as a debug tool by allowing developers to draw simple shapes using them. We'll add a DEBUG bool to TargetCamera, and if it's checked, `OnDrawGizmos()` will draw information about each shot in the Scene pane.

Add the following code to the end of the TargetCamera class:

```
public class TargetCamera : MonoBehaviour {
    …

    // OnDrawGizmos() is called ANY time Gizmos need to be drawn, even when
    //  Unity isn't playing!
    public void OnDrawGizmos() {
        List<Shot> shots = Shot.shots;
        for (int i=0; i<shots.Count; i++) {
            Gizmos.color = Color.green;
            Gizmos.DrawWireSphere(shots[i].position, 0.5f);
            Gizmos.color = Color.yellow;
            Gizmos.DrawLine( shots[i].position, shots[i].target );
            Gizmos.color = Color.red;
            Gizmos.DrawWireSphere(shots[i].target, 0.25f);
        }
    }
}
```

Now, when you play the scene, you should see little gizmos pop up in the Scene pane like the ones shown in Figure 34.9 showing a green wireframe sphere where the camera was positioned when the shot was taken and a smaller red sphere where the `Physics.Raycast()` from the camera hit an object. If you see a shot that has a red sphere back at the point 0,0,0 (in the bottom-right corner of the map near where _FPC starts), that means that the `Physics.Raycast()` didn't hit anything, and that shot should be replaced.

Speaking of replacing shots, right now, we don't have a way to delete the entry in PlayerPrefs. To do this, we'll use another feature of `OnDrawGizmos()`. As mentioned in the code listing comments, `OnDrawGizmos()` is called any time that the scene draws gizmos, so we can take advantage of that to run a little code even when Unity is not playing.

1. Add the following `DeleteShots()` method to the end of the Shot class:

```
public class Shot { // Shot does not extend MonoBehaviour
    …
    // Delete Shots from Shot.shots and PlayerPrefs
    static public void DeleteShots() {
        shots = new List<Shot>();
        if (PlayerPrefs.HasKey(prefsName)) {
            PlayerPrefs.DeleteKey(prefsName);
            Utils.tr("PlayerPrefs."+prefsName+" has been deleted.");
```

```
    } else {
        Utils.tr("There was no PlayerPrefs."+prefsName+" to delete.");
    }
  }
}
```

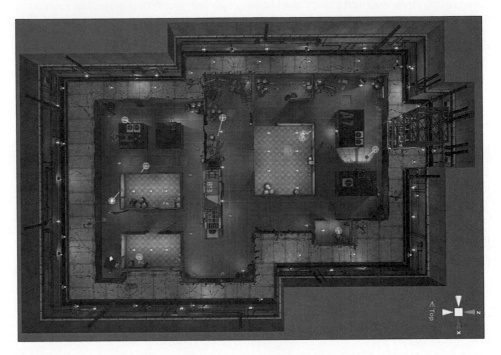

Figure 34.9   Gizmos showing the location of the eight shots from around the scene. Note that the image has been rotated 90° clockwise to better fit the page.

2. Next, add a `checkToDeletePlayerPrefs` bool field to the top of TargetCamera and the bold lines to the end of `TargetCamera.OnDrawGizmos()`:

```
public class TargetCamera : MonoBehaviour {
    …

    public GameObject        fpCamera; // First-person Camera

    public bool              checkToDeletePlayerPrefs = false;

    public bool              _____;
    …

    // OnDrawGizmos() is called ANY time Gizmos need to be drawn, even when
    //  Unity isn't playing!
    public void OnDrawGizmos() {
```

```
            ...
            // If checkToDeletePlayerPrefs is checked
            if (checkToDeletePlayerPrefs) {
                Shot.DeleteShots(); // Delete all the shots
                // Uncheck checkToDeletePlayerPrefs
                checkToDeletePlayerPrefs = false;
                shotNum = 0; // Set shotNum to 0
            }
        }
}
```

Now, even when Unity is not playing, if you check the box in the Inspector next to the Target-Camera field `checkToDeletePlayerPrefs`, Unity will run the code to delete the prefs from PlayerPrefs, notify you that it has been done in the console, and then uncheck `check-ToDeletePlayerPrefs` in the Inspector. You need to be very careful if you choose to use this kind of feature, but it can be really useful in situations like this.

If you tested checkToDeletePlayerPrefs (as you should), you now need to go take some more shots and save them before continuing.

Replacing Individual Shots

Now, you can delete all the shots together, but what if you want to just replace a single shot?

1. Add the following static method to the end of the `Shot` class:

```
public class Shot { // Shot does not extend MonoBehaviour
    ...
    // Replace the shot
    static public void ReplaceShot(int ndx, Shot sh) {
        // Make sure there's a Shot at that index to replace
        if (shots==null || shots.Count <= ndx) return;
        // Remove the old Shot
        shots.RemoveAt(ndx);
        // List<>.Insert() adds something to the list at a specific index
        shots.Insert(ndx,sh);

        Utils.tr("Replaced shot:", ndx, "with", sh.ToXML());
    }
}
```

2. Now make the changes to TargetCamera shown here. This will involve making several changes to the // `Mouse Input` section of the code so I have included that entire section:

```
public class TargetCamera : MonoBehaviour {
    ...

    void Update () {
        Shot sh;
```

```
// Mouse Input
// If Left or Right mouse button is pressed this frame…
if (Input.GetMouseButtonDown(0) || Input.GetMouseButtonDown(1)) {
    sh = new Shot();
    // Grab the position and rotation of fpCamera
    sh.position = fpCamera.transform.position;
    sh.rotation = fpCamera.transform.rotation;
    // Shoot a ray from the camera and see what it hits
    Ray ray = new Ray(sh.position, fpCamera.transform.forward);
    RaycastHit hit;
    if ( Physics.Raycast(ray, out hit) ) {
        sh.target = hit.point;
    }

    if (editMode) {
        if (Input.GetMouseButtonDown(0)) {
            // Left button records a new shot
            Shot.shots.Add(sh);
            shotNum = Shot.shots.Count-1;
        } else if (Input.GetMouseButtonDown(1)) {
            // Right button replaces the current shot
            Shot.ReplaceShot(shotNum, sh);
            ShowShot(Shot.shots[shotNum]);
        }
    }

    // Position _TargetCamera with the Shot
    // ShowShot(sh);                        // Comment out or delete this line

}

// Keyboard Input
…
}
…
}
```

3. Play the scene and walk around.

Now, as long as editMode is checked in the _TargetCamera Inspector, you can right-click to replace any of the shots you don't particularly like. Then, when you want to save the updated list of shots, press Shift+S.

Maximizing the Target Window

You may have noticed in your development that it's somewhat difficult to see the Target window at its small size. You can adjust a camera's on-screen window at runtime by changing its Camera.rect value. Try adding the following code to TargetCamera. Note that this will still show the tiny _Crosshairs_12 in the middle of the screen; can you think of a way to hide it when the target window is enlarged?

```
public class TargetCamera : MonoBehaviour {
    …

    public bool                 _____;

    public Rect             camRectNormal; // Pulled from camera.rect

    …

    void Start() {
        …
        Screen.showCursor = false;

        camRectNormal = camera.rect;
    }

    void Update () {
        …

        // Keyboard Input
        …
        if (editMode && Input.GetKey(KeyCode.LeftShift)) { … }
        // Hold Tab to maximize the Target window
        if (Input.GetKeyDown(KeyCode.Tab)) {
            // Maximize when Tab is pressed
            camera.rect = new Rect(0,0,1,1);
        }
        if (Input.GetKeyUp(KeyCode.Tab)) {
            // Return to normal when Tab is released
            camera.rect = camRectNormal;
        }
    }

}
```

Now it's time to add the mode that players will see.

Comparing Shots

Because we're asking players to take the same shots as we have, it's critical to write a good Shot comparison function to compare the player's Shot to the target Shot. The method we will use compares both the location of the camera when taking the Shot and the location of the `Physics.Raycast()` hit that is generated by the ray shooting from the camera. We will not compare the rotation of the two Shots because if the player is not standing in exactly the right position, she will have to rotate differently from the original Shot to get the correct objects in view. This is shown in Figure 34.10.

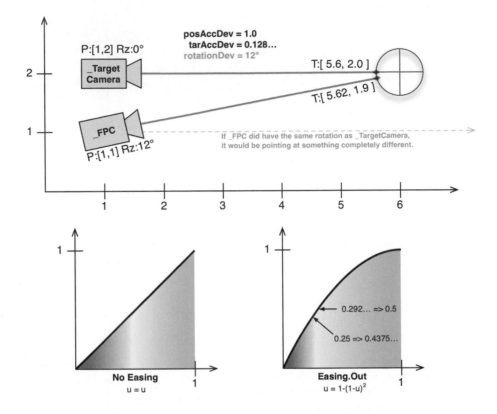

Figure 34.10   A 2D demonstration of why we are comparing camera position and target position rather than camera rotation. Also shows the effects of using Easing.Out on accuracy percentage.

You'll see in the following code that we also make use of the `Easing.Ease()` function to perform an Easing.Out on the accuracy percentage before it is returned. While Easing is most often used for interpolation and movement, it can be used to curve or alter any number that tends to sit between 0 and 1 (like the percentage accuracy that we're calculating). As shown in Figure 34.10, using Easing.Out (which is the function $u = 1 - (1 - u)^2$) will curve the results as shown in the bottom right of the figure. This will make a larger area get a good percentage score while still dropping the percentage to 0 at the same point as the original, accommodating the extreme difficulty in getting the camera in the exact right position while still limiting the radius of the deviation from the correct position to `maxPosDeviation` and `maxTarDeviation`. I personally use easing a *lot* in my game design work. You can read more about it in the "Interpolation" section of Appendix B, "Useful Concepts."

Add the following static method to the end of the `Shot` class to compare the two shots. This code is going to reference some fields that we'll set on _TargetCamera in the Inspector, so later we'll add a singleton to TargetCamera to make this easy:

```
public class Shot { // Shot does not extend MonoBehaviour
    …

    // Compare two Shots. 1 is a perfect match, while <0 is not valid
    public static float Compare(Shot target, Shot test) {
        // Get the positinal deviation of both the camera and the Raycast hit
        float posDev = (test.position - target.position).magnitude;
        float tarDev = (test.target - target.target).magnitude;

        float posAccPct, tarAccPct, posAP2, tarAP2; // Accuracy percentages
        TargetCamera tc = TargetCamera.S;

        // Get a value for accuracy where 1 is perfect and 0 is barely ok
        posAccPct = 1-(posDev/tc.maxPosDeviation);
        tarAccPct = 1-(tarDev/tc.maxTarDeviation);

        // Curve the value so that it's more forgiving. This uses the same
        //  Easing that we do for motion. You can curve ANY value between
        //  0 and 1, not just Interpolation values.
        posAP2 = Easing.Ease(posAccPct, tc.deviationEasing);
        tarAP2 = Easing.Ease(tarAccPct, tc.deviationEasing);

        float accuracy = (posAP2+tarAP2)/2f;

        // Remember that you can use Utils to format numbers nicely as strings
        string accText = Utils.RoundToPlaces(accuracy*100).ToString()+"%";
        Utils.tr("Position:",posAccPct,posAP2,"Target:",tarAccPct,tarAP2,
            ➥"Accuracy",accText);

        return(accuracy);
    }
}
```

Now, add the bolded code to TargetCamera to make use of the `Slot.Compare()` function:

```
public class TargetCamera : MonoBehaviour {
    static public TargetCamera S;

    public bool              editMode = true;
    public GameObject        fpCamera; // First-person Camera
    // Maximum deviation in Shot.position allowed
    public float             maxPosDeviation = 1f;
    // Maximum deviation in Shot.target allowed
    public float             maxTarDeviation = 0.5f;
    // Easing for these deviations
    public string            deviationEasing = Easing.Out;

    public bool              checkToDeletePlayerPrefs = false;

    public bool              _____;
```

```csharp
public Rect           camRectNormal; // Pulled from camera.rect
public int            shotNum;
public GUIText        shotCounter, shotRating;
public GUITexture     checkMark;
public Shot           lastShot;

void Awake() {
    S = this;
}

…

void Update () {
    …
    if (Input.GetMouseButtonDown(0) || Input.GetMouseButtonDown(1)) {
        …

        if (editMode) {
            if (Input.GetMouseButtonDown(0)) {
                // Left button records a new shot
                Shot.shots.Add(sh);
                shotNum = Shot.shots.Count-1;
            } else {
                // Right button replaces the current shot
                Shot.ReplaceShot(shotNum, sh);
                ShowShot(Shot.shots[shotNum]);
            }
            // Reset information about the player when editing shots
            ResetPlayerShotsAndRatings();
        } else {
            // Test this shot against the current Shot
            float acc = Shot.Compare( Shot.shots[shotNum], sh );
            lastShot = sh;
        }
    }
    …
}

…

// OnDrawGizmos() is called ANY time Gizmos need to be drawn, even when
//   Unity isn't playing!
public void OnDrawGizmos() {
    …

    // Show the player's last shot attempt
    if (lastShot != null) {
        Gizmos.color = Color.green;
```

```
            Gizmos.DrawSphere(lastShot.position, 0.25f);
            Gizmos.color = Color.white;
            Gizmos.DrawLine( lastShot.position, lastShot.target );
            Gizmos.color = Color.red;
            Gizmos.DrawSphere(lastShot.target, 0.125f);
        }
    }
}
```

Be sure to set `TargetCamera.editMode` to false in the Inspector for _TargetCamera, and then press Play. You should be able to walk around and select various target shots with the *Q* and *E* keys. Line yourself up with the target shot and click the left mouse button to take a test shot. The Console pane will show you information on your accuracy, and a new gizmo should appear in the Scene pane that shows the last shot you took. If you are consistently inaccurate on a specific shot, you can use this to see whether it's your position or your aim that is causing the problem. You can then adjust `maxPosDeviation` and `maxTarDeviation` to something that works better for you.

Recording and Displaying Player Progress

Now that shots are being compared properly, it's time to show the player how she is doing in the game. Add the bolded code shown here to TargetCamera:

```
public class TargetCamera : MonoBehaviour {
    …
    public string          deviationEasing = Easing.Out;
    public float           passingAccuracy = 0.7f;
    …
    public Shot            lastShot;
    public int             numShots;
    public Shot[]          playerShots;
    public float[]         playerRatings;

    …

    void Start() {
        …
        // Load all the shots from PlayerPrefs
        Shot.LoadShots();
        // If there were shots stored in PlayerPrefs
        if (Shot.shots.Count>0) {
            shotNum = 0;
            ResetPlayerShotsAndRatings();
            ShowShot(Shot.shots[shotNum]);
        }
        …
    }
```

```csharp
void ResetPlayerShotsAndRatings() {
    numShots = Shot.shots.Count;
    // Initialize playerShots & playerRatings with default values
    playerShots = new Shot[numShots];
    playerRatings = new float[numShots];
}


void Update () {
    ...
    if (Input.GetMouseButtonDown(0) || Input.GetMouseButtonDown(1)) {
        ...
        if (editMode) {
            if (Input.GetMouseButtonDown(0)) {

                ...
                ShowShot(Shot.shots[shotNum]);
            }
            // Reset information about the player when editing shots
            ResetPlayerShotsAndRatings();
        } else {
            // Test this shot against the current Shot
            float acc = Shot.Compare( Shot.shots[shotNum], sh );
            lastShot = sh;
            playerShots[shotNum] = sh;
            playerRatings[shotNum] = acc;
        }

    }

    // Update the GUITexts
    shotCounter.text = (shotNum+1).ToString()+" of "+Shot.shots.Count;
    if (Shot.shots.Count == 0) shotCounter.text = "No shots exist";
    // ^ Shot.shots.Count doesn't require .ToString() because it is assumed
    //   when the left side of the + operator is a string
    // shotRating.text = ""; // This line is now commented out

    if (playerRatings.Length > shotNum && playerShots[shotNum] != null) {
        float rating = Mathf.Round(playerRatings[shotNum]*100f);
        if (rating < 0) rating = 0;
        shotRating.text = rating.ToString()+"%";
        checkMark.enabled = (playerRatings[shotNum] > passingAccuracy);
        // ^ the > comparison is used to generate true or false
    } else {
        shotRating.text = "";
        checkMark.enabled = false;
    }
}
...
}
```

Now, when you press Play, taking a shot will show you a shot rating in the lower-right corner of the target window, and if that rating is above the _TargetCamera's `passingAccuracy`, a check mark will appear in the upper-right corner as well.

Adding a Snapshot Sound and Visual Effect

To make this seem more like the player is taking pictures, we're going to add a shutter sound and visual effect.

Adding the Audio Source

Select _TargetCamera in the Hierarchy, and from the menu bar choose *Component > Audio > Audio Source*. As its name would imply, an Audio Source component generates sound in your scene. In the Audio Source component that has now appeared in the Inspector, click the target icon to the right of the Audio Clip field and choose the only audio clip in our Project Assets: *camera-shutter-click-03*. You will see now that below the Audio Clip field, Unity tells you "This is a 3D Sound."

Unity has both 3D and 2D sounds. 2D are normal stereo sounds that you're used to dealing with (like when listening to music). 2D sounds will sound the same to the player regardless of where the Audio Source is in the scene. 3D sounds, in contrast, change based on how far they are from the Audio Listener (which is the component on FPCamera that acts like a microphone in this game), and they will even have a Doppler effect when moving toward or away from the Audio Listener (like how a car siren will change pitch as it is moving toward or away from you). 3D sounds are fantastic in some games, but we really don't want one for this prototype; we want the camera shutter to sound the same regardless of where the player is.

So, click the name *camera-shutter-click-03* in the Inspector to highlight it in the Project pane. Then select it in the Project pane to show import settings for *camera-shutter-click-03*. Uncheck the box next to *3D Sound* (setting it to false) and click *Apply*. Now, select _TargetCamera in the Hierarchy, and the Audio Source component will now tell you that *camera-shutter-click-03* is a 2D sound. In the Audio Source component, make sure that *Bypass Effects* is checked and *Play On Awake* is *not* checked. (If *Play On Awake* were true, it would cause the camera sound to play immediately when the scene started.)

Adding the Shutter Visual Effect

In the Project pane, select the Texture named _*White* in the Textures folder. Then choose *Game Object > Create Other > GUI Texture* from the menu bar. This will make a new GUITexture in the Hierarchy named _White. Rename it to *WhiteOut* so that It Is not confused with the _White already in the Hierarchy. Then, set it as follows:

WhiteOut (GUITexture)	P:[0.5,0.5,0]	R:[0,0,0]	S:[1,1,0]
Layer:	_TargetCamera		
Pixel Inset:	[x:0, y:0, w:0, h:0]		

This should completely fill the Target window with white. Any time the shot in the Target window changes, this WhiteOut will flash to draw the player's attention.

Audio and Visual Effect Code

Add the following code to the `TargetCamera` class to use the Audio Source and WhiteOut. Note the two different strategies that we use for delaying an action: `Invoke()` and yielding a coroutine.

```
public class TargetCamera : MonoBehaviour {
    …
    public Shot[]          playerShots;
    public float[]         playerRatings;
    public GUITexture      whiteOut;

    void Start() {
        // Find the GUI Components
        …
        checkMark = go.GetComponent<GUITexture>();
        go = GameObject.Find ("WhiteOut");
        whiteOut = go.GetComponent<GUITexture>();
        // Hide the checkMark and whiteOut
        checkMark.enabled = false;
        whiteOut.enabled = false;

        …
    }

    void Update () {
        Shot sh;

        // Mouse Input
        // If Left or Right mouse button is pressed this frame…
        if (Input.GetMouseButtonDown(0) || Input.GetMouseButtonDown(1)) {
            …

            if (editMode) {
                …
            } else {
                // Test this shot against the current Shot
                float acc = Shot.Compare( Shot.shots[shotNum], sh );
                lastShot = sh;
                playerShots[shotNum] = sh;
                playerRatings[shotNum] = acc;
                // Show the shot just taken by the player
                ShowShot(sh);
                // Return to the current shot after waiting 1 second
                Invoke("ShowCurrentShot",1);
            }
```

```
            // Play the shutter sound
            this.GetComponent<AudioSource>().Play();
        }
        ...
    }

    public void ShowShot(Shot sh) {
        // Call WhiteOutTargetWindow() and let it handle its own timing
        StartCoroutine( WhiteOutTargetWindow() );
        // Position _TargetCamera with the Shot
        this.transform.position = sh.position;
        this.transform.rotation = sh.rotation;
    }

    public void ShowCurrentShot() {
        ShowShot(Shot.shots[shotNum]);
    }

    // Another use for coroutines is to have a fire-and-forget function with a
    //  delay in it as we've done here. WhiteOutTargetWindow() will enable
    //  whiteOut, yield for 0.05 seconds, and then disable it. Compare this
    //  method of delay to the Invoke("ShowCurrentShot",1f) used above
    public IEnumerator WhiteOutTargetWindow() {
        whiteOut.enabled = true;
        yield return new WaitForSeconds(0.05f);
        whiteOut.enabled = false;
    }

    ...
}
```

Now, when you play the scene, it should feel more like taking photos. When you snap a shot, the shutter sound is played, WhiteOut blinks, the shot you just took is shown for a second, WhiteOut blinks again, and then the target shot is shown with a rating for how well you did.

Summary

Although the coding in this tutorial was simpler than previous chapters, I hope you appreciated the chance to see the kind of powerful visual technology that is included in Unity (even in Unity Free). Most of the tutorial projects in this book are meant to be prototypes, and as such, they look like prototypes. With this project, I wanted to give you the chance to make something beautiful.

The tutorial in the next chapter returns to prototype-style graphics, but it includes the most complex user interaction and reading of XML files. It also makes further use of the multicamera tricks that you learned in this chapter.

Next Steps

This prototype introduced you to a lot of new concepts and showed how to get beautiful graphics out of Unity. Here are some additional things you can add to make it a more interesting game:

1. Add a timer in the top right of the main window that counts down the amount of time the player has to find all eight photographs.

2. Change the environment or create a new environment for the game. The current environment has a flat floor, but there's no need for that to be the case.

3. If you do change the environment (or even in this environment), you might want to consider adjusting the `maxTarDeviation` of a shot comparison based on the distance of the `Shot.target` from the `Shot.postion`. If the two are far apart, you should allow more `maxTarDeviation`. This would be particularly important in a large outdoor environment.

4. Put moving creatures in the environment that the player must find and photograph. Give the player points for the location and size of the creature in the shot. Something similar to this was a really fun photography side quest in *Beyond Good & Evil* by Ubisoft.

   Hint: Use GameObject.Rendere.Bounds to get the 3D bounding volume around the creature, and then call `Camera.WorldToViewportPoint()` on the Bound's center and extents to find where they would be in the viewport. If the object is centered and fills a decent amount of the frame, give the player points. You might even give them more points for following the rule of thirds (search for "photography rule of thirds" online).

   If you do add dynamic objects moving through the scene, and you're using Unity Pro, be sure to look at the Mesh Renderer component of the Inspector for the dynamic objects and set *Use Light Probes* to true. This will enable you to use the light probe information shown in Figure 34.2 on the dynamic objects.

5. Add roving guards or lights that the player must hide from. Information about this can be found in the original Unity Stealth tutorial that this environment was pulled from. Search for "Unity Stealth tutorial" online, and you should find it easily.

CHAPTER 35

PROTOTYPE 8: OMEGA MAGE

Omega Mage is a game prototype that mixes the dungeon exploration of *The Legend of Zelda* or *Rogue* with element-based spell-casting and an interface that works for either mouse or touchscreen (Android, iOS, and so on).

This is the last prototype of the book and therefore the most complex. At the end, you'll have a nice skeleton for an action-adventure game.

Getting Started: Omega Mage Prototype

The unitypackage for this project includes a number of assets, materials, and scripts. Because you already have experience with building objects in Unity out of simple shapes (as you did in the SHMUP prototype), I do not ask you to do so in this chapter. Instead, you import a series of prefabs that will serve as the artwork in this game.

Game Overview

Omega Mage is a dungeon crawler in the vein of classics like *The Legend of Zelda* and *Rogue*. However, in this game, the main character is a magic user who can call upon the four elements to defeat her enemies.

Figure 35.1 shows what Omega Mage will look like at the end of the prototype. The _MainCamera on the left 3/4 of the screen shows the action from a top-down camera angle, and the right 1/4 of the screen contains a simple inventory for selecting elements.

Figure 35.1   An example of what Omega Mage will look like

Omega Mage was designed with touch-based tablets like the iPad and Android in mind, so the interactions will work equally well through either mouse or touch interface.

The player will click or tap on the ground in the main area to cause her character to walk to the tapped point. Tapping on one of the four elements in the inventory area will select it (and the player will see it orbiting around the Mage). Tapping the black "none" element in the middle of the others clears the element selection.

Clicking and dragging with no element selected causes the Mage to continuously move toward the player's cursor (or touch) until she releases the mouse or lifts her finger, at which point, the Mage will stop. If she has an element selected, clicking and dragging on the ground will cast a ground spell (like the fire spell shown in Figure 35.1).

Tapping on an enemy will attack it. If the player has an element selected, the Mage will cast a spell of that element type. If she has no element selected, the tap will push the enemy away slightly.

Changes to ProtoTools in the Unitypackage

For this prototype, I've added a couple of new scripts to the ProtoTools directory:

- **PT_MonoBehaviour:** This simple script just adds some shortcuts to nested fields that we change often, including position, localPosition, rotation, scale, material, and color. If your scripts extend this instead of MonoBehaviour, they'll gain this small added functionality.
- **PT_Mover:** This more complex script allows an object to move in a time-based way using Bézier curves that affect position, rotation, scale, and color of the primary material. This is a child of PT_MonoBehaviour, so if your scripts extend this, they will gain both the PT_MonoBehaviour and PT_Mover functionalities.

SET UP THE PROJECT FOR THIS CHAPTER

Following the standard project setup procedure, create a new project in Unity. If you need a refresher on the standard project setup procedure, see Appendix A, "Standard Project Setup Procedure." When you are creating the project, you will be asked if you want to set up defaults for 2D or 3D. Choose 3D for this project.

- **Project name:** OmegaMage
- **Download and import package:** Find Chapter 35 at http://book.prototools.net
- **Scene name:** __OmegaMage_Scene_0
- **Project folders:** These are all imported from the unitypackage
- **C# script names:** Just the imported scripts in the ProtoTools folder
- **Remember:** Change the name of Main Camera to _MainCamer

The texture images for the ground and wall blocks that are in the _Textures & Materials/ cartoon6r.free.fr folder were created by Philippe Cizaire and are used and included in the unitypackage with his permission. To see more of his work, check out his website at http://cartoon6r.free.fr.

Building the Scene

Unlike the previous prototype, this game uses Extensible Markup Language (XML) and a series of 3D tiles to build the game environment. Double-click the *Rooms.xml* file inside the Resources folder to see what I mean. The layout of these rooms using text was inspired by the classic adventure game *Rogue*, which became one of the first "graphical" games by displaying the player, enemies, and dungeons as ASCII art that looked much like the text in the Rooms.xml file.

In this prototype, we need to read the XML data from Rooms.xml and the parse that into information to build a room from 3D tiles (using TilePrefab in the _Prefabs folder). This will be accomplished by a LayoutTiles script on _MainCamera in concert with a small Tile script on the TilePrefab. The textures for the tiles will be defined using fields in the _MainCamera:LayoutTiles Inspector.

To start, create a new C# script in the __Scripts folder named *Tile* and attach it to TilePrefab in the Prefabs folder. Open the Tile script in MonoDevelop and enter the following code:

```
using UnityEngine;
using System.Collections;

public class Tile : PT_MonoBehaviour {
// public fields
    public string         type;

// Hidden private fields
    private string        _tex;
    private int           _height = 0;
    private Vector3       _pos;

// Properties with get{} and set{}

    // height moves the Tile up or down. Walls have height=1
    public int height {
        get { return( _height ); }
        set {
            _height = value;
            AdjustHeight();
        }
    }

    // Sets the texture of the Tile based on a string
    // It requires LayoutTiles, so it's commented out for now
    /*                                                              // 1
    public string tex {
        get {
            return( _tex );
        }
        set {
            _tex = value;
```

```
        name = "TilePrefab_"+_tex; // Sets the name of this GameObject
        Texture2D t2D = LayoutTiles.S.GetTileTex(_tex);
        if (t2D == null) {
            Utils.tr("ERROR","Tile.type{set}=",value,
              "No matching Texture2D in LayoutTiles.S.tileTextures!");
        } else {
            renderer.material.mainTexture = t2D;
        }
    }
}
*/                                                        // 2


// Uses the "new" keyword to replace the pos inherited from PT_MonoBehaviour
// Without the "new" keyword, the two properties would conflict
new public Vector3 pos {
    get { return( _pos ); }
    set {
        _pos = value;
        AdjustHeight();
    }
}


// Methods
    public void AdjustHeight() {
        // Moves the block up or down based on _height
        Vector3 vertOffset = Vector3.back*(_height-0.5f);
        // The -0.5f shifts the Tile down 0.5 units so that it's top surface is
        //  at z=0 when pos.z=0 and height=0
        transform.position = _pos+vertOffset;
    }
}


}
```

1. This is the beginning of a multiline comment that hides the property `tex` from the compiler for now.

2. This is the end of the multiline comment that hides `tex`.

You'll notice that the `tex` property is commented out. This is because it requires the LayoutTiles script to be in place to compile properly. After you have entered the preceding code and made sure that it all compiles, create a new script named *LayoutTiles* in the __Scripts folder and attach it to _MainCamera. Then, remove the multiline comments (/* and */) from before and after the `tex` property. Unity will throw a compiler error (Assets/__Scripts/Tile.cs(31,53): error CS0117: 'LayoutTiles' does not contain a definition for 'S'), but we'll rectify that now by writing the LayoutTiles script. Open LayoutTiles in MonoBehaviour and add the following code:

```
using UnityEngine;
using System.Collections;
using System.Collections.Generic;
```

```csharp
[System.Serializable]
public class TileTex {
    // This class enables us to define various textures for tiles
    public string          str;
    public Texture2D       tex;
}

public class LayoutTiles : MonoBehaviour {
    static public LayoutTiles S;

    public TextAsset       roomsText; // The Rooms.xml file
    public string          roomNumber = "0"; // Current room # as a string
    // ^ roomNumber as string allows encoding in the XML & rooms 0-F
    public GameObject      tilePrefab; // Prefab for all Tiles
    public TileTex[]       tileTextures; // A list of named textures for Tiles

    public bool _____;

    public PT_XMLReader    roomsXMLR;
    public PT_XMLHashList  roomsXML;
    public Tile[,]         tiles;
    public Transform       tileAnchor;

    void Awake() {
        S = this; // Set the Singleton for LayoutTiles

        // Make a new GameObject to be the TileAnchor (the parent transform of
        //  all Tiles). This keeps Tiles tidy in the Hierarchy pane.
        GameObject tAnc = new GameObject("TileAnchor");
        tileAnchor = tAnc.transform;

        // Read the XML
        roomsXMLR = new PT_XMLReader(); // Create a PT_XMLReader
        roomsXMLR.Parse(roomsText.text); // Parse the Rooms.xml file
        roomsXML = roomsXMLR.xml["xml"][0]["room"]; // Pull all the <room>s

        // Build the 0th Room
        BuildRoom(roomNumber);
    }

    // This is the GetTileTex() method that Tile uses
    public Texture2D GetTileTex(string tStr) {
        // Search through all the tileTextures for the proper string
        foreach (TileTex tTex in tileTextures) {
            if (tTex.str == tStr) {
                return(tTex.tex);
            }
        }
        // Return null if nothing was found
```

```
        return(null);
}

// Build a room from an XML <room> entry
public void BuildRoom(PT_XMLHashtable room) {
    // Get the texture names for the floors and walls from <room> attributes
    string floorTexStr = room.att("floor");
    string wallTexStr = room.att("wall");
    // Split the room into rows of tiles based on carriage returns in the
    //  Rooms.xml file
    string[] roomRows = room.text.Split('\n');
    // Trim tabs from the beginnings of lines. However, we're leaving spaces
    //  and underscores to allow for non-rectangular rooms.
    for (int i=0; i<roomRows.Length; i++) {
        roomRows[i] = roomRows[i].Trim('\t');
    }
    // Clear the tiles Array
    tiles = new Tile[ 100, 100 ]; // Arbitrary max room size is 100x100

    // Declare a number of local fields that we'll use later
    Tile ti;
    string type, rawType, tileTexStr;
    GameObject go;
    int height;
    float maxY = roomRows.Length-1;

    // These loops scan through each tile of each row of the room
    for (int y=0; y<roomRows.Length; y++) {
        for (int x=0; x<roomRows[y].Length; x++) {
            // Set defaults
            height = 0;
            tileTexStr = floorTexStr;

            // Get the character representing the tile
            type = rawType = roomRows[y][x].ToString();
            switch (rawType) {
            case " ": // empty space
            case "_": // empty space
                // Just skip over empty space
                continue;
            case ".": // default floor
                // Keep type="."
                break;
            case "|": // default wall
                height = 1;
                break;
            default:
                // Anything else will be interpreted as floor
                type = ".";
```

```
                break;
            }

            // Set the texture for floor or wall based on <room> attributes
            if (type == ".") {
                tileTexStr = floorTexStr;
            } else if (type == "|") {
                tileTexStr = wallTexStr;
            }

            // Instantiate a new TilePrefab
            go = Instantiate(tilePrefab) as GameObject;
            ti = go.GetComponent<Tile>();
            // Set the parent Transform to tileAnchor
            ti.transform.parent = tileAnchor;
            // Set the position of the tile
            ti.pos = new Vector3( x, maxY-y, 0 );
            tiles[x,y] = ti; // Add ti to the tiles 2D Array

            // Set the type, height, and texture of the Tile
            ti.type = type;
            ti.height = height;
            ti.tex = tileTexStr;

            // More to come here…
        }
    }
}
```

This should all compile fine (and now you'll no longer have the error from Tile), but you need to add some things in the _MainCamera:LayoutTiles Inspector before it will actually work. Click _MainCamera in the Hierarchy and enter the data shown in Figure 35.2.

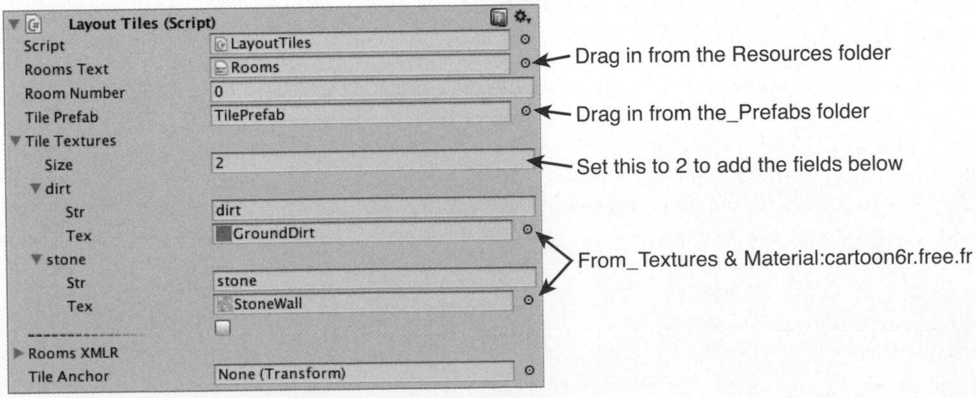

Figure 35.2   Inspector settings _MainCamera:LayoutTiles

After you have done this, press Play, and a room will be built for you. If you like, you can stop, change `_MainCamera:LayoutTiles.roomNumber` in the Inspector to another valid number (0–8), and press Play again to see other rooms in the dungeon. Be sure to stop playback and set `roomNumber` back to 0 when you're done looking around.

You'll notice that the room is pretty dark now, but that's okay; our Mage character will carry a torch.

Oh, and save your scene. Always remember to save your scene!

The Mage Character

Drag _Mage from the _Prefabs folder into the Hierarchy pane. This is the GameObject for the player character in Omega Mage. You can see that _Mage comes complete with a Rigidbody and Capsule Collider as well as a placeholder human model and an overhead spotlight.

Create a new C# script in the __Scripts folder named *Mage* and attach it to _Mage in the Hierarchy. Open the Mage script in MonoDevelop and enter the following code:

```
using UnityEngine;
using System.Collections;
using System.Collections.Generic;    // Enables List<>s
using System.Linq;                   // Enables LINQ queries

// Mage is a subclass of PT_MonoBehaviour
public class Mage : PT_MonoBehaviour {
    static public Mage S;

    void Awake() {
        S = this; // Set the Mage Singleton
    }
}
```

Of course, we'll add a lot more to this later, but for now, we need to properly position _Mage in the room. Open LayoutTiles in MonoBehaviour and add the following bold code to the BuildRoom() method just above where it currently has "`// More to come here…`":

```
public class LayoutTiles : MonoBehaviour {
    …

    // Build a room from an XML <room> entry
    public void BuildRoom(PT_XMLHashtable room) {
        …

        // These loops scan through each tile of each row of the room
        for (int y=0; y<roomRows.Length; y++) {
            for (int x=0; x<roomRows[y].Length; x++) {
```

```
            …
            ti.tex = tileTexStr;

            // If the type is still rawType, continue to the next iteration
            if (rawType == type) continue;

            // Check for specific entities in the room
            switch (rawType) {                                           // 1
            case "X": // Starting position for the Mage
                Mage.S.pos = ti.pos; // Uses the Mage Singleton
                break;
            }

            // More to come here…
        }
    }
}
```

1.   In the previous version of this code listing, it would treat any `rawType` char it didn't recognize as a '.' (ground). Here, the code checks to see if that unrecognized `rawType` char was an 'X' (the char for the start position of the Mage).

This will properly position the _Mage where the *X* is in Room 0 of the Rooms.xml file. Now, it's time to make _MainCamera follow _Mage. Create a new C# script in the __Scripts folder named *CameraFollow* and attach it to _MainCamera. Open CameraFollow in MonoDevelop and enter the following code:

```
using UnityEngine;
using System.Collections;

public class CameraFollow : PT_MonoBehaviour {
    public static CameraFollow S;

    public Transform        targetTransform;
    public float            camEasing = 0.1f;
    public Vector3          followOffset = new Vector3(0,0,-2);

    void Awake() {
        S = this;
    }

    void FixedUpdate() {
        Vector3 pos1 = targetTransform.position+followOffset;
        pos = Vector3.Lerp(pos, pos1, camEasing);
    }
}
```

Now, return to Unity and select _MainCamera in the Inspector. You need to set `targetTransform` in the _MainCamera:CameraFollow Inspector. Click the disclosure triangle next to _Mage in the Hierarchy; then open the disclosure triangle next to CharacterTrans. You'll see that Spotlight is a child of CharacterTrans. Drag Spotlight into the `targetTransform` field in the _MainCamera:CameraFollow Inspector. This will cause the _MainCamera to be slightly ahead of _Mage because Spotlight is always positioned slightly ahead of where the _Mage is looking. Press Play, and you should see this result. If you select _Mage in the Hierarchy while the scene is playing and adjust the transform.rotation.z value in the _Mage Inspector, you should see the camera follow the pool of light that is just in front of the _Mage.

Mouse Interaction

Because we want this game to be playable on either a computer or touch-based mobile device, all of the interactions are going to be based on simple mouse gestures. This works for tablets because Unity automatically converts single touches on a tablet into mouse gestures.

The mouse interaction code will be added to the Mage script, and it's going to take a decent amount of coding to get the initial pieces working. Add the following to the Mage script:

```
using UnityEngine;
using System.Collections;
using System.Collections.Generic;    // Enables List<>s
using System.Linq;                   // Enables LINQ queries

// The MPhase enum is used to track the phase of mouse interaction
public enum MPhase {
    idle,
    down,
    drag
}

// MouseInfo stores information about the mouse in each frame of interaction
[System.Serializable]
public class MouseInfo {
    public Vector3      loc;        // 3D loc of the mouse near z=0
    public Vector3      screenLoc;  // Screen position of the mouse
    public Ray          ray;        // Ray from the mouse into 3D space
    public float        time;       // Time this mouseInfo was recorded
    public RaycastHit   hitInfo;    // Info about what was hit by the ray
    public bool         hit;        // Whether the mouse was over any collider

    // These methods see if the mouseRay hits anything
    public RaycastHit Raycast() {
        hit = Physics.Raycast(ray, out hitInfo);
        return(hitInfo);
    }

    public RaycastHit Raycast(int mask) {
        hit = Physics.Raycast(ray, out hitInfo, mask);
        return(hitInfo);
    }
```

```
}

// Mage is a subclass of PT_MonoBehaviour
public class Mage : PT_MonoBehaviour {
    static public Mage S;
    static public bool DEBUG = true;

    public float              mTapTime = 0.1f; // How long is considered a tap
    public float              mDragDist = 5; // Min dist in pixels to be a drag

    public float              activeScreenWidth = 1; // % of the screen to use

    public bool _____;

    public MPhase             mPhase = MPhase.idle;
    public List<MouseInfo>    mouseInfos = new List<MouseInfo>();

    void Awake() {
        S = this; // Set the Mage Singleton
        mPhase = MPhase.idle;
    }

    void Update() {
        // Find whether the mouse button 0 was pressed or released this frame
        bool b0Down = Input.GetMouseButtonDown(0);
        bool b0Up = Input.GetMouseButtonUp(0);

        // Handle all input here (except for Inventory buttons)
        /*
        There are only a few possible actions:                          // 1
        1. Tap on the ground to move to that point
        2. Drag on the ground with no spell selected to move to the Mage
        3. Drag on the ground with spell to cast along the ground
        4. Tap on an enemy to attack (or force-push away without an element)
        */

        // An example of using < to return a bool value
        bool inActiveArea = (float) Input.mousePosition.x / Screen.width <
          ➥activeScreenWidth;

        // This is handled as an if statement instead of switch because a tap
        //  can sometimes happen within a single frame
        if (mPhase == MPhase.idle) { // If the mouse is idle
            if (b0Down && inActiveArea) {
                mouseInfos.Clear();  // Clear the mouseInfos
                AddMouseInfo();      // And add a first MouseInfo

                // If the mouse was clicked on something, it's a valid MouseDown
                if (mouseInfos[0].hit) {    // Something was hit!
```

```
                    MouseDown();              // Call MouseDown()
                    mPhase = MPhase.down;     // and set the mPhase
                }
            }
        }

    if (mPhase == MPhase.down) { // if the mouse is down
        AddMouseInfo(); // Add a MouseInfo for this frame
        if (b0Up) {        // The mouse button was released
            MouseTap(); // This was a tap
            mPhase = MPhase.idle;
        } else if (Time.time - mouseInfos[0].time > mTapTime) {
            // If it's been down longer than a tap, this may be a drag, but
            //  to be a drag, it must also have moved a certain number of
            //  pixels on screen.
            float dragDist = (lastMouseInfo.screenLoc -
                                mouseInfos[0].screenLoc).magnitude;
            if (dragDist >= mDragDist) {
                mPhase = MPhase.drag;
            }
        }
    }

    if (mPhase == MPhase.drag) { // if the mouse is being drug
        AddMouseInfo();
        if (b0Up) {
            // The mouse button was released
            MouseDragUp();
            mPhase = MPhase.idle;
        } else {
            MouseDrag(); // Still dragging
        }
    }
}

// Pulls info about the Mouse, adds it to mouseInfos, and returns it
MouseInfo AddMouseInfo() {
    MouseInfo mInfo = new MouseInfo();
    mInfo.screenLoc = Input.mousePosition;
    mInfo.loc = Utils.mouseLoc; // Gets the position of the mouse at z=0
    mInfo.ray = Utils.mouseRay; // Gets the ray from the Main Camera through
                                //   the mouse pointer
    mInfo.time = Time.time;
    mInfo.Raycast(); // Default is to raycast with no mask

    if (mouseInfos.Count == 0) {
        // If this is the first mouseInfo
        mouseInfos.Add(mInfo); // Add mInfo to mouseInfos
    } else {
```

```
            float lastTime = mouseInfos[mouseInfos.Count-1].time;
            if (mInfo.time != lastTime) {
                // if time has passed since the last mouseInfo
                mouseInfos.Add(mInfo); // Add mInfo to mouseInfos
            }
            // This time test is necessary because AddMouseInfo() could be
            //  called twice in one frame
        }
        return(mInfo); // Return mInfo as well
    }

    public MouseInfo lastMouseInfo {
        // Access to the latest MouseInfo
        get {
            if (mouseInfos.Count == 0) return( null );
            return( mouseInfos[mouseInfos.Count-1] );
        }
    }

    void MouseDown() {
        // The mouse was pressed on something (it could be a drag or tap)
        if (DEBUG) print("Mage.MouseDown()");
    }

    void MouseTap() {
        // Something was tapped like a button
        if (DEBUG) print("Mage.MouseTap()");
    }

    void MouseDrag() {
        // The mouse is being drug across something
        if (DEBUG) print("Mage.MouseDrag()");
    }

    void MouseDragUp() {
        // The mouse is released after being drug
        if (DEBUG) print("Mage.MouseDragUp()");
    }

}
```

1. As you can see in the multiline comment, only a few different kinds of possible mouse interactions are possible:

    1. Tap on the ground to move to that point.
    2. Drag on the ground with no spell selected to move to the Mage.
    3. Drag on the ground with a spell selected to cast along the ground.
    4. Tap on an enemy to attack (or force-push away without an element).

After you have added this code, you can press Play and see the results. If you click the mouse on nothing (the background), nothing happens. Clicking any object will produce a "Mage.Mouse-Tap()" message in the Console window. Clicking and holding (or dragging) will produce "Mage. MouseDrag()" messages followed by a "Mage.MouseDragUp()" message when you release the button.

The `if (DEBUG) print();` statements will only print if the static `Mage.DEBUG` bool is set to true. That way, you can easily turn these comments off when you no longer need them.

Of the four mouse interactions listed in note `// 1`, we'll handle the two types of movement first.

Movement

When the player taps on the ground, the Mage should move there. First we'll add code to control the Mage movement using the Rigidbody (which will make collision happen properly). Add the following bold code to the `Mage` class. This will allow a tap to move the _Mage:

```
public class Mage : PT_MonoBehaviour {
    …
    public float           activeScreenWidth = 1; // % of the screen to use

    public float           speed = 2; // The speed at which _Mage walks

    public bool _____;

    public MPhase          mPhase = MPhase.idle;
    public List<MouseInfo> mouseInfos = new List<MouseInfo>();

    public bool            walking = false;
    public Vector3         walkTarget;
    public Transform       characterTrans;

    void Awake() {
        S = this; // Set the Mage Singleton
        mPhase = MPhase.idle;

        // Find the characterTrans to rotate with Face()
        characterTrans - transform.Find("CharacterTrans");
    }

    …

    void MouseTap() {
        // Something was tapped like a button
        if (DEBUG) print("Mage.MouseTap()");
```

```
        WalkTo(lastMouseInfo.loc); // Walk to the latest mouseInfo pos
    }

    void MouseDragUp() {
        // The mouse is released after being dragged
        print("Mage.MouseDragUp()");
    }

    // Walk to a specific position. The position.z is always 0
    public void WalkTo(Vector3 xTarget) {
        walkTarget = xTarget;     // Set the point to walk to
        walkTarget.z = 0;         // Force z=0
        walking = true;           // Now the Mage is walking
        Face(walkTarget);         // Look in the direction of the walkTarget
    }

    public void Face(Vector3 poi) { // Face toward a point of interest
        Vector3 delta = poi-pos; // Find vector to the point of interest
        // Use Atan2 to get the rotation around Z that points the X-axis of
        // _Mage:CharacterTrans toward poi
        float rZ = Mathf.Rad2Deg * Mathf.Atan2(delta.y, delta.x);
        // Set the rotation of characterTrans (doesn't actually rotate _Mage)
        characterTrans.rotation = Quaternion.Euler(0,0,rZ);
    }

    public void StopWalking() { // Stops the _Mage from walking
        walking = false;
        rigidbody.velocity = Vector3.zero;
    }

    void FixedUpdate () { // Happens every physics step (i.e., 50 times/second)
        if (walking) { // If Mage is walking
            if ( (walkTarget-pos).magnitude < speed*Time.fixedDeltaTime ) {
                // If Mage is very close to walkTarget, just stop there
                pos = walkTarget;
                StopWalking();
            } else {
                // Otherwise, move toward walkTarget
                rigidbody.velocity = (walkTarget-pos).normalized * speed;
            }
        } else {
            // If not walking, velocity should be zero
            rigidbody.velocity = Vector3.zero;
        }
    }

    void OnCollisionEnter( Collision coll ) {
        GameObject otherGO = coll.gameObject;
```

```
            // Colliding with a wall can also stop walking
            Tile ti = otherGO.GetComponent<Tile>();
            if (ti != null) {
                if (ti.height > 0) { // If ti.height is > 0
                    // Then this ti is a wall, and Mage should stop
                    StopWalking();
                }
            }
        }
    }
}
```

Now, when you press Play, your Mage will walk to a point on the ground that you click. However, it would be nice to give the player a little more feedback about the tap.

Adding a Tap Indicator

Create a new C# script in the __Scripts folder named *TapIndicator* and drag it onto the
TapIndicator in the _Prefabs folder. Then open the TapIndicator script in MonoDevelop and
enter this code:

```
using UnityEngine;
using System.Collections;
using System.Collections.Generic;

/*
TapIndicator makes use of the PT_Mover class from ProtoTools. This allows it to
 use a Bezier curve to alter position, rotation, scale, etc.

You'll also notice that this adds several public fields to the Inspector.
*/

public class TapIndicator : PT_Mover {

    public float       lifeTime = 0.4f; // How long will it last
    public float[]     scales; // The scales it interpolates
    public Color[]     colors; // The colors it interpolates

    void Awake() {
        scale = Vector3.zero; // This initially hides the indicator
    }

    void Start () {
        // PT_Mover works based on the PT_Loc class, which contains information
        //  about position, rotation, and scale. It's similar to a Transform but
        //  simpler (and Unity won't let us create Transforms at will).

        PT_Loc pLoc;
        List<PT_Loc> locs = new List<PT_Loc>();
```

```
        // The position is always the same and always at z=-0.1f
        Vector3 tPos = pos;
        tPos.z = -0.1f;

        // You must have an equal number of scales and colors in the Inspector
        for (int i=0; i<scales.Length; i++) {
            pLoc = new PT_Loc();
            pLoc.scale = Vector3.one * scales[i];    // Each scale
            pLoc.pos = tPos;
            pLoc.color = colors[i];                   // and each color

            locs.Add(pLoc);                            // is added to locs
        }

        // callback is a function delegate that can call a void function() when
        //  the move is done
        callback = CallbackMethod;        // Call CallbackMethod() when finished

        // Initiate the move by passing in a series of PT_Locs and duration for
        //  the Bézier curve.
        PT_StartMove(locs, lifeTime);
    }

    void CallbackMethod() {
        Destroy(gameObject);         // When the move is done, Destroy(gameObject)
    }

}
```

As you can see from the code, this creates a fire-and-forget object. It is instantiated, sets up a Bézier curve to interpolate both scale and color (we'll set the values for this in the Inspector next), and when the PT_Mover is done, it calls the `CallbackMethod()` and destroys its own GameObject.

Click on TapIndicator in the _Prefab folder of the Project pane and enter the values shown in Figure 35.3 into the Inspector.

Now, open Mage in MonoDevelop and add the following code to instantiate the TapIndicator:

```
public class Mage : PT_MonoBehaviour {

    …

    public float            mTapTime = 0.1f; // How long is considered a tap
    public GameObject        tapIndicatorPrefab; // Prefab of the tap indicator

    …

    void MouseTap() {
        // Something was tapped like a button
```

```
        if (DEBUG) print("Mage.MouseTap()");

        WalkTo(lastMouseInfo.loc);  // Walk to the latest mouseInfo pos
        ShowTap(lastMouseInfo.loc); // Show where the player tapped
    }

    …

    void OnCollisionEnter( Collision coll ) {
        …
    }

    // Show where the player tapped
    public void ShowTap(Vector3 loc) {
        GameObject go = Instantiate(tapIndicatorPrefab) as GameObject;
        go.transform.position = loc;
    }
}
```

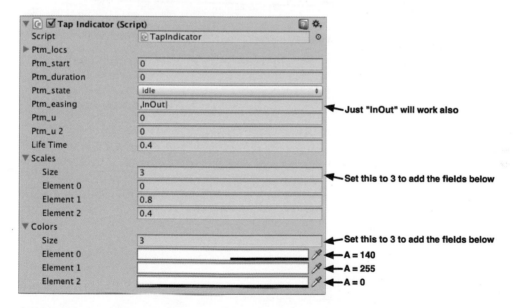

Figure 35.3   Inspector settings TapIndicator:TapIndicator

The last step in implementing the TapIndicator is to set the `tapIndicatorPrefab` field in the _Mage:Mage Inspector. Drag TapIndicator from the _Prefabs folder into the `tapIndicatorPrefab` field on _Mage:Mage, and then press Play. You should now see an indicator whenever you tap, as shown in Figure 35.4.

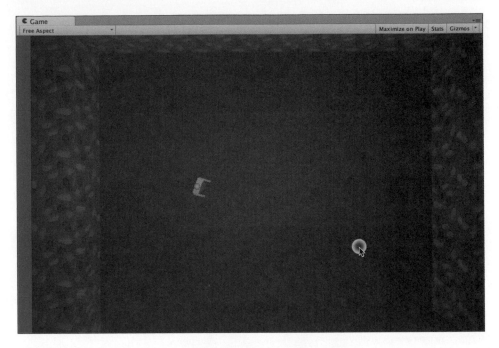

Figure 35.4   The Game pane showing current progress on Omega Mage

Moving When Dragging

The second type of mouse interaction previously listed was "Drag on the ground with no spell selected to move to the Mage." This should also be easy to add. All we need to do is to call `WalkTo()` with a new location whenever the player is dragging the mouse. We also need to tell the Mage to `StopWalking()` when `MouseDragUp()` is called. Otherwise, the Mage will continue moving toward the last location of the players mouse, which doesn't feel right following the continuous motion of leading the Mage with the drag. Add the following bolded code to Mage in MonoDevelop:

```
public class Mage : PT_MonoBehaviour {
    …
    void MouseDrag() {
        // The mouse is being drug across something
        if (DEBUG) print("Mage.MouseDrag()");

        // Continuously walk toward the current mouseInfo pos
        WalkTo(mouseInfos[mouseInfos.Count-1].loc);
    }

    void MouseDragUp() {
        // The mouse is released after being dragged
        if (DEBUG) print("Mage.MouseDragUp()");
```

```
              // Stop walking when the drag is stopped
              StopWalking();
          }
          …
      }
}
```

This mouse interaction was easy, but the remaining two are a little more difficult because they have to do with casting spells. For casting spells, we need an inventory.

The Inventory and Selecting Elements

In Figure 35.1 (at the beginning of the chapter), you saw that the right 1/4 of the screen contains an interface for selecting elements. It's time to build that interface.

Start by adding an `ElementType` enum to the top of the Mage script between `enum MPhase` and class `MouseInfo`. This will allow us to refer to elements by name or number. (You can convert from an enum to an int with a typecast, as you'll see in the next script.)

```
using UnityEngine;
using System.Collections;
using System.Collections.Generic;     // Enables List<>s
using System.Linq;                    // Enables LINQ queries

// The MPhase enum is used to track the phase of Mouse interaction
public enum MPhase {
    …
}

// The ElementType enum
public enum ElementType {
    earth,
    water,
    air,
    fire,
    aether,
    none
}

// MouseInfo stores information about the mouse in each frame of interaction
[System.Serializable]
public class MouseInfo {
    …
}

// Mage is a subclass of PT_MonoBehaviour
public class Mage : PT_MonoBehaviour {
    …
}
```

Create a new C# script in the __Scripts folder named *ElementInventoryButton*. Open it in MonoDevelop and enter the following code:

```
using UnityEngine;
using System.Collections;

public class ElementInventoryButton : MonoBehaviour {

    public ElementType            type;

    void Awake() {
        // Parse the first character of the name of this GameObject into an int
        char c = gameObject.name[0];
        string s = c.ToString();
        int typeNum = int.Parse(s);

        // typecast that int to an ElementType
        type = (ElementType) typeNum;
    }

    void OnMouseUpAsButton() {
        // Tell the Mage to add this element type
        //Mage.S.SelectElement(type);
    }

}
```

Once that is saved and compiles properly, switch back to Unity and drag _InventoryCamera from the _Prefabs folder into the Hierarchy. It should situate itself at P:[-100,0,0] R:[0,0,0] S:[1,1,1].

Open the disclosure triangle next to _InventoryCamera in the Hierarchy, and then attach the ElementInventoryButton script to the child GameObjects *0_Earth*, *1_Water*, *2_Air*, *3_Fire*, and *5_None*. When you press Play, you should see that the ElementInventoryBytton.type of each of these buttons assigns itself due to the Awake() method. You could assign these yourself in the Inspector, of course, but I felt that it was important for you to know that it is possible to convert from stringes to chars to integers to enums.

Adjusting the Two Cameras

As you can see, the _InventoryCamera includes a camera that covers the right 1/4 of the screen and is rendered above the image from _MainCamera. This is controlled by the Viewport Rect and Depth fields in the _InventoryCamera.Camera Inspector. You can see the Inspectors for both _MainCamera and _InventoryCamera in Figure 35.5. _InventoryCamera has a depth of 0, which is greater than the default _MainCamera depth of –1, so the _MainCamera is rendered in the background. However, _MainCamera is still centered in the middle of the screen with 1/4 of its image hidden by _InventoryCamera. Change the Viewport Rect settings of _Main-Camera to those shown in Figure 35.5, and _MainCamera will now only attempt to fill the left 3/4 of the screen. This would also be a good time to choose a different background color for _MainCamera. (I recommend [R:48, G:64, B:48] in the color picker; the alpha setting for a background color is ignored by Unity.)

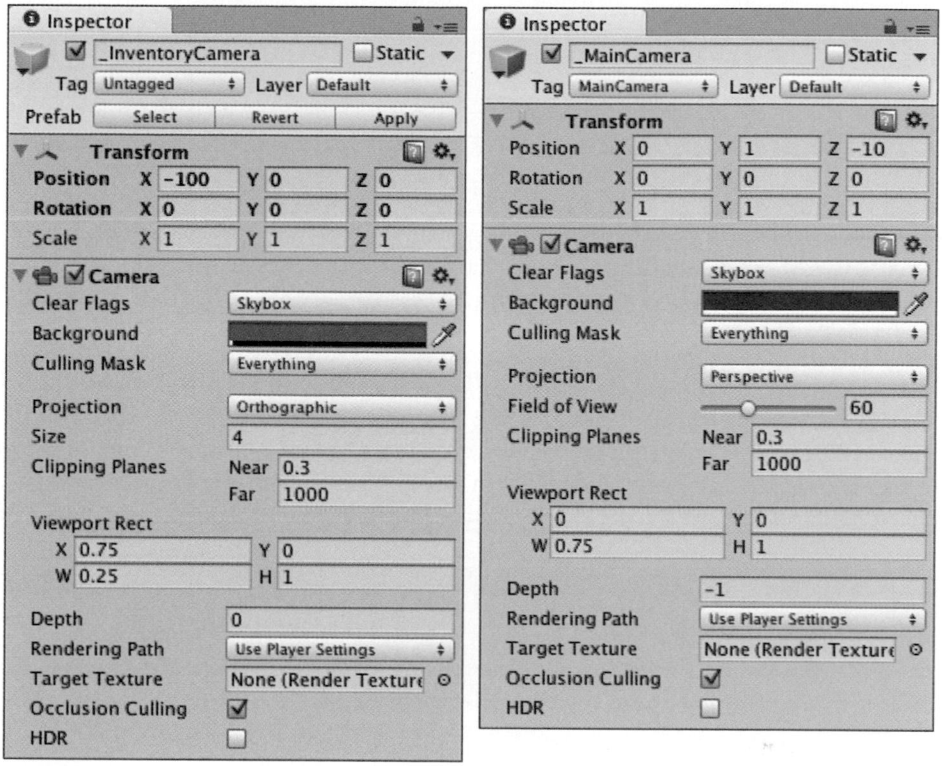

Figure 35.5 Camera Inspectors for _InventoryCamera and _MainCamera

Because this prototype is designed with an iPad in mind, the main screen is meant to be viewed at a 4x3 aspect ratio (the original iPad resolution was 1024x768, while the iPad Air and iPad Mini Retina both have a screen resolution of 2048x1536). To see what this will look like in Unity, choose *4:3* from the aspect ratio pop-up menu in the top-left corner of the Game pane. (If you choose something like 16:9, you will see gray bars on either side of the wooden inventory background.)

The final adjustment you need to do to is to make Mage ignore any clicks or taps in the right 1/4 of the screen. Select Mage in the Hierarchy and set the `activeScreenWidth` field of the *Mage (Script)* Inspector to *0.75*.

Selecting Elements

As you could see in the code for ElementInventoryButton, we need to add a `SelectElement()` method to Mage that will choose an element and cause it to circle the Mage's head. However, before doing that, we need to make the `Element` class and prepare the Element_Sphere GameObject prefabs that will circle the Mage. Create a new C# script in the __Scripts folder named *Element* and enter this code:

```
using UnityEngine;
using System.Collections;

public class Element : PT_MonoBehaviour {
    public ElementType    type;
}
```

As you can see, there's not much to it, but it does extend the PT_MonoBehaviour class, which gives us access to several shortcuts for modifying Element.gameObjects, and it attaches an ElementType field named `type` to each prefab.

Now, in Unity's Project pane, find the four Element_Spheres in the _Prefabs folder. Click *Element_Sphere_Air* and then Shift-click *Element_Sphere_Water* so that they're all four selected. From the menu bar, choose *Component > Scripts > Element*. This will simultaneously add the Element script to all four prefabs. Now, individually select each prefab and choose the appropriate `Element.type` in the Inspector pane for that prefab (for example, set the `type` of Element_Sphere_Air to *air*).

In further iterations of this game (beyond the scope of this book), multiple elements can be selected simultaneously to create different mixed spells as is done in the game *Magicka* by Paradox Interactive—and the code you're about to add to Mage will reflect that possible expansion—but for now, we will only allow the selection of a single element at a time. Add the following bolded code to Mage to implement element selection:

```
public class Mage : PT_MonoBehaviour {
    ...
    public float              speed = 2; // The speed at which _Mage walks

    public GameObject[]       elementPrefabs; // The Element_Sphere Prefabs
    public float              elementRotDist = 0.5f;    // Radius of rotation
    public float              elementRotSpeed = 0.5f;   // Period of rotation
    public int                maxNumSelectedElements = 1;

    public bool  _____;

    ...
    public Transform          characterTrans;

    public List<Element>      selectedElements = new List<Element>();

    ...

    void Update() {
        ...
        if (mPhase == MPhase.down) { // if the mouse is down
            AddMouseInfo(); // Add a MouseInfo for this frame
```

```
        if (b0Up) {
            …

        } else if (Time.time - mouseInfos[0].time > mTapTime) {
            …

            if (dragDist >= mDragDist) {
                mPhase = MPhase.drag;
            }

            // However, drag will immediately start after mTapTime if there
            //   are no elements selected.
            if (selectedElements.Count == 0) {
                mPhase = MPhase.drag;
            }
        }
    }

    if (mPhase == MPhase.drag) {
        …
    }


    OrbitSelectedElements();
}

…


// Show where the player tapped
public void ShowTap(Vector3 loc) {
    GameObject go = Instantiate(tapIndicatorPrefab) as GameObject;
    go.transform.position = loc;
}

// Chooses an Element_Sphere of elType and adds it to selectedElements
public void SelectElement(ElementType elType) {
    if (elType == ElementType.none) {    // If it's the none element…
        ClearElements();                 //   then clear all Elements
        return;                          //   and return
    }

    if (maxNumSelectedElements == 1) {
        // If only one can be selected, clear the existing one…
        ClearElements(); // …so it can be replaced
    }

    // Can't select more than maxNumSelectedElements simultaneously
    if (selectedElements.Count >= maxNumSelectedElements) return;

    // It's okay to add this element
    GameObject go = Instantiate(elementPrefabs[(int) elType]) as GameObject;
    // ^ Note the typecast from ElementType to int in the line above
```

```
        Element el = go.GetComponent<Element>();
        el.transform.parent = this.transform;

        selectedElements.Add(el); // Add el to the list of selectedElements
    }

    // Clears all elements from selectedElements and destroys their GameObjects
    public void ClearElements() {
        foreach (Element el in selectedElements) {
            // Destroy each GameObject in the list
            Destroy(el.gameObject);
        }
        selectedElements.Clear(); // and clear the list
    }

    // Called every Update() to orbit the elements around
    void OrbitSelectedElements() {
        // If there are none selected, just return
        if (selectedElements.Count == 0) return;

        Element el;
        Vector3 vec;
        float theta0, theta;
        float tau = Mathf.PI*2; // tau is 360° in radians (i.e. 6.283…)

        // Divide the circle into the number of elements that are orbiting
        float rotPerElement = tau / selectedElements.Count;

        // The base rotation angle (theta0) is set based on time
        theta0 = elementRotSpeed * Time.time * tau;

        for (int i=0; i<selectedElements.Count; i++) {
            // Determine the rotation angle for each element
            theta = theta0 + i*rotPerElement;
            el = selectedElements[i];
            // Use simple trigonometry to turn the angle into a unit vector
            vec = new Vector3(Mathf.Cos(tvheta),Mathf.Sin(theta),0);
            // Multiply that unit vector by the elementRotDist
            vec *= elementRotDist;
            // Raise the element to waist height.
            vec.z = -0.5f;
            el.lPos = vec;     // Set the position of the Element_Sphere
        }
    }
}
```

Once this has been saved and compiled, return to Unity and select _Mage in the Hierarchy. You will see that the new fields have been added to the *Mage (Script)* Inspector. Open the disclosure triangle next to the `elementPrefabs` field and set its `Size` to *4*. Then drag each of the

Element_Sphere prefabs into the `elementPrefabs` array in the same order as the enum: Earth, Water, Air, and Fire. When finished, your _Mage.Mage (Script)_ Inspector should look like that in Figure 35.6.

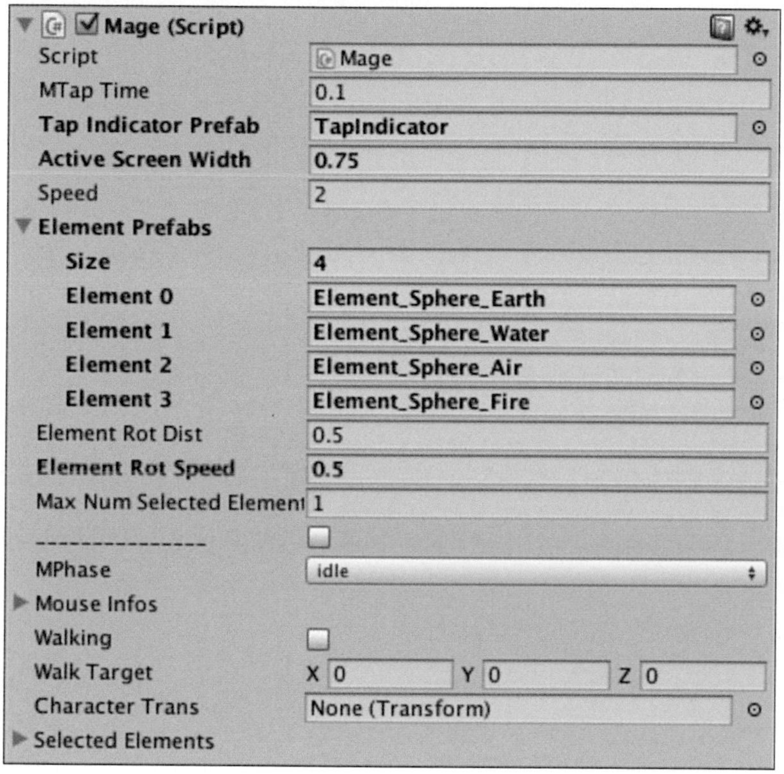

Figure 35.6   Mage (Script) Inspector for _Mage showing elementPrefabs

Open the ElementInventoryButton script in MonoDevelop and remove the comment (`//`) on the line that calls `Mage.S.SelectElement()`:

```
void OnMouseUpAsButton() {
    // Tell the Mage to add this element type
    Mage.S.SelectElement(type);
}
```

Now, when you press Play, you can select a single element, and that element will orbit around the Mage. Clicking the black none element will clear your selection. If you want, you can set `maxNumSelectedElements` in the _Mage (Script)_ Inspector to a higher number (like 4) to see how multiple Element_Spheres would orbit the Mage, but for the purposes of this chapter, set `max-NumSelectedElements` back to 1 when you're done checking that out.

Now that you can select elements, let's do something with them. The game is designed to be able to handle two kinds of spells:

- *Ground spells* are cast on the ground itself and are used for area-of-effect damage to or protection from enemies.
- *Attack spells* are cast directly at a single enemy.

In this chapter, you will be building the fire ground spell.

Casting the Fire Ground Spell

The spell we'll be creating is the fire ground spell. To cast this spell, the player will select a single element and then draw a colored path on the ground that the spell will follow, sprouting a line of flame to discourage enemies.

For this to work, we need more information about where the player initially started the mouse interaction or touch: Was it over the ground, an enemy, or the Mage? This information will change how the rest of the mouse gesture is interpreted. This will be accomplished by adding tags to various GameObjects (including the Mage, the TilePrefab, and various enemies) and then using the `Utils.FindTaggedParent()` function from the SHMUP prototype. However, because `Utils.FindTaggedParent()` will return null if nothing in the parent Hierarchy is tagged, that case needs to be handled as well.

Add the bolded code to the Mage C# script:

```
public class Mage : PT_MonoBehaviour {
    …
    public MPhase          mPhase = MPhase.idle;
    public List<MouseInfo> mouseInfos = new List<MouseInfo>();
    public string          actionStartTag; // ["Mage", "Ground", "Enemy"]

    public bool            walking = false;

    …

    void MouseDown() {
        // The mouse was pressed on something (it could be a drag or tap)
        if (DEBUG) print("Mage.MouseDown()");

        GameObject clickedGO = mouseInfos[0].hitInfo.collider.gameObject;
        // ^ If the mouse wasn't clicked on anything, this would throw an error
        //    because hitInfo would be null. However, we know that MouseDown()
        //    is only called when the mouse WAS clicking on something, so
        //    hitInfo is guaranteed to be defined.

        GameObject taggedParent = Utils.FindTaggedParent(clickedGO);
        if (taggedParent == null) {
```

```
            actionStartTag = "";
        } else {
            actionStartTag = taggedParent.tag;
            // ^ this should be either "Ground", "Mage", or "Enemy"
        }
    }

    void MouseTap() {
        // Something was tapped like a button
        if (DEBUG) print("Mage.MouseTap()");

        // Now this cares what was tapped
        switch (actionStartTag) {
        case "Mage":
            // Do nothing
            break;
        case "Ground":
            // Move to tapped point @ z=0 whether or not an element is selected
            WalkTo(lastMouseInfo.loc);  // Walk to the first mouseInfo pos
            ShowTap(lastMouseInfo.loc); // Show where the player tapped
            break;
        }
    }

    void MouseDrag() {
        // The mouse is being drug across something
        if (DEBUG) print("Mage.MouseDrag()");

        // Drag is meaningless unless the mouse started on the ground
        if (actionStartTag != "Ground") return;

        // If there is no element selected, the player should follow the mouse
        if (selectedElements.Count == 0) {
            // Continuously walk toward the current mouseInfo pos
            WalkTo(mouseInfos[mouseInfos.Count-1].loc);
        }
    }

    void MouseDragUp() {
        // The mouse is released after being drug
        if (DEBUG) print("Mage.MouseDragUp()");

        // Drag is meaningless unless the mouse started on the ground
        if (actionStartTag != "Ground") return;

        // If there is no element selected, stop walking now
        if (selectedElements.Count == 0) {
            // Stop walking when the drag is stopped
            StopWalking();
```

```
        }
    }
    ...
}
```

Once this code is done, the tags need to be added to a couple of objects. Because of the `Utils.FindTaggedParent()` method, only the topmost parent needs to have the tag, which will help a lot with complex objects—like the Mage—that have several colliders on them.

Select _Mage in the Hierarchy and choose *Add Tag* from the Tag pop-up menu at the top of the _Mage Inspector. In the Tags array, add tags for *Mage*, *Ground*, and *Enemy*. Once this is complete, select _Mage in the Hierarchy again and set its tag to *Mage*. Select *TilePrefab* in the _Prefabs folder of the Project pane and set its tag to *Ground*. Now save your scene and press Play.

You should see now that tapping on _Mage or dragging from _Mage to anywhere else doesn't do anything. Tapping on the ground still moves _Mage like normal, and dragging on the ground causes _Mage to follow only if no elements are selected.

Using a LineRenderer to Cast a Ground Spell

When an element is selected, we want to draw a line on the ground in the color of that element and then cast an elemental ground spell (in this case, a fire spell). The line can be drawn through the use of a LineRenderer, which is the same standard Unity component that is used for the built-in TrailRenderer. However, the LineRenderer is a little bit lower level and more controllable.

Only one line needs to be drawn at a time, so we only need a single LineRenderer component. Select _Mage in the Hierarchy and from the menu bar select *Component > Effects > Line Renderer*. You'll see that there is now an ugly pink line segment near your _Mage. We'll soon make it look much nicer.

You'll also notice that there is now a LineRenderer component in the _Mage Inspector. Open the disclosure triangle next to `Materials` in the LineRenderer Inspector and click the little circle to the right of Element 0. This will bring up a list of all the materials in the project. Choose *Default-Particle* from the end of the list (it's one of the few default materials included in every Unity project). This material works particularly well for lines, trails, and simple particles. The line should now look a lot nicer.

Uncheck the boxes next to *Cast Shadows* and *Receive Shadows* in the LineRenderer Inspector. Open the disclosure triangle next to *Parameters* and set both *Start Width* and *End Width* to *0.2*. Finally, now that the LineRenderer is ready, uncheck the box next to LineRenderer to disable it. (We'll enable it through code when needed.) When finished, your LineRenderer settings should look like those in the left image of Figure 35.7.

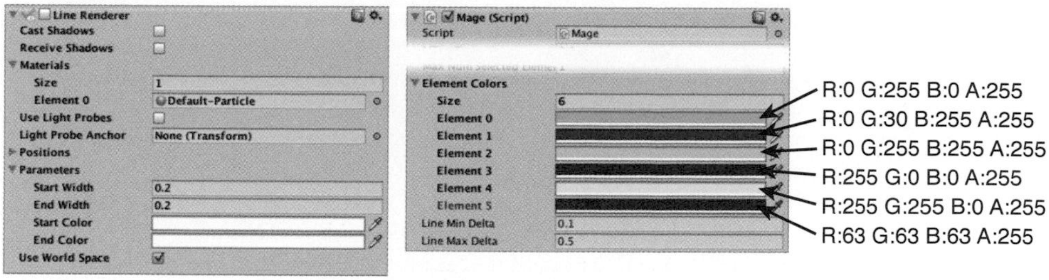

Figure 35.7 _Mage:LineRenderer settings and _Mage:Mage.ElementColor settings

Open the Mage script in MonoDevelop and add the bolded code that follows to implement the line renderer:

```
public class Mage : PT_MonoBehaviour {
    …
    public int            maxNumSelectedElements = 1;
    public Color[]        elementColors;

    public bool _____;

    public List<Vector3>    linePts; // Points to be shown in the line
    protected LineRenderer  liner; // Ref to the LineRenderer Component
    protected float         lineZ = -0.1f; // Z depth of the line
    // ^ protected variables are between public and private.
    //     public variables can be seen by everyone
    //     private variables can only be seen by this class
    //     protected variables can be seen by this class or any subclasses
    //     only public variables appear in the Inspector
    //     (or those with [SerializeField] in the preceding line)
    public MPhase         mPhase = MPhase.idle;
    …

    void Awake() {
        S = this; // Set the Mage Singleton
        mPhase = MPhase.idle;

        // Find the characterTrans to rotate with Face()
        characterTrans = transform.Find("CharacterTrans");

        // Get the LineRenderer component and disable it
        liner = GetComponent<LineRenderer>();
        liner.enabled = false;
    }

    …
```

```
void MouseDrag() {
    …
    // If there is no element selected, the player should follow the mouse
    if (selectedElements.Count == 0) {
        // Continuously walk towards the current mouseInfo pos
        WalkTo(mouseInfos[mouseInfos.Count-1].loc);
    } else {
        // This is a ground spell, so we need to draw a line
        AddPointToLiner( mouseInfos[mouseInfos.Count-1].loc );
        // ^ add the most recent MouseInfo.loc to liner
    }
}

void MouseDragUp() {
    …
    // If there is no element selected, stop walking now
    if (selectedElements.Count == 0) {
        // Stop walking when the drag is stopped
        StopWalking();
    } else {
        //TODO: Cast the Spell

        // Clear the liner
        ClearLiner();
    }
}

…

void OrbitSelectedElements() {
    …
}


//--------------- LineRenderer Code ---------------//

// Add a new point to the line.
void AddPointToLiner(Vector3 pt) {
    pt.z = lineZ; // Set the z of the pt to lineZ to elevate it slightly
                  //  above the ground

    linePts.Add(pt);
    UpdateLiner();

}

// Update the LineRenderer with the new points
public void UpdateLiner() {
```

```
        // Get the type of the selectedElement
        int el = (int) selectedElements[0].type;

        // Set the line color based on that type
        liner.SetColors(elementColors[el],elementColors[el]);

        // Update the representation of the ground spell about to be cast
        liner.SetVertexCount(linePts.Count);  // Set the number of vertices
        for (int i=0; i<linePts.Count; i++) {
            liner.SetPosition(i, linePts[i]); // Set each vertex
        }
        liner.enabled = true;                   // Enable the LineRenderer
    }

    public void ClearLiner() {
        liner.enabled = false;  // Disable the LineRenderer
        linePts.Clear();        // and clear all linePts
    }

}
```

Once you save and compile this, you're going to need to set up the elementColors array in the _Mage:Mage (Script)_ Inspector. Fill the 6 elements of elementColors with the colors shown in the right image of Figure 35.7. Save your scene and press Play. Now, when you select an element and drag on the ground, a line shows where the spell will be cast. However, the line probably looks a little glitchy now. This is because some points in the line are too close together, and others are too far apart. The following changes to the Mage class code will improve this. It will also add a maximum total line length, after which point, the line will no longer draw. This will prevent players from casting ridiculously long spells.

```
public class Mage : PT_MonoBehaviour {
    …
    public Color[]            elementColors;

    // These set the min and max distance between two line points
    public float              lineMinDelta = 0.1f;
    public float              lineMaxDelta = 0.5f;
    public float              lineMaxLength = 8f;

    public bool _____;

    public float              totalLineLength;
    public List<Vector3>      linePts; // Points to be shown in the line

    …
```

```
//--------------- LineRenderer Code ----------------//

// Add a new point to the line. This ignores the point if it's too close to
//   existing ones and adds extra points if it's too far away
void AddPointToLiner(Vector3 pt) {
    pt.z = lineZ; // Set the z of the pt to lineZ to elevate it slightly
    //   above the ground

    //linePts.Add(pt);            // COMMENT OUT OR DELETE THESE TWO LINES!!!
    //UpdateLiner();              // COMMENT OUT OR DELETE THESE TWO LINES!!!

    // Always add the point if linePts is empty…
    if (linePts.Count == 0) {
        linePts.Add (pt);
        totalLineLength = 0;
        return; // …but wait for a second point to enable the LineRenderer
    }

    // If the line is too long already, return
    if (totalLineLength > lineMaxLength) return;

    // If there is a previous point (pt0), then find how far pt is from it
    Vector3 pt0 = linePts[linePts.Count-1]; // Get the last point in linePts
    Vector3 dir = pt-pt0;
    float delta = dir.magnitude;
    dir.Normalize();

    totalLineLength += delta;

    // If it's less than the min distance
    if ( delta < lineMinDelta ) {
        // …then it's too close; don't add it
        return;
    }

    // If it's further than the max distance then extra points…
    if (delta > lineMaxDelta) {
        // …then add extra points in between
        float numToAdd = Mathf.Ceil(delta/lineMaxDelta);
        float midDelta = delta/numToAdd;
        Vector3 ptMid;
        for (int i=1; i<numToAdd; i++) {
            ptMid = pt0+(dir*midDelta*i);
            linePts.Add(ptMid);
        }
    }
```

```
        linePts.Add(pt); // Add the point
        UpdateLiner();   // And finally update the line
    }
    …
}
```

Now the line should display much more smoothly, and it should stop drawing at the point that it's about 8 meters long (that is, 8 Unity units long).

The Fire Spell

Now that we can see the line where the spell will go, It's time to cast a spell. Drag FireGround-SpellPrefab from the _Prefabs folder of the Project pane into the scene, and you can get a preview of what the spell will look like. You can also take this time to examine its *Particle System* component, which is generating all of the fire particles. Once you're done exploring it, delete the instance from the Hierarchy (though not from the Project pane, of course).

Open the Mage script and add the following code:

```
public class Mage : PT_MonoBehaviour {
    …

    public GameObject          fireGroundSpellPrefab;

    public bool _____;

    protected Transform        spellAnchor; // The parent transform for all spells

    …

    void Awake() {
        …
        liner.enabled = false;

        GameObject saGO = new GameObject("Spell Anchor");
        // ^ Create an empty GameObject named "Spell Anchor". When you create a
        //    new GameObject this way, it's at P:[0,0,0] R:[0,0,0] S:[1,1,1]
        spellAnchor = saGO.transform; // Get its transform
    }

    …

    void MouseDragUp() {
        …
        // If there is no element selected, stop walking now
        if (selectedElements.Count == 0) {
            // Stop walking when the drag is stopped
            StopWalking();
        } else {
```

```
                CastGroundSpell();
                // Clear the liner
                ClearLiner();
            }
        }


    void CastGroundSpell() {
        // There is not a no-element ground spell, so return
        if (selectedElements.Count == 0) return;

        // Because this version of the prototype only allows a single element to
        //   be selected, we can use that 0th element to pick the spell.
        switch (selectedElements[0].type) {
        case ElementType.fire:
            GameObject fireGO;
            foreach( Vector3 pt in linePts ) { // For each Vector3 in linePts…
                // …create an instance of fireGroundSpellPrefab
                fireGO = Instantiate(fireGroundSpellPrefab) as GameObject;
                fireGO.transform.parent = spellAnchor;
                fireGO.transform.position = pt;
            }
            break;
//TODO: Add other elements types later
        }

        // Clear the selectedElements; they're consumed by the spell
        ClearElements();
    }
    …
}
```

Save the Mage script and return to Unity. You will now see a `fireGroundSpellPrefab` field on the *_Mage.Mage (Script)* Inspector. Drag the FireGroundSpellPrefab from the _Prefabs folder of the Project pane into this field and save your scene. Now, when you play the scene, you can choose a fire element and cast a fire spell on the ground. However, that spell lasts forever right now.

Fire-and-Forget Spells

One of the aspects of the way this game is designed is that spells should be able to be cast by the Mage script and then forgotten. Rather than the Mage script managing the duration, damage, and behavior of the spell, the individual spell prefabs can manage themselves. To accomplish this for the fire ground spell, create a new C# script in the __Scripts folder named *FireGroundSpell* and attach it to the FireGroundSpellPrefab in the _Prefabs folder. Open the script in MonoDevelop and enter this code:

```csharp
using UnityEngine;
using System.Collections;

// Extends PT_MonoBehaviour
public class FireGroundSpell : PT_MonoBehaviour {

    public float         duration = 4; // Lifetime of this GameObject
    public float         durationVariance = 0.5f;
    // ^ This allows the duration to range from 3.5 to 4.5
    public float         fadeTime = 1f; // Length of time to fade
    public float         timeStart; // Birth time of this GameObject

    // Use this for initialization
    void Start () {
        timeStart = Time.time;
        duration = Random.Range(duration-durationVariance,
                                duration+durationVariance);
        // ^ Set the duration to a number between 3.5 and 4.5 (defaults)
    }


    // Update is called once per frame
    void Update () {
        // Determine a number [0..1] (between 0 and 1) that stores the
        //   percentage of duration that has passed
        float u = (Time.time-timeStart)/duration;

        // At what u value should this start fading
        float fadePercent = 1-(fadeTime/duration);
        if (u>fadePercent) { // If it's after the time to start fading…
            // …then sink into the ground
            float u2 = (u-fadePercent)/(1-fadePercent);
            // ^ u2 is a number [0..1] for just the fadeTime
            Vector3 loc = pos;
            loc.z = u2*2; // move lower over time
            pos = loc;
        }

        if (u>1) { // If this has lived longer than duration…
            Destroy(gameObject); // …destroy it
        }
    }


    void OnTriggerEnter(Collider other) {
        // Announce when another object enters the collider
        GameObject go = Utils.FindTaggedParent(other.gameObject);
        if (go == null) {
            go = other.gameObject;
```

```
        }
        Utils.tr("Flame hit",go.name);
    }

//TODO: Actually damage the other object

}
```

Now, when you play the scene, you will see that after you cast the fire ground spell, each spurt of fire lasts for about 4 seconds and dies out. In addition, if you make the Mage walk through the fire, the "Flame hit" announcement will appear in the Console. The Mage's spells won't damage her of course, so let's give her a way to look for some enemies that she can damage.

Changing Rooms

As a kindness to our Mage, the first room doesn't have any monsters in it, but there will certainly be some throughout the dungeon. The Mage needs a way to move from room to room. This will be accomplished with the PortalPrefab in the _Prefabs folder and some scripting. If you inspect the PortalPrefab, note that it is in the *Ignore Raycast* layer. Unity automatically includes this layer in every project, and we're using it here to ensure that the `Physics.Raycast()` done by MouseInfo ignores the PortalPrefab and falls through to the Tile beyond it.

Create a new C# script named *Portal* and place it in the __Scripts folder. Then, attach it to the PortalPrefab prefab in the _Prefabs folder. Open the Portal script in MonoDevelop and enter the following code:

```
using UnityEngine;
using System.Collections;

public class Portal : PT_MonoBehaviour {

    public string    toRoom;
    public bool      justArrived = false;
    // ^ true if _Mage has just teleported here

    void OnTriggerEnter(Collider other) {
        if (justArrived) return;
        // ^ Since the Mage has just arrived, don't teleport her back

        // Get the GameObject of the collider
        GameObject go = other.gameObject;
        // Search up for a tagged parent
        GameObject goP = Utils.FindTaggedParent(go);
        if (goP != null) go = goP;

        // If this isn't the _Mage, return
        if (go.tag != "Mage") return;
```

```
        // Go ahead and build the next room
        LayoutTiles.S.BuildRoom(toRoom);
    }

    void OnTriggerExit(Collider other) {
        // Once the Mage leaves this Portal, set justArrived to false
        if (other.gameObject.tag == "Mage") {
            justArrived = false;
        }
    }

}
```

The `justArrived` bool is important because it keeps the Mage from immediately being tele-ported back to the previous room. If `justArrived` wasn't there, the Mage appearing in the new room (above the Portal) would invoke `OnTriggerEnter()` and be sent back to the previous room.

Now, we need to make several changes to the LayoutTiles script to allow it to build rooms more than once (and to allow it to destroy the old room Tiles that are being replaced). Open Layout-Tiles and edit the code as shown in bold here:

```
public class LayoutTiles : MonoBehaviour {
    …
    public TileTex[]        tileTextures; // A list of named textures for Tiles
    public GameObject       portalPrefab; // Prefab for the portals between rooms

    public bool _____;

    private bool            firstRoom = true; // Is this the first room built?
    public PT_XMLReader     roomsXMLR;
    …

    public Texture2D GetTileTex(string tStr) {
        …
    }

    // Build a room based on room number. This is an alternative version of
    //  BuildRoom that grabs roomXML based on <room> num.
    public void BuildRoom(string rNumStr) {
        PT_XMLHashtable roomHT = null;
        for (int i=0; i<roomsXML.Count; i++) {
            PT_XMLHashtable ht = roomsXML[i];
            if (ht.att("num") == rNumStr) {
                roomHT = ht;
                break;
            }
        }
        if (roomHT == null) {
```

```
            Utils.tr("ERROR","LayoutTiles.BuildRoom()",
                    "Room not found: "+rNumStr);
            return;
        }
        BuildRoom(roomHT);
    }


    // Build a room from an XML <room> entry
    public void BuildRoom(PT_XMLHashtable room) {
        // Destroy any old Tiles
        foreach (Transform t in tileAnchor) { // Clear out old tiles
            // ^ You can iterate over a Transform to get its children
            Destroy(t.gameObject);
        }


        // Move the Mage out of the way
        Mage.S.pos = Vector3.left * 1000;
        // ^ This keeps the Mage from accidentally triggering OnTriggerExit() on
        //   a Portal. In my testing, I found that OnTriggerExit was being called
        //   at strange times.
        Mage.S.ClearInput(); // Cancel any active mouse input and drags

        string rNumStr = room.att("num");

        // Get the texture names for the floors and walls from <room> attributes
        ...
        float maxY = roomRows.Length-1;
        List<Portal> portals = new List<Portal>();

        // These loops scan through each tile of each row of the room
        for (int y=0; y<roomRows.Length; y++) {
            for (int x=0; x<roomRows[y].Length; x++) {
                ...
                ti.tex = tileTexStr;

                // Check for specific entities in the room
                switch (rawType) {
                case "X": // Starting position for the Mage
                    // Mage.S.pos = ti.pos;              // COMMENT OUT THIS LINE!
                    if (firstRoom) {
                        Mage.S.pos = ti.pos; // Uses the Mage Singleton
                        roomNumber = rNumStr;
                        // ^ Setting roomNumber now keeps any portals from
                        //     moving the Mage to them in this first room.
                        firstRoom = false;
                    }
                    break;
```

```
            case "0":  // Numbers are room portals (up to F in hexadecimal)
            case "1":  // This allows portals to be placed in the Rooms.xml file
            case "2":
            case "3":
            case "4":
            case "5":
            case "6":
            case "7":
            case "8":
            case "9":
            case "A":
            case "B":
            case "C":
            case "D":
            case "E":
            case "F":
                // Instantiate a Portal
                GameObject pGO = Instantiate(portalPrefab) as GameObject;
                Portal p = pGO.GetComponent<Portal>();
                p.pos = ti.pos;
                p.transform.parent = tileAnchor;
                // ^ Attaching this to the tileAnchor means that the Portal
                //    will be Destroyed when a new room is built
                p.toRoom = rawType;
                portals.Add(p);
                break;

            }

        // More to come here…

        }
    }


// Position the Mage
foreach (Portal p in portals) {
    // If p.toRoom is the same as the room number the Mage just exited,
    //  then the Mage should enter this room through this Portal
    // Alternatively, if firstRoom == true and there was no X in the
    //  room (as a default Mage starting point), move the Mage to this
    //  Portal as a backup measure (if, for instance, you want to just
    //  load room number "5")
    if (p.toRoom == roomNumber || firstRoom) {
        // ^ If there's an X in the room, firstRoom will be set to false
        //    by the time the code gets here
        Mage.S.StopWalking(); // Stop any Mage movement
        Mage.S.pos = p.pos; // Move _Mage to this Portal location
        // _Mage maintains her facing from the previous room, so there
```

```
                      //  is no need to rotate her in order for her to enter this room
                      //  facing the right direction.
                      p.justArrived = true;
                      // ^ Tell the Portal that Mage has just arrived.
                      firstRoom = false;
                      // ^ Stops a 2nd Portal in this room from moving the Mage to it
                  }
              }

              // Finally assign the roomNumber
              roomNumber = rNumStr;
          }
      }
```

For this code to compile properly, you need to add a few lines to Mage as well. Open Mage in
MonoDevelop and add the `ClearInput()` method to the end of the `Mage` class:

```
public class Mage : PT_MonoBehaviour {
    …
    public void ClearLiner() {
        liner.enabled = false;    // Disable the LineRenderer
        linePts.Clear();          // and clear all linePts
    }

    // Stop any active drag or other mouse input
    public void ClearInput() {
        mPhase = MPhase.idle;
    }
}
```

Save and switch back to Unity. Select _MainCamera in the Hierarchy and find the _MainCamera.
LayoutTiles (Script) Inspector. Drag PortalPrefab from the _Prefabs folder in the Project pane into
the `portalPrefab` field of the LayoutTiles (Script) Inspector. Now is a good time to also make
sure that the `roomNumber` field is set to 0 so that your Mage starts in the correct room.

Save your scene, press Play, and you'll see that the Mage can now walk from room to room
by walking into portals. Try exploring the entire dungeon if you like. Now that the Mage can
explore, it's time to give her some enemies.

Spawning Enemies

In addition to storing information about the Tile layout of the room, the Rooms.xml file also
includes information about two different kinds of enemies: bugs and spikers. These are
represented in the Rooms.xml file by a b for the bug and a ^, v, {, or } for the spikers (because
the spikers need to have an initial direction set for them). Note that the < and > angle brackets
couldn't be used because they are special reserved characters in XML files.

All Enemies

All enemies in the game will share certain traits. Each will have some sort of simple movement. Most will be damaged by spells. Each will damage the Mage if they collide with her. Each will have a collider of some sort that is used to determine what it is colliding with.

Because so many aspects of all enemies are shared, it makes sense to handle them in some sort of hierarchical, object-oriented way. In the SHMUP prototype, we implemented an `Enemy` superclass with several subclasses. For this prototype—to demonstrate something different—we'll implement an *interface* instead. Look at the "Interfaces" section in Appendix B, "Useful Concepts," for an introduction to the concept.

Briefly, an interface declares methods or properties that will later be implemented by a class. Any class that implements the interface can then be referred to in code as that interface type rather than as the specific class. This differs from subclassing in several ways, one of the most interesting of which is that a class may implement several different interfaces simultaneously, whereas a class can only extend a single superclass.

We will also create a *factory* to instantiate the various enemy types for us. This will be an adaptation of the classic Factory Pattern described in the book *Design Patterns* by the "Gang of Four."[1] When the `LayoutTiles.BuildRoom()` method encounters a character that it doesn't understand (like the b, ^, v, {, or }), it will pass it to the `EnemyFactory.Instantiate()` method to see whether an enemy should be created. A diagram of this concept is shown in Figure 35.8. `EnemyFactory.Instantiate()` is a "factory" because it can create any number of different classes and return them to LayoutTiles as long as they all implement the `Enemy` interface. For more information about other design patterns, see the "Software Design Patterns" section of Appendix B.

There are two ways to approach designing something like this. One is to think really hard about it ahead of time and try to foresee all the possible parts of each Enemy type's behavior that you want to abstract into the interface. The other is to just build a couple of enemies, see what methods they have in common, and then add those to the interface. The second method is much more akin to the iterative process of design that is used throughout this book, though it can lead to less flexibility and extensibility. Most of the time, I do a mixture of the two methods with a weighting toward the second. I try to just start coding something with both the knowledge that I will have to refactor some of the code later and a weather eye toward things that I will want to abstract into an interface or superclass later. With that in mind, let's make the EnemyBug work.

---

[1] Erich Gamma, Richard Helm, Ralph Johnson, and John Vissides. *Design Patterns: Elements of Reusable Object-Oriented Software.* Reading, MA: Addison-Wesley, 1994. The Factory Pattern is one of many described in the book. Others include the Singleton Pattern that has been used in many of the tutorials in this book.

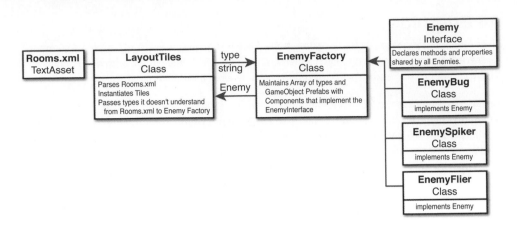

Figure 35.8 Conceptual structure of EnemyFactory

EnemyBug

Bugs are a very basic kind of enemy. They will simply move toward the Mage if she's in the same room with them. Bugs have no knowledge of walls or the layout of the room and will therefore happily walk into a wall rather than navigating around to get to the player. (If you want to make them more intelligent later, you can add A* pathfinding (pronounced "A-star") or use Unity's navigation mesh.) Bugs are damaged by—but unafraid of—fire and will damage the Mage if they touch her.

Let's start by making the EnemyBug chase after the player. Create a new C# script named *EnemyBug*, and place it in the __Scripts folder. Then drag it on to EnemyBug in the _Prefabs folder.

Next, drag an instance of EnemyBug from the _Prefabs folder into the Hierarchy. Ensure that its position is P:[8,4,0], which will place it in the same room with the player once LayoutTiles has built the 0th room (but still keep it far enough away that you have lots of time to cast a spell on it before it reaches you). If you explore EnemyBug in the Hierarchy, you can see that it is constructed very much like _Mage, with a top-level GameObject (EnemyBug) that contains a Rigidbody and CapsuleCollider. EnemyBug parents a child named CharacterTrans that is used to parent and rotate a child named View_Bug that actually has the model of the Bug seen by the player. As with View_Character, View_Bug also has individual colliders on each of its body parts. This is more important with View_Bug than View_Character because View_Bug's legs stick out farther than the boundary of the CapsuleCollider on EnemyBug.

Open the EnemyBug script and enter the following code. As you can see, it's almost entirely cut and pasted from Mage. In general, when you're coding large systems, you don't want to cut and paste code like this. However, when prototyping, it's very useful to copy and paste at first and then—once you know exactly what you want—you can abstract the code later.

```
using UnityEngine;
using System.Collections;
using System.Collections.Generic;
```

```
public class EnemyBug : PT_MonoBehaviour {
    public float            speed = 0.5f;

    public bool _____;

    public Vector3          walkTarget;
    public bool             walking;
    public Transform        characterTrans;


    void Awake() {
        characterTrans = transform.Find("CharacterTrans");
    }

    void Update() {
        WalkTo (Mage.S.pos);
    }

    // --------------- Walking Code ----------------
    // All of this walking code is copied directly from Mage

    // Walk to a specific position. The position.z is always 0
    public void WalkTo(Vector3 xTarget) {
        walkTarget = xTarget;      // Set the point to walk to
        walkTarget.z = 0;          // Force z=0
        walking = true;            // Now the EnemyBug is walking
        Face(walkTarget);          // Look in the direction of the walkTarget
    }

    public void Face(Vector3 poi) { // Face towards a point of interest
        Vector3 delta = poi-pos; // Find vector to the point of interest
        // Use Atan2 to get the rotation around Z that points the X-axis of
        //   EnemyBug:CharacterTrans towards poi
        float rZ = Mathf.Rad2Deg * Mathf.Atan2(delta.y, delta.x);
        // Set the rotation of characterTrans (doesn't actually rotate Enemy)
        characterTrans.rotation = Quaternion.Euler(0,0,rZ);
    }

    public void StopWalking() { // Stops the EnemyBug from walking
        walking = false;
        rigidbody.velocity = Vector3.zero;
    }

    void FixedUpdate () { // Happens every physics step (i.e., 50 times/second)
        if (walking) { // If EnemyBug is walking
            if ( (walkTarget-pos).magnitude < speed*Time.fixedDeltaTime ) {
                // If EnemyBug is very close to walkTarget, just stop there
                pos = walkTarget;
                StopWalking();
```

```
            } else {
                // Otherwise, move towards walkTarget
                rigidbody.velocity = (walkTarget-pos).normalized * speed;
            }
        } else {
            // If not walking, velocity should be zero
            rigidbody.velocity = Vector3.zero;
        }
    }

}
```

Press Play, and you'll see that your Mage will now be chased by an EnemyBug. If you cast a fire spell on the ground and the bug walks through it. You will also get a message about it in the Console pane. However, the fire doesn't actually hurt the bug yet.

Damaging the EnemyBug

We need to add a function that allows the bug to be hurt. Add the following code to EnemyBug:

```
public class EnemyBug : PT_MonoBehaviour {
    public float            speed = 0.5f;
    public float            health = 10;

    public bool _____;

    private float           _maxHealth;
    public Vector3          walkTarget;
    public bool             walking;
    public Transform        characterTrans;

    void Awake() {
        characterTrans = transform.Find("CharacterTrans");
        _maxHealth = health; // Used to put a top cap on healing
    }

    …

    void FixedUpdate () { // Happens every physics step (i.e., 50 times/second)
        …
    }

    // Damage this instance. By default, the damage is instant, but it can also
    //  be treated as damage over time, where the amt value would be the amount
    //  of damage done every second.
    // NOTE: This same code can be used to heal the instance
    public void Damage(float amt, bool damageOverTime=false) {
        // If it's DOT, then only damage the fractional amount for this frame
        if (damageOverTime) {
```

```
        amt *= Time.deltaTime;
    }

    health -= amt;
    health = Mathf.Min(_maxHealth, health); // Limit health if healing

    if (health <= 0) {
        Die();
    }
}

// Making Die() a separate function allows us to add things later like
//  different death animations, dropping something for the player, etc.
public void Die() {
    Destroy(gameObject);
}
}
```

Now that the EnemyBug has the ability to be damaged, it's time to make the FireGroundSpell do so. Open FireGroundSpell and enter the following code:

```
public class FireGroundSpell : PT_MonoBehaviour {
    …
    public float        timeStart; // Birth time of this GameObject
    public float        damagePerSecond = 10;

    …

    void OnTriggerEnter(Collider other) {
        …
    }

    void OnTriggerStay(Collider other) {
        // Actually damage the other
        // Get a reference to the EnemyBug script component of the other
        EnemyBug recipient = other.GetComponent<EnemyBug>();
        // If there is an EnemyBug component, dmage it with fire
        if (recipient != null) {
            recipient.Damage(damagePerSecond, true);
        }
    }
}
```

Save, press Play, and cast a fire spell on the ground between _Mage and EnemyBug. You'll see that the bug disappears shortly after touching the fire. However, if you pay attention, you'll notice that the bug actually dies too quickly. The fire spell does 10 damage/second, and the EnemyBug has 10 health, so it should take 1 second to die, but it's happening faster than that. This is because the bug is touching multiple individual FireGroundSpellPrefab instances, and each one is damaging it individually. The way that damage is done to the EnemyBug needs to be modified so that the bug doesn't take compound damage from multiple instances of the same spell. We need to modify the `Damage()` method of EnemyBug so that it also takes information on the type of damage that is done and treats different types of damage differently. First, replace the `recipient.Damage()` line you just added to the end of FireGroundSpell with this one:

```
// If there is an EnemyBug component, damage it with fire
if (recipient != null) {
    recipient.Damage(damagePerSecond, ElementType.fire, true);
}
```

Then, edit EnemyBug as shown in the following code. Note that you'll be replacing most of the `Damage()` method:

```
public class EnemyBug : PT_MonoBehaviour {
    …
    public Transform          characterTrans;
    // Stores damage for each element each frame
    public Dictionary<ElementType,float>    damageDict;
    // ^ NOTE: Dictionaries do not appear in the Unity Inspector

    void Awake() {
        characterTrans = transform.Find("CharacterTrans");
        _maxHealth = health; // Always starts with max health
        ResetDamageDict();
    }

    // Resets the values for the damageDict
    void ResetDamageDict() {
        if (damageDict == null) {
            damageDict = new Dictionary<ElementType, float>();
        }
        damageDict.Clear();
        damageDict.Add(ElementType.earth, 0);
        damageDict.Add(ElementType.water, 0);
        damageDict.Add(ElementType.air,   0);
        damageDict.Add(ElementType.fire,  0);
        damageDict.Add(ElementType.aether,0);
        damageDict.Add(ElementType.none,  0);
    }

    …

    // Damage this instance. By default, the damage is instant, but it can also
    //  be treated as damage over time, where the amt value would be the amount
    //  of damage done every second.
    // NOTE: This same code can be used to heal the instance
    public void Damage(float amt, ElementType eT, bool damageOverTime=false) {
        // If it's DOT, then only damage the fractional amount for this frame
```

```
        if (damageOverTime) {
            amt *= Time.deltaTime;
        }


        // Treat different damage types differently (most are default)
        switch (eT) {
        case ElementType.fire:
            // Only the max damage from one fire source affects this instance
            damageDict[eT] = Mathf.Max ( amt, damageDict[eT] );
            break;


        case ElementType.air:
            // air doesn't damage EnemyBugs, so do nothing
            break;


        default:
            // By default, damage is added to the other damage by same element
            damageDict[eT] += amt;
            break;
        }

    }


    // LateUpdate() is automatically called by Unity every frame. Once all the
    //  Updates() on all instances have been called, then LateUpdate() is called
    //  on all instances.
    void LateUpdate() {
        // Apply damage from the different element types

        // Iteration through a Dictionary uses a KeyValuePair
        // entry.Key is the ElementType, while entry.Value is the float
        float dmg = 0;
        foreach ( KeyValuePair<ElementType,float> entry in damageDict ) {
            dmg += entry.Value;
        }


        health -= dmg;
        health = Mathf.Min(_maxHealth, health); // Limit health if healing

        ResetDamageDict(); // Prepare for next frame

        if (health <= 0) {
            Die();
        }
    }

    ...


}
```

Now, it takes a full second of fire damage for the bug to die. If you want to double-check that the timing works properly, you can increase the bug's damage to 100 and see that it does indeed take 10 seconds for it to die.

Showing Damage

Right now, there is no indication to the player that the bug is actually being damaged until it dies. Many games flash something red when it's damaged (we did this in the SHMUP prototype), but color already has a lot of meaning in this game, so we should alter something other than color when a character is damaged. Instead of flashing red, we'll scale the model slightly using the CharacterTrans. Add the following code to EnemyBug to do so:

```
public class EnemyBug : PT_MonoBehaviour {
    public float          speed = 0.5f;
    public float          health = 10;
    public float          damageScale = 0.8f;
    public float          damageScaleDuration = 0.25f;

    public bool _____;

    private float         damageScaleStartTime;
    …

    void LateUpdate() {
        // Apply damage from the different element types

        // Iteration through a Dictionary uses a KeyValuePair
        // entry.Key is the ElementType, while entry.Value is the float
        float dmg = 0;
        foreach ( KeyValuePair<ElementType,float> entry in damageDict ) {
            dmg += entry.Value;
        }

        if (dmg > 0) { // If this took damage…
            // and if it is at full scale now (& not already damage scaling)…
            if (characterTrans.localScale == Vector3.one) {
                // start the damage scale animation
                damageScaleStartTime = Time.time;
            }
        }

        // The damage scale animation
        float damU = (Time.time - damageScaleStartTime)/damageScaleDuration;
        damU = Mathf.Min(1, damU); // Limit the max localScale to 1
        float scl = (1-damU)*damageScale + damU*1;
        characterTrans.localScale = scl * Vector3.one;

        health -= dmg;
        health = Mathf.Min(_maxHealth, health); // Limit health if healing
```

```
        ResetDamageDict(); // Prepare for next frame

        if (health <= 0) {
            Die();
        }
    }
    ...
}
```

Now, when the EnemyBug takes damage, it will pop to a smaller size (80% its original scale) and then interpolate back up to 100% over 0.25 seconds. Save your scene, press Play, and test it with the fire spell.

Damaging the Mage

The last thing for the EnemyBug to do is damage the Mage on contact. Contact with any enemy will cause the Mage to jump backward, lose some health, and blink for 1 second of invincibility. This will be done by switching the Mage into a different mode for 1 second that controls all of these factors. Open the Mage script and edit the code as shown:

```
public class Mage : PT_MonoBehaviour {
    ...
    public GameObject        fireGroundSpellPrefab;

    public float             health = 4; // Total mage health
    public float             damageTime = -100;
    // ^ Time that damage occurred. It's set to -100 so that the Mage doesn't
    //     act damaged immediately when the scene starts
    public float             knockbackDist = 1;    // Distance to move backward
    public float             knockbackDur = 0.5f;  // Seconds to move backward
    public float             invincibleDur = 0.5f; // Seconds to be invincible
    public int               invTimesToBlink = 4;  // # blinks while invincible

    public bool _____;

    private bool             invincibleBool = false; // Is Mage invincible?
    private bool             knockbackBool = false; // Mage being knocked back?
    private Vector3          knockbackDir; // Direction of knockback
    private Transform        viewCharacterTrans;

    protected Transform      spellAnchor; // The parent transform for all spells

    ...

    void Awake() {
        ...
        // Find the characterTrans to rotate with Face()
        characterTrans = transform.Find("CharacterTrans");
        viewCharacterTrans = characterTrans.Find("View_Character");
        ...
```

```
    }

    …


    void FixedUpdate () { // Happens every physics step (i.e., 50 times/second)
        if (invincibleBool) {
            // Get number [0..1]
            float blinkU = (Time.time - damageTime)/invincibleDur;
            blinkU *= invTimesToBlink; // Multiply by times to blink
            blinkU %= 1.0f;
            // ^ Modulo 1.0 gives us the decimal remainder left when dividing
                  ➥blinkU
            //    by 1.0. For example: 3.85f % 1.0f is 0.85f
            bool visible = (blinkU > 0.5f);
            if (Time.time - damageTime > invincibleDur) {
                invincibleBool = false;
                visible = true; // Just to be sure
            }
            // Making the GameObject inactive makes it invisible
            viewCharacterTrans.gameObject.SetActive(visible);
        }


        if (knockbackBool) {
            if (Time.time - damageTime > knockbackDur) {
                knockbackBool = false;
            }
            float knockbackSpeed = knockbackDist/knockbackDur;
            vel = knockbackDir * knockbackSpeed;
            return; // Returns to avoid walking code below
        }


        if (walking) { // If Mage is walking
            …
        }
    }

    void OnCollisionEnter( Collision coll ) {
        GameObject otherGO = coll.gameObject;

        // Colliding with a wall can also stop walking
        Tile ti = otherGO.GetComponent<Tile>();
        if (ti != null) {
            if (ti.height > 0) { // If ti.height is > 0
                // Then this ti is a wall, and Mage should stop
                StopWalking();
            }
        }
```

```
    // See if it's an EnemyBug
    EnemyBug bug = coll.gameObject.GetComponent<EnemyBug>();
    // If otherGO is an EnemyBug, pass otherGO to CollisionDamage()
    if (bug != null) CollisionDamage(otherGO);
}

void CollisionDamage(GameObject enemy) {

    // Don't take damage if you're already invincible
    if (invincibleBool) return;

    // The Mage has been hit by an enemy
    StopWalking();
    ClearInput();

    health -= 1; // Take 1 point of damage (for now)
    if (health <= 0) {
        Die();
        return;
    }

    damageTime = Time.time;
    knockbackBool = true;
    knockbackDir = (pos - enemy.transform.position).normalized;
    invincibleBool = true;
}

// The Mage dies
void Die() {
    Application.LoadLevel(0); // Reload the level
    // ^ Eventually, you'll want to do something more elegant
}

// Show where the player tapped
...

}
```

That's it for the EnemyBug at this point. Make sure that all your work gets passed to the version of EnemyBug in the _Prefabs folder by clicking the *Apply* button to the right of Prefab in the top section of the EnemyBug Inspector. This applies all the changes you've made back to the EnemyBug Prefab. Just to be sure everything worked properly:

1. Save your scene.
2. Delete EnemyBug from the Hierarchy.
3. Drag a new instance of EnemyBug into the Hierarchy from the _Prefabs folder.
4. Make sure that it works the same way.

If everything works fine, you can delete the new EnemyBug instance from the Hierarchy and save the scene. If anything went wrong, you can revert back to the saved version of the scene and try applying the changes again. If for some reason this still doesn't work, drag the working version of EnemyBug from the Hierarchy into the _Prafabs folder. This will make a new prefab named *EnemyBug 1*. Then delete the old EnemyBug prefab and rename EnemyBug 1 to *EnemyBug*.

EnemySpiker

The next kind of enemy we'll implement is the EnemySpiker. The spiker moves back and forth patrolling a line. It's not affected by any spells, and it damages the Mage on contact.

Create a new C# script named *EnemySpiker* and place it in the __Scripts folder. Attach this script to the EnemySpiker prefab in the _Prefabs folder. Open the EnemySpiker script and enter the following code:

```csharp
using UnityEngine;
using System.Collections;
using System.Collections.Generic;

public class EnemySpiker : PT_MonoBehaviour {
    public float          speed = 5f;
    public string         roomXMLString = "{";

    public bool _____;

    public Vector3        moveDir;
    public Transform      characterTrans;

    void Awake() {
        characterTrans = transform.Find("CharacterTrans");
    }

    void Start() {
        // Set the move direction based on the character in Rooms.xml
        switch (roomXMLString) {
        case "^":
            moveDir = Vector3.up;
            break;
        case "v":
            moveDir = Vector3.down;
            break;
        case "{":
            moveDir = Vector3.left;
            break;
```

```
        case "}":
            moveDir = Vector3.right;
            break;
        }
    }

    void FixedUpdate () { // Happens every physics step (i.e., 50 times/second)
        rigidbody.velocity = moveDir * speed;
    }

    // This has the same structure as the Damage Method in EnemyBug
    public void Damage(float amt, ElementType eT, bool damageOverTime=false) {
        // Nothing damages the EnemySpiker
    }

    void OnTriggerEnter(Collider other) {
        // Check to see if a wall was hit
        GameObject go = Utils.FindTaggedParent(other.gameObject);
        if (go == null) return; // In case nothing is tagged

        if (go.tag == "Ground") {
            // Make sure that the ground tile is in the direction we're moving.
            //  A dot product will help us with this (see the Useful Concepts
            //  Reference).
            float dot = Vector3.Dot(moveDir, go.transform.position - pos);
            if (dot > 0) { // If Spiker is moving towards the block it hit
                moveDir *= -1; // Reverse direction
            }
        }
    }
}
```

Making EnemySpiker Hurt Mage

The EnemySpiker uses a trigger (instead of a normal collider) so that collisions with other objects don't cause the spiker to go off course due to collisions. However, this also means that it currently passes harmlessly through the Mage. Make the following code edits to Mage to make EnemySpiker able to hurt her:

```
public class Mage : PT_MonoBehaviour {
    …

    void OnCollisionEnter( Collision coll ) {
        …
    }
```

```
    void OnTriggerEnter(Collider other) {
        EnemySpiker spiker = other.GetComponent<EnemySpiker>();
        if (spiker != null) {
            CollisionDamage(other.gameObject);
        }
    }

    void CollisionDamage(GameObject enemy) {
        ...
    }

    ...
}
```

To test the new EnemySpiker, complete the following steps:

1. Drag an EnemySpiker from the Project pane to the Hierarchy pane to add an instance of EnemySpiker to the scene. Be sure to position it somewhere that it will be about 1 meter (1 Unity unit) above the floor and between some walls.

2. Save the scene.

3. Play the scene to test everything and see the EnemySpiker behavior.

4. If everything seems to be working fine, delete the EnemySpiker instance from the Hierarchy and save your scene again.

Now we have two different kinds of enemies in the game that have their own behaviors and can each damage the Mage; however, if we wanted them to do different amounts of damage to the Mage—for example: if we wanted the EnemySpiker to only remove 0.5 health from the Mage instead of the 1 health that's removed by the bug—there's not a way to do that right now because then even if each of the enemies had a touchDamage field, there is no elegant way to pass it into the CollisionDamage method (which only takes a GameObject as input). It's times like these when an interface can help.

Abstracting the Enemy Interface

As mentioned earlier, an interface is a great way to abstract out the commonalities of two different classes. For EnemyBug and EnemySpiker to both properly interact with the Mage when they touch her, we really only need to know two things about them:

1. Where the enemy is located so the Mage can get knocked back

2. The amount of damage the enemy does to the Mage when she touches it

As you will read in the "Interfaces" section of Appendix B, an interface is like a promise that any class that implements the interface will implement specific methods and properties. Although interfaces cannot contain information about fields, that functionality can easily be handled by properties.

Create a new C# script named *Enemy* and put it in the __Scripts folder. Open it and enter this code:

```
using UnityEngine;
using System.Collections;

public interface Enemy {
    // These are declarations of properties that will be implemented by all
    //  Classes that implement the Enemy interface
    Vector3     pos { get; set; } // The Enemy's transform.position
    float       touchDamage { get; set; } // Damage done by touching the Enemy
}
```

Interfaces are usually very short because they only declare methods and properties that will be implemented later. Now it's time to make use of the Enemy interface. Make the following changes to the beginning of the EnemyBug script:

```
public class EnemyBug : PT_MonoBehaviour, Enemy {
    [SerializeField]
    private float           _touchDamage = 1;
    public float            touchDamage {
        get { return( _touchDamage ); }
        set { _touchDamage = value; }
    }
    // The pos Property is already implemented in PT_MonoBehaviour

    public float            speed = 0.5f;
    …
}
```

The EnemyBug : PT_MonoBehaviour, Enemy tells C# that EnemyBug extends the PT_MonoBehaviour class *and* implements the Enemy interface. If there is more than one interface implemented or if there is a class and one or more interfaces, they are separated by a comma. This change to EnemyBug implements the promised touchDamage property, while the promised pos property is already implemented by PT_MonoBehaviour. The [SerializeField] attribute causes the private field _touchDamage to appear in the Inspector (even though it's private).

Now, add similar code to the beginning of EnemySpiker:

```
public class EnemySpiker : PT_MonoBehaviour, Enemy {
    [SerializeField]
    private float           _touchDamage = 0.5f;
    public float            touchDamage {
        get { return( _touchDamage ); }
        set { _touchDamage = value; }
    }
    // The pos Property is already implemented in PT_MonoBehaviour
```

```
    public float            speed = 5f;
    …
}
```

Now, both EnemyBug and EnemySpiker class instances can be treated as instances of the
Enemy interface. Make the following changes to Mage to see how this works:

```
public class Mage : PT_MonoBehaviour {
    …

    void OnCollisionEnter( Collision coll ) {
        …

        // See if it's an EnemyBug
        EnemyBug bug = coll.gameObject.GetComponent<EnemyBug>();
        // If otherGO is an EnemyBug, pass bug to CollisionDamage(), which will
        //  interpret it as an Enemy
        if (bug != null) CollisionDamage(bug);
        // if (bug != null) CollisionDamage(otherGO);  // COMMENT OUT THIS LINE!
    }

    void OnTriggerEnter(Collider other) {
        EnemySpiker spiker = other.GetComponent<EnemySpiker>();
        if (spiker != null) {
            // CollisionDamage() will see spiker as an Enemy
            CollisionDamage(spiker);
            // CollisionDamage(other.gameObject);       // COMMENT OUT THIS LINE!
        }
    }

    void CollisionDamage(Enemy enemy) {

        // Don't take damage if you're already invincible
        if (invincibleBool) return;

        // The Mage has been hit by an enemy
        StopWalking();
        ClearInput();

        health -= enemy.touchDamage; // Take damage based on Enemy
        if (health <= 0) {
            Die();
            return;
        }

        damageTime = Time.time;
        knockbackBool = true;
        knockbackDir = (pos - enemy.pos).normalized;
        invincibleBool = true;
```

```
    }

    …
}
```

Even though EnemyBug and EnemySpiker share very little code, they can both be handled by the `CollisionDamage()` method because they both implement the Enemy interface. It's important to note that even though EnemyBug and EnemySpiker share a lot of fields (for example, gameObject, transform, and so on); as far as `CollisionDamage()` is concerned it can only access the two properties `pos` and `touchDamage` that are declared in the Enemy interface.

Making an EnemyFactory

The abstraction of the two enemies into the Enemy interface also gives us the ability to make a factory that can be used to generate enemies if passed the string representation from Rooms.xml. As described earlier in the chapter, a factory is a class or method that can create instances of different classes that all implement the same interface. It will be useful for us in this game because after it's implemented, adding new enemies to the factory will be as simple as editing an array in the _MainCamera.LayoutTiles Inspector.

First, you need to add a few more lines to the Enemy interface. Open Enemy in MonoDevelop and edit it as follows:

```
public interface Enemy {
    // These are declarations of properties that will be implemented by all
    //  Classes that implement the Enemy interface
    Vector3     pos { get; set; } // The Enemy's transform.position
    float       touchDamage { get; set; } // Damage done by touching the Enemy
    string      typeString { get; set; } // The type string from Rooms.xml

    // The following are already implemented by all MonoBehaviour subclasses
    GameObject   gameObject { get; }
    Transform    transform { get; }
}
```

Make these changes to the EnemyBug script:

```
public class EnemyBug : PT_MonoBehaviour, Enemy {
    [SerializeField]
    private float            _touchDamage - 1;
    public float             touchDamage {
        get { return( _touchDamage ); }
        set { _touchDamage = value; }
    }
    // The pos Property is already implemented in PT_MonoBehaviour
    public string            typeString {
        get { return( roomXMLString ); }
```

```
        set { roomXMLString = value; }
    }

    public string          roomXMLString;
    public float           speed = 0.5f;
    ...
}
```

And these changes to the EnemySpiker script:

```
public class EnemySpiker : PT_MonoBehaviour, Enemy {
    [SerializeField]
    private float          _touchDamage = 0.5f;
    public float           touchDamage {
        get { return( _touchDamage ); }
        set { _touchDamage = value; }
    }
    // The pos Property is already implemented in PT_MonoBehaviour
    public string          typeString {
        get { return( roomXMLString ); }
        set { roomXMLString = value; }
    }

    public float           speed = 5f;
    public string          roomXMLString = "{";

    public bool _____;
    ...
}
```

Now, open the LayoutTiles script in MonoDevelop and make the following code changes:

```
[System.Serializable]
public class TileTex {
    ...
}


[System.Serializable]
public class EnemyDef {
    // This class enables us to define various enemies
    public string     str;
    public GameObject go;
}

public class LayoutTiles : MonoBehaviour {
    ...
    public GameObject      portalPrefab; // Prefab for the portals between rooms
    public EnemyDef[]      enemyDefinitions; // Prefabs for Enemies

    public bool _____;
```

…

```
public void BuildRoom(PT_XMLHashtable room) {
    …

    // These loops scan through each tile of each row of the room
    for (int y=0; y<roomRows.Length; y++) {
        for (int x=0; x<roomRows[y].Length; x++) {
            …

            // Check for specific entities in the room
            switch (rawType) {
            …
            case "F":
                …
                portals.Add(p);
                break;

            default:
                // Try to see if there's an Enemy for that letter
                Enemy en = EnemyFactory(rawType);
                if (en == null) break; // If there's not one, break out
                // Set up the new Enemy
                en.pos = ti.pos;
                // Make en a child of tileAnchor so it's deleted when the
                //   next room is loaded.
                en.transform.parent = tileAnchor;
                en.typeString = rawType;
                break;
            }

        }
    }
    …
}

public Enemy EnemyFactory(string sType) {
    // See if there's an EnemyDef with that sType
    GameObject prefab = null;
    foreach (EnemyDef ed in enemyDefinitions) {
        if (ed.str == sType) {
            prefab = ed.go;
            break;
        }
    }
    if (prefab == null) {
        Utils.tr("LayoutTiles.EnemyFactory()","No EnemyDef for: "+sType);
        return(null);
    }
```

```
        GameObject go = Instantiate(prefab) as GameObject;

        // The generic form of GetComponent (with the <>) won't work for
        //  interfaces like Enemy, so we must use this form instead.
        Enemy en = (Enemy) go.GetComponent(typeof(Enemy));

        return(en);
    }

}
```

All that's left to do is add the different EnemyDefs to _MainCamera.LayoutTiles. Select _MainCamera in the Hierarchy. Open the disclosure next to enemyDefinitions in the *LayoutTiles (Script)* Inspector and set its length to *5*. Set the five Str fields to *b*, *^*, *v*, *{*, and *}*. Drag EnemyBug from the _Prefabs folder into the first Go field and EnemySpiker into the remaining four. When you're done, it should look like Figure 35.9.

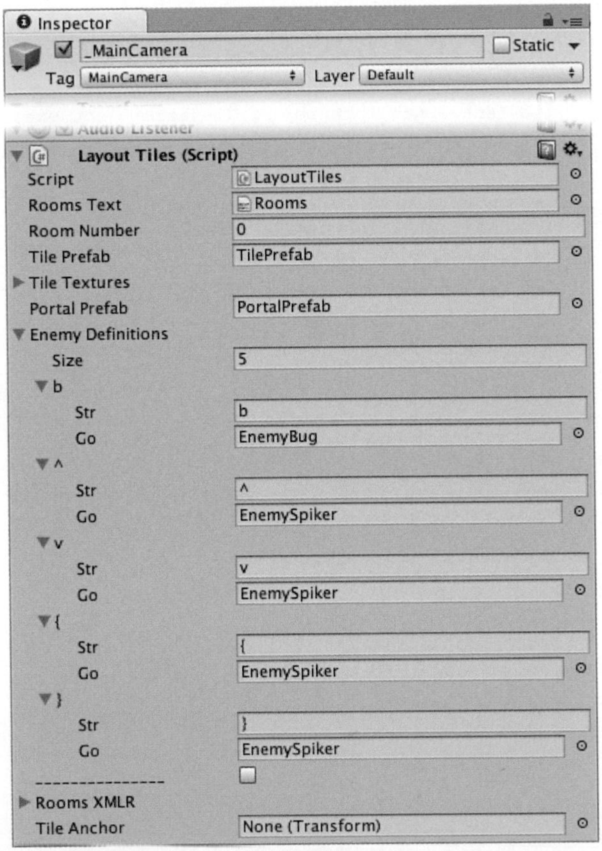

Figure 35.9   Settings for _MainCamera:LayoutTiles.enemyDefinitions

Now, as you walk through the dungeon, you will encounter both kinds of enemies. Because of the four different characters for an EnemySpiker, the spikers will be initialized facing the proper direction.

Summary

That's it for the final tutorial. This prototype introduced you to a lot of new concepts like interfaces and the Factory Pattern. I'm personally going to continue working on this prototype and see where it goes as a game. I invite you to do the same or, just like any of these, use it as the foundation on which to build your own fantastic game.

Next Steps

If you do continue with this project, here are some additional things you can add to make it a more interesting game:

1. Add direct spells. These would be cast by choosing an element and then tapping on an enemy.

2. Make more enemies. There is a prefab in the _Prefabs folder for an EnemyFlier that could hover around and then swoop to attack, but there wasn't room in the chapter for the code.

3. Add spells for each element and also a direct spell for when no element is selected. (As discussed earlier in the chapter, this could push the enemy back.)

4. Make the elements a resource. Maybe there are fountains around the dungeon where the Mage can restore her supply of elements. Maybe killing enemies releases elements. In the inventory on the right, the element buttons could show how many of that element the Mage has collected. You'd also want a top limit on how many elements of each type she could carry.

5. Add more interesting ground and wall tiles. If you don't let the player walk off a cliff, you could make a dropoff tile that was lower than the others but still had a collider up where the Mage would collide with it, and it would look a little more interesting but still act just like a wall tile.

6. Use physics layers to more specifically manage your collisions.

7. Following in the footsteps of *Rogue*, make a procedurally generated dungeon so that you had a new, never-before-seen dungeon every time you played.

Thanks!

Thank you again for reading this book. I sincerely hope that it helps you to achieve your dreams.

PART IV

APPENDICES

STANDARD PROJECT SETUP PROCEDURE

Many times throughout the book, you are asked to create a new project and then given code to try. This is the standard procedure that you should follow each time to create a new project, set up a scene, create a new C# script, and attach that script to the Main Camera of the scene. Instead of repeating these instructions throughout this book, they are collected here.

Setting Up a New Project

Follow these steps to set up a new project. The screenshots show the procedure on both OS X and Windows:

1. From the menu bar, choose *File > New Project* (see Figure A.1).

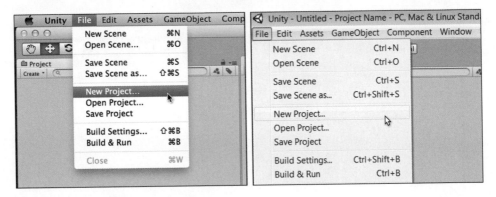

Figure A.1   Choosing New Project from the File menu on OS X and Windows

2. This opens the Unity Project Wizard (as shown in Figure A.2). In the wizard, click *Set* (*Browse* on Windows) to choose the location for your new project. This brings up a standard file dialog box enabling you to set the location of your project folder (see Figure A.3).

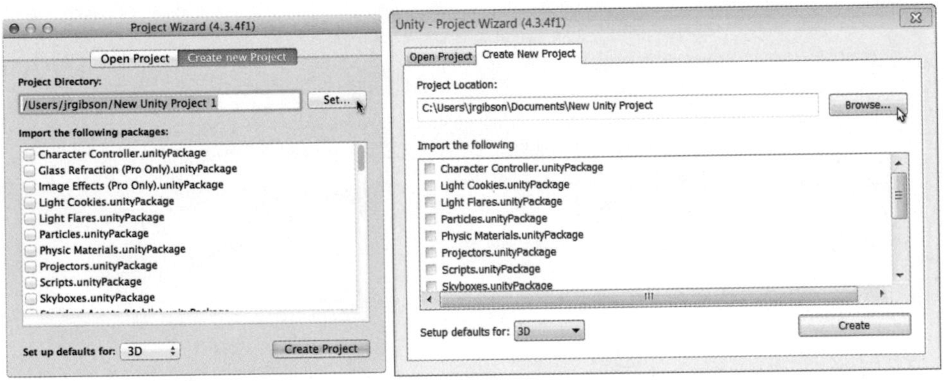

Figure A.2   The Project Wizard

3. In this step, the instructions for OS X and Windows differ, although both involve creating a new folder for the Unity project (see Figure A.3). In Figure A.3, the project is named *Project Name*, but you'll obviously want to choose a more appropriate name. I tend to store all of my Unity projects inside a folder named *Unity Projects*, as shown.

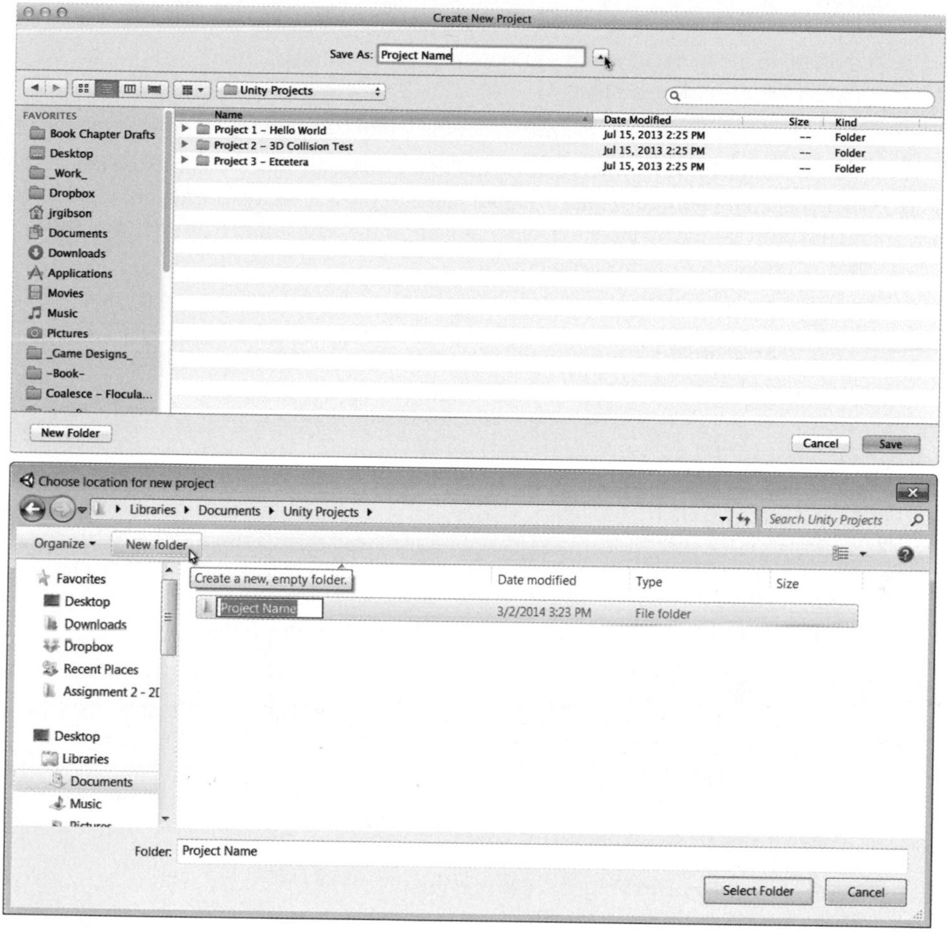

Figure A.3   The *Create New Project* (OS X) and *Choose location for new project* (Windows) dialog boxes

- **OS X:** On OS X, you do *not* need to create a new folder to hold your project; Unity will automatically create one:

  a. If you do not see the full-size version of the standard file navigation dialog box that is shown in Figure A.3, click the disclosure triangle (shown under the black mouse cursor to expand the dialog box.

  b. Navigate to the location where you would like to place the new project folder (which is the *Unity Projects* folder in the example).

  c. Type the name of the project (shown as *Project Name* in the top image of Figure A.3) into the *Save As* field at the top of the window.

  d. Click the *Save* button in the bottom right of the dialog box.

- **Windows:** On Windows, you must create a new folder to hold your new project:
  a. Navigate to the folder in which you want to place you project folder (which is the *Unity Projects* folder in the example).
  b. Click the *New Folder* button (shown under the white cursor in Figure A.3).
  c. Type the name of your project (shown as *Project Name* in Figure A.3) into the new folder name field (highlighted in blue in Figure A.3) and press Enter on the keyboard. This should both set the name of the folder and enter the new folder name into the *Folder* field at the bottom of the dialog box.
  d. Click the *Select Folder* button in the bottom right of the dialog box.

4. After completing step 3, you will be returned to the Project Wizard, and the path in the *Project Directory* field will be replaced by the path to the new project folder.

> **note**
>
> **PROJECT WIZARD OPTIONS**   Unity gives you the option to import a number of packages as part of the Project Wizard. I generally avoid this for three reasons:
>
> - **Project bloat:** If you import every possible package, the size of the project will bloat to 1,000 times its original size (from ≈300Kb to ≈300MB)!
> - **Project pane clutter:** Importing all the packages will also add a huge number of items and folders to your Assets folder and Project pane.
> - **You can always import them later:** At any time in the future, you can choose *Assets > Import Package* from the menu bar to import any of the packages listed in the Project Wizard.
>
> In addition, starting with Unity 4.3, you are also given the option to "set up defaults" for 3D or 2D. This option has very little effect on the project, so I usually leave 3D selected.

5. In the Project Wizard, click the *Create Project* button shown in Figure A.2 (labeled *Create* on Windows). Unity will appear to close and relaunch, presenting you with the blank canvas of your new project. This relaunch may take a few seconds, so be patient.

Getting the Scene Ready for Coding

The new project you just created comes with a default scene. To get ready for coding, follow these instructions (though they are not required for all projects):

1. Save the scene.

   The first thing you do in a project should *always* be to save the scene. Choose *File > Save Scene As* from the menu bar and choose a name. (Unity will automatically navigate to the correct folder in which to save the scene). I tend to choose something like _Scene_0, which is easily enumerable as I create more scenes in the future. The underscore at the beginning of the name will sort the scene to the top of the Project pane.

2. Create a new C# script (optional).

   Some chapters ask you to create one or more C# scripts before beginning the project. To do so, click the *Create* button in the Project pane and choose *Create > C# Script*. A new script will be added to the Project pane, and its name will be highlighted for you to change. Name this script whatever you like as long as there are no spaces or special characters in the name, and then press the Return or Enter key to save the name. In Figure A.4, the script is named HelloWorld.

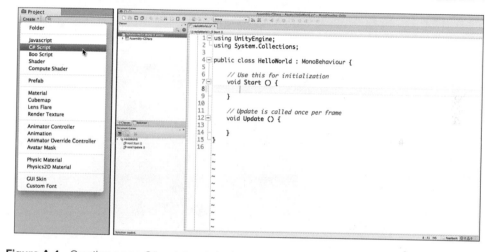

Figure A.4   Creating a new C# script and viewing that script in MonoDevelop

> ## warning
>
> ### Changing a script name after it has been created can cause problems
>
> When you set the name of a script as part of the creation process, Unity will automatically change the name in the class declaration as well (on line 4 in Figure A.4). However, if you choose to change the name of your C# script after that initial process, you need to change its name not only in the Project pane but also in the class declaration line of the script itself. In Figure A.4, this class declaration is on line 4, where *HelloWorld* would need to be changed to the new script name.

3. Attach the C# script to the scene's Main Camera (optional).

   Some chapters request that you *attach* one or more of the new scripts to the Main Camera. Attaching a script to a GameObject like Main Camera will make that script a *component* of the GameObject. All scenes will start with a Main Camera already included, so that's a fantastic place to attach any basic script that you want to run. Generally, if a C# script is not attached to a GameObject in the scene, it will not run.

This next part's a bit tricky, but you'll soon be used to it because it is so frequently done in Unity. Click the name of the new script, drag it onto the name of the Main Camera in the Hierarchy pane, and release the mouse button. It should look like what is shown in Figure A.5.

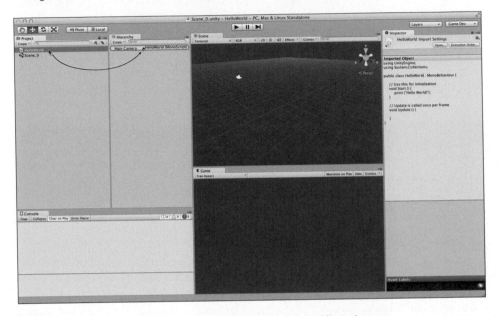

Figure A.5   Dragging the C# script onto the Main Camera in the Hierarchy pane

The C# script is now attached to the Main Camera and will appear in the Inspector if the Main Camera is selected. To begin editing the code of the C# script in MonoDevelop, simply double-click the script's name in the Project pane.

USEFUL CONCEPTS

This appendix is full of concepts that will help you be a better and more effective prototyper and programmer. Some of these are code concepts, others are methodologies. These are collected here in an appendix to make them easier for you to reference later when you look back at this book in the coming years.

Topics Covered

This appendix covers several different topics, categorized into four distinct groups and sorted alphabetically (rather than attempting to sort them conceptually). Many of these include Unity code examples, and others point you to specific parts of the book where the concept is used.

C# and Unity Coding Concepts

This section covers elements of C# coding that you may want to look back at for a refresher after you've finished the book. There are also some here that, though important, didn't fit well into one of the regular chapters. For convenience, these have all been collected into this appendix.

Bitwise Boolean Operators and Layer Masks

As you learned in Chapter 20, "Boolean Operations and Conditionals," a single pipe (|) can be used as a non-shorting conditional OR operator, and a single ampersand (&) can be used as a nonshorting conditional AND operator. However, when dealing with ints, they have another important feature. | and & can be used to perform bitwise operations on integers, and are therefore sometimes referred to as *bitwise OR* and *bitwise AND*.

In a bitwise operation, the individual bits of an integer are compared using one of the 6 bitwise operators included in C#. The following list of them includes the effect that they would have on an 8-bit byte (a simple integral type of data that can hold numbers from 0 to 255). The operations work the same way on a 32-bit int (but 32-bits wouldn't have fit on this page).

&	AND	`00000101 & 01000100` returns `00000100`
		OR	`00000101	01000100` returns `01000101`
^	Exclusive OR	`00000101 ^ 01000100` returns `01000001`
~	Complement (bitwise NOT)	`~00000101` returns `11111010`
<<	Shift Left	`00000101 << 1` returns `00001010`
>>	Shift Right	`01000100 >> 2` returns `00010001`

In Unity, bitwise operations are most often used to manage LayerMasks. Unity allows developers to define up to 32 different layers, and a LayerMask is a 32-bit integer representation of which layers to consider in any physics engine or raycast operation. In Unity, the variable type LayerMask is used for LayerMasks, but it is just a wrapper for a 32-bit int with a little additional functionality. When using a LayerMask, any bit that is a 1 represents a layer that is seen, and any bit that is a 0 represents a layer that is ignored (that is, masked). This can be very useful if you want to check collision against only a specific layer of objects or if you wish to specify a layer to ignore. (For example, the built-in layer 2, named *Ignore Raycast*, is automatically masked out for all raycast tests.)

Unity has eight reserved "built-in" layers, and all GameObjects are initially placed in the zeroth (0th) layer, which is named *Default*. The remaining layers, numbered 8 through 31, are referred to as *User Layers*, and giving one of these a name will place it in any pop-up menu of layers (for example, the Layer pop-up menu at the top of each GameObject Inspector).

Because the layer numbers start at zero, the bitwise LayerMask representation of not masking the zeroth layer is a 1 in the farthest-right position of the LayerMask. (See the variable `lmZero` in the following code listing.) This can be a bit confusing (because the integer value of this representation is 1, not 0), so many Unity developers use the bitwise shift left operator (`<<`) to assign LayerMask values. (For example, 1<<0 generates the value 1, which is the zeroth layer, and 1<<4 generates a 1 in the proper place to mask all but the fourth physics layer.) The following code listing includes more examples:

```
 1 LayerMask lmNone = 0;       // 00000000000000000000000000000000 bitwise    // 1
 2 LayerMask lmAll = ~0;       // 11111111111111111111111111111111 bitwise    // 2
 3 LayerMask lmZero = 1;       // 00000000000000000000000000000001 bitwise
 4 LayerMask lmOne = 2;        // 00000000000000000000000000000010 bitwise    // 3
 5 LayerMask lmTwo = 1<<2;     // 00000000000000000000000000000100 bitwise    // 4
 6 LayerMask lmThree = 1<<3;   // 00000000000000000000000000001000 bitwise
 7
 8 LayerMask lmOneOrThree = lmZero | lmTwo;                                    // 5
 9            // This creates 00000000000000000000000000000101 bitwise
10
11 LayerMask lmZeroThroughThree = lmZero | lmOne | lmTwo | lmThree;
12            // This creates 00000000000000000000000000001111 bitwise
13
14 lmZero = 1 << LayerMask.NameToLayer("Default");                             // 6
15            // This creates 00000000000000000000000000000001 bitwise
```

1. When all bits are set to 0, the LayerMask will ignore all layers.

2. When all bits are set to 1, the LayerMask will interact with all layers.

3. The integer value of a 1 in the second place of a LayerMask is 2, which demonstrates how it can get confusing to assign LayerMask values by integer value.

4. Using the shift left operator makes more sense in this case because the 1 is shifted two places to the left for the second physics layer.

5. A bitwise OR is used to collide with either layer 0 or layer 2.

6. The static method `LayerMask.NameToLayer()` will return a layer number when it is passed a layer name. This is used as shown on line 14.

Coroutines

A coroutine is a feature of C# that allows a method to pause in the middle of execution, allow other methods to execute, and then return to execution. This is used in the "Dice Probability" section of this appendix because the function to calculate all the possible outcomes of rolling many dice could take so long to execute that it would appear to the user that the computer was frozen. Coroutines can also be used as timers for tasks that you want to happen on a certain schedule (as an alternative to using an `InvokeRepeating` call).

Unity Example

In this example, we want to print the time every second. If we used the `Update()` method to print the time, it would print dozens of times per second, which is far too many.

Create a new Unity project. Then create a C# script named *Clock*, attach it to Main Camera, and enter this code:

```
using UnityEngine;
using System.Collections;

public class Clock : MonoBehaviour {

    // Use this for initialization
    void Start () {
        StartCoroutine(Tick());
    }

    // All coroutines have a return type of IEnumerator
    IEnumerator Tick() {
        // This infinite while loop will keep the print happening until the
        //  coroutine is halted or the program is stopped
        while (true) {
            print(System.DateTime.Now.ToString());
            // This yield statement tells the coroutine to wait about 1 second
            //  before continuing. Coroutine timing is not perfectly exact.
            yield return new WaitForSeconds(1);
        }
    }

}
```

There are a few different kinds of `yield` statements:

```
yield return null;                     // Will continue as soon as possible

yield return new WaitForSeconds(10);   // Will wait 10 seconds

yield return new WaitForEndOfFrame();  // Will wait until the next frame

yield return new WaitForFixedUpdate(); // Will wait until the next fixed update
```

Coroutines are used in the prototypes for Chapters 33–35.

Enum

Enum is a simple way to declare a type of variable that only has a few specific options, and it is used throughout the book. Enums are declared outside of class definitions.

```
public enum PetType {
    none,
    dog,
    cat,
    bird,
```

```
        fish,
        other
}

public enum Gender {
        unspecified
        female,
        male
}
```

Later, a variable within a class can be declared using the enum's type (for example, `public PetType` in the following code listing). The various options for an enum are referred to by the enum type, a dot, and the enum option (for example, `PetType.dog`):

```
public class Pet {
        public string    name = "Flash";
        public PetType    pType = PetType.dog;
        public Gender    gender = Gender.male;
}
```

Enums are actually integers masquerading as other values, so they can be cast to int (as shown on lines 7 and 8 in the following code listing). This also means that an enum will default to the 0th option if not explicitly set. For example, using the preceding definition of the enum `Gender`, declaring a new variable `Gender gen;` would automatically assign `gen` the default value of `Gender.unspecified`.

```
 1 public class Pet {
 2      public string    name = "Flash";
 3      public PetType    pType = PetType.dog;
 4      public Gender    gender = Gender.male;
 5
 6      void Awake() {
 7          int i = (int) PetType.cat; // i would equal 2            // 1
 8          PetType pt = (PetType) 4;  // pt would equal PetType.fish  // 2
 9      }
10 }
```

1. The code `(int)` shown on line 7 is an explicit typecast that forces `PetType.cat` to be interpreted as an int. This is similar to the `as GameObject` keyword and type that is used as part of `Instantiate()` statements in Unity, but the explicit typecast is more low-level and can be used on simple data types like ints. (The `as` keyword can only be used on instances of classes.)

2. Here, the int literal `4` is explicitly typecast to a PetType by the code `(PetType)`.

Enums are often used in `switch` statements (as you've seen throughout this book).

Function Delegates

A function delegate is most simply thought of as a container for similar functions (or methods) that can all be called at once. Delegates can be used to implement a *strategy pattern,* which is a software design pattern frequently used by game developers to define different AI strategies to be used by the same artificial intelligence (AI) agent when it encounters disparate circumstances. Strategy pattern is described in the "Software Design Patterns" section of this appendix.

The first step of using a function delegate is to define the type of the delegate. The type sets the parameters and return values for both the delegate and the functions it will contain.

```
public delegate float FloatOperationDelegate( float f0, float f1 );
```

The preceding line creates a `FloatOperationDelegate` delegate definition that takes two floats as input and returns a single float. Once the definition is set, you can define target methods that fit this delegate definition:

```
using UnityEngine;
using System.Collections;

public class DelegateExample : MonoBehaviour {
    // Create a delegate definition named FloatOperationDelegate
    // This defines the parameter and return types for target functions
    public delegate float FloatOperationDelegate( float f0, float f1 );

    // FloatAdd must have the same parameter and return types as
    //   FloatOperationDelegate
    public float FloatAdd( float f0, float f1 ) {
        float result = f0+f1;
        print("The sum of "+f0+" & "+f1+" is "+result+".");
        return( result );
    }

    // FloatMultiply must have the same parameter and return types as well
    public float FloatMultiply( float f0, float f1 ) {
        float result = f0 * f1;
        print("The product of "+f0+" & "+f1+" is "+result+".");
        return( result );
    }
}
```

Now, a variable of the type `FloatOperationDelegate` can be created, and either of the target functions can be assigned to it. Then, this delegate variable can be called just like a function (see the delegate field `fod` in the following syntax).

```
public class DelegateExample : MonoBehaviour {
    public delegate float FloatOperationDelegate( float f0, float f1 );

    public float FloatAdd( float f0, float f1 ) { … }
    public float FloatMultiply( float f0, float f1 ) { … }

    // Declare a field "fod" of the type FloatOperationDelegate
    public FloatOperationDelegate fod; // A delegate field

    void Awake() {
        // Assign the method FloatAdd() to fod
        fod = FloatAdd;

        // Call fod as if it were a method; fod then calls FloatAdd()
        fod( 2, 3 ); // Prints: The sum of 2 & 3 is 5.

        // Assign the method FloatMultiply() to fod, replacing FloatAdd()
        fod = FloatMultiply;

        // Call fod(2,3); it calls FloatMultiply(2,3), returning 6
        fod( 2, 3 ); // Prints: The product of 2 & 3 is 6
    }
}
```

Delegates can also be *multicast*, which means that more than one target method can be assigned to the delegate. This is the ability we count on to fire our weapons in the Chapter 30, "Prototype 3: Space SHMUP," prototype where a single call to the `fireDelegate()` delegate in turn calls all of the `Fire()` methods of the weapons on the player's ship. If the multicast delegate has a return type that is not void (as in our example), the final target method called will be the one to return a value. However, if a delegate is called without having any functions attached, it will throw an error. Prevent this by first checking to see whether it is null.

```
void Awake() {
    // Assign the method FloatAdd() to fod
    fod = FloatAdd;

    // Add the method FloatMultiply(), now BOTH are called by fod
    fod += FloatMultiply;

    // Check to see whether fod is null before calling
    if (fod != null) {
        // Call fod(3,4); it calls FloatAdd(3,4) & then FloatMultiply(3,4)
        float result = fod( 3, 4 );
        // Prints: The sum of 3 & 4 is 7.
        // then Prints: The product of 3 & 4 is 12.

        print( result );
        // Prints: 12
```

```
        // Thie result is 12 because the last target method to be called
        //    is the one that returns a value via the delegate.
    }
}
```

Interfaces

An interface declares methods and properties that will then be implemented by a class. Any class that implements the interface can be referred to in code as that interface type rather than as its actual class type. This differs from subclassing in several ways, one of the most interesting of which is that a class may implement several different interfaces simultaneously, where a class can only extend a single superclass.

Unity Example

Create a new project in Unity. In that project, create a C# Script named *Menagerie* and enter the code that follows:

```
using UnityEngine;
using System.Collections;
using System.Collections.Generic;

// Two enums to set specific options for fields in classes
public enum PetType {
    none,
    dog,
    cat,
    bird,
    fish,
    other
}

public enum Gender {
    female,
    male
}

// The Animal interface declares two public properties and two public methods
//    that all Animals must have
public interface Animal {
    // Public Properties
    PetType      pType { get; set; }
    Gender       gender { get; set; }

    // Public Methods
    void         Move();
    string       Speak();
}
```

```
// Fish implements the interface Animal
public class Fish : Animal {
    private PetType       _pType = PetType.fish;
    private Gender        _gender;

    public PetType pType {
        get { return( _pType ); }
        set { _pType = value; }
    }

    public Gender gender {
        get { return( _gender ); }
        set { _gender = value; }
    }

    public void Move() {
        Debug.Log("The fish swims around.");
    }

    public string Speak() {
        return("…!");
    }
}


// Mammal is a superclass that will be extended by Dog and Cat
public class Mammal {
    protected Gender      _gender;

    public Gender gender {
        get { return( _gender ); }
        set { _gender = value; }
    }
}

// Dog is a subclass of Mammal AND implements Animal
// Because Dog is a subclass of Mammal, it inherits the protected field _gender
//   and the public property gender. If _gender had been private, Dog would not
//   have been able to inherit it.
public class Dog : Mammal, Animal {
    private PetType        _pType = PetType.dog;

    public PetType pType {
        get { return( _pType ); }
        set { _pType = value; }
    }

    public void Move() {
        Debug.Log("The dog walks around.");
    }
```

```
    public string Speak() {
        return("Bark!");
    }
}

// Cat is a subclass of Mammal AND implements Animal
public class Cat : Mammal, Animal {
    private PetType       _pType = PetType.cat;

    public PetType pType {
        get { return( _pType ); }
        set { _pType = value; }
    }

    public void Move() {
        Debug.Log("The cat stalks around.");
    }

    public string Speak() {
        return("Meow!");
    }
}

// Menagerie is a subclass of MonoBehaviour
public class Menagerie : MonoBehaviour {
    // This list can take instances of ANY class that implements Animal
    public List<Animal>      animals;

    void Awake () {
        animals = new List<Animal>();

        Dog d = new Dog();
        d.gender = Gender.male;
        // When d is added to Animal, it is added as an Animal, not a Dog
        animals.Add( d );
        animals.Add( new Cat() );
        animals.Add( new Fish() );

        // In this loop, all Animals are treated the same way, even though they
        //   work differently
        for (int i=0; i<animals.Count; i++) {
            animals[i].Move();
            print("Animal #"+i+" says: "+animals[i].Speak());
            switch (animals[i].gender) {
            case Gender.female:
                print("Animal #"+i+" is female.");
                break;
            case Gender.male:
                print("Animal #"+i+" is male.");
```

```
                    break;
                }
            }
        }
    }
}
```

As you can see in the code, having the Animal interface allows the `Cat`, `Dog`, and `Fish` classes to all be treated in the same way and stored in the same `List<Animal>` even though two are subclasses of Mammal and one is a class that doesn't extend anything. For an example of how this is used in a project, take a look at Chapter 35, " Prototype 8: Omega Mage."

Naming Conventions

Naming conventions were initially covered in Chapter 19, "Variables and Components," but they're important enough to repeat here. The code in this book follows a number of rules governing the naming of variables, functions, classes, and so on. Although none of these rules are mandatory, following them will make your code more readable not only to others who try to decipher it but also to yourself if you ever need to return to it months later and hope to understand what you wrote. Every coder follows slightly different rules—my personal rules have even changed over the years—but the rules I present here have worked well for both me and my students, and they are consistent with most C# code that I've encountered in Unity:

1. Use *camelCase* for pretty much everything. In a variable name that is composed of multiple words, camelCase capitalizes the initial letter of each word (except for the first word, in the case of variable names).
2. Variable names should start with a lowercase letter (e.g., `someVariableName`).
3. Function names should start with an uppercase letter (e.g., `Start()`, `FunctionName()`).
4. Class names should start with an uppercase letter (e.g., `GameObject`, `ScopeExample`).
5. Private variable names can start with an underscore (e.g., `_hiddenVariable`).
6. Static variable names can be all caps with *snake_case* (e.g., `NUM_INSTANCES`). As you can see, snake_case combines multiple words with an underscore in between them.

Operator Precedence and Order of Operations

Just as in algebra, some operators in C# take precedence over others. One example that you are probably familiar with is the precedence of * over + (for example, 1 + 2 * 3 is 7 because the 2 and 3 are multiplied before the 1 is added to them). Here is a list of common operators and their precedence. An operator that is higher in this list will happen before one that is lower.

`( )`	Operations grouped by parentheses will always take precedence
`F()`	The calling of a function
`a[]`	The access of an array
`i++`	Post-increment

`i--`	Post-decrement
`!`	NOT
`~`	Bitwise NOT (complement)
`++i`	Pre-increment
`--i`	Pre-decrement
`*`	Multiply
`/`	Divide
`%`	Modulus
`+`	Add
`-`	Subtract
`<<`	Shift left
`>>`	Shift right
`<`	Less than
`>`	Greater than
`<=`	Less than or equal to
`>=`	Greater than or equal to
`==`	Equal to (the comparison operator)
`!=`	Not equal to
`&`	Bitwise AND
`^`	Bitwise exclusive OR (XOR)
`|`	Bitwise OR
`&&`	Conditional, shorting AND
`||`	Conditional, shorting OR
`=`	Assignment

Race Conditions

Unlike many of the other topics in this section, a race condition is something that you definitely *don't* want in your code. A race condition occurs when it is necessary in your code for one thing to happen before another, but it's possible that the two things could happen out of order and cause unexpected behavior or even a crash. Race conditions are a serious consideration when designing any code that is meant to be run on multiprocessor computers, multithreaded operating systems, or networked applications (where different computers around the world could possibly end up in a race condition with each other), but they can also be an issue in the simple Unity games that we write.

Let's create an example.

Unity Example
Follow these steps:

1. Create a new Unity project named *Unity-RaceCondition*. Create a C# script named *SetValues* and enter this code:

```
1 using UnityEngine;
2 using System.Collections;
3
4 public class SetValues : MonoBehaviour {
5     static public int[]        VALUES;
6
7     void Start() {
8         VALUES = new int[] { 0, 1, 2, 3, 4, 5 };
9     }
10
11 }
```

2. Create a second script named *ReadValues* and enter this code into it:

```
1 using UnityEngine;
2 using System.Collections;
3
4 public class ReadValues : MonoBehaviour {
5
6     void Start() {
7         print( SetValues.VALUES[2] );
8     }
9
10 }
```

3. Create two cubes in the scene and name them *Cube0* and *Cube1*. Attach the SetValues script to Cube0 and the ReadValues script to Cube1.

    Now, when you try to play the scene as we've created it, you will most likely encounter an error message in the Console pane. I say "most likely" because one of the things that makes race conditions difficult is the unpredictability of them occurring one way or another. If you don't get the error, try moving SetValues to Cube1 and ReadValue to Cube0. Even if you're not seeing the error, please continue reading.

    NullReferenceException: Object reference not set to an instance of an object ReadValues.Start () (at Assets/ReadValues.cs:7)

    If you double-click the error message, it should take you to line 7 of ReadValues.cs. (Your line number may differ slightly.)

    ```
    print( SetValues.VALUES[2] );
    ```

4. Let's use the debugger to learn more about what's causing the error. Add a breakpoint next to the print line of ReadValues.cs and attach the debugger to Unity. If you need a refresher on the debugger, read Chapter 24, "Debugging."

5. When you run the project (in Unity) with the debugger attached, it will freeze on your breakpoint immediately before executing that line. We know that something's wrong with this line, and as a NullReferenceException, we know that we're trying to access some variable that isn't yet defined. Let's look at each variable and see what's happening. Open the Watch pane in MonoDevelop (*View > Debug Windows > Watch* from the menu bar; there should be already a check mark next to it, and selecting it again will bring the Watch pane to the front). The only variable used in this line is SetValues.VALUES, so type *SetValues. VALUES* into a line of the Watch window, and you'll be able to see its value. As we expected, VALUES isn't defined; that is, it's currently null. But we know that VALUES is supposed to be defined in `SetValues.Start()`. You can see the code that does so just a few lines above. The only way that VALUES could not be defined is if `SetValues.Start()` hasn't run yet, and that's exactly what has happened.

This is a race condition. `SetValues.Start()` defines `SetValues.VALUES`, but `ReadValues.Start()` is possibly trying to use that field before it has been set. We know that `Start()` is called on each GameObject before the first `Update()` the GameObject receives, but it is unclear in what order various objects are called. I believe that it might happen in the order that the objects are added to the Hierarchy, but I'm not certain of that. In fact, I'm not even sure if you're encountering the same error that I am because it's possible that your `Start()` methods may be called in a different order from mine.

This is the major problem with race conditions. The two `Start()` functions are racing against each other. If one is called first, your code works fine, but when the other is called first, every-thing breaks. Regardless of whether your code happens to be working, this is an issue that you need to resolve.

This is one reason that there is a difference between the `Awake()` and `Start()` methods in a MonoBehaviour. `Awake()` is called immediately when a GameObject is instantiated, whereas `Start()` is called immediately before the first `Update()` that the GameObject receives. This can be a difference of several milliseconds, which for a computer program is a very long time. Even if you have a number of objects in your Hierarchy, you can be guaranteed that `Awake()` will be called on all of them before `Start()` is called on any of them. `Awake()` will always happen before `Start()` as long as both objects are added to your scene in the same frame (or are there from the beginning as Cube0 and Cube1 are).

Knowing this, take a look back at the original error. The error is happening because of the race between the two `Start()` functions. To fix this, move the one that needs to happen first into an `Awake()` method instead. Replace line 7 of the SetValues script as shown in the following code listing. You will need to click the Stop button in the MonoDevelop debugger (or select *Run > Stop* from the MonoDevelop menu bar) as well as stop playback in Unity before changing the SetValues code:

```
1 using UnityEngine;
2 using System.Collections;
3
4 public class SetValues : MonoBehaviour {
5     static public int[]        VALUES;
```

```
 6
 7     void Awake() {
 8         VALUES = new int[] { 0, 1, 2, 3, 4, 5 };
 9     }
10
11 }
```

Now, the `SetValues.Awake()` method will definitely be called before the `ReadValues.`
`Start()` method, and the race condition is resolved.

Recursive Functions

A function that is designed to call itself repeatedly is known as a recursive function. One simple
example of this is calculating the factorial of a number.

In math, 5! (5 factorial) is the multiplication of that number and every other natural number
below it:

$$5! = 5 * 4 * 3 * 2 * 1 = 120$$

It is a special case that 0!=1, and the factorial of a negative number will be 0 for our purposes:

$$0! = 1$$

We can write a recursive function to calculate the factorial of any integer:

```
 1 void Awake() {
 2     print( fac (-1) );    // Prints 0
 3     print( fac (0)  );    // Prints 1
 4     print( fac (5)  );    // Prints 120
 5 }
 6
 7 int fac( int n ) {
 8     if (n < 0) {          // This keeps it from breaking if n<0
 9         return( 0 );
10     }
11     if (n == 0) {         // This is the "terminal case"
12         return( 1 );
13     }
14     int result = n * fac( n-1 );
15     return( result );
16 }
```

When `fac(5)` is called in the preceding code, and the code reaches the 14th line, `fac()` is called
again on n-1, which is now 4. This process continues with `fac()` called four more times until it
reaches the terminal case at `fac(0)` and then begins to return values. The chain of recursion
resolves something like this:

```
fac(5)
5 * fac(4)
5 * 4 * fac(3)
5 * 4 * 3 * fac(2)
5 * 4 * 3 * 2 * fac(1)
5 * 4 * 3 * 2 * 1 * fac(0)
5 * 4 * 3 * 2 * 1 * 1
5 * 4 * 3 * 2 * 1
5 * 4 * 3 * 2
5 * 4 * 6
5 * 24
120
```

The best way to really understand what's happening in this recursive function is to place a breakpoint at line 14, connect the MonoDevelop debugger to the Unity Process, and use *Step In* to watch the recursion happen step by step. (If you need a refresher on the debugger, read Chapter 24.)

A Recursive Function for Bézier Curves

Another fantastic example of a recursive function is the Bézier curve interpolation static method (named `Bezier`) that is included in the ProtoTools Utils class as part of the unitypackage imported at the beginning of Chapters 31 through 35. This function can interpolate the position of a point along a Bézier curve composed of any number of points. The code for the `Bezier` function is listed at the end of the "Interpolation" section of this appendix.

Software Design Patterns

In 1994, the "Gang of Four" (Erich Gamma, Richard Helm, Ralph Johnson, and John Vissides) released the book *Design Patterns: Elements of Reusable Object-Oriented Software,*[1] which described various patterns that could be used in software development to create effective, reusable code. This book uses two of those patterns and refers to a third.

Singleton Pattern

The Singleton Pattern is the most commonly used in this book and can be found in Chapters 26, 27, and 29–35. If you know that there will only ever be a single instance of a given class in the game, you can create a *singleton* for that class, which is a static variable of that class type that can be used to reference it from anywhere in code. The following code listing shows an example:

---

[1] Erich Gamma, Richard Helm, Ralph Johnson, and John Vissides, *Design Patterns: Elements of Reusable Object-Oriented Software* (Reading, MA: Addison-Wesley, 1994). The Factory Pattern is one of many described in the book. Others include the Singleton Pattern, which is used in many of the tutorials in this book.

```
1 public class Hero : MonoBehaviour {
2     static public Hero S;                                     // 1
3
4     void Awake() {
5         S = this;                                             // 2
6     }
7 }
```

```
1 public class Enemy {
2
3     void Update() {
4         public Vector3 heroLoc = Hero.S.transform.position;   // 3
5     }
6
7 }
```

1. The static public field `S` is the singleton for hero. I personally name all of my singletons `S`.

2. Because there will only ever be one instance of the `Hero` class, it is assigned to `S` on `Awake()`, when the instance is created.

3. Because `S` is both public and static, it can be referenced anywhere in code via the class name as `Hero.S`.

Factory Pattern

Factory Pattern is used and described in Chapter 35. In short, Factory Pattern uses an interface to define a group of similar classes, and then a *factory* function is created that can return one of those objects based on the arguments passed into it. In *Omega Mage*, this is used to choose from amongst different possible enemy types that can be placed in a level. The enemies are very different classes, but they both implement the same `Enemy` interface, so the factory can return any of them. To learn more about interfaces, see the "Interfaces" section in this appendix. To see how Factory Pattern is used in a project, look at Chapter 35.

Strategy Pattern

As mentioned in the "Function Delegates" section of this appendix, the Strategy Pattern is often used in AI and other areas where you may want to change behavior based on conditions yet still only call a single function delegate. In the Strategy Pattern, a function delegate is created for a type of action that the class can perform (for example, taking an action in combat), and an instance of that delegate is given values and called based on the situation. This avoids complicated switch statements in the code, because the delegate can be called in a single line:

```
1 using UnityEngine;
2 using System.Collections;
3
4 public class Strategy : MonoBehaviour {
5     public delegate void ActionDelegate();                    // 1
6
7     public ActionDelegate act;                                // 2
8
```

```
 9      public void Attack() {}                                    // 3
10          // Attack code would go here
11      }
12
13      public void Wait() { … }
14      public void Flee() { … }
15
16      void Awake() {
17          act = Wait;                                            // 4
18      }
19
20      void Update() {
21          Vector3 hPos = Hero.S.transform.position;
22          if ( (hPos - transform.position).magnitude < 100 ) {
23              act = Attack;                                      // 5
24          }
25
26          if (act != null) act();                                // 6
27      }
28 }
```

1. The `ActionDelegate` delegate type is defined. It has no parameters and a return type of void.

2. `act` is created as an instance of `ActionDelegate`.

3. The `Action()`, `Wait()`, and `Flee()` functions here are placeholders that are meant to show that various actions would be defined that matched the parameters and return type of the `ActionDelegate` delegate type.

4. The initial strategy for this agent is to `Wait`.

5. If the hero singleton comes within 100 meters of this agent, it will switch its strategy to `Attack` by replacing the target method of the `act` function delegate.

6. Regardless of which strategy is selected, `act()` is called to execute it. It is useful to check that `act != null` before calling it because calling a null function delegate (that is, one that has not yet had a target function assigned to it) will cause a runtime error.

Variable Scope

The *scope* of variables is an important concept in any programming language. A variable's scope refers to how much of the code is aware of the variable's existence. *Global scope* would mean that any code anywhere could see and reference the variable, whereas *local scope* means that the variable's scope is limited in some way, and it can't be seen by everything else in the code. If a variable is local to a class, then only other things within the class can see it. If a variable is local to a function, then it only exists within that function and is destroyed once the function has completed.

The following code demonstrates several different levels of scope for different variables within a single class. Numbered comments after the code explain what is happening on important lines.

```
using UnityEngine;
using System.Collections;

public class ScopeExample : MonoBehaviour {

    // public fields (public class variables)
    public bool              trueOrFalse = false;                      // 1
    public int               graduationAge = 18;
    public float             goldenRatio = 1.618f;

    // private fields (private class variables)
    private bool             _hiddenVariable = false;                  // 2
    private float            _anotherHiddenVariable = 0.5f;

    // protected fields (protected class variables)
    protected int            partiallyHiddenInt = 1;                   // 3
    protected float          anotherProtectedVariable = 1.0f;

    // static public fields (static public class variables)
    static public int        NUM_INSTANCES = 0;                        // 4
    static private int       NUM_TOO = 0;                              // 5

    void Awake() {
        trueOrFalse = true; // Works: assigns "true" to trueOrFalse   // 6
        print( trueOrFalse ); // Works: prints "true"
        int ageAtTenthReunion = graduationAge + 10; // Works          // 7
        print( _anotherHiddenVariable ); // Works                     // 8
        NUM_INSTANCES += 1; // Works                                  // 9
        NUM_TOO++; // Works                                           //10
    }

    void Update() {
        print( ageAtTenthReunion ); // ERROR                         //11
        float ratioed = 1f; // Works
        for (int i=0; i<10; i++) { // Works                          //12
            ratioed *= goldenRatio; // Works
        }
        print( ratioed ); // Works
        print( i ); // ERROR                                         //13
    }
}

public class SubScopeExample : ScopeExample {                         //14
    void Start() {
        print( trueOrFalse );           // Works: prints "true"      //15
```

```
        print( partiallyHiddenInt );   // Works: prints "1"        //16
        print( _hiddenVariable );      // ERROR                    //17
        print( NUM_INSTANCES );        // Works                    //18
        print( NUM_TOO );              // ERROR                    //19
    }
}
```

1. **Public fields:** The three variables here are all public fields. All fields are class variables, meaning that they are declared as part of the class and are visible to all functions within that class. Because these fields are public, the subclass SubScopeExample also has a public variable `trueOrFalse`. Public variables can also be seen by anything else in code that has a reference to an instance of ScopeExample. This would allow a function with the variable `ScopeExample se` to see the field `se.trueOrFalse`.

2. **Private fields:** These two variables are private fields. Private fields can only be seen by this instance of ScopeExample. The subclass SubScopeExample does not have a private field `_hiddenVariable`. A function with the variable `ScopeExample se` would not be able to see or access the field `se.hiddenVariable`.

3. **Protected fields:** A field marked protected is between public and private. The SubScopeExample subclass does have a protected field `partiallyHiddenInt`. However, a function with the variable `ScopeExample se` would not be able to see or access the field `se.partiallyHiddenVariable`.

4. **Static fields:** A static field is a field of the class itself, not the instances of the class. This means that `NUM_INSTANCES` is accessed as `ScopeExample.NUM_INSTANCES`. This is the closest thing to global scope that I use in C#. Any script in my code can access `ScopeExample.NUM_INSTANCES`, and `NUM_INSTANCES` is the same for all instances of ScopeExample. A function with the variable `ScopeExample se` could not access `se.NUM_INSTANCES`, but it could access `ScopeExample.NUM_INSTANCES`. The SubScopeExample subclass of ScopeExample can also access `NUM_INSTANCES`.

5. `NUM_TOO` is a private static class variable, which means that all instances of ScopeExample share the same value of `NUM_TOO`, but no other class can see it or access it. The SubScopeExample subclass cannot access `NUM_TOO`.

6. The `// Works` comment means that this line executes without any errors. `trueOrFalse` is a public field of ScopeExample, so this method of ScopeExample can access it.

7. This line declares and defines a variable named `ageAtTenthReunion` that is locally scoped to the method `Start()`. This means that once the `Start()` function has finished executing, the variable `ageAtTenthReunion` will cease to exist. Also, nothing outside of this function can see or access `ageAtTenthReunion`.

8. As a private field `_anotherHiddenVariable` can only be seen by methods within instances of this class.

9. Within a class, static public fields can be referred to by their name, meaning that the `Start()` method can reference `NUM_INSTANCES` without needing the class name before it.

10. `NUM_TOO` can be accessed anywhere within the ScopeExample class.

11. This line throws an error because `ageAtTenthReunion` was a local variable of the method `Start()` so it has no meaning in `Update()`.

12. The variable `i` declared and defined in this `for` loop is locally scoped to the `for` loop. This means that `i` ceases to have meaning when the `for` loop has completed.

13. This line throws an error because `i` has no meaning outside of the preceding `for` loop.

14. This line declares and defines SubScopeExample as a subclass of ScopeExample. As a subclass, SubScopeExample has access to the public and protected fields of ScopeExample but not to the private fields. Because SubScopeExample does not have its own `Awake()` or `Update()` functions defined, it will run the versions defined in its base class, ScopeExample.

15. `trueOrFalse` is public, so SubStaticField has inherited a `trueOrFalse` field. Additionally, because the base class (ScopeExample) version of `Awake()` has run by the time `Start()` is called on SubScopeExample, `trueOrFalse` has been set to `"true"` by the `Awake()` method.

16. SubScopeExample also has a protected `partiallyHiddenInt` field that it inherited from ScopeExample.

17. `_hiddenVariable` was not inherited from ScopeExample because it is private.

18. `NUM_INSTANCES` is accessible by SubScopeExample because as a public variable, it is inherited from the base class ScopeExample. Additionally, the two classes share the same value for `NUM_INSTANCES`, so if one instance of each class were instantiated, `NUM_INSTANCES` would be 2 regardless of whether it were accessed from ScopeExample or SubScopeExample.

19. As a private static variable, `NUM_TOO` is not inherited by SubScopeExample. However, it's worth noting that even though `NUM_TOO` is not inherited, when SubScopeExample is instantiated and runs the base class version of `Awake()`, the `Awake()` method can access `NUM_TOO` without errors then because the base class version is running within the scope of the ScopeExample class even though it's actually running on an instance of SubScopeExample.

These 19 notes have include both very simple and very complex examples of variable scope. If some if it didn't make sense to you, that's okay. You can come back and read it later once you've used C# some more and have more specific scope questions.

XML

XML (Extensible Markup Language) is a file format that is designed to be both flexible and human-readable. Here is an example of some XML from Chapter 31, " Prototype 4: Prospector Solitaire." Additional spaces have been added to make it a little more readable, but that is okay because XML will generally treat any number of spaces or line breaks as a single space.

```xml
<xml>
    <!-- decorators are the suit and rank in the corners of each card. -->
    <decorator type="letter" x="-1.05" y="1.42"  z="0" flip="0" scale="1.25"/>
    <decorator type="suit"   x="-1.05" y="1.03"  z="0" flip="0" scale="0.4" />
    <decorator type="suit"   x="1.05"  y="-1.03" z="0" flip="1" scale="0.4" />
    <decorator type="letter" x="1.05"  y="-1.42" z="0" flip="1" scale="1.25"/>
    <!-- A list of all cards that defines where pips are placed. -->
    <card rank="1">
        <pip x="0" y="0" z="0" flip="0" scale="2"/>
    </card>
    <card rank="2">
        <pip x="0" y="1.1"  z="0" flip="0"/>
        <pip x="0" y="-1.1" z="0" flip="1"/>
    </card>
</xml>
```

Even without knowing much at all about XML, you should be able to read this somewhat. XML is based on *tags* (also known as the *markup* of the document), which are the words between the two angle brackets (for example, `<xml>`, `<card rank="2">`). Most XML *elements* have an *opening tag* (e.g., `<xml>`) and a *closing tag* that contains a forward slash immediately after the opening angle bracket (e.g., `</xml>`). Anything between the opening and closing tags of an element is said to be the *content* of that element.

There are also *empty-element tags*, which are tags that serve as both the opening and closing tag with no content between them. For example,
`<card rank="1" />` is a single empty-element tag. In general, XML files should start with `<xml>` and end with `</xml>`, so everything in the XML document is content of the `<xml>` element.

XML tags can have *attributes*, which are like fields in C#. The empty-element `<pip x="0" y="1.1" z="0" flip="0"/>` that is seen in the XML listing includes x, y, z, and `flip` attributes.

In an XML file, anything between `<!--` and `-->` is a *comment* and is therefore ignored by any program that is reading the XML file. In the preceding XML listing, you can see that I use them the same way that I use comments in C# code.

There is a robust XML reader included in C# .NET, but I have found it to be very large (it adds about 1 MB to the size of your compiled application, which is a lot if you're making something for mobile) and unwieldy (using it is not simple). So, I've included a much smaller (though not at all as robust) XML interpreter called PT_XMLReader in the ProtoTools scripts that are part of the unitypackage imported at the beginning of Chapters 31 through 35. For an example of its use, take a look at Chapter 31.

Math Concepts

A lot of people cringe when they hear the word *math,* but that really doesn't need to be the case. As you'll see throughout this book, there are some really cool things that can be done with math. Here in this appendix, I cover just a few great math concepts that can help you in game development.

Sine and Cosine (Sin and Cos)

Sine and cosine are functions that convert an angle value Θ (theta) into a point along a wave shape that ranges from -1 to 1. They are shown in Figure B.1.

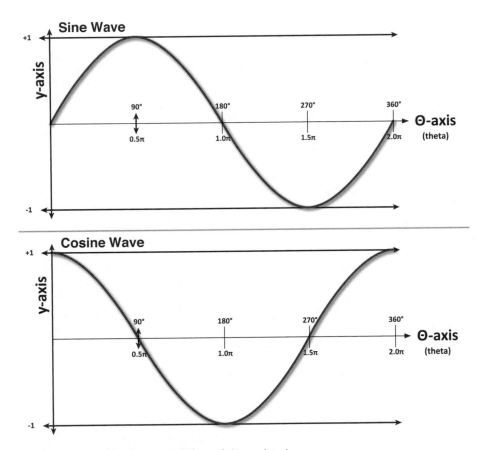

Figure B.1   The traditional representations of sine and cosine

But sine and cosine are much more than just waves; they're descriptions of the relationship of x and y when going around a circle. I'll demonstrate what I mean with some code.

Unity Example
Follow these steps:

1. Open Unity and create a new scene. Create a new sphere in the scene (*GameObject > Create Other > Sphere*). Set Sphere's transform to P:[0,0,0], R:[0,0,0], S:[0.1, 0.1, 0.1]. Add a TrailRenderer to Sphere. (Select Sphere in the Hierarchy and choose *Component > Effects > Trail Renderer* from the menu bar.)

2. Open the disclosure triangle next to Materials in the *Sphere:TrailRenderer* Inspector and click the circle to the right of Element 0 to select *Default-Particle* as the texture for the Trail-Renderer. Set `Time` = 1, `StartWidth` = 0.1, and `EndWidth` = 0.1 as well.

3. Create a new C# script named *Cyclic*. Attach it to Sphere in the Hierarchy. Then open the Cyclic script in MonoDevelop, and enter this code:

```csharp
using UnityEngine;
using System.Collections;

public class Cyclic : MonoBehaviour {
    public float        theta = 0;
    public bool         showCosX = false;
    public bool         showSinY = false;

    public bool _____;

    public Vector3      pos;
    public Color[]      colors;

    void Awake() {
        // Define some Colors to use
        colors = new Color[] {
            new Color(1f,   0f,    0.0f),
            new Color(1f,   0.5f,  0.0f),
            new Color(1f,   1f,    0.0f),
            new Color(0.5f, 1f,    0.0f),
            new Color(0f,   1f,    0.0f),
            new Color(0f,   1f,    0.5f),
            new Color(0f,   1f,    1.0f),
            new Color(0f,   0.5f,  1.0f),
            new Color(0f,   0f,    1.0f),
            new Color(0.5f, 0f,    1.0f),
            new Color(1f,   0f,    1.0f),
            new Color(1f,   0f,    0.5f),
            new Color(1f,   0f,    0.0f)  };
    }

    void Update () {
        // Calculate radians based on time
        float radians = Time.time * Mathf.PI;
        // Convert radians to degrees to show in the Inspector
        // The "% 360" limits the value to the range from 0-359.9999
```

```
        theta = Mathf.Round( radians * Mathf.Rad2Deg ) % 360;
        // Reset pos
        pos = Vector3.zero;
        // Calculate x & y based on cos and sin respectively
        pos.x = Mathf.Cos(radians);
        pos.y = Mathf.Sin(radians);

        // Use sin and cos if they are checked in the Inspector
        Vector3 tPos = Vector3.zero;
        if (showCosX) tPos.x = pos.x;
        if (showSinY) tPos.y = pos.y;
        // Position this.gameObject (the Sphere)
        transform.position = tPos;
    }

    void OnDrawGizmos() {
        if (!Application.isPlaying) return;

        // Choose the color based on where we are in the circle
        float cIndexFloat = (theta/180f)%1f * (colors.Length-1);
        int cIndex = Mathf.FloorToInt(cIndexFloat);
        float cU = cIndexFloat % 1.0f; // Get just the decimal bit
        Gizmos.color = Color.Lerp( colors[cIndex], colors[cIndex+1], cU );
        // Show individual Sin and Cos aspects using Gizmos
        Vector3 cosPos = new Vector3( pos.x, -1f-(theta/360f), 0 );
        Gizmos.DrawSphere(cosPos, 0.05f);
        if (showCosX) Gizmos.DrawLine(cosPos, transform.position);

        Vector3 sinPos = new Vector3( 1f+(theta/360f), pos.y, 0 );
        Gizmos.DrawSphere(sinPos, 0.05f);
        if (showSinY) Gizmos.DrawLine(sinPos, transform.position);
    }
}
```

4. Before pressing Play, set the Scene pane to 2D by clicking the *2D* button at the top of the Scene pane. Press Play, and you will see that the sphere doesn't initially move, but there are colored circles moving below and to the right of the sphere. (You may need to zoom out to see them.) The circle on the right follows the wave defined by Mathf.Sin(theta), and the circle below follows the Mathf.Cos(theta) wave.

If you check showCosX in the *Sphere:Cyclic (Script)* Inspector, Sphere will start moving in the X direction following a cosine wave. You can see how the X motion of Sphere is connected directly to the cosine motion of the bottom wave. Uncheck showCosX and check showSinY. Now, you can see how the Y motion of Sphere is connected to the sine wave. If you check both showCosX and showSinY, Sphere will move in the circle defined by combining x = cos(theta) and y = sin(theta). A full circle is 360°, or 2π radians (that is, 2 * Mathf.PI).

This connection is also shown in Figure B.2, which uses the same colors as those in the Unity example.

This means that you can use sine and cosine for all sorts of circular or cyclic behavior!

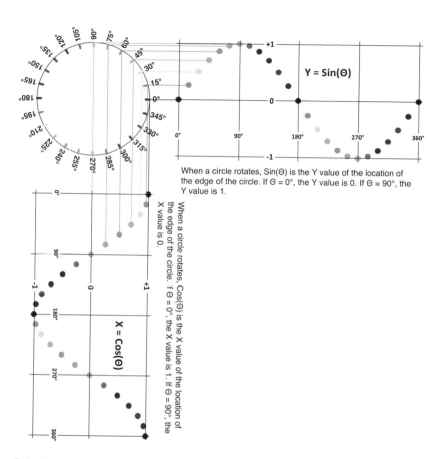

Figure B.2   The relationship of sine and cosine to a circle

These properties of sine and cosine are used in the Chapter 35, *Omega Mage*, game prototype to orbit the element around the Mage's head and in the Chapter 30 *Space SHMUP*, prototype to define wavy movement for the Enemy_1 enemy type and to adjust the linear interpolation easing of the Enemy_2 type (see the "Interpolation" section in this appendix for information about linear interpolation and easing).

Dice Probability

Chapter 11, "Math and Game Balance," covered Jesse Schell's Rule #4 of probability: Enumeration can solve difficult mathematical problems. Here is a quick Unity program that will enumerate all the possibilities for any number of dice with any number of sides. However, beware that each die you add drastically increases the number of calculations that must be done (for example, 5d6 [five six-sided dice] take six times longer to calculate than 4d6 and 36 times longer to calculate than 3d6).

Unity Example

Follow these steps to create an example:

1. Start a new Unity project. Create a new C# script named *DiceProbability* and drag it onto the Main Camera in the Scene pane. Open DiceProbability and enter this code:

```csharp
using UnityEngine;
using System.Collections;

public class DiceProbability : MonoBehaviour {

    public int        numDice = 2;
    public int        numSides = 6;
    public bool        checkToCalculate = false;
    // ^ When you set checkToCalculate to true, this will start calculating
    public int        maxIterations = 10000;
    // ^ The maximum number of iterations to perform in a single cycle of the
    //    CalculateRolls() coroutine
    public float    width = 16;
    public float    height = 9;

    public bool _____;

    public int[]    dice;  // An array of the values of each die
    public int[]    rolls; // An array storing how many times a roll has come up
    // ^ For 2d6 this would be [ 0, 0, 1, 2, 3, 4, 5, 6, 5, 4, 3, 2, 1 ],
    //    meaning that a 2 was rolled once while a 7 was rolled 6 times.

    void Awake() {
        // Set up the main camera to properly display the graph
        Camera cam = Camera.main;
        cam.backgroundColor = Color.black;
        cam.isOrthoGraphic = true;
        cam.orthographicSize = 5;
        cam.transform.position = new Vector3(8, 4.5f, -10);
    }

    void Update() {
        if (checkToCalculate) {
            StartCoroutine( CalculateRolls() );
            checkToCalculate = false;
        }
    }

    void OnDrawGizmos() {
        float minVal = numDice;
        float maxVal = numDice*numSides;
```

```csharp
        // If the rolls array is not ready, return
        if (rolls == null || rolls.Length == 0 || rolls.Length != maxVal+1) {
            return;
        }


        // Draw the rolls array
        float maxRolls = Mathf.Max(rolls);
        float heightMult = 1f/maxRolls;
        float widthMult = 1f/(maxVal-minVal);

        Gizmos.color = Color.white;
        Vector3 v0, v1 = Vector3.zero;
        for (int i-numDice; i<=maxVal; i++) {
            v0 = v1;
            v1.x = ( (float) i - numDice ) * width * widthMult;
            v1.y = ( (float) rolls[i] ) * height * heightMult;
            if (i != numDice) {
                Gizmos.DrawLine(v0,v1);
            }
        }
    }


public IEnumerator CalculateRolls() {
    // Calculate max value (the maximum possible value that could be rolled
    //   on the dice (for example, for 2d6 maxValue = 12)
    int maxValue = numDice*numSides;
    // Make the array large enough to hold all possible values
    rolls = new int[maxValue+1];

    // Make an array with an element for each die. All are preset to a value
    //   of 1 except for the first die which is set to 0 (to make the
    //   method RecursivelyAddOne() work properly)
    dice = new int[numDice];
    for (int i=0; i<numDice; i++) {
        dice[i] = (i==0) ? 0 : 1;
    }

    // Iterate on the dice.

    int iterations = 0;
    int sum = 0;

    // Usually, I avoid while loops because they can lead to infinite loops,
    //   but because this is a coroutine with a yield in the while loop, it's
    //   not as big of a problem.
    while (sum != maxValue) {
    // ^ the sum will == maxValue when all dice are at their maximum value

        // Increment the 0th die in the dice Array
        RecursivelyAddOne(0);
```

```
        // Sum all the dice together
        sum = SumDice();
        // and add 1 to that position in the rolls array
        rolls[sum]++;

        // add to iterations and yield
        iterations++;
        if (iterations % maxIterations == 0) {
            yield return null;
        }
    }
    print("Calculation Done");

    string s = "";
    for (int i=numDice; i<=maxValue; i++) {
        s += i.ToString()+"\t"+rolls[i]+"\n";
    }

    int totalRolls = 0;
    foreach (int i in rolls) {
        totalRolls += i;
    }
    s += "\nTotal Rolls: "+totalRolls+"\n";

    print(s);

}


// This is a recursive method, meaning that it calls itself. You can read
//   about recursive methods more later in this appendix.
public void RecursivelyAddOne(int ndx) {
    if (ndx == dice.Length) return; // We've exceeded the length of dice
    //   Array, so just return

    // Increment the die at position ndx
    dice[ndx]++;
    // If this exceeds the capacity of the die…
    if (dice[ndx] > numSides) {
        dice[ndx] = 1;                  // then set this die to 1…
        RecursivelyAddOne(ndx+1);    // and increment the next die
    }
    return;
}

public int SumDice() {
    // Sum the values of all the dice in the dice array
    int sum = 0;
    for (int i=0; i<dice.Length; i++) {
        sum += dice[i];
    }
```

```
        return(sum);
    }
}
```

2. To use the DiceProbability enumerator, press Play and then select Main Camera in the Hierarchy pane. In the *Main Camera:Dice Probability (Script)* Inspector, you can set `numDice` (the number of dice) and `numSides` (the number of sides for each die) and then click `checkToCalculate` to calculate the probability of any specific number coming up on those dice. Unity will enumerate all the possible results and then output the results to the Console pane. Try it first with 2 dice of 6 sides each (2d6) and you'll get these results in the console (you will have to select the console message to see more than the first two lines):

```
2       1
3       2
4       3
5       4
6       5
7       6
8       5
9       4
10      3
11      2
12      1


Total Rolls: 36

UnityEngine.MonoBehaviour:print(Object)
<CalculateRolls>c__Iterator0:MoveNext() (at Assets/DiceProbability.cs:110)
UnityEngine.MonoBehaviour:StartCoroutine(IEnumerator)
DiceProbability:Update() (at Assets/DiceProbability.cs:34)
```

3. Next, try 8d6. You'll see that this takes a lot longer to calculate and that the results (and the curve graph) progressively update each time the coroutine yields (see the "Coroutines" section in this appendix).

Now, any time you want to know the probability of something like rolling a 13 on 8d6, you can figure it out through enumeration. (It's 792/1,679,616 = 11/23,328 ≈ 0.00047 ≈ 0.05%.) In addition, this code could be tweaked to choose random rolls every time and give you a practical probability instead of the theoretical probability that is currently produced.

Dot Product

Another extremely useful math concept is the dot product. A dot product of two vectors is the result of multiplying the respective x, y, and z components of each vector together and adding the results as shown in the following pseudocode listing:

```
1 Vector3 a = new Vector3( 1, 2, 3 );
2 Vector3 b = new Vector3( 4, 5, 6 );
3 float dotProduct = a.x*b.x + a.y*b.y + a.z*b.z;                    // 1
```

```
4 // dotProduct = 1*4 + 2*5 + 3*6
5 // dotProduct = 4 + 10 + 18
6 // dotProduct = 32
7 dotProduct = Vector3.Dot(a,b); // This is the real way to do it in C#     // 2
```

1. Line 3 shows a manual calculation of the dot product of Vector3s a and b.

2. Line 7 shows the same calculation performed using the built-in static method `Vector3.Dot()`.

At first, this may not seem very important, but it has another extremely useful property: The float that the dot product returns is also equivalent to a.magnitude * b.magnitude * Cos(Θ) where Θ is the angle between the two vectors, as shown in Figure B.3.

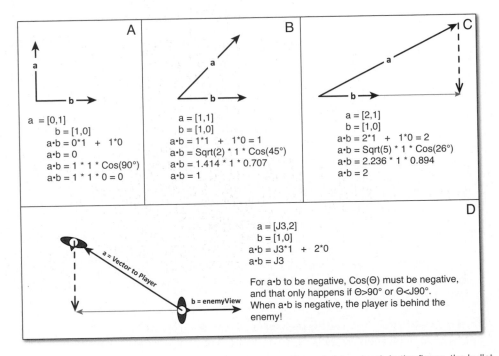

Figure B.3   Dot product examples (decimal numbers are approximate values). In the figure, the bullet • denotes the dot product operation.

As you see in Figure B.3.D, this can be used to tell whether an enemy is facing the player character (which can be useful in stealth games). There are several other places that this can be used, and it's very common in computer graphics programming. In *Omega Mage*, this is used in `EnemySpiker.OnTriggerEnter()` to tell whether the EnemySpiker is moving toward or away from the trigger that it hit.

Interpolation

An *interpolation* refers to any mathematical blending between two values. When I was working as a contract programmer after college, I feel that one of the major reasons I got a lot of job offers was because the motion of elements in my graphics code looked smooth and juicy (to use Kyle Gabler's term). This was accomplished through the use of various forms of interpolation, easing, and Bézier curves, all of which are presented in this section of the appendix.

Linear Interpolation

A *linear interpolation* is a way of mathematically defining a new value or position by stating that it is in between two existing values. All linear interpolations follow the same formula:

$$p01 = (1-u) * p0 + u * p1$$

In code, this would look something like this:

```
1 Vector3 p0 = new Vector3(0,0,0);
2 Vector3 p1 = new Vector3(1,1,0);
3 float    u  = 0.5f;
4 Vector3 p01 = (1-u) * p0  +  u * p1;
5 print(p01); // prints: ( 0.5, 0.5, 0 ) the point half-way between p0 & p1
```

In the preceding code listing, a new point p01 is created by interpolating between the points p0 and p1. The value u ranges in value between 0 and 1. This can happen with any number of dimensions, though we will usually be interpolating Vector3s in Unity.

Time-Based Linear Interpolations

In a time-based linear interpolation, you are guaranteed that the interpolation will complete in a specific amount of time because the u value is based on the amount of time that as passed divided by the total desired duration of the interpolation.

Unity Example

To create a Unity example, do the following:

1. Start a new Unity project named *Interpolation Project*. Create a cube in the Hierarchy (*GameObject > Create Other > Cube*). Select *Cube* in the Hierarchy pane and attach a TrailRenderer to it (*Components > Effects > Trail Renderer*). Open the Materials array of the TrailRenderer and set Element 0 to the built-in material *Default-Particle*. (Click the circle to the right of Element 0, and you will see *Default-Particle* in the list of available materials.)

2. Create a new C# script in the Project pane named *Interpolator*. Attach it to Cube and then open it in MonoDevelop to enter this code:

```
using UnityEngine;
using System.Collections;

public class Interpolator : MonoBehaviour {
    public Vector3      p0 = new Vector3(0,0,0);
    public Vector3      p1 = new Vector3(3,4,5);
    public float        timeDuration = 1;
    // Set checkToCalculate to true to start moving
    public bool         checkToCalculate = false;

    public bool _____;

    public Vector3      p01;
    public bool         moving = false;
    public float        timeStart;

    // Update is called once per frame
    void Update () {
        if (checkToCalculate) {
            checkToCalculate = false;

            moving = true;
            timeStart = Time.time;
        }

        if (moving) {
            float u = (Time.time-timeStart)/timeDuration;
            if (u>=1) {
                u=1;
                moving = false;
            }

            // This is the standard linear interpolation function
            p01 = (1-u)*p0 + u*p1;

            transform.position = p01;
        }

    }
}
```

3. Switch back to Unity and press Play. In the *Cube:Interpolator (Script)* component, check the box next to checkToCalculate, and Cube will move from p0 to p1 in 1 second. If you adjust timeDuration to another value and then check checkToCalculate again, you will see that Cube will always move from p0 to p1 in timeDuration seconds. You can also change the location of p0 or p1 while Cube is moving, and it will update accordingly.

Linear Interpolations Using Zeno's Paradox

Zeno of Elea (ca. 490–430 BCE) was a Greek philosopher who proposed a set of paradoxes all having to do with the philosophical impossibility of everyday, commonsense motion.

In Zeno's Dichotomy Paradox, the question is posed of whether a moving object can ever reach a stationary point. Imagine that a frog is hopping toward a wall. Every hop, he covers half of the remaining distance to the wall. No matter how many times the frog hops, it will still have covered only half of the distance remaining to the wall after its last hop, so it will never reach the wall.

Ignoring the philosophical implications of this, we can actually use a similar concept along with linear interpolation to create a smooth motion that eases toward a certain point. This is used throughout this book to make cameras that smoothly follow various points of interest.

Unity Example

Continuing the same *Interpolation Project* from before, now add a sphere to the scene (*GameObject > Create Other > Sphere*) and move it somewhere away from Cube. Create a new C# script in the Project pane named *ZenosFollower* and attach it to Sphere. Open ZenosFollower in MonoDevelop and enter this code:

```csharp
using UnityEngine;
using System.Collections;

public class ZenosFollower : MonoBehaviour {

        public GameObject          poi; // Point Of Interest
        public float               u = 0.1f;
        public Vector3             p0, p1, p01;

        // Update is called once per frame
        void Update () {
                // Get the position of this and the poi
                p0 = this.transform.position;
                p1 = poi.transform.position;

                // Interpolate between the two
                p01 = (1-u)*p0 + u*p1;

                // Move this to the new position
                this.transform.position - p01;
        }
}
```

Save the code and return to Unity. There, set the `poi` of Sphere:ZenosFollower to be Cube (by dragging Cube from the Hierarchy pane into the `poi` slot of the *Sphere:ZenosFollower (Script)* Inspector). Save your scene!

Now, when you press Play, the sphere will move toward the cube. If you select the cube and check the `checkToCalculate` box, the sphere will continue to follow the cube. You can also move the cube around in the Scene window manually and watch the sphere follow.

Try changing the value of u in the *Sphere:ZenosFollower* Inspector. Lower values will make it follow more slowly while higher values will make it follow more rapidly. A value of *0.5* would make the sphere cover half of the distance to the cube every frame, which would exactly mimic Zeno's Dichotomy Paradox (but in practice, this follows far too closely). It is true that with this specific code, the sphere will never get to exactly the same location as the cube, and it's also true that because this code is not time based, the sphere will follow more closely on fast computers and follow more slowly on slow ones, but this is just meant to be a very quick, simple following script.

Interpolating More Than Just Position

It's possible to interpolate almost any kind of numeric value. In Unity, this means that we can very easily interpolate values like scale, rotation, and color among others.

Unity Example

This can either be done in the same project as the previous interpolation examples or in a new project:

1. Create two new cubes in the hierarchy named *c0* and *c1*. Make a new material for each (*Assets > Create > Material*) and name the materials *Mat_c0* and *Mat_c1*. Apply each material to its respective cube by dragging it on top of it. Select c0 and set its position, rotation, and scale to anything you want (as long as it's visible on screen). Under the *c0:Mat_c0* section of the Inspector, you can also set the color to whatever you want. Do the same for c1 and the color of Mat_c1, making sure that c1 and c0 have different positions, rotations, scales, and colors from each other.

2. Add a third cube to the scene, leave it in the default position, and name it *Cube01*.

3. Create a new C# script named *Interpolator2* and attach it to Cube01. Enter this code into Interpolator2:

```
using UnityEngine;
using System.Collections;

public class Interpolator2 : MonoBehaviour {
    public Transform    c0, c1;
    public float        timeDuration = 1;
    // Set checkToCalculate to true to start moving
    public bool         checkToCalculate = false;

    public bool         _____;

    public Vector3      p01;
    public Color        c01;
```

```
public Quaternion    r01;
public Vector3       s01;
public bool          moving = false;
public float         timeStart;

// Update is called once per frame
void Update () {
    if (checkToCalculate) {
        checkToCalculate = false;

        moving = true;
        timeStart = Time.time;
    }

    if (moving) {
        float u = (Time.time-timeStart)/timeDuration;
        if (u>=1) {
            u=1;
            moving = false;
        }

        // This is the standard linear interpolation function
        p01 = (1-u)*c0.position + u*c1.position;
        c01 = (1-u)*c0.renderer.material.color +
                u*c1.renderer.material.color;
        s01 = (1-u)*c0.localScale + u*c1.localScale;
        // Rotations are treated differently because Quaternions are tricky
        r01 = Quaternion.Slerp(c0.rotation, c1.rotation, u);

        // Apply these to this Cube01
        transform.position = p01;
        renderer.material.color = c01;
        transform.localScale = s01;
        transform.rotation = r01;
    }

}
}
```

4. Back in Unity, drag c0 from the Hierarchy pane into the c0 field of the *Cube01:Interpolator2 (Script)* Inspector. Do the same for c1 and the c1 field. Press Play and then click the check-ToCalculate check box in the *Cube01:Interpolator2* Inspector. You'll see that Cube01 now interpolates much more than just position.

Linear Extrapolation

All the interpolations we've done so far have had u values that ranged from 0 to 1. If you allow the u value to go beyond this range, you get *extrapolation* (so named because instead of interpolating between two values, it is now extrapolating data outside of the original two points).

Given the initial two points 10 and 20, an extrapolation of u=2 would work as shown in Figure B.4.

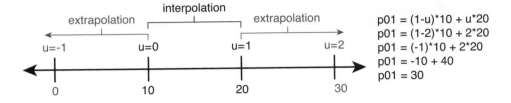

Figure B.4   An example of extrapolation

Unity Example

To see this in code, make the following modifications to Interpolator2:

```
using UnityEngine;
using System.Collections;

public class Interpolator2 : MonoBehaviour {
    public Transform    c0, c1;
    public float        uMin = 0;
    public float        uMax = 1;
    public float        timeDuration = 1;
    // Set checkToCalculate to true to start moving
    public bool         checkToCalculate = false;

    public bool _____;

    public Vector3      p01;
    public Color        c01;
    public Quaternion   r01;
    public Vector3      s01;
    public bool         moving = false;
    public float        timeStart;

    // Update is called once per frame
    void Update () {
        if (checkToCalculate) {
            checkToCalculate = false;

            moving = true;
            timeStart = Time.time;
        }
```

```
if (moving) {
    float u = (Time.time-timeStart)/timeDuration;
    if (u>=1) {
        u=1;
        moving = false;
    }
    // Adjust u to the range from uMin to uMax
    u = (1-u)*uMin + u*uMax;
    // ^ Look familiar? We're using a linear interpolation to do so!

    // This is the standard linear interpolation function
    p01 = (1-u)*c0.position + u*c1.position;
    c01 = (1-u)*c0.renderer.material.color +
            u*c1.renderer.material.color;
    s01 = (1-u)*c0.localScale + u*c1.localScale;
    // Rotations are treated differently because Quaternions are tricky
    r01 = Quaternion.Slerp(c0.rotation, c1.rotation, u);

    // Apply these to this Cube01
    transform.position = p01;
    renderer.material.color = c01;
    transform.localScale = s01;
    transform.rotation = r01;
    }


  }
}
```

Now, if you just press Play and click the `checkToCalculate` box on Cube01, you'll get the same behavior as before. But, try changing `uMin` to -1 and `uMax` to 2 in the *Cube01:Interpolator2 (Script)* Inspector. Now, click `checkToCalculate`, and you'll see that the color, position, and scale all extrapolate and go beyond the original range that you set. However, rotation will not extrapolate beyond the rotation of c0 or c1 due to a limitation of the `Quaternion.Slerp()` method (which does a spherical linear interpolation for rotations). If `Slerp()` is passed any number below 0 as its u value, it still treats it as 0 (and any number above 1 is treated as 1). If you look at the documentation for Vector3, it also has a `Lerp()` method that can interpolate between Vector3s, but I never use that function because it also clamps the values of u to the range from 0 to 1 and doesn't allow extrapolation.

Easing for Linear Interpolations

The interpolations we've been doing so far are pretty nice, but they also have a very mechanical feel to them because they start abruptly, move at a constant rate, and then stop abruptly. Happily, there are several different *easing functions* that can be used to make this movement more interesting. This is most easily explained with a Unity example.

Unity Example
Open Interpolator2 in MonoDevelop and make the following modification:

```
using UnityEngine;
using System.Collections;

public enum EasingType {
    linear,
    easeIn,
    easeOut,
    easeInOut,
    sin,
    sinIn,
    sinOut
}

public class Interpolator2 : MonoBehaviour {
    public Transform    c0, c1;
    public float        uMin = 0;
    public float        uMax = 1;
    public float        timeDuration = 1;
    public EasingType   easingType = EasingType.linear;
    public float        easingMod = 2;
    public bool         loopMove = true; // Causes the move to repeat
    // Set checkToCalculate to true to start moving
    public bool         checkToCalculate = false;

    …

    void Update () {
        …

        if (moving) {
            float u = (Time.time-timeStart)/timeDuration;
            if (u>=1) {
                u=1;
                if (loopMove) {
                    timeStart = Time.time;
                } else {
                    moving = false;
                }
            }
            // Adjust u to the range from uMin to uMax
            u = (1-u)*uMin + u*uMax;
            // ^ Look familiar? We're using a linear interpolation to do so!

            // Easing functions
            u = EaseU(u, easingType, easingMod);
```

```
                    // This is the standard linear interpolation function
                    p01 = (1-u)*c0.position + u*c1.position;
                    …

            }
    }

    public float EaseU(float u, EasingType eType, float eMod) {
        float u2 = u;

        switch (eType) {
        case EasingType.linear:
            u2 = u;
            break;

        case EasingType.easeIn:
            u2 = Mathf.Pow(u, eMod);
            break;

        case EasingType.easeOut:
            u2 = 1 - Mathf.Pow( 1-u, eMod );
            break;

        case EasingType.easeInOut:
            if ( u <= 0.5f ) {
                u2 = 0.5f * Mathf.Pow( u*2, eMod );
            } else {
                u2 = 0.5f + 0.5f * (  1 - Mathf.Pow( 1-(2*(u-0.5f)), eMod )  );
            }
            break;

        case EasingType.sin:
            // Try eMod values of 0.16f and -0.2f for EasingType.sin
            u2 = u + eMod * Mathf.Sin( 2*Mathf.PI*u );
            break;

        case EasingType.sinIn:
            // eMod is ignored for SinIn
            u2 = 1 - Mathf.Cos( u * Mathf.PI * 0.5f );
            break;

        case EasingType.sinOut:
            // eMod is ignored for SinOut
            u2 = Mathf.Sin( u * Mathf.PI * 0.5f );
            break;
        }

        return( u2 );
    }
}
```

Save Interpolator2 and switch back to Unity. In the *Cube01:Interpolator2 (Script)* Inspector, set uMin back to 0 and uMax back to 1. Press Play and click checkToCalculate. Now, because loopMove is checked as well, Cube01 will continuously interpolate between c0 and c1.

Try playing around with the different settings for easingType. easingMod will affect the *easeIn*, *easeOut*, *easeInOut*, and *sin* easing types. For the *sin* type, try an easingMod of *0.16* as well as one of *-0.2* to see the flexibility of the Sin-based easing type.

In Figure B.5 you can see a graphical representation of the various easing curves. In this figure, the horizontal dimension represents the initial u value, while the vertical dimension represents the eased u value (u2). You can see that in every example when u=1, u2 also equals 1. Because of this, if the linear interpolation is time based, the value will always move completely from p0 to p1 in the same time regardless of the easing settings.

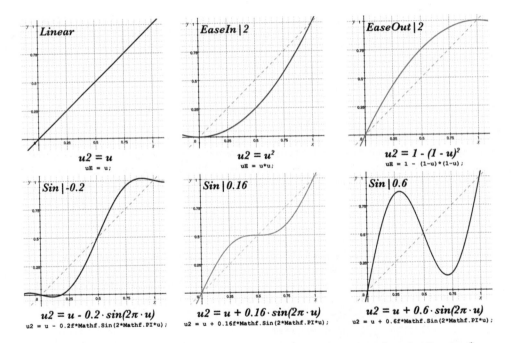

Figure B.5   Various easing curves and their formulae. In each case, the number after the pipe (|) represents the easingMod value.

The *Linear* curve shows no easing (u2 = u). In each of the other curves shown, the u2=u line remains as a dashed diagonal line to show normal, linear behavior. If the vertical component of a curve is ever below the dashed diagonal, the movement is happening more slowly than a linear curve. Conversely, if the vertical component of the curve is ever above the dashed diagonal, the eased curve is ahead of where the linear movement would have been.

The *EaseIn* curve will start slowly and then move faster toward the end (u2 = u*u). This is known as *easing in* because the first part of the motion is "easy" and slow before it then speeds up.

The *EaseOut* curve is the opposite of the *EaseIn* curve. With this curve, the movement starts quickly and then slows at the end.

The three *Sin* curves on the bottom of the diagram all follow the same formula (u2 = u + n * sin(u*2π), where n is a floating-point number (the variable `easingMod` in our code). The multiplication of u * 2π inside of the sin() ensures that as u moves from 0 to 1, it passes through a full sine wave (moving center, up, center, down, and back to center). If n=0, the sine curve has no effect on the curve (that is, the curve remains linear), as n moves further from zero in either direction, it has more of an effect.

The curve *Sin|-0.2* is an ease-in-out with a bounce. The n value of *-0.2* adds a negative sine wave to the linear progression, causing a moving object to back up a bit from p0, move quickly toward p1, overshoot a bit, and then settle at p1. An n value closer to zero of *Sin|-0.1* would cause the object to ease-in to full speed at the center point and then slow as it approached p1 without the extrapolation bounce at either end.

In the curve *Sin|0.16,* a slight sine curve is added to the linear u progression, causing the curve to get ahead of linear, slow in the middle, and then catch up. If moving an object, this will bring it to the center point, slow it in the middle to "feature" it for a while, and then move it out.

The curve *Sin|0.6* is the easing curve that is used by Enemy_2 in Chapter 30. In this case, enough positive sine wave has been added to cause the object to shoot past the center point to a point about 80% of the way to p1, then move back to a point 20% of the way to p1, and then finally move to p1.

Bézier Curves

A Bézier curve is a linear interpolation between more than two points. Just as with a normal linear interpolation, the base formula is p01 = (1-u) * p0 + u * p1. The Bézier curve just adds more points and more calculations.

Given three points: p0, p1, and p2

> p01 = (1-u) * p0 + u * p1
> p12 = (1-u) * p1 + u * p2
> p012 = (1-u) * p01 + u * p12

As is demonstrated in the preceding equations, for the three points p0, p1, and p2, the location of the point of the Bézier curve is calculated by first performing a linear interpolation between p0 and p1 (called p01), then performing a linear interpolation between p1 and p2 (called p12), and finally performing a linear interpolation between p01 and p12 to obtain the final point, p012. A graphical representation of this is shown in Figure B.6.

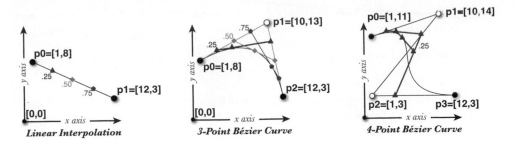

Figure B.6   A linear interpolation and 3-point and 4-point Bézier curves

A four-point curve requires more calculations to accommodate all four points:

$$p01 = (1-u) * p0 + u * p1$$

$$p12 = (1-u) * p1 + u * p2$$

$$p23 = (1-u) * p2 + u * p3$$

$$p012 = (1-u) * p01 + u * p12$$

$$p123 = (1-u) * p12 + u * p23$$

$$p0123 = (1-u) * p012 + u * p123$$

Four-point Bézier curves are used in many drawing programs as a way of defining very control-lable curves, including: Adobe Flash, Adobe Illustrator, Adobe Photoshop, The Omni Groups' OmniGraffle, and many others. In fact, the curve editors used in Unity for animation and audio processing uses a form of four-point Bézier curves.

Unity Example

Follow these steps to create a Bézier curve example in Unity. When writing code, I don't use the accented é in Bézier because code tends to be written without any accented characters.

1. Create a new scene in your Unity project named _BezierScene. Add four cubes named c0, c1, c2, and c3. Set the transform.scale of all cubes to S:[0.5, 0.5, 0.5]. Position the cubes in various positions around the scene and adjust your Scene view so that you can see all of them. Next, add a sphere to the scene, attach a TrailRenderer to it, and set the material of the TrailRenderer to *Default-Particle* (as described in step one of the *Unity Example* for the "Time-Based Linear Interpolation" section earlier in this appendix).

2. Create a new C# script named *Bezier* and attach it to Sphere. Open Bezier in MonoDevelop and enter the following code:

```
using UnityEngine;
using System.Collections;

public class Bezier : MonoBehaviour {
    public Transform    c0, c1, c2, c3;
    public float        timeDuration = 1;
```

```
// Set checkToCalculate to true to start moving
public bool          checkToCalculate = false;

public bool _____;

public float         u;
public Vector3       p0123;
public bool          moving = false;
public float         timeStart;

void Update () {
    if (checkToCalculate) {
        checkToCalculate = false;
        moving = true;
        timeStart = Time.time;
    }

    if (moving) {
        u = (Time.time-timeStart)/timeDuration;
        if (u>=1) {
            u=1;
            moving = false;
        }

        // 4-point Bezier curve calculation
        Vector3 p01, p12, p23, p012, p123;

        p01 = (1-u)*c0.position + u*c1.position;
        p12 = (1-u)*c1.position + u*c2.position;
        p23 = (1-u)*c2.position + u*c3.position;

        p012 = (1-u)*p01 + u*p12;
        p123 = (1-u)*p12 + u*p23;

        p0123 = (1-u)*p012 + u*p123;

        transform.position = p0123;
    }

    }
}
```

3. Back in Unity, assign each of the four cubes to their respective fields in the *Sphere:Bezier (Script)* Inspector. Then press Play and click the `checkToCalculate` check box in the Inspector. Sphere will trace a Bézier curve between the four cubes. It's important to note here that Sphere only ever touches c0 and c3. It is influenced by but does not touch c1 and c2. This is true of all Bézier curves. The ends of the curve will always touch the first and last points, but no points in-between are ever touched. If you're interested in looking into a kind of curve where the midpoints are touched, look up "Hermite spline" online (as well as other kinds of splines).

A Recursive Bézier Curve Function

As you saw in the previous section, the additional calculations for adding more control points to a Bézier curve are pretty straightforward conceptually, but it takes a while to type all the additional lines of code. The following code listing includes an elegant recursive function to calculate a Bézier curve of any number of points. This is included in the ProtoTools `Utils` class that is part of the initial unitypackage for Chapters 31 through 35:

```
// Remember that these three "using" lines will be needed by your code
using UnityEngine;
using System.Collections;
using System.Collections.Generic; // Needed for the List<>s in these functions

public class Utils {
    // There are many lines in Utils prior to the Bezier methods
    …

    // The standard Vector Lerp functions in Unity don't allow for extrapolation
    //   (i.e., u is clamped to 0 <= u <= 1), so we write our own Lerp function
    static public Vector3 Lerp (Vector3 vFrom, Vector3 vTo, float u) {
        Vector3 res = (1-u)*vFrom + u*vTo;
        return( res );
    }


    // While most Bezier curves are 3 or 4 points, it is possible to have
    //   any number of points using this recursive function
    // This uses the Lerp function above because the Vector3.Lerp function
    //   doesn't allow extrapolation
    static public Vector3 Bezier( float u, List<Vector3> vList ) {
        // If there is only one element in vList, return it
        if (vList.Count == 1) {
            return( vList[0] );
        }

        // Create vListR, which is all but the 0th element of vList
        // e.g., if vList = [0,1,2,3,4] then vListR = [1,2,3,4]
        List<Vector3> vListR =  vList.GetRange(1, vList.Count-1);

        // And create vListL, which is all but the last element of vList
        // e.g., if vList = [0,1,2,3,4] then vListL = [0,1,2,3]
        List<Vector3> vListL = vList.GetRange(0, vList.Count-1);

        // The result is the Lerp of the Bezier of these two shorter Lists
        Vector3 res = Lerp( Bezier(u, vListL), Bezier(u, vListR), u );
        // ^ The Bezier function recursively calls itself here to split the
        //     lists down until there is only one value in each
```

```
        return( res ); // Return the result
    }


    // This version allows an array or a series of Vector3s as input which is
    //  then converted into a List<Vector3>
    static public Vector3 Bezier( float u, params Vector3[] vecs ) {
        return( Bezier( u, new List<Vector3>(vecs) ) );
    }


    …
}
```

Roleplaying Games

There are many good roleplaying games (RPGs) out there. The most popular is still probably *Dungeons & Dragons* by Wizards of the Coast (D&D), which is now in its fifth edition. Since the third edition, D&D has been based on the d20 system, which uses a single twenty-sided die in place of the many complex die rolls that were common in prior systems. I like D&D for a lot of things, but I have found that my students will often get bogged down in combat when attempting to run D&D as their first system; it has a lot of very specific combat rules, especially in the fourth edition.

My personal recommendation for a first RPG system is *FATE* by Evil Hat Productions. *FATE* is a simple system that allows players to contribute directly to the narrative much more than other systems allow. (Other systems give all power over events to the person running the game.) You can learn about *FATE* at the website http://faterpg.com, and you can read the free *FATE* system reference document (SRD) at http://fate-srd.com.

Tips for Running a Good Roleplaying Campaign

Running a roleplaying campaign can do wonders for your abilities as both a game designer and storyteller. If you try running a campaign yourself, here are some tips that I've found to be very useful when my students start running campaigns:

1. **Start simple:** There are a lot of different roleplaying systems out there, and they vary greatly in the complexity of their rules. I recommend starting with a simple system like *Dungeons & Dragons*. Initially released in 1974, D&D was the first roleplaying system and has continued to be the most popular system over the last 40 years. While the complete rules of D&D are anything but simple, the basic rule set that covers most situations is really pretty straightforward, and you can then add more rulebooks as you get deeper into the system.

   As described in the preceding section, another fantastic possibility for new role-players is the *FATE* system, which has much simpler rules for combat and contests of will than D&D. In addition, *FATE* has specific game mechanics that allow players to make storytelling suggestions to the game master, which makes the storytelling of *FATE* games more collaborative than other systems.

2. **Start short:** Rather than starting with the first episode of a campaign that you expect to take a full year of play to complete, try starting with a simple mission that can be wrapped up in a single night of play. This will give your play group a chance to try out their characters and the system and see if they like both. If not, it's easy to change to something else, and it's much more important that the players enjoy their first experience roleplaying than that you kick off an epic campaign.

3. **Help the players get started:** Unless the other players in your campaign have prior experience roleplaying, it would be a very good idea for you to create their characters for them. This gives you the chance to make sure that the characters have complementary abilities and stats to make up a good team. A standard roleplaying party is composed of the following characters:

   - A warrior to absorb enemy damage and fight up close
   - A wizard to do long-range damage and detect magic
   - A thief to disarm traps and make sneak attacks
   - A cleric to detect evil and heal the other party members

   However, if you're going to create characters for your players, you should get early buy-in from them by asking them to tell you about the kind of play experience they would like and the kind of abilities that they want their character to have. Early buy-in and interest is one of the keys to getting your players past the rough patches that can happen at the beginning of a game.

4. **Plan for improvisation:** Your players will frequently do things that you don't expect. The only way to plan for this is to prepare yourself for flexibility and improvisation. Be ready with things like maps of generic spaces, a list of names that could be used for NPCs (non-player characters) that the party may or may not encounter, and a few generic monsters of various difficulties that you can conjure at will. The more you have ready beforehand, the less time you'll have to spend looking through your rulebooks in the middle of the game.

5. **Be willing to make rulings:** If you can't find the answer to a question in the rules after 10 minutes of looking, just make a ruling using your best judgment and agree with the players that you'll look it up after the game session is over. This will keep the game from bogging down due to esoteric rules.

6. **It's the players' story too:** Remember to allow the players to go off the beaten path. If you've prepared too narrow a scenario, you might be tempted to not let them do so, but that would run the risk of killing their enjoyment of the game.

7. **Remember that constant optimal challenge isn't fun:** In the discussion of flow in games in the first part of the book, you read that if players are always optimally challenged, they get exhausted quickly. This is also true in RPGs. Boss fights should always optimally challenge your players, but you should also have fights where the players win easily (this helps demonstrate to them that their characters are actually getting stronger as they level up) and sometimes even fights that the players need to flee from to survive (this is usually not expected by players, and can be really dramatic for them).

If you keep these tips in mind, it should help your roleplaying campaigns be a lot more fun for you and your players.

User Interface Concepts

Axis and Button Mapping for Microsoft Controllers

While most of the games included in this book use a mouse or keyboard interface, I'm guessing you might want to eventually hook up a gamepad controller to your games. Generally, the easiest controller to get working on a PC, OS X, or Linux is the Microsoft Xbox 360 Controller for Windows. You can get it in either a wired or wireless version, and the wireless version comes with a receiver that allows up to four Xbox controllers to be connected to one machine at a time.

However, it is unfortunately true that each platform (PC, OS X, and Linux) interprets the controllers differently, so you'll need to set up an Input Manager that adapts to how the controller works on each platform.

Alternatively, you could save yourself a lot of trouble and choose an input manager from the Unity Asset Store. Several of my students have used *InControl* by Gallant Games, which maps input from not only Microsoft controllers but also Sony, Logitech, Ouya, and many others to the same input code in Unity.

> http://www.gallantgames.com/pages/incontrol-introduction

If you do wish to configure the Unity InputManager yourself, Figure B.7 contains information from the Unify community's page about the Xbox 360 controller.[2] The numbers in the figure indicate the joystick button number that can be accessed by the *InputManager Axes* window. The axes are designated with the letter *a* before them (for example, aX, a5). If working with multiple joysticks on the same machine, you can designate a specific joystick in the InputManager Axes by using *joystick # button #* (for example, "joystick 1 button 3"). The same Unify page also includes a downloadable InputManager setup for four simultaneous Microsoft controllers.

On PC, the driver for the controller should install automatically. On Linux (Ubuntu 13.04 and later), it should be included as well. For OS X, you need to download the driver from TattieBogle at http://tattiebogle.net/index.php/ProjectRoot/Xbox360Controller/OsxDriver.

Right-Click on OS X

Throughout this book, there are many times when I ask you to right-click on something. However, many people don't know how to right-click on a Macintosh because it's not the default setting for OS X trackpads and mice. There are actually several ways to right-click, and the one you use depends on how new your Mac is and how you prefer to interact with your machine.

---

[2] The Unify community's page for this is: http://wiki.unity3d.com/index.php?title=Xbox360Controller

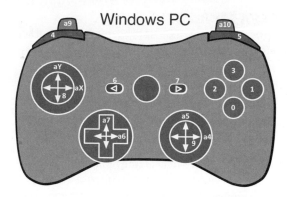

This is using the Tattie Bogle
Driver for Mac OSX
http://tattiebogle.net/index.php/ProjectRoot/
Xbox360Controller/OsxDriver

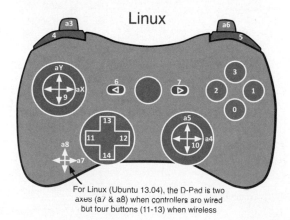

For Linux (Ubuntu 13.04), the D-Pad is two
axes (a7 & a8) when controllers are wired
but four buttons (11-13) when wireless

Figure B.7   Xbox controller mapping for PC, OS X, and Linux

Control-Click = Right-Click

Near the bottom-left corner of all modern OS X keyboards is a Control key. If you hold down the Control key and then left-click (your normal click) on anything, OS X treats it as a right-click.

Use Any PC Mouse

You can use almost any PC mouse that has two or three buttons on OS X. I personally use a Razer Orochi.

Set Your OS X Mouse to Right-Click

If you have an OS X mouse made in 2005 or later (the Apple Mighty Mouse or Apple Magic Mouse), you can enable right-clicking by going into *System Preferences > Mouse*. Select the *Point & Click* tab at the top of the screen. Check the box next to *Secondary click* and then choose *Click on right side* from the pop-up menu directly below *Secondary Click*. This will make a click on the left side of the mouse left-click and a click on the right side right-click.

Set Your OS X Trackpad to Right-Click

Similar to the Apple Mouse, any modern Apple laptop trackpad (or the Bluetooth Magic Track-pad) can be configured to right-click. Open *System Preferences > Trackpad* and choose the *Point & Click* tab at the top of the window. Check the box next to *Secondary Click*. If you choose *Click or tap with two fingers* from the pop-up menu directly below *Secondary Click*, it will make tapping with one finger the standard left-click and tapping with two fingers the right-click. There are also other right-click trackpad options if you prefer.

ONLINE REFERENCE

Whereas many online references would just give you a list of websites to check out, I thought it would be more useful for me to use this appendix to tell you a bit about how I tend to look for answers online when I need them. Appropriately, this includes a few basic links, but it also includes strategies for tracking down information and answers to problems that you might encounter.

I recommend reading this straight through once (it's very short) and then returning to it when you encounter an issue.

Tutorials

Unity has created a series of tutorials over the years that can be very useful to check out. This book focused on short gameplay tutorials to help you understand how to program game mechanics, whereas the tutorials created by Unity tend to spend an equal amount of time on art assets, animation, building scenes, and visual effects in addition to scripting. This book is about you learning how to design and prototype games; their tutorials are about learning all the different features of the Unity engine.

Be aware when looking at these that many were made with older versions of Unity, and they sometimes don't update the tutorials to match the new version of the engine (meaning that sometimes the elements of the Unity interface that the tutorial describes have changed). In addition, some of these tutorials are written in JavaScript rather than C#. This should be fine for you—especially once you've read and understood the code in this book—but it will mean reading and writing code in an additional language.

Unity Website: Learn Section

On Unity's website, there is a *Learn* section that is meant to introduce you to Unity through several different tutorials. This link will take you to that page. Choose a topic that you would like to learn about, and you can view a video tutorial to help you do so:

- http://unity3d.com/learn/tutorials/modules

Demo Projects

Many of Unity's old tutorials are now located in the *Demo Projects* section of their website. Several of these require you to open them via the *Asset Store* window in Unity itself. Because all of these are considered "complete projects," they will overwrite the contents of any project you have open when you import them, so you should create a new project before doing so:

- http://unity3d.com/gallery/demos/demo-projects

Unity Resources

Once you have some experience with Unity under your belt, you may want to look at some more advanced resources. These are good if you want to learn the best practices of Unity development (the best way to use XML, the best way to implement animations, and so on).

Unity Gems

A few resources online specifically focus on Unity development, and Unity Gems is one of the best. They have tutorials on artificial intelligence, finite state machines, shaders, and more:

- http://unitygems.com

Will Goldstone's Websites

Goldstone was one of the first people to write a book on Unity, and he has continued to create and update resources on his websites:

- http://www.unity3dstudent.com/
- http://learnunity3d.com/
- http://learnunity2d.com/

Programming

As you delve further into programming Unity, you'll find that the documentation for programming Unity with C# is primarily located in two places: Unity's scripting documentation and the Microsoft C# reference. The Unity scripting documentation does a fantastic job of documenting Unity-specific features, classes, and components, but it doesn't cover any of the core C# classes (such as List<>, Dictionary<>, and so on). For these, turn to Microsoft's C# documentation. I recommend first looking for something in the Unity documentation available on your computer, and if it's not there, then look in the Microsoft docs.

Unity Scripting Reference

Unity scripting references include the following:

- **Online:** http://docs.unity3d.com/Documentation/ScriptReference/
- **Local:** From within Unity, choose *Help > Scripting Reference* from the menu bar. This brings up a version of the reference that is stored locally on your computer. Even if you don't have an Internet connection, this reference is available. (I use it while traveling all the time.)

Microsoft C# Reference

Search Bing.com for *Microsoft C# Reference*. The first hit should be what you're looking for. As of the time of writing this book, the URL is

> http://msdn.microsoft.com/en-us/library/618ayhy6.aspx.

Stack Overflow

Stack Overflow is an online community of developers helping developers. People post questions, and other members of the site answer them. In a bit of gamification, those who give the best answers (as voted by other members) earn experience points and prestige on the site:

> http://stackoverflow.com

Often, when I'm trying to figure out how to do something new or unusual, I'll end up finding a good answer on Stack Overflow. For instance, if I want to know how to sort a List<> using LINQ, I enter *c# LINQ sort list of objects* into Google, and as I write this, the top four hits are Stack Overflow questions. I usually find myself there via a Google search rather than starting on Stackoverflow.com, but when a hit comes up on the site, it's my first choice for finding good answers.

Learning More C#

I highly recommend two additional books for learning more about C#:

- **For beginners:** Rob Miles's *CSharp Yellow Book,* 2014.pdf, http://www.csharpcourse.com

  Rob Miles, a lecturer at the University of Hull, has written a fantastic book on C# programming that he updates often. You can find the current version on his website (shown here). It is witty, clear, and comprehensive.

- **For reference:** *C# 4.0 Pocket Reference, 3rd Edition,* http://shop.oreilly.com/product/0636920013365.do

  Although there is now a C# 5.0 version of this reference, Unity is still using the C# 4.0 standard (well, it's most of C# 4.0; there are actually a few bits missing), so this is the reference for you. Any time I have a C# question, this is the first place I turn. It's a truncated version of the information in O'Reilly's *C# in a Nutshell* book, but I actually find the pocket reference more useful.

Searching Tips

Any time you want to search for something having to do with C#, make *C#* the first term in your search. If you just search for *list,* the first thing to come up has nothing to do with coding. Searching for *C# list* will get you to the right place immediately.

Similarly, if you want to find anything related to Unity, be sure to make *Unity* your first search term.

Finding Assets

The following sections provide advice on finding various art and audio assets.

The Unity Asset Store

The Asset Store is accessed by opening the Asset Store window in Unity (choose *Window > Asset Store* from the menu bar) or by going to the following website. The Asset Store has a huge collection of models, animations, sounds, code, and even complete Unity projects that you can download. Most of the assets are available for a small fee, but some of the assets on the site are even free. Some things are very pricey, but they are often worth it and can save you hundreds of hours of development:

- https://www.assetstore.unity3d.com/

Models and Animations

These sites are some places to look for 3D models. Some will be free, but many will be paid. Also, be aware that many of the free ones are for noncommercial use only:

- **TurboSquid:** http://www.turbosquid.com
- **Artist3D:** http://artist-3d.com/
- **Google 3D Warehouse:** http://sketchup.google.com/3dwarehouse/

  Be aware that nearly all the assets on the Google 3D Warehouse site are in SketchUp or Collada formats, neither of which import into Unity very well. You can watch this Unite 2013 talk for information on how to make the imports work better:

  http://www.youtube.com/watch?v=Zj727ov9Pe0.

Fonts

Nearly all the fonts on these sites are free for noncommercial use, but you will often need to pay to use them on commercial projects:

- http://www.1001fonts.com/
- http://www.1001freefonts.com/
- http://www.dafont.com/
- http://www.fontsquirrel.com/
- http://www.fontspace.com/

Educational Software Discounts

If you are a student or faculty member of a university, you qualify for many discounts on software.

- **Unity Technologies:** Unity offers educational versions of Unity Pro through Studica.

  http://www.studica.com/us/en/unity

- **Adobe:** Adobe offers the entire Creative Cloud suite of their tools to students for $19.95 per month. This includes Photoshop, Illustrator, Premier, and many others.

  http://www.adobe.com/products/creativecloud/students.edu.html

- **AutoDesk:** AutoDesk gives students and educators a free 36-month license for almost any of their tools, including 3ds Max, Maya, Motionbuilder, Mudbox, and more.

  http://www.autodesk.com/education/student-software

- **Blender:** Blender is a free, open source tool for modeling and animation. It includes many of the capabilities of software like Maya and 3ds Max but is entirely free and can be used for commercial purposes. However, its interface is quite different from what you may be used to from other modeling and animation software.

  http://www.blender.org/

INDEX

Numbers

3D animation/model resources, 854-855

3D printing, touch as an Inscribed Layer aesthetic, 47-48

A

A Pattern Language, 45

AAA (top) games, costs in developing, 213

Achiever player type (diamonds), 67

acquaintances as playtesters, 145

action, five-act dramatic narrative structures
 falling action (Act IV), 51
 rising action (Act II), 51

action games
 Omega Mage
  changing rooms, 764-768
  creating an inventory, 747-754
  creating the game environment, 730-735
  customizing setup, 789
  damaging enemies, 772-777
  damaging players, 777-782
  enemy factories, 785-789
  enemy interfaces, 782-785
  EnemyBug GameObjects, 770-780
  EnemySpiker GameObjects, 780-782
  example of play, 728-729
  fire ground spell, 754-762
  fire spell, 761-762
  fire-and-forget spells, 762-764
  ground spell, 756-761
  importing Unity asset packages, 729
  Mage GameObject (player character), 735-737
  mouse interaction, 737-747
  project setup, 729
  selecting elements from inventory, 749-754
  spawning enemies, 768-782
 puzzles in, 188
  boss fights, 195
  chain reaction puzzles, 194
  physics puzzles, 194
  sliding blocks/position puzzles, 193
  stealth puzzles, 194
  traversal puzzles, 194

action lists (GameObjects), *Apple Picker* game analysis, 231-232

actions
 discernable actions (meaningful play), 64
 integrated actions (meaningful play), 64-65
 tracking and reacting to (empathetic characters versus avatars), 57

Activision, *Kaboom!* game analysis (systems thinking), 229-234

Adkinson, Peter
 innovation and the design process, 97-98
 RoboRally, 97-98

ADL (Automated Data Logging) and playtesting, 151

Adobe software, educational software discounts, 855

Aeon of Strife, game mods and cultural mechanics, 81-82

aesthetics
 Cultural Layer (Layered Tetrad), 82
  cosplay, 82
  defining, 35
  fan art, 82
  gameplay as art, 83
 Dynamic Layer (Layered Tetrad), 70
  defining, 34
  environmental aesthetics, 70, 73-74
  procedural aesthetics, 70-73

F

J

Q

R

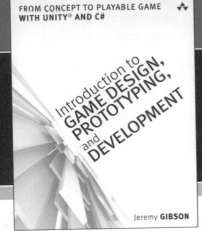

FROM CONCEPT TO PLAYABLE GAME
WITH UNITY® AND C#

Introduction to GAME DESIGN, PROTOTYPING, and DEVELOPMENT

Jeremy **GIBSON**

FREE
Online Edition

Safari
Books Online

Your purchase of *Introduction to Game Design, Prototyping, and Development* includes access to a free online edition for 45 days through the **Safari Books Online** subscription service. Nearly every Addison-Wesley Professional book is available online through **Safari Books Online**, along with over thousands of books and videos from publishers such as Cisco Press, Exam Cram, IBM Press, O'Reilly Media, Prentice Hall, Que, Sams, and VMware Press.

Safari Books Online is a digital library providing searchable, on-demand access to thousands of technology, digital media, and professional development books and videos from leading publishers. With one monthly or yearly subscription price, you get unlimited access to learning tools and information on topics including mobile app and software development, tips and tricks on using your favorite gadgets, networking, project management, graphic design, and much more.

Activate your FREE Online Edition at
informit.com/safarifree

STEP 1: Enter the coupon code: VOBAXWA.

STEP 2: New Safari users, complete the brief registration form.
Safari subscribers, just log in.

If you have difficulty registering on Safari or accessing the online edition,
please e-mail customer-service@safaribooksonline.com